To inspire ambition, to stimulate the imagination, to provide the inquiring mind with accurate information told in an interesting style, and thus lead into broader fields of knowledge—such is the purpose of this work

The New
BOOK OF KNOWLEDGE
Volume Seven

Other Famous Works
of
Popular Instruction
by
the Same Editor

✦✦✦

PRACTICAL KNOWLEDGE FOR ALL
Six Vols.

NEW UNIVERSAL ENCYCLOPEDIA
Ten Vols.

UNIVERSAL HISTORY OF THE WORLD
Eight Vols

THE SECOND GREAT WAR
Nine Vols

PEOPLES OF ALL NATIONS
Two Vols

COUNTRIES OF THE WORLD
Two Vols

WONDERS OF THE PAST
Two Vols.

MANNERS AND CUSTOMS OF MANKIND
Three Vols

OUR WONDERFUL WORLD
Four Vols.

WORLD'S GREAT BOOKS IN OUTLINE
Seven Vols.

MASTERPIECE LIBRARY OF SHORT STORIES
Twenty Vols.

MADE AND PRINTED IN GREAT BRITAIN BY THE AMALGAMATED PRESS, LTD.

SOME UNIVERSITY HOODS AND COATS OF ARMS

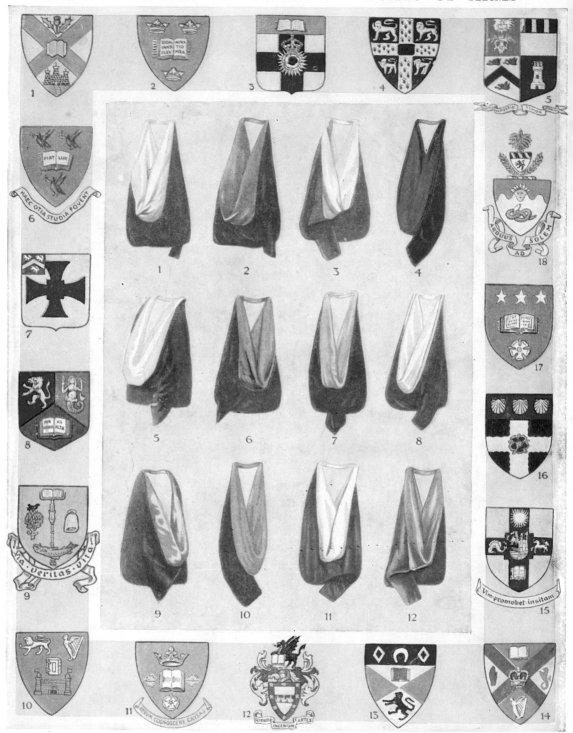

Painted specially for this work by FRANK COLLINS

The frame enclosing the hoods shows the coats of arms of the following universities : 1, Edinburgh. 2, Oxford. 3, London. 4, Cambridge. 5, Aberdeen. 6, Liverpool. 7, Durham. 8, Birmingham. 9, Glasgow. 10, Dublin. 11, Sheffield. 12, Wales. 13, St. Andrews. 14, Belfast. 15, Bristol. 16, Reading. 17, Leeds. 18, Manchester. Hoods are worn by graduates on ceremonial occasions to show the nature of their degree, and are usually of cloth or silk. 1, B.Sc. (Bachelor of Science), London. 2, B.Sc. Aberdeen. 3, B.Mus. (Bachelor of Music), London. 4, M.A (Master of Arts), Oxford. 5, M.A., Cambridge. 6 M.Com (Master of Commerce), Durham. 7, M.Sc. (Master of Science), Birmingham. 8, M.Arch. (Master of Architecture), National University of Ireland. 9, M.A., Wales. 10, D.Sc. (Doctor of Science), Edinburgh. 11, D.D. (Doctor of Divinity), St. Andrews. 12, Ph.D. (Doctor of Philosophy), Birmingham. In some universities hoods are of a standard colour, combined with another colour or colours to denote the degree. For instance, all hoods of the University of Leeds are of a green shade, which may be dark, medium, or light green. In some countries a scarf is worn instead of a hood. The hood is worn in such a way as to show the lining.

The NEW BOOK OF KNOWLEDGE

A Pictorial Treasury of Reading & Reference for Young and Old

Edited by
SIR JOHN HAMMERTON

COMPLETE IN EIGHT VOLUMES
Alphabetically Arranged

OVER SIX THOUSAND ILLUSTRATIONS
OVER 600 IN COLOUR AND GRAVURE

VOLUME SEVEN
SOU–ZWI

THE WAVERLEY BOOK COMPANY LTD.
Farringdon Street, London, E.C.4

HERE AND THERE IN THIS VOLUME

When you are just looking for 'something interesting to read,' this list will help. With it as a guide, you may wander through storyland, visit far-away countries, meet famous people of ancient and modern times, review history's most memorable incidents, explore the marvels of Nature and science—in short, find whatever suits your fancy at the moment

HOW MANY QUESTIONS CAN YOU ANSWER?

Here are a few only of the unnumbered thousands which are answered in each one of our eight volumes. You can use this page as a test of your own knowledge, or you can draw up from it a set of 'posers' with which to puzzle your friends. But odd scraps of knowledge are of little value compared with the result of organized study, and you should refer to the Study Outlines in the Eighth Volume for a reading guide.

COLOUR AND GRAVURE PLATES AND PAGES
IN THIS VOLUME

WHEN YOU ARE IN NEED OF READY REFERENCE

In using THE NEW BOOK OF KNOWLEDGE *as a work of reference, Volume Eight is indispensable. As regards its contents that particular volume is unique, for it is at once a complete Index to the preceding Seven Volumes and an Encyclopedia in itself. Its purpose is fourfold, as indicated below.*

(1) **Through the Year with the N.B.K.** Its opening section takes the form of a Calendar of the Year, giving for each day all the chief events and matters of interest, with references to the pages of THE NEW BOOK OF KNOWLEDGE in which full particulars concerning the event, personality, or other interest of the day may be found. By the intelligent use of this section (a) the young reader can have the daily delight of reading about topics that have special association with the particular day of the year on which he may be making his reference ; (b) father or mother can suggest what would be the most appropriate reading for the day ; and (c) the school teacher can set the lessons for the day with a genuine topical appeal.

(2) **Study Outlines.** This large and important section of the volume provides a simple method of study which should enable any of our young readers to become expert in using THE NEW BOOK OF KNOWLEDGE as an auxiliary manual of home study ; and thus what is learnt in school may be amplified, brought home more vividly, and more securely fixed in the memory.

(3) **The Fact-Index.** Actually this is in itself a complete Encyclopedia. In addition to providing many thousands of references to contents of Volumes One to Seven, it records many more thousands of facts in biography, geography, history, science, the arts, etc., that are not mentioned in its seven predecessors. Therefore, if you look in vain for any subject in the alphabetical order of Volumes One to Seven, turn to Volume Eight and you will almost certainly find it there.

It is a good plan, when using THE NEW BOOK OF KNOWLEDGE *as a work of reference, always first to look up any subject in the Fact-Index of Volume Eight.*

(4) **Thousands of Additional Entries.** In the main body of the work all important terms are explained as they arise ; but the scientist in every field of learning uses a "shorthand" of words and terms to convey a more precise meaning and to save repetition. Such words and terms are included in the Fact-Index so as to free the reading pages from a burden of thousands of brief cross-references which a more strict following of the full encyclopedic method would involve. When in doubt, therefore, about the significance of a term, *look it up in the Fact-Index* ; often you will find all the information you want there, but if further explanation is required the Fact-Index will give you page references to that more complete account in the main volumes. Remember that apart from its role as a never-failing source of recreative and entertaining reading, THE NEW BOOK OF KNOWLEDGE is designed to make your school and college learning of treble value by fitting that learning into its place in daily life.

KEY TO PRONUNCIATION

Most of the subject-headings in THE NEW BOOK OF KNOWLEDGE require no special indication of the way in which they should be pronounced. There are also many for whose proper pronunciation it is only necessary to know which syllable is stressed ; in these cases the stress is shown *after* the syllable, thus, Armadil'lo. Where further guidance is necessary the following signs are employed.

ah = a as in father
aw = a as in ball
ê = vowel sound in fern, word, girl, curl
ow = vowel sound in now, bout
oi = vowel sound in noise, boy

Unmarked vowels have their **short sound,** as a in hat, e in bet, i in bit, o in not, u in but, oo in book

Marked vowels have their **long sound,** as in hāte, bē. bīte. nōte. tūne, bōōn

Vowels in italics have a slurred or obscure sound as in abet (*a*-bet'), recent (rē'-se*n*t),conform (k*o*n-form'), nation (nā'-sh*u*n), tailor (tā'-l*o*r)

th = first sound in thing, thank
th = first sound in the, that
zh = s in measure, leisure
g = hard g, as in good, girl
j = soft g, as in gem, ginger
kh = guttural in loch

LIST OF ABBREVIATIONS

The abbreviations most commonly used in this work are noted below ; longer lists of abbreviations often met with in reading or conversation are given under the heading Abbreviations in Volume One and also in the Fact-Index that is contained in Volume Eight.

A.D., *Anno Domini* (in the year of our Lord, of the Christian era)
a.m., *ante meridiem* (before noon)
b., born
B.C., before Christ
C., Centigrade
c., *circa* (about)
Co., county, company
d., died
e.g., *exempli gratia* (for example)
etc., *et cetera* (and so forth)
et seq., *et sequens* (and following)
F., Fahrenheit
h.p., horse-power

i.e., *id est* (that is)
lb., pound, pounds (weight)
m., miles
MS., MSS., manuscript, manuscripts
oz., ounce, ounces
p.m., *post meridiem* (after noon)
Pop., population
Pron., pronunciation
q.v., *quod vide* (which see)
sq. m., square miles
St., Saint
U.S.A., United States of America
viz., *videlicet* (namely)
yd., yard

The STORY of SOUND and its MARVELS

Beyond the range of the human ear there are 'sounds' which some animals can hear. Then there are air waves which are classed as Ultrasonics, farther still outside the range. Here is an account of Sound, its recording and its reproduction.

Sound. The tick of a watch, the rumble of thunder or the crack of an exploding aerial bomb; the chirp of a cricket, the croak of a frog, the song of the thrush and the roar of a lion—all are "sounds." What is the character which unites them all in one class of natural phenomena? It is that they are produced by a vibrating object.

The old-fashioned watchman's rattle has a toothed wooden cog which pushes out a flexible tongue of wood; the natural spring of the wood returns it to its former position. Wood-wind musical instruments such as the clarinet, oboe and bassoon cause musical notes by the vibration of a reed of thin cane or similar material when the player blows into the mouthpiece; some organ pipes, too, have reeds which are vibrated when the organist presses a key and allows air to rush in. Toy whistles, when blown, direct a stream of air through a narrow slit (not unlike that of the organ pipe illustrated in Fig. 2), causing the air to pulsate. Other whistles are constructed in such a way that when they are blown the air causes a pea or small ball to flutter to and fro and produce a rolling note.

The string of a violin or of a violoncello vibrates when the player draws his bow across it or, as he sometimes does, plucks the string with a finger. By "stopping" the string at different lengths the player, in effect, shortens the string and gets a higher note than that given out by the "open" (unshortened) string.

The wood-wind instrumentalist opens or closes holes drilled in the pipe of his oboe or clarinet, and shortens or lengthens the vibrating column of air in that way. The brass instrument player usually opens or closes valves which bring into use, or shut off, loops of tube—though you may see the trombonist actually extend or shorten *his* instrument by an arrangement of telescoping tubes, as he works the slide to and fro.

You may bang a metal tea-tray to produce another type of sound; in fact, if it is fairly flexible, you need not strike it, and you can "make a row" by merely pushing the centre out and letting it flex back again.

The diaphragm of a telephone transmitter does something like this when you speak into the mouthpiece; some types of motor-car horn have a metal diaphragm which is pushed out by a toothed wheel and springs back again—a version of the watchman's rattle. The human voice is produced by the vibration of the vocal cords in the larynx when we send a stream of air against them; the pitch depends on the tightness or looseness of the cords, and on the pressure of the air stream.

Sounds made near enough to us can be heard because the air disturbance (in wave form) set up by the sound impinges upon our ear drums and makes them vibrate; the hidden ear mechanism and the brain interpret these vibrations, and we identify them for what they are.

Sound vibrations also travel in wood, in metal and in water. You can use a wooden rod as a "stethoscope"; the waterworks inspector, looking for a hidden leak, may put one end of his staff to the ground and apply his ear to the opposite end. Try using a rod in this way, to hear the ticking of a small watch placed on a soft mat;

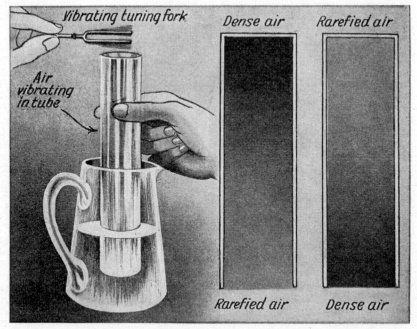

Vibrating tuning fork

Dense air

Rarefied air

Air vibrating in tube

Rarefied air

Dense air

SOUND VIBRATIONS AND THE WAVES THEY CAUSE

Fig. 1. These diagrams show the cause of sound waves in organ pipes. Left, a tuning fork has been set in vibration by striking it. It sets up sympathetic vibrations in the column of air in the tube, and if the tube is raised or lowered in water to alter the length of the empty part, the vibrations of the tuning fork and those of the air in the tube can be made to synchronise. The air column is traversed by waves having an up-and-down motion. If the top of the tube is closed (right-hand pictures) an air column set in vibration will be alternately compressed and rarefied : the tube corresponds to a closed organ pipe.

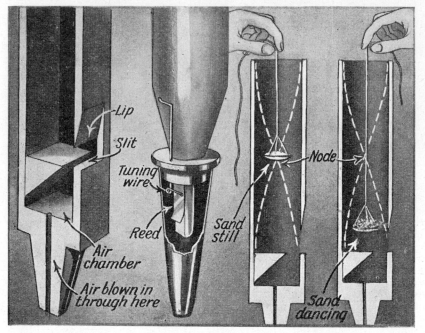

HOW AIR VIBRATIONS PRODUCE MUSICAL NOTES

Fig. 2. We see in the left-hand diagram the lower part of a wooden organ pipe. Air from the bellows enters by the narrow aperture at the bottom, expands in the air chamber, and then is forced through the slit, past the sharp edge of the lip. This sets the air column vibrating. In the second diagram from the left, a reed pipe is shown : the air must set the reed (a metal tongue) vibrating before it can make its way out. The tongue imparts its movements to the air column ; it can be tuned by the wire resting on it. The third and fourth diagrams show an experiment with sand on a rubber membrane (*see* text).

then try using a metal rod, and note how much better metal conducts the sound than does wood.

Get someone to strike an iron railing, or a long iron pipe, while you place your ear near to it at some distance from the place where your friend applies the blow. You will probably hear the sound *twice*—once conducted through the metal and, somewhat later, a second time through the air. The velocity of sound in air is about 350 metres per second; through iron it is 5,000 metres per second; and through water about 1,500 metres in a second. The temperature makes a difference to the velocity, and at a temperature of 0° Centigrade the velocity through air is 331 metres: for every degree by which the temperature rises, the velocity increases by 60 centimetres per second. When the temperature is 20° Centigrade, sound waves through the air have a velocity of 343 metres per second—just over 1,100 feet. It is possible to estimate the distance you are from a thunderstorm, if you time the interval between seeing the lightning flash and hearing the thunder. You can take it that sound will travel roughly a mile in five seconds.

The physiological definition of sound is that it is the sensation we receive in our ears, and interpret with our brain, when air waves from a vibrating source reach the ears. Sounds have loudness, pitch, and something which for want of a better term we can call quality. The *loudness* depends on the *intensity* of the waves—i.e. their energy of motion—and on the extent to which the waves are checked, broken up, or " absorbed " in passing through inter-

vening mediums such as air, brick walls, plaster partitions, or the artificial insulating substances by which builders try to exclude noise.

The *pitch* of a sound depends upon the *frequency* with which the originating vibrating body gave out its pulsations. As we have noted, the musical instrument player can produce, at will, notes of different pitch by altering the length of the vibrating string, or column of air, of his violin or wood-wind or brass instrument. The note A above middle C has a frequency of 438 vibrations per second (Philharmonic pitch) — when the temperature is 68° F. ; musical instruments for orchestras are tuned by this standard. So a body vibrating 438 times per second produces the note we know as A.

Now for " quality ": Most sounds are made up of many tones having different frequencies. The lowest one is called the *fundamental*, and the pitch is named by the frequency of this fundamental. In addition there are higher-frequency tones known as *overtones*. Many of these overtones have frequencies which are simple multiples of the fundamental frequency, and they are known as *harmonics*. Quality is the effect which sounds produce upon the hearing mechanism, and is the result of the intensity, the frequency, and the number of the tones which characterize the sound in question. To quality we owe the varying " colour " of the sound produced by different instruments of an orchestra.

Figs. 1 and 2 illustrate how vibrations can be set up in open and closed organ pipes, and how a metal tongue or reed can be used to impart a desired " colour " to a musical note. The experiment shown on the right of Fig. 2 discloses that sand particles suspended on a rubber membrane in an organ pipe will " dance " when the fundamental note of the pipe is sounded—but only if the sand is placed either above or below a " node." A node is a point at which the vibrating body—air in this case—is at rest, between two waves. Because the air is still, the sand particles on the membrane are not set in vibration.

If we define sound strictly by the physiological meaning we must exclude vibrations which some animals can receive and which we cannot. Did you know that whistles can be made which sound a " note " to which a dog will respond but which his master cannot hear ? And that other " silent " sound waves are used to make tiny particles of the pigment carbon black collect together in groups, so that they can be recovered when natural gas is burned in the experimental manufacturing process ? Ultrasonics is the name given to these vibrations which are beyond the range of human hearing.

Bats, besides making an audible cry or squeak, also send out an ultrasonic one; the latter is considered to enable them to avoid obstacles, by the animal automatically registering the reflection of the ultrasonic pulsation when this strikes an object. Other experimental uses of ultrasonic waves, besides those instanced, are in killing silkworm parasites, sterilizing milk, and killing bacteria.

The range of sound frequencies audible to Man is from about 20 to 15,000 vibrations per second; the range varies with different individuals, but beyond 20,000 can be classed as ultrasonic. The bat's silent cry goes up to about 70,000 per second; and some of the ultrasonic vibrations used experimentally have the shortness of light waves.

SOUND REPRODUCTION AND RECORDING

SOUND waves in air die away rapidly—we cannot either " store " sound, or transmit it long distances, without the help of some other medium. For sound transmission, we call in electricity to help us. If we wish to produce a comparatively small volume of sound at a considerable distance away we use the telephone (*q.v.*); and for producing a large volume of sound at a comparatively short distance we use a " public address system," with loud-speakers. Both of these problems differ in detail, but they have much in common.

In the story of the Microphone we explain how the vibrations caused by sound can be used to cause variations in an electric current, which can then be transmitted along a pair of wires. Now we wish to reproduce them as sound waves again, and the simplest possible arrangement is the ordinary telephone receiver (Fig. 3). This has a thin iron diaphragm supported near to the poles of a permanent magnet, around which are wound coils of wire through which the rapidly-varying or " speech-modulated " current (often simply termed speech

current) is passed. Variations in this cause corresponding changes in the magnetic field acting on the diaphragm, which " waggles " in sympathy, and its movements generate sound waves which approximately correspond to the sounds picked up by the microphone. One can only say " approximately " because a thin metal diaphragm clamped at its edges cannot possibly have an even response to all sound frequencies, and distortion is bound to occur. But this kind of receiver is quite satisfactory for speech purposes when the sound levels required are not high—i.e., when the receiver is placed close to the ear. The response of a telephone receiver to music is disappointing, since amongst other defects, it " chops " the lower frequencies.

Loud-speakers, such as are used for public address systems, present different problems—they are not placed near the ear, and have, therefore, to produce very much larger sound outputs. Larger types of the telephone earpiece, fitted with horns, were used as early loud-speakers; but they were in many ways unsatisfactory. To produce a lot of sound requires

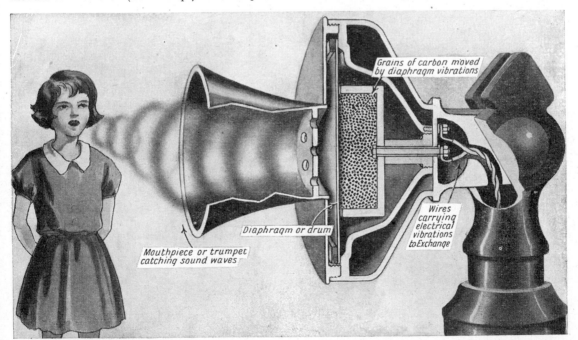

Grains of carbon moved by diaphragm vibrations

Diaphragm or drum

Mouthpiece or trumpet catching sound waves

Wires carrying electrical vibrations to Exchange

AN EVERYDAY ' MIRACLE ' : FROM LIPS TO TELEPHONE RECEIVER

Fig. 3. When we speak into a telephone microphone, the words have been formed by air vibrations in our throat and near-by parts. Passing from the mouth, these air vibrations travel as sound waves through the air. Impinging on the flexible diaphragm of the microphone, the air waves press the carbon granules together, and then allow these granules to relax again. These movements cause variations in the electrical resistance of the telephone circuit ; traversing the wires, the variations move the diaphragm of the telephone receiver, and the original sounds are reproduced.

a large diaphragm, and a lot of movement, which is not easy to arrange. We therefore use a "moving coil" type of speaker (Fig. 4), the construction of which is similar in principle to that of the moving coil microphone. (*See* Microphone).

A large non-metallic diaphragm (usually made of stout paper) has attached to it a coil of thin wire through which the speech current is passed. The coil is located in the strong magnetic field of a circular ("pot") magnet, either permanent or electro-magnet, and variations in the current in the coil cause it to move in the magnetic field. Thus it moves the diaphragm, which can be of quite large size—up to 18 inches or larger. This, coupled with the fact that the diaphragm is not rigidly clamped at the edges, and can therefore move freely, gives a high sound output, with a much better frequency response. Types of speaker used in cinemas are shown in Fig. 6.

Fig. 4

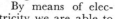

By means of electricity we are able to amplify the microphone currents by the use of valve amplifiers (*see* Electronic Devices), and thus to produce sound levels many times larger than the original source. Considered as engineering devices, both the moving coil microphone and the moving coil speaker are so inefficient that without the use of amplifiers no sound could be produced at all. But by the use of amplifiers a person with a microphone can, without raising his voice, address a vast crowd of people through a number of loud-speakers. Loud-speakers are used by the million in ordinary wireless sets, in addition to public address work both indoors and outdoors, railway station announcing, mobile units on cars, cinema and theatre work. A special form, known as the "loud hailer," is used at sea, and elsewhere. This last is a special design of speaker which is highly directional—instead of producing a comfortable level of sound all round it is made to produce a very high sound level over a narrow beam. Producing very little sound outside its actual beam, the loud hailer has to be "sighted" like a gun, and it is possible even in bad weather to produce intelligible speech at a mile or more. The sound pressures produced by the diaphragm of the hailer are so high that, if it is operated at full power with its waterproof canvas cover in position, the diaphragm will actually be punctured.

Since sound cannot be stored as sound, it follows that the only way of reproducing sounds except at the instant of their occurrence is to use them to make a record of themselves which can be reproduced later—to "write them down," as it were, as with the ordinary gramophone disk (*see* Gramophone) or the dictating machine cylinder, both of which carry a mechanical pattern cut in them, this pattern corre-

Fig. 4. The loud-speaker has a field magnet with poles (S, S) and pole-piece (N); it is energised by current in the field coil (F). The resulting magnetic flux is varied by tiny currents passing through the 'speech coil' (MC) from a radio receiver, and thus the cone-shaped diaphragm is moved in and out.

sponding with sound vibrations. The pattern is caused to vibrate a needle and reproduce the sounds (1) either directly, by mechanical coupling of the needle to a diaphragm; or (2) by the use of an electric "pick-up" to reproduce them electrically, via an amplifier and a loud-speaker.

There are other methods than these. The sound can be photographically recorded on a film, for example, by the use of a "light valve." This is a very delicate mechanism by which variations in microphone current open or close a tiny slit through which light falls upon a moving photographic film. When developed and printed, this film gives us a "sound track" which records the variations in microphone current by variations in either the width or the density of the silver image on the film (*see* Fig. 5). This sound track is afterwards "scanned" by a tiny spot of light which passes through the moving sound track, and falls on a photo-electric cell (*see* Photo-electric Devices). This cell re-translates the variations in light into variations in current; then, suitably amplified, these current variations operate a loud-speaker and reproduce the original sounds. The above method is used in every cinema, and every talking film carries its sound track printed along one side of it.

Fig. 5

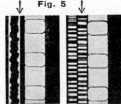

Photographic recording has other uses, in addition to talking pictures. One is for other recordings which are played frequently, since

Western Electric Co., Ltd., and British Thomson Houston Co., Ltd.

SOUND-ON-FILM AT THE CINEMA

Figs. 5 and 6. The cinema film carries a sound 'autograph' on a narrow track (shown by an arrow) alongside the pictures. This track may be in terms of variable width (top left), or variable density (top right). The electrical variations set up by the track give again speech and music, through high- and low-frequency loud-speakers of the type here seen.

the sound track does not wear, like a gramophone record, through the scratch of a needle. One of the best-known examples is the Post Office "Speaking Clock" which gives the time to telephone subscribers in the London area when they dial TIM. This device uses sound tracks recorded on glass disks (*see* illus. in page 2576). The disks, being self-supporting, are practically free from wear of any sort, offering a great advantage over a sound track on a film, since a film wears through being constantly wound and unwound.

More than 50 years ago a Dane by the name of Valdemar Poulsen discovered that a length of hard steel wire, run near a magnet coil carrying speech currents, became variably magnetised so that a sound record was impressed upon it in the form of what might be termed a "pattern" of magnetism; the sounds could be reproduced by running the wire close to another coil which was connected to a telephone receiver. This was because of the variation in the magnetic field of the wire "cutting" the conductors of the coil, and generating variable currents, like a tiny dynamo (*q.v.*). The sounds produced were very faint, since the valve amplifier did not then exist, and "Poulsen's Telegraphone," as it was called, was little more than a curiosity.

With the arrival of the valve amplifier the idea of magnetic recording took on a new lease of life, and finds very wide uses. A considerable advantage has been given to it in the last few years by the use, instead of steel wire or tape, of new high-efficiency magnetic materials in powder form embedded in a paper or plastic tape.

The broad principles of the modern magnetic recorder are shown in Figs. 7 and 8. The tape is unwound from one reel and passes through the recording head (connected to the microphone circuit),

and is then wound on to another reel. It is then rewound (since otherwise it would be played backwards), and run through the reproducing head, which is connected to a loud-speaker circuit. The record can be reproduced as often as desired—it neither wears nor deteriorates—or can instantly be erased and the tape used for another recording. Erasing is done by

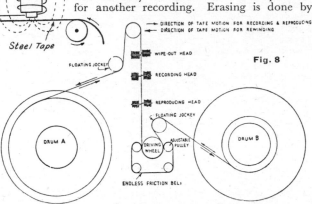

Marconi's Wireless Telegraph Co., Ltd.

SOUND RECORDED ON METAL TAPE

Fig. 7. **The principle of the Blattnerphone is shown simply at top. Current variations from an amplifier vary the magnetic flux in the coil, and so a 'pattern' of these changes is impressed in varied magnetism on the steel tape as the latter passes the magnet. The Marconi-Stille system (Fig. 8) is shown in more detail, with recording head, reproducing head, and wipe-out head. (See text).**

running the tape over a permanent magnet (or any source of a steady magnetic field) situated in a "wipe-out head." The magnetic recorder can be used for long recordings—an hour or more—and the length is limited only by the size of spool used.

Magnetic recording has been applied to sound films, in place of photographic recording. It will not supplant the ordinary gramophone record, since there is no way of making thousands of copies easily and cheaply, as is the case with the moulded type of disk we know so well.

From CONGO to CAPE of GOOD HOPE

In the land of veld and bush, Briton and Boer, once enemies, now work in harmony, building together a Dominion of the British Commonwealth. There are also other territories in South Africa, not included in the Union.

South Africa. The story of South Africa—now a self-governing Dominion of the British Commonwealth, 790,219 square miles in area—is one of bold explorers and hardy settlers on unfriendly coasts, of battles against pygmy Bushmen using poisoned arrows, and against Kaffirs and Zulus, wielding huge shovel-headed spears. It tells of conflicts with wild beasts, of the discovery of gold and diamonds, of the clash of Boer and Briton in the wilderness, of missionaries who carried civilization into desert and jungle, and at last of the establishment of peace and prosperity.

The land in which this stirring drama was played is shut off from the ocean by hills that rise from low-lying coasts step upon step, with barren terraces (karoos) between. The hills ascend until suddenly the whole vast region opens out into a plateau from 4,000 to 6,000 feet above the sea, stretching far to

the northward. Here is the treeless, grass-covered, rolling "veld," and the rough scrub or "bush," where stunted acacias, dwarf mimosas, and aloes fight for life in the dry soil.

Sheltered from the moist ocean breezes, the climate is bracing and healthful. Game of all kinds was formerly plentiful, and if lions and leopards made travel dangerous, there were numberless antelopes—including the springbok, modern symbol of the Union—buffaloes, zebras and giraffes to provide meat for the hunter. In the more tropical regions along the east coast the elephant, the hippopotamus and the rhinoceros are still found in small numbers. There are several game reserves, including the huge Kruger National Park in the eastern Transvaal. (*See also* the article on Africa).

Minerals form the greatest source of South Africa's wealth. Gold is found chiefly in the Transvaal Province and diamonds are produced in quantity from the Kimberley and Pretoria fields. Large coal deposits in the Transvaal and Natal yield millions of tons every year, and the copper mines of the Cape of Good Hope are famous.

On the sloping terraces and plateaux called the veld· and the karoo the finest breeds of sheep graze, and since the days of the early Boer shepherds wool-growing has been the leading agricultural pursuit. Angora goats are raised for mohair. The cattle and dairy industry received a strong impetus from the First World War (1914–18) and butter became an important article of export. A picturesque, though dying, branch of the livestock industry is ostrich farming, which is carried on in the Cape Province. Until irrigation was undertaken in 1877, the cultivation of grains and fruits was confined to the better-watered area. Since that date irrigation has

Extent.—(Including the Territory of S.W. Africa) 790,219 square miles. Total population 11,418,350. The Provinces of the Union of South Africa are Cape of Good Hope (277,113 sq. m. ; pop. 4,016,800), Natal (35,284 sq. m. ; pop. 2,182,700), Orange Free State (49,647 sq. m. ; pop. 875,550), Transvaal (110,450 sq. m. ; pop. 4,183,800). Native Protectorates (not within the Union) : Basutoland (11,716 sq. m. ; pop. 556,400), Bechuanaland Protectorates (275,000 sq. m. ; pop. 285,000), Swaziland (6,705 sq. m. ; pop. 186,880).

Physical Features.—Great interior plateau of "veld" country, with mountains close to and parallel with the coast. Series of gradually rising terraces—the Karoos. Drakensberg Range (rising to 11,000 ft.) between Natal and Orange Free State. Chief rivers : Vaal, Orange, Limpopo.

Principal Products.—Wool ; maize, sugar, cotton, tobacco, citrus fruits ; gold, diamonds, coal, copper, tin ; wines ; ostrich feathers ; motor vehicles and other engineering products ; leather goods ; clothing and textiles ; tinned foods.

Chief Cities.—Johannesburg (Transvaal) population 762,910 ; Cape Town (Cape Province) 383,890 ; Durban (Natal) 338,817 ; Pretoria (Transvaal) 167,649 ; Port Elizabeth (Cape Province) 147,544 ; Pietermaritzburg (Natal) 63,160.

been steadily extended, and the waters of the rivers spread over thousands of acres of what were formerly desert land.

The largest crop is "mealies" (Indian corn), but wheat is making rapid strides. Oats, Kaffir corn, forage crops, and fruits are grown in the south, while on the coast of Natal sugar-cane, tea, and other semi-tropical crops flourish. Because of the drought-resisting properties of cotton, increasing areas are devoted to it.

Conditions brought about by the First World War greatly stimulated manufacturing, which had previously been confined chiefly to flour, meats, tobacco, wines, and brandy. Now the tanning of leather and making of tanning extract from wattle bark are becoming important, as is the manufacture of cement, clay products, vehicles and furniture. In 1934 the first steel works in Pretoria was built. The whole of the railways (over 13,000 miles) of the

South African Railways

IN SOUTH AFRICA'S GREAT GAME RESERVE

The Kruger National Park had its origin in a sanctuary for game which was founded in 1898 by Paul Kruger (1825–1904), President of the South African Republic (Transvaal), and was then known as the Sabi Reserve. It was later considerably enlarged, and in 1926 was constituted a national park. The reserve measures about 220 miles by 40 miles, and lies along the South African Union side of the Portuguese East African border. Above are seen zebras and wildebeests drinking at a water-hole. Elephants, lions, giraffes and hippopotamuses also abound in the park.

SOUTH AFRICA: LAND OF VELD, MOUNTAIN AND FOREST

The mountain ridges skirting the eastern coast of South Africa cause abundant rain to fall in the coastal belt, leaving the interior and the west coast arid. With the exception of the two Portuguese colonies of Angola and Mozambique, and the fragment of the Belgian Congo, all the territory shown on the map above is included within the British Commonwealth.

Union were taken under Government control by 1922. Since 1932 a through air service for passengers and mail has operated between Cape Town and London, and there are connexions between Cape Town and the other main cities of the Union by the air liners of South African Airways.

Geographically, South Africa extends from the borders of the Belgian Congo to the Cape of Good Hope, and includes, in addition to the Provinces of the Union, Rhodesia (q.v.), South-West Africa (q.v.), and the native Protectorates of Basutoland, Bechuanaland Protectorate and Swaziland. These three territories are now under the administration

of a single High Commissioner, with a Resident Commissioner in each. There are very few Europeans in the Protectorates, and the tribes largely govern themselves with little outside help.

BASUTOLAND, which occupies an area to the south-east of the Orange Free State, is a mountainous country, varying in altitude between 5,000 and 11,000 feet, but it has the best grain lands and excellent pasturage for cattle and sheep. It has been British territory since 1868, when Moshesh, the first "paramount" chief of Basutoland, appealed for protection. Many thousand Basuto have left their own country to work in the mines.

South African Government

ZULU WOMAN AT THE HAIRDRESSER'S

A favourite way of doing the hair among Zulu women is to twist it
into tight strands, which are then daubed with clay to secure them.
A tedious process, it takes several hours to complete.

suffers from the dry, hot climate. The largest
town is Serowe (population 15,900).

SWAZILAND, lying at the south-east corner
of the Transvaal, provides winter grazing
for flocks of sheep from that Province. The
capital of Swaziland is Mbabane.

South Africa was found in the 15th century
by Europeans who were seeking an ocean
highway to the rich commerce of India.
Bartholomew Diaz, the Portuguese navigator
who discovered the Cape of Good Hope in
1488, and Vasco da Gama, who reached India
by that route 10 years later, as well as the
scores who followed in their wake, looked upon
this vast southern projection of the "Dark
Continent" merely as something they had to
go round on their way to the "land of spices
and silk." They stopped only for wood and
water or to repair the damage done by the
Cape storms.

It took a shipwreck to bring about the first
settlement. Dutch sailors, driven ashore in
Table Bay, near the Cape of Good Hope, in
1648, were compelled to forage for themselves for several months. Rescued and returned to Holland, they gave such a good
account of their discoveries that in 1652 Jan
van Riebeek, for the Dutch East India Company, established a fort and a plantation in
the shadow of Table Mountain. More settlers
followed, and in 1687 some French Huguenots
threw in their lot with the Dutch colonists.

or on the farms of the Union. The chief town is
Maseru, situated near the Caledon river.

BECHUANALAND PROTECTORATE, by far the largest
of these areas, should not be confused with British
Bechuanaland, which is part of Cape Province. The
greater part of the Protectorate, which was declared
British in 1885, consists of the Great Kalahari
desert, where big game is plentiful. There is swamp
and grass-land farther north but the whole country

The pioneers of Table Bay soon tired of the petty
tyrannies of the Dutch East India Company. By
1720 they had begun their treks or migrations. They
pushed over the northern hills or followed the
mountains towards Natal, as the south-east coast
had been called by Vasco da Gama when he discovered it on Christmas Day (Jesus's "Natal Day')'
in 1497, setting themselves up as independent
farmers, vine-growers, and cattle-raisers.

A FERRY ON THE TUGELA RIVER IN NATAL

A cable stretching from one bank to another keeps the ferry on its course while the boatman poles his flat-bottomed craft
across. The Tugela, 300 miles long, is one of the swift-flowing rivers which rise in the Drakensberg Mountains in western
Natal and flow east into the Indian Ocean. It was the scene of much fighting during the Boer War (1899–1902).

F. Hudson

GRANDEUR OF THE VICTORIA FALLS

Among the many natural wonders and beauties of Southern Rhodesia the most spectacular is beyond doubt the Victoria Falls, on the Zambezi river. Here is the section, over 500 yards wide, known as the Rainbow Fall, where the waters, falling into a vast chasm, throw up clouds of spray in which a perpetual rainbow is seen.

To face page 3016

Union of South Africa

MEMORIAL TO THE DUTCH FOUNDER OF CAPE TOWN, THE GATEWAY OF SOUTH AFRICA

This statue of Jan van Riebeek, the Dutch surgeon who, in 1652, founded the first white settlement at the Cape of Good Hope, stands on the esplanade at Cape Town, looking out over Table Bay. Towering above the city is Table Mountain, generally covered by a great white cloud, called locally ' the table-cloth.' The city lies in an amphitheatre between Table Mountain and the Lion's Rump. the northernmost of the hills of the Cape Peninsula.

In the Cape region the colonists had encountered the Hottentots, a friendly, easy-going race of blacks, many of whom were soon enslaved. But as they reached farther into the interior they came upon natives of an entirely different spirit. In the western part of the great plateau lived the Bushmen, a race of dwarfs, shrewd and freedom-loving. The colonists ill-treated these little people, and many white men died from their poisoned arrows. The Bushmen were hunted down, but they refused to make peace, and today scattered remnants of them live in remote parts.

Towards the east coast were the Kaffirs, giants in stature, strong, intelligent, and well organized. Once aroused to the fact that the white men were trying to seize their territory, these Kaffirs hurled themselves upon the intruders with their great assegai spears and fought with a courage and ferocity never surpassed among savages.

Meanwhile the Napoleonic wars in Europe had made Great Britain and Holland enemies, and the British seized Cape Colony in 1795, returned it to the Dutch in 1803, but took it back again in 1806. Finally, in 1814, Holland, for the sum of £6,000,000, surrendered all claim upon Cape Colony.

There were at that time in the Cape region about 27,000 " Boer " settlers, as the colonists of Dutch descent were called from the Dutch word for "farmer." Most of them strongly objected to their new rulers. Great Britain, in 1820, settled 4,000 of her own citizens in the colony, and British missionaries interfered with the harsh treatment of the natives by the Boers. In 1834 slavery was abolished by the British Parliament, and bitter resentment at this loss to their prosperity spread among the Boers.

South African Railways

THE 'GREAT HOLE' AT KIMBERLEY

Formerly the most extensive open diamond mine in the world, the ' Great Hole ' at Kimberley, Cape Province, is almost a mile in circumference and a quarter of a mile deep. Mining has been discontinued there since 1909, owing to the sides falling in.

In 1836 began the " Great Trek," when 7,000 Boers emigrated from Cape Colony into the great plains beyond the Orange river, and across into

JOHANNESBURG : CENTRE OF THE GOLD-MINING INDUSTRY

The largest city of Transvaal Province and of the South African Union, Johannesburg is situated on the world's most extensive goldfields. Founded in 1886, the city contains some fine buildings, but the mining quarter (above) looks much like any other mining town. Johannesburg is the main centre of the diamond cutting industry outside the Netherlands.

A KRAAL AND RURAL INDUSTRIES IN SOUTH AFRICA

South African Railways

The beehive-shaped huts of a Zulu village or kraal (top) are grouped around a central open space, into which the tribe's cattle are herded at night to protect them from wild beasts. Ostriches (centre photograph) are still bred on farms, where the birds are given a free run over a large expanse of open ground. The feathers, of which the white plumes of the male are the most valuable, are cut two inches from the socket in such a way that birds feel no pain during the operation. The lower photograph shows a citrus plantation in the province of Natal; the Union of South Africa exports large quantities of fruit, including oranges, peaches, plums, grape fruit and grapes.

Natal, and beyond the Vaal river. There these farmers and cattle-raisers set up independent republics, the Orange Free State and the Transvaal. In Natal they failed, for this province had been colonized some years before by the British, and it was officially declared a colony of Great Britain in 1843.

After recognizing the independence of the Transvaal in 1852 the British attempted to annex it in 1877, partly on the ground of internal anarchy and the danger from the formidable military power of the Zulu chief Cetawayo (1836–84), and partly to forward the federation of all South Africa into one British dominion. Three years later the Boers took up arms. On February 27, 1881, they defeated the British forces at Majuba Hill, killing the general in command. Thereupon Gladstone (1809–98), who had become Prime Minister, withdrew the British claims to the Transvaal, and the Boers regained self-government under British suzerainty. The British, in 1879, had fought and conquered King Cetawayo and his trained army of 40,000 Zulus. The conflict shook the foundations of British rule in South Africa, but in the end the British were victorious and the Zulu military system was broken up.

In 1869 the Kimberley diamond-fields were discovered on the western border of the Orange Free State, and in 1886 came the discovery of the goldfields of the Witwatersrand in the Transvaal, the richest and most productive goldfield in the world. There was a frantic rush to these regions by adventurers, gamblers, promoters, young men seeking their fortunes and older men looking for serious investments.

Thriving industrial centres suddenly grew up in the midst of the wilderness at Kimberley, Johannesburg (*q.v.*) and other places. Their population increased rapidly, and South Africa saw the spectacle of these energetic progressive settlements of "uitlanders" (foreigners) surrounded on all sides by the old-fashioned primitive Boers, who were opposed to change and asked only to be allowed to continue their free life of patriarchal simplicity on the open veld. Meanwhile, the commanding figure of Cecil Rhodes (1853–1902) appeared in South African politics (*see* Rhodes, Cecil) with his dream of a great empire under British rule extending northward into Central Africa. The Boers, however, under Paul Kruger (1825–1904), President of the Transvaal, organized anti-British sentiment into the "Afrikander Bond"—Afrikander, or Afrikaner, being the term applied to whites of Dutch descent born in South Africa.

Rhodes, who had already established British authority over that vast central portion of South Africa north-west of the Transvaal known as Bechuanaland, now organized the British South Africa Company, which took over Mashonaland in 1890 and conquered Matabeleland, taking it from the native chiefs in 1893. These regions today lie in Southern Rhodesia, between the Limpopo and Zambezi rivers. The Boers were thus hemmed in.

South African Railways

THE HOME OF CECIL RHODES

Groote Schuur, his home at Rondebosch, near Cape Town, was left by the British statesman, Cecil Rhodes (1853–1902) in trust to be the official residence of the Prime Minister of the Union of South Africa, although the Union was not established until eight years after his death.

The non-Boers on the "Rand" (as the Witwatersrand is popularly called) complained that the laws of the Transvaal Boers discriminated against them in many ways and made it virtually impossible for any foreigner to obtain any voice in affairs. Then Joseph Chamberlain (1836–1914) became British Colonial Secretary, and aided by Rhodes he supported the British claims to participate in the Government.

In 1895 Dr. L. S. Jameson (an officer of the British South Africa Company and an associate of Rhodes) organized a force of some 500 men to invade the Transvaal simultaneously with a rising of Uitlanders in Johannesburg. The raid was unsuccessful, but the wave of resentment which it aroused eventually led the Transvaal and the Orange Free State to take up arms against Britain. Hostilities broke out in October 1899, and only after two and a half years of hard fighting were the British victorious. (*See* Boer War).

Out of this conflict there came a period of reconstruction and the gradual growth of friendly feeling between the British and the Boers. This resulted in the granting of self-government to the Boers in 1906; and in 1910 the Union of South Africa was formed, which included the Provinces of the Cape of Good Hope, Natal, the Transvaal and the Orange Free State. The Union was given self-governing powers under a Governor-General appointed by the British Sovereign.

In the First World War (1914–18) South African troops gave valuable help in clearing the Germans out of their colonies in Africa, and afterwards the Union was given a mandate over South-West Africa, which had formerly been one of Germany's colonial possessions.

In the Second World War (1939–45) the Union of South Africa sent its troops to aid the Allies in East and North Africa and in Italy; nearly 400,000 South Africans (all of them volunteers) served in the armed forces.

From 1910 to 1948 the Union Government was in the hands of three generals who had fought against Great Britain in the Boer War—Louis Botha (1862–1919), J. B. M. Hertzog (1866–1942), and J. C. Smuts (1870–1950). The attitude of those successive Governments was friendly towards Great Britain, and the relations between the two countries continued to be close. At a General Election held in 1948, however, the Smuts Government was defeated, and the Nationalist-Afrikaner Party, led by D. F. Malan (born 1874), a former minister of the Dutch Church, took office. The Malan Government was less inclined to maintain close relations with Great Britain and tended to make South Africa more independent and self-supporting.

The population of South Africa is 11,418,350, about one-fourth being white. The capital of the Union is Pretoria, but the Parliament meets at Cape Town. The capitals of the four provinces are Cape Town (Cape of Good Hope), Pietermaritzburg (Natal), Pretoria (Transvaal), and Bloemfontein (Orange Free State). English and Afrikaans (q.v.) are both official languages, but the common law is the Roman-Dutch law of the Boers. (See also South-West Africa and separate articles on the Provinces and the chief cities.)

South African Literature.

The Literary compositions of South Africa are comprised under two heads—those written in English and those written in Afrikaans. With regard to the English section, much that is not strictly by South Africans was written from the early 17th century onwards by travellers, naturalists, explorers, and missionaries. David Livingstone's Missionary Travels and Researches in South Africa (1857) is perhaps the best known.

Of South African writers properly so called, undoubtedly the most noted in fiction is Olive Schreiner (1862–1920). Her Story of an African Farm (1883), brought to England by the author and submitted to the poet and novelist George Meredith (1828–1909), who was then reader to a publishing firm, achieved an immediate success upon publication. This vivid and sensitive study of South African life far exceeded in literary quality any of her later writings.

Later popular novelists included Gertrude Page, who died in 1922, and whose novels dealt chiefly with farm life in Rhodesia. Sarah Gertrude Millin's God's Stepchildren (1924) portrays for Europeans the inevitable problems created by the contact of white races with coloured. Her biography of General Smuts (1936) was notable, and she wrote also a life of the South African pioneer Cecil Rhodes.

South Africa figures prominently in some of the best-known novels of Sir Rider Haggard (1856–1925). It was from his sojourn in that country that the impulse came to him to compose his Zulu stories, tales such as King Solomon's Mines (1885),

Jess (1887), and Nada the Lily (1892). His masterpiece She (1887) also has an African setting.

Pauline Smith displayed sympathy and sincerity. She published a volume of short stories under the title of The Little Karoo (1925), and also to her name are The Beadle (1927) and Platkops Children (1935). William Plomer (born 1903), who lived as a young man in Zululand, published a vivid study of South African life in I Speak of Africa (1927). Many of his stories and poems have an African setting.

A well-known book of the 1920s was The Life and Works of Alfred Aloysius Horn (Trader Horn) edited for this hardy and whimsical " old-timer " of South Africa's wilds by Ethelreda Lewis (1927). Another vivid study is Turning Wheels (1937), Stuart Cloete's first novel of Boer life, which became a best-seller in the United States and Britain. His later works included Congo Song (1943) and The Third Way (1946).

Vivid Portrayals of Desert and Veld

The father of South African poetry was Thomas Pringle (1789–1834). His poem Afar in the Desert (1828) was considered by Samuel Coleridge to be one of the three or four most perfect lyrics in the English language. Pringle's love of Nature, his passion for freedom, and his full understanding of the spirit of the South African native mind, vividly shine in poems such as those entitled The Lion Hunt, and The Bechuana Boy.

Of younger poets Roy Campbell (born 1901) has a strong sense of literary colour, almost primitive vitality, and a faculty of self-criticism and objectivity. He achieved fame with The Flaming Terrapin (1924) ; then followed, among other volumes, Adamastor (1930) and The Georgiad (1931). Other poems of his, portraying the veld and its untamed life, are The Zebras, and A Veldt Eclogue: the Pioneers. An outstanding later work was Talking Broncho. The Centenary Book of South African Verse (1925) edited by F. C. Slater, contains the poems of 68 writers.

There is a sense in which Rudyard Kipling (1865–1936) has been regarded as one of the foremost English poets of South Africa, for he spent much time in the country and knew it well, and his feeling for South Africa was revealed in his poems of life there.

Noteworthy for its profundity and world-wide reputation as a contribution to modern philosophy is the Holism and Evolution (1926) of General Smuts (q.v.), one of South Africa's most prominent figures. In the field of autobiographical adventure Trekking On (1936), Commando, and No Outspan, by Deneys Reitz (1882–1944), were notable examples.

In Afrikaans, South African literature received its special impetus after the Boer War (1899–1902). Before this, the Afrikaner poetry of F. W. Reitz was highly praised by Kipling. Then came a new generation of poets, some of outstanding merit in the lyric style: Jan Celliers (Die Vlakte, 1906); Totius (By Die Monument, 1908); Louis Leipoldt (Oom Gert Vertel en Ander Gedigte, 1911); C. J. Langenhoven; and A. G. Vissen. Langenhoven (1873–1932) whose initiative later led to the recognition of Afrikaans as an official language by the Union Government in 1918, is also one of the foremost novelists and prose writers, with a wide appeal among the Afrikaans-reading public. Another

IMPRESSIVE SCENIC WONDERS OF SOUTH AFRICA

South African Railways

Off the steep and rocky headland of Cape Point (upper), which is 850 feet high and not far from the naval port of Simon's Town in Cape Province, two oceans—the Atlantic and the Indian—meet. The promontory is part of a national park, to be preserved as an open space for all time. Near Howick in Natal are the falls of the Great Umgeni river (lower), over a precipice 364 feet high. When swollen by rain this is one of the most imposing waterfalls in the world. Though a hydro-electric power plant is operated by the Falls their beauty remains unspoilt.

well-known prose writer is A. A. Pienaar, whose Uit Oerwoud en Vlakte, published under the pseudonym of Sangiro, is a sensitive piece of work on the tragedy of animal life in Africa's forests. It appeared in English as The Adventures of a Lion Family. In addition to Langenhoven, amongst novelists and short story writers are J. H. H. der Waal (born 1871) and D. F. Malherbe (born 1881) both with established reputations.

Also to the high credit of Afrikaans authorship is that semi-scientific, highly original story, The Soul of a White Ant, by Eugene Marais (1872–1936). It was translated into English by Winifred de Kok and most of the critics paid tribute to the genius of its author, who was a voluminous contributor to Land and Volk for many years. His poem, Winter Nag, is described by his son as the herald of the new Afrikaans movement.

SOUTHERN HALF *of the* NEW WORLD

Continent of mighty rivers, vast forests and far-stretching plains, South America can boast of almost unlimited natural resources; and yet the development of this immense area has scarcely begun.

South America. Shaped like a huge triangle, this continent tapers to a point at the south and spreads out wide in the north, in the tropics, where four-fifths of its whole area lies. It is traversed by a mountain chain from north to south near the western coast—the Andes. This is the highest mountain mass on the globe, with the exception of the Himalayas; and Mount Aconcagua, on the boundary between Chile and Argentina, is the highest peak in the Western Hemisphere. Very rich in minerals, the Andes have one big drawback: volcanic eruptions and earthquakes are frequent among them, and sometimes destroy whole cities.

On the eastern side of the continent are the Brazilian highlands; and between the western and eastern ranges is a vast plain, drained by the River Amazon (*q.v.*). The valley of the Amazon in the tropics is mostly an unexplored jungle covered with forests of valuable woods. The Amazon basin once supplied nearly all the world's rubber, but this industry is now of small importance there.

Large parts of South America, though lying in the torrid zone, are so cold that little will grow there, for it is height above sea-level, rather than nearness to the Equator, that determines their temperature. Some regions in the heart of the tropics are so high that the mountains are covered with snow. The temperate regions lie farther south. Enormous quantities of wheat and other grains are grown on farms in Argentina, and herds of cattle, sheep and horses roam the treeless plains or "pampas." There the seasons of the Northern Hemisphere are reversed because, owing to the tipping of the earth's axis, the South Pole points to the sun when the North Pole is turned from it. The heavens are also different: the North Star, which is visible in northern latitudes, is not seen below the Equator, while the Southern Cross is a beautiful constellation that people in the north never witness.

At the southern end of South America is a bleak and sparsely inhabited region known as Patagonia, with large sheep farms. Between Patagonia and Tierra del Fuego is the Strait of Magellan, the route taken by most steamers going round the continent. The main island of Tierra del Fuego is the largest island near the continent, and, in fact, the only one of any importance, except Trinidad (one of the West Indies), north of Venezuela, and the group of Falkland Islands, about 300 miles east of Magellan Strait, both of which belong to Britain.

South America has a remarkably regular coastline except in southern Chile where the coast reminds one of the fiords of Norway. The lack of good harbours is a disadvantage to commerce, making it necessary in some places for ships to load and unload some distance from the shore by means of lighters. This lack of harbours is partly compensated for by the river systems, which are navigable for thousands of miles. There is, moreover, no finer harbour in the world than that of Rio de Janeiro, on the Atlantic coast.

Belem, formerly known as Pará, in northern Brazil, exported quantities of wild rubber before rubber plantations were established in Malaya. At São Salvador or Bahia, on the east coast, the chief exports are tobacco, cacao and sugar; and from Santos, just south of Rio de Janeiro, huge amounts of coffee are sent abroad. From Punta Arenas, in Chilean Patagonia, boats take cargoes of wool. Travelling up the coast of Chile you see ships waiting for cargoes of nitrate, to be used as fertilizer, and in the manufacture of explosives and iodine. From Peru come copper, oil, cotton and sugar; and from Ecuador are exported thousands of tons of cacao (from which chocolate and cocoa are made), and nuts and timber.

Of all the South American cities, only Buenos Aires, Rio de Janeiro, São Paulo, Montevideo and Valparaiso have much manufacturing. Industrial development has been hampered by the lack of conveniently situated supplies of iron ore and by the poor quality of the coal.

No section of the world holds greater opportunities for the future than South America. Its vast agricultural areas are but awaiting development. Transport, too, is backward. Most of the

---

Extent.—About 7,310,800 sq. m. Pop. about 90 millions.

Natural Features.—Mountains: Andes, lower coastal mountains of Brazilian and Guiana highlands. Highest peak, Aconcagua, 23,081 feet. Largest rivers: Amazon, Paraguay-Paraná, São Francisco, Orinoco. Largest lake, Titicaca: estimates vary upwards from about 3,200 sq. m.

Principal Products.—Sugar-cane, cotton, coffee, tobacco, wheat, cacao, nuts; gold, silver, nitrate, copper, oil, tin, diamonds; wool, meat and hides.

Political Divisions.—Republics: Argentina (capital, Buenos Aires), Bolivia (Sucre and La Paz), Brazil (Rio de Janeiro), Chile (Santiago), Colombia (Bogotá), Ecuador (Quito), Paraguay (Asunción), Peru (Lima), Uruguay (Montevideo), Venezuela (Carácas). Colonies: British Guiana (Georgetown), Dutch Guiana (Paramaribo), French Guiana (Cayenne).

SOME SOURCES OF WEALTH IN SOUTH AMERICA

Top left and bottom, E.N.A.

The southern half of the New World contains immense natural resources mostly undeveloped, largely owing to lack of transport. Among the products are Brazil nuts, which are obtained not only in the country of that name but also in the Guianas and Venezuela. Before being washed and sorted for export the rough-shelled triangular nuts have to be removed from the thick woody casing (top left). Brazil is one of the principal sources of the diamonds used in industry; they are found in the beds of streams near Diamantina in the State of Minas Geraes, and the photograph at top right shows workers 'diamond washing' there. Lower, chilled beef is being loaded on a steamer at Ensenada, the port of La Plata in Argentina, whence immense quantities of meat are sent abroad.

people who live in the mountains travel on foot or by mule, and goods are carried by llamas. Of recent years, however, transportation has improved considerably, and every country has at least one railway. Railways cross the Andes at three points, connecting Argentina with Chile and Bolivia. Improvement in transport and communication with North America has helped in the development of South America's resources. The Panama Canal brought the riches of the west coast thousands of miles nearer to the markets of eastern America and Europe. The aeroplane has shortened to hours or days former journeys of weeks or months over mountains, through steaming forests, or across pathless plains. International air services connect all the republics with the United States and Europe; Buenos Aires can be reached in four days from the United States, whereas the journey of almost 6,000 miles by sea takes nearly three weeks.

South America abounds in minerals. Most of them are found in the Andes, along the entire western coast, though many occur in the Brazilian plateau. Since the arrival of the Spaniards in the 16th century an enormous amount of silver has been taken from the mines of South America, and this is still one of the most abundant of the metals in the Andes. Gold, too, is found in several places, although not in large quantities. Copper abounds in Bolivia, Peru, and Chile. The three Guianas supply gold, diamonds and aluminium ore.

The nitrate deposits in northern Chile long supplied practically all the world with fertilizer, nitric acid, and iodine. Colombia furnishes most of the world's emeralds and much platinum. Diamonds, manganese and thorium are found in Brazil; tin, nickel, bismuth, and borax are mined in Bolivia; and vanadium and wolframite in Peru. The asphalt lakes of Trinidad and Bermudez, in Venezuela, are unparalleled. There are also vast deposits of petroleum, Venezuela, Colombia and Peru being the chief producers. The present mineral output of South America, however, gives only a hint of her future productivity.

The population of South America is a mixture of European (mainly Spanish and Portuguese), African and native Indian elements. People of pure European ancestry are not in the majority, yet European influence and character are predominant, and a civilization of a decidedly Spanish type, modified by local conditions, has evolved. Most of the people are of mixed Indian and white blood and are called mestizos (half-breeds); but in Brazil there is a larger admixture of African blood than in any of the other States. Spanish is the universal language except in Brazil, where Portuguese is spoken.

The Indians of South America can be divided into those of the tropical forests; the hunting Indians of the plains and forests of the temperate zone; the primitive fisherfolk of the far south; and the highland Indians of the Andes. In the tropical forests of the Amazon, Orinoco and the northern coast, the Indians build houses along the river banks on the highest land they can find, to avoid floods. For food the men catch fish, snare turtles and hunt game. A number of tribes practise a primitive agriculture, growing yams, maize, and cassava (from the roots of which last tapioca is prepared).

The Indians of the plains have almost disappeared, and the remnants of the tribes now lead a settled life in villages. The most warlike of the plains Indians were the Araucanians from the cool forests of southern

Dorien Leigh

A DISTANT GLIMPSE OF THE ANDES

The volcanic range of the Andes varies in character from snow-capped masses to wooded alpine country and barren plateaux. Aconcagua is the highest peak (extreme left background) and is on the frontier between Argentina and Chile. In the foreground are weird-looking cactus plants which flourish in desert land and grow to a height of forty or fifty feet.

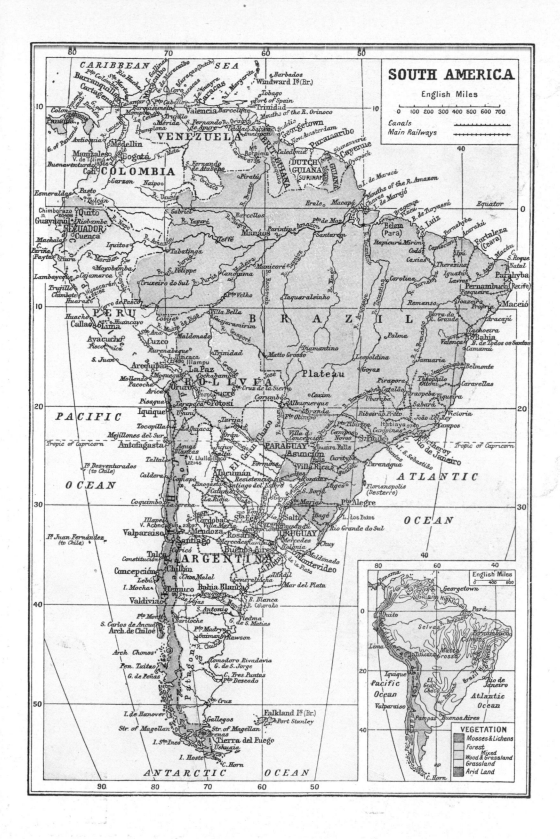

SOUTH AMERICA

English Miles

FACTS YOU SHOULD KNOW ABOUT SOUTH AMERICA

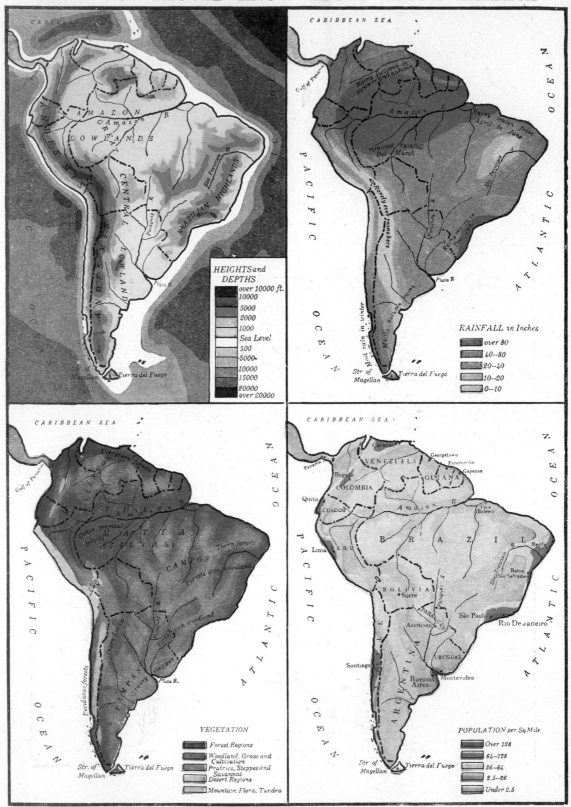

Nature seems to have followed, in a measure, the same pattern in building both North and South America. On the west are the young rugged mountains, in the east the old worn-down ranges, with plateaux and lowlands between. Notice how the densest vegetation occurs in the regions of heavy rainfall, and how the most thickly-peopled districts are scattered on or near the eastern and western coasts, while enormous areas are very sparsely populated.

To face page 3025

F. W. Bond; W. S. Berridge; The Times

SOUTH AMERICAN ODDITIES

At the top left is a toucan. Above, a family of peccaries, members of the pig tribe. Lower left, a white rhea, an ostrich-like bird found only in South America. Below, a tree boa which squeezes its prey to death.

Chile, who were never conquered by the Spaniards or the Chileans. Formerly they lived by hunting and fishing, but now they breed livestock and grow cereals and vegetables.

In the extreme south on the Strait of Magellan and near-by islands live the surviving members of the Yahgan and Ona Indians, but these tribes have almost disappeared. These people lived in the most primitive fashion; for shelter in that cold, wet region they had mere windbreaks of branches covered with guanaco (species of llama) hides, and their only garment was a fur cloak. Their food was guanaco flesh, fish, berries and fungi.

In contrast to these primitive folk were the Indians of the Andes; chief of these were the Incas (*q.v.*). In a number of ways these people were as civilized as the early Egyptians and excelled in building with stone without the use of cement. Most of the Indians of Peru and Bolivia are descendants of the Incas, but they do not display the same high level of intelligence. Except in remote regions of the continent, much of which is almost unknown to white men, the Indians perform all the manual labour for the half-breeds and white population.

The mainland of South America was discovered by Columbus in 1498. The rumour in Mexico of a rich empire to the south aroused the ambition of the Spaniards, and caused Francisco Pizarro (*q.v.*) to invade Peru with a few followers in 1532. There he discovered the Incas. Finding the kingdom in the throes of a civil war, the Spaniards had little difficulty in conquering it.

With the exception of Brazil, which was a Portuguese possession, the greater part of South America was under the rule of Spain from the 16th to the 19th century. In 1810 the Spanish colonies began their struggles for independence. The enthusiasm of Simon Bolivar (1783–1830) and the heroism of José de San Martin (1778–1850) helped to bring them to a successful conclusion by 1826. Brazil, which had severed its connexion with Portugal in 1822, remained an independent monarchy until a revolution in 1889 made it a republic. Thus were born 10 republican States—Argentina, Bolivia, Brazil, Colombia, Ecuador, Chile, Paraguay, Peru, Uruguay and Venezuela. The Guianas are now the only places on the mainland remaining under European control.

Though the South American republics have used the United States government as a model, their institutions have not worked with the smoothness found in the northern nation. Dictatorships and revolutions have frequently occurred. There is no educated middle class in most of these countries to provide a steadying weight of public opinion, and the politicians of the upper class have often been

VARIED TYPES OF SOUTH AMERICAN RACES

1. Most of the people of Chile are half-breeds, of mixed Spanish and Indian blood; this is the family of a prosperous farmer. 2. An Indian flower-seller of Caracas, the capital of Venezuela. 3. The Chuncho Indians, a forest tribe of Brazil, paint their faces; the chief is scraping some pigment from his finger. 4. The gauchos (cowboys) of Argentina wear massive silver belts with their gala attire. 5. A peculiar headdress is worn by the Aymara Indians of the Bolivian highlands, flaps protecting the ears from the biting winds. 6. Indian women of Peru carry their babies in a shawl on their backs. 7. Cigars produced in Paraguay are made by women—who smoke them, too.

able to exploit the government and the ignorant Indian peasants for their own profit. Hence it has frequently happened that a dictator and his party have ruled a nation until they were forced out of power by revolution.

In international affairs South American countries have shown a tendency to submit their disputes to arbitration. They were among the first to join the League of Nations and later the United Nations. Closer relations between the South American countries and other nations of the Western Hemisphere are promoted by the work of the Pan-American Union (official organization of the 21 republics of the Western Hemisphere for the development of closer co-operation among these nations), which was established at Washington in 1890, and arranges for Pan-American Conferences to be held every five years.

South American Literature.

Spanish is the predominating language of South America, and when people speak of South American literature Spanish-American is generally implied. This had its origin about 400 years ago in the letters and reports of the conquest of Spanish America sent back to Spain and Portugal by both missionaries and by the " conquistadores," as the early conquerors of the land were termed.

By the end of the 16th century Mexico and the Peruvian city of Lima had become centres of intellectual activity, and an epic poem by the Chilean Pedro de Oña (born 1571), entitled Arauco domado, was published at Lima in 1596. The 17th century was notable for the plays of the Mexican Juan Ruiz de Alarcon (c. 1581–1639), and the mystical poetry of Sor Juana Ines de la Cruz (1651–95). Little of outstanding importance was produced during the 18th century, but it is interesting to note that the El periquillo sarniento of José Joaquin de Lizardi (1774–1827) is considered the first authentic American novel.

The numerous revolutions of the early part of the 19th century produced a flood of patriotic verse, such as La Victoria de Junin (1825), by José Joaquin Olmedo (1780–1847), and the Himno del desterrado, of the Cuban José Maria Heredia (1803–39). Once the revolutionary period had passed, the poets, detesting all things Spanish, turned their attention to native themes. Towards the latter half of the century the " Gaucho (cowboy) poetry " made its appearance in the Argentine, and the life of the gaucho became valuable literary material.

With more recent times two forces have modified the course of Spanish-American literature. One is the " modernista " movement, seeking to enrich poetry; and the other " Americanismo " or " Criollismo," which deals with nationalism. Its prophet was the Uruguayan José Enrique Rodó (1872–1917), known as the " Latin Emerson."

Among modern South American writers the best known included the Nicaraguan Rubén Darío (1867–1916), poet in the classic tradition and a critic whose worth is acknowledged by the entire Spanish world. Gabriele Mistral (born 1889), a Chilean poet and educationist, established her reputation with Desolación in 1922. Much of her early work, such as La Voz de Elqui (1908), was widely read in South America. Later volumes included Nubes Blancas (1923) and Tala (1938). She was awarded the Nobel prize for literature in 1945. Some of her poetry showed an affinity with Buddhist thought. Other noted writers are Florencio Sanchez (1875–1910), the Argentine dramatist; and the novelists Gonzalo Febres, Carlos Reyles, Martin Aldao, and Manuel Galvaz.

Southampton.

At the head of Southampton Water, with the Isle of Wight sheltering it from the open English Channel, the town of Southampton in Hampshire is primarily concerned with the trade of the British Commonwealth and passenger shipping to North America. From its

The Times

SOUTHAMPTON: ENGLAND'S GATEWAY IN THE SOUTH

At the head of Southampton Water, seventy-nine miles south-west of London, Southampton is one of Britain's busiest and most progressive ports. Some of its docks are seen in this photograph. Primarily concerned with passenger traffic to and from North America and with the trade of the British Commonwealth, the port is also one of the largest oil storage centres in the United Kingdom. Its numerous industries include engineering and flour-milling.

vast acreage of docks, which can accommodate the largest liners, much of Great Britain's import trade travels by railway 79 miles north-east to London; and exports—especially textiles and hardware—start on their journey to foreign markets. Southampton is also an airline terminus and a flying-boat base.

The town lies on a peninsula between the Rivers Itchen and Test. The district was occupied in the Stone Age, and in ancient Roman days the settlement of Clausentum (a link in Roman communications with the Continent) was not far away. It was, however, probably after the Danish invasions of the 11th century that the site of the present town was first developed. The Bar Gate (erected just after the Norman Conquest of 1066) is the most noteworthy part remaining of the ancient walls. In Southampton, too, is the world's oldest bowling-green, dating from 1299. The pride of the modern town is the Civic Centre, including town hall, art gallery and library.

The natural harbour is one of the finest in the kingdom, and has the unusual advantage of a double tide, caused by the tidewater reaching the port by two routes, on either side of the Isle of Wight. Under an extension scheme, carried out during 1927-34, more than 400 acres of land to the west of the original docks were reclaimed and added to the available dock and industrial area. In 1933 King George V opened at Southampton the largest dry dock in the world. During the Second World War (1939-45) the port was one of the main embarkation spots from which British and Allied soldiers went to the Continent. Here, also, some of the components of Mulberry Harbours (q.v.) were built and assembled. German aircraft repeatedly bombed the port and town, over 1,000 air-raid warnings being given in Southampton between 1940 and 1945; and considerable damage was done. The population of the town is 170,000.

South Australia.

The greater part of this State, forming the southern central section of the Australian Commonwealth and bordering all the other States except Tasmania, is waterless desert, but in the north-east is the extraordinary underground waterway system of "Lakes" Eyre, Frome, and Torrens, which are almost dried-up salt beds well below sea-level; while in the south-east are grazing lands and the lower reaches of the Murray.

Adelaide (q.v.), the capital of the State, lies between the Gulf of St. Vincent and the sea and Mount Lofty (2,234 feet). From the shores of Spencer Gulf, the principal inlet, which is situated farther west, can be seen the peaks of the main Flinders Range and the Hummocks. Profitable settlement is possible only over a small proportion of the State, but the farmers of South Australia are proud of the quality and quantity of their crops, while fruit growing and flour milling are on the increase. Sheep-farming, for both wool and mutton, is the occupation of a large proportion of South Australians. The vineyards in the Adelaide district are famous, providing a flourishing wine industry. Copper and iron are two of the minerals exported. Uranium (q.v.) has been found.

South Australia was founded as a British colony in 1836, when Capt. Hindmarsh, R.N., the first Governor, landed near the site of Adelaide. Matthew Flinders (1774-1814), explorer and navigator, had surveyed the coast 34 years previously. The desert Northern Territory, occupying that part of the continent to the north of South Australia, was at one time under the control of that State, but it was officially handed over to the Commonwealth Government in 1911. The State has a Parliament of two houses, and is administered by a Governor appointed by the Crown and assisted by an Executive Council.

Railways have done much to solve the transport problems of this wide area. The Trans-Continental (East-West) Railway runs westward across the desert to Kalgoorlie (Western Australia) from Port Augusta, on Spencer Gulf, with an extension to near Port Pirie (population 12,750), the second largest town in the State. In addition there is a line running north from Port Augusta to Alice Springs in the Northern Territory ; it is intended to extend this to Port Darwin.

Southey,

ROBERT (1774-1843). To have written some of the finest biographies and some of the most enchanting letters in the English language is no small achievement for any man, though even his main ambition was to win lasting fame as a poet.

Southey's Life of Nelson is regarded as a model of what a short biography should be, and the same is true of his life of Wesley. But of his poems few are now remembered, with the exception of some of the ballads, such as The Inchcape Rock, The Battle of Blenheim and Lord William.

The son of a linen draper, Southey was born at Bristol on August 12, 1774, and was educated at Westminster School, London, and at Balliol College, Oxford. By 1803 he had decided to earn his living by writing and went to live at Keswick, Cumberland, in order to be near his friend the poet Samuel Taylor Coleridge (1772-1834). In 1813 he was appointed Poet Laureate. Southey's output was prodigious and years of overwork so affected his health that when he died on March 21, 1843, he had been insane for three years.

Extent—380,000 square miles. Population (excluding aborigines) 646,000.

Physical Features.— Featureless desert in north and west. Flinders and other mountain ranges in the east, rising to over 3,000 feet (highest peak Mount Woodroffe, 5,200 ft.), and surrounded by pastoral lowlands. Lakes Eyre (4,000 sq. miles), Torrens, etc., form central drainage system of Australia. Rivers include the Murray.

Principal Products.—Wheat, barley, and other crops ; fruit, wine ; meat, wool ; flour ; copper, iron, gypsum ; dairy produce.

Chief City.—Adelaide (capital) 390,000.

South Pole.

At the centre of the Antarctic Circle, a region lying within a circle drawn at 66 degrees 30 minutes S., is the South Geographical Pole. The South Magnetic Pole does not coincide with the geographical pole, and Sir Douglas Mawson in 1914 established the position of the Magnetic South as Latitude 71 degrees 10 minutes S. ; Longitude 150 degrees 41 minutes E.

For an account of the exploration of the south polar region see Antarctica and Polar Exploration. An explanation of magnetic phenomena and the poles is given in our story of Magnetism. (See also Compass; North Pole).

South-West Africa.

This flat and largely infertile territory covers an area of about 317,725 square miles. It lies between Angola on the north and Cape Province on the south. To the east lies Bechuanaland Protectorate and to the west the Atlantic Ocean; the coastline is 800 miles long. The principal occupations are stock-raising and the mining of diamonds, though small quantities of tobacco, maize and cotton are grown.

The capital of South-West Africa, Windhoek (population about 15,000), is in the centre of the territory, about 180 miles from the sea. Walvis Bay, the chief port, is an integral part of Cape Province in the Union of South Africa, though it is administered as part of South-West Africa.

From 1884, when it was annexed by Germany, until the First World War (1914–18) it was known as German South-West Africa. In 1915 the Germans there surrendered, and from 1919 it was administered by the Union of South Africa under mandate from the League of Nations. In 1925 a constitution, with a parliamentary assembly, was given to the country. In 1946 the Union submitted to the General Assembly of the United Nations a

South African Railways

CAPITAL OF SOUTH-WEST AFRICA

Situated 180 miles inland from the port of Swakopmund, Windhoek is the capital of South-West Africa, a former German colony, which from 1919 has been administered by the Union of South Africa. The town is noted for its medicinal springs. Lead, copper, silver and salt are found near by.

request from the majority of the inhabitants of South-West Africa that the territory should be incorporated in the Union. This request was refused, but from 1947 South-West Africa has sent representatives to the Union Parliament. The population is 352,000, of which about one-tenth are Europeans.

Soya Bean. An annual herb of the family *Leguminosae*, the soya plant (*Glycine soja*) is bushy and two to four feet tall, with branching stems; and the small lilac flowers mature into pods containing from two to five beans. Stems, leaves and pods are covered with stiff reddish hairs. A native of Asia, it has been an important crop in the Far East from very early times, but it is only since the 20th century that western civilization realized the importance of the soya, which is said to have more uses than any other plant.

Like other members of the pea family it puts nitrates back into the soil through the action of bacteria on its roots, and at the same time the entire plant can be used as green fodder or silage. The discovery of the several other possible uses of the soya bean was the work of chemists and food specialists. The beans contain all the vitamins and twice as much protein and fat as beef. They are almost free of starch and sugar, and so can be eaten by people suffering from diabetes. They yield a " milk " more digestible than that of a cow; their other food products include coffee substitutes, macaroni, cheese, flour, sausage filling, lard and butter substitutes, salad and cooking oil. In Asiatic countries, where rice is an important food, the diet is balanced with soya beans, which provide the protein otherwise lacking in a meatless diet.

In industry soya bean oil is taking the place of cottonseed and linseed oils and is used in paints, varnishes, enamels, soaps, linoleum and printing ink. The protein from the bean resembles the casein from cow's milk and is used in the making of paints, paper sizing, glue, and waterproofing for textiles. This protein, combined with formaldehyde, is used in plastics (*q.v.*) and rayon (*q.v.*). The meal or " cake " remaining after the oil has been extracted is an excellent cattle food.

E.N.A

LOADING SOYA BEAN CAKE

On the wharfside at the port of Dairen, Manchuria, being loaded on to junks, are piles of what look like grindstones but are really cakes of compressed soya beans after the oil has been extracted. These cakes make excellent cattle food.

SUNSHINE and SHADOW in SPAIN

A natural and historical link between Europe and North Africa, Spain still bears many traces of six centuries of Moorish occupation. It is a land of striking contrasts, in climate, colour and character.

Spain. It has been said that Europe ends at the Pyrenees and that there Africa begins. Spain, now separated from her colony in Morocco only by the narrow strait of Gibraltar (*q.v.*), was until late geological times united with it. In its formation as well as in its people the Iberian peninsula suggests the northern coast of Africa. Here is the same smooth coastline, the indentations of which, apart from the fiord-like inlets along the Bay of Biscay to the north and round the north-west corner where Spain touches the Atlantic, might almost be numbered on one hand—the bays of Cadiz, Algeciras, Malaga, and the harbours of Barcelona and Cartagena. Spain has a central plain, high, mountainous, and dry, where mule trains plodding across the waste suggest the Sahara ; and there is a fertile rim studded with flourishing cities.

The central table-land, rising to an average height of nearly 2,700 feet, and punctuated by

---

Extent —190,112 square miles ; with Balearic and Canary Islands 194,942 square miles. Population 27,729,000. Colonies (in Africa) 134,700 sq. m. ; pop. 1,494,600.

Physical Features.—Pyrenees and Cantabrian Mountains separating Spain from France ; Sierra de Guadarrama, Sierra de Gredos, Sierra de Gata, Montes de Toledo, Sierra Morena, dividing and bounding the central plateau ; Sierra Nevada to the south (highest point, Mulahacen, about 11,420 feet). Chief rivers the Ter, Llobregat, Ebro, Guadalaviar, Jucar, and Segura, flowing into the Mediterranean ; and the Minho, Douro, Tagus, Guadiana, and Guadalquivir, flowing into the Atlantic Ocean.

Products.—Wheat, barley, other cereals ; cotton, sugar-cane, vegetables, grapes and wine, olives and olive oil, oranges and other fruits, nuts ; silk ; sheep and goats, wool, other live-stock ; sardines, tunny, cod ; coal, lead, iron, copper, mercury, silver, salt ; cotton and woollen goods, paper, corks, glass, sugar, leather goods, tobacco products.

Chief Cities.—Madrid (1,413,690), Barcelona (1,225,318), Valencia (520,213), Seville (375,060), Saragossa (262,042), Malaga (287,080) ; Bilbao, Murcia, Granada, Cordoba, Cartagena (each more than 100,000).

---

sharply-peaked mountain ranges or sierras—occupies over half the actual area of the land. None of the great cities are there, except Madrid (the capital), and a few whose interest is chiefly historic. Toledo, the "hundred-towered" city, on its rock surrounded on three sides by the River Tagus, and on the other by medieval fortifications, presents long lines of palaces and convents terraced around the rocky slope, an army of belfries piercing the sky, and the huge square mass of the Moorish Alcazar on the topmost crest. Although no longer the capital of a kingdom, as it was under the Visigoths from the 5th to the 8th century, Toledo is still the Church capital and seat of the Primate of all Spain. Saragossa, once the capital of the independent kingdom of Aragon, is a flourishing modern city. Like Toledo, it has a Gothic cathedral and a Moorish castle, and a university founded in 1474. Salamanca, on the Tormes, is the oldest and most famous of Spain's university towns, and the one which introduced Arabic learning into Europe. Burgos, at the foot of the mountains to the north, is dominated by a Gothic cathedral, the most elaborate in all Spain, and by romantic memories of that famous 11th century warrior the Cid.

The chief industry of this dreary plateau is represented by the sheep that roam all the summer long in flocks of up to 10,000. The sheep of Spain can be numbered in millions. Scarcely a tree is to be seen in these regions, for ruthless cutting, practised through the centuries, has stripped all but six per cent of the land of the forests

SPAIN WITH ITS NEIGHBOUR, PORTUGAL

MODERN SPANISH PORTS OF CORUNNA AND BILBAO

On the Atlantic coast Corunna, or La Coruña as it is called by the Spaniards, has an extensive harbour (upper) and exports tinned fish, chiefly sardines, and agricultural produce. The capital of the province of Vizcaya (Biscay), Bilbao is on the River Nervion, which is spanned by five bridges, the one in the lower photograph being the Puente de la Merced. The town exports large quantities of iron ore from the neighbouring mines and has iron-foundries.

that once covered it. Windswept, dusty, exposed to extremes of cold and heat, this plateau is one of the most thinly populated regions of Europe.

But the coast regions of Spain tell a different story. There are found numerous large cities and active industries. A traveller crossing the Pyrenees from France on the west—there are now railways at both ends of the mountain range—will come out on the lands bordering the Bay of Biscay, which are the wettest in Europe, just as those on the central plateau are the driest. Here the air is mild all the year round and roses bloom at Christmas as in midsummer. Here is a scene of active coal and iron mining. The three Basque provinces at the foot of the Pyrenees produce more than half the iron that is mined in Spain. And they have other industries—grape-growing for wine, apples for cider, and fishing. The most valuable fish caught is the sardine. The largest fish found around the coasts is the tunny.

The Basques themselves are a mysterious people, about whose origin scholars have long speculated. Their characteristics distinguish them even when they migrate with other Spaniards or Frenchmen to America, and their language differs from neighbouring tongues not only in its words but in the very type of its grammar. Most students believe that the Basques are a remnant of an early race that the Greeks and Romans found in Spain and called Iberians. The Basques in France and Spain today number about 600,000.

Crossing the Pyrenees at their eastern end, the traveller comes upon Barcelona, metropolis of Catalonia, and other densely populated coast towns, where manufacturing, particularly the weaving of cotton and wool, goes on. The Balearic Islands (q.v.) are a centre of the shoe industry.

Farther south on this coast lies what has been called the garden region of Spain, centring in Valencia. The climate is hot and dry, but by means of irrigation channels introduced centuries ago by the Moors the fertile soil is made to yield in tropical luxuriance grains, sugar-cane, oranges, lemons, figs, dates, pomegranates, tomatoes, melons and grapes. Mulberries, too, grow in abundance, making Valencia the chief area of the silk industry.

The southern provinces of Spain, known as Andalusia, form the beautiful region of which poets

sing. Here is the picturesque Moorish city of Granada, the splendid capital of the Moorish province which held out for 200 years after the Moors had been driven from the rest of Spain. It was once a city of 400,000 inhabitants; now it is not much more than one-fourth of that size. Its chief glory is the palace of the Alhambra (q.v.), the most perfect remaining relic of Moorish art. Cordoba, or Cordova, once one of the leading commercial centres of the world, is still famed for its leather and olive oil. Cadiz, said to be the oldest town of continuous existence in Europe, was founded about 1100 Before Christ by the Phoenicians under the name of Gadir. It remained an important city for thousands of years, having its final burst of splendour in the 18th century when it held the monopoly of trade with Spanish America.

The south of Spain is also the country of famous wines, malaga and sherry, although wine is to a great extent an industry of all the 50 Provinces. Even the central plateau in places is irrigated for grape-growing. In these tropical regions there are to be seen lizards sometimes three feet long, and scorpions, and there grow forests of cork oak, the bark of which is one of the country's chief products.

Next to agriculture, mining is the greatest source of Spain's wealth, though not developed to anything like its full extent. Its mountains yield copper, iron, lead, manganese, zinc, antimony, fluorspar, pyrites and potash. Spain has the world's largest and richest deposits of mercury, and its coal and anthracite reserves are vast. The bulk of the mineral production is exported to other countries. Coal, however, is not mined in sufficient quantities to satisfy the domestic requirements, and there are considerable imports of it. Water-power is being developed slowly. Railways are still too few for the needs of the country, and in the remoter parts ox teams and mule trains are often the only means of transport. The leading manufactures are iron and steel, cotton goods, paper, glass, sugar, cork products, and silk.

Spain's industrial backwardness, despite its natural wealth, is due to the character of its surface and its people. The great barrier of the Pyrenees, passable only in a few places, has kept the country from becoming a crossroads of commerce between Africa and the rest of Europe; while its ranges of

E.N.A.

SAN SEBASTIAN'S FRONT

On the Bay of Biscay eleven miles from the French frontier, San Sebastian is one of the most fashionable seaside resorts in Spain. Before the country became a republic, in 1931, the town was the summer residence of the Court.

Neville Hardy

A ·CARMEN' OF MODERN SPAIN

Before it became a tragic battlefield in 1936 Spain was a 'and where the romance of
olden times lingered long and was displayed in many a charming shape; at Granada,
in particular, the spirit of the colourful past was very evident in place and people.
In the picture above we see a gypsy girl of this region dancing an old-time measure.

John Bushby

ROCKY GORGE IN ANDALUSIA

Beneath the Tolox and Estepona hills, Ronda, seen above, lies on a lofty plateau
rent in twain by the awesome chasm of the Guadalevin. Andalusia. a region of
southern Spain, with its lingering sense of the East and its old cities recalling the
Moorish occupation, is plainly different from the rest of the country

To face page 3033

of the British Isles, it has only half as many inhabitants. The country's economic progress has also been greatly retarded by the fact that the people were largely uneducated. Until the 20th century two-thirds of the Spaniards were unable to read, but this proportion is being slowly reduced. Spain has 11 universities—Madrid the largest, Salamanca the oldest, Granada, Seville, Valencia, Santiago, Saragossa, Valladolid, Murcia, Oviedo, and Barcelona.

The pageant of Spain's past is as picturesque and full of contrasts as the country itself. About 1000 B.C. the greatest seamen of the ancient world, the Phoenicians, sought its shores in their small ships for iron and tin. Five hundred years later Carthage colonized the land and held it until Rome's galleys and armies drove out the Carthaginians in 201 B.C. Then came six centuries of Roman colonization and government. The bull fight, Spain's most popular diversion today, is really a survival from the Roman wild beast shows.

With the 5th century A.D. began 300 years of subjection to barbarian conquerors—the Vandals, who gave their name to Andalusia (Vandalusia), the Suevi, and the Visigoths. The Visigothic period (415–711) ends with the battle of Jerez de la Frontera (711), in which Moorish invaders from Africa overthrew the Goths and established a Mahomedan power which lasted for a period of over seven centuries.

The Moorish period represents a stage in the pageant of Spanish history almost richer than the time of the Romans, and the development that the Moors gave the land has persisted to our own day. They cultivated the arid soil of Spain, and the old Roman cities, rebuilt on Arabic lines, began to show palaces and vast mosques with domes and minarets. Fine metal work and silk and leather work as beautiful as any from the

E.N.A.

THE ALCAZAR IN SEVILLE
On the left bank of the Guadalquivir river 54 miles from the Atlantic, Seville contains several structures built by the Moors, among them being the Alcazar (above) which has been the palace of both Moorish and Spanish kings.

east-to-west interior mountains and its largely unnavigable streams have isolated its people into sharply differentiated groups, speaking different dialects and languages. It was not until the 16th century that political unification was accomplished; and even today the differences of customs, sentiment, and economic organization are so marked that Spain is a nation in some respects regionally divided against itself.

Other factors have handicapped Spain— the rigours of the Inquisition (q.v.), which, while primarily religious, stamped out individual initiative; the neglect of trade and industry in the quest of gold for the New World; unwise monetary policies; and the depopulation resulting from long warfare.

Spain is as thinly populated as Ireland: with twice the area

OLD TRANSPORT SERVING MODERN SPAIN
In some respects Spain is still very backward compared with most European countries. Above, in a cobbled street in Corunna, is a bullock-cart of an old type that is still used all over the land. Lack of good roads hinders the introduction of motor transport.

WHERE THE MIDDLE AGES LIVE ON IN SPAIN

H. Felton; E.N.A.

Capital of the province of the same name, Avila (upper) is situated on the Adaja river and is a splendid example of a medieval walled city, with its well-preserved granite walls, 86 towers and nine gateways. Its notable buildings include the Gothic Cathedral and a Moorish castle. In the city of Santiago de Compostela, 32 miles from the port of Corunna, is the Cathedral (lower) containing the shrine of the patron saint of Spain—the apostle Saint James or Sant' Iago. The structure, of early Romanesque architecture, was founded in 1078 on the site of an earlier church destroyed by the Moors in 997. The superb cloisters are considered the finest in Spain. The town, much visited by pilgrims, contains numerous churches and chapels, and was a centre of Christian art in the Middle Ages.

THE OLD AND THE NEW IN SPANISH CITIES

On a hill 2,785 feet high, Burgos is a picturesque old city with a magnificent Gothic Cathedral (upper). The 13th-century edifice contains 44 altars, 60 sculptured tombs and 100 statues (*see also* page 3041). The city trades in agricultural produce, and manufactures leather goods and paper. In Valencia (lower) the business section is modern; the thoroughfare seen is the Avenida de Blasco Ibañez, named after the novelist who died in 1928. The third largest city of Spain, Valencia is a thriving Mediterranean port two and a half miles from the mouth of the Guada-laviar; its exports include rice, fruit, wines, silk and olive oil. According to tradition the first printing press in Spain was established there in 1474. Valencia suffered considerable damage during the Civil War of 1936–39

Dorien Leigh

BLOOD-SPORT PERHAPS DERIVED FROM ROMAN WILD BEAST SHOWS

Bull-fights take place in an arena which is surrounded by a barrier to protect spectators from the bull and over which the fighters can clamber to safety if necessary. A trumpet-call announces the beginning of a contest, and a bull rushes into the ring, where it is confronted by mounted *picadores* (pikemen), with attendant footmen. The *picadores* try to prod the bull with a short-pointed lance ; the footmen may endeavour to distract the beast's attention by waving red cloaks. In the second act, darts are planted in the animal's shoulders by men on foot, called *banderilleros*. Last the bull is attacked by the *espada* (swordsman) or *matador*, who should kill it with a sword thrust between the shoulder blades.

East came out of Spain, and a Toledo sword blade became as desirable as one from Damascus.

Christian kingdoms meantime were formed in the northern mountains and were gradually detaching sections of the Moorish domains. The kingdom of Asturias on the Bay of Biscay, which later expanded into the kingdom of Leon and Castile, was the cradle of Spanish liberty. Soon Aragon, Navarre, and the county of Barcelona (Catalonia), at the foot of the Pyrenees, and Portugal on the Atlantic, arose to join in the battle to free Spain from Mahomedan rule. In the battle of the plains of Tolosa (1212) Castile and Leon broke the Moorish power and drove the Moors into the small kingdom of Granada.

From this period came tales of chivalry. Among these are the songs and stories of the Christian knight the Cid (meaning " the lord "—his real name was Rodrigo Ruy Diaz de Bivar), who in the 11th century was the hero of Spanish romance.

With the marriage in 1469 of Ferdinand of Aragon and Isabella of Castile, most of Spain was united under a single rule. In 1492—the year Columbus gave the New World to the Spanish Crown—came the final expulsion of the Moors from Spain through the conquest of Granada.

Under the grandson of Ferdinand and Isabella, Charles I of Spain—better known as Charles V,

emperor of the remains of the Holy Roman Empire —Spain became mistress of most of the known world. With his son Philip II, self-appointed champion of the Catholic faith, the Inquisition spread its baneful influence over Spain. Moors and Jews were expelled from the country, and Protestants and even Catholic Spaniards suspected of heresy were tortured and burned at the stake, these executions being known as *autos da fé* or acts of faith. At the same time the resources of the kingdom were permanently impaired in the vain attempt to suppress Protestantism in other lands. (*See* Armada, Spanish).

After the time of Philip II Spain steadily declined in power. The War of the Spanish Succession (1701–14) cost it most of its outlying possessions in Europe and seated a French prince on its throne. From 1714 to the outbreak of the French Revolution Spain was little more than a satellite of France. In 1808 Napoleon placed his brother Joseph on the throne of Spain, and the outraged Spaniards revolted. Aided by the British, they freed the country from Bonaparte rule in the Peninsular War (1808–14). At the same time a liberal con-stitution was adopted (1812), but Ferdinand VII withdrew it when he returned to the throne in 1814. By the end of his reign—he died in 1833— Spain had lost all its vast empire in the New World except Cuba and Porto Rico, and these were lost in the Spanish-American War of 1898.

As the old absolutist Spain decayed, a new and more liberal Spain was emerging. Conflicts between liberals and reactionaries brought alternate periods of revolutionary movement and constitutional government. From 1873 to 1875 Spain was a republic, but in 1875 the monarchy was restored. In 1876 a new constitution was adopted. A powerful military organization was saddled upon the people, and Church control was strongly entrenched. Both the Army and the Roman Catholic Church were staunch supporters of the monarchy.

During the First World War (1914–18) Spain remained neutral, but there was widespread unrest. Violent strikes paralysed industry; a movement for the independence of Catalonia threatened to disrupt the kingdom. Uprisings of the Riff tribesmen in Spanish Morocco seemed likely to drive the Spanish from northern Africa.

General Primo de Rivera, following the example of Mussolini (q.v.) in Italy, seized power in 1923, suspended the constitution, suppressed political parties, and set up a form of dictatorship. With French aid he put down the Moroccan revolt. He made strikes illegal, helped to found new industries, built new highways, and attempted other reforms. For a time conditions improved. But the renewed and world-wide trade depression after 1929 brought fresh troubles to Spain. Primo de Rivera attempted to reform the inefficient Spanish Army, thus losing its support and that of the King. He resigned in 1929, dying in 1930.

Opposition to the dictatorship now turned into opposition to the monarchy. Republican parties won an overwhelming victory in the municipal elections of 1931. King Alfonso XIII fled, and Spain became a republic.

Now had to be devised effective methods of modernizing a country which had fallen far behind in the march of progress. Most difficult were the problems of the farmers. Three-quarters of the Spanish people got their living directly from agriculture. Yet Spanish farming methods had changed little since the Middle Ages.

The almost medieval nature of Spanish land-ownership was a great obstacle to the improvement of farming methods. In the south, huge estates were owned by wealthy families who lived in Madrid or abroad and took no interest in their

R. Gorbold; E.N.A.; Dorien Leigh

SPANISH PEOPLE GRAVE AND GAY

Much of the soil of Spain is poor, and peasants are prematurely aged (top left) by the toil involved in wresting a living from such land. The mantilla, a headdress of black silk lace (top right), is worn by the women when going to church. Dancing is exceedingly popular, particularly in Andalusia ; and in Seville it is not unusual to encounter groups (lower) performing in the street to the sound of castanets and guitars.

E.N.A.

SEGOVIA CATHEDRAL : ONE OF SPAIN'S GOTHIC FANES

Built upon a narrow ridge of rock in the valley of the Eresma river in central Spain is the ancient city of Segovia, of which the outstanding landmark is the Gothic Cathedral. Founded in 1521 and completed in 1577, the edifice con-tains some fine stained glass windows. Another relic of the past is a magnificent aqueduct, dating from the time of the Roman Emperor Trajan (c. A.D. 56–117), which is still in use and brings water from the Rio Frio, ten miles away.

land. In the north and north-west, the land was divided into such small holdings that the farmer could not gain a living for his family and was unable to improve his methods. Furthermore, the ordinary Spaniard, son of a hot sultry climate, had never been noted either for his energy or for his industry.

As its first step in attacking its difficult problems, the young Republic adopted a new Constitution, drawn up by Spanish legal and other experts who had studied the governments of other nations. This constitution provided for a single House of Parliament, the *Cortes* ; a President elected every six years and subject to removal by the Cortes, and a Cabinet under a Premier who was responsible to the Cortes and could be removed by it. It gave

the vote to everyone over 23, provided for the separation of Church and State, made education for all free and compulsory, and guaranteed freedom of speech, of religion, and of the Press. It renounced war as an instrument of national policy, and it promised to establish government by " workers of all classes."

But dissatisfaction and unrest continued to grow, and two new parties came into prominence: the Fascists led by José Primo de Rivera, nephew of the former dictator; and the Catholic Action party led by José María Gil Robles. When Gil Robles was admitted to the Cabinet, workers in the north feared that he would seize power as Hitler had done in Germany, and therefore revolted. Moorish troops brought over from Africa suppressed the revolt with much cruelty, especially against the miners in Asturias. More than 25,000 people were imprisoned. Thoroughly alarmed, the opposition parties united into a " Popular Front " and won a sweeping victory in the election of February 1936.

Before the new Popular Front Cabinet had done much to carry out its programme a military revolt broke out. General Francisco Franco led a Moorish army across to Spain from Morocco ; in the north of the country General Emilio Mola headed a force of rebel officers and their men. As the civil war progressed, extremists took control on both sides. Conservatives mostly joined the Fascist rebels, together with landowners, industrialists, and the Church authorities, and Liberals, together with peasants and workers, supported the new war Cabinet headed by the Socialist leader, Francisco Largo Caballero. Bravery and cruelty were exhibited on both sides as the terrors of civil war took great toll of life, destroyed enormous quantities of property, and aroused hatreds which would embitter the land for years to come. Thus, while the conflict solved none of Spain's underlying problems and made more difficult their ultimate solution, it split the country into two armed camps, one tending towards Fascism, the other towards Socialism or to Communism.

Rebel or " Nationalist " troops under Franco had found their first foothold at Spain's southern tip, to which they ferried native Moorish troops and army supplies across the Strait of Gibraltar from Morocco. The second rebel army under General Mola (later killed in an air crash) was formed around Pamplona and Saragossa in the north. These two armies fought their way across Spain towards Madrid, cutting off the city's rail and highway communication with the coast as they approached. A line of communication between Franco's and Mola's armies was opened in August 1936, and the convergence on Madrid was then hastened.

Franco's forces rescued a rebel army garrison besieged in the ancient Alcazar fortress in Toledo, and then pressed on, reaching the outskirts of Madrid early in November 1936. The government moved to Valencia, and, in 1937, to Barcelona, leaving the city's defence to the untrained militia, which maintained a stubborn resistance. Rebel leaders set up headquarters in Burgos and claimed that Franco was the head of the legitimate government of Spain. This claim was speedily recognized by the governments of Portugal, Germany and Italy.

The last two had supported Franco from the first (Italian aircraft had

PRIMO DE RIVERA SPEAKING
The first Dictator of Spain, General Primo de Rivera, supported by the Army and Navy, seized supreme power in the country in 1923 and became Prime Minister in 1925. Increasing unpopularity compelled him to resign in 1929, and he died on March 16, 1930.

GENERAL FRANCO
Successful rebel leader during the Spanish Civil War (1936–39), General Franco formed his own Government in 1938 and assumed dictatorial powers. In 1947 he announced that Spain was to become a monarchy at his death or disability.

indeed landed in Spanish territory within a few hours of the start of the revolt), because of their sympathy for his political aims, their fear that his defeat would mean a victory for Communism, and their belief that a Spanish government sympathetic to them would prove strategically important in case of a general European war. Germany and Italy sent arms, ammunition, bombing planes, and trained " volunteers " to aid the rebel cause. Soviet Russia thereupon aided the loyalist side by sending munitions and helping, through the Communist International, to organize within Spain an " International Brigade " of anti-Fascist volunteers from other lands. Such foreign participation made the Spanish struggle a miniature world war, and further embittered the siege of Madrid, which was marked by repeated bombing raids. Great Britain and France attempted to set up a " non-inter-vention " committee, but a pact produced by this body was largely ignored.

In the spring of 1938 the balance turned firmly in General Franco's favour, for in spite of the grim resistance and occasional successes of the Government troops their opponents succeeded in isolating Catalonia and cutting off communications with Madrid. The Civil War dragged on until early in 1939, when the eventual victory of General Franco was foreshadowed by his capture of Barcelona and the rest of Catalonia. At the end of February 1939 the British and French Governments recognized Franco's government as the official rulers of Spain. Madrid fell to Franco's forces in March of the same year, and the war was over.

Spain declared her neutrality in the Second World War (1939–45), but in June 1940 announced that she was a "non-belligerent"—a term which might mean almost anything, but did not hide her intention to aid Germany and Italy as far as her own interests counselled her. The Franco Government then annexed the so-called "international zone" of Tangier, which bordered on Spanish Morocco; and throughout the war Spain assisted Germany and Italy by a variety of means, short of actual fighting. This, combined with the harshness of the Fascist methods of Franco, led to Spain's exclusion from the United Nations (q.v.). In 1946 all countries belonging to the United Nations withdrew their ambassadors in protest from Madrid. In the following year a law was passed declaring that Spain was again to be regarded as a monarchy, but that until Franco's death there was to be no King. A Regency Council was, however, appointed to help Franco, who remained head of the State, and to select a successor in the event of his death.

SPAIN'S *Great* LEGACY *of* BEAUTY

*M*any styles of past ages are to be observed in the art and architecture of Spain,
from the highly ornamented palaces of the Moors to the grotesques of Goya
and the haunting beauties of El Greco.

Spanish Art and Architecture.

First the Romans, then the Visigoths from what is now Rumania, and after them the Moors, con-quered and left their mark in Spain, so that it is comparatively late in history that this harassed land developed any artistic and architectural style of its own. The Moors left an enduring impression, especially in the centre and south. Among the fine examples of Moorish art are the mosque of Cordoba, with its hundreds of inter-lacing, superimposed arches (*see* page 3043); the Alcazar, or Palace, at Seville (*see* illus. page 3033); and the world-famous Alhambra (q.v.) of Granada, a large series of buildings of which the most exquisite is the Court of the Lions. Much of this Moorish work is, to our eyes, rather over-ornamented and exotic, but it constitutes none the less an important aspect of art.

National Gallery; photo, Mansell
Noted for paintings of peasants and urchins, such as this Peasant Boy, Murillo (1617–82) began as a street artist.

As the Moors were gradually driven out of Spain the Romanesque style began to filter in from the north, where it was pure, to the centre and south, where it was often mixed with the Moorish style. The first large Romanesque building was the cathedral of Spain's patron saint, St. Iago (James) de Compostela, in the town of Santiago. This form spread until the 12th century, and then Gothic architecture appeared gradually throughout Spain, following much the same sequence as elsewhere in Europe. (*See* Architecture).

By the beginning of the 13th century, Gothic was the prevalent style in all but the southern regions. Moreover, Gothic lasted longer in Spain than elsewhere on account of the comparative remoteness of the country from outside influences. Eventually the influence of the Renaissance began to be felt, producing architecture of various types; there were, *e.g.*, the *plateresque*, in which the chief feature was a tremendous wealth of extraneous sculptural decoration; the *herrera*, named after Juan Herrera (*c.* 1530–1597), who built the Escorial near Madrid—a grand yet severe and simple style; and the *churrigueresque* style, named after José Churriguera (died 1725)—a highly exaggerated form of the Baroque style of Italy and central Europe. The finest examples of these styles are to be seen in the cathedrals of Spain—in which, indeed, the whole history of the country's architecture can be traced.

Whereas the earliest native Spanish sculptures were quite crude compared with those of other lands, as Gothic styles came in the Gothic sculpture of France came with them. But the artists were for the most part foreigners—German, French or Italian. The last brought with them the ideas of the Renaissance, and were responsible for the *plateresque* style previously referred to. One Spaniard who became eminent as a worker in the manner of Michelangelo (q.v.) was Alonzo Berruguete (died 1561). Spanish sculptors, however, practised wood-carving on a very large scale for decorative work in cathedrals, two leading exponents of this art being Gaspar Becerra (1520–70) and Gregorio Hernandez (*c.* 1576–1636). Neither of these sculptors was so outstanding as Martinez Montanes (died 1649), " the great carver," whose fine figure sculptures, such as the " Christ " of Seville, are masterpieces. Many of these wood carvings were painted by Francisco Pacheco (1571–1654), who thus linked this art with that of painting, for he was also the teacher of Velazquez.

Painting in Spain was at first under the influence of Byzantine art, as the extant Spanish " primitives " show, though there was, too, the inevitable

W. F. Mansell

Perhaps the finest Gothic structure in Spain, the cathedral of Burgos was founded in 1221—curiously enough, by an Englishman—but it was not completed until some three hundred years later. In consequence it shows a wide range of Gothic styles. In this picture the earlier work is visible in the lower half of the building, while the spires and pinnacles show the influence of a German architect who was responsible for the 15th-century parts. This ornateness largely spoils the fine effect of the façade, designed two hundred years earlier. Within the church are 44 altars.

Anderson

THE ESCORIAL—VAST PILE OF ROYAL AND RELIGIOUS BUILDINGS

Built by Juan Herrera, to the order of Philip II, this huge building—for it may be considered as a single whole, so unified is its design—dates from the middle of the 16th century. It contains a cathedral church, a royal palace and apartments, library and picture-gallery, and a monastery with its college attached. Yet it is none the less a compact, well-knit structure, perhaps a little grim in general appearance, but a change indeed from the ornateness of the German-Gothic manner of Burgos (overleaf) or the wonderful intricacy of the Moorish buildings of Cordoba (opposite page). The Escorial is said to contain over 2,500 windows, 1,200 doors, and about 90 fountains. Built of grey granite in the severest Doric style, it is situated on rising ground some 34 miles north-west of Madrid, and commands a magnificent stretch of country.

Anderson

One of the finest Moorish monuments of Spain is the great mosque at Cordoba, and in the lower photograph is a general view of the hypostyle, with its red and white columns and arches. Originally there were 1,420 of these, but a number have disappeared. There is a good deal of superb ornament in other parts of the mosque, such as the glorious example seen in the upper photograph. For sheer intricacy of design this can hardly be matched, and it has a beauty totally different from anything ever produced by European artists. The edifice has been a cathedral since 1236.

WEIRD BRILLIANCE OF EL GRECO'S DESIGN

Anderson

One of three fine El Greco paintings preserved for many years at Toledo, this Burial of Count Orgaz shows that artist's style to perfection. With a curious, tortured sense of rhythm he combines an extraordinary skill in the use of brilliant light and shade and a most original range of colours. Here, the realism of the human scene is strangely matched by and cunningly linked with the Divine one; notice the use of the torch-flames and the Cross (extreme right centre) to hold the two parts of the picture together, by linking its two complementary motifs.

Anderson

Like other very great painters, Velazquez, in his last period, was able to produce the most brilliant effects with the minimum of effort, and this famous painting, Las Meninas (the Maids of Honour), is a fine example of this. For the unaffected grace of the figures—those of the Infanta Margarita and her ladies—as well as for the particularly pleasant self-portrait, this has long been a favourite example of the work of the greatest of all Spanish artists. One of his last important works, it is among the treasures of the Prado Gallery in Madrid.

A MONTANES MASTERPIECE CARVED FROM WOOD

Almost the only sculptor who could achieve in wood the effects usually sought in stone, Montanes must be ranked as one of Spain's greatest artists. Indeed, it is hard, when one considers the quality of most wood-carvings of any size, to realize that this glorious St. John is in that medium at all. No wonder that the artist was referred to by his contemporaries simply as 'the great carver'; yet when it came to colouring his masterpieces he was not too proud to rely on the skill of other artists of his day. This superb example of his art can be seen in the Seville Museum.

Anderson

Often called 'brutal' and 'coarse,' Goya was by no means always a painter of unpleasant things of life, as the lower of these two paintings shows. Entitled The Parasol, it has in it much of the feeling one associates with the work of French 18th-century painting, and none of the grim mysticism so typical of Spanish art. The snow scene in the top picture is nearer to the Spanish tradition, and gives an almost uncannily real effect of bitter cold. Notice the use, in each picture, of a wind-blown tree to add movement to the scene, and the effective lighting of the background.

SUPERB MODERN SPANISH PAINTING

One of the greatest modern Spanish painters was Ignacio Zuloaga (1870–1945), of whose work this study is an example. Although it shows the influence of the French schools of the late 19th century, it is unmistakably Spanish, both in subject and in atmosphere ; and, indeed, Zuloaga was hailed as the reviver of truly national Spanish painting. Brilliantly portrayed against a typical landscape of their homeland, these three smiling ladies are as essentially Spanish as is their costume.

Zwemmer Collection

Moorish influence. Later, Flemish, French and German influences were predominant, especially after the visit of Jan Van Eyck to Spain in 1428. Spanish artists were also affected by Italian art, beginning with one Starnina (born 1354), and this trend became ever more important, Michelangelo and Raphael being the artists especially attractive to Spanish painters. Among these, the chief were Luis de Morales (1509–68), Luis de Vargas (1502–68), and various members of the school of Valencia, of whom Francisco Ribalta (1551–1628) is an important example. All of these painted religious pictures; and, indeed, the strange religious fanaticism which is so characteristic of Spain, together with the Spaniard's sombre outlook, is a governing factor in the art of this country. A Spaniard who worked chiefly in England is Antonis Mor; whereas a Greek who worked in Spain was the Cretan Domenicos Theotocopoulos (c. 1544–1614), world-famous under his nickname " El Greco." Working under Tintoretto as a young man in Venice and absorbing much that was finest in the Venetian school, he later evolved a highly individual manner imbued by a deep sense of Catholicism. His finest paintings, such as The Burial of Count Orgaz, Ascension of the Virgin, and the Dream of Philip II, are in Spanish galleries, but he is represented in the National Gallery, London, by his Christ's Agony in Gethsemane.

It was in the 17th century that Spain produced her three finest painters, in all of whose works may be seen that sombre colour, depth of shade and brilliantly contrasted light and that intensity of feeling which characterize Spanish painting.

The first of the trio was Francisco Zurbaran (1598–1664), who worked a good deal at Seville, and who was painter to King Philip IV. Above all things a realist, he was consequently apt to make his figures coarse and unimaginative, especially when he incorporated peasants and urban types in his religious paintings. He was influenced to a considerable extent by contemporary Italians, such as Caravaggio and Guercino, and by his countryman José de Ribera (1588–1652), who was also known as Lo Spagnoletto. The latter, despite his nationality, was, as a painter, more Italian than Spanish.

Second in time, but the most gifted of Spain's painters, was Velazquez (q.v.). Ranking as one of the foremost artists of all time, he was pre-eminent alike as portraitist, landscape painter and painter of groups and historic scenes. He did but few religious paintings, and even in them he used as his models the men and women of his own time. To this realism he brought an imagination, a colouring, and a genius for design that have never been surpassed. His Venus in the National Gallery in London is considered to be one of the world's most beautiful paintings; while his portrait of Philip IV on a prancing charger, his group Las Meninas (The Dwarfs) and some of his historical pieces are notable masterpieces. He spent much time in Italy, studying Michelangelo, Raphael and Tintoretto especially, but his own genius was enough to surmount any one influence.

Last of the trio is Esteban Murillo (1617–82), a deeply religious painter, who, apart from some delightful studies of urchins and peasants, was chiefly concerned with the reproduction in paint of the lives of the saints and martyrs. Where

Seville Museum; photo, Anderson

PAINTING BY ZURBARAN

Among the finest painters that Spain produced in the 17th century, Francisco Zurbaran (1598–1664) was apt to make his figures too realistic and unimaginative. His picture Jesus Crowning Saint James (above) is relieved by the detail in which the flowers have been painted.

Zurbaran and Velazquez painted reality, Murillo envisaged idealized types, raised above the spiritual levels of mere humanity by their religious experience (*see also* Murillo, Esteban). Like Velazquez, he left a number of imitators, some of whose works can scarcely be distinguished from his own. At Madrid, however, a strong independent school continued, its chief artist being Claudio Coello (1630–93), by many considered the last great Spanish painter. Francisco de Goya (1746–1828), the satirist and portrait painter, differing from all who had preceded him, scoffed at ecclesiastical life; his bitter satire showed the miseries of war and poverty. Among his nudes is the celebrated Maja. As an etcher he ranks supreme.

Goya's reactions to the horrors of the Peninsular War (1808–14), experienced at Madrid and Saragossa, have come down to us in his dramatic Disasters of War, a series of etchings executed during 1810–13, of which the first complete edition appeared in 1863. Others of his etchings include the two series Bull-fight, and Proverbs. It has been said of the latter that they approximate to the most amazing etched pictures by an artist since the time of Rembrandt. Among Goya's last works are his lithographs, of which the most notable are Woman Spinning, The Duel, and four bull-fight scenes entitled the Toros de Bourdeos. (*See* Goya).

Of the modern school, Mariano Fortuny (1838–74) was a skilled painter of wedding groups, the

Prado, Madrid; photo, Anderson

ONE OF THE FINEST PRODUCTS OF VELAZQUEZ' ART

Few subject pictures have ever been so successfully wrought as this masterpiece by Velazquez (1599–1660), entitled The Surrender of Breda—the latter being a city of the Netherlands which capitulated to the Spaniards in 1625. On account of the number of those weapons which heightens the warlike atmosphere of the work it is also known as The Lances. Observe how the expression of each face has been rendered with the exactness of an individual portrait.

interiors of churches, and of Court ceremonies. Ignacio Zuloaga (1870–1946) presented truth in all its stern austerity and became noted for his studies of bull-fighters and dwarfs, and portraits of celebrities. His art was essentially Spanish and was marked by richness of colour. Pablo Picasso (*q.v.*), by birth a Spaniard and the most influential painter of the 20th century, belongs to an international group deriving inspiration from French rather than Spanish art.

Spanish Literature.

The Romans gave the Spaniard his language, but it was the Iberians (the original inhabitants of the country), Jews, Celts, Vandals, Visigoths, and Arabs as well, who gave him his character. It is this character—proud, dignified, mystic, gracious, elegant and sometimes cruel—together with the isolation and wars of Spain, which have formed the traits of Spanish literature. The language, an outgrowth of Latin, is a less uniform speech than its sister tongues, French, Portuguese and Italian. The official language and literary tongue is Castilian, a dialect softened by Arabic. Catalonia, a district in the north-east, has a language—Catalan—and a literature of its own.

The earliest known work in Spanish is the Poema del Cid (Poem of the Cid) by an unknown author and dating from 1140. The Cid ("lord") was Rodrigo Ruy Diaz de Bivar, who died in 1099. Though he had often helped Moslems against Christians, the poem presents him as a dauntless champion of Christianity against the Moors and leaves a graphic record of the life of the times. Another work of the 12th century is the religious drama, El Auto de los Reyes Magos (Mystery of the Magian Kings), a play of the Three Wise Men.

Spanish energies were sapped by eight centuries of struggle with the Moors, and the year 1492, when the Moors were expelled, saw the discovery of America, opening new outlets and interests to Spain. Conspicuous writers of the 15th century included the Marquess of Santillana, with his famous Serranillas and poems; Juan de Mena, with The Labyrinth of Fortune; Jorge Manrique, with his Coplas, or verses, on the death of his father. The 17th century was the "golden age" of Spanish literature as it was of national glory.

In 1605 appeared the first part of Don Quixote, bringing fame to poverty-stricken Miguel de

Cervantes Saavedra (see Cervantes). Satire though it is, its most notable result was to project kindliness and human warmth into literature, and its influence was felt all over Europe. Two other attacks on hollow chivalry were made in Mateo Alemán's (c. 1547–c. 1614) novels, Guzmán de Alfarache, and Atalaya de la Vida Umana (The Watchtower of Human Life), the first of that purely Spanish invention, picaresque literature (which was to exert so great an influence throughout Europe), dealing with the *picaro* or rogue.

Four notable dramatists appear in this same period. The two best-known are Lope Félix de Vega Carpio (1562–1635) and Pedro Calderón de la Barca (1600–81), better known as Lope de Vega and as Calderón. The prolific Lope wrote his first play at the age of 12, and produced altogether over 1,000. His rapid improvisations lack finish but glow with genius. Cervantes called him " a monster of naturalness." All was grist to his mill ; probably no dramatist drew inspiration from so many sources.

Calderón, on the other hand, might be called " a monster of ingenuity." He is at his best in " cloak-and-sword " plays. His one good philosophical drama, La Vida es Sueño (Life is a Dream), retells an Oriental story, The Awakened Sleeper. The third dramatist, Gabriel Téllez, popularly known as Tirso de Molina, gained fame by dramatizing the old legend of a certain Don Juan, who was supposed to have been trapped by some friars in their monastery and murdered. The fourth dramatist is Juan Ruiz de Alarcón (c. 1580–1639), a Mexican hunchback, student of Salamanca, and rich business man. Mocked for his deformity, he rebuked cruelty and other vices by presenting character types. During the 18th century the theatre, which had fallen into decadence, was revived and revolutionized by the plays of Leandro F. de Moratin and Ramón de la Cruz. At the beginning of the 19th century, two noteworthy poets appeared, Quintana and Gallego.

An outstanding novelist of the 19th century is Benito Pérez Galdós (1845–1920), who

CALDERÓN DE LA BARCA
Better known simply as Calderón, Pedro Calderón de la Barca (1600–81) wrote numerous plays of which more than 100 are extant. Among the best known of those translated into English are the philosophical drama entitled Life's a Dream, and the Fairy Lady.

wrote a brilliant series of historical novels. Pedro Antonio de Alarcón (1833–91) set the world laughing with his El Sombrero de tres picos (The Three-Cornered Hat). José María de Pereda hated cities and the middle class, and created fine peasant types.

First Spanish dramatist to win the Nobel Prize was the Basque writer José Echegaray (1833–1916), whose play El gran Galeoto had considerable success. He was the leading Spanish playwright from 1873 to the 90s.

Angel Ganivet and Joaquin Costa started the movement of " the generation of 1898," resulting in a new flowering of literature. Ramón Pérez de Ayala (born 1880) has been called best of modern Spanish poets, with sensitive, melancholy Juan Ramón Jiménez (born 1881) perhaps second among them.

A leader of Spanish drama was Jacinto Benavente (born 1866), winner of the Nobel Prize for literature in 1922, and who revolutionized the drama. His tragedy of peasant life, La Malquerida (The Passion Flower), was a tremendous success. Delightful comedies were written by the brothers Serafin (1871–1938) and Joaquín (1873–1944), Alvarez Quintero; and delicate, poetic novels and plays by Gregorio Martínez Sierra (born 1881). From the beginning of the 20th century there was a revival in all fields of Spanish literature, which, however, came abruptly to an end in 1936 with the outbreak of the Civil War. Garcia Lorca (c. 1898–1936) was the most representative poet and dramatist of the 1930s.

Famous abroad for his novel, Los Cuatro Jinetes del Apocalipsis (The Four Horsemen of the Apocalypse), Vicente Blasco Ibáñez (1867–1928) was a highly popular novelist of but little literary importance. Pío Barója (born 1872) poured out novels in a forceful, formless cataract; and Ramón Maria del Valle-Inclán (1870–1936) was a powerful, startling stylist. Another stylist, leading critic of Spain, was José Martínez Ruiz (born 1874), called Azorín, who showed equal skill as poet and novelist.

The greatest intellectual force in recent years was Miguel de Unamuno (1864–1936), philo-

E.N.A.
RAMÓN PÉREZ DE AYALA
Born in 1880, Señor de Ayala is one of the outstanding writers of modern Spain, and some of his books have been translated into English. One of his popular novels is Belarmino y Apolonio, the story of two cobblers, one with an artistic and the other with a philosophic ideal.

G. W. Teager

COMMON HOUSE SPARROW
Although it is hardly a favourite in agricultural districts of Britain—for it is sometimes destructive of crops—the house sparrow is popular in the cities, where its cheery chirp and enterprising ways endear it especially to those who seldom visit the country. This specimen is country-bred, for no sooty sparrow 'townee' has such bright plumage.

sopher, poet and novelist. Individualism was strong in his work, The Tragic Sentiment of Life, just as it has always been a vital trait of the Spaniards and their literature. The conflict between faith and reason, which is the essence of Unamuno's work, is at the root of Spanish philosophy.

Sparrow. Of the finch family, the house sparrow (*Passer domesticus*) is perhaps the best known. A small black-streaked brown bird, it is found throughout the British Isles, except the outermost islands of the Hebrides, and in almost every region where Man dwells. The bulky and untidy nest is made of whatever materials are handy—hay, straw, roots, rags, bits of paper—but is always lined with feathers. The eggs are white tinged with blue or green, with brown or black speckles, and there are three or four broods a year. Though sometimes destructive to crops, the sparrow eats insects and is a useful scavenger.

The tree sparrow (*P. montanus*) is essentially a bird of the open country and is slightly smaller than the house species. It has brown plumage, with a white collar round the throat and two white bars on the wing, and occurs locally in England

and Scotland, but is rare in Wales and Ireland. Usually it nests in hollow trees or in holes in rocks; the eggs are browner than those of the house sparrow.

The so-called hedge sparrow, or accentor, is not related to the foregoing birds but is a member of the warbler family. Its plumage is dusky brown, with a reddish back and bluish-grey head and neck. It is often mottled with white, and pure white specimens are sometimes seen. The eggs are blue, without spots. (*See* colour plate facing page 440).

Sparta. The most formidable rival of Athens in ancient Greece was the city-state of Sparta, whose race of warriors has given us the adjective "spartan." More like a group of straggling villages than a city, Sparta prided itself, not like Athens on art or learning or splendid buildings, but on its valiant men. Although Athens, with her beautiful temples and statues, her poetry and philosophy, dominated the intellectual life of the Hellenic world, it was Sparta which in the end snatched from its cultured opponent political supremacy.

The Spartan government was founded on the principle that the life of every individual from the moment of birth belonged absolutely to the State. The elders of the city inspected the new-born infants and ordered the weak and unhealthy to be carried to a near-by chasm and left to die. By this practice Sparta made sure that only those who were physically fit should survive.

The children who were allowed to live were brought up under a rule of iron. At the age of seven Spartan boys were removed from the control of their parents and organized into small bands, over which the strongest and most courageous were made captains. They slept in public dormitories

Courtesy of the British School at Athens

WHERE ONCE STERN SPARTANS LIVED
Few relics are left of ancient Sparta, the city that ruled the Peloponnesus in southern Greece from 405 to 379 B.C. The hardy warriors of the city-state gave us the adjective 'spartan.' Part of the site of the old city is occupied by the modern Sparta (above), which is the capital of the Greek department of Laconia.

on hard beds of rushes, ate coarse and meagre fare, and wore only the simplest and scantiest clothing. They were drilled each day in gymnastic and military exercises, and were taught to endure pain and hardship without complaint and to obey orders without question.

They were allowed to feel the pinch of hunger and encouraged to supplement their fare by pilfering food for themselves. This was not done to cultivate dishonesty but to develop shrewdness and enterprise. If they were caught, they were whipped for their awkwardness. Once, it is said, a Spartan boy, having stolen a young fox for his dinner, allowed the animal, which was hidden under his cloak, to gnaw out his vitals rather than disclose his theft by crying out. The girls were educated in classes under a similar but less rigorous system.

All Spartan male citizens between the ages of 20 and 60 served in the army, and, though they were allowed to marry, all had to belong to a men's dining club and to eat and sleep in public barracks. They were forbidden to possess gold and silver, their money consisting of iron bars. War-songs were their only music, and their literary education was slight. No luxury was allowed, even in the use of words. They spoke shortly and to the point, in the manner which we have come to call " laconic," from Laconia, the name of the district of which Sparta was the capital.

There were three classes of citizens in Laconia. First, the Spartan citizens (*Spartiates*) who lived in the city itself and who alone had a voice in the government. Second, the *Perioeci*, or " dwellers round," who lived in the surrounding villages, were free, but had no political rights. They were the tradesmen and mechanics—occupations not allowed to the Spartans. Third, the *Helots*, who were serfs, or slaves, and were forced to cultivate the soil for the citizens, their masters, who owned the land.

Another strange feature of Sparta was that the government was headed by two kings, who ruled jointly, serving as high priests as well as leaders in war. Each king acted as a check upon the other. There was a sort of cabinet composed of five *ephors*, or overseers, who exercised a general control over law and custom, and came in later times to have greater power than the kings. The legislative power was vested in a senate or council of elders, which was chosen from men over the age of 60.

The Spartan armies were all but irresistible. Each citizen soldier was inspired by the resolve to win or die. The Spartan mother, when she gave her son his shield, used to say: " Bring back this shield yourself or be brought back dead upon it."

The Spartan constitution is said to have been founded by Lycurgus (*q.v.*). Under the rigid discipline of its laws Sparta extended its conquests

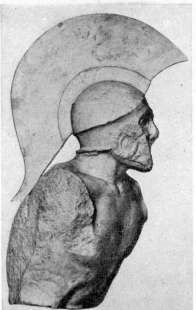

A SPARTAN WARRIOR
Bred to be soldiers, the male Spartans were contemptuous of pain and death and of the luxuries of life. They wore a helmet with a high crest and large cheek pieces.

over the neighbouring states until it gained control of most of the Peloponnesus in southern Greece. Sparta's prowess naturally brought rivalry with Athens, the leader of the northern States and for a time of all Greece. This rivalry culminated in the Peloponnesian War (431–405 B.C.), which resulted in Athens's ruin and Sparta's supremacy. But the tyranny of the Spartans aroused rebellion, and the jealous limitations of citizenship gradually cut down the number of specially trained warriors. After about 30 years of Spartan domination, the people of the city of Thebes revolted and defeated Sparta in 371 B.C. With the rest of Greece, Sparta was conquered by the Macedonians in 338 B.C., and eventually became a part of the Roman Empire. (*See* Greece).

The modern town of Sparta, built after the Greek War of Independence with the Turks in 1834, covers part of the ancient site, near the River Iri (the ancient Eurotas) and about 15 miles from the Gulf of Messenia. The population of the town is 6,000.

Spartacus (died 71 B.C.). The danger of an uprising of slaves was constantly in the minds of the ancient Romans, for there were in the Empire about three slaves to every free man. Several such rebellions did occur, and the most formidable was that headed by the Thracian, Spartacus, in 73 B.C. Escaping from the school of gladiators at Capua he fled to Mount Vesuvius, where he collected an army of runaway slaves like himself.

For two years he terrorized Italy, defeating army after army sent against him from Rome and laying the land waste from the foot of the Alps to the southern tip of the peninsula. But the insurrection was crushed, Spartacus was slain, and 6,000 of his followers were crucified along the Appian Way leading to Rome.

At the close of the First World War (1914–18) the name " Spartacists " was applied to the extremists of the German Socialists, whose leader, Karl Liebknecht, had written under the pen-name of " Spartacus." The Spartacists aimed at establishing a workers' republic, and there was fierce fighting in 1919 before they were suppressed. Liebknecht was killed in January 1919.

Specific Gravity. You may have heard the saying: " A pint of water weighs a pound," and if you knew that an Imperial gallon of water actually weighed 10 lb. you probably wondered how such a loose statement came to be used. But we have not always measured liquids by the present gallon, and in wine measure we still have the " Winchester " gallon, equal only to 0·833 of an Imperial gallon. This measure dates back to the time of Queen Anne, and is still the standard measure for liquids in the United States of America. Probably the old saying we have mentioned arose in days when the now obsolete Winchester measure was the usual one, and was a fair approximation, since a pint would weigh $\frac{8\cdot33}{8}$ lb.

In 1824, during the reign of George IV, the present Imperial Standard Gallon was introduced : it was defined as containing 227·274 cubic inches. This figure was arrived at by taking the volume of 10 lb. of distilled water when the barometer stood at 30 inches of mercury, and the temperature was 62 degrees Fahrenheit. The legal definition also stated that the water was to be weighed with brass weights in arriving at this standard volume. As you will know if you have read our stories of Gravitation and Physics, the *density* of a substance— that is, the closeness with which its particles are packed together—depends on the temperature and atmospheric pressure at the time. That is why these two conditions were stipulated by the scientists who drew up the factors for the standard gallon.

Specific gravity is the ratio between the density of water and that of other substances. You will see that in the following table of common substances we have printed Water in bold type, with its specific gravity as " 1," and its weight per cubic foot as 62·4 lb. This weight is approximate : the figure generally accepted is 62·36 lb., but for all ordinary calculations 62·4 is near enough.

Substance	Specific gravity	Density in lb. per cubic foot
Cork	0·25	15·6
Timbers	0·5 to 0·8	30 to 50
Alcohol	0·8	50
Water	**1**	**62·4**
Sea water	1·025	64
Glass	2·6	162
Aluminium ..	2·7	168
Copper	8·9	555
Lead	11·37	709
Gold	19·32	1205
Osmium	22·5	1404

Metals and alloys differ in density according to their chemical composition. Cast metals also differ from drawn, extruded, or otherwise worked metals.

You will see that specific gravity does not tell us directly the weight of a given volume of material, but only how this material compares with water. We have to use the formula:

Specific gravity of substance × weight of similar volume of water

to ascertain the unit density. For example:

Alcohol (s.g. 0·8) × 62·4 lb. = 49·92 lb. per cu. ft.
(taken as 50 lb.)

In the case of gases the unit substance by which others are compared is Air, which is taken as 1. Examples are Acetylene, s.g. 0·920; Chlorine, s.g. 2·423; Oxygen, s.g. 1·106. The specific gravity of liquids is measured with an instrument called a hydrometer (*q.v.*).

Spectacles.

These were probably first worn by the Chinese, who used enormous rimless spectacles with flat rock crystal windows. The Emperor Nero is said to have used a large cabochon emerald as a lens, holding this before the eye when wishing to see more clearly at a distance.

Early lenses to aid vision were held between the thumb and finger, before the eye. Later they were mounted in rims of various material as single lenses. Still later, two lenses were hinged together so as to clamp on to the nose, leaving the hands more or less free. Then sides were added— after the style of the early Chinese spectacles—but conforming to the facial measurements.

Lenses, too, underwent a considerable change. People needing glasses selected from a number of crude simple lenses those which enabled them to see best, either for distance or near sight. Two half-lenses were fitted into a frame, using the top half for distance and the lower half for near. This formed the first " bifocal spectacles "—usable for reading as well as for distance.

Bifocal spectacles were further improved by cementing a small lens on to the lower half of the distance lens; and later by fusing two, sometimes three, lenses together so as to form solid bifocal and trifocal lenses.

The forms of the lenses were made different to counteract distortion caused when looking obliquely through them. The quality of the glass was also improved by adding certain metals to its com-

Walter H. Thompson

PREPARING A SPECTACLE LENS FOR GRINDING

Defects of vision are counteracted by looking through lenses, which a spectacle-maker produces from specially prepared optical glass by grinding. The lens blank is dabbed with warm pitch (left) to make it adhere to the grinding machine on which (right) it is then placed. To correct short sight a concave lens is used ; a person with long sight will need a convex one. Prismatic lenses are suitable for double vision and for the correction of a squint.

position that prevented harmful radiations passing through.

"Contact lenses," a recent development, are worn under the lids, close to the eyeball, and maintained in position by suction. They have some advantages over ordinary spectacles, but a drawback is that they have only a single focus.

Lenses are also made of plastic material instead of glass, both for spectacles and contact wear. They are quite good in many respects but are lacking in hardness of surface, and have not the chemical composition of glass.

The ophthalmoscope and the retinoscope make it possible to examine the eye in detail, both externally and internally. Thus the ophthalmist is able to determine whether the cause of eye ailments is physiological or pathological in origin. And he can prescribe lenses to correct errors of refraction. (*See* Lens).

Spectroscope AND

Spectrograph. The spectrum, or band of colours, given off by an incandescent body tells us a great deal about the nature of that body. If a beam from the sun is observed through a spectroscope, its white light is seen to be split up into the seven colours red, orange, yellow, green, blue, indigo and violet—a "rainbow" band. If, instead of "analysing" sunlight, we use a Bunsen burner to heat a block of ordinary kitchen salt, and look at the flame through the spectroscope, we see only one colour—bright yellow.

Fox

PREPARING A CONTACT LENS
Made of plastic material, contact lenses (taking the place of ordinary spectacles) fit under the lids close to the eyeball and before insertion are moistened with a liquid resembling tear fluid (above), which acts as a shock absorber between the lens and the eye.

The green-blue light from a mercury-vapour lamp gives a five-colour spectrum, composed of two shades of yellow, and of the colours green, blue and violet. These colours each give images of the slit in the collimating telescope (Fig. 1): two yellow lines, a green line, a blue one, and two violet lines. Spectra such as those from sodium and mercury-vapour lights are called *line spectra*.

As explained under Spectrum, differing colours are due to different wavelengths. Sunlight has all the colours which make up white light, and these colours are spread according to their respective wavelengths along the band. The light from sodium atoms (in the kitchen salt) is practically mono-chromatic, or one-coloured ; it is seen in the eyepiece of the spectroscope as two close lines of yellow.

The mercury-vapour light is not monochromatic, and is made up of lights of various colours and frequencies, so that the slit-images are spaced out in a band. When the light from an incandescent lamp is viewed with the spectroscope we see a band of colour, or continuous spectrum—from red to violet, denoting that light of all wavelengths is emitted.

The spectroscope has three main parts (*see* Fig. 1): collimator, prism and observing telescope. The slit of the collimator is directed towards the light to be viewed; the lenses are adjusted to bring the rays parallel. The beam then passes through the

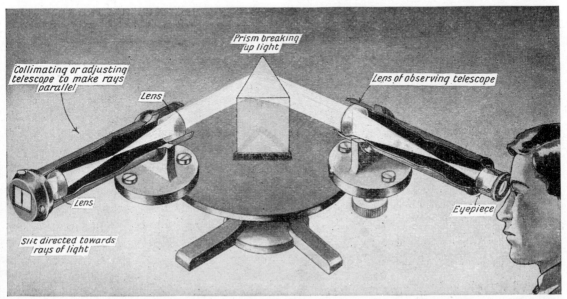

HOW SUNLIGHT IS ANALYSED WITH A SPECTROSCOPE
Fig. 1. The French mathematician René Descartes (1596-1650) and Sir Isaac Newton (1642-1727) found that a prism could split up the white light of the sun into a rainbow-hued band of colour. Joseph Fraunhöfer (1787-1826) used a telescope to view the image produced by the prism, and so made a spectroscope. This simplified diagram explains its working.

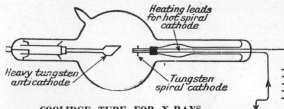

COOLIDGE TUBE FOR X-RAYS

Fig. 2.   W. D. Coolidge (b. 1873) introduced this form of vacuum tube for generating X-rays. A low-voltage current from the battery indicated at the right warms the cathode, made of tungsten wire, and the wire emits a stream of electrons.   They are driven down to the anti-cathode by a high-potential current applied between cathode and anti-cathode; when they strike the latter they produce the X-rays.

prism, where the rays are bent towards the base of the prism, each according to its colour and wavelength—the red being bent least, and the violet most.   An image of the spectrum forms at the focus of the telescope, and the eyepiece of that instrument enlarges the image.   (*See* Lens).

The spectroscope is sometimes called a " spectrometer," and such an instrument, when adapted for *measuring* instead of merely viewing spectra, would really be a " meter."   Another type also named a spectrometer is used for taking photographs of spectra, and the name *spectrograph* is more appropriate here, because a record is made.   At the end of an instrument like the viewing telescope a photographic plate is arranged, and on it the various spectral lines are brought to a focus at different points, according to their wavelength separation. Yet a third type of spectrometer (also alternatively termed a spectrograph) is that employed in X-ray analysis (Fig. 3).

Sir Lawrence Bragg, who, with his father, Sir William Bragg (1862–1942), shared the Nobel Prize for Physics in 1915, has said that the X-ray spectrometer opened up a new world. The pioneer instrument of this kind was constructed by Sir William Bragg; father and son worked together on the investigation and analysis of crystals with the spectrometer from 1913 onwards.   The reason that these rays were chosen was that, being so short (0·1 millimicron, as compared with light waves, which are 400 millimicrons in length), they would penetrate into the interstices of a crystal.

Light (*q.v.*) travels in straight lines; and in passing through a tiny opening, or between the bars of a " grating " ruled with lines set very close together, on glass, the waves are diffracted or spread (*see* page 1941). Some of the light beams go straight on through the opening; others are so diffracted that

they diverge at an angle with the straight-through beam.   Diffracted beams can be produced only when the lines of the grating are farther apart than the length of the wave of light which we are using. The same thing happens if X-rays are directed upon the face of a crystal: the atoms in the crystal are arranged in a pattern—varying according to the substance we are dealing with—and these atoms act as a diffraction grating, scattering and diffracting the X-rays in a distinctive pattern.

By studying the angles of these diffracted beams reflected back from the crystal face, scientists can get an idea of the pattern which the atoms make in the substance.   The rays are invisible to the eye, but the pattern they make can be photographed. The intensity of the reflected rays is measured by the amount of ionisation which they produce in an ionisation chamber.   X-ray analysis of structure is used to examine metals and other minerals, chemi-

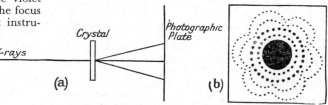

AN EARLY EXPERIMENT IN X-RAY ANALYSIS

Fig. 3.   A narrow beam, directed upon the crystal as at (a), produces upon the photographic plate a pattern like that at (b).   The rays, diffracted by the molecules in the crystal, write their ' autograph.'

cal compounds, and even some of the organic substances such as proteins.   Amorphous (non-crystalline) substances also give distinctive patterns (Fig. 4, lower), and research into plastics and synthetic textile fabrics depends a good deal upon the spectrometer.

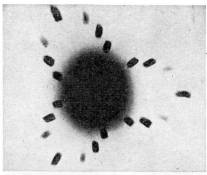

X-RAY SPECTROGRAPHS

Fig. 4.   The crystal structure of the diamond is shown by the top photograph ; the symmetrical pattern of dots is a clue to the molecular arrangement.   In the lower photo we see a spectrograph of paraffin.

It was a German scientist, Max von Laue, who in 1912 conceived the idea that the atoms in a crystal might be made to act like a diffraction grating, provided that a source of radiation of sufficiently short wavelength was used as the " light." First he arranged a photographic plate so that any beams reflected by the crystal would be intercepted by the plate.   This not proving successful, he next placed the plate behind the crystal, and obtained a photo which proved the correctness of his theory.   The Braggs followed up this pioneer work and, with other scientists, made X-ray analysis into an exact tool of research and experiment.   This use of X-rays is quite distinct from that in which the intense penetrating power of the rays is employed to give a photograph through opaque substances.   In the case of X-ray analysis it is the extreme shortness of the waves which is the useful property.

BRIGHT COLOURS FROM THE SUN'S PAINT-BOX

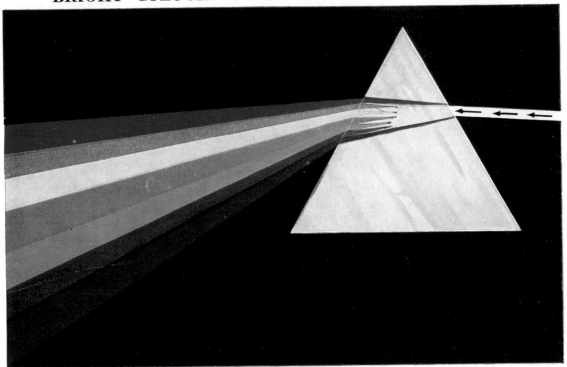

When a narrow beam of sunlight passes through a prism the light is split up into components of different wavelength, which are bent more or less away from the line of incidence, according to their wavelength. Hence the coloured rays spread out, as shown. From the top downwards, the colours of the spectrum are Red, Orange, Yellow, Green, Blue, Indigo and Violet. They can easily be memorised by the word 'Vibgyor,' reading from the violet upwards in this case. (In some books you may find them classed as six colours only, with indigo-blue treated as a single colour.)

Spectrum. No doubt you have often seen little "rainbows" projected from the bevelled edges of a plate glass mirror. Did you guess that you held the key to one of the most wonderful secrets of Nature—the breaking up of white light into its component coloured band which we call the spectrum? The vivid play of colour shown in our picture above is what we see in a spectroscope when a beam of sunlight is "analysed."

The portion of the sun's spectrum which is visible as "light" is only a part of the complete spectrum. Rays of *shorter* wavelength include the ultra-violet ("beyond-the-violet") rays. Those having waves *longer* than those visible include the infra-red ("below-the-red") rays. See overleaf where is a diagram (not to scale) showing the electro-magnetic spectrum. This spectrum includes wire-less waves at one end, and radium emanations at the other, besides other rays which are mentioned in the story of Radiation.

Sir Isaac Newton (1642–1727) has recounted how, in 1666, he "procured a triangular glass prism to try therewith the celebrated phenomena of colours." René Descartes (1596–1650) had arrived at the theory that the colours of the rainbow were due to refraction; he also had tried experiments with a prism upon which he let a beam of sunlight fall. Newton made a hole in the window shutter of a

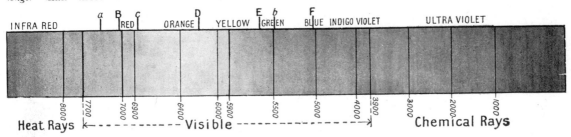

THE SPECTRUM OF VISIBLE AND INVISIBLE RAYS

The colours in the spectrum are in order of decreasing wavelengths, those at the red end being longer than those at the violet end. Wavelengths are usually expressed in 'Ångström units,' which represent one ten-millionth of a millimetre. At opposite ends of the spectrum are the invisible rays—the heat rays, or infra-red radiation, and the very much shorter actinic rays, or chemically active ultra-violet radiation. The letters at the top mark 'Fraunhöfer's lines.'

darkened room, and allowed a beam of sunlight to pass through. In the path of this beam he placed a glass prism; at the opposite side of the room he placed a white screen—and found that on the screen there appeared a band of colours, much longer than it was broad.

This lengthening of the image of the small hole in the shutter puzzled Newton for a long time. Try how he would, he could not prevent it. At length he determined that the spreading of the band was due to the different angles through which the rays of various colours were bent by the prism. Then Newton re-combined coloured lights into white light. He did this by using a large convex lens to bring all the coloured rays to a single focus, and found that then the colours disappeared, and only a white light emerged.

The reason for this spreading is explained more fully in the preceding story, of the Spectroscope. All luminous flames (e.g. that of a lamp) give *continuous* spectra, resembling that of sunlight, and the spectrum is produced by tiny carbon particles which are burning in the flame. A piece of platinum wire held in the white flame of a Bunsen burner, and so made white hot, will yield a similar continuous band of colours.

Another kind of spectrum is the *line* spectrum. Using the same Bunsen flame as before, and dipping

tinuous spectrum which has two vacant places in it. The gaps are in the positions where the yellow lines appeared in the line spectrum of sodium chloride. Now they show up as black lines. The missing lines represent coloured light, of certain wavelengths, which have been absorbed by the sodium flame through which the white light was first passed before reaching the spectrometer.

When placed in front of an incandescent body, a gas or vapour *absorbs* the same lights (of same wavelengths) which it will itself *send out* when made incandescent. So the black absorption lines in a spectrum are a sure indication of the absence, in the light being investigated, of radiations of certain frequencies. By comparing certain dark lines in the solar spectrum with colour lines in the line spectra of different chemical elements, it has been demonstrated that these elements exist also in the sun.

" But, if they exist in the sun," you may ask, " why are their colours absent from its spectrum ? " The answer is that chemical vapours in the sun's surrounding atmosphere " filter out " or absorb these wavelengths: if the sodium line is absent from the sun's spectrum, it is because sodium vapour in the atmosphere abstracts the sodium yellow from the spectrum.

Three names stand out in the story of the dark lines: Dr. William Hyde Wollaston (1766–1828), probably the first to report them, in 1802; Joseph Fraunhöfer (1787–1826), who studied and mapped them, and after whom they are still called "Fraunhöfer's lines "; and Gustav Robert Kirchoff (1824–87). Kirchoff, along with Bunsen, found that the dark lines could be produced by passing white light from oxy-

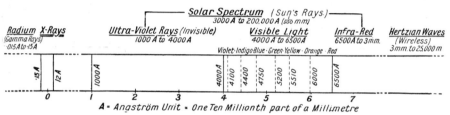

Radium X-Rays (Gamma Rays) .015 A to .15 A

Ultra-Violet Rays (Invisible) 1000 A to 4000 A

Solar Spectrum (Sun's Rays) 3000 A to 200,000 A (1/200 mm)

Visible Light 4000 A to 6500 A

Violet · Indigo Blue · Green Yellow · Orange · Red

Infra-Red 6500A to 3mm.

Hertzian Waves (Wireless) 3mm. to 25,000 m

A = Angström Unit = One Ten Millionth part of a Millimetre

BEYOND THE SOLAR SPECTRUM AT BOTH ENDS

The main purpose of this diagram is to show the relation of the very short and the very long rays to those with which we are more familiar—the rainbow-hued band into which the spectroscope splits up sunlight. The Ångström unit was named after a Swedish scientist, Anders Jonas Ångström (1814–74). Compare with the similar diagram overleaf.

the platinum wire into a solution of common salt (sodium chloride) before placing the wire in the flame, we shall get a yellow flame of sodium. There will be no band, but only an image of the slit in the collimator, and perhaps two closely set lines, but more often only one, unless a good spectroscope is used and carefully adjusted.

If a platinum wire previously dipped in a solution of lithium chloride is put in the flame, two coloured lines will appear—red and yellow. If calcium chloride is used, the colours of the slit-images will be green and red; strontium chloride will yield red and blue lines. (The platinum wire must be kept down low enough to prevent it giving a spectrum.) Robert Wilhelm Bunsen (1811–99), inventor of the burner mentioned, used this method of analysing substances, by seeing which spectral lines they emitted when made incandescent.

A third kind of spectrum is the *absorption* spectrum. Let us go back to our experiment with sodium chloride. Two yellow lines close together are seen in a good spectrometer, as we have said. But if we direct white light into the spectrometer, and on its way this light is made to traverse a cooler flame containing salt, we shall see in the eyepiece a con-

hydrogen lime-light through the vapour from an incandescent metal, before directing the white light into a spectroscope. (This is the same method as that described in the absorption experiment with sodium chloride vapour above.) Sir Henry Roscoe, an eminent English chemist (1833–1915), did much to make spectroscopic analysis a precise method of research, and a number of new chemical elements were discovered by its aid. Helium (from Greek *helios*, " sun ") was discovered in the sun before its existence on earth was known.

Today the spectrum can be spread out until it extends around an arc about 100 feet in length. In order to photograph any desired portion of the long spectrum, one or more photographic plates are affixed to a circular track not unlike that of a model railway. Besides the prism spectroscope (also called spectrometer and spectrograph when used for measuring or for making records), there is the diffraction type of instrument. This latter uses a grating ruled on clear glass or on metal or mirror-glass. Parallel lines, perhaps as closely set as 20,000 to the inch, are engraved with a diamond point. It was Fraunhöfer who made the first diffraction grating. (*See* Spectroscope.)

Spelling. Quite a lot has been said and written about the difficulties of English spelling—much of which is not true. Learning to spell, of course, like everything else worth while, requires effort. But it need not be a " bogey." Everyone can learn to spell if he goes about it in the right way.

Many have said that English is not a phonetic language, that is, it is not spelt as it is pronounced. Let us try to discover if this is correct. Investigation has shown that some 22 per cent of the words in common use are non-phonetic, but that leaves 78 per cent that are spelt as they sound and are pronounced as they look. An authority on word study calls attention to the fact that " six of every seven syllables of our (the English) language are phonetic." Such difficulties as there are, then, must lie in the 22 per cent non-phonetic words, and with one syllable in seven. English, therefore, is mainly a phonetic language.

It has been estimated that the average person can read and understand between 8,000 and 10,000 words. The average writing vocabulary is much smaller; from 4,000 to 5,000 words are enough for most people.

To compile a scientific spelling list we evidently need to separate our writing from our speaking vocabulary, or, in other words, to find out just what words we use in writing. Elaborate investigations have been made to discover what are the common words used in writing by school children and adults. While no one of the several investigations has given us a list which we may regard as final, a composite one made up of the words that appear in the majority of these lists may be accepted as a writing vocabulary approximating to that used by most people of average education.

Some of the investigators have carried out tests to determine the relative spelling difficulty of the " commonest words," and have made groupings to indicate the school ages at which they should be learned. The following list of 100 words is widely cited as containing the most difficult of those which are in ordinary use:

which	writing	ready	choose	very
their	heard	forty	tired	none
there	does	hour	grammar	week
separate	once	trouble	minute	often
niece	would	among	any	whole
meant	siege	busy	much	seize
business	sure	built	beginning	cough
many	loose	colour	blue	piece
friend	lose	making	though	raise
some	Wednesday	dear	coming	ache
been	country	guess	early	read
since	February	says	instead	said
used	know	having	easy	hoarse
always	could	just	through	shoes
where	seems	doctor	every	tonight
women	Tuesday	whether	they	wrote
done	wear	believe	half	enough
hear	answer	knew	break	truly
here	two	laid	buy	sugar
write	too	tear	again	straight

An examination of these words shows that one-third of them are *homophones* (words that are sounded alike but spelt differently, such as *there, their* ; *two, too*). It is obvious that we cannot spell any homo-phonous word until we know which one of the pair or group it is; that is, we must know its meaning.

The other difficulties in English spelling are due chiefly to the confusion in the formative days of the language between the phonetic standards of Anglo-Saxon and Norman-French; in part to the retention of old spellings after pronunciations had changed; to the introduction of new spellings based on mis-taken analogies and etymologies; and to the borrow-ing by English from many other languages.

It saves time to learn the spelling, pronunciation, meaning and use of a word all at once. One of the serious mistakes of schools in the past was that they required pupils to spell words which were altogether beyond their understanding. The practice of the modern school is different.

The first step in seeking to know a word is to *see* it exactly. Much, perhaps most, of misspelling is due to *half*-seeing words. The second step is to pronounce the word precisely as it should be pro-nounced. If you say the word correctly, you will not write *prespiration* for *perspiration*, or *suprised* for *surprised*. You must form two images of the word—the visual (the *look* of it) and the auditory (the *sound* of it)—and these two images must be closely associated in your mind.

Remembering Peculiar Spellings

Next, centre your attention on the critical point in its spelling by asking yourself, " What is the particular thing to remember about the form of this word ? " The only difficult point about the word *thumb* is the silent *b* at the end. Fix your mind on that, connecting it with such words as *climb, comb, lamb*. You will never forget how to spell *separate* if you associate it with *parade*, which has the same Latin root. Then analyse the word; divide it into parts; put together the meanings of these parts to see what the word originally meant, or literally means; try to explain how the present or derived meaning comes from the original one.

For example, take the word *conductor*. From a dictionary we learn that it comes from the Latin *con* (with or together) + *ducere* (to lead) + *or* (instrument or thing that acts). A conductor, then, is one who leads or directs other people. A knowledge of the derivation of a word frequently helps us to remember a peculiar spelling, as *Wednesday*, from *Woden*. Then comes the meaning of the word ; this includes definition and use, or uses. There should be prac-tice in the use of words in sentences, in all the various senses a given word may have.

The best type of spelling book not only makes its selection of words by a comparative study of the lists and scales of the investigators, but it *organizes* these words according to scientific teaching principles. Derivative forms are grouped so that pupils may ob-serve the system by which they are built up. Homo-phones are presented first in illustrative phrases or short sentences. Words phonetically similar are brought together, so as to make use of the principle of association. Interest is stimulated by the use of every proper device.

While it is true that only a few rules for spelling English words are really helpful, those few do help, particularly when the pupil perceives them for himself after studying groups of illustrative words. The addition of the suffix -*ing* to *write, ache, guide, desire, bruise, increase, prepare*, enables the rule for dropping the final silent *e* before suffixes beginning with a vowel to be formulated.

By adding *-ed* or *-ing* to *mar, confer, refer, submit, acquit, control,* we learn that monosyllables and words accented on the last syllable, ending in a single consonant preceded by a single vowel, double the final consonant before a suffix the first letter of which is a vowel.

Such words as *deny, comply, query, verify, dusty, muddy, homely, pretty, jolly,* and others ending in *y* preceded by a consonant, change *y* to *i* before *-ed, -er, -est,* or *-able.* Thus: *denied, complied, dustier, muddiest, prettiest, verifiable.* But note the forms *denying, complying, studying.*

The final *e* is dropped before an ending beginning with a vowel (as *seize, seizure* ; *conceive, conceivable*), but retained before an ending beginning with a consonant (as *achievement, encouragement*). The *e* is also retained when needed to keep the identity of a word (as *dyeing, shoeing, hoeing*), or to keep the soft pronunciation of a *g* or *c* (as *peaceable* and *changeable*). (*G* and *c* before *a, o* and *u* are pronounced as in *gave* and *cat* ; before *e, i,* and *y* they are pronounced as in *gentle* and *centre,* though not invariably so in the case of *g*).

Most plurals are formed by adding *s* to the singular. But words ending in *s, x, z, ch, sh,* form the plural by adding *es.* Thus : *circuses, taxes, churches.* Singular forms ending in *y* preceded by a consonant form the plural by changing *y* to *i* and adding *es.* Thus : *salaries, factories, remedies, cherries, libraries.*

To avoid confusion between *ei* and *ie,* keep in mind the word *Alice,* in which you have *li* and *ce* to remind you that *i* follows *l,* and *e* follows *c.* This will help with words like *believe, relieve, receive, perceive* ; but it applies only when the sound is long *e.* Otherwise *ei* is the more usual spelling, as in *deign, vein, rein, freight, height, sleight, foreign, counterfeit, heifer.* An old jingle by which to remember this is " Use *i* before *e* except after *c,* or when it's like *a* as in neighbour or weigh." But do not forget the exceptions: *financier, seize, weird, either, neither, leisure, inveigle.*

If you are confused about whether to end a word in *-able* or *-ible,* try to think whether there is a noun related to it ending in *-ation.* If a word has a noun ending in *-ation,* the adjective generally also has *a* in its suffix, and ends in *-able.* Thus *accuse* has the noun *accusation,* and the adjective *accusable;* and we have *limitation, limitable; duration, durable; detestation, destestable,* etc. If there is no noun ending in *-ation,* the adjectives usually end in *-ible,* as *collectible, digestible, repressible.*

There have been many attempts to introduce simplified spellings. The first was that of Noah Webster, who, in his American Dictionary (1828) dropped the *u* from such words as *favour, honour, mould, colour,* and changed the French-derived *metre, centre, theatre,* etc., to *meter, center, theater,* etc. These simpler spellings have largely taken the place of the others in the United States of America.

In the 19th and 20th centuries there were demands for spelling reform in the English language, varying from suggested modifications to lessen deviations from the common rule, from the poet Robert Bridges (1844-1930), to the proposal for a new phonetic alphabet by the Irish dramatist and author George Bernard Shaw (1856–1950).

Spenser, EDMUND (1552-99). An Elizabethan poet, Spenser will be remembered for all time by his allegorical poem in praise of moral goodness entitled The Faerie Queene.

In its verses fair ladies, courtly knights, magicians and fearsome monsters are portrayed, with the idealized form of Queen Elizabeth as the principal character (Gloriana). Although the poem often becomes little more than a series of more or less disconnected episodes, the enchantment of Spenser's inimitable verbal music runs through it all.

From a portrait owned by the Earl of Kinnoull
EDMUND SPENSER
Despite objections to his tedious use of allegory, the Elizabethan poet Edmund Spenser is admired as the creator of a world of fantasy and beauty in The Faerie Queene.

The poet was born in London and was educated at Merchant Taylors' School, London, and at Pembroke Hall, Cambridge. Early introduced at Court, for his services as secretary to the Lord Deputy of Ireland he was rewarded with an estate of 3,000 acres in County Cork. While at his Irish seat, Kilcoman Castle, in 1589 he read part of The Faerie Queene to his friend Sir Walter Raleigh, who persuaded Spenser to bring the poem to London, where he was received in audience by Queen Elizabeth. In 1597 Kilcoman Castle was burned and sacked in an Irish rebellion. The poet died in London on January 16, 1599, and was buried in Westminster Abbey.

His other works include The Shephearde's Calendar (*see* page 1211); the pastoral Colin Clout's Come Home Again, describing his visit to London after nine years' absence in Ireland; the marriage songs, Prothalamion, with its refrain, Sweet Thames, run swiftly till I end my song, and Epithalamion; Astrophel, an elegy on the death of his friend, Sir Philip Sidney (1554–86); and, in prose, View of the State of Ireland. Spenser had the gift of making verbal music, and the Spenserian stanza in which The Faerie Queene was written was a notable contribution to English metrical verse, used by Byron in Childe Harold's Pilgrimage, and by Keats in The Eve of St. Agnes.

Sphinx. Chiselled from solid rock probably some 2,800 years before the birth of Christ, the Great Sphinx of Gizeh in Egypt is the oldest example of this form of art. It has the body and paws of a lion, but its head is a portrait of King Khafra (ruler of Egypt *c.* 2867–2811 B.C.), who built it and placed it before his pyramid tomb. It

THE GREAT SPHINX BY DAYLIGHT AND FLOODLIGHT

Khafra, Pharaoh of Egypt from about 2867 to 2811 B.C., perpetuated his memory and features by having his portrait carved from the rock as the head of the Great Sphinx at Gizeh, near Cairo, Egypt. The face is 14 feet wide, and the creature's body is 187 feet long. In 1926 the sand between the paws was cleared away, revealing an open-air temple (upper). The lower illustration shows Khafra's features, once painted red, lit up by floodlighting.

was worshipped as the sun-god, Harmachis, and there are remains of an open-air temple between the paws, with an altar of Roman date.

Grains of sand caught up by the winds of the desert have scratched and rasped the rock until all sharpness of angles and lines has melted away. The beard and nose have gone; the " graceful smile " described by visitors of old has vanished, leaving the strange inscrutable look which led the Arabs to call it the " Father of Terrors." But the huge mass of the body remains in crumbling outline, defying time and men.

The head of the Sphinx measures 19 feet from top of forehead to bottom of chin, and the shoulders and the upper portion of the paws extend forward 56 feet. The body is 187 feet in length, while the height from the ground to the top of the head is 66 feet. These dimensions were discovered in 1926, when the Egyptian government succeeded in digging away the surrounding sand, revealing the complete body of sculptured rock and the paws of built-up stone. Smaller sphinxes exist elsewhere in Egypt, often standing in pairs at a temple entrance.

A series of sphinxes was exacavated on the site of the ancient Egyptian city of Thebes in March 1949. The figures, each carved from a single block of sandstone and about nine feet long, form a continuation of the avenue of sphinxes which connects the temple of Ammon at Karnak with the temple of Luxor, nearly two miles away, and each bears the head of King Nechtanebis, who reigned about 400 B.C.

From the Egyptians the Greeks borrowed their idea of a sphinx, which they conceived as a winged lion with a female bust. According to legend, the sphinx that lived on a hill above the city of Thebes in Boeotia, Greece, put a riddle to all those who passed by, and devoured all who failed to guess the answer. After many had died in this way, the Theban hero, Oedipus, succeeded in solving the riddle and so caused the monster's death. (*See* illustration in page 2425).

Spices AND CONDIMENTS.

In medieval England the customary winter diet consisted of bread and coarse salt meat, which became unpalatable by spring. So spices were in enormous demand to lend some savour to this monotonous and tasteless fare. Cinnamon, cloves and pepper were worth their weight in gold, and for centuries these condiments were among the most important articles of commerce. The spice trade was a leading factor in determining the rise and fall of States, in provoking wars, and in discovery and exploration. It was chiefly the desire to discover new ways of reaching the spice-producing countries that led to the finding of sea routes to the East in the early 15th century, and the discovery of America.

Arabia was at first the distributing centre for spices, which were brought overland, chiefly from India, by camel caravans. Venice rose to world power in the 14th and 15th centuries through her control of the Mediterranean trade in spices and other imports from the East. When Venice lost command of this trade at the end of the 15th century, as the result of the discovery of new sea routes to the East round the Cape of Good Hope, first Portugal, then Holland, rose to wealth and power largely through their monopoly of the spice trade. It was mainly to break the Dutch monopoly that the English East India Company was formed in 1600, and granted a charter by Queen Elizabeth.

A number of these aromatic substances have other uses besides that as flavouring agents. Some, such as vanilla, cloves and pepper, are valuable in perfumery, sweetmeats, and scented soaps, or in the manufacture of incense, as cinnamon. Others—cardamom, ginger, nutmeg, oil of cloves—are utilized in medicines. Turmeric is used as a yellow dye, especially by the natives of the sub-continent of India and of China.

It is a remarkable fact that a large proportion of the spices are successfully grown only on islands or near the sea. Nutmegs, cloves, vanilla, cinnamon and cardamom may be termed island plants, and long before " spice islands " are in sight sailors know that they are near—by the fragrance which is borne to them on the land breeze.

Egyptian Travel Bureau

KARNAK'S AVENUE OF SPHINXES
The ancient Egyptian city of Thebes lay along the east bank of the Nile, the northern half of its ruins being now known as Karnak, and the southern as Luxor. At Karnak are three vast brick enclosures, wherein temples once stood, and towards the northernmost of these runs this remarkable avenue of small sphinxes, still well preserved after thousands of years.

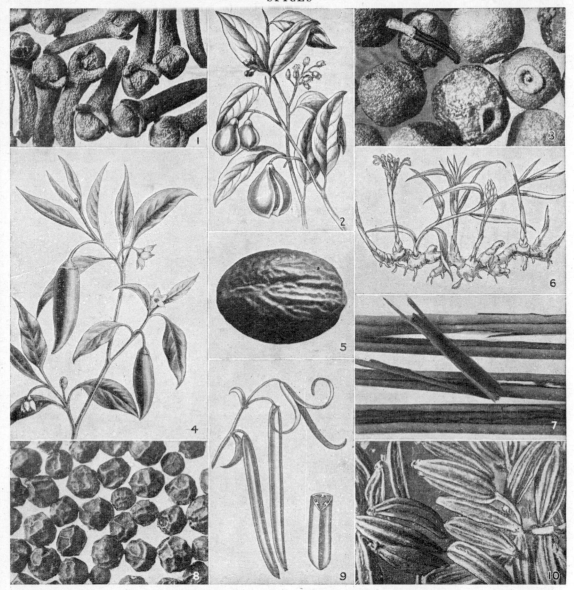

HOW SPICES AND CONDIMENTS GROW

Different types of plants give us the spices and condiments used in food. 1. Cloves, twice natural size. 2. Nutmeg tree branch, much reduced, with flowers, leaves and fruit. 3. Allspice berries, much magnified. 4. Red pepper branch, with flowers and fruit. 5. Nutmeg. 6. Ginger plant—a growing root. 7. Cinnamon bark. 8. Black pepper berries, somewhat magnified. 9. Vanilla beans—the pods are seven or eight inches long. 10. Caraway seeds, highly magnified.

The flavour of spices is due to the presence of aromatic oils secreted in the plant, and these oils are strongest in different parts of the various plants. In cloves and capers it is the flower-buds which are particularly aromatic; in coriander, capsicums and pepper it is the fruit. The ginger, liquorice and turmeric of commerce are roots or underground stems, and cinnamon and cassia are the inner bark of trees. In most of the savoury herbs—sage, mint, thyme, marjoram, parsley—the leaves are richest in these essential oils, while nutmegs, caraway and anise are seeds. Mace is the outer fibrous coat of the nutmeg seed.

When flower-buds are utilized they are plucked just before they are ready to break into blossom.

The whole clove is the dried flower-bud of a small bushy tree; the four petals are closed into a tight ball, held by four fleshy sepals. Capers are the salted and pickled buds of the caper plant, a trailing shrub which grows wild on mountainous slopes bordering the Mediterranean Sea; the flower is " sensitive," opening when the sun strikes it, and must, therefore, be gathered very early in the morning while it is still unopened.

Cinnamon is the dried inner bark of a small ever-green tree, which grows best in Ceylon. It has long been popular, having been highly prized in Biblical times. Resembling it in flavour is its close relative, cassia bark. Several species of cassia yield medicinal substances, the most widely known being senna, consisting of leaflets and seed-pods, from which a purgative drink is made.

Pimento or allspice, also known as Jamaica pepper, consists of the small unripe fruits of a tree belonging to the myrtle family, which resembles the clove. The spice takes its name allspice from its resemblance in perfume and taste to a mixture of cinnamon, cloves and nutmeg. The word pimento comes from the Spanish *pimienta*, meaning pepper.

Coriander is one of the oldest known spices. It is the fruit of a small herb growing on the shores of the Mediterranean, and also largely cultivated in the sub-continent of India. It is valued as an ingredient in confectionery, is used to disguise unpleasant tastes in medicines, and is one of the components of curry powder. Another of the spices often used in curry is cumin, which is also used as a substitute for caraway seeds in seed cakes.

Mustard (*q.v.*), from which the condiment is obtained, will grow almost anywhere, the best white variety (*Brassica alba*) being grown in England. The mustard of commerce is a mixture of black and white mustard, the seeds being ground, mixed with wheat flour, and coloured yellow with turmeric.

The SPIDER *Alert in her* 'PARLOUR'

There are people who shudder at the mere sight of a spider. Yet the ways of these creatures are of absorbing interest once the observer can overcome his or her instinctive repugnance.

Spiders. In their struggles for existence, spiders have developed strange habits for concealing themselves, protecting their young, and capturing their prey. This last is of the utmost importance, for all spiders are carnivorous, that is, they feed upon creatures that they are able to catch.

The web of the garden spider appears in all its delicate tracery when it is outlined in dew as here.

Except in the Arctic regions and on the tops of high mountains, where there is little insect life as food supply, spiders are found in all parts of the world, even in remote islands. Some catch their prey by speed of foot, some by leaping from ambush, a great many by means of silken webs which they spread in their victim's path.

Spider webs are of several kinds and shapes. Some are funnel-shaped, others are closely woven sheets which look like fine tissue paper. The most beautiful and elaborate structures are the wheel-shaped webs, woven with geometrical precision, of the so-called orb spinners.

The common garden spider (*Epeira diademata*) is among the most skilful of these. You can find a web in almost any garden, stretched across a fence corner or between the branches of shrubs. The female, distinguishable by her big, rounded, brown or green body, with regular white markings, sits in the middle of the web waiting for visitors. If the web is touched lightly, or if a small object is thrown into it, she rushes at it, ready to attack the intruder; it is by the trembling of the web that she knows that something has been caught.

When hard rain or wind comes along, the web may be wrecked. Then the spider may be watched as she builds it again. She drops, or jumps, from one support to another, paying out a silk cable behind her, and fastening it wherever she can. Soon she has an irregular space enclosed. These lines are so fine that it would be necessary to lay four or five thousand of them side by side to make a ribbon an inch wide. Round these lines she runs, pulling them with her hind foot to test their strength. If one breaks she spins another.

Soon she has her space divided into four nearly equal parts. Then she spins other spokes across the centre. The many crossings make a stout hub. Starting at this hub, she weaves a spiral line, crossing the spokes and glueing the joints. The spiral is carried round four or five turns. This is in effect the temporary scaffolding, made of tough threads like the spokes. This stage in construction is shown in the fourth illustration in the opposite page.

H. E. Cowley

HOW THE WEB IS WOVEN
In this close-up photograph it can be seen just how the spider manages to spin its web. One strand is coming from the spinneret in the end of the spider's body, and others are being dealt with by the last two pairs of legs.

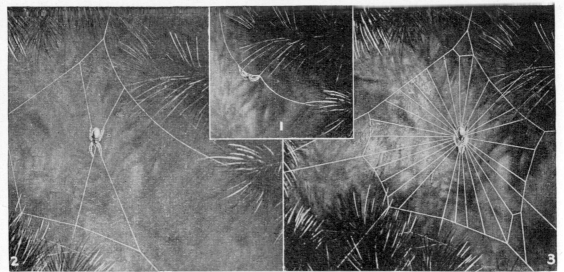

About four and a half hours
elapsed during the taking of these
photographs, but the spider did
not work for the whole of the
time. The actual building of the
web took a little over an hour.

Now she starts near the outside edge and circles in spiral fashion round towards the centre. This time she uses a much thinner and finer silk, studded with small sticky beads. It is this thread that catches and holds the feet of unwary insects. As she travels back to the central hub, the spider cuts the scaffolding away. When the new sticky spiral is complete, she spins new support lines from the outer rim of the web to the supporting branches and pulls them tight, until the whole structure is taut. It takes less than an hour to make the web. If it is destroyed, the spider has plenty of material to build another, for in the hind part of her body are the little "spinnerets" from which it is woven. These may have as many as 100 holes through which the silky material is ejected. The web starts as a liquid, which quickly solidifies on contact with air.

It is the female who does this work and she nearly always lives alone. The male is very much smaller than she is. The female spider barely tolerates her mate and even eats him if other food is scarce. She builds her house, catches her food, looks after her

A SPIDER WORKS AT NIGHT
These photographs of the web of a garden spider
in course of construction were taken by flashlight.

After hanging the first cable (1),
she built a frame (2) into which
she fitted a series of spokes (3). A
spiral was then added (4) to hold
the spokes in position, and soon
the web had been completed (5).

family, and lives most of the time in a state of busy solitude.

Centuries ago the work of the spider was looked upon as magic and the Greeks made a story about her. The spider, they said, was a maiden named Arachne, who challenged the goddess Athena (q.v.) to a contest in weaving, and proved herself more skilful. Enraged that a mortal should be more clever than herself, the goddess tore Arachne's work to pieces, and the disconsolate maiden tried to hang herself. But Athena in her mercy changed the rope into a cobweb and Arachne into a spider, telling her to spend the rest of her days in making webs. It is because of this story that the scientific name *Arachnida* was given to the spider and its relatives.

Sometimes a spider's web stretches across a small stream. How was the first thread carried across? The spider merely waited until the wind was in the right direction and then climbed on a high branch and released a long free thread. This was carried over by the breeze, became entangled in the shrubs on the other side, and was then drawn tight and fastened. Provided with this first cable

J. J. Ward

A SPIDER LIES IN WAIT

After constructing its web the spider retires to a hiding-place near by, taking with it a single thread by which it remains in communication with its gossamer fly-trap. In this photograph we see a female garden spider resting outside her snare, with her hind-leg clutching the communication cord.

rushes out, fastens a broad band around the big floundering insect and with a few dexterous kicks rolls it over two or three times until it is unable to move. Then a quick bite with her poison jaws completes the work.

Spiders use their silken threads for purposes other than spinning webs. A cocoon is woven to contain the eggs, and is either fastened to a leaf or twig or is carried about by the mother underneath her body until the young hatch. Some species then transport the baby spiders on their backs until the youngsters are old enough to look out for themselves. The young spiders are miniature versions of the adult; they do not undergo metamorphosis (drastic change in shape) as the insects do, but merely grow rapidly.

The trap-door spiders dig holes in the ground and conceal the openings with hinged covers, lining the inside of their tunnels with a layer of silk. The door may be a simple flap of silk and earth, or it may have the edges accurately cut to fit the opening, so that when it is shut one cannot distinguish it from the surrounding earth. On the inner surface of the door are tiny holes and grooves, which receive the claws and jaws of the spider when it is holding the door closed against its enemies. These spiders lie in wait, with the door just propped open, and dart out to seize any passing prey they may see.

path across the stream, the spider found it easy to stretch the other lines and spin the web around them.

Some kinds of spiders do not live on their webs, but hide in small woven nests near by. From the centre of the web they stretch a tight line to their den. This acts like a door-bell. A grasshopper, perhaps, jumps into the net. Quickly the spider

The raft-spider builds a boat of leaves and twigs lashed together with silken cables, launched on the surface of a pond. Wishing to make a raid upon water insects, the spider leaves the raft and runs out over the surface of the pool to catch them. Even more ingenious is the true water spider (*Argyroneta aquatica*), which lives among the plants at the bottom of clear, quiet ponds. There it builds a thimble-shaped dome of waterproof silk, fastened

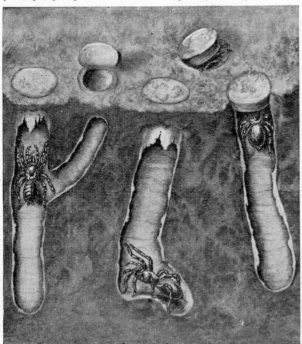
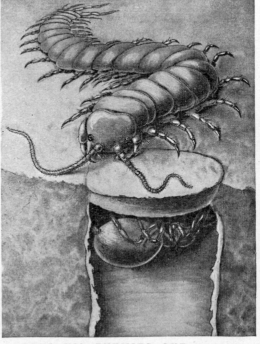

A TRAP-DOOR LETS HIM IN AND KEEPS HIS ENEMIES OUT

On the left are trap-door spiders in the security of their burrows. The doors, neatly hinged and carefully bevelled to fit the entrances, open at the slightest touch from below, and spring shut again when pressure is removed. On the right is a spider safe in the hole, holding down the door so that the centipede cannot get in. Both are shown magnified.

GIANT SPIDER WITH ITS HUMMING-BIRD PREY

Edward Step

me of the giant members of the spider group, found in tropical ions, have earned the name of bird-eating spiders, and here 1 see one of them at its feathered repast. Although birds not actually the main items of their diet, these horrid creatures—sometimes as much as eight inches from leg-tip to leg-tip—are able to catch small birds by lying in wait just inside their holes (you can see one in the background of this picture) and then springing on their unsuspecting victim.

STUDYING THE SPIDER WITH THE MICROSCOPE

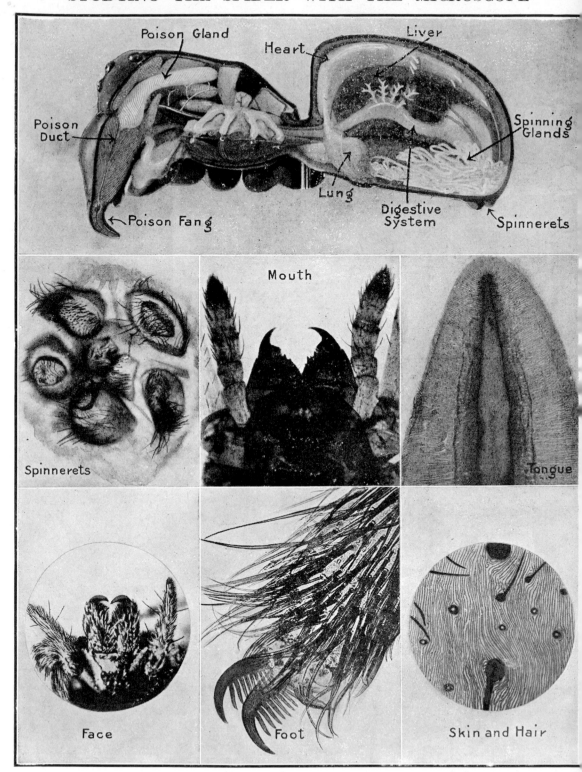

These photographs are many times magnified, so that you may see exactly how a spider is built. The noteworthy features of the internal structure are the poison ducts, which end in the curved claw in front of the mouth, and the spinning glands, which terminate in the spinnerets. All that part of the head which is visible directly from the front is called the face. The spider can swallow only liquid foods. After it wounds its prey with its claws and kills it by the poison flowing from the duct in the under side of the claw, the spider sucks the victim dry, and casts aside the hard parts.

mouth downward to the stem of a plant or wedged in the crevice of a stone. Then it goes to the surface and catches air bubbles on its hairy body and carries them down, brushing them off into its cell until it is filled to the brim with air. To this home the water spider brings whatever prey it catches. Here, too, its eggs are laid and hatched. (*See* series of pictures in page 2287).

Young spiders have a method of aerial navigation. On a hot day the spider climbs to the top of a bush or a fence post, or merely to the summit of a clod of earth. There it lifts up its abdomen and spins out a thread, which is carried upward by the air rising from the warm ground. Other threads are added to the first one, and perhaps spun together into a fluffy cloud of gossamer. The breeze tugs at the " aircraft," the spider lets go of the launching platform, hanging by a slender thread, and away it sails. When it wants to descend it spins out a drop-cord until it reaches the landing-place.

Certain crab-spiders (*Thomisidae*) hide in flowers and seize insects that come for honey. The wandering wolf spider (*Lycosa*) runs down its prey in an open race. It is to this family that the poisonous tarantula of southern Europe belongs.

The poison of a spider is rarely, if ever, directly fatal to Man. It destroys cells near the point of the bite and thus may bring about a fatal general infection of " blood poisoning." The " black widow," " hourglass," or " shoe-button " spider scientifically known as *Lactrodectus mactans*, has a bad reputation in the United States for causing deaths in this manner. The female is the dangerous one. She is about half an inch long, and coal black, marked with red or yellow or both. She usually has on the underside a patch of colour shaped like an hour-glass, and red spots on the back. The male is half the size of the female and more conspicuously marked. These spiders are found under logs and stones and around outbuildings.

Male spiders are often much smaller than the females, and frequently brilliantly coloured; and in some species they per-

J. J. Ward
LIFE OF A HUNTING SPIDER
The hunting spider carries its cocoon of eggs about with it (top photo) as it spins the nest in which it will be placed (centre). When the young spiders hatch (bottom) they burst the cocoon open and swarm out, able at once to fend for themselves.

form extraordinary antics before the females, leaping and swaying and displaying their beauty. Usually these dancers remain at a safe distance, or approach with great caution, for if they fail to find favour they are likely to be pounced upon by the female and eaten.

Spiders vary greatly in shape and size. Some are no bigger than the head of a pin, while others, like the giant bird-eating spiders (*Mygale*) of South America, sometimes have bodies measuring up to three inches in length and legs expanding to seven inches. These giants are usually hunters, leaping on their prey from a nest or burrow in a rotten tree trunk; they may eat small mammals and reptiles as well as birds.

The thread which spiders produce is stronger than silk, but it cannot be obtained in sufficient quantities for cloth making. It is sometimes used for the delicate cross-hairs in telescopes and other optical instruments, where extra fine strands of great strength are needed.

Spiders belong to the order *Araneida* of the class *Arachnida*, which also includes scorpions. The *Arachnida* in turn are included in the sub-kingdom of the *Arthropoda* (creatures with jointed legs), which also contains the insects, the crustaceans, the centipedes and the millipedes.

They are not insects, for they have eight legs, whereas insects have only six (*see* Insects). Also, the head and thorax of spiders are consolidated in one segment, called the *cephalothorax*, which is connected with the abdomen by a slender waist. The number of eyes the spider has varies from two to eight, according to the species.

Spinning. Among the wonders of modern industry are the great textile mills, turning out miles and miles of beautiful fabrics; and the machines which they employ are marvels of inventive genius. Fundamentally, cloth-making involves two processes: spinning and weaving. Both processes had been discovered long before Man had learned to write and before recorded history began.

Spinning consists in drawing out and twisting the fibres of flax, cotton, wool, silk, or other materials (including the synthetic ones), so as to form a yarn suitable for weaving. Weaving, in turn, is the art of interlacing lengthwise yarns ("warp") with crosswise yarns ("weft" or "woof") so as to produce cloth. (The story of weaving is told under the headings Jacquard Loom; Loom; and Weaving).

For thousands of years the only means of spinning were the spindle and distaff. The prepared fibres were loosely bound to the end of the "distaff" (a short stick), which was held in the left hand or stuck in the spinner's belt. The notched end of the spindle was then caught in some of the fibres on the distaff; these were drawn out by the spinner's hands, and twisted into yarn by rotating the dangling spindle, a "whorl" of stone or clay being attached to its opposite end to weight the spindle and assist this operation. When a yard or so of yarn was thus spun, it was wound about the shaft of the spindle and fastened, and the operation was repeated. Threads of wonderful fineness have been fashioned in this primitive way. The cobweb-like muslins of India were woven of thread so fine that 253 miles of it were spun from a single pound of cotton. The spindle used was of bamboo, about as long as a darning-needle, and lightly weighted with clay.

Later came the spinning wheel. The principle of this is identical with that used in spinning with the hand spindle—twisting, combined with stretching—but the spindle is mounted in bearings and given a uniform motion by being attached to a wheel driven by a pedal and crank. During the 18th century several notable inventions completely revolutionized spinning, by enabling the operator to spin many threads at the same time.

James Hargreaves produced the spinning jenny (see page 1578), which enabled a worker to spin 20 threads at once. Sir Richard Arkwright invented the spinning frame, which could be driven by machinery and turned out work equal to that of the spinning wheel (see page 235). Samuel Crompton (q.v.), in his spinning mule, combined some of the principles of the machines made by Hargreaves and Arkwright. Today factories with power-driven "mule spinners" and "ring spinners" enable a single operative to spin more yarn or thread in the

course of a day than was possible with thousands of spinning wheels before 1750.

The production of the artificial textile fibres such as rayon or nylon is on the lines of those used by the spider and the silkworm. A viscous solution is forced through tiny holes in a "spinneret" so as to make long, continuous threads, which are then hardened by various processes. These threads are afterwards spun in much the same way as other textile fibres to make yarns of the required sort. (See Rayon.)

Spirits.

The term "spirits" is generally used to describe alcoholic liquors, having above a certain alcohol content, which are obtained by distillation of fermented liquors. The name is thus applied to brandy, rum, whisky and industrial alcohol.

Brandy is made by distilling certain wines or fermented grape juice. Rum is made by distilling the alcohol resulting from the fermentation of molasses by yeast (see Sugar). In Britain

Metropolitan Museum of Art, New York; British Museum; Victoria & Albert Museum
SPINNING BY HAND IN OLDEN TIMES
1. Models of women of ancient Egypt spinning flax with distaffs ; others are weaving linen cloth on horizontal looms. 2. Weaving and spinning in medieval times : the woman seated in the centre is holding two crude combs for carding (combing) the threads. 3. Carved walnut spinning-wheel of the 18th century.

most of the industrial alcohol is also manufactured by distilling fermented molasses.

Barley, rye and other grains are used in making whisky. The grain is steeped in water and left for about three weeks on the malting floor, where it germinates and the starch in the grain is converted into sugar. The germinated grain, called " malt," is mashed with hot water, and the filtered solution containing the dissolved sugars is fermented by adding yeast. The main product of the fermentation, apart from the carbon dioxide given off, is alcohol. This is concentrated by distillation. The resulting liquor, containing 40 to 50 per cent alcohol by volume, is called whisky. It has to mature in special casks before it is in a fit state for consumption.

Whisky, brandy and rum all contain about the same amount of alcohol, the differences in their characters being due to the small amounts of " secondaries " produced in the fermentation, and distilled with the alcohol.

The production of spirits is closely supervised in Britain by the Excise authorities, the Excise duty being an important source of revenue which helps to " pay the nation's bills."

The tax on spirits is based on the " proof " gallon. There is an interesting story behind this. It was found, many years ago, that when a spirit was poured on gunpowder, if the spirit was over a certain strength (called proof strength), then the gunpowder could be lit. With a more dilute spirit, the powder could not be made to burn when ignited. This was an uncertain standard, and later the amount of alcohol in proof spirit was based on the density of the solution as determined by a hydrometer (q.v.). On this definition, proof spirit contains 49·28 per cent of alcohol by weight, or 57·1 per cent by volume, at a temperature of 60° F. Pure alcohol is 175·1 per cent proof. A whisky containing 40 per cent alcohol by volume is 70 per cent proof, or 30 degrees " under proof." An 80 per cent alcohol solution would be 140 per cent proof, or 40 degrees " over proof." In the United States, proof spirit is defined as 50 per cent alcohol by volume, and pure alcohol would in this classification be 200 per cent proof.

Industrial alcohol is made from various materials according to availability. In the United States maize is used; in Sweden and Canada wood waste; in Germany and Eastern Europe potatoes; and in sugar-producing countries the alcohol is distilled from molasses. Methylated spirits is described under alcohol.

The word " spirit " is applied to various solutions, such as " spirit of salt " for hydrochloric acid solution, and " spirit of hartshorn " for a solution of ammonia. Petrol is also known as motor spirit. (See Alcohol).

Spitsbergen.
An Arctic archipelago 360 miles north of Norway (see map in page 223), the chief islands of Spitsbergen are Mainland or West Spitsbergen, North East Land, Prince Charles Foreland, Edge Island, Barents Land, King Karl's Land, Hope Island and Bear Island. There are numerous smaller islands, and the area of the group, which is also known as Svalbard, is 24,294 square miles. It is a dependency of Norway.

All the islands are mountainous, with peaks reaching a height of from 3,000 to 5,000 feet, and there are numerous glaciers. The coast of Mainland is deeply indented by fiords, which give access to the heart of the country ; most of the other islands have good natural harbours. The winters are severe, but from July to September the temperature is well above freezing point.

Owing to the climate, vegetation is scanty. Land animals include the fox, reindeer and polar bear. Whales and seals occur in the neighbouring waters. Coal is the principal product, and there are several mining camps inhabited all the year round.

The Norwegians claim to have discovered the group in 1194, and it was certainly visited by the Dutch navigator Willem Barents (died 1597) in 1596, and by the English explorer Henry Hudson (died 1611) in 1607. Norway's sovereignty over the islands was recognized in 1920, but that country did not take formal possession of Spitsbergen until 1925.

During the Second World War (1939–45) a raid was made in 1941 by Canadian, British and Norwegian troops to forestall a German plan to seize the rich coal mines on West Spitsbergen. The Allies brought 700 Spitsbergen miners and their families to Great Britain, dynamited the mines and set fire to the stocks of coal. In 1943 German naval forces made an attack on the archipelago, but did little damage.

Sponges.
Though sponges have been known for thousands of years it was not until the 19th century that they were proved to be animals and not plants, forming a division of the animal kingdom called the *Porifera*. Like plants they are always fixed and have no eyes or other sense organs, or legs, or any of the internal organs that we usually think of as belonging to animals. Yet they have the mode of feeding, and type of egg cells and development that belong to animals. And in other obscure ways they resemble animals and not plants. Of course this refers to *living* sponges. The washing

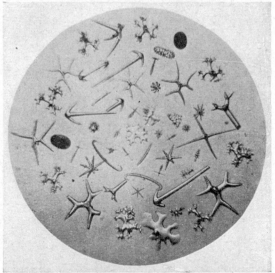

H Bastin

SPONGE SPICULES
Seen under a microscope a piece of sponge is hardly recognizable, for it is found to consist of a mass of variously-shaped pieces of limy or flinty material called spicules, which go to make up the skeleton. Here is a selection of spicules, taken from different types of sponge.

sponge is only the skeleton of a colony of sponges; in life it was filled in and covered with the soft jelly-like flesh of living cells.

Sponges of all kinds always live in water. Most of them are sea forms, but one family is common in fresh water in most parts of the world. The marine forms live mostly in fairly shallow water, down to a few hundred feet deep; but some live in the deepest seas.

They are of many sizes, forms and colours. One is very simple, an inch or less in length, and branching like a delicate bit of seaweed. Another is like a small vase half an inch long. Others take the form of vases a foot or more in diameter. "Finger-sponges" often grow on oyster beds and look somewhat like a many-fingered hand. The wonderful "Venus's flower-basket" (*Euplectella aspergillum*) of the Philippine Islands is about the size and shape of a banana. Ordinary bath sponges when living have much the size and shape that we know from their skeletons, with the firmer smooth end attached to the ocean bed, stone or shell

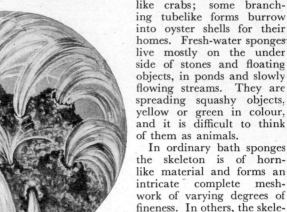

A SPONGE FEEDING

The minute particles of animal and vegetable matter on which the sponge feeds are obtained from the water which enters its body through pores. The used water, containing waste products, pours out through larger openings as shown above.

of some creature, and the softer rough end tree. Some sponges live only attached to other animals like crabs; some branching tubelike forms burrow into oyster shells for their homes. Fresh-water sponges live mostly on the under side of stones and floating objects, in ponds and slowly flowing streams. They are spreading squashy objects, yellow or green in colour, and it is difficult to think of them as animals.

In ordinary bath sponges the skeleton is of horn-like material and forms an intricate complete mesh-work of varying degrees of fineness. In others, the skeleton consists of rods and fibres of limy material (spicules), interlocked in intricate ways. In others, again, the fibres and rods are of flinty material. The beautiful skeleton of the "Venus's flower-basket" is of flinty fibres interwoven in ways so delicate and complicated one wonders that such a lowly creature as a sponge could have formed it and had it for its skeleton. When we refer to a skeleton we do not mean that it is all to be compared with that of a human

HUGE SPONGES FROM THE GULF OF MEXICO

Among the world's most important sponge fisheries are those off the west coast of Florida, United States, in the Gulf of Mexico. Above is part of one day's catch landed at Tarpon Springs, Florida, which is the centre of the trade in the United States. These large sponges are coarser, harder and not so durable as those obtained in the Mediterranean and are not usually sold for toilet purposes, being more suitable for such uses as cleaning windows or machinery.

being—only that it serves to give support and protection to the sponge. Although sponges are in most ways very simple animals, they are rather difficult to understand, for they are so different from other animals.

One simple type is just a small narrow tube half an inch long, attached at one end, with the outer or free end open. Numerous invisible pores admit water to the chamber within. This chamber is lined with peculiar cells, each one provided with a lash which keeps the water moving in through the small pores and out through the larger ones. This water contains oxygen for breathing, and very minute particles of food which are swept into the cells to be digested. In large sponges millions of pores admit water to systems of branched channels on the inside, which have tiny chambers lined with feeding cells. The channels lead to larger openings and so to the outside. It is these large holes that are seen in ordinary sponges.

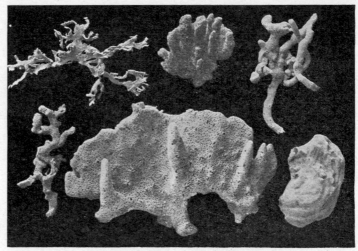

SPONGES OF STRANGE SHAPES

Though the sponge fisheries of Western Australia are not of much commercial importance they yield numerous varieties, from small sponges that look like seaweed or a cluster of worms to the larger ' glass ' type—the latter so named because their skeleton contains much silica, a constituent of glass.

Sponges are not single animals, but colonies of many individuals. The original small single sponge produces buds, much like the growth of twigs on plants. Each bud is a new sponge, but soon all are so closely knit together that it is difficult to distinguish the separate animals. Small sponges, three or four inches in diameter, may consist of a dozen or more individuals.

Sponges also hatch as larvae from egg cells only a thousandth of an inch in diameter. The larva swims away from the parent, anchors itself and begins to grow. In 25 years it may be a two-and-a-half-foot sponge. Possibly because of its peculiar odour a sponge is hardly ever eaten by other creatures, but numbers of them die of a fungus disease.

The world's chief sponge fisheries are the Gulf of Mexico off the west coast of Florida in the United States; the Caribbean Sea around Cuba and the Bahamas; and the coastal waters of the central and eastern Mediterranean. To obtain the chief American sponge, the soft yet durable " sheep's wool " (*Hippospongia gossypina*), crews may sail 50 to 80 miles out from shore and send deep-sea divers down 60 to 120 feet or more. Encased in a suit and helmet, the diver carries a knife to fight off barracudas and sharks, and a hook to tear the big sponges from their beds. For any period up to two hours he collects sponges and puts them into net baskets lowered by rope from the boat.

The crew members kill the collected sponges on deck by walking barefoot upon them. They are then hung over the side of the boat to dry. Next, they are scraped and beaten to rid them of dead tissue. Then the sponges are washed in tubs of sea water and strung up, ready for market when the boat reaches port.

From the eastern Mediterranean come the finest toilet sponges, including the Turkey cup (*Euspongia mollissima*). In the Mediterranean, most of the divers wear a diving-suit, but there are also naked divers who can go straight down 100 feet by holding heavy stones in their hands. Having let go the

stones and gathered his sponges, the diver is pulled up by a rope attached to his wrist.

To re-stock depleted beds, small pieces of live sponge are attached to sticks or tiles and planted in the sea-bed. They grow fast, and can be gathered in from two to three years.

At times there have been shortages of animal sponges, and this has encouraged the use of substitutes. One of these is the loofah, which is the mass of fibres from the inside of a loofah gourd; these plants grow in Japan, China, the sub-continent of India, Central America and the West Indies. Rubber sponges are also widely used. Others, very similar to animal sponges in physical properties, are made by fluffing up viscose rayon while it is still in the fluid state and then hardening it.

Spring. When water which has sunk into the ground issues from beneath the surface through a natural opening in sufficient quantity to make a distinct current, it is called a spring.

In general, springs are due to water seeping underground through porous rock or soil and accumulating on top of a layer of impervious rock or soil. In such cases the water must find some outlet, which may occur in a valley or upon a hillside. In a valley, it may be at a point where the land dips below the level of the impervious layer; and on a hillside it will probably be where the water runs along the slope of a bed of rock or clay to a place where the bed " outcrops " or comes to the surface.

When the water is forced up under pressure it is called an artesian spring. Artesian wells, so called from *Artesium*, the Roman name of Artois, in France, where such a well was first sunk, are Man-made springs (*see* Artesian Wells). Springs that rise from a considerable depth are generally permanent, but many springs are intermittent, ceasing to flow during long spells of dry weather.

Mineral springs, which contain mineral salts in solution, often become health resorts and fashionable " watering places," such as Spa, in Belgium (where woods for its weight but possesses considerable shock-absorbing qualities. Spruce is in constant demand for general building purposes.

Squash Rackets. A very strenuous game, squash rackets is played in a small court with four walls, roof, and a wooden floor, usually illuminated by electric lights. The general idea of the game is the same as in " fives " (*q.v.*), the object of each of the two players being to score a point by striking the ball with the small, long-handled racket either before it reaches the ground or on the first bounce in such a way that his adversary is unable to return it correctly and so loses a point.

The server must stand with at least one foot in the service " box," and serve in such a way that the ball (it is a small, black, rubber sphere, the size of a " fives " ball) strikes the front wall of the court above the " service line " and falls within the service court in which his opponent is standing. As in lawn tennis two services are normally allowed, and if both are faults the server must surrender the service to his

H. Bastin

DECORATIVE AND USEFUL SPRUCE
Belonging to the order *Coniferae*, the spruce is an evergreen found in Europe, Asia and North America. It is especially well-known in the countries of northern Europe, because there young spruces are commonly used as 'Christmas trees'.

the use of the name " spa " for such a resort originated) ; Baden, in Germany ; Karlsbad (Karlovy Vary), Czechoslovakia ; Bath, England ; and Saratoga Springs in New York State.

When hot springs occur far from any volcano it is probable that water has sunk deep into the interior of the earth, where it has been warmed by the earth's internal heat, and forced back to the surface by pressure. A hot spring which throws up columns of water and steam is called a geyser (*q.v.*).

Spruce. As " Christmas trees " spruces are known to children and grown-ups all over the northern parts of Europe. Widely distributed in Europe, Asia and North America, they are distinguished from the firs in having curved needles set all round the smaller branches instead of in flat rows, and in having hanging instead of erect cones. These evergreen trees belong to the family *Coniferae*.

The finest of all European species is the Norway spruce (*Picea excelsa*), attaining a height of 80 to 150 feet. In Britain it is an ornamental as well as a timber tree. The most important North American species are the white, black, and red, the blue or Colorado, the Engelmann and the Sitka spruce.

Spruce timber is highly valued in shipbuilding, for it combines strength, lightness and elasticity. It is also the chief wood from which paper pulp and cellulose are obtained. It was used for aeroplane construction, because it is not only the toughest of soft

Sport & General

A GAME OF 'SQUASH'
Played by two people in a small court with four walls and a roof and a wooden floor, squash racquets, or ' squash,' is a very strenuous game. The diagram (upper) shows the lay-out of the court, which is usually illuminated by electric light.

J. Kearton

A RED SQUIRREL FEEDING
The agile alertness of the red squirrel is obvious in this photograph of one on a tree stump busy with a nut. Squirrels always sit upright on their haunches to eat, holding the food daintily with their front paws.

opponent. The services are delivered from the two boxes alternately. When the ball is in play the rally continues until one or the other fails to make a good return. During a rally the ball may hit any of the other walls before it hits the front one, and any part of them except the metal strip between the in-play line and the floor. Game consists of nine points, only the server scoring. It is always advisable to stand well back in the court as it is easier to run forwards than backwards.

Rackets is similar to squash but is played on a much larger court and usually by four persons.

Squirrel. Belonging to the order of rodents, members of the squirrel family (*Sciuridae*) are found in almost every part of the world, except Australia and Madagascar.

The so-called red squirrel (*Sciurus vulgaris*), which occurs throughout Europe, including Great Britain, and Northern Asia, varies greatly in colour in different localities. In northern and western Europe they are bright reddish-brown, like those of British woodlands; in the mountains of southern Europe they are greyish-black; in Siberia and Russia they are pale grey (it is the skins of this grey squirrel that are in such demand for fur). The British squirrel is about eight inches long in body, with a tail, thick and bushy in winter, of seven inches.

Squirrels live in trees and leap from bough to bough with extraordinary agility. Their nests, called " dreys," are made of leaves, grass and moss, and are built in branches of trees or in hollow trunks. Three or four young are born at a time. Their food consists chiefly of pine cones, nuts, acorns, fruits and fungi, but they occasionally eat birds' eggs. They always sit up on their haunches to eat, holding the food in their front paws. They store nuts and acorns as winter food-supply but do not really hibernate, though they may sleep for considerable periods if the winter is severe.

The grey squirrels (*S. carolinensis*), now more common in England than the native red squirrel, were introduced from North America and have become a pest; for they eat eggs and young birds and also drive out the weaker red squirrels.

The flying squirrels of North America, Asia and eastern Europe, have a peculiar extension of skin connecting the fore and hind legs. This is loose and forms a kind of parachute when the legs are extended, enabling them to make gliding leaps of nearly 20 yards. They vary in colour from bluish-grey to brown, and are nocturnal in habit.

Staffa, SCOTLAND. An uninhabited volcanic island of the Inner Hebrides, seven miles from the island of Mull, Staffa is an egg-shaped tableland about three-quarters of a mile long, one-third of a mile wide and 71 acres in area. In the north-east there is a shelving shore, but otherwise the coast has formidable cliffs with numerous caves, the faces and walls of which in most cases are formed of colonnades of black hexagonal and pentagonal basaltic pillars; hence the island's name, which is a Scandinavian word meaning pillar island.

The most remarkable cave is Fingal's, which was discovered in 1772 by Sir Joseph Banks, and is Scotland's nearest approach to Ireland's Giant's Causeway (*q.v.*). The cave is 227 feet long, 42 feet wide and 66 feet high. The entrance is an arch supported by basalt columns, and from it to the end of the cave there is a pavement of broken columns. The composer Mendelssohn (*q.v.*) was inspired by Fingal's Cave in writing his overture The Hebrides. Other caves are the Scallop or Clamshell Cave, the Boat Cave, and Mackinnon's or Cormorants' Cave. Not far from the Scallop Cave is a rock shaped like a shepherd's cap and known as " the Herdsman."

Fred W. Hardie

CAVE OF COLUMNS IN STAFFA
Fingal's Cave, at the southern end of the isle of Staffa in the Inner Hebrides, is world famous. The symmetry of the multitude of basalt pillars ranged along the front and sides is astonishing, and the cave, which is 66 feet high, is remarkable for its lovely stalactites.

Staffordshire. One of the midland counties of England, Staffordshire has an area of 1,153 miles. Its surface is low or undulating except in the north where the Pennines enter it. In the centre of the county another stretch of high ground is Cannock Chase, once a royal hunting ground, now a coalfield.

The chief river, the Trent, the third longest in England, rises in the county. In the north of Staffordshire are the Potteries, the centre of the English china and pottery industry, which is carried on chiefly in the "Five Towns" of Tunstall, Burslem, Hanley, Stoke-upon-Trent, and Longton—now forming the county borough of Stoke. In the south of the county is part of the Black Country, which extends also into Warwickshire, with its coalfields and iron and steel works. Elsewhere the county is agricultural, cattle-breeding, dairy farming, and the cultivation of wheat, barley and oats being carried on.

The county town, Stafford, is an important railway centre, and has boot and shoe factories and engineering works. Salt is made from a brine spring in the district. Stafford (population 30,000) has been a borough since 1206, and the beautiful cruciform 12th-century church of St. Mary is the most notable building. Stafford Castle occupies the site of a Norman stronghold. There are several larger industrial centres within the county that are more populous, including Wolverhampton, Walsall, Smethwick, West Bromwich, and Wednesbury. Burton-on-Trent (*q.v.*) in the extreme east of the county is the most important brewery centre in England. Among smaller places of historic interest is Lichfield (*q.v.*), with its Cathedral (*see* illustration in page 726), perhaps the most beautiful of the smaller English ones. The town has also Staffordshire's most interesting literary associations. The English poet and angler Izaak Walton (1593–1683) was born in Stafford. Arnold Bennett (1867–1931) was born near Hanley, and the scene of his most important novels is laid in the Potteries. The population of the county is 1,431,400.

Stalin, JOSEPH VISSARIONOVITCH (born 1879). Commander-in-Chief of the armed forces and Chairman of the Council of Ministers of the Soviet Union, Stalin was born on December 21, 1879, the son of a peasant of Gori in Georgia, Caucasia, named Djugashvili. Stalin is one of the adopted names he used during his long career as a revolutionary. *Stal* is Russian for steel, and the name presumably was originally intended to symbolise his strong character.

JOSEPH V. STALIN

The real name of the leader of the Soviet Union is Djugashvili. Stalin (meaning 'man of steel') is one of the names he used during his career as a revolutionary. He came to power in 1927 and succeeded in crushing all opposition groups and individuals.

In his youth he became a rebel against the Tsarist regime, and as he grew older his political activities began to be noticed by the police; in 1902, as a member of the Social Democratic Party, he was arrested and exiled to Siberia. Until the Russian Revolution of 1917 he suffered repeated arrest and exile to Siberia, but always managed to escape.

He became a member of the Bolshevik Central Committee and editor of the newspaper, Pravda (Truth), which later became the chief organ of the Bolshevik Government. When the Bolsheviks gained power in October 1917, Stalin served against Russian Royalist forces who were attempting to overthrow the Revolutionary Government, and the Poles, winning considerable fame by his defence of Tsaritsyn (renamed Stalingrad) against Tsarist troops. After the campaign he became People's Commissar for State Control, and a member of the Revolutionary Military Council, 1920–23.

Then began a long struggle for supremacy between Stalin and Trotsky, who was second only to the Russian leader Lenin (*q.v.*) in the Bolshevik Government. After the death of Lenin in 1924, Stalin gradually obtained the ascendancy, and in 1927 he succeeded in overthrowing Trotsky, who was exiled in 1928, and all other possible rivals and establishing himself in supreme power. As Secretary-General of the Communist Party, Stalin introduced his first Five-Year Plan, which was intended to make Russia self-supporting, as well as agriculturally. By the aid of foreign capital and foreign technicians factories and engineering works were built in many parts of the country, hydro-electric plant was installed to supply power, and towns sprang up in new industrial areas.

In 1931 Stalin found it necessary to modify the strictly Communistic principles which underlay the Five-Year Plan, and he introduced certain changes providing for greater individual responsibility and for reward in proportion to services rendered. In addition he provided for the mass transference of peasants to industrial occupations, and offered opportunities for Russian technicians to return to the new country he was building. The results of the first Five-Year Plan and similar Plans launched in 1933 and 1937 were obscured by the Second World War (1939–45).

In 1939 he concluded a non-aggression pact and trade treaty with Germany, for which he was widely criticized in western Europe and the United States. Later events suggested that he did this to strengthen

Russia's position in preparation for the coming struggle with Germany that he felt to be inevitable. In May 1941 he became Chairman of the Council of People's Commissars—in effect, Prime Minister.

When German armies suddenly invaded Russia on June 22, 1941, Stalin took over the direction of Russia's war effort in all its aspects—military, economic, political and diplomatic. He welded the enormous resources of the country into a colossal military machine that first halted the advance of the Germans and then drove them back into their own country. In November 1943 he travelled to Teheran, Persia, for a conference with Mr. Winston Churchill, the British Prime Minister, and President Roosevelt of the United States. In February 1945 he met President Roosevelt and Mr. Churchill at Yalta in the Crimea to discuss war and post-war problems. In July 1945 he conferred in Berlin with Mr. Harry S. Truman (who succeeded Roosevelt as President), Mr. Churchill, and Mr. Attlee (British Premier in July 1945 in place of Mr. Churchill).

After the war Stalin, in the fourth Five-Year Plan of 1946, launched an ambitious programme to rehabilitate the war-devastated regions of Russia and to increase her industrial capacity.

Stalingrad. A city of the Russian Soviet Federal Socialist Republic, Stalingrad is on the River Volga, 240 miles from its mouth, and is the chief town of the region of the same name. Formerly called Tsaritsyn, in 1918 it was the scene of the defeat of a Tsarist force by Bolshevik troops under command of Joseph Stalin (q.v.) and its name was changed in his honour. Between 1922 and 1942 Stalingrad developed enormously, becoming one of the largest industrial centres of the Soviet Union. It produced tractors and other agricultural machinery, lorries, motor-vehicles, tanks, and it had oil refineries and sawmills.

In the spring of 1942, during the Second World War, the Germans determined to capture Stalingrad in order to control traffic on the Volga, which was one of the most important lines of communication remaining to the Russians. By the middle of September the Germans had reached the outskirts of the city. Concentrated artillery and aerial bombardments reduced most of it to rubble, and street fighting was continuous. Every standing stone building became a fortress, defended with the utmost ferocity floor by floor, from street level to rooftop and back again. Such battles sometimes went on for days.

Though the Germans forced back the defenders almost to the river they failed to gain command of the waterway. In the meantime the Russians had estab-

HIGH-WATER MARK OF THE GERMAN WAR-TIDE IN RUSSIA
The turning point of the campaign in Russia during the Second World War (1939–45) was the failure of the Germans to capture Stalingrad in the winter of 1942–43. The broken line on the map indicates the limit of the German advance in November 1942 ; the solid line marks the front to which the Germans had been forced back by the Russians by February 16, 1943.

lished themselves on the west bank of the river both north and south of Stalingrad, and had assembled new armies. On November 19, 1942, the Russians attacked the German and satellite forces north-west and south of Stalingrad, cutting two of the railway lines on which the Germans depended for supplies and reinforcements. On November 24 a third Russian army attacked fortified German positions north of the city, and by the beginning of the following month the German 6th Army had been encircled by the Russians. Large German forces managed to escape to the west, but by February 2,

1943, the German 6th Army had ceased to exist —330,000 of its men had been wounded, killed or taken prisoner.

The heroic defence of Stalingrad, which lasted for about five months, was the turning point of the war in Russia, and King George VI presented a sword of honour to the Russian people to mark British admiration for their valiant feat of arms. The weapon was handed to Stalin by Mr. Winston Churchill at Teheran, Persia, in December 1943. The population of Stalingrad before the Second World War was 445,500.

The ROMANCE of the POSTAGE-STAMP

*The fascination of stamp-collecting needs no explanation, but its value as a
source of education and information is sometimes forgotten : from stamps
we learn geography and history in the most interesting way possible.*

Stamps AND STAMP - COLLECTING. Stamp-collecting, or philately, is a favourite hobby in all lands, and it creates an important trade in many countries. It owes its charms to the immense variety of stamps in existence, the diversity of their designs, and the glimpses they bring us of peoples and places all over the world.

Even in its most elementary stages it has an educative value, increasing one's knowledge of geography and history; while in its commercial aspect there is always the possibility of one's stamps increasing in value, and of a rare specimen

being discovered. Some of the rarest stamps in the world (*see* illustration page 3075, and under Mauritius in page 2121) are worth a fortune.

The postage-stamp is not a thing of great antiquity. It was first produced by Great Britain in 1840, at the suggestion of Sir Rowland Hill, and, small as it is, this little piece of paper worked one of the wonders of the civilized world. It used to be a very costly matter to get letters by post in the old days, and instead of receiving them free, as one does today, one had to pay the postage to the postman on delivery.

Courtesy of the Postmaster-General

STAMPS BY THE THOUSAND BEING PRINTED AND PACKED

British postage-stamps are printed by a private firm at High Wycombe, Buckinghamshire. At the left, rolls of them are coming off the presses. The ink is tested frequently for colour and to see if it is affected by moisture. Other classes of stamp, such as National Health Insurance and Entertainment Tax, are issued by Somerset House, London, to the various post offices : at the right, sheets of newly-printed stamps of this kind are being checked and packed.

Courtesy of Stanley Gibbons, Ltd.

SOME PHILATELIC CURIOSITIES AND COMMEMORATIVE STAMPS

1. A stamp without inscriptions ; Brazil, 1844. 2. One of the famous blue ' Post Office Mauritius ' ; this specimen is in the collection of King George VI. 3. A quaint stamp of 1870 from Afghanistan. 4. The rarest stamp in the world, a one-cent British Guiana; it was last sold for £10,000 and is the only one known. 5. From the Kingdom of Naples, 1858 ; this extinct State was incorporated with Italy in 1861. 6 and 10. Modern stamps of the Netherlands and Finland in which a part of the face-value goes to a welfare fund for children. 7. One of the stamps issued for the Allied Occupation of Germany. 8. A Cape of Good Hope stamp of 1853, one of the most popular stamps of the 19th century. 9. A million-dollar stamp, but worth only a few pence; a high value of 1948 due to the collapse of the Chinese dollar. 11. A stamp of Great Britain issued in 1948 in honour of the Silver Wedding of King George VI and Queen Elizabeth. 12. Stamps of South Africa, 1948, made small to save paper; as with all South African stamps, one is inscribed in English and the other in Afrikaans. 13. Shakespeare honoured on a stamp of Hungary.

One can imagine what a lot of time and trouble there would be if postmen had to wait at the door to collect the small amounts payable on all the letters, postcards, papers and parcels, to say nothing of the extra work at the post offices to keep accounts of the moneys collected. All that was simplified by issuing adhesive stamps which one can buy at any post office and use to prepay the postage. The stamp is like a magic talisman. Stick it on the letter, drop the letter in the pillar-box, and it is carried off to wherever one wishes it to go. The stamp shows that the Post Office has received its due payment. (*See* page 2661).

The idea of using stamps to prepay postage caught on at once in England, but it was some years before it began to be realized abroad that the system was deserving of universal adoption. The United States did not issue stamps until 1847, France and Germany (Bavaria) not until 1849. Beginning with the 'fifties, the system began to spread rapidly throughout Europe and the British Empire, and now there is no civilized nation and no organized colony that does not issue postage-stamps.

The first postage-stamps of Great Britain, issued in 1840, bore a portrait of the then young Queen Victoria. Why did they bear a portrait ? There were several reasons, but the most important was because it was a safeguard against forgery, as any change in a familiar face is quickly detected. The corner letters you see on these stamps were designed for the same purpose.

During her long reign Queen Victoria's portrait appeared on just over 3,000 different stamp issues of Great Britain and the Colonies. After her death the portrait of King Edward VII, and later that of King George V, appeared on most stamps of the British Empire. In 1935 over 200 varieties were issued to commemorate the Silver Jubilee ; in 1936 stamps bearing the head of King Edward VIII were issued, and in the following year came the King George VI stamps, including the special Coronation issue.

Perhaps the most popular portraits have been those of Princesses Elizabeth and Margaret. Several appeared on the stamps of the African Dominions and Colonies visited by the Royal Family in 1947, and a delightful portrait was issued in Canada to celebrate Princess Elizabeth's marriage to the Duke of Edinburgh in 1948.

Other countries followed Britain's example in using portraits for their stamp designs. Some have studies of natives, local scenery, birds, beasts and fishes, heraldic emblems, and even mythological subjects. As you turn the pages of a stamp album you traverse continents with giant strides

The date for the issue of the One Penny Black was fixed for the 6th of May 1840, though the stamps were circulated several days before the time appointed for their use. There were eleven plates used Nos. 1 to 11; the stamps were printed in sheets of 240 (rows of twelve)

Plate xi   *Guide lines in N.E. square of all four stamps*   *Plate xi*

Courtesy of F. H. Vallencey

A PAGE FROM A SPECIALIST'S STAMP ALBUM

The first of all postage-stamps was the ' penny black ' of Great Britain, and above is a page from a specialist's album showing specimens of this stamp. At the top are three ' mint ' ones— unused, with the gum on the back. In the centre is a stamp on a ' cover,' as an envelope is termed. At the bottom are two single examples and a strip of four. At the top of the page are written details of the date of issue, watermark, the plate numbers and how the stamps were printed. Thus the page gives the history of the stamps thereon.

The more advanced philatelist needs other apparatus, such as a magnifying glass, in order to study variations of perforation, colouring, watermark, and so on. An unused or a "mint" stamp is usually worth more than a used one of the same issue and denomination, but this rule is by no means without exceptions.

The wise collector, once he has amassed a good-sized collection, concentrates on some class of stamps that appeals to him; he does not attempt to spread his collection over the whole of the philatelic field. Clean or lightly marked stamps in perfect condition are more to be desired than mere numbers. Moreover, a stamp collection of any pretensions should always include with every series that is at all fully represented a neatly written history or other description. The collector must know his stamps, or half his pleasure is lost.

Such a collection should be mounted in a loose-leaf album, whose pages can be added to or rearranged at will; and its compilation and arrangement entail the use of a catalogue or even a monograph on the specialized subject. A popular development in specialized collecting is air mail philately. "Flown covers" sent by air on a "first flight" or on some record-breaking journey are often quite valuable. The word philately is derived from two Greek words meaning "love of tax-free (i.e. prepaid) things."

Stanley, SIR HENRY MORTON (1841–1904). "The river was calm, and broad and brown. Armies of parrots screamed overhead as they flew across the river ; legions of monkeys sported in the branchy depths; howling baboons alarmed the solitudes; crocodiles haunted the sandy points and islets; herds of hippopotami grunted thunderously at our approach; elephants bathed their sides by the margin of the river; there was unceasing vibration from millions of insects throughout the livelong day; from the shores came the unearthly cry of the relentless cannibals." Such was the description

and everywhere get glimpses of the life and customs of the people. History, too, is portrayed in these little pieces of paper, for wars and revolutions, and even changes of government, produce their provisionals, their surcharges (in which the value of the stamp is altered), or their overprints (when there is a new legend printed on the stamp).

Stamp collecting, to be worth while, must be pursued with due regard to the condition of the stamps and the method and neatness of arranging them. You should not put dirty or damaged specimens into the album at all, because one black sheep will spoil the appearance of a whole page of stamps. The stamps should be mounted in the album with specially prepared hinges made of gummed paper and should be handled only with stamp tweezers. Never tear a stamp haphazard off an envelope, but soak it off carefully.

given by the explorer Stanley, of the River Congo in Africa, when, the first white man to visit that part of Africa, he travelled 2,000 miles to its mouth. Far in the interior he had embarked on its waters, without knowing what river it was or where it would lead him. Livingstone (*q.v.*), who had discovered the stream near its headwaters, thought it was the Nile because it flowed northward; but Stanley found that presently the river turned westward, and he began to suspect that the mighty stream upon which he was voyaging might be the Congo, whose mouth on the west coast was already known.

Stanley had entered Africa from the east coast, from Zanzibar, so that when he arrived at the Congo's mouth he had crossed the equatorial belt of Africa from east to west, opening up this vast region to the world. The expedition took three years (1874–77), and cost the lives of all three of his white companions, and those of a number of the native porters.

The results of this expedition were enormous, for it led directly to the formation of the Congo Free State by King Leopold of Belgium and the exploitation of the region. Stanley himself, after England had refused to interest herself in the new territory, returned to Africa and under the patronage of King Leopold directed the opening of the country to commerce, establishing trading posts and river navigation. The abuses which sprang up later under Leopold's rule were in no way Stanley's fault, as he was always the friend of the natives and worked for their good.

Stanley's interest in equatorial Africa had been first aroused some years before when, as the correspondent of a New York newspaper, he had been sent to Africa to find the missionary explorer David Livingstone, who had at that time been lost in the interior of Africa for five years. Stanley set out from Zanzibar for the interior on March 21, 1871. After overcoming almost insuperable difficulties and travelling for nearly eight months he came to an Arab town named Ujiji on Lake Tanganyika. He had heard rumours from the natives that a white man with a white beard was in this town, and he marched into it. Good fortune was with him, for he found Livingstone—old, ill, and with scanty supplies. When he actually saw before him the man for whom he had been searching so long all Stanley found to say was, " Dr. Livingstone, I presume! "

Staying in Ujiji four months, Stanley became a devoted admirer of Livingstone, but was unable to persuade him to leave his work and return to civilization. After the elderly missionary's death Stanley determined to continue his work of exploring the interior of Central Africa. The expedition down the Congo was the result. After Livingstone's death a monument was erected on the spot where he and Stanley had met, and this was replaced by a new memorial unveiled on November 15, 1946.

Stanley's life throughout was an adventurous one. His name was originally John Rowlands and he was born at Denbigh in Wales on June 29, 1841. After a youth of extreme poverty he ran away to sea and landed in New Orleans, United States, where he was adopted by a merchant named Stanley, whose name he took. He fought first with the Confederates (Southerners) and later with the Federals in the American Civil War (1861–65), and later became a newspaper correspondent. In this capacity he accompanied the British expeditionary force to Kumasi in Ashanti in 1873.

In 1887 Stanley led another expedition across Africa, this time travelling from west to east. The object of his journey was to rescue Emin Pasha, a German agent of the Egyptian Government who had been cut off in equatorial Africa by a native rebellion. He succeeded in bringing Emin Pasha back to civilization. Also he discovered the Ruwenzori mountains and Lake Edward Nyanza.

His later years were spent in England, where he was elected to Parliament, and was knighted by Queen Victoria in 1899. He died on May 10, 1904, and was honoured with a public funeral in Westminster Abbey, London.

COUNTLESS STARS *that* FILL *the* SKY

*I*t *is believed that there are at least a thousand million fixed stars, some at distances so vast that the imagination reels in the contemplation of them and of their mysteries. Our Earth itself is a satellite of a star—the sun.*

Star. Without a telescope fewer than 2,500 stars can be seen by the observer in the Northern Hemisphere—or in both hemispheres about 4,400—looking up at the heavens on the clearest night. And not every one of these is certain to be a "star." At least four or five may be planets (*q.v.*). The stars are in reality great balls of fire like our sun, and it is only because of their immense distance from the earth that they do not overwhelm us with a blaze of heat and light.

With modern high-power telescopes it is possible to see and photograph at least one hundred million stars, and even this does not exhaust the extent of the starry universe. For some years astronomers have been systematically photographing the heavens through their telescopes, bit by bit, and the camera is able to record on the photographic plates stars so faint as to be undetected by the human eye even with the aid of the most powerful telescope. It is calculated that those plates will show about a thousand million fixed stars, and that altogether there may be 15 to 100 times as many stars as there are people now in the world.

There is no way of seeing whether these other stars have planets circulating round them as our sun has. But quite recently astronomers have found that two of the nearest stars are moving through space not in quite straight lines, but in the rather sinuous curves that would be expected if planets were periodically pulling them off course. If this is the reason it is unlikely that planetary systems are very rare, so that in many places in the universe there may exist worlds like our own— worlds where plants and animals and thinking beings grow and develop in much the same way as they do on the earth.

Even if the beings on these supposed worlds should develop wireless systems capable of communicating across interstellar space, it would take years and in some cases centuries for their messages to travel to us, in spite of the fact that wireless waves travel at the same speed as light—186,000 miles a second. It takes over four years for light to reach us from the nearest visible star, which is Alpha Centauri (not visible in northern latitudes), while the rays of light that are now coming to us from some of the most distant stars undoubtedly started on their journey before the birth of Christ.

How is it possible for men to measure these enormous distances that separate us from the stars? It is done by determining what is called the " annual parallax " of the star. This process consists in observing the star from one position in the earth's orbit, and then, six months later, from the opposite side of the orbit, and computing the resulting angle. The distances are so great that the angle is very small, and the measurements must be so delicate that the parallax of only about 5,000 stars has been determined with approximate accuracy. The nearer the star, however, the easier it is to measure this angle, so we know that most of the stars which are still unmeasured lie at a greater distance than those for which the parallax has been measured. The first parallax determination was made by Bessel in 1838.

Our universe, as astronomers conceive it, consists of thousands of millions of galaxies distributed at random throughout unbounded space. Each galaxy contains thousands of millions of stars, interspersed with clouds of dust and gas, and gathered together into forms varying from globe-like clusters to flattened disks showing a

spiral structure. Our own Galaxy is probably of this latter kind, and when from the earth—a tiny satellite attached to an insignificant star called the sun near the edge of the disk —we look out towards the rim of the disk, we see the Milky Way.

If we look at the stars at a particular time at night, and then again an hour or so later, we see that they have changed their apparent positions in the heavens, with the single exception of the Pole Star. This change is due solely to the rotation of the earth on its axis. The ancients realized that at any particular hour on any particular night of the year the stars always present the same picture, and so they called them " fixed stars," as opposed to the planets, which they named the " wanderers."

But the stars are not really fixed, any more than the earth and the sun and the moon are fixed. They are moving among themselves with enormous velocity and, so far as we now know, almost in straight lines. Our sun, which is itself a star, is moving with the whole solar system in the direction of the first-magnitude star Vega at the rate of 700 miles a minute, but even at this terrific speed it will take 400,000 years to arrive, if nothing interferes to change its direction or retards its progress.

Some of the other stars move so fast that it seems certain they will some day escape from our Galaxy altogether, going out into space or nothingness, or perhaps toward other galaxies. These " runaway stars," as they are called, have in some cases a velocity as high as 200 miles a second, which means that they could go completely round the earth in a little more than two minutes.

Stars are ordinarily classified by " magnitudes," in the order of their brightness. In the " first magnitude " are placed the 20 brightest stars— Sirius, *Canopus, *Alpha Centauri, Vega, Capella, Arcturus, Rigel, Procyon, Achernar, *Beta

DISTANCES OF THE NEARER STARS
Thirty of the nearer stars at their proportionate distances from the Earth are shown, but not in relative positions. The number of years the light from each takes to reach the Earth (L.Y. or Light Years) is a measure of their distance.

POLLUX
50 L.Y.

CAPELLA
49 L.Y.

GAMMA VIRGINIS
48 L.Y.

BETA CASSIOPEIA
46 Light Years

ARCTURUS
44 L.Y.

CASTOR
48 L.Y.

DELTA HERCULIS
42 L.Y.

GAMMA PEGASI
40 L.Y.

ALPHA CEPHEI
39 Light Years

ALPHA OPHIUCHI
37½ L.Y.

BETA VIRGINIS
31 L.Y.

DELTA CASSIOPEIA
30 L.Y.

BETA LEONIS
31 L.Y.

ZETA SAGITTARII
28½ L.Y.

ZETA HERCULIS
29 L.Y.

ETA HERCULIS
26⅓ L.Y.

VEGA
26½ L.Y.

FOMALHAUT
23½ Light Years

XI BOÖTES
18 L.Y.

XI URSA MAJORIS
18½ L.Y.

ETA CASSIOPEIA
17 L.Y.

ALTAIR
15 L.Y.

61 CYGNI
11 L.Y.

EPSILON ERIDANI
10 L.Y.

PROCYON
10½ L.Y.

TAU CETI
10¼ L.Y.

SIRIUS
8¾ L.Y.

BARNARD'S STAR
6 L.Y.

ALPHA CENTAURI
4⅓ L.Y.

PROXIMA CENTAURI
4 Light Years

EARTH

Centauri, Betelgeuse, Altair, *Alpha Crucis, Aldebaran, Pollux, Spica, Antares, Fomalhaut, Deneb, and Regulus. (Those marked with an asterisk (*) cannot be seen in northern latitudes.) In the second group are 50 stars, including the Pole Star as well as the two Pointers.

In the third group we have 160; in the fourth 500; in the fifth 1,500; in the sixth 4,000; and so on, until in the magnitudes between the 16th and 17th there are supposed to be more than 50 million stars, none of which, of course, can be seen without the most powerful telescopes. The stars seem to twinkle because of the effect produced on the light waves by the earth's own atmosphere. The human eye unaided cannot see stars fainter than the sixth magnitude.

The larger groups or constellations which the stars seem to form in the sky have been given various fanciful or legendary names — for example: Ursa Major (the Great Bear), Lyra (the Harp), Taurus (the Bull), and Orion (the Warrior). In our system of cataloguing, it is usual to designate the stars in each constellation by Greek letters in the order of their brilliance. Thus the pointer star nearest Polaris is named Alpha Ursae Majoris (brightest star of the Great Bear).

Let us consider some of the brighter stars. The one most important to navigators and explorers is Polaris (the Pole Star) which, though it appears to us as a somewhat dim star of the second magnitude, is seen through great telescopes as a triple sun—three stars instead of one, but so far away that they cannot be separated by the naked eye.

The most brilliant of all stars is Sirius, the

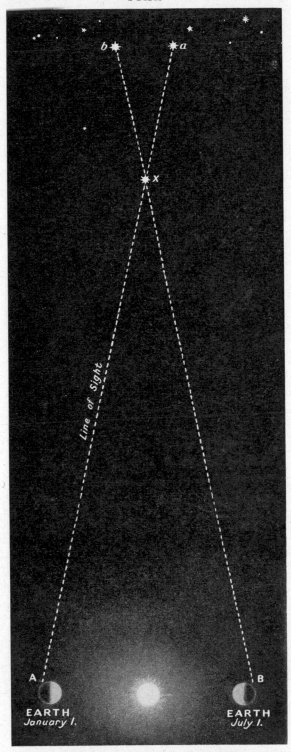

MEASURING STELLAR DISTANCES
The star X, when observed from a position A on January 1, appears, in relation to the much more distant stars, to be at *a*. By July 1, when the earth is at B, at the other side of its orbit, and 186,000,000 miles distant from A, the star X will appear to be at *b*. The distance from A to X can then be calculated easily by the astronomer.

3079

Dog Star, best observed in the evening in spring. This great sun is more than 25 times as bright as our own. The English astronomer Edmund Halley (1656–1742) was the first to suspect that Sirius was not behaving exactly as it should, but it remained for F. W. Bessel in 1844 to work out the facts, though they could not then be demonstrated for lack of powerful enough instruments. He declared that Sirius had an unseen companion star, about half as big, and that the two revolved about the same centre of gravity. In 1862 the American lens-maker Alvan G. Clark found this companion star with a new telescope he had constructed, and thus Bessel's computations were completely verified.

Sirius is comparatively near to us, being the fifth in distance from the sun. Just to give some idea what " near " in this connexion means, let us set down the figures. Sirius is 51,000,000,000,000 miles from our earth! If Sirius were travelling in our direction about six times as fast as the fastest projectile that ever left the muzzle of a great gun, it would not reach us in much less than a quarter of a million years.

The companion of Sirius does not interfere with the light it sends to the earth; but in the case of Algol, which also has a companion star, a regular eclipse occurs. Algol, " The Demon," was so called by the Arabs because it shines with the brightness of the Pole Star for about two and a half days, when suddenly its light is reduced by two-thirds; then in a few hours it regains its intensity. This is due to Algol's companion, which, in circling about, gets between the star and the earth and shuts off part of the light which we receive from it. Over 250 eclipsing " variables " of the Algol type are known, and it is estimated that one star in every four has a partner or companion star. More than 25,000 such stars have been observed.

Vega is interesting not only because the solar system is travelling towards it, but because in about 12,000 years it will become the north star instead of Polaris. This is due to what is called the " precession of the equinoxes," which causes the true north-and-south axis of the earth to move in a circle with respect to the stars, like the upper part of a spinning top.

Sometimes stars explode. A star which is ordinarily so dim that it can be seen only with a powerful telescope, if at all, may suddenly flare up and become so bright that it is visible to the naked eye. Some of these *novae* (new stars) flare more than once, but they all eventually decline to their former magnitudes. One of the brightest novae appeared in the summer of 1918 in the constellation Aquila, blazing out as brightly as Sirius, then becoming invisible to the naked eye. Another one, Nova Herculis, flared up twice between December 1934 and June 1935. Novae are not the same as "shooting stars." (*See* Meteors and Meteorites).

The stars are of different colours—white, blue, yellow or red. By means of the spectroscope (*q.v.*) we can ascertain the chemical elements of which the stars are composed. Nor is that all; for spectra differ with temperature, so the spectroscope can tell us how hot a star is. This knowledge, coupled with what we know about the structure of matter and

its behaviour under different temperatures, enables us to compute the approximate size of a star as soon as we know how bright it is absolutely, that is, how much energy it sends us.

Thanks to this knowledge scientists now believe that stars are either " giants " or " dwarfs." A giant is a young star, just a mass of rarefied gas, which is contracting and getting hotter because of the contraction. Arcturus and other bright stars are in this class. In a dwarf, internal processes giving out heat allow the star to remain stable, with a density nearly that of water, radiating heat into space like our sun. Eventually it cools rapidly, giving a reddish light, and dies. The Sirius companion is in this phase, and has contracted to so dense a mass that one cubic inch of it would weigh a ton. A peculiar class of stars more recently discovered contains the Cepheids— variable stars, formerly supposed to have companions. The spectroscope indicates that they expand and contract.

A recent achievement of astronomy has been the invention of a method for determining the diameter of stars, by the American physicist Albert A. Michelson (1852–1931). The stars are so far away that they appear as points in the telescope, no matter whether large or small, and so cannot be measured by any previously known method. Professor Michelson found, however, that if a plate containing two parallel slits be placed over the objective of the telescope, the image of a star viewed through the slits would be crossed by stripes of light and darkness, because of " interference " (*see* Light). Then as the slits are moved apart

THE ' MILK ' IN THE MILKY WAY

That long irregular belt of white across the sky, called the Milky Way, or Galaxy, is made up of myriads of stars which are so far away they look like a misty band. It may be seen, on a clear night, stretching in a tremendous arc from horizon to horizon. Stars are grouped more thickly in it than anywhere else in the heavens.

the bars disappear. The amount of separation required to cause this disappearance depends upon the distance and diameter of the star. Using this method, members of the Mt. Wilson observatory staff found the diameter of Betelgeuse, the brightest star in the constellation Orion, to be about 250 million miles—so great, indeed, that if its centre were placed at the centre of the sun its outer edge would lie just inside the orbit of Mars, thus engulfing nearly half of the whole solar system. (Along with another American physicist, Edward W. Morley (1838–1923), Michelson was responsible for the famous experiments to find out the velocity of light.)

One of the most perplexing problems of modern astronomy is to discover the source of energy that maintains light and heat in the stars. Long ago it was suggested that the source of the sun's heat was contraction, but we now know that this could not possibly give sufficient energy to maintain the heat of the sun and other stars for any considerable length of time. Consequently we must look for other sources. One of the most promising of these sources is the "destruction" of matter itself. It is now believed that matter and energy are so very closely related to each other that a certain amount of energy is equivalent to a certain amount of matter and, conversely, that, accompanying the total destruction of matter, immense stores of energy are set free. (*See* Energy).

The sun, for example, if it should *all* radiate away by this process, should last another 15,000,000,000 years. Where the mass came from in the first place, or whither the radiation is bound, no one can say. All the processes of stellar evolution, as we now conceive them, are downhill processes. We seem to be on a slow but determined downward journey to an energyless and perhaps massless solitude. But it is cheering to know that the end is probably billions of years away.

Let us imagine we are given the power of departing from the earth and the solar system, and of moving endlessly outward in a straight line through space. When we get far enough out to view the galaxy to which the solar system belongs, we notice that it is a very fine watch-shaped cluster of stars about five times as great in diameter as in thickness, the large dimension being some 100,000 light-years. Its 30,000,000,000 or more stars have patches of nebular material scattered through them, though this is relatively small. (*See* Nebulae).

If our path carries us in the direction of the Great Nebula of Andromeda, where we arrive after a journey of some 900 thousand light-years, we discover this to be another galaxy, rather similar to the one we left, containing an immense number of stars and a hot gaseous material from which stars will probably develop later. Looking back towards our former home we see it as a dim spiral patch in space, for it, too, seems a well-developed spiral nebula.

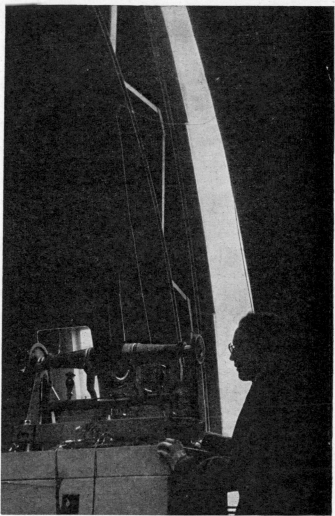

G.P.A.

TELLING TIME BY STARS
The checking and measurement of time is an important function of an observatory. Above an observer is using a special telescope by means of which the exact time is determined by the passage of a star across the intersecting point of two threads in the lens. The broad strip of light in the background is the opening in the dome of the observatory.

Then, if we continue our journey, we shall probably pass near a few other such islands-in-space, and see many more in the distance. These are the "island universes." Our galaxy is but one of them. Remote from each other, yet each colossal in itself, these smoky catherine-wheels of light dot the empty void we call "space" or "nothingness."

Einstein (*q.v.*) has proposed that a "straight" journey prolonged for an immense span of time might end where it started, for if matter is not infinitely far spread out in space, then space itself should be curved around matter so that our path would slowly be bent back like that of an ant crawling inside a great hollow glass globe.

When we think how long men have studied the stars, and yet how great are the marvels revealed in the past hundred years, there seems almost no limit to the hopes we may have of yet further knowledge of these mysterious worlds.

Starch. This is a poly-saccharide (*see* Sugar), the molecule being composed of a large number of glucose molecules joined together, with the elimination of water. The seeds, bulbs, tubers and fruit of many plants contain starch which acts as a reserve supply of food (*see* Photo-synthesis). It occurs in small grains or granules, which differ in size and shape in each species of plant. Starch is found especially in cereals, in potatoes, in carrots and other root vegetables, and in sago and tapioca. Potatoes contain about 20 per cent starch, and cereal grains contain 65–80 per cent.

Commercially, starch is usually obtained from potatoes, and from grains such as maize. To extract starch from potatoes, they are grated and washed with cold water on a sieve which permits the starch granules to pass but retains the pulp. The granules settle, and fibres and other impurities are washed away. The starch is then dried. From maize, starch is made by soaking the grain, removing the germ in special mills, and grinding the residue. The separated starch and gluten (protein) are then washed through bolting (sifting) cloths, and the starch is separated from the gluten in centrifugal separators.

As usually prepared, starch is a white or yellowish-white powder. The granules form a suspension in cold water, but on boiling they burst, and a clear paste is formed which sets to a jelly on cooling. This paste is used for stiffening linen at the laundry, and as a substitute for gum. When tested with iodine, it gives a fine blue colour.

On boiling with acid solutions, starch is hydrolised (decomposed by water), first into dextrin (a gum-like substance), and finally to maltose and glucose, which are sugars. Commercial " liquid glucose," used in making boiled sweets, is made in this way, and is a mixture of dextrin, maltose and glucose. A similar breaking down of starch into sugar also occurs in the mouth, where it is brought about by an enzyme present in the saliva.

Although starch is not formed in the animal body, a similar substance called glycogen exists as a reserve carbohydrate in the liver (*q.v.*) and muscles of animals.

Starfish AND SEA-URCHINS. Though they seem so different at first sight these creatures belong to the same group, the *Echinodermata* (" spiny-skins "), one of the most ancient in the animal kingdom.

A well-grown starfish of the common type, such as the *Asterias rubens* of British coasts, has the shape of a regular five-pointed star, about six inches across and one inch thick in the centre. It is brown in colour and covered with a mosaic of limy plates and rows of points, and near the centre is a small sieve-like opening. This is its dorsal (back or upper) surface. The lower or ventral side shows a furrow, broadening from the tip of each of the five arms towards the centre, where a circular opening (the mouth) is closed by five pointed teeth meeting at the centre. The mouth opens into a loose bag-like stomach, whose folds extend out into the arms; and round it is a system of water-tubes, blood-vessels, egg-producing organs and so forth.

When a captive starfish crawls up the glass side of an aquarium, showing its underside, it is possible to see, pushed out from rows of tiny holes in the ray, many tubes each ending in a sucker by which the animal clings to the glass. They are swollen

F. Martin Duncan

A STARFISH TAKES A WALK ON THE SAND

One of the common starfish found round the coasts of Britain is *Asterias rubens* (above), which looks like a brown five-pointed star and is about six inches across. It is not often seen in motion, but it pulls itself along by means of the suckers on the undersides of the five ' arms.' The trail of this specimen is visible in the wet sand. At the right is a deep imprint made when it rested. The starfish feeds mainly on bivalve (twin-shell) molluscs, whose shells it pulls open.

with water sucked in through the sieve in the creature's back, and it is by these " feet " that the starfish moves over the sea floor.

Starfish are of several kinds and varied shapes. Some are very thick, with short fat arms; others are small and round and flat, with snaky arms (brittle stars); others have many-branched arms (basket-fish). If a starfish loses a ray it grows another, and if it is cut into halves each piece grows into a new individual. Starfish are tremendous eaters and do much damage to oyster beds, crawling over the oysters and slowly pulling open their shells in order to eat the occupant.

The spined sea-urchins are as varied in shape as the starfish. Some are flat, and if you rub off the velvet-like skin you find on the lower side a five-pointed pattern of holes for tube-feet, precisely as in a starfish. Another kind is the shape and size of a bun, like the common British sea-urchin (*Echinus esculentus*); and here, again, under the spiny coat of its flat lower side, you can see the five furrows. The heart urchins are heart-shaped, and are often found as fossils in chalk cliffs. In the spherical or egg-shaped sea-urchins the furrows extend up the sides, and the tube-feet, which come out along them, are longer than those of the star-fishes. By means of these and its spines the animal is able to move.

Most sea-urchins move very little, hoping to be overlooked in their dull green or purplish coat by the big fishes and other enemies who consider their soft insides good eating. Their bristling spines protect them against small fishes and crabs. In among the spines, which are mounted on a sort of hinge and can be waved about, are scattered flexible appendages ending in a sort of finger and thumb. With these the urchin (which is a name derived from the French hérisson, meaning hedge-hog) picks off and throws away particles of dirt that get entangled in the spines. All live either by scooping up mud from which the stomach extracts nourishment in the form of the minute life it contains, or by nibbling edible things which adhere to rocks and weeds.

Starfishes and sea-urchins produce enormous quantities of eggs every summer, most of which are eaten by other marine creatures. From the eggs that survive hatch curious little objects not in the least like adult urchins or starfish, but they eventually settle on the sea bed and " grow up." All echinoderms go through a long and curious metamorphosis (change of form) of this type. To this group also belong the sea-lilies, or crinoids, which show the same five-rayed symmetry and are like tall, many-branched plants; yet even these start life as swimming creatures.

Starling. With its beautiful black plumage brightly shot with purple, green, and steel blue, and most of its feathers tipped with buff, the common starling (*Sturnus vulgaris*) of Britain and Europe generally, is a very active bird, remarkable for the way in which it mimics the notes of other birds and any sound that takes its fancy.

About eight inches long, it spends much of the time on the ground probing with its slender bill for worms and grubs. The nest, composed of grass, twigs and moss, is placed in a hole in a tree or old building, or under the eaves of a house.

Schensky

BRISTLY SEA-URCHINS
Related to the starfish, and of about the shape and size of a bun, the common British sea-urchin bristles with spines, each of which is mounted on a sort of hinge and can be waved about. These protect it from hungry fishes and crabs.

From four to seven pale blue eggs are laid, and there are two, sometimes three, broods a year (*see* Eggs colour plate facing page 440). In winter starlings migrate to southern Europe and north Africa in enormous numbers. Introduced into Australia and New Zealand, starlings have become a pest there, eating grain and fruit and driving native birds from their breeding-places.

The rose-coloured starling (*Pastor roseus*), a crested bird with rose-pink back, shoulders, breast and under parts, black elsewhere, is an occasional visitor to England.

State, Great Officers of. There were formerly nine Great Officers of State, who were Ministers of the British Crown. They were the Lord High Steward, the Lord High Chancellor, the Lord High Treasurer, the Lord President of the Council, the Lord Privy Seal, the Lord Great Chamberlain, the Lord High Constable, the Earl Marshal, and the Lord High Admiral.

At the present day only three of these are still members of the Government—the Lord Chancellor, the Lord President of the Council, and the Lord Privy Seal. Except that the Lord President presides at the rarely-held full meetings of the Privy Council, the two last-named offices carry no special duties and are often held in conjunction with other appointments. The offices of the Lord High Treasurer and the Lord High Admiral are not now held by individuals, the duties being performed by the Lords of the Treasury and the Lords of the Admiralty.

The Lord Great Chamberlain has charge of the Palace of Westminster, as the Houses of Parliament are officially called, and when the Sovereign opens Parliament in person the Lord Great Chamberlain makes all the arrangements. He appoints a peer to carry the Sword of State and walks next to him in the procession. He also assists at the introduction of peers on their creation and has special functions at Coronations.

The Lord High Steward is an office to which an appointment is made only for special events, such as a Coronation. The Lord High Constable originally commanded the King's Army, but that office is now in abeyance and is only revived for a Coronation. The Earl Marshal is the head of the College of Arms, or Heralds College, which makes grants of coats of arms to those entitled to them, and he appoints the Kings of Arms, Heralds and Pursuivants. He attends the Sovereign when the latter opens Parliament in person, and arranges Coronations and other state ceremonies such as Royal marriages and funerals. Since 1672 the office has been hereditary in the family of the Howards, Dukes of Norfolk.

Steam. When a liquid is heated, its molecules are quickened in motion, and those which have acquired the most velocity will tend to spring up from the surface of the liquid and mount into the space above. When water is raised to the boiling point in a vessel to which air at normal pressure is allowed to have access, we cannot make the water hotter than the temperature of the boiling point. At ordinary atmospheric pressure, and at sea-level, this temperature is 212° F., or 100° C.

In evaporating, a liquid loses heat energy, and its temperature drops until its heat-loss is balanced by the heat input from the gas ring or electric hot-plate on which the kettle or pan of water is standing. We cannot make the water hotter than 212° F.— so long as the vessel is open to the atmosphere.

The temperature of boiling water is ordinarily high enough for cooking meat and vegetables; but if we take our stove and saucepan to the summit of a high mountain we shall find that water boils there at a lower temperature than at sea-level, and we have to cook our potatoes for a longer time to make them soft. People who live at high altitudes sometimes get over this difficulty by using a pressure cooker. This device was invented long ago by Denis Papin (1647-1710). It is a strongly made cooking vessel with a lid which can be clamped down tightly so as to be steam-tight.

A small amount of water is put into the cooker and the meat and vegetables, or pudding, are placed inside. The lid is screwed down, and the cooker is put over a gas ring or hot-plate in the usual way. What happens now? The molecules spring up from the water into the space above, but they cannot escape, as before, into the atmosphere. So the pressure inside rises, and with it the temperature —for the two are linked together. When a pressure of 5 lb. per square inch is developed inside the cooker, the temperature is 228° F. instead of 212°. At a pressure of 15 lb. per square inch, the temperature is almost 250° F. The result is that foods cook more quickly, and certain joints which are tough by ordinary cooking methods are made tender.

It is the *change in pressure* which alters the boiling point. In an open vessel the liquid is subject only to atmospheric pressure—roughly 14·7 lb. per square inch. What will happen if we use a closed air-tight vessel, and lower the pressure inside it below that of the atmosphere? We should expect the water to boil at a lower temperature, and this is what it does, in fact.

You probably know that a high temperature in cooking alters or even spoils the flavour of some food stuffs. Condensed milk and evaporated milk are ordinary milk from which part of the contained water has been driven off by evaporation. This process is carried out in " vacuum pans " where a lower than usual pressure is maintained, with the result that the water comes off at a lower temperature in the form of steam. Thus the flavour and other qualities of the milk are preserved. Sugar is boiled in vacuum pans at a pressure of about 5 lb. per square inch in order to make the liquid crystallize; the boiling temperature is then between 150° F. and 160° F. A higher temperature would cause part of the sugar to change chemically.

Steam is an invisible gas. As it comes from the spout of a kettle it condenses on meeting the cooler air, and a white plume of water droplets is what we see. But if you look more closely at the kettle spout, when the water is boiling briskly, you will probably notice that the plume does not start right from the end of the spout, but begins to appear a little way from it. In between is a space in which we can see nothing, although we can detect air movement. This "empty" space is filled with real steam, in the gaseous state before it starts to condense.

We have noted that water takes up heat energy when it boils; it gives up this same " latent " energy when it condenses again into water. This is how buildings are warmed by steam pipes: the energy gained in the furnace and boilers is given up to the air of the rooms by the pipes and radiators.

Outlets for Steam's Restless Energy

In the reciprocating steam engine the heat energy of the steam is used to move pistons in and out, and to turn wheels for machinery. In the steam turbine a many-bladed wheel is driven round by steam jets, and the shaft on which the wheel is mounted turns a ship's screw, or drives other machinery. In the boilers, water is evaporated much as it is in a pressure cooker. In both appliances a safety valve can be set to blow off at a given pressure; so the steam gets hotter and hotter until this pressure is attained.

When steam is let into the cylinders of an engine it forces out the pistons, transforming heat energy into mechanical energy. In most locomotives the steam, after expending energy upon the piston, is released to the atmosphere. But most engines of other kinds pass the used steam to a condenser, in which a pressure below that of the atmosphere is produced by a pump. So instead of the piston having to work against a back-pressure of 14·7 lb. per square inch, this back-pressure is reduced to a pound or two, and more energy is able to be taken from the steam. Steam turbines would be very wasteful (*see* Power Stations, page 2673) if they exhausted their spent steam directly to the air, instead of to a condenser.

If a steam engine has only a single cylinder in which the steam can exert its " push," much of the energy is wasted. So there are compound engines, with pairs of cylinders connected together. The first to receive the steam is the high-pressure cylinder; leaving the exhaust pipe of this, the steam goes then to a larger (low-pressure) cylinder, in which it does more work, mainly by expanding against the piston. Three and even four sets of cylinders are compounded, forming triple-expansion and quadruple-expansion engines, to ensure that all possible use is made of the heat energy of the steam. James Watt (*q.v.*) discovered the "expansive" use of steam by shutting off steam from the engine cylinder when the piston had carried out part only of its stroke, and letting the expansion of the steam in the cylinder drive it for the remainder.

Engineers measure the quantity of steam in pounds : a pound of steam is the amount produced by the evaporation of a pound of water. At the pressure of the atmosphere, a cubic inch of water produces nearly a cubic foot of steam when evaporated. (*See* Steam Engine).

How MAN first PUT STEAM to WORK

Until James Watt built his ' rotative ' engines the only source of power to drive machinery was wind or water. Here is the early story of the reciprocating Steam-engine ; that of the Steam Turbine is told under Turbine.

Steam Engine. Man's first attempts to use the energy of steam were in pumping water. Giambattista della Porta (1538–1615) sketched and described a very small apparatus in which steam from a boiler forced water out of a tank. He is notable also because he pointed out another way of moving liquids—by filling a vessel with steam, and then condensing the steam into water, so that it took up very much less space. Water could be drawn up into this airless space from a reservoir.

Here we have the germ of the two first practical steam engines : (1) the "atmospheric engine," in which the steam merely allowed a partial vacuum to be brought about in a cylinder containing a piston, and the weight of the atmosphere forced down the piston; and (2) the "real" steam engine, in which steam pressure drove the piston.

Denis Papin (1647–1712) had shown the way to use the second method, but never put it to practical use. His cylinder acted also as boiler; it was closed at the bottom, and he put a little water in and applied heat beneath. Steam was generated, and forced up the piston; a spring latch held the piston-rod when at the top of its stroke. When Papin released the latch, atmospheric pressure drove the piston down again.

After this many inventors published schemes or took out patents for raising water by means of steam; few got beyond "paper" schemes. Thomas Savery, however, built practical engines for pumping water. He had a workshop near Fleet Street, in London. Savery (1650?–1715) used a spherical boiler, with fire beneath; steam was led to a second closed metal vessel (steam receiver), and when this was full, the steam tap was shut.

'Modern' Look Achieved by Newcomen

Now a stream of cold water was poured over the outside of the steam receiver, cooling the steam and condensing it. The next operation was to open a tap on a pipe leading from a well or river below and entering the steam receiver; the lower pressure in the receiver allowed atmospheric pressure outside to drive up water into it. By working the taps in the proper manner, successive lifts of water were obtained.

Savery's machine looked nothing like a modern engine, but the engines built by Thomas Newcomen (1663–1729) began to take on a "modern" look. Newcomen used the atmospheric method, letting steam into a vertical cylinder, cooling the cylinder by a spray of cold water entering the cylinder near the bottom, and allowing the greater pressure on top of the piston (it was open to the air) to drive it down to the bottom of the cylinder again. Thus Newcomen achieved a steady to-and-fro (reciprocating) action, with considerable power.

The engine was not unlike later "beam engines" (*see* illustration in page 3086). There was a long wooden beam, pivoted above, which dipped and rose, see-saw fashion. At the inner end was attached by a chain the free end of the piston-rod; at the outer end, jutting through the wall of the engine-house, above the opening of a mine shaft, was attached by another chain the top end of a long wooden pump-rod which descended into the mine to work pumps at different levels.

Efficient But Wasteful of Steam

The pump-rod was so heavy that it pulled down the outer end of the beam—and pulled up the piston to the top of the cylinder. By filling the cylinder with steam, then cooling it, Newcomen emptied it of air and lowered the pressure below that of the atmosphere (14.7 lb. per square inch). This outside pressure overcame the weight of the pump-rod and pulled up that rod, giving a stroke to the pumps below. The joint between the piston and the wall of the cylinder was sealed by a shallow pool of water on top.

For half a century Newcomen engines drained mines of water, and pumped drinking water to towns. There were about a hundred of them working in England and Scotland by the time that James Watt (1736–1819) began to turn his attention to improving the Newcomen engine. He had been asked to repair a model engine for the College of Glasgow, and found that the atmospheric principle was very wasteful of steam, because the cylinder had first to be made very hot, and then it had to be cooled down again. "Why not keep it always hot," said Watt to himself, "and do the condensing in a separate chamber which could be kept always cold ? " We must mention that John Smeaton (1724–92) had made some improvements in Newcomen engines, but without altering the working principles.

First working alone, and later in partnership with Matthew Boulton of Birmingham, Watt persevered with his plan for a separate condenser. It was in 1765 that he had begun to tackle the problem ; not until eleven years later were practical engines built to his design. A single-acting engine was built, with steam pressure driving down the piston, and a state of vacuum below it. By means of an equilibrium valve, steam was now admitted to *both*

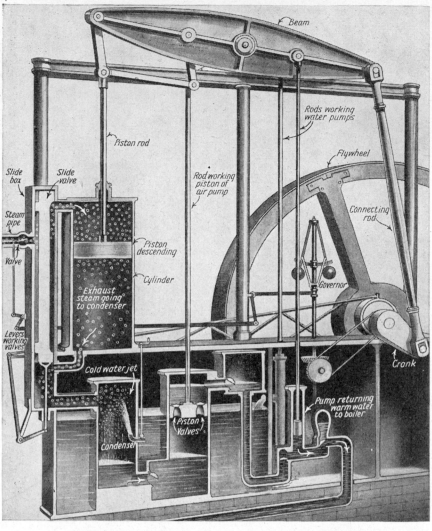

SIMPLIFIED DIAGRAM OF AN EARLY BEAM ENGINE

This type of steam engine was evolved from the early double-acting engines built by Boulton and Watt, and continued in use for nearly a century. The slide-valve admits steam alternately above and below the piston, forcing it down and up and causing the crank to turn the flywheel. The engine itself works the slide-valve, the air-pump for the condenser, and the water-pump to feed the boiler. The centrifugal governor regulates the speed by controlling the steam throttle valve. A jet of cold water in early condensers cooled and condensed the steam. Power was taken off for machinery by a belt on a pulley on the flywheel shaft.

acting rotative engine which Boulton and Watt built in 1783 used a queer method of securing rotary movement from a reciprocating piston. Since a competitor had secured a patent which legal opinion considered to cover the use of a crank, Watt was barred from driving his flywheel in this way; instead he employed a "sun-and-planet motion," which you can see in the Science Museum, London, on a later engine built in 1788 for use at Boulton and Watt's Birmingham works.

The engines of this date used "dropvalves," opened and shut automatically by an arrangement of rods and trip-levers. William Murdock (1754–1839) patented a slide-valve in 1799, while an employee of Boulton and Watt. This did away with the three separate valves needed hitherto. The slide was moved to and fro over openings in the cylinder wall by a rod connected to a kind of crank called an "eccentric." This comprised an eccentric pulley rotating in a strap fixed to a rod. The pulley was attached to the engine crank-shaft not at the centre of the disk, but a little away from the centre; the rod joining the slide-valve to the eccentric pulley went to the strap embracing the outside of the disk, so that when the engine shaft turned round, it turned the pulley and worked the slide to and fro.

George Stephenson's son Robert, when he came to build the locomotives on his father's design, utilised a shifting link motion invented by Christopher Howe in 1843. The shifting link was a curved one, like a slotted quadrant; the end of the rod from the slide-valve was pivoted in a block which could slide in the slot of the curved link. To each end of the link was attached the end of an eccentricrod, and there were two eccentrics. Now, by working a hand lever attached to the shifting link, either eccentric could be brought in line with the end of the valve rod, and the engine could be made to run either forwards or backwards.

sides of the piston, equalising the pressure so that the weight of the pump-rod could raise the piston to the top of the cylinder again. Spent steam from the cylinder was led to the separate condenser (in a position somewhat like that shown in the beam engine, seen above). Here a water spray condensed the steam; and an air pump (1) drew away the water, and (2) maintained lowered pressure inside the condenser. There are a few ancient pumping engines, working at Cornish tin-mines, which are not unlike those built by Watt.

Watt next worked at making a "rotative" engine, which should turn wheels for machinery. (The earlier method had been to use a pumping engine to deliver water to the paddles of a waterwheel, and to take off the power-drive from the water-wheel for various machines). A double-

Stephenson's locomotives opened new paths of design for stationary engines as well as self-propelling ones. As we tell in the story of the Locomotive, the design of that type of steam-engine remains today much as it was left by Stephenson and other early constructors. At first most stationary engines had vertical cylinders, and the beam engine was a favourite pattern. Some were still in use about half a century ago. Higher-pressure steam began to be used; the compound principle (*see* Steam) was applied by adding a second cylinder towards the flywheel-end of the beam. The " grasshopper " type was evolved, having a " half-beam " pivoted at one end instead of at the middle. But all these engines were cumbersome and took up much space, so that the more compact horizontal type soon began to challenge them.

Eventually, most engines were made with a horizontal cylinder arrangement. At our great museums in London or the provinces you can see a cavalcade of the different types evolved by a hundred years of invention, improvement and simplification. By the time that James Watt and the Stephensons had achieved success in their respective spheres, the steam-engine had shed its swaddling clothes, and had taken on the form it was to keep, in the main. (*See* Locomotives; Railways; Stephenson, George; Trevithick, Richard; Watt, James).

Steel.

Any malleable iron obtained from the liquid state is now classed as steel. Until fairly recently " steel " meant an iron containing less carbon than does cast iron (not more than 2 per cent), and more carbon than does wrought iron. Another distinguishing quality was the property of being " tempered "—made hard by heating and then cooling. These definitions are still true of certain types of steel, but they have had to be widened and enlarged. Today cast irons are made with properties which formerly were possessed only by steels, and the old-time steel is now classed as high-carbon steel. (*See* Alloys; Iron and Steel).

Stephen, KING OF ENGLAND (1097 ?–1154).

The 19 years that Stephen, grandson of William the Conqueror, reigned over England were one prolonged contest for the crown, with the result that conditions grew more confused year by year, and the people were kept in poverty and oppression.

In the lifetime of Henry I the barons had sworn loyalty to and had recognized as heir his daughter Matilda, widow of the German Emperor Henry V. After Henry's death, however, in 1135, they chose as King of England and Duke of Normandy the easy-going Stephen of Blois, son of Henry's sister Adela, daughter of William the Conqueror. Stephen thereupon claimed the throne.

Matilda did not let her inheritance slip without a struggle. Her husband, Geoffrey of Anjou, successfully asserted her claim to Normandy, in France; and after his death their son, young Henry of Anjou, the future Henry II of England, took up the contest. In 1153 Stephen, wearied by the long struggle and saddened by the death of his eldest son Eustace, agreed to the Treaty of Wallingford, by which Henry agreed to leave Stephen undisturbed on condition that he himself should succeed to the throne after Stephen's death. Stephen died on October 24, 1154.

Stephenson, GEORGE (1781–1848).

Few great inventors had as humble a beginning as Stephenson, who was born on June 9, 1781. His father was fireman of a pumping-engine in the coal-mining village of Wylam, near Newcastle-on-Tyne, Northumberland. One room in a cottage near the pit-mouth—a cottage which also sheltered three other families—was the home of his parents and their six children. School was not to be thought of. Bread was not always to be had in sufficient quantity. In this grimy village he spent his babyhood; childhood saw him looking after the cattle at a near-by farm. At 14 he became his father's assistant, and for this work he received the wage of a shilling a day. At 21 he himself was an engine-man at two shillings, with his father under him as a fireman.

Eager to add to his knowledge of engines and steam, Stephenson at 18 entered a village school which held evening classes. It was only at the age of 19 that he could write his own name. Most of his spare time was devoted to work and study, and his self-improvement brought him steady promotion. At

G. STEPHENSON
Pioneer of British railways, George Stephenson designed and used his first locomotive in a colliery in 1814.

31 he was " engine-wright " (builder and erector of stationary engines) at Killingworth Colliery and earning £100 a year—equal to nearly £500 nowadays—which enabled him to send his son to a Newcastle school. He first became known to the general public by the invention of a miner's safety-lamp, which he perfected about the same time as Sir Humphry Davy produced his. There was a violent controversy as to whose invention was really first, but there was no doubt of the independence of their discoveries, though the two lamps worked on the same general principle. Stephenson was granted £1,000 for his lamp in 1818. Meanwhile, his position permitted him to experiment with the construction of steam-engines.

It was then the practice in such places as the Killingworth Colliery to lay wooden or iron plates as tracks for the wheels of horse-drawn coal-trucks to run on (*see* Railways). Why not use steam instead of horses to pull the trucks? This idea, in fact, was " in the air," and after seeing experiments of the kind which had been carried out by others Stephenson persuaded his employer to back such a project at Killingworth.

His first locomotive, completed in 1814, ran successfully at about four miles an hour; in the second locomotive he improved the original principle, by turning the exhaust steam into the chimney to make a forced draught, thus increasing the speed of burning of the fire and improving efficiency. This " steam-blast " was one of his outstanding contributions to the progress of locomotives. Another was his tubular boiler (*see* Boiler), in which the hot gases from the furnace in front were led through a number of tubes running lengthwise through the water space of the boiler.

Stephenson's engine, " Locomotion No. 1 " (*see* illustration page 2735), run over the Stockton and Darlington Railway at its opening in 1825, was the first ever used to draw both goods and passengers. His " Rocket," four years later, won the £500 prize offered by the Liverpool and Manchester Railway for the best locomotive engine (see Locomotive). He was now recognized as an outstanding engineer, and, though he often had to fight opposition to railway development he was soon leading consultant of railway companies, not only in England but in all Europe. He surveyed routes, designed bridges and tunnels, and supervised these pioneer works in railway engineering. George Stephenson died on August 12, 1848.

His son Robert (1803–59) inherited his father's outstanding abilities. After helping in the preliminary survey of the Stockton to Darlington route in 1821 he studied engineering in all its branches, and soon became a noted civil engineer. Among his works were several railways, including the London-Birmingham line (built 1833–38), and famous bridges in various parts of the world. These included the tubular bridge over the Menai Strait between Anglesey and Caernarvonshire, Wales, which is over 1,800 feet long, and the Victoria Bridge over the St. Lawrence River at Montreal, Canada. He helped to develop his father's locomotive factory at Newcastle, and later made his firm the leading locomotive manufacturers in the world. The present-day descendant of this firm built a full-size replica of the " Rocket " locomotive for the Science Museum, London. Along with the historic original " Rocket," it is on view, as well as personal relics of George Stephenson.

Robert Stephenson died on October 12, 1859, and was buried in Westminster Abbey, London. Both father and son had been offered the honour of knighthood, but, simple, unostentatious men as they were, had declined it.

Stereoscope. Try this little experiment. Hang a finger ring or a small curtain ring by a length of thread so that the ring is about on a level with your nose. Stand at arm's length away, and try to poke a longish piece of stiff wire, bent into a U-shape, through the ring. If you close one eye, you will find it much more difficult to achieve than if you use both eyes. The U of the wire should be large enough to require a fairly accurate pass before it will transfix the ring. The use of both eyes makes a good deal of difference in estimating distance from an object, and the angle one object makes with another. There is another very important property of two-eyed viewing, which you will probably never appreciate unless by misfortune you have to make-do with a single eye.

Perhaps you have thought until now that both eyes see the same object in exactly the same way, but this is by no means the case. For the right eye sees more of the right side of an object, and the left eye more of the left side, as you may observe by looking at an object with one eye closed, then the other. And in focusing the two eyes upon a point midway between them, they view the object from angles which differ slightly. The brain puts these two images together and we see them as one object. That is how we get our impressions of depth, solidity, or relief. This applies only to " binocular " or two-eye vision, such as persons have who are normal-sighted.

The ordinary camera has only one " eye " or lens —consequently photographs appear flat. The principle of the stereoscope is to endow the camera with binocular vision, and to view the pair of photos (of the same object or scene), taken with this camera, through a pair of prismatic lenses which combine the two images in one. Two photographs are taken simultaneously with a stereoscopic camera, so arranged that one lens photographs it from an angle slightly to the right and the other from an angle to the left. These photographs (stereographs) are then mounted side by side.

The stereoscope itself is an instrument with a similar pair of lenses for looking at such photographs. The two images are so blended by the brain that we see a single picture, in which every part stands out solid with life-like effect.

The principle of the stereoscope (from the Greek words, stereos, " solid," and skopein, " to view ") is used in binoculars, field-glasses, and in opera glasses. There are also binocular microscopes and telescopes ; and attempts have been made to apply the principle to motion pictures and to television.

The stereoscope is a comparatively modern invention, the first of the kind having been devised by Sir Charles Wheatstone (1802–75), the English physicist, in 1838. The stereoscope invented by Wheatstone was greatly improved upon by Sir David Brewster, who in 1849 devised a lens-stereoscope, which became very popular. The open form of stereoscope was devised in 1861 by an American, Oliver Wendell Holmes.

Stereotyping. In the process of letter-press printing, the surface of the type becomes gradually worn down and flattened. The fine hairlines of some letters become thickened and in time would be broken. The quality of illustration blocks also suffers if large numbers of copies are run off from them. For these reasons it is unusual to print direct from type except for quite small runs.

Instead, the page, or group of pages, of type (with the accompanying illustration blocks if any) are duplicated by making type-metal replicas called stereotypes. These " stereos "—the common abbreviation—are metal plates about an eighth of an inch thick. They are mounted on wooden blocks to make them the same height as printing type, or they are held by clips on metal blocks for the same purpose. Should the printer be required to produce, say, 100,000 copies of a leaflet, he can prepare eight sets of stereos, and mount them together side by side and in rows. Then, by using a press of suitable size, he need merely run off 12,500 copies, making 100,000, which can be cut from the larger sheet.

When the type-matter and illustrations have been arranged in pages, and a proof has shown everything to be correct, the page or set of pages are " locked up " in a steel frame : a sheet of papier mâché or some similar plastic material is pressed down on to the type so that its under side makes a moulded reproduction of the type, etc. Then this " matrix " is placed in a shallow rectangular mould and molten stereo-metal is poured over its embossed face. As a result, when the metal cools, we have a plate reproducing all the characters of the type from which the matrix was made. If the printing is to be done on a rotary press—in which the printing surface is a cylinder—the stereo plate will next be bent to the correct radius to fit the cylinder (in two halves). Or the plates may be cast to the cylindrical form in one operation in the first place, by use of a caster semi-cylindrical in form.

In order to make harder-wearing stereo plates, these may be faced with some more durable metal such as nickel. In electro-typing (*q.v.*) the printing face of the plate is made of copper or another metal deposited by an electro-plating process on to a matrix made somewhat as for stereotyping. This copper layer is about as thick as a sheet of stout paper, and is thickened up with a backing of a lead-tin alloy. (*See* Books ; Printing).

'R.L.S.'—GREAT TELLER *of* TALES

The Samoan natives among whom Robert Louis Stevenson spent his last years called him ' Tusitala,' The Teller of Tales ; for to them, as to us, he was the beloved weaver of romantic yarns of adventure.

Stevenson, ROBERT LOUIS BALFOUR (1850-94). Born on November 13, 1850, at number 8, Howard Place, Edinburgh, he was the only child of Thomas Stevenson, civil engineer, whose father, Robert, was a famous lighthouse engineer. As a novelist, Stevenson chose to alter the spelling of his second name from Lewis to Louis and to drop the third, and eventually became world-renowned as " R.L.S."

He was a delicate child, and suffered intermittently from illness all his life; so that the volume and finished excellence of his work are a monument to his courage and tenacity. From the age of eight to 17 he attended various

Scottish novelist, Robert Louis Stevenson was perhaps the best-loved literary figure of the 19th century.

schools, and in his 17th year entered Edinburgh University, where he studied law. He formed a friendship with the poet, William Ernest Henley, in 1875, a friendship which, despite certain quarrels, was to last until his death in 1894.

In 1875, too, Stevenson was called to the Bar, though he never practised as a lawyer. Already he had published collections of essays under the titles of Familiar Studies of Men and Books and *Virginibus Puerisque*, and as a result of travels in Belgium and France he wrote An Inland Voyage, and Travels With a Donkey in the Cevennes. By 1879 he had published Will o' the Mill, a fantasy, one of the finest pieces he ever wrote. A disagreement with his father left him dependent for his living upon his own exertions, at a time when he was unknown to the general public and earned but little by his pen.

An important phase of his life began with his visit to California in the United States, where he lived at San Francisco. Here he developed tuberculosis and would have died but for Mrs. Osbourne, an American widow who nursed him back to health, and whom he married in 1880. Stevenson returned with his

wife and step-children to Scotland, where they were welcomed into his father's house. The step-son, Lloyd Osbourne (1868–1947) collaborated with Stevenson in some of his stories, notably a farce entitled The Wrong Box (1889), The Wrecker (1892), and The Ebb Tide (1894), the latter a story of the South Seas. While in Scotland Stevenson wrote Thrawn Janet, and The Merry Men. And during 1882 he completed one of his most popular and best-known adventure stories—Treasure Island, originally entitled The Sea-Cook—a tale which established his reputation and which remained a favourite children's book; it was first published as a serial in a boys' periodical.

To the years 1884–86 belong the autobiographical A Child's Garden of Verses. Then, in The Strange Case of Dr. Jekyll and Mr. Hyde, he achieved his second popular success. Other adventure stories in the style of Treasure Island included Kidnapped, and its sequel Catriona; these tales had Scottish backgrounds and derived in part from the romanticism of Sir Walter Scott (*q.v.*). On his father's death in 1887, Stevenson, who could not endure the severe climate of Scotland, left Britain, never to return. With his wife, mother and step-son, he went to the United States, where he began The Master of Ballantrae.

After cruising among the Pacific Islands, he bought an estate at Apia in Samoa, which he

STEVENSON'S GRAVE IN SAMOA
On his death on December 4, 1894, Stevenson was buried according to his wish on the summit of Mount Vaea on the Samoan island of Upolu in the South Pacific. His body was carried to the grave by the natives, who called him Tusitala, or The Teller of Tales.

named Vailima, and there he settled. Of his life there he wrote eloquently in the Vailima Letters. In 1893 during an acute attack of illness Stevenson dictated St. Ives, afterwards completed by Sir Arthur Quiller-Couch (1863–1944). The following year he began The Weir of Hermiston. On December 4, 1894, he died as the result of an apoplectic stroke from which he never regained consciousness.

The natives, who regarded him as a beloved chief, and called him Tusitala, The Teller of Tales, carried his body to Mount Vaea, cutting a path to the summit with their knives and axes. There they buried him, and there he lies today in the green place of trees and birds and wind-swept solitude, with the verses of his Requiem for an epitaph:

> Under the wide and starry sky,
> Dig the grave and let me lie.
> Glad did I live and gladly die,
> And I laid me down with a will.
> This be the verse you grave for me;
> " Here he lies where he longed to be;
> Home is the sailor, home from sea,
> And the hunter home from the hill."

Stevenson's optimistic outlook and courageous spirit are expressed in much of his poetry. A magnificent artist, he evolved a perfectly balanced, harmonious style by dint of hard schooling and industry. As an essayist he created some of the most delightful studies in the language. His critics have insisted that his thought lacked profundity, but as a story writer he was primarily concerned in telling an adventurous and absorbing tale. His brave philosophy of life was expressed in his poem Celestial Surgeon:

> If I have faltered more or less
> In my great task of happiness;
> If I have moved among my race
> And shown no glorious morning face;
> If beams from happy human eyes
> Have moved me not; if morning skies,
> Books, and my food, and summer rain
> Knocked on my sullen heart in vain:—
> Lord, thy most pointed pleasure take
> And stab my spirit broad awake;
> Or, Lord, if too obdurate I,
> Choose thou, before that spirit die,
> A piercing pain, a killing sin,
> And to my dead heart run them in!

THE STORY OF TREASURE ISLAND

IT all began when the old sailor who called himself " Captain " Billy Bones came to live at the inn kept by Jim Hawkins's father. Billy Bones had a perpetual fear of being visited by a one-legged sailor, and when he died, after a visit from a blind beggar named Pew, he had been given " the black spot," a signal that the pirate gang were after him. Before they had time to search his old sea-chest, Jim Hawkins discovered in it the chart of Treasure Island, and took it to his friend, Doctor Livesey, and to Squire Trelawney. It was the squire who fitted out the Hispaniola, the schooner in which they sailed from Bristol to seek the treasure, with Captain Smollett in command and one-legged Long John Silver as ship's cook.

The voyage to Treasure Island was uneventful, but just as they were arriving, Jim overheard a conversation between Long John and another man, which confirmed the captain's suspicions that Long John and almost all the crew were members of the old pirate crew of Captain Flint, the original owner of the treasure. The crew came near to mutiny, and, playing for time, Captain Smollett gave them all leave to go ashore. Six mutineers remained in the ship, while Jim Hawkins also slipped ashore. Terrified, he later saw one of the faithful sailors murdered by Silver, while cries showed that another had been killed. Jim Hawkins then discovered a marooned man on the island, Ben Gunn, an old shipmate and enemy of Silver, who promised help.

Meanwhile, the captain's party, consisting of himself, Trelawney, Doctor Livesey, and Trelawney's three servants, had left the ship, joined by Abraham Gray, one of the sailors who decided to remain true to them. They had established themselves in a stockade discovered on a sandy hill near the shore, containing a hut which was built round a spring. In making a final journey from the ship they lost their boat, and also one of Trelawney's servants, though not without mortally

wounding one mutineer and killing another. While the pirates were demolishing the boat, Jim Hawkins found his way to the stockade.

In the morning the pirates attacked the stockade, but were beaten off, losing five men; the defenders lost Trelawney's other two servants and the captain was wounded. Later in the day the doctor set off to find Ben Gunn, while Jim Hawkins went off on his own. Jim discovered Ben Gunn's boat and made his way to the ship, which he cut adrift: but he himself was then swept away by the tide, and, worn out, he went to sleep. When he woke up he had drifted a long way, but he re-discovered the schooner, its sails set but no one in control.

Jim boarded it and found that the two men left on board had fought: one was dead, the other badly hurt. But he revived this man, and with his help grounded the ship in a safe place; they then fought, Jim having to shoot him to save his own life. Eventually he went ashore, but when he once more reached the stockade, in the middle of the night, he stumbled among the pirates, now in possession of it, and was taken prisoner. The captain's party, it seemed, had deserted the hut, leaving Silver and his five remaining men in possession: but Silver was now having great difficulty with the others, who wished to put Jim to death at once. The upshot of it was, they sent Silver " the black spot," the sign that his own turn had come. Silver quietened them, however, by pointing out that Jim made a useful hostage, and by suddenly producing the plan of the island, which the doctor had evidently given him.

The pirate party set off for the treasure hunt, taking Jim with them and following the chart. This first led them to a skeleton, a grisly sign arranged by Captain Flint; and then they were terrified by a voice repeating from the undergrowth Flint's last words. It was the voice of Ben Gunn, but none of them believed he was alive. When they reached the spot where the treasure but it usually dies as it has lived, by violence. The male stickleback seems always to be seeking a fight. Yet he combines with his ferocious qualities a domestic virtue unusual among the fishes. It is he who builds the nest in which the female lays her eggs, and he guards it for three weeks or so until the young are hatched.

Sticklebacks are found throughout Northern and Central Europe, Northern Asia, and North America. The common British three-spined species (*Gasterosteus aculeatus*) are fresh-water fish, and grow to be, at the most, three or four inches long. They have spines or thorns on their backs (hence the name), and these are sharp weapons. During the first year of their lives they gather in small, apparently friendly groups, but with the coming of the next summer each male selects a territory which he fiercely defends against all comers.

Once established as master of his territory, the male builds a tunnel-shaped nest, using as building materials sticks and leaves cemented together with a sticky material which he secretes. By the time it is finished he has assumed brilliant tints of blue and red. The female stickleback then lays her eggs in the nest, and when it is filled the male mounts guard over it. If another fish or even a man's hand comes within reach, he sallies forth with spines erect to give battle in defence of his home and his young.

The 10-spined stickleback (*G. pungitius*) is also a fresh-water species, slightly smaller than *G. aculeatus*. The sea stickleback (*Spinachia vulgaris*), which reaches a length of about seven inches, is armed with 15 spines.

Courtesy of Messrs. Cassell & Co., Ltd.

LONG JOHN SILVER ON TREASURE ISLAND

Having tried unsuccessfully to induce the captain's party to surrender, one-legged Long John Silver threatens Doctor Livesey. 'Before an hour's out,' he cries, 'ye'll laugh on the other side!'

should have been, there was only an empty pit. Then the quarrel between Silver and his men came to a head; at the critical moment the captain's party appeared, killing two of the men, while the other three fled, and all was over. Long John Silver, having saved Jim Hawkins's life, was forgiven by the rest of the captain's party. The bulk of the treasure, which Ben Gunn had long ago discovered and hidden in his cave, was eventually loaded on board the schooner, provisions were left for the three deserted pirates, and, with a fair wind behind them, the adventurers saw the last of Treasure Island.

Stickleback. The life of this small fish is short but full of excitement. At the age of about three or four years it has lived out its time;

W. S. Berridge

TEN-SPINED STICKLEBACK

Although this specimen shows only nine spines it is none the less a ten-spined stickleback, for sometimes one of the spines is missing. This fish is slightly smaller than the common three-spined species, but is just as pugnacious.

Stirlingshire. This is one of the larger Scottish counties, comprising 451 square miles. It is part-Highland, part-Lowland, for in the north-west area is Ben Lomond (3,192 feet), a well-known Scottish mountain, and in the south-east mixed farming is carried on and coalfields supply fuel for industry. The ironworks at Carron near Falkirk have long been famous, and calico-printing, bleaching, tanning, paper-making and brewing are among the other industries. Grangemouth, on the Forth, is the chief port. The battles of Stirling Bridge (1297), Falkirk (1298), and Bannockburn (1314), which achieved Scottish independence, all took place in the county of Stirlingshire.

The town of Stirling, county town of Stirlingshire, grew up around the castle that crowns the precipitous hill on the right bank of the Forth, 35 miles north-west of Edinburgh. The castle is still the most prominent feature of the town. The exact age of it is unknown ; but Alexander I died there in 1124, and other Scottish monarchs have been closely associated with it. James II and James V were born in the castle. Near by is the parish church, in which Mary Queen of Scots and

W. F. Taylor

GREATER STITCHWORT

In Britain during spring the greater stitchwort (*Stellaria holostea*) produces its pure white blooms. A plant of the hedgerows, it straggles over other growths, its stems being very weak.

James VI were crowned. The population of the town is 28,500, of the county 186,000.

Stitchwort. One of the common plants of early spring in Britain, lining roadsides and hedge-bottoms with its starry white flowers, the stitchwort sprawls over other herbage. For its brittle, grass-like stems are scarcely able to support themselves, and, as they grow quickly, they must take advantage of every support they can find. The flowers of the greater stitchwort (*Stellaria holostea*) are over half an inch across, pure white in colour, with five deeply cleft petals. The narrow, simple leaves and lateral shoots are in opposite pairs, and this and other features show the plant's relationship to the campions (*q.v.*), in the order *Caryophyllaceae*. There are six other species of the genus *Stellaria* native to Britain, including the lesser stitchwort (*S. graminea*), in which the petals are so deeply cleft as to appear as ten instead of five in number. One species (*S. media*) is the chickweed common in waste and cultivated places.

Stockholm. Sometimes called the "Venice of the North," the capital of Sweden (*q.v.*) lies on a group of hilly islands and peninsulas in the midst of fiords and bays, streams and straits. One-

M. O. Henchoz

STOCKHOLM : SWEDEN'S STATELY CAPITAL

Situated at the point where Lake Mälar empties into the Baltic Sea, Stockholm is built on several islands as well as on the mainland, and in travelling from one part of the city to another one is as likely to go by ferry as by tram or bus. Above, the old town on Staden Island, and part of the Slussen crossing, are seen from Södermalm.

seventh of the space within its limits is occupied by water, and in travelling from one part of the city to another one is as likely to go by water as by road. Many of the streets are so precipitous that flights of steps are necessary to get from one to another.

The city falls into three principal sections, as we see from the Norrbro (north bridge), the handsome granite structure which links the modern business quarter to the north (Norrmalm), with the island Staden, where the old city was, according to tradition, founded in 1255. Between Staden and the northern district, with its fine public buildings, lies the little Island of the Holy Ghost, on which are the Houses of Parliament, built between 1898 and 1905. On the bank of Lake Mälar is the Town Hall, designed by Professor R. Ostberg. When completed in 1923, after twelve years' work, this building was recognized as one of the most important architectural achievements of the age.

Looking south towards Staden, we see in a corner of the island the Royal Palace, built during 1697–1754. Near the palace is the oldest church in Stockholm, founded in 1264 and dedicated to St. Nicholas, and beyond this is the Stortorg (great market). West of Staden, on a little island, is Sweden's chief temple of fame, the 13th-century Riddarholm Church; since the time of Gustavus Adolphus (1594–1632) this church has been the burial-place of the royal family.

From the south end of Staden a wide bridge leads to Södermalm, the old southern quarter, whose steep rocky heights rise 120 feet above the water's edge. Traffic difficulties led to the complete reconstruction of this point, known as Slussen —the most direct highway from the centre of the city to the southern suburbs. Here, where thousands of vehicles and people cross daily, a three-loop elevated crossing on the American " cloverleaf " plan has been devised (see illus., page 3092). Farther west, bridges across Lake Mälar afford improved communication to outer Stockholm.

Looking east from the Norrbro we see another island, Skeppsholm, the headquarters of the Swedish Navy. Beyond it rise the wooded heights of the island of the Djurgarden or Deer Park.

Stockholm is the chief cultural as well as the industrial and commercial centre of Sweden. It is the seat of the principal learned societies and royal academies, and of the Caroline Institute, the leading medical school, and the University of Stockholm. There are technical schools for agriculture, forestry, mining, engineering, and so on; museums of art, antiquities, natural history, and anthropology; a Royal Opera House and a Concert House, built in 1926—the last another of Stockholm's remarkable contributions to architecture.

The city has a good harbour, kept open by ice-breakers during the winter. It is noted for its iron and steel products, including such varied things as dairy machinery, bridges, engines, turbines, telephone equipment and pneumatic tools. Other industries include shipbuilding, tanning, manufacturing of paper, textiles and pottery. The population of Stockholm is 703,000.

Stocks and Shares
When a company is formed or " floated " certain people undertake to supply the money or " capital " to provide the business with premises, equipment and so on. The total sum needed is divided into a great number of equal parts, called shares; e.g., a total capital of £10,000 divided into 10,000 equal shares of £1 each, or perhaps 100,000 shares of 2s. each. Those furnishing the money are called shareholders. They " subscribe " for a set number of shares.

The original money needed by companies is nowadays usually subscribed privately; but when a private company has grown it may be changed into a public company, so that the general public can be invited to become members. Those " prospectuses " and other large advertisements of companies you may see from time to time in the newspapers are either invitations to the public to provide additional money for a company or announcements intended to interest people in buying existing shares that the present owners want to sell. When shares have been issued and all the money due on them has been paid by the shareholders, the company can " convert " the shares into stock. Some kinds of stock are therefore really fully paid shares of companies.

But most stocks represent money borrowed by a company or a government or other public authority. A stock may be issued at par; then the lender has to pay £100 for a £100 stock certificate. Or it may be issued at a discount or below par (e.g., £98 for a £100 stock certificate), or at a premium, or above par (e.g., £102). Similarly, stock may be redeemable at a premium; then the stockholder would receive more than £100 in cash for each £100 stock certificate that he held.

Meaning of Gilt Edged Securities
Stock and share certificates are sometimes called *securities*. Securities such as British Government stocks, which involve little risk that the interest will not be paid or the loan repaid, are sometimes called gilt edged securities, because originally the names of stockholders were entered at the Bank of England in books with gilt edges.

Instead of issuing shares, companies often finance extensions of their business by borrowing. The lenders receive debenture certificates, which state how much they have lent, how much interest they are to be paid, and usually when the loan is repayable. Debentures are therefore not shares. There is no such thing as a debenture share. The shareholder risks his money in the success of the business of the company, and shares in any profits that may be made. His part of the profits is called dividend. If the company does not make a profit there is nothing to be shared, and hence no dividend.

Some people are more cautious than others. To induce different types of people to invest, the total share capital of most public companies is divided into various classes of shares, according to the right they give to a share in the profits. Preference shares have the first claim to a dividend; but this right is usually limited to a stated percentage; say, 5 or 6 per cent. Then comes the right of the ordinary shares, on which the dividend may be higher; e.g., 10 per cent or more. These may be followed by deferred shares, which would be entitled to what remained of the distributable profit after the claims of the other kinds of shares had been met.

Further, preference shares may be divided into first and second preference, cumulative preference, etc. In 1929 a new class of share was introduced:

redeemable preference shares. These may be repaid at the discretion of the company out of accumulations of profit. All other kinds of shares, when once issued, continue until the company is dissolved or " wound up."

An unpretentious building in Throgmorton Street, London, is the home of a world-famous institution: the London Stock Exchange. This is the principal place in England where marketable securities—the shares and stocks of companies and the loan stocks of the British Government, of other governments, of municipalities and public authorities of all kinds at home and abroad— are bought and sold. There is a rather larger stock exchange in Wall Street, New York, and there are similar stock exchanges (or bourses) in most of the capital cities of Europe. Such stock exchanges enable people to invest their money in stocks and shares and to sell securities they may own.

The London Stock Exchange is a private institution, similar to an exclusive club, established in 1802, and managed by a Council elected by the members. This Council is responsible for maintaining the Stock Exchange building and organization, and for controlling the professional activities of its members by an elaborate code of rules and regulations. The members number about 4,000, grouped in about 600 firms.

Difference Between Jobbers and Brokers

On the London Stock Exchange, though not on other stock exchanges, members are rigidly divided into two classes—jobbers (or dealers) and brokers. Only brokers deal direct with the public, for whom they act as agents in the buying and selling of securities, receiving for this service commission according to a fixed scale. Jobbers are traders in particular kinds of securities, and they buy from and sell to brokers, who are thus an essential link between jobbers and the members of the public. Jobbers make their living from the difference between the prices at which they buy and sell, called the " jobber's turn."

A broker receiving an order to buy, say, £500 4 per cent Funding Loan, an important British Government stock, would go to the " gilt edged " section of the House, and ask one of the jobbers to " make a price," without telling him whether he wanted to buy or sell. The jobber would quote a double price, say, 114⅞—115⅛, indicating that he is willing to buy at £114 17s. 6d. for £100 stock and to sell for £115 2s. 6d. If satisfied with this price the broker will accept, and both jobber and broker will enter the amount in their dealing book. If not satisfied, the broker would go to another jobber, and if necessary to another.

Having bought stock for his client, the broker sends him a bought contract note. Transactions are normally settled at the end of the fortnightly account, Stock Exchange settlement days occurring roughly at fortnightly intervals. The buyer on receiving a contract note would send a cheque to the broker, who would in due course secure and send to him a stock or share certificate. Similarly, the seller of stock receives a sold contract note from his broker, and must send him before the end of the account the certificate of the stock he has sold.

Sometimes people buy securities, believing that the price will rise and they will be able quickly to sell them at a profit. Such " speculators for the rise " are called " bulls." Conversely, some people sell shares they have not got, thinking the price will fall and they will be able to buy the shares at a lower price before they have to send the share certificate to their broker. They are called " bears." Such speculation is now much less than it was before 1939.

Stomach. When a mouthful of food is swallowed, the first stopping-place of that food is the stomach. This is an irregular cone-shaped bag, some 10 by four inches in measurement, which is one of the principal digestive organs of the body. When it is empty, it hangs almost vertical ; when it is filled, it swings obliquely or crosswise in the abdomen (see upper illustration in page 150).

Four layers of tissues form this bag. From inside to outside they are the mucous, submucous, muscular, and serous coats. The muscular coat makes this bag very elastic. The stomach has two openings; one at the top, opening from the gullet (or oesophagus), and the other—a very important one —opening into the small intestine, and called the pylorus, from the Greek word for a watchman.

In the mucous lining of the stomach are found certain cells or glands, whose business it is to manufacture the gastric juice. This is one of the major digestive fluids, and is made up largely of salts, hydrochloric acid, pepsin, and rennin. The powerful churning movement of the stomach mixes the food with this liquid, which dissolves and also changes certain parts of food; thus the gastric juice splits fat, attacks protein, curdles milk, and alters sugar chemically. The juice is very acid, and so kills germs. When the contents of the stomach are sufficiently acid a very delicate mechanism, both nervous and chemical in its action, causes the pylorus to relax, and to let the stomach contents pass forwards (see illustration in page 1016).

" Indigestion " may result from too much gastric juice being formed or from too little. In the first instance the doctor prescribes an alkali to relieve the distress ; in the second case he gives dilute hydrochloric acid along with pepsin. Gastric ulcer is a common complaint but the cause, as yet unknown, is probably nervous and due to the quickened pace of living. If medical treatment fails to cure it, the new surgery removes part of the acid-bearing area of the stomach as well as the ulcer, to prevent recurrence of the trouble.

Stone Age. This is a rather artificial division used by archaeologists to describe the period during which Man's tools and implements were ones adapted or fashioned from stone. It thus marks off a stage of culture before men learnt the use of metals. Following it came the Age of Copper, the Age of Bronze, and the Age of Iron. Or we might perhaps more properly include all three as the Age of Metal, since the phases cannot be accurately dated, and those in which Man utilised these various primary metals overlapped a good deal.

The Age of Stone was not the same in date in various countries and regions; indeed, the phase of stone implements still continues in some remote regions. Generally the progress of culture in Europe is taken as a datum. First there was the Eolithic Age (these terms are explained in pages 2080–81) ; the implements appear sometimes to be naturally shaped stones, and there is even doubt if any so-called "arte-facts," or stones worked by Man, belong to this age. In the next or Palaeolithic Age we find the oldest undoubtedly man-made implements. This phase is sub-divided into Upper, Middle and Lower Palaeolithic, with reference to the position of geological layers in which the implements have been found.

Progressively, as we come nearer the age of civilization, the tools and implements improve in workmanship. The older palaeoliths were roughly shaped pieces of quartz or flint from which flakes had been struck off by the use of a stone as a hammer. In the later phases the flaking was done more by pressure, and the workmanship was much finer. Tools of bone, ivory, and horn came into use.

The Mesolithic or middle Age, while it shows a decline in workmanship, is noteworthy because pebbles painted with simple designs are found. This suggests belief in magic, or the beginnings of religion. The Neolithic Age, which followed, is marked by finer and better-made implements, often polished and more specialised in use. Pottery was made during this phase; the bow and arrow were used; linen was woven; and animals were domesticated. Some of these advances belong also to the Meso-

Frith

STONE AGE BURIAL: A KENT DOLMEN

Burial chambers dating from the Stone Age and consisting of an unhewn capstone supported by uprights are known as dolmens. The body was placed in the chamber and the whole heaped over with earth. A number of them have become exposed, as is Kit's Coty House (above), a dolmen near Aylesford, Kent.

lithic Age, for this age was one of change, during which the improvements noted began to appear. In our story of Man (pages 2081–2084) there is a reasonable reconstruction of the life of our primitive ancestors as far as archaeologists can piece the evidence together.

BRITTANY'S RIDDLE OF THE STONE AGE

Near the village of Carnac in Brittany, France, are remarkable rows of menhirs, or standing stones, relics of the Stone Age. In the alignments at Ménec (above) there are 1,169 stones, arranged in eleven rows; the rocks are of the granite of the district and are coated with white lichen.

They vary in height from 18 feet down to two feet. There are gaps in some of the rows where stones have been removed to be used in local buildings. The object and origin of these monuments are still uncertain. In addition to the menhirs there are several dolmens and grave-mounds.

Stonehenge. On Salisbury Plain, in Wiltshire, about seven miles north of the city of Salisbury, stands Stonehenge, the most important remaining monument of antiquity in the British Isles. It is composed of an encircling earthwork or ditch 300 feet across, and the remains of four groups of stones, two circular and built around the same centre, and two inner groups roughly horseshoe-shaped and also concentric. The outer circle of stones, from which many are now missing, has a diameter of 100 feet and is represented by 16 stones standing some 13½ feet above the ground and weighing each some 26 tons. These are joined at the top by heavy capstones.

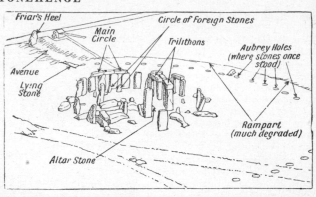

This outer ring is composed wholly of *sarsens*, a name usually given to sandstone when it occurs on chalky downs, as it does in Wiltshire. Nine feet within the outer ring is another ring, also incomplete, which is nowadays represented by a number of bluestones about six feet high. Then come the two horseshoe-shaped groups, the two largest members of which rise to 22 feet and are joined by a gigantic capstone.

Central Aerophoto Co., Ltd.; Fox

MIGHTY RELICS OF BRITAIN'S STONEHENGE

Of unknown antiquity, though it has been suggested that it was erected about 1680 B.C., Stonehenge stands on Salisbury Plain, Wiltshire. The component parts of this ancient British monument are indicated in the diagram at the top. The white dots in the centre illustration are the Aubrey holes—named after the antiquary John Aubrey (1626-97)—where once stood the outermost ring of stones. The trilithons (bottom) consist of blocks of enormous weight.

Within the inmost group lies the so-called altar stone, a slab of sandstone 16 feet long, now broken in two. Near by are the "slaughter stone," so-called because it was long thought, probably incorrectly, that it had been associated with human sacrifice in the distant past; and the "hele stone," which takes its name from *helios*, the Greek word for the sun. The stone derived its name from the fact that the rising sun on Midsummer Day casts a direct shadow from the hele stone on to the altar stone.

Stonehenge was long regarded as a complete mystery, but excavation and photography from the air have added much to our knowledge of this fascinating monument. But when and by whom it was built are still matters of which little is known, although scientists have argued about the matter for centuries. Geologists say that the sarsens or sandstone blocks came from the Marlborough Downs, 14 miles away, and that the bluestones are identical with those of Pembrokeshire, South Wales, which is 200 miles from Stonehenge. Obviously it must have taken a great deal of time and labour for primitive men without mechanical resources to convey such heavy weights over such a distance. It has, however, been suggested that the bluestones, the so-called "foreign" stones of our key diagram, may have been transported on some huge glacier ages ago.

In the past it was thought by some authorities that Stonehenge contained the last remains of a Druidical temple, and this view gained popular support. In modern times at daybreak on Mid-summer Day a rite has been carried out there by people who style themselves modern Druids (*q.v.*). But there is no conclusive evidence for associating Stonehenge with the Druids—the priests of the religion of the Ancient Britons. It seems likely that the site on which the stones now stand was a burial ground and that funeral ceremonies were carried out there thousands of years ago.

As to its date, the most reasonable theory seems to be that the surrounding ditch was dug late in the Old Stone Age, and that the stone groups were added in the New Stone Age. The building could not have taken place any later, as no signs of metal tooling have been found.

The site of Stonehenge was purchased in 1915 by Sir Cecil Chubb, who presented it to the nation three years later. Since then it has come under the care of the Ministry of Works, which has caused various fresh excavations to be carried out at intervals since 1920.

NATURE'S STILT-WALKERS *of* BIRD-LAND

*D*istinguishing features of these striking birds are very long necks and legs and
bills—specialised equipment enabling them to catch living food in ponds,
lakes and marshes, which are their normal habitat.

Storks, HERONS AND THEIR KIN. One peculiarity of the stork is its habit of building its nest on a house-top, or a church spire, or at the top of a tall tree. One species—the common or white stork (*Ciconia ciconia*)—returns year after year to the same nest and adds each season to the pile of sticks until the nest becomes several feet high. In some parts of Europe, especially in the Netherlands and Germany, it is a common practice for a large box or improvised platform of some kind to be placed on a roof to induce a stork to nest there. It is protected by law in several countries, because it acts as a scavenger and keeps down vermin, which is the main reason why people like it to nest on their homes. Its food usually consists of frogs, insects, mice, lizards, snakes and fish.

The migratory white stork seen here just alighting, is a familiar bird in most European countries, from Sweden to Spain.

Storks have no voice, and during the mating season when other birds express themselves in song they go through a grotesque dance, leaping from the ground with extended wings flapping wildly and making a clattering noise with their beaks.

The migratory white stork is common in most parts of continental Europe, and it occurs occasionally in the eastern counties of England. It is found during the breeding season from southern Sweden to Spain and Greece, and it winters in Africa. It is about three and a half feet in length. The head, neck and body are white; the wings partly black; the bill and legs red. The eggs, of which there are usually four or five, are white tinged with buff. It has been celebrated from ancient times for the affection which it displays towards its young, which have also had the reputation (not so well founded) of showing great regard to their parents. The black stork (*C. nigra*) is a smaller, darker bird and much less common. Found in central and southern Europe, in Asia and some parts of Africa, it is a rare visitor to Britain.

The adjutant stork (*Leptoptilus dubius*) of the sub-continent of India stands nearly five feet high, and the extended wings often measure 15 feet from tip to tip. It received its name from its supposedly military gait. The plumage is slate-coloured above and greyish white beneath. In the villages and towns of the sub-continent the bird walks freely about the streets, acting as a scavenger. (*See* illustration in page 27).

A close relative of the adjutant is the marabou (*L. crumeniferus*) of Africa, very similar to the Indian species in size, appearance and habits. The soft white coverts of its underparts and tail furnish the marabou feathers used for trimming various articles of women's clothing.

Another African stork is the shoe-bill (*Balaeniceps rex*), which frequents dense swamps of the White Nile. Five feet in height, it has grey plumage, the head is surmounted by a small curled tuft of feathers, and the large bill, shaped somewhat like the forepart of a shoe, is tipped with a formidable hook. Its food consists of small animals and carrion. The nest is a hole in the ground, roughly lined with herbage, and may contain as many as 12 white eggs, though sometimes only two are laid.

Closely related to the storks are the ibises, distinguished by their long, curved beaks. Numerous species are found in the warm countries of both hemispheres. The Egyptian ibis (*Ibis aethiopica*) was revered by the ancient Egyptian and was the subject of many superstitions. At death it was mummified, and numbers of bodies of these birds have been found in old tombs. Though now very rare in Lower Egypt it still breeds in other parts of Africa.

The wood ibis (*Mycteria americana*), about 40 inches long, has white plumage with glossy black wing and tail feathers, and breeds in large colonies along the coast of the United States from Texas to South Carolina. The birds have a curious way of obtaining their food. The whole flock appears to be dancing as they stir up the mud of a marsh or pond with their feet, and when a disturbed fish or frog rises to the surface the nearest bird kills it with a snap of the bill. After the

W. S. Berridge

EXTRAORDINARY SHOEBILL
The general build of the shoebill is much like that of other members of the stork family ; but it has a cumbersome-looking beak, the shape of which is indicated by the bird's name. The beak is adapted to food-getting in the Nile mud.

booming trumpet-like call that can be heard long after the bird is out of sight. The European crane (*Grus grus*) is ashy-grey, with blackish throat and face, and stands about four feet high. The brown eggs, with dark spots, are laid in a nest built on tufts of coarse marsh grass.

The demoiselle crane (*Anthropoides virgo*) is an African and Asiatic species, but visits Greece and other parts of southern Europe. Three and a half feet high, its plumage is generally grey ; the sides of the head are adorned with two white tufts, and the breast bears long blackish feathers. It differs from

"dance" has ended and the water has cleared the ibises feed on the slaughtered prey floating on the surface.

The spoonbill (*Platalea leucorodia*), a relative of the ibis, has a long flat and black beak which widens out at the yellow tip somewhat like a spoon. The bird is about 32 inches long, has white plumage with a tinge of buff round the neck, and is common throughout central and southern Asia and Europe. Formerly it bred in Great Britain, where it now occasionally occurs as a visitor to Norfolk. They feed upon small fish, snails and frogs.

Other relatives of the storks are the cranes, which are found on dry land as well as in marshes. They feed on fish, frogs, lizards, mice, grasshoppers and grain and are among the wariest of birds. In flight the crane utters a

SACRIFICED TO FASHION
Egret feathers became less fashionable when the cruelty shown in these photographs was known to the public. 1. Mother egret keeping her young birds warm. 2. The mother bird shot by a plume hunter. 3. The motherless nestlings crying for food. 4. On the point of dying of hunger.

other cranes in that the head and neck are completely feathered and the beak is no longer than the head. The European and demoiselle species occasionally visit Great Britain.

The egrets (*Egretta*) are small white herons with a tufted head plume. They frequent south-eastern Europe and parts of Asia, and during the mating season the birds have a magnificent train of plumes, which are the aigrettes or "ospreys" of the feather trade. At one time egrets were slaughtered for these plumes, the importation of which into the United Kingdom is now forbidden.

The only member of the stork group native to Great Britain is the European or common heron (*Ardea cinerea*). It stands three feet high. The plumage is grey on the upper parts, with

While there are some superficial differences in the habits of the various members of the stork family, the resemblances between them are sufficient to show their relationship. An artist has here given his impressions of episodes in the lives of these interesting birds. 1. Common herons in flight from a feeding ground; these are the only members of the stork family native to Great Britain. 2. Cranes from the continent of Europe flying in wedge formation at the time when they are leaving the cold north for a warmer climate. 3. A white stork feeding her young. In the background may be seen others, each standing on one leg. 4. Adjutant stork of southern Asia, about to pounce upon a hooded crow. 5. Egyptian ibis capturing a frog. The ibis, worshipped by the ancient Egyptians, is now rare in lower Egypt but is found from the Upper Nile to South Africa.

greyish white below; the forehead, sides of the face and breast feathers are white; the pointed beak is yellow. It feeds upon fish, frogs, snakes, small animals and birds, and it nests in colonies or heronries. The nest, made of sticks and lined with grass, is large and flat and is usually built in the top of a tall tree. The eggs are large and bluish. (*See* colour plate facing page 440).

Sometimes, where there is little fear of being molested by Man, herons breed in low trees, or even among reeds in a lake. The bittern (*q.v.*) is a relative of the heron and is also found in Britain.

Storms. Unusually violent weather is called a storm; and high winds are a conspicuous feature of these disturbances. When the wind rises to over 40 miles an hour it is known as a gale. A storm with wind over 75 miles an hour is called a hurricane. In Chinese waters such a storm is known as a typhoon. Among the signs which give warning of a hurricane are a dull red sunset caused by a thin haze of clouds; hot humid air; an unexpectedly high barometer, accompanied by a dying down of the wind; and, if at sea, a growing swell. Then, suddenly, the barometer drops; a rain cloud rushes forward from the horizon; and a deluge seems to fill the air with water, while the wind blows with terrific force.

These hurricanes are intense cyclonic storms, with winds blowing toward a central region of low atmospheric pressure. The winds blow spirally, instead of straight toward the centre, because they are deflected by the rotation of the earth, anti-clockwise in the northern hemisphere and clock-wise in the southern. Sailing ships avoid the dangerous central region of low pressure by taking

W. S. Berridge

SPOONBILL OF THE STORK TRIBE
Once numbered amongst birds which bred in Great Britain the spoonbill is now only a rare visitor. About 32 inches long, it has white plumage, with a tinge of buff at the neck, and the long and flat black bill widens out at the tip some-what like a spoon—hence its name.

the wind from starboard, or right, in the northern hemisphere, and from port or left in the southern. The vessel then sails toward calmer weather at the edge of the storm. Sometimes a ship passes through a storm into an area where all seems calm and serene, and then runs into the storm again. The region of deceptive calm was the centre, or " eye," of the storm.

Tropical cyclones do terrific damage to shipping, crops, trees and buildings. They cause waves which sometimes flood cities and result in considerable loss of life. The power required to keep such a storm going probably comes from the heat which is released when moisture is condensed to rain within the storm. This heat keeps the air pressure low at the centre of the storm, and as long as the low pressure persists the storm continues. A typical hurricane may generate over a hundred thousand million horse-power.

Thunderstorms are caused by moist air rising, cooling, and condensing its moisture. They com-

K.L.M

TREES LAID FLAT BY A STORM
The results of a tornado must be seen to be believed ; its force is overwhelming. When such a storm struck the Dutch province of Gelderland in 1927 it snapped the trunks of substantial trees as if they were matchsticks, and laid them flat, as seen here.

SACRED IBISES, CLOSE RELATIVES OF THE STORK

Capt. C. W. R. Knight

hese wonderful birds, with their black, white and crimson umage, are the famous sacred ibises of Egypt. In that untry, however, they are now very rare, and indeed are so early extinct as to have been driven to a few isolated places as breeding haunts, in one of which this picture was taken; it shows the wings with a patch of crimson plumage on the underside, the curved bill, long neck and long, black legs of these strange birds—all indications of their relationship with the storks.

L. J. Langford

HANDSOME HERON AND CURIOUS CRANE

THE two birds which you see here look so much alike that you might well take it for granted that they are closely related. But while the heron (above) is a member of the same order as that which includes the storks and the ibises, the crane (left) belongs to a quite different group. It has, however, the long neck, long, slender legs, and dagger-like bill which characterize so many members of the stork group.

The heron is the only stork-like bird which breeds at all frequently in Britain, and it makes, as seen here, a huge platform of sticks in which to rear its family. These birds are sociable, and nest together—sometimes as many as fifty pairs inhabiting the same heronry. The nests are nearly always high up in the tree tops, and the nesting season begins very early in the spring of the year.

To face page 3101

monly occur late in hot afternoons, when the towering clouds build themselves into masses that rise in billowing curves above a flat base, and get darker and heavier with moisture, as they rise higher and higher. (*See* Clouds).

Most people have watched the various stages of a thunderstorm—the heavy nimbus cloud, the torrential rain, the squall caused by the rise and fall of the air in front of the cloud, and the broken clouds following the storm centre. Hail accompanies these storms as a general rule. The power that is represented by them is tremendous—a one-inch rainfall over 10 square miles represents as much as 232,300,000 cubic feet of water. To evaporate and condense this water at 50° Fahrenheit during the lifetime of a storm takes more than 36 million horse-power. In the tropics it is common for some regions to have thunder showers on 200 days during the year. The path of a thunderstorm is far shorter and narrower than that of a hurricane or cyclonic storm, and its duration is usually only a few hours. The British Air Ministry estimates that some 1,800 thunderstorms are in progress in various parts of the world at any given moment.

Tornadoes arise when the conditions that cause thunderstorms are unusually violent. By centrifugal action air is forced away from the centre, thus leaving a core of low pressure—perhaps only 1/10th of normal. Because of the suction in this low-pressure core, houses collapse and roofs are carried off; corks are drawn from bottles and window panes fall outward. Around the edge of the funnel-shaped cloud, which almost touches the ground and projects from the main cloud-mass, the wind may blow at 200 miles an hour. The storm is accompanied by a deafening roar, as it passes onward at 25 to 40 miles an hour. Fortunately a tornado is only a few thousand feet wide.

A waterspout is a tornado at sea, sucking in water at its base, and carrying the water spirally upward with the wind to the overhanging cloud.

Stratford-upon-Avon.

In this ancient Warwickshire town, situated on the River Avon, the Elizabethan poet William Shakespeare (*q.v.*) was born, and there he died. Both he and Anne Hathaway, his wife, lie buried in the church of the Holy Trinity. On the slab over his grave is the well-known inscription, said to have been selected by Shakespeare himself :

> Good friend, for Jesus' sake forbeare
> To digg the dust encloased heare ;
> Bleste be ye man that spares thes stones,
> And curst be he that moves my bones.

Though commercialized, the town is not entirely spoilt. The reputed house of Shakespeare's parents in Henley Street, which contains the small white-washed room in which he is said to have been born, is still preserved. On the walls of this room appear signatures of numerous distinguished visitors. The house serves in part as a museum, containing a collection of books and pictures illustrating the life and times of Shakespeare. A Shakespeare memorial building, including a theatre, a gallery of paintings, and a library of his books, was burnt down in 1926. A fine new Memorial Theatre on the banks of the Avon was opened in 1932. The little thatched cottage in which Anne Hathaway was born is at Shottery, about a mile from Stratford. At Wilmcote is the cottage of Shakespeare's mother, Mary Arden. The population of Stratford is 14,260.

The Times

SHAKESPEARE MEMORIAL THEATRE AT STRATFORD-UPON-AVON

The series of annual Shakespeare Festivals held at Stratford-upon-Avon began on April 23, 1879, when the first Memorial Theatre was opened. It was burned down in 1926, and the new theatre (above), designed by Miss Elizabeth Scott, was opened in 1932, again on April 23, the date thought to be the birthday of the poet. These memorial productions run for some months, and most distinguished Shakespeare players and producers have taken part in them.

Strathcona AND MOUNT ROYAL, DONALD ALEXANDER SMITH, 1ST BARON (1820–1914). " The Grand Old Man of Canada," as he was called in the later years of his long and brilliant career— the man to whom in large measure western Canada owes its splendid and rapid economic development —was born on August 6, 1820, in a little stone cottage at Archiestown in Morayshire, Scotland.

Before he was quite 18, Donald Alexander Smith left his home to seek his fortune in Canada, and he entered the service of the Hudson's Bay Company, which at that time controlled most of what is now the Dominion of Canada. For 13 years he roughed it in the wilds of Labrador; then he spent 10 more in the Canadian North-West. He mastered the workings of the fur trade, found time to read and study, and eventually became resident governor of the Company, with headquarters in Montreal.

Fur traders, Indians, and half-breeds all respected and trusted Donald Smith, and when a rebellion led by a half-breed named Louis Riel broke out on the Red river in 1869, the Canadian Government appointed Donald Smith special commissioner to deal with the rising, and he did much to bring the revolt to an end. When, in 1870, the Province of Manitoba was formed, he was elected to its first legislative assembly, and he was for a number of years a member of the Canadian House of Commons.

A man of understanding and vision, he saw that if Canada was to become a prosperous and powerful country, if the distant parts of this vast territory were to be knit to the centre, it must have a trans-continental railway. It was largely through his financial and administrative ability, and the use of his own fortune, that the Canadian Pacific Railway was completed in 1885.

Of his vast wealth he gave huge sums to McGill University at Montreal and to other institutions. During the Boer War of 1899–1902 he raised and equipped at his own expense a regiment of 600 men—Strathcona's Horse.

Donald Smith was knighted by Queen Victoria in 1886, and in 1897 he was made a Baron of the United Kingdom with the title of Lord Strathcona and Mount Royal. In 1896 he was appointed High Commissioner for Canada in London, and from that time until his death on January 21, 1914, he was a prominent public figure. Few men did more than he to strengthen the bonds between Canada and Great Britain.

Stratosphere. The outer layer of the earth's atmosphere, above the highest clouds, where the air is thin and is not carried from one level to another by currents, is called the Stratosphere.

Thermometers carried in aircraft or balloons making high flights show that the air becomes steadily colder as the height increases. In England, if the temperature is 50° F. on the ground it is probably just about freezing (32°) a mile up, about 40° below zero five miles up, and about 70° below zero seven miles up. Then this steady fall of temperature stops, and this is where the stratosphere begins. It may get a few degrees warmer in the next mile or two, but generally the temperature remains at this low figure up to heights of 20 miles or even more.

Then, for some reason as yet unknown, the temperature rises again, until at 40 miles the air, now very thin indeed, is as hot as boiling water. Above this, again, the temperature falls once more until the cold of interplanetary space is reached. The height at which any particular temperature occurs depends to some extent on the place above which it is measured. It is an extraordinary fact that the hottest part of the stratosphere is above the poles, which are the *coldest* points on the earth's surface.

Up to now we have learned very little about the stratosphere by direct observation. The highest aeroplane flight ever made only reached just over 10½ miles, and even the stratosphere balloon Explorer II got no higher than about 13¼ miles. Unmanned balloons carrying recording instruments, or sending automatic signals by radio to tell meteorologists on the ground what the upper-air conditions are like, have reached over 20 miles, but even this is really only the lower part of the stratosphere. (*See* illustration page 89).

Above this we have to rely on indirect means in guessing at the temperature and pressure; for instance, measuring the speed of sound from explosions, estimating the resistance met by meteors, and studying the reflections of radio waves. But we do know that the density of the air drops steadily with height, showing no such peculiar reversals as the temperature does. Half the air is contained in the first 3½ miles above the surface. Only about a quarter of the air is left to be spread out over a hundred miles of the stratosphere, and the pressure drops so quickly that in the hot region it is not much more than exists between the walls of a so-called " vacuum " flask used to keep drinks hot.

At a height of 60 miles the density is only one millionth what it is at ground level. It is here that radio waves are reflected and so enabled to travel round the world. Here, too, the aurora is produced by particles shot out from the sun, and meteorites begin to encounter sufficient resistance to make them luminous. The only man-made objects to reach heights like this are the V2 rockets used during the Second World War (1939–45) to bombard London and now used to increase our knowledge of conditions in the upper air. (*See* Air ; Rocket ; Bomb.)

Strauss, JOHANN (1825–99). The man who was to set the people of Vienna, the Austrian capital, and the world dancing in waltz time was the eldest son of another noted Johann Strauss (1804–49), who himself wrote dance music and was probably the most popular conductor of his time.

Strauss (pron. strows) the elder forbade his sons to take up his profession, but Johann, after passing a few miserable years as a clerk, in 1844 defied his father by conducting his own orchestra in a public restaurant, and including his own compositions in the programme. After his father's death in 1849, Johann succeeded him as conductor of his orchestra, and in 1863 became conductor of the Viennese Court balls. As a composer he gained world-wide fame with such astonishingly successful waltzes as The Blue Danube (1867), Voices of Spring, and Tales from the Vienna Woods. His light operas, full of flowing and rhythmic melodies, were equally successful and popular: they included Die Fledermaus (The Bat), 1874, his masterpiece in this style ; A Night in Venice (1883), and The Gipsy Baron (1885). The acknowledged master of waltz composition in the Viennese tradition,

RICHARD STRAUSS CONDUCTS
In addition to being one of the foremost German composers since Johannes Brahms (1833–97), Strauss was also an eminent conductor, and it was as a conductor of the Munich opera in Germany that he first became known. He is here seen at an open-air performance in Athens, Greece.

Strauss composed nearly 400 waltzes, all of a uniform high standard, as well as polkas, mazurkas and galops. He died in Vienna on June 3, 1899.

Johann Strauss was not related to the German composer Richard Strauss (q.v.).

Strauss, RICHARD (1864–1949). The most celebrated composer of the early 20th century, Richard Strauss (pron. strows) was born in Munich, Germany, on June 11, 1864, and was educated at Munich University. As a child he displayed considerable musical precocity, and at 10 had composed his first two works. His Symphony in D minor was first performed in 1881, and his remarkable F minor symphony was given at New York in 1884. But it was as a conductor of the Munich opera that he first became known. In 1885 he came under the influence of the German composer Richard Wagner (1813–83), and his youthful enthusiasm for that master is exemplified in his tone poems, Don Juan (1889), and Death and Transfiguration (1890). Both these works foreshadowed the composer's mastery of orchestral technique and revealed his realistic yet extravagant style.

Till Eulenspiegel's Merry Pranks (1895) and Don Quixote (1898) displayed to the full Strauss's high degree of skill as an orchestral writer. His highly evolved and complex style represented the climax of 19th century orchestral development, and his operas caused a sensation chiefly on account of their experimental nature and unaccustomed harmonies. They included Feuersnot (1901), Salomé (1905), Elektra (1909), and Der Rosenkavalier (1911). The last named, with its enchanting Viennese waltzes, proved Strauss's most popular opera.

He not only worked for effects beyond those of Wagner but added specially made instruments to imitate certain sounds. He could write melodies worthy of the most talented composers, as shown especially in his songs, of which Morgen (Morning) and Serenade are two of the most beautiful.

Strawberry. The luscious, rich-red strawberry fruits which one picks in summer from the garden, or which one enjoys in the form of strawberry jam, are, the botanists tell us, the swollen and pulpy receptacles of the white flowers (which appear in spring) and in which the seeds are embedded. As it ripens, the so-called berry becomes red and filled with the sweet juice for which strawberries are famous. (See colour plate facing page 1401).

During late spring and summer each plant sends out a number of " runners "—thin and lengthy stems which trail flat on the ground and at intervals develop tiny plants. The latter secure a grip on the soil, produce roots, and the following year bear fruit in the same way as their parents. It may be on account of this " straying " habit that the plant received its name of straw(stray)berry.

A forerunner of the several garden varieties is the wild strawberry (Fragaria vesca) of Britain's woodlands and hedgerows. The fruit of this is very small but no less relishable than that of the cultivated kinds. A British relative of the wild strawberry, known as the barren strawberry (Potentilla fragariastrum), is somewhat similar in leaf and flower but the inconspicuous and dry fruit of this species is quite dissimilar.

These are all perennial plants—that is, they live on from year to year.

Streptomycin. This substance is a first cousin of penicillin (q.v.) and, like it, is a wonder-drug of the present age. It is prepared from the mould Streptomyces griseus, which is grown in commercial quantities and conditions. It takes on where penicillin leaves off ; for penicillin is helpless against the bacillus of tubercle, whereas this bacillus is the special target of streptomycin. Its challenge is most successful when the bacillus of tubercle has attacked the meninges, or covering membranes of the brain, causing their inflammation in the dangerous condition called tubercular meningitis. Like penicillin, streptomycin does

WILD STRAWBERRIES
Although very much smaller than the cultivated kinds the fruit of the wild strawberry plant, found growing in British woodland clearings and on shady banks, is delicious. The white flowers appear during April–May.

not kill the enemy germ, but antagonizes its reproduction in the tissues. It holds up the invading organisms until the " host "—the patient—gets the advantage again and can fight and win the battle.

Stuart. A Royal family, some of whose members reigned over Scotland and others over both Scotland and England, bore this name. Robert II (ruled 1371–90), the son of Walter Stewart and Marjory (daughter of Robert the

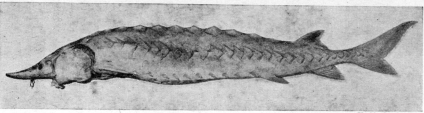

'ARMOUR-PLATED' STURGEON

H. H. Goodchild

An irregular visitor to the estuaries and rivers of Great Britain, the sturgeon, from eight to nine feet long, has the head and body encased in large bony plates. The snout projects far beyond the small toothless mouth, and between snout and mouth hang four barbels or feelers. From the salted and dried roe caviare is made ; and isinglass is obtained from the swim bladder.

Bruce), was the first Scottish ruler of the line. Robert III, James I, II, III, IV, and V, and Mary followed him. The spelling of the name has varied at different periods, but Stuart came into general use from the time of Mary Queen of Scots (1542–87).

James VI of Scotland, Mary's son, on the death of Queen Elizabeth became king of England as James I (reigned 1603–25), thus uniting England and Scotland under one crown, though the two countries remained independent in other respects. Charles I (1625–49) followed James I. The Stuart succession in England was interrupted by the Commonwealth, but was resumed (1660) at the Restoration with Charles II (1660–85).

The remaining rulers of the house were James II (1685–88), his daughter Mary, who ruled jointly with her husband William III from 1688 to 1694, and Anne (1702–14), Mary's sister, who became

Queen upon the death of William in 1702. The attempt to put back the Stuarts on the British throne caused the Jacobite Rebellions of 1715 and 1745. The last male in the house of Stuart was a Cardinal of the Roman Catholic Church, who died in 1807. (*See* Jacobites ; Pretender).

Sturgeon. Caviare and one of the best sorts of isinglass are two valuable products of the sturgeon. Caviare, which is usually considered a great delicacy to eat, is prepared from the eggs (roe) taken from the female sturgeon ; and isinglass, used for making jellies and for clarifying wines and beers, is made from the inner membrane of the fish's swim-bladder.

The sturgeon (*Acipenser sturio*) is a large bulky fish with a body usually eight or nine feet long, a skin covered with five rows of large bony plates, a conical and tapering snout by means of which it obtains its food—mainly worms, for which it searches in the sand and mud. It is a member of the group with a gristly, not bony, skeleton (*see* Sharks), and remains of its ancestors are found in some of the oldest rocks.

There are about 25 species, which vary greatly in size. One species, of the Black and Caspian Seas, may reach a length of 24 feet and a weight of 2,000 lb. Others, such as the sterlet, rarely exceed a length of three feet. Most species live in the sea a great part of the year, ascending rivers to spawn, though a few are entirely fresh-water fishes. In Great Britain, where it is an occasional visitor, the sturgeon is a " royal " fish, any caught in territorial (within three miles of the British coast) waters belonging to the Crown, as a result of an Act of Parliament passed in the reign of Edward II.

SHIPS *of* WAR *that* SINK *and* SWIM

*M*any inventions have gone to the making of the modern underwater craft
whose role is such a deadly one, though we may smile at some of the early
ingenious ideas that were actually tried.

Submarines. The idea of attacking enemy warships from below the surface has attracted the minds of inventors almost continuously from the middle of the 16th century and long before that at intervals. In the early days the absence of any engines to propel the ship was an insurmountable difficulty to efficient work, but all sorts of ingenious ideas were put forward for propulsion by hand.

The next problem was how to sink the enemy when the submarine had come up to her; and the solutions to that ranged from a clockwork-operated mine, to be attached to her hull, to a huge gimlet, worked by a crank inside the submarine, to bore holes in her. None of these ideas was successful.

During the American Civil War in the 1860s a Confederate submarine, after several fatal experi-

ments, did contrive to sink a Federal man-of-war by means of an explosive charge on the end of a long pole, but the shock of the explosion loosened the submarine's timbers as well, and she went down with her whole crew alongside her victim. The publication of Jules Verne's novel Twenty Thousand Leagues Under the Sea in 1870 incited inventors to all sorts of ingenious under-water vessels, some of which drowned their crews on trials.

Some were forced below the water by horizontal screws, like a helicopter's, but the great trouble was that steam could not be stored for more than a very short run below water. Moreover, until the invention of the periscope (*q.v.*) the only means of finding the target was through bulls-eyes in the conning tower projecting above the surface, which made the submarine very vulnerable.

SUBMARINES

The really practical submarine was invented by two Americans, John P. Holland and Simon Lake. The latter intended his boat to run along the bottom of the sea on wheels and release divers who would salve treasure from sunken wrecks, and only later did he adapt it to war needs.

The perfection of the electric motor permitted submarines to run submerged for much longer periods; the motor acted as a generator when the submarine was on the surface and, coupled to the internal combustion engines used for surface propulsion, charged the accumulators to supply itself when it was used to drive the ship along. That is the principle which is still used, although any number of improvements have been made in details.

It was at the beginning of the 20th century that the submarine became really practical, although she was still quite small. The first five built for the British Navy in 1901 and 1902 to Holland's design were only 63 feet long, with a crew of seven. On the surface they were driven by a petrol engine similar to that of a motor-car, and as the fumes were dangerous in an enclosed space the Admiralty ordered that every submarine should carry white mice on board; these little animals would immediately detect fumes, and squeak. But the authorities forgot that the bluejacket was so fond of animals that he immediately put his pets as far away from danger as he could !

The invention of the Diesel engine, working on heavy oil which does not give off dangerous fumes, made all the difference. Although some efforts have been made to drive submarines (generally particularly fast ones) on the surface by steam, the Diesel is still the prime mover in practically all.

Submarines are now built up to 350 feet in length, with a displacement of 2,500 tons—several have been built even bigger—but the principles are still the same. As the pressure of water increases rapidly the deeper they dive, the pressure hull has to be built circular or oval (the best shapes for strength against pressure) ; otherwise it would be crushed. But submarines, when cruising on the surface, have to be given a flat deck. To avoid the deck being crushed the space under it is open to the sea, so that there is the same pressure on both sides of the deck.

The ship is navigated from a conning tower amidships with a small bridge over it, and the steering gear and so on is duplicated inside the hull. Through this tower the periscopes pass; when the ship is

submerged only a short length of periscope shows above the surface and cannot easily be detected, although if she is travelling at any speed it raises a feather of white spray which can be dangerous.

The submarine is fitted with big tanks for water ballast, which can be adjusted to such a nicety that her buoyancy will be reduced to practically nil, and a ton or so will decide whether she comes to the surface or sinks to the bottom. In that condition her hydroplanes, or horizontal rudders, are used and they can force her down or bring her up as required. They will, of course, only work if she is going ahead; if she has to stop her engines—generally because she is being pursued with listening gear— a little more ballast is taken in and she sinks slowly towards the bottom until the danger is passed. To bring her up again compressed air stored in steel bottles is admitted into the tanks to expel the water.

Until well into the Second World War (1939-45) the submarine had to come to the surface to charge her accumulators with her Diesel engines; they demand a great deal of air, and they could not get

New York Times; Central News

SUBMARINES OF THE ROYAL NAVY
Seen here stripped of her guns and other deck equipment, H.M.S. Seraph (upper) carries seven 21-inch torpedo tubes and a crew of 44 ; she was completed in 1944. H.M.S. Ambush (lower), completed in 1947 and 280 feet long, made a special cruise in northern waters in 1948 to test her equipment and that of the crew under severe Arctic conditions.

ON DUTY IN A SUBMARINE OF THE BRITISH NAVY

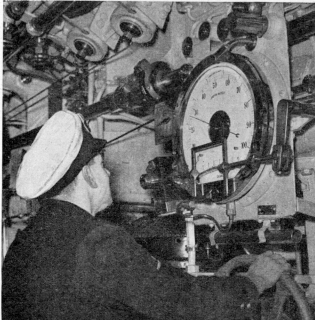

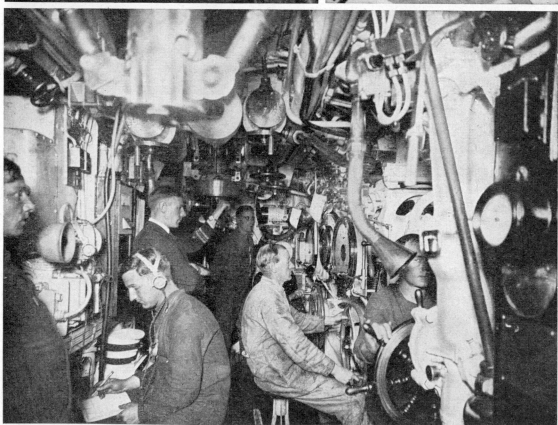

Fox; Keystone

The interior of a submarine is, to the novice, a bewildering mass of machinery. At the top left, the coxswain at the controls of the hydroplane (movable horizontal fins on the outside of the hull) is keeping an eye on the depth gauge as the vessel submerges. Top right, a torpedo is being loaded into a tube for firing. Lower, the crew at action stations preparatory to submerging. Seated on the left is the wireless operator, who sends and receives messages while the vessel is on the surface; beyond him an officer is looking through the periscope; on the right is the helmsman at the wheel, and a rating operating the trimming tanks to regulate the depth of the dive made by the vessel.

this from the inside of the boat while submerged. That was generally done at night, but hostile aircraft with powerful lights gave little warning of their approach and destroyed quite a number. The Germans therefore introduced what they called the "schnorkel gear," sending a tube up to the surface and drawing down air while the ship was safely submerged, so that they could remain under water for a long period. Some form of this device has been adopted by the British and other navies. Another very important advantage is that the submarine can be propelled submerged by her Diesels (drawing engine air from the surface), at a much higher speed than is generally possible with electric motor propulsion from batteries.

P.A.-Reuter

BRITISH SUBMARINES IN A NAVAL DOCKYARD
Of the same class as H.M.S. Ambush (see illustration in page 3105), Alaric and Alderney (right) each carry a 4-inch gun. The inlets by which the superstructure can flood freely, thereby maintaining the same water pressure inside and outside the hull, can be clearly seen in the decking of H.M.S. Alderney.

The submarine still normally depends on her torpedoes (q.v.), as she has for years past, but they are expensive. Therefore many underwater craft carry a gun on deck for use on the surface. Others carry mines in vertical tubes which let them drop while the ship is submerged. The sudden release of the weight of a mine or torpedo would upset the balance of the boat, and make her break surface, were she not fitted with tanks to admit the right amount of water when the torpedo is fired or the mine dropped.

The modern submarine carries numerous auxiliary machines which take up a lot of space in her awkwardly shaped hull and make the crew uncomfortable. That does not deter a great number of men from volunteering, and the Submarine Branch of the Royal Navy has its pick of the finest officers and men in the Service.

Subtraction. Suppose we wish to know the distance between Carlisle and Glasgow. We find that Carlisle is 299 miles from London by railway, while Glasgow is 401 miles from London. To obtain the solution of this problem we must compare these two distances with a view to finding the *difference* between them, or, looking at it in another way, to finding how much greater 401 is than 299. To help us solve this problem let us first consider some simple examples of subtraction.

1. If a sheet of paper is 6 inches wide and 9 inches long, how may it be cut to make it square? Since we know from our study of addition that 9=6+3, we cut off 3 inches from the longer side. When we place a 6-inch line beside a 9-inch line we find that 3 inches must be added to the 6-inch line to make it 9 inches long, or that 3 inches must be taken from the 9-inch line to make it equal to the 6-inch line. In other words, 3 is the *difference* between 6 and 9.

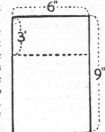

The Times

ESCAPE FROM A SUBMARINE
Taken at the training establishment for submarine crews at Portsmouth, Hampshire, this photograph shows how men in a sunken submarine are able to escape. Wearing a Davis breathing apparatus, a rating is rising through the replica of a submarine's escape hatch placed in a water-tank.

2. One basket of grapes weighs 9 lb., another 14 lb. How much more does the heavier one weigh? Five pounds is the *difference* in weight.

3. It is 10 o'clock. How many more hours to

12 o'clock? Two hours is the *difference* in time.

In the paper problem given, the difference can be measured directly. In the weight and time problems that follow it, the difference can be found by counting from 9 up to 14 or from 10 up to 12, as the case may be; for example, 10, 11, 12, 13, 14 (5 numbers counted, then 14 is 5 greater than 9). Differences, however, need not be counted if the *addition* facts are known. For example, since 9+5=14, when 9 is given, it follows that, to make it into 14, 5 more are needed.

4. If from a rope 15 feet long a piece 8 feet long is cut, how much rope remains?

Solution: Here we may count the numbers from 8 to 15 and find that there are 7 of them. Hence the *remainder* is 7 feet. A better way is to remember that if 8 is one of the two numbers whose sum is 15, the other is 7. It is clear that a remainder left after taking away part of a number is found just as an excess or a difference in value is found between two numbers.

5. Henry had 17 marbles and lost 9. How many had he left? We may count from 9 up to 17 and conclude that Henry had 8 marbles left; or we may set out 17 counters, then remove or subtract 9 of them and count the number left. The first method is adopted for further treatment of this subject.

To compute *differences* or *remainders*, it is necessary to know 81 elementary subtraction facts or combinations, as follows :

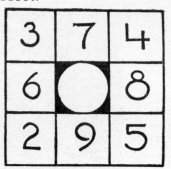

chart for subtraction. Draw it on a large sheet of paper, put in the centre some number between 10 and 20, with other lower numbers in squares around it, and give quickly the difference between this and the other numbers as they are indicated.

Change the number in the centre frequently.

COMPUTING. Cut strips of paper, 10 inches long and one inch wide for the tens, and squares one inch long for the ones.

1. How much more than 23 is 35?

Solution: (a) 3 and what make 5? (Set down the 2).

  35   (b) 2 tens and what make 3 tens? (Set
  23   down the 1 ten).
  ――

  12   (c) Then 23 and what make 35?

2. What is the difference between 43 and 75?

Solution: (a) 3 and what = 5? (Set down the 2).

  75   (b) 4 tens and what = 7 tens? (Set
  43   down the 3 tens).
  ――

  32   (c) Then 43 and what makes 75?

3. How many more is 61 than 34? To understand the solution better, look at this addition:

$$\begin{array}{r} 34 \\ 27 \\ \hline 61 \end{array}$$

Omit the lower number, but keep the sum.

$$\begin{array}{r} 34 \\ +\ \text{what} \\ \hline =\ 61? \end{array}$$

Eleven must have been the sum of the first column. Then what was the missing figure under the 4 ? Four and what make 11? When the 1 was set down, 1 was also carried to the tens column. What was the missing figure under the 3? 4 tens and what = 6 tens? Then what was the missing number?

Solution: (a) Since 4 is greater than 1, we count up from 4 to 10 and then 1 more. 4 and what = 11? (*See* diagram below). Set down the 1. Carry 1 ten to 3 tens.

  61
  34
  ――

  27   (b) 4 tens and how many = 6 tens?
       (c) Then 34 and what = 61?

Answer: The difference is 27.

We may now solve the problem set at the beginning, about the distance between Carlisle and

The thirty-six combinations on the right of the heavy lines are usually learned in second stage.

The forty-five combinations on the left of the heavy lines are usually learned in the first stage.

These must become thoroughly familiar, but they should require little practice if the addition facts are well remembered. Since 4 + 5 = 9, then it follows as a consequence that 9 − 5 = 4; also 9 − 4 = 5. If 4 and 5 put together make 9, then, when either is present, the other is needed to make 9.

It is easy to make a drill

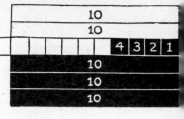

Glasgow. We know that Carlisle is 299 miles from London, and Glasgow is 401 miles from London. To find the distance between Carlisle and Glasgow we subtract the former number from the latter.

Answer: The distance is 102 miles from Carlisle to Glasgow, because Glasgow is situated 102 miles farther away from London.

In a subtraction problem the number *diminished* or the greater of the two numbers compared is called the *minuend;* the number subtracted or the smaller number of the two compared is called the *subtrahend;* the number left after subtraction is called the *remainder;* the number by which the greater number exceeds the lesser is called the *difference.*

864 *minuend*
218 *subtrahend*
———
646 *remainder or difference*

1. Add the subtrahend and remainder or difference. If the work is correct, the sum equals the minuend.

864 *minuend*
218 *subtrahend*
———
646 *difference*
———
864 *minuend*

2. Subtract the difference from the minuend. The result should be the subtrahend.

864 *minuend*
646 *difference*
———
218 *subtrahend*

Accuracy and speed in subtraction are secured (1) by mastering the "fundamental facts"; (2) by using as few words as possible in computing; (3) by forming the habit of testing the correctness of each answer.

Sudan. The region of Africa stretching south from the Sahara Desert and Egypt to the central equatorial zone, and from Cape Verde on the Atlantic coast to the Red Sea and the Abyssinian highlands on the east, is called the Sudan or Soudan, the name being derived from the Arabic *Beled-es-Sudan,* meaning "country of the blacks."

A district of no definite boundaries, it is divided into three parts—the Western Sudan, containing

Ewing Galloway; Sudan Railways
SUDANESE TOWN AND A SHEIKH
On the left bank of the Nile opposite Khartum, capital of the Anglo-Egyptian Sudan, is Omdurman, whose dwellings are mostly mud huts with awnings of grass mats over the entrance (upper). The mounted sheikh or headman (lower) has the Negroid features which are often met with amongst the Sudanese.

the basins of the rivers draining into the Atlantic; the Central Sudan, with the rivers flowing into Lake Chad; and the Anglo-Egyptian Sudan. Most of Western and Central Sudan is French territory.

French Sudan is one of the eight colonies of French West Africa and is situated north of the Senegal and Niger rivers, with an area of 479,783 square miles. A number of the inhabitants are

IRRIGATING THE SUDAN WASTES
Flood waters from the Abyssinian highlands are trapped by the Sennar Makwar dam (above) on the Nile and used to irrigate several million acres of soil. The wedges of granite break the tremendous fall of water.

Topical

nomads (wanderers) whose wealth consists of cattle, horses, asses, sheep, goats and camels; the settled peoples grow millet, rice, maize, ground-nuts and cotton. Important irrigation schemes have been carried out in the Ségou district on the north bank of the Niger, making thousands of hitherto barren acres suitable for cultivation.

The capital of French Sudan is Bamako (population 70,500). Other towns are Kayes, Ségou, Sikasso and Gao. A railway 760 miles long runs from Kulikoro via Bamako and Kayes to the Atlantic coast at Dakar, the capital of French West Africa. There is air connexion with Dakar and Brazzaville in French Congo. The population, mostly Negroes, is 3,778,370.

The Anglo-Egyptian Sudan is bounded on the north by Egypt, on the east by Abyssinia and the Red Sea, on the south by Uganda and the Belgian Congo, on the west by French Equatorial Africa. It has an area of 967,500 square miles and includes most of the Nile valley. The territory is divided into eight provinces—Blue Nile, Darfur, Kassala, Khartum, Kordofan, Northern, Upper Nile and Equatoria, each under a Governor. In the north is the Nubian Desert, and much of the north-west is also barren. The south is heavily forested.

In the north, where the Sennar dam irrigates several million acres, cotton is grown, and millet, the staple food of the Sudanese. The forests in Kordofan, Blue Nile and Kassala yield gum arabic, which is used in the manufacture of adhesives and in confectionery. Forests along the Blue Nile yield tanning material. In the upper reaches of the White Nile there is a vast amount of papyrus (*q.v.*). The

wandering tribes, who live chiefly in the north, breed cattle, sheep, goats and camels. Gold mines are worked at Gabait and at other places in the Red Sea hills. Salt pans (deposits above ground) at Port Sudan supply the needs of the whole country, and much salt is exported. Other products include senna leaves and pods, ground-nuts, dates, hides and skins, beans, maize and ivory.

The capital of the Anglo-Egyptian Sudan is Khartum (population 61,800). Among other large towns are Omdurman, Port Sudan, Suakin, Wady Halfa, El Obeid and Kassala. There are 2,000 miles of railway, and regular steamer services on the Nile. Internal air services link the principal towns, and there are connexions with Egypt and Europe.

The rule of Egypt in the Sudan, after having been gradually extended in the course of 60 years, was interrupted in 1882 by the revolt of the Sudanese leader known as the Mahdi, who, with his successor, the Khalifa, held the country from 1885 to 1898. In 1896 an Anglo-Egyptian army commenced operations for the recovery of the lost territory, and on September 2, 1898, the overthrow of the Khalifa was completed at the battle of Omdurman. An Anglo-Egyptian treaty, signed in 1899 and reaffirmed in 1936, provided for the administration of the Sudan by a Governor-General appointed by Egypt on British recommendation.

In 1948 a Legislative Assembly and an Executive Council of Sudanese were set up under British guidance, giving the Sudanese a greater share in their own government. The Egyptians disagreed with this as they thought that Egypt should have sovereignty over Sudanese territory. The population is about 7,547,500. (*See* Africa ; Egypt).

Suez Canal.

(Pron. sōō′-ez). The idea of a canal across the Isthmus of Suez to connect the Red Sea and the Medi-

SUEZ CANAL
English Miles
0   5   10

MEDITERRANEAN SEA
Port Said

Bay of Tina

Tina

El Kab
Bir ed Dueidar
to Gaza

El Kantara

Bir Abu Aruk
El Ferdan

Ismailia
Lake Timsa

Tussum
Serapeum

Faid
Great Bitter Lake

Little Bitter Lake

Shalluf

Kubri

Suez
Port Tewfik
to Akaba

Roads ———
Railways ++++

30

SUEZ CANAL
Cut through the isthmus of Suez, the Suez Canal connects the Red Sea with the Mediterranean.

THE LOW AND SANDY BANKS OF THE SUEZ CANAL

Vessels passing through the Suez Canal have to proceed very slowly in order to create as little wash as possible, the banks being low and sandy and therefore easily damaged. Here a huge floating dock is being taken through the water-way by tugs, all other traffic being suspended during the operation. The Canal is 103 miles long and the least width is just under 197 feet. It was opened in 1869. Construction occupied ten years, at a cost of about £17 million.

terranean occupied the minds of men for ages, from the time (about 1300 B.C.) when the Pharaoh Seti I had connected the Nile with the Red Sea, until the 19th century when the French engineer Ferdinand de Lesseps, having obtained the necessary permission from the Turkish Viceroy of Egypt, began the construction of the present canal on April 25, 1859.

The canal was opened on November 17, 1869. It is 103 miles long, with a minimum width of 196 feet 10 inches. The maximum draught allowed for vessels is 34 feet. The average time for passing through the waterway is 11 hours 30 minutes, navigating by night as well as day.

It shortens the journey from Britain to the port of Bombay in the republic of India by 5,000 miles, and is used by between 5,000 and 6,000 vessels annually in normal times. A swing bridge, completed in 1940, crosses the canal at El Kantara to connect Cairo by rail with Beirut in Syria.

The management of the canal is normally under the direction of an international Board representing the Suez Canal Company, on which the French have the largest number of members. Britain has 10 members, three for the Government and seven for shipping interests. The rights of the Company expire in 1968, when the Suez Canal and all its accessories will become the property of Egypt.

The canal is of immense importance to Britain in time of war as a route to and from the Orient and Australasia, and control of the waterway is essential to the defence of Egypt. In the Second World War (1939–45) it was closed to all but Allied shipping, and although it was attacked by German and Italian aircraft in 1941 and 1942 it suffered only slight damage. Under the terms of an agreement concluded in 1946 with the Egyptian Government, Britain maintained troops and aircraft in the vicinity of the Canal for its protection until 1949.

Suffolk. (Pron. suf'-ok). A maritime county of England, with an area of 1,482 square miles, Suffolk has a coast-line of about 62 miles on the North Sea. It is bounded on the north by Norfolk, on the south by Essex, on the west by Cambridgeshire. The surface is generally flat, but there are hills in the north-west. The rivers include the Waveney, Stour and Orwell. In the north are Oulton Broad and other sheets of water, parts of the Norfolk Broads.

Agriculture is the chief industry, but fishing is also important. Barley, oats and wheat are grown ; cattle, sheep and horses (especially the breed known as Suffolk Punches) are bred. The county town is Ipswich (pop. about 102,450), which has a number of engineering works. Lowestoft (a fishing port),

Southwold, Aldeburgh (a fishing centre) and Felixstowe (named after the 7th century Bishop Felix of Dunwich) are popular seaside resorts.

Other towns include Bury St. Edmunds, named after St. Edmund the Martyr, King of East Anglia (841–870); Saxmundham, Stowmarket, Bungay and Beccles, the two latter being centres of the printing trade. The county has several fine churches of flint and stone. Towards the Essex border is the district known as Constable's country, after John Constable (1776–1837), a native of East Bergholt, who became famous for his landscape paintings of East Anglia.

For purposes of local government the county is divided into two portions—East Suffolk and West Suffolk, each with its county council. The population of Suffolk is about 416,000.

The ADVENTURES of a LUMP of SUGAR

In one form or another sugar is one of the essential ingredients in a balanced diet, as a producer of energy. Here is told how it journeys from plantation and beet-field to consumer.

Sugar. From the commercial point of view this indispensable sweetener is a comparatively modern product. The ancient Greeks and Romans had no sugar, and used honey instead for sweetening. Sugar was probably produced first in India, as early as the 1st century of our era, but for many centuries it was used only as a medicine or as a rare delicacy at feasts.

The Arabs, who gave Europe so many wonderful things, brought the sugar-cane plant from India. They introduced the cultivation of the plant into Egypt, Sicily, and Spain, and also gave us its name—" sugar " is from the Arabic word *sukkar*. It was not until the time of the Crusades (12th and 13th centuries) that sugar became generally known in Europe. The earliest record we find of sugar in England was at the beginning of the 14th century—and then it was used only for medicinal purposes.

By the close of the 14th century Europe had developed a flourishing trade in sugar and other Oriental products by the overland route. Venice remained the great central market of this trade until the beginning of the 15th century, when Vasco da Gama made his memorable voyage round the south of Africa and discovered an ocean route to India. Columbus, too, was seeking a water route for the trade in sugar and spices when he made his discovery of the New World.

The Nations in Search of New Sources

The sugar and spice trade was immensely valuable. One of the chief motives which impelled Spain, France, England, and other European nations to reach out after tropical and subtropical colonies was to obtain their own sugar supply.

Up to the time of the Napoleonic wars practically the whole of the world's sugar supply came from the sugar-cane. In 1747 Andreas Sigismund Marggraf (1709–82), a German chemist, had discovered that the juice of beet contained the same sugar (sucrose) as cane; and Napoleon, finding his sugar supplies threatened by the Allied blockade, gave bounties to beet-sugar producers. At a later date in Germany beet-sugar production was stimulated by the Government and, by selective breeding, beets with a higher sugar content were grown. At one time beet-sugar seriously threatened the cane-sugar industry. In the last 25 years between a quarter and one-third of the world's sugar has come from beet grown in the temperate regions of Europe and the U.S.A.

Cuba, Java, India, the Philippine Islands, the United States and Puerto Rico are the main producers of cane sugar. Beet sugar is grown chiefly in Russia, Germany, France, Czechoslovakia and the United States. Beet sugar production is becoming of increasing importance in Great Britain, and during the Second World War (1939–45) it furnished the domestic sugar ration.

Extracting the Sugar from Sugar-Cane

Sugar-cane is a tall grass having numerous bamboo-like stems which grow up to 20 feet high. It is a tropical plant but has been grown in sub-tropical climates like those of Natal, Florida and Egypt. When they are ripe the canes are cut and stripped of their leaves. They contain about 70 per cent water and 10–15 per cent of sugar. They are torn in a " shredder " before being passed through a series of mills each consisting of three rolls, one on top and two underneath. The rollers are grooved to allow the juice to drain out, and the pressure put on the rollers increases as the crushed canes pass through the series. After extracting the juice, water is added to the canes ; and on further milling a more dilute juice is obtained. The final pulp, called " bagasse," is used for fuel or for making compressed boards.

The extracted juice is strained to remove dirt and pieces of cane, and is then clarified by adding milk of lime and heating to boiling. Calcium salts of the acids present, with protein and other substances, are precipitated together. The filtered syrup is now evaporated in vacuum pans to a thick syrup of 50 per cent sugar content. The evaporation used to be done in open pans, but boiling in vacuum pans is quicker and is mostly used today. The syrup is now crystallised in another vacuum pan. It is here evaporated until it is supersaturated with sugar, and is now allowed to crystallise, while more syrup is added and water is evaporated off. The whole process is carefully controlled so that crystals of the required size are formed. Part of the syrup (the " mother-liquor ") does not crystallise and remains clinging to the crystals.

The mixture of sugar crystals and mother-liquor, called the " massecuite," is put into great whirling drums, called " centrifugals," where most of the syrup is forced out through perforations in the drum while the raw sugar remains inside. The syrup called " first molasses " is reboiled once or twice to give further crops of sugar crystals

Courtesy of the Tourist and Exhibitions Board of Trinidad and Tobago

OBTAINING SUGAR FROM THE CANE IN THE WEST INDIES

Much sugar still reaches Britain from the West Indies, including the island of Trinidad. 1. At the railhead the cutdown canes are weighed and loaded into trucks to be taken to the sugar-mill. 2. A conveyor belt passes the canes to the crushers, which extract the juice. 3. Water is evaporated from the juice in vacuum pans and the liquid transformed into a thick syrup. This process is carefully controlled, both by observation through windows in the side of the pan and by sampling. 4. Dark sugar, which contains impurities, is exported in bags, ready for refining.

less pure than the first. The final molasses is called " blackstrap." Yellow " Demerara " sugar is obtained from the first crystallisation and is exported from the country of origin without further refining. In some cases the cane juice goes through a more complicated process than that described here, resulting in plantation white sugar which, like Demerara, is not further refined. The less pure " raw " sugar, containing 96 per cent sugar and many impurities which give it a dark colour, is usually shipped in bags to refineries in more highly industrialised countries than those in which the sugar-cane grows.

Blackstrap molasses is a dark treacly liquid containing about 50 per cent sucrose and other sugars. In some countries it is burned with the bagasse, but it is a valuable by-product. It can be used as cattle feed, or can be diluted and fermented to give alcohol and other products such as acetone and citric acid. The " first molasses " can be used for edible purposes.

The raw sugar goes through a number of processes. " Affination " involves washing the crystals with strong syrup, to remove the layer of molasses left clinging to them. By using a small amount of strong syrup instead of water, the crystals do not dissolve. The sugar is then dissolved in water, a process inaccurately but generally known as remelting, and the impurities are precipitated by lime and phosphoric acid. The solution is often filtered through " bone-char " in large cylinders, a process which removes the colour and many impurities. Bone-char consists largely of calcium phosphate, and after use can be revived by washing and heating strongly. The sugar solution is sometimes treated with active charcoal, only about 1 per cent being required to remove the coloured impurities.

The purified syrup is now evaporated, crystallised and centrifuged in much the same way as was the raw sugar. The sugar remaining in the drums is pure white granulated sugar and after being dried and packed is ready for the market. The molasses from the refinery is much more pure than that resulting from raw sugar production, and is used for cooking purposes.

Up to a generation ago the liquor from the vacuum pans (known as the massecuite), was poured directly into large conical moulds about 18 inches deep, the molasses drained away through the apex of the cone and the crystallised sugar turned out in the once familiar " sugar-loaves." Today cube sugar has replaced it, and is usually made by moulding moistened granulated sugar. Caster sugar and icing sugar are obtained by grinding the best grades of granulated sugar and sifting them through bolting silks. Brown sugar may be a poorer grade of sugar, but it is also made from white sugar by adding a dye. Golden syrup is manufactured from sugar by " inverting " part of it (see later), which prevents sugar crystallising from the 80 per cent solution.

Making Sugar from Beet

Sugar beet is a white root of the same group as the red beet of the garden. It contains about 15 per cent of sugar. The whole process of extraction and refining of sugar from beets is conducted in a single factory, as beets are grown in the temperate climate of highly industrialised countries within reach of the factories. Sugar-cane has to be processed soon after it is cut, so that extraction plants are very busy for a limited period and idle for the rest of the time. Beets can be stored, and the processing can be spread over a longer period.

At one time the juice was extracted from the beets by pressure, but now a diffusion process is used. After washing, the beets are cut by sharp rotating knives into little pieces called " cossettes." These are soaked in hot water in a " diffusion battery " made up of 10–12 tanks each holding from 2–4 tons. The process is arranged on the " counter-current " principle so that fresh cossettes are extracted by strong syrup while nearly exhausted cossettes come into contact with fresh water. Thus a uniformly strong syrup is produced, while the minimum of sugar is left in the exhausted beets. The residual pulp left at the finish is used for cattle food.

The clarification of the beet syrup is usually done by the carbonation process. The juice is heated to 90° C., and excess of lime is added. Carbon dioxide is passed in, in stages, and the sludge of calcium carbonate and impurities is filtered off after each stage. Finally, sulphur dioxide is used, which bleaches the liquid. After a final filtration the syrup is evaporated in vacuum pans, as for cane-sugar, and the sugar is separated in centrifugals. Further crops of sugar crystals are obtained from the first molasses, as in the case of cane-sugar.

In the United States a new method is being used for purification of beet juice before evaporation. This is called " ion-exchange " and the principle is the same as that of water-softening (in which the salts causing the hardness of water are removed by percolating through special clays or zeolites). In the case of beet juice the inorganic salts are removed, together with many other impurities. The process of purification means that 95 per cent of the sugar of the beet is obtained, as against 90 per cent obtainable by ordinary methods. The resulting molasses is also purer.

Different Kinds of Sugars

The molasses thrown off in the centrifugals in beet sugar making, unlike cane-sugar molasses, is not suitable for the manufacture of rum, but it is easier to extract more sugar from it. In the Steffens process the sugar is extracted from diluted molasses by precipitating a compound of sugar with lime. The sugar can then be obtained from the precipitate by treatment with carbon dioxide. In the United States the Steffens " waste "—the molasses with all the sugar extracted from it—is sometimes used to make sodium glutamate, which is a valuable new flavouring material for soups, and a number of other processed foods.

Sugars are about the most valuable of energy-producing foods as they are absorbed quickly and completely in the body and there is no waste. They occur in nearly all fruits. The sugar beet is merely one of several sugar-storing roots, and the sugar maple is not the only plant with sugar in its juice, though it has a very high proportion of sugar. (See Maple).

There are many substances called sugars, of which sucrose (cane or beet sugar) is the most familiar. They are carbohydrates, being composed of carbon, hydrogen and oxygen. Mono-saccharides are sugars all having the formula $C_6H_{12}O_6$. Although they all have the same formula, and the same atoms in the molecule, they differ because in each sugar these atoms are arranged differently. Mono-saccharides include glucose or grape sugar, which is found in crystalline lumps in raisins (dried grapes), and fructose or fruit sugar, which is used as a substitute for cane sugar in the diet of diabetic patients. Fructose is made from artichokes. A mixture of glucose and fructose, called " invert sugar," is found in honey and many sweet fruits. Glucose and fructose are also called dextrose and laevulose—from Latin dexter, "right" : and laevus, "left"—because one rotates polarised light (see Light) to the right and the other rotates it to the left.

Di-saccharides are sugars having the formula $C_{12}H_{22}O_{11}$. A di-saccharide molecule is made up of two molecules of a mono-saccharide, the same or different, with the elimination of water. The sucrose molecule is thus made up of one of glucose and one of fructose. On heating with dilute acids, it is split up or hydrolysed, because one molecule

ON THE WAY FROM SUGAR BEET TO SUGAR BOWL

In the upper left-hand corner is a sugar beet, ready to be sliced into 'cossettes' and yield its juices. Next you see the top of a battery of diffusion tanks, arranged in a circle. Each new lot of cossettes is packed into one of the tanks, and hot water or a supply of syrup already extracted is turned on. The water or syrup absorbs the sugar in the cossettes, and passes to the purifying tanks, where it is treated, first with milk of lime and then with carbonic acid gas. The lime seizes upon impurities, and the gas precipitates the lime. The liquid enters the vacuum filter, where the precipitate is removed, and goes to the evaporator, which reduces the liquid to a thick syrup. After being subjected to sulphur dioxide, which bleaches it, the thickened liquid passes through filter presses, and is ready for the crystallizing process. This is conducted in huge vacuum pans. These are heated by steam coils, and an air pump maintains a partial vacuum within them, in order to permit boiling at low temperature. The crystals are removed from the liquid by the centrifugal drier, the last moisture is driven out by the hot-air drier, and the sugar is graded for size, weighed and packed. The product from both sugar-cane and beetroot is the form known as sucrose. It was Napoleon I 's desire to be free of oversea supplies which encouraged beet-sugar production.

of water is taken up per molecule of sucrose, into glucose and fructose in equal quantities.

$$C_{12}H_{22}O_{11} + H_2O = C_6H_{12}O_6 + C_6H_{12}O_6$$
sucrose   *glucose*   *fructose*

This hydrolysis is known as "inversion," and the mixture of glucose and fructose is called "invert sugar"; because whereas the sucrose rotates polarised light to the right, the mixture of glucose and fructose rotates it to the left—i.e. the direction is reversed or inverted.

Maltose, a sugar formed by the action of malt on starch, is a di-saccharide, each molecule being made up of two of glucose. Lactose or milk-sugar occurs in milk, and is another di-saccharide. It is the foundation used in making many pills. Commercially, the name glucose is given to corn syrup which contains glucose and other substances. (*See* Starch).

When sucrose is heated with a little water until it melts and begins to turn yellow it forms, on cooling, a hard glassy mass called "barley sugar." If heated still more, it partially decomposes, leaving a soluble brown material called "caramel," which is used to colour food and beverages.

Saccharin is a white powder made from toluene, one of the components of coal-tar. It is 550 times as sweet as cane sugar but has none of the energy-producing food value of sugars. Here the bee, at least, is not misled, for saccharin does not taste sweet to her!

Sulpha Drugs. With penicillin and streptomycin this group marks the most spectacular and brilliant achievement of chemistry in recent years against *Streptococci* and *Staphylococci*—the germs causing pneumonia, boils, inflammation of bone and many other ills. It is interesting to note that the sulpha group does not act by destroying the germs; rather it holds up their capacity to breed in the tissues of their victim, so that he, rested and fed and nursed, can fight the enemy with success.

In 1908 the chemist Gelmo originated the simplest member of the group. With an irony not peculiar to chemistry he did not realize what he had found. In 1935 the German chemist Domagk, experimenting with the aniline dyes for which Germany was so famous, chanced upon the fact that the substance, until then used in dyeing, would cure streptococcal blood-poisoning in mice. His much-loved small daughter, the story goes, was at the time desperately ill from a streptococcal infection and he tried the mouse-cure on her. She recovered. Forthwith the chemists and physicians of the world were in hot chase after the new remedy. Nowadays there are numerous sub-divisions of the group, each of which exercises its own special function against a specific disease.

Sulphur. Gathered from the throats of volcanoes and forming compounds that smell unpleasantly, sulphur is sometimes indeed a nuisance. Silver teaspoons tarnish when used with eggs because the sulphur in the egg forms a blackish silver sulphide over the surface of the spoon. That same sulphur forms an alliance with hydrogen to produce the offensive odour of rotten eggs (hydrogen sulphide or sulphuretted hydrogen). The pungent odour of cabbage, onions, turnips, and mustard is due to sulphur compounds.

Sulphur is an exceedingly active substance. But its activities are so varied, useful, and indeed indispensable to us that we can afford to overlook its peccadilloes. Modern industry could scarcely "carry on" without sulphur and its compounds, particularly one invaluable acid (*see* Sulphuric Acid). Sulphur enters into most of the proteins, those remarkable complex substances which are so important in animal tissues and in many vegetable structures. Human hair contains the exceptionally high proportion of 5 per cent sulphur.

It occurs free in volcanic regions all over the earth and still more widely diffused in compounds. The world's commercial supply used to come almost entirely from Sicily, but now the United States is the chief producer. The Texas-Louisiana deposits occur in rock formations overlying salt domes. These deposits lie buried under from 500 to 1,500 feet of soft material—clay, shale, sand and gravel. Since 1903 they have been successfully mined by an ingenious process. Several steel pipes, of sizes ranging from 13 inches to 1 inch in diameter, are driven, one within the other, deep into the sulphur bed. Water, heated far above the boiling point, is pumped down the outer pipes. Melted sulphur, heavier than water, collects in a pool around the lower end of the pipes. Air, compressed to a pressure of about 250 pounds to the square inch, is forced down the central 1-inch pipe, and the melted sulphur, more than 99 per cent pure, rises to the surface through the next encircling pipe.

Sulphur assumes at least six well-known disguises or "allotropic modifications," and some others which are in doubt as being possibly not pure sulphur. It crystallizes in two forms, the rhombic (ordinary form) and monoclinic; it has several amorphous (shapeless or non-crystalline) states, some soluble and some insoluble.

Sulphur is a non-metallic element, with an atomic weight of 32. The symbol is S. It melts at 235° F. (113° C.); hence the water used in mining it has to be heated *above* the boiling point. When melted it becomes a clear yellow liquid, but as the temperature is further raised it darkens and thickens, until at about 256° F. (180° C.) it is too solid to be poured; heated still further, it liquefies again, reaching the boiling point at 832° F. (444° C.).

It is sold in several forms: as a light yellow odourless and tasteless powder; in solid rolls or cones, known as "roll sulphur" or "roll brimstone"; and in very finely powdered forms, one, known as "flowers of sulphur" or "sublimed sulphur," obtained by cooling sulphur vapours in a large room so that they condense and "snow down" in fine crystals, and another, known as "milk of sulphur," "lac sulphuris," or "precipitated sulphur," obtained by precipitation from solution. "Roll brimstone" is sometimes burned in old buildings to kill vermin. Precipitated sulphur and sublimed sulphur are used in medicine.

Among the more important sulphur compounds, apart from sulphuric acid, are sulphur dioxide (SO_2), bleach and insecticide; the poisonous and explosive liquid carbon bisulphide (CS_2), solvent, disinfectant, and insecticide; ferrous sulphate (green vitriol or copperas), mordant for dyes, insecticide, water purifier, used in the manufacture of inks and pigments; copper sulphate (blue vitriol), mordant and germicide; sodium thiosulphate, commercially known as hyposulphite of soda, used in photography, tanning, dyeing and bleaching; and the alums, complex double sulphates, used in dyeing, paper-making and tanning, and generally as astringents. Of the sulphur compounds occurring in Nature, some are valuable ores, as cinnabar (mercuric sulphide) and galena (lead sulphide); iron pyrites or " fool's gold " (iron disulphide) is sometimes used as a source of sulphur.

Sulphuric Acid.

Few chemicals affect our lives as widely as does sulphuric acid. From the time we get up in the morning to put on clothes dyed and bleached by the acid of sulphuric acid, until we are lighted to our beds at night by electricity conducted over wires of copper which have been refined by the aid of sulphuric acid, we are constantly depending on this powerful and active servant.

Sulphuric acid is never satisfied, chemically speaking, with things as they are; it must always tear other compounds apart and make new ones by combining with them. In doing so it chars paper, cloth and wood, eats into flesh, acts as a violent poison, and is generally dangerous and destructive. It is a good servant, though a bad master; the same qualities which are so dangerous uncontrolled make it invaluable when we want to break up a refractory chemical compound and rebuild it into something else. Sulphuric acid (H_2SO_4) is, for instance, the main reagent in the Leblanc soda process (*see* Sodium) for splitting sodium chloride or common salt into sodium and chlorine so that soda or sodium carbonate may be made from the one and hydrochloric acid from the other.

The old name for sulphuric acid, " oil of vitriol," is now strictly applied only to the 93·5 per cent acid, a colourless, oily-looking liquid, very greedy of moisture and therefore used as a drying agent. The ordinary acid, containing from 30 to 38 per cent water, is known as " chamber acid " from the lead chambers in which it is made.

The manufacture of sulphuric acid is one of the great chemical industries. There are two important processes of manufacture. In the old lead-chamber process—to give a mere skeleton of some rather complicated reactions— sulphur in the form of " brimstone " or pyrites or other compound is burned, giving sulphur dioxide. These fumes then pass through a series of lead chambers in which they react with steam and certain oxides of nitrogen to form the diluted chamber acid which may be evaporated to obtain a more concentrated acid. In the newer contact or catalytic process, the presence of a catalyst induces sulphur dioxide to unite directly with oxygen from the air to form sulphur trioxide. This is dissolved in previously made acid, and water is added. The water and the trioxide unite to form sulphuric acid; in this reaction, $H_2O + SO_3$ becomes H_2SO_4.

Sumatra.

Part of the Republic of Indonesia and the sixth largest island in the world, Sumatra has an area of 165,000 square miles. It is situated in the Malay Archipelago, separated from the Malay Peninsula by the Strait of Malacca and from the island of Java by Sunda Strait. Sumatra is mainly mountainous, the Barisan range running for 1,000 miles along the western coast, with volcanic peaks from 5,000 to 12,000 feet high.

The rivers along the west coast are mostly unnavigable; but those on the east are the best means of communication. The largest streams are the Asahan, which drains Lake Toba and the Rokan, Kampar, Jambi and Musi.

Sumatra is bisected by the Equator and the climate is hot and damp, the rainfall everywhere being at least 60 inches. In immense forests of teak, palms, camphor trees, ebony and myrtles are found elephants, tigers, tapirs and rhinoceroses, and the orang-utan. Crocodiles infest the river mouths.

Unlike its neighbour Java, Sumatra was mostly left unaffected by Dutch rule, except in the south-east and certain small areas along the coasts. Rice, the staple food of the native population, is the main crop; other products are sugar, coffee, pepper and rubber. Excellent tobacco is grown at Deli, and copra (dried coconut " meat "), sisal and tea are exported. Minerals include gold, silver, sulphur, tin, lead, coal and oil. The chief

Courtesy of the Netherlands Information Bureau

RIVERSIDE TOWN ON THE ISLAND OF SUMATRA
One of the few towns in Sumatra is Kuta Raja (above), on the Achin river. Vast areas of the huge tropical island, which is separated from Java by the Sunda Strait, are still virgin forest—because it has not been so extensively developed as the rest of Indonesia, largely owing to lack of communications.

towns are on the coast and include Padang, Palembang, Belawan and Sabang. There are 1,233 miles of railway and nearly 16,000 miles of roads. Air services are maintained between Palembang and Java and Singapore.

Different tribes of the Malay family inhabit the island, and they vary considerably in language and civilization. Most of them are farmers; but the Menangkabans, who are the most advanced, are noted for architecture, silver work and weaving. The prevailing religion is Mahomedanism.

Civilized first by the Hindus in the 7th century of the Christian era, Sumatra came under the influence of the Mahomedan Arabs six centuries later. In 1508 the Portuguese explorer Lopez de Figuera visited the island, and trading settlements were soon established on the coast. Towards the end of the 16th century the Portuguese were driven out by the Dutch, Sumatra being eventually incorporated in the Netherlands East Indies.

In February 1942, during the Second World War (1939–45), Japanese forces landed on Sumatra and occupied the western shores of Sunda Strait. They remained in possession of the island until the surrender of Japan to the Allied nations on August 14, 1945. In 1946 a native State, called the Republic of Indonesia, was established in Java, whose territory included Sumatra. Later the States of South and East Sumatra were formed, the rest of the island remaining part of the Indonesian Republic. In 1949 the Netherlands East Indies, with the exception of Dutch New Guinea, were granted self-government by the Netherlands. In 1950 South and East Sumatra were again merged with the Indonesian Republic. The population of Sumatra is over 8,000,000.

Our GIANT SUN and Its GIGANTIC TASKS

Besides giving us all our food and heat and light, the sun makes and distributes our weather, keeps the waterfalls falling and the winds blowing, and holds big and little worlds in their appointed paths.

Sun AND THE SOLAR SYSTEM. A modern astronomer calls us all children of the sun. Centuries ago the Incas of Peru also called themselves children of the sun and performed strange ceremonies in worship of the king of the heavenly bodies. They were mistaken in thinking the sun was a god, but they were right in believing that there would be no earth—at least as we know it—and no people on the earth if it were not for the sun. If the light of the sun were suddenly shut off, we should soon perish from cold and starvation.

In point of fact, if the heat of the sun were reduced by only 10 per cent the whole of the temperate zone, the zone now inhabited by the majority of the human race, would be converted into frozen wastes. Perhaps we might keep warm for a while with the stock of coal still in the mines; but in the meantime our food supply would give out and there would be no way of replenishing it, for in such cold nothing would grow.

The very coal that we burn is a gift of the sun, for coal was formed from giant ferns and other primitive plants which long ago stored up the rays of sunlight for our use today. From coal we get most of our power, but we also get power from windmills and waterfalls. Yet neither the windmill

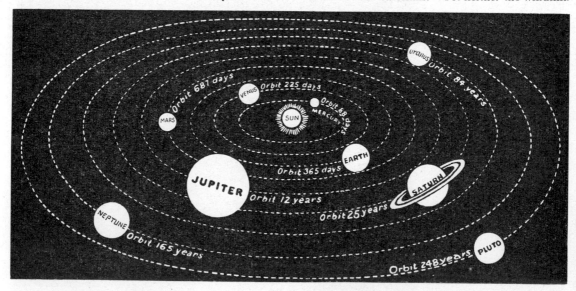

HOW THE PLANETS REVOLVE ABOUT THE SUN

The nine large planets (of which the earth is one) and the sun, which constitute our solar system, are shown in this diagram. All these bodies move round the sun in an elliptical path, being held in their orbits by the gravitational force of the sun and of one another. The planets differ greatly in size and orbit ; whereas Mercury goes around the sun in 88 days, Pluto takes 248 years, because it is a vast distance from the sun—some 3,700 million miles.

nor the waterfall would give us any power if it were not for the sun.

It is because the sun heats some regions of the atmosphere to a higher degree than others that we have winds, and it is because the sun vaporizes the water of the oceans and raises it to the hill and mountain tops that we have rivers and waterfalls.

Attempts have been made to construct "solar engines" worked by the direct heat of the sun's rays. A solar motor in actual use consists of a 33-foot reflector with 1,788 small mirrors that concentrate sunlight upon a boiler. There is plenty of heat to be harnessed, for the sun sends hurtling out into space so much heat that every square centimetre of space at the earth's distance receives enough to raise the temperature of a gramme of water 1·93 degrees Centigrade in one minute (this unit of heat is the "solar constant"). About an hour of bright sunlight produces steam enough to develop about 12 horse-power. The apparatus is moved by clockwork so that the reflector always exactly faces the sun.

The sun's influence is also exerted in the enormous force of gravitation by which it holds the entire solar system together. *Sol* is the Latin word for "sun," and the phrase "solar system" means the group of heavenly objects which are actually held in captivity by the sun. These objects include the nine large planets (of which the earth is one), a great number of asteroids (little brothers of the planets), and a much greater number of very small bodies which appear nearly every night as meteors or "shooting stars." All these bodies move in elliptical but almost circular paths round the sun, simply because they can't get away. It is chiefly the power of gravity exerted by the sun which keeps the earth from flying off on a straight course into space. (*See* Meteors and Meteorites; Planets).

The force of the sun's attraction as exerted upon Pluto, the farthest of the planets, in its path round the sun is equal to the strength of a column of steel many hundreds of miles thick and 3,675 millions of miles long, for that is the estimated distance of Pluto from the sun. In comparison, we on the earth are near neighbours of the sun, only 93 millions of miles away ! The ancient Greeks estimated the sun's distance as only four and a half million miles, although they calculated the moon's distance correctly.

The temperature of the sun is believed to be at least 10,000° Fahrenheit, which is 8,000° higher than any temperature ever obtained in any electrical furnace. Every known substance on the earth, even the hardest stone or metal, would instantly turn to gas under such intense heat. This

Paul Popper

PROBING THE SECRETS OF THE SUN

Known as a coelostat, the above apparatus is at London University Observatory at Mill Hill, London. It aids in the study of the sun's physical and chemical properties. Two mirrors, one rotated by a driving mechanism, reflect the sun's rays down into a laboratory where they are analysed with scientific precision by means of a spectroscope.

is one of the reasons why we believe that the sun is not a solid but is largely made up of gases.

What causes such intense heat? If the sun were actually burning it would soon be reduced to dust and ashes. Its fire would begin to go out within less than 1,500 years. So the "combustion theory" cannot be accepted.

One theory, for long favoured, is based on the fact that when gases contract they create heat. It is generally supposed that the sun, being composed mostly of gases, is slowly contracting, and in this way continues to give off such immense quantities of heat and light. Yet the sun is so enormous that if contraction were the only source of its energy it would still radiate warmth for 10 million years.

The most modern theory is that the vast energy radiated is released when matter is "destroyed," or mass is converted into energy. (*See* Star, page 3081).

The diameter of the sun is 865,400 miles, or about 109 times that of the earth, and if we could put the sun in a pair of scales we should have to use 333,420 globes like the earth to bring the scales to a balance. In other words, the mass or weight of the sun is 333,420 times that of the earth. A small pea beside a large pumpkin gives some idea of the relative sizes of the earth and sun.

When we look at the sun through a telescope we see it as a broad round white disk, marked here and there with little black splotches that look like holes or caverns in the surface. These are the sun spots, which are still a great mystery. When light from the spots is examined with the spectroscope (*q.v.*) the lines are seen to be doubled. This is known as the "Zeeman effect," and is obtained in the laboratory by passing light through a strong magnetic field. From this it is assumed that the spots mark great magnetic storms. The form of these spots is constantly changing, yet they last long enough for us to be able to determine that the sun rotates on its axis in a period of about 25 days. As in the case of the planet Jupiter, the equatorial regions of the sun rotate in a shorter period than the polar regions.

The invention of the spectroscope revolutionized the study of the sun, because it made it possible for astronomers to discover at least a great number of the materials composing the sun. Practically all the elements which have been found in the earth's crust are to be found in the sun also. This might be a reason for believing that at some time in the past the earth split off from the sun, except that most stars show this same chemical composition.

The white surface of the central body of the sun is called the *photosphere* (light sphere). This is surrounded by a layer of incandescent gases, the *chromosphere* (colour sphere). From the chromosphere, or even the photosphere itself, vast eruptions shoot up to heights ranging from 20,000 to 300,000 miles. These *prominences* are of enormous extent and often shoot up to a height of 200,000 miles in an hour. Beyond the prominences is a halo of light, the *corona*, visible only at the time of an eclipse of the sun. (*See* Eclipse).

Sundew.

There is something almost human —or perhaps it would be more exact to say inhuman—about the way this plant ensnares its insect prey. The upper surface of each leaf is covered with numerous hairlike projections or "tentacles," and these are provided with glands which give out a sticky fluid attractive to insects. Each leaf seems to be covered with hundreds of glistening dewdrops; hence the name of the plant.

If an insect touches the tentacles it sticks, and all the neighbouring tentacles begin to bend toward the centre of the leaf, holding the insect and making the leaf look like a small closed fist. As soon as the prey is caught the fluid secreted by the tentacles becomes acid, containing digestive properties which make soluble all the nitrogenous parts of the insect's body.

After the insect is digested —usually in about two days —the tentacles all straighten out and the leaf trap is set for another visitor.

Three species of the genus, *Drosera*, are found in Britain —the round-leaved (*D. rotundifolia*), the narrow-leaved (*D. intermedia*) and the long-leaved (*D. anglica*). They grow in boggy ground, and in spite of their small dimensions their red and green glistening foliage makes them conspicuous. In summer they send up stems bearing a number of small white flowers. Several other marsh plants, such as butterwort and bladderwort, catch and digest insects. (*See* Pitcher Plants; Venus's Fly-trap).

Sunfish.

All head and no body—that is the sunfish! Above and underneath the part that would correspond to the neck are two big triangular fins, and just at the

SUNDEW SNARES   *A. W. Dennis*
The numerous sticky-tipped hair-like projections which cover the upper surface of each leaf of the sundew plant are shown plainly here. The sticky liquid attracts insects to their death. The specimen is the round-leaved species.

place where it should begin to widen out like most other fish it stops altogether. Its outline is roughly circular. Specimens eight feet long and weighing nearly a ton have been caught.

The sunfish, which seems to have got its name from its habit of basking in the sun on the surface of the ocean, is not good for food, but is sometimes caught for the oil it yields. It is apparently a stupid creature, because it will allow men in boats to approach quite close, and it is, therefore, easily harpooned. Often it puts up a tremendous fight, dragging the craft of its assailants through the water at considerable speed.

It is found in almost all parts of the Atlantic and Pacific oceans, and one species (*Mola mola*) occasionally occurs off the coasts of Great Britain.

Sunflower.

When the French explorer Samuel de Champlain (*q.v.*) visited the Indians on the eastern shore of Lake Huron, one of the Great Lakes of North America, early in the 17th century, he found them cultivating the large common sunflower, the best-known of the several species of this plant. They had probably brought it from its native prairies beyond the Mississippi. Its stalks furnished the red men with a textile fibre, its leaves served as fodder, its flowers yielded

W. S. Berridge
THE STRANGE SUNFISH
Here is a strange travesty of the fishy form! Its body is so short that it seems to consist only of a large head with a tail immediately attached to it. The sunfish is sometimes as much as eight feet long.

IMMENSE ERUPTION OF A SOLAR PROMINENCE

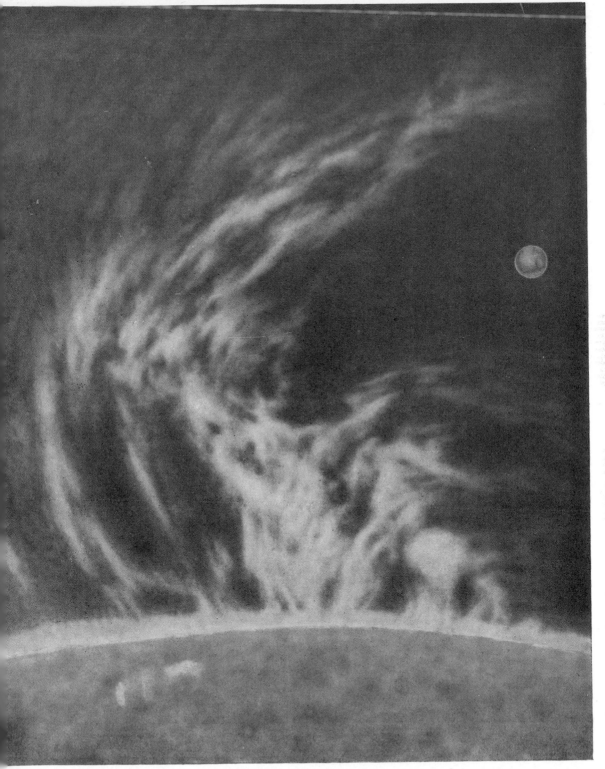

activity of the sun is well seen in the outpourings of luminous
⋯s and vapours known as prominences, one variety of which
⋯sociated with sun-spots. These vapours are largely made up
⋯calcium and hydrogen. A calcium prominence viewed
⋯ugh the spectroscope is seen at two positions in the violet
region, the more brilliant of which is near the end of the visible
spectrum. It is by this violet light, which sees only the glowing
calcium vapours, that the photograph on which this illustration
is based was taken at Mount Wilson Observatory, California.
The small green sphere represents the earth on the same scale

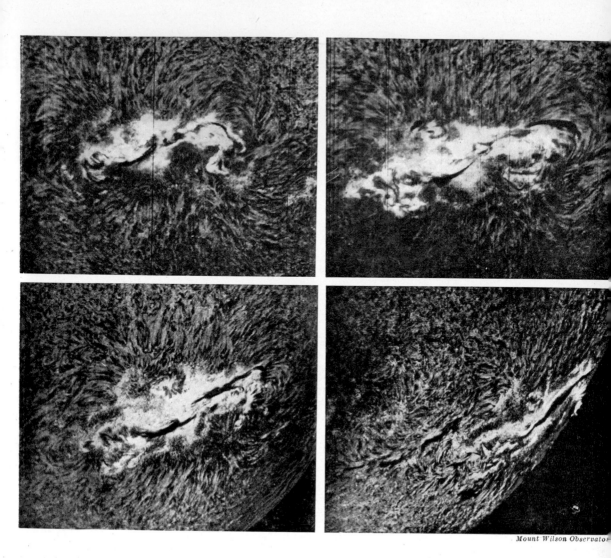

Mount Wilson Observatory

SEVEN DAYS IN THE LIFE OF A SUN-SPOT

THESE four photographs, which were taken by Dr. Hale through a spectroheliograph by hydrogen light, show the movement on August 3, 5, 7 and 9, in 1915, of a large sun-spot, and its changes in form. In the last it is disappearing round the edge, or limb, of the sun's disk. This motion of sun-spots, due mainly to the sun's rotation, was first discovered by Galileo. The life of a spot, which is really a vast vortex of flaming gases, slightly cooler than the body of the sun, is usually measured in days.

To face page 31.

a yellow dye, and its seeds provided both food and oil. Early European settlers in Canada were quick to appreciate the usefulness of this plant and sent seed home to Europe. It was introduced into Britain in 1596 and it is now grown as a commercial crop in southern Europe, in the sub-continent of India, and in Egypt.

The common annual sunflower (*Helianthus annuus*) is a giant of the family *Compositae*, with large, coarse heart-shaped leaves, brown-centred golden blossoms often measuring nearly a foot across, and sometimes attains a height of 10 feet. Each " head " produces a large number of seeds, rich in fat and protein, which are fed to poultry and livestock or are crushed for their oil. In some countries the seeds are roasted and eaten. In Queensland, Australia, about 500,000 acres were to be devoted to the growing of sunflowers and millets to provide food for pigs, which, in turn, would help to feed Great Britain. Experiments were being carried out in Tanganyika, British East Africa, in 1948, with a view ultimately to alternating sunflowers and ground-nuts (*q.v.*) as large-scale oil-producing crops.

Garden species and varieties grown in Britain for their decorative value include both annuals and perennials, the latter spreading rapidly by means of their long, roaming roots which send up new plants from the tips.

Surface Tension.

Have you ever floated a steel sewing needle on the surface of water? Strange as it may seem, this can be done if the needle is placed on gently, so as not to break through the water surface. No doubt you have at some time or other seen mercury spilled on to a flat surface: the mercury takes the form of a spherical droplet, and if you try to break this shape you succeed only in making smaller globules. Bring two globules close together, and they will combine to form a single larger globule.

These are manifestations of surface tension. We all know that when we pour water into a vessel it flows to the bottom and stays there, rising higher or lower in the vessel according to the amount. But we seldom realize the essential difference between a liquid, such as water, and a gas, such as hydrogen. If we cause a gas to enter a vessel, it *fills* the vessel, regardless of the amount of gas we admit. It is spread out more thinly if in small quantity; and is packed more closely if a larger quantity is forced in. The reason for this different behaviour is that the molecules of a liquid cohere, or stick together, because the force of attraction between them is comparatively so much stronger than that between gas molecules.

THE COMMON SUNFLOWER
The brown-centred golden heads of the tall-growing sunflower produce a large number of seeds, which are fed to poultry or livestock or are crushed for their oil.

Upon looking through a glass vessel partly filled with water, the line where the water stops and the air begins seems a sharp one. But in the topmost portion of the water surface there is a horizontal region in which the liquid is changing into a vapour under the influence of evaporation. Perhaps this layer is only one molecule in thickness at the " interface " (the junction of the two layers, liquid and gas). Here, in this very thin boundary region, resides the strange property called surface tension. We can explain it roughly by comparing the region to a thin sheet of rubber tightly stretched across the vessel. (But whereas the rubber gets its tension from being stretched, the tension in the interfacial region between a liquid and a gas, or that between water and oil, has nothing to do with any stretching of the film). This state of tension is the reason why we can float a needle; why liquids assume a globular form; why oil poured on troubled waters calms the waves; why the pond-skater can stride over the

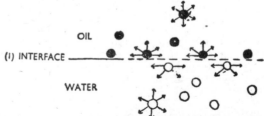

OIL

(1) INTERFACE

WATER

Penguin Books Ltd.
The dark circles represent oil molecules, the light circles water ones. The arrows on some of them indicate the directions in which they are attracted by each other. The shape of a soap molecule (with fat-soluble and water-soluble " ends ") is shown in the small diagram immediately below.

WATER SOLUBLE. ➔ ◖▬▬ ← FAT SOLUBLE

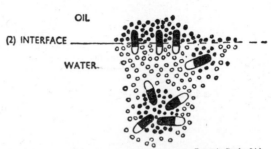

OIL

(2) INTERFACE

WATER.

Penguin Books Ltd.
SOAP MOLECULES AND SURFACE TENSION
When soap molecules are present in the water with oil, some lie across the interface in both oil and water phases and draw groups of oil molecules into the water. (*See* text).

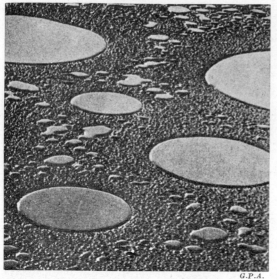

G.P.A.

SURFACE TENSION AT WORK

Oil poured on water does not mix with it, for oil is not soluble in water and the surface tension of the two liquids keeps them apart. This state of tension is the reason why oil released on a stormy sea calms the waves.

surface of a pool; and why we use soap to wash clothes and hands and so on.

The purpose of soap (*q.v.*) or detergents (*q.v.*) is to lower the interfacial tension so that a lather can be formed which carries off the greasy dirt. If a little oil be poured on top of water it will form rounded patches which do not mix with the water, for oil is not soluble in water. If we shake a bottle containing oil poured on top of water, the oil is dispersed in tiny droplets, so that we get what is called an emulsion.

Perhaps you have seen the floating " ducks " made of light material, which skim about in a realistic manner if you attach a small piece of camphor behind them. The camphor dissolves in the water and lowers the surface tension a great deal. The tug-of-war between the unbalanced tensions drives the ducks hither and thither.

Surface tension is due to the greater energy of the molecules at the surface, as compared with those in deeper layers. If two liquids which will not mix are forming a boundary layer—oil on water, for example—there is attraction between the molecules of the one and the other, as well as between the molecules of the same liquid. As explained in our story of Detergents, the molecules of the chemicals in soaps and like agents have two " portions "; one portion with an affinity for water, and another with an affinity for oily substances. Thus they are able to bring together the grease and the water, or to " wet " the grease, and out comes the dirt.

Surrealism. In painting and literature Surrealism may be described as the expression of dreams, both waking and sleeping, their symbols, and deep fantasies of the subconscious. There is nothing essentially new in this form of art; indeed its exponents claimed as Surrealists such painters as the 16th century Flemish artists Bosch and Brueghel. But whereas the older painters linked the subconscious life with the conscious, Surrealists chose their subject matter from symbolism provided by the subconscious.

Like several other revolutionary art movements, Surrealism originated in France during the 1920s, though many of the most prominent Surrealist painters were not French; these included the Italian Giorgio de Chirico (born 1888), the Spaniards Salvador Dali (born 1904), and Joan Miro (born 1893), and the Russian Marc Chagall (born 1887). Other notable Surrealists included the German Max Ernst (born 1891) and the Swiss Paul Klee (1879–1940).

The earlier examples of Surrealism sought to get away from all previous forms and to lay the foundations for a new development of painting and sculpture. The Frenchman Jean Lurçat, especially in his " dream-landscapes," foreshadowed later Surrealism. These, to the eyes of ordinary people, did indeed remind one of dreams, with that brilliant clarity and colour, and that strange grouping of apparently unrelated objects, which came later to be taken as an authentic sign of Surrealist painting.

In later developments of this style the painting invariably contained a number of objects which had no connexion with one another, although the design as a whole was frequently pleasing and the composition emotionally expressive. Yet no indication of the meaning was given, and the casual spectator examining such a picture put his own interpretation on what he saw.

The first important Surrealist exhibition in Britain was held in London in 1936, when the paintings and sculptures aroused much controversy. Besides objects of art in the accepted sense it contained a number of " arrangements " in which all kinds of objects were hung on pieces of canvas or wood and given incongruous titles. These were of little artistic merit.

At the beginning of the Second World War (1939–45) Surrealism as a pioneer art movement had fulfilled its purpose. A number of the best Surrealist artists modified their style in favour of what became known as " abstract " painting— a form of design which was entirely independent of " representational " meaning (no attempt was made to reproduce the physical appearance of an object), but corresponded to the subjective states of feeling in the artist. Among the most brilliant of the British Surrealist artists were Paul Nash (1889–1946), Ben Nicholson, Eileen Agar and John Tunnard.

The Surrealist movement in literature was most marked in France, where it had a considerable vogue during the 1920s and '30s. Its leaders were Louis Aragon and André Breton, the latter of whom published in 1924 a Manifesto of Surrealism. This movement was essentially romantic, and was preoccupied with " fantasies," and individual associations of places and emotions.

Surrey. An inland county of England, with an area of 722 square miles, Surrey is bounded on the north by the Thames and the county of London, by Kent on the east, by Hampshire and Sussex on the south, by Hampshire and Berkshire on the west. The chief rivers are the Wey and Mole, tributaries of the Thames, and the Eden, which flows into the Medway. The North Downs extend across the county, the highest point being Leith Hill (965 feet). The county is noted for its heaths and commons, and is well wooded in the Thames valley.

Wheat and oats are grown, and there are hop gardens around Farnham. Market-gardening is an important industry, and sheep are grazed on the Downs. The county town is Kingston-upon-Thames (population 39,500), where the coronation stone on which were crowned a number of the Anglo-Saxon kings of England is preserved in the market-place. Other important centres are Guildford, Reigate, Woking and Godalming. Croydon, Richmond (noted for its park) and Wimbledon (headquarters of lawn tennis in Britain) are boroughs on the outskirts of London. At Epsom is the racecourse on which the Derby is run. Places widely known for their beauty include Hindhead, Box Hill, Virginia Water and Friday Street. The population of the county of Surrey is 1,180,900.

Will F. Taylor

OLD SURREY TOWN OF GUILDFORD

On the London–Portsmouth road, at the foot of a ridge called the Hog's Back, Guildford was formerly a centre of the woollen industry, but is now mainly an agricultural market centre. In the photograph we are looking down the High Street towards the Hog's Back, with the 16th-century Guildhall and its clock on the right.

Sussex. Originally the kingdom of the South Saxons, this maritime county of southern England has an area of 1,457 square miles and for the purposes of local government is divided into two counties, East Sussex and West Sussex, each with its council. It is bounded on the north by Surrey and Kent, on the east by Kent, on the south by the English Channel, on the west by Hampshire. Crossing Sussex from the Hampshire border to Beachy Head is the range of hills known as the South Downs, the highest point being Ditchling Beacon (813 feet). North of the Downs is the plain called the Sussex Weald. The principal rivers are the Adur, Arun, Ouse and Rother.

The county is celebrated for its breed of sheep— the Southdown. Horses and cattle also are reared. Wheat is the most important cereal; there are hop gardens in the east and many market gardens. There was once a prosperous iron industry near Mayfield. Along the coast are a number of large watering-places—Brighton, Worthing, Hastings and Eastbourne; smaller resorts are Rye, Winchelsea, Bexhill, Littlehampton and Bognor Regis. The county town of East Sussex is Lewes (population 11,000); and Chichester (population 14,000) is the capital of West Sussex. Market towns include Midhurst and Horsham. Newhaven is a port for France.

The county contains the ruins of Pevensey, Bodiam and Hurstmonceux (now the Royal Observatory) castles, and of Bayham and Battle abbeys. At Arundel is Arundel Castle, the seat of the Duke of Norfolk; near Lewes is the Glyndebourne Opera House. There are early British earthworks on the Downs. The population is 769,900.

Sutherlandshire. In the extreme north-west of Scotland, this county has an area of 2,028 square miles, and is bounded on the north by the Atlantic Ocean, on the east by Caithness

J. Dixon-Scott

OLD SUSSEX FORTRESS

Ruins of the castle in which Henry III (1207–72) was imprisoned by Simon de Montfort are still to be seen at Lewes, the county town of East Sussex. Above is the barbican of the castle, built shortly after the Norman Conquest of 1066.

and the North Sea, on the south by Ross and Cromarty, on the west by the Atlantic. The coast on the north and north-west is very rugged, Cape Wrath rising to a height of 523 feet.

Much of Sutherlandshire is wild and mountainous, and there are several peaks over 3,000 feet high, Ben More Assynt (3,273 feet) being the highest. Loch Shin is the largest of numerous lakes, others being Assynt, Naver and More. The main rivers are the Oykell, Helmsdale, Brora, Shin and Fleet.

The county is noted for its grouse moors and deer forests. The water-falls at Escuallin are among the finest in Britain. The chief industries are the rearing of sheep and fishing. The county town is Dornoch (population 2,670). Other centres are Golspie, Tongue, Scourie and Lochinver. The population is 14,400.

Swallows, MARTINS AND SWIFTS.

Long, narrow, pointed wings and forked tail are characteristics of these birds, as is the habit of feeding entirely on insects, which are caught on the wing. They winter in warm southern climes, usually in Africa, and arrive in Britain at the end of March or the beginning of April.

The common or chimney swallow (*Hirundo rustica*) is blue-black on the upper parts, save for a patch of russet red on the forehead; the under surface is generally cream, with a deep collar of blue-black across the throat. The bill is broad and flat, and the tail deeply forked, more so in the male than the female. Adult birds frequent the same haunts season after season, and if the old nest has not been destroyed they will repair it; otherwise they

build a new one under the eaves or against the beams or chimneys of a house or outbuilding.

The nest of the common swallow is made of mud mixed with grass and straw and is lined with fine grass and feathers. The eggs are white, spotted with reddish brown (*see* colour plate facing page 440), and generally there are two broods each year. The young birds and their parents begin to assemble in flocks at the end of August or early in September, though it may be another six weeks before they fly south.

The blue and white house-martin (*Delichon urbica*) is much smaller than the swallow, and the

SWALLOW, MARTIN AND SWIFT
Lined with grass and feathers, a swallow's nest (top left) is made of mud mixed with grass and straw. The sand-martin builds its home at the end of a tunnel in a sandy bank (top right). The swift (centre), whose plumage is black and glossy, never perches but clings to walls and trees. The house-martin constructs a nest of hundreds of little pellets of mud, with an entrance at the side (bottom).

hind-parts are covered with white feathers. In Britain the nest is nearly always built against the side of a building, and is rounded and covered with little pellets of mud, with the entrance at the side. The brown sand-martin (*Riparia*) digs with its bill a very long tunnel to his nest, which is placed in sandy banks or railway cuttings. Like the swallow, the martin is migratory. flying southward from Britain in autumn.

The swift (*Micropus apus*) belongs to a different order, but it resembles the swallow in general appearance and habits. It arrives in Britain at about the same time of year as the swallow and martin, and it builds a rather primitive nest of straw, grass and feathers. Usually two white eggs are laid. The swift, whose plumage is sooty black and glossy, never perches, its short feet and hook-like claws enabling it only to cling to walls and trees. It lives on insects and hunts in companies, filling the air with its screams.

One species of Oriental swift (*Collocalia fuciphaga*), breeds in caves and constructs nests which are considered a rare table delicacy, yielding the "bird's nest soup" of which the Chinese and the inhabitants of Borneo are so fond.

Swan. In England the swan was formerly a royal bird—no subject might possess one without a licence from the Crown. The British Sovereign and the London Livery Companies of the Dyers and Vintners still keep swans on the upper Thames, and every July the young birds have their bills nicked with a penknife to denote their ownership—a process known as "swan upping." The largest swannery in England, already established in Tudor times, is at Abbotsbury, inside the Chesil Bank, Dorset, and is the property of Lord Ilchester.

Swans belong to the same group as geese and ducks, and are large birds characterized by long, graceful necks, short legs, and the absence of feathers from the eye to the bill. The plumage is generally pure white, sometimes dark about the head. In 1697 black swans were discovered in Australia, where they are still found.

The male swan is called a cob; the female a pen; and the young are styled cygnets (*see* illustration in page 449). The call note of the male of some species is loud and trumpet-like, but the mute swan is almost silent, its voice normally being little more than a hiss. The latter species is the common swan of Europe (*Cygnus olor*). It reaches a length of five feet and a weight of 30 lb. Its plumage is spotless white, the bill is orange-red surmounted by a black knob (the "berry") and the legs are black. Semi-domesticated swans of this species have lived in Britain for centuries; in its wild state it is found in eastern Europe and in Asia as far south as the sub-continent of India.

The trumpeter or whistling swan (*C. buccinator*) is mainly an Arctic species, but it often visits Britain in winter. It is much like the mute swan, except

Fox

SWAN UPPING ON THE RIVER THAMES

Every year in July the young swans or cygnets on the upper Thames are marked to denote their ownership, the operation being known as swan upping. The birds may belong to the Sovereign, to the Vintners or to the Dyers Livery Companies of the City of London, and the claimant's mark is made on the side of the bill with a penknife. In the photograph representatives of the King and of the Companies are at work at Teddington on the cygnets, or 'clear-bills.' Ownership is determined by that of the parent birds, and when the parents have different markings the brood is divided.

John H. Stone

SWAN WITH HER CYGNETS

Young swans, or cygnets, have greyish-brown feathers until the second
year when they are shed for white plumage.   The adult bird may be as
much as five feet in length and weigh 30 pounds.   (*See also* page 449).

for its lemon-yellow bill tipped with black and its
loud, harsh note.   Another northern species, the
smaller Bewick's swan (*C. bewickii*), is an occasional
visitor to Britain; it has less yellow on the beak and
is much smaller than the trumpeter.

The nest of the swan is a large
untidy pile of reeds and water-plants,
and usually contains about six greenish-
white eggs.   The male bird defends the
nest ferociously and will attack any
animal or person that approaches.   The
birds feed on the stems, seeds and roots
of water plants, and on insects and
molluscs.

Swansea.   This Welsh town,
second in size only to Cardiff, is situated
in the county of Glamorgan at the
mouth of the Tawe.   The chief industries
include the manufacture of tinplate and
the smelting of copper, zinc, silver and
other metals.   Oil is refined, and there
are engineering works and flour mills.
Coal is exported.   There are few old
buildings in the town, though some parts
of the Norman castle (rebuilt in 1330)
still stand.   Swansea is the seat of a
university and has a grammar school
founded in 1682.   In the Guildhall
are panels painted by the British artist
Sir Frank Brangwyn, R.A. (born 1867).
During the Second World War (1939–45)
Swansea was heavily damaged by German air raids
on the nights of February 19, 20 and 21, 1941,
much of the principal shopping district being
destroyed.   The population is about 158,800.

SWEDEN'S *Lovely* LAND *and* *Sturdy* PEOPLE

*Once an extremely warlike nation, the Swedes have been at peace longer than any
other European race except the Swiss.   They have created one of the most
democratic societies in the world by gradual reforms, not by revolution.*

Sweden.   Occupying the eastern and larger
part of the Scandinavian peninsula, Sweden has
an area about 1½ times that of the British Isles.   It
is separated from Norway on the west by a high
plateau, studded with the lofty peaks of the Kiolen or
Keel Mountains, from which the land slopes
steeply to the east and more gradually to the south
(for map, *see* Norway, page 2395).   Its northern
extremity, separated from Finland on the north by
the River Tornio, lies beyond the Arctic Circle;
its southern limit, nearly 1,000 miles away, lies
upon the Skagerrak, the
Kattegat and the Baltic.

On the east the land
ends in low, sandy and
often marshy s h o r e s
along the Gulf of Both-
nia, becoming more
rocky in the southern
part bordering on the
Baltic.   On the south-
western coast low sandy
shores alternate with
steep cliffs, which, how-
ever, are rarely more
than 30 feet high.   The
coast is studded with is-
lands, the largest of them
Öland and Gottland off
the south-east coast.

With its enormous coast-line, more than 1,400
miles in length, and its numerous good harbours,
Sweden has large maritime interests and a mercantile
marine of over 2,000 vessels.   Herring and other fish
abound in the sheltered sounds between the islands
and the coast, and contribute an important part to
the national wealth.

Sweden is divided into three parts or provinces—
Norrland, Svealand, and Götaland—which together
cover an area of more than 170,000 square miles,
and have a population of nearly 7,000,000.   Svealand, in the middle, the
original Sweden proper,
is a region of lakes and
birch woods, of pros-
p e r o u s f a r m s a n d
flourishing towns.   Here
is Stockholm (*q.v.*), the
capital and largest city.
Lovely Lake Siljan, the
" Eye of Dalecarlia,"
one of the beauty spots
of Sweden, is in this
province.   The peasants
of D a l e c a r l i a (" the
Valleys ") still sometimes
wear their picturesque
costumes, and here we
may see midsummer
festivities in their most

Extent.—North to south, about 1,000 miles : east to
west, about 250 miles.   Area 173,000 square miles.
Population about 6,842,000.

Physical Features.—Surface in general an undulating
plateau falling in terraces from the west to the low
Baltic plain on east and south.   Chief mountain range
the Keel (or Kiolen), which separates Sweden from
Norway; highest peak, Kebnekaise (7,000 feet).   Many
lakes and rivers, occupying together more than 8 per
cent of the area.   Largest lakes : Väner (2,149 square
miles) ; Vätter, Mälar, Hjelmar.   Rivers : Dal, Klar,
Ljusne, Tornio, Kalix, Lule, Skellefte, Ume, Windel.

Products.—Oats, rye, barley, potatoes, sugar-beet, wheat,
hay, flax ; cattle, sheep, goats, reindeer ; dairy products ;
fish ; iron, zinc, manganese, lead, coal ; iron and steel
products ; timber, furniture, matches, wood pulp, and
other wood products ; paper, porcelain, glass ;
machinery.

Principal Cities.—Stockholm (capital, about 703,000) ;
Göteborg 337,000 ; Malmö 181,000 ; Norrköping
82,000 ; Hälsingborg 70,000.

SWEDEN'S CLEAN AND STATELY CAPITAL CITY

M. O. Henchoz; Swedish Travel Bureau

Moored in the harbour at Stockholm (upper) are fishing-boats drying their curiously-shaped nets. The city is built on a number of islands as well as on the mainland; and ferry-boats, some of which can be seen alongside the quay in the background, supplement the city's tram and omnibus services. On the shore of Lake Mälar, the Stadshus or City Hall (lower) took 12 years to build. It was completed in 1923. A very fine example of modern Swedish architecture, it has a roof of copper plates, and the walls and massive tower are of wine-coloured bricks.

charming and romantic setting. The old customs are still carried out, including folk-dances round the Maypole and bonfires on the hilltops.

The short summer, coming in with a sudden burst of green, is the busiest time of Sweden's year, for sowing and harvesting must be done in a few months before the long, dark winter again descends. Sweden lies so far north, one seventh of it being within the Arctic Circle, that the summers are very short and the winters from seven to nine months long, with little spring and autumn between.

Since the western mountains shut off the warm winds from the Atlantic, the extremes of temperature are greater than in Norway. The ports on the Gulf of Bothnia are frozen for six months in the year, and except in very mild winters navigation is impeded by ice along the northern and central parts of the Baltic. In summer there are only two or three hours of darkness in each 24 hours, and in winter only two or three hours of daylight. In the northernmost regions the sun does not set for a month during the summer; and for a month during the winter it does not rise above the horizon.

Away from this northern region, but a little to the north of Stockholm, in the middle province of Svealand, is the university town of Uppsala, the chief seat of learning of the country. In ancient times Uppsala was the seat of the Swedish kings and of the worship of the Norse gods, Odin, Thor and Freya. It now contains the cathedral (begun in the 13th century) of the archbishop of the Swedish Lutheran Church and the University founded in 1477. In this same district are the prosperous iron-mines of Danemora.

Götaland, or Gothland, south of Svealand, was the ancient home of the Goths; thence, too, came many of the Vikings, who explored widely in the 9th and 10th centuries. Götaland is the richest agricultural and industrial region, fully three-fourths of its area being under cultivation and providing the chief industry of the country. Its frontage on two seas, with its numerous ports, makes it also the chief maritime district.

Apart from Stockholm, the country's largest centres of population are in this southern province. Göteborg, Hälsingborg, and Malmö on the west coast, Karlskrona and Norrköping on the east coast, are all important cities. Malmö, the third largest in the country, is almost at the southern-most tip of Sweden and 16 miles due east across the Sound from Copenhagen in Denmark.

The chief port of Sweden, and the second largest city, is Göteborg (Gothenburg), whose steamers carry iron, steel, and timber to the far corners of the earth. The total value of Sweden's exports amount annually to about £200,000,000 and a great part of this goes through the port of Göteborg. In addition, Göteborg is important as a railway centre and as the starting-point of the famous Göta Canal, the lengthy inland navigation system across southern Sweden, which connects Göteborg and Stockholm.

The 240-mile journey through the Göta Canal, occupying three days, is a favourite with tourists. Passing the beautiful Trollhättan Falls, climbing to a height of more than 300 feet above the sea and descending again by means of 58 locks, we traverse the lakes Väner, Vätter and Mälar between wooded hills and lovely pastures, with here and there an ancient castle, a picturesque red farmhouse or a tiny village. But the Göta Canal is not merely a sight for travellers; it is an important artery of trade through which pass thousands of vessels each year.

Norrland, north of Svealand, is larger than the two other provinces combined. It is a region of virgin forests, high mountains, and broad rivers, whose vast wealth in timber, iron ore and water-power has only recently been developed.

Here is the flourishing iron-mining town of Kiruna, more than 100 miles inside the Arctic Circle. We may sometimes see an encampment of Lapps with their herds of reindeer, though

M. O. Henchoz

YOUNG SWEDEN IN GALA DRESS
At a festival held in Skansen, near Stockholm, the youngsters wear the gay costumes of the district called Dalecarlia, in which the dress of the peasants varies from village to village.

BLONDE BEAUTIES OF THE 'HEART OF SWEDEN'

The 'heart of Sweden' is the district of Dalecarlia, or Dalarne, and here old ways and old costumes are still cherished. Peasant dress varies from village to village, and the beautifully embroidered aprons of these happily-smiling girls indicate that they hail from Leksand. a village widely renowned for its prepossessing inhabitants.

Swedish Travel Bureau

The most prosperous industries of Sweden are the production of timber and the mining of iron. The leading saw-mills of the country lie along the shores of the Gulf of Bothnia. In the upper photograph tree-trunks are being transported from the forest where they have been felled to the mill, drawn by a caterpillar tractor. In the far north of Sweden, well within the Arctic Circle, are the mines of the Malmberg, a mountain of iron ore near Gellivare, which yields immense quantities of the metal, much of which is exported to other countries. A general view of the Malmberg is given in the lower photograph. A railway which runs from Gellivare and reaches the coasts of both Sweden and Norway—at Lulea and Narvik respectively—is one of the most northerly railways in the world.

it to drive his threshing machine and milking machine, and for other operations. It is also used to heat the soil for the forced cultivation of vegetables.

In spite of the increase in manufacturing and other industries, nearly half the people are still engaged in agriculture, " the mother industry." Little of the land, however, is suitable for cultivation, only about 10 per cent being under crops. Oats, rye, and barley are the principal cereals, and there is some wheat. Potatoes and sugar-beet are grown in large quantities, and the making of sugar is a thriving industry. Much live-stock is raised, and dairy products are extensively exported.

Both the fresh- and salt-water fisheries of Sweden are important. Salmon, pike, trout, char and perch abound in the lakes and streams; and herring, cod, mackerel and sprat are caught in the Baltic.

The Swedes are a happy, sturdy and healthy people. The winter is not a season of gloom for them, for their outdoor sports make it a period of delight. Then the whole country is one vast expanse of hard crisp snow, over which people glide on sleds or skis. Most Swedish boys and girls, as well as the older folks, take their daily recreation in this way. The farmer drives his sleigh straight across the country, for most barriers lie buried deep beneath the snow; and lakes and rivers are frozen deep, offering wonderful opportunities for skating, ski-ing and sleighing—sports in which the Swedes are expert. This bracing winter air is stimulating and healthy, and Sweden's death-rate is only eight per 1,000.

Education is free and compulsory for children between seven and 14, and there are excellent schools and colleges. Besides the State University at Uppsala, there is another smaller State University at Lund, in Götaland, as well as higher institutions of learning at Stockholm and Göteborg. The Swedes are a highly cultured people. They have a special aptitude for scientific pursuits, and have produced some famous scientists, including Linné (Linnaeus), remembered for his classification of plants and animals, and Alfred Nobel, the inventor of dynamite, who established the Nobel Prizes (see Linné, Carl von ; Nobel Prizes). Among noteworthy Swedish writers are the playwright August Strindberg 1849–1912) and the novelist Selma Lagerlöf (1858–1940), who was awarded the Nobel Prize for literature in 1909.

Lapps and Finns were met with in Sweden at an early date, and about the beginning of the Christian era the Goths dwelt there also. But, like Denmark and Norway, the land was first organized as a state by the Scandinavian "Northmen," the terror of Europe, in the 10th century (see Northmen; Scandinavia). Christianity was not fully established until the 11th century. Sweden united with Norway and Denmark in the Union of Kalmar in 1397, but in 1524 it revolted under the leadership of Gustavus Vasa against Danish rule and became an independent kingdom. Under Gustavus Adolphus, the grandson of Gustavus Vasa, in the early 17th century, the country became one of the great powers of Europe (see Gustavus Adolphus). It championed the Protestant cause in Germany in the Thirty Years' War (1618–48), and wrested territory from Russia, Poland and Prussia, so that it became the mistress of the Baltic, ruling the eastern as well as the western shore of that sea.

But collapse came in the 18th century under Charles XII (q.v.) and after. For a time this boy-king was able to hold off his enemies, Russia, Poland and Denmark. And in 1709 the ascendancy of Sweden was lost by the defeat of Charles XII by Peter the Great at Poltava, in southern Russia.

Little by little her conquests were taken from her. In 1810 one of Napoleon's marshals, Bernadotte, was elected Crown Prince, and the present reigning Swedish house is descended from him. In 1815 Finland, which had been ceded to Russia in 1809, was officially transferred to Russian rule, but by way of recompense Norway was joined to Sweden under the Swedish King.

In 1905 the Norwegian Parliament declared this union dissolved and chose a King of their own. The Swedish King, Oscar II, protested but accepted its decision. The son of Oscar II was Gustavus V, who reigned 43 years (1907–50).

As long ago as 1909 the right to vote, without restrictions concerning ownership of property or size of income, was granted to all men 23 years of age or over; and 10 years later the same privilege was extended to women. The Government of Sweden is a limited hereditary monarchy, with a King, a Cabinet and a Parliament or Riksdag, consisting of an upper house of 150 members, one-eighth of whom are elected each year, and a lower house, for which a General Election is held every four years. Lutheranism is the State religion, to which more than 90 per cent of the people belong.

During both World Wars (1914–18 and 1939–45) Sweden remained neutral. In the period 1940–45 the country gave a home to thousands of refugees driven from the other Scandinavian countries by the Germans, and the Swedish Government also assisted in the exchange of wounded prisoners-of-war between Germany and the Allies. The population is about 6,842,000.

Swedenborg, EMANUEL (1688–1772). Scientist, philosopher and mystic, Swedenborg was born in Stockholm, Sweden, on January 29, 1688, the son of a Swedish pastor. He was educated at the University of Uppsala, and travelled widely to extend his knowledge, studying at Oxford, Utrecht and Paris. In his youth he showed unusual brilliance in scientific matters, and in later

EMANUEL SWEDENBORG
One of the most brilliant scientists of his day, Swedenborg in 1747 decided to devote himself to things spiritual. His writings on religion had a deep influence on the development of thought.

years became an authority on natural science, natural philosophy and engineering subjects. In 1716 he was given the post of assessor in the Swedish Royal College of Mines, and his duties necessitated his visiting the mines of Austria, Bohemia and Saxony, besides those of his own country.

In addition to being a scientist of considerable distinction, Swedenborg was a prolific writer and an inventor. He evolved, for example, a device for curing smoky chimneys, and an ear-trumpet. He was the first to employ mercury for the air-pump, and he worked out a system for determining longitude at sea by observation of the moon among the stars. For many years he continued his scientific research work, and it is a remarkable fact that when his writings came to be examined about a century after his death it was found that much knowledge attributed to later scientists was actually due to him. It is to Swedenborg, for instance, that we are indebted to some extent for our knowledge of aviation, for among his experimental models was that of a flying machine. He knew, however, that it would not fly.

This remarkable Swede is chiefly remembered by the work that he did after middle life. He believed that in the year 1745 he had received a divine commission to interpret the spiritual meaning of the Scriptures, and, abandoning his scientific work, he devoted the rest of his life to meditation and writing. He did not found a sect, but his views attained wide popularity, and in 1787 the New Jerusalem Church was organized; congregations of this New (Swedenborgian) Church still exist in Britain and elsewhere. He died on March 29, 1772, in London, where he had spent several years of his life.

Swift, JONATHAN (1667–1745). To most

people Swift is known only as the author of Gulliver's Travels, a book widely read by children for its lively adventures. The story, however, was written with a more serious purpose than that of amusement. It was meant as a satire, to lay bare the faults of Man, and with special allusion to the politics of the time. If one understands the inner meaning of Gulliver's Travels one gains an insight into Swift's character and purpose.

Swift was born on November 30, 1667, in Dublin, of English parents, and was educated at Trinity College, Dublin. When he was 20 years old he became secretary to a retired English statesman, Sir William Temple, and spent much of the next 10

years on his employer's estate in England, using his leisure in reading, and in writing several books, which laid the foundation of his literary reputation. Through Sir William Temple's interest he took his Master of Arts degree at Oxford in 1692.

In 1695, four years before his employer's death, Swift became a clergyman of the Church of England, and was soon appointed to a church in Ireland. Because most of the Irish people were Roman Catholics his congregation rarely consisted of more than 15 persons, and often when only he and the parish clerk were present Swift was said to have begun the exhortation with the words, "Dearly beloved Roger!"

But his new position gave Swift enough money on which to live, and from time to time to visit London, where he stayed from 1700 to 1713. There he became intimate with Addison (q.v.) and Steele and other leading literary men of his day. He became well known, too, in English political circles. He allied himself with the Tory party, wrote brilliant political pamphlets in defence of its policies and became a power to be reckoned with. The Whigs feared the lash of his satire, and the Tories feared to lose his support, and he was so courted and flattered that he became unbearably arrogant. As a reward for his services he was appointed, in 1713, Dean of St. Patrick's Cathedral, Dublin.

It is evident from Swift's life that he used his skill in writing largely as a means to an end—as a correction of abuses. Whether he is trying to relieve distress in Ireland, or tilting at the corruption of politicians, in every case he matches folly with folly. In other words, he is a satirist—one of the greatest of all time. The brightest and darkest spot in the life of this proud ironical genius was his long and tender friendship for the lady whom he called "Stella" (her real name was Esther Johnson). He first met her while he was a member of Sir William Temple's household, and she a girl eight years old. He taught her to write and gave her advice as to her reading. His Journal to Stella, which was not published in its entirety until 1948, records the most intimate side of his life, as well as his gossipy comment on men and events. Whether or not Swift married her is not known, though their marriage was thought to have taken place about 1715.

To Stella and to another lady, Esther Vanhomrigh ("Vanessa"), Swift caused great unhappiness, for, although he was capable of the

National Portrait Gallery

DEAN SWIFT

Outstanding as a satirist, Jonathan Swift, Dean of St. Patrick's, Dublin, wrote some of the finest English prose. Gulliver's Travels is his masterpiece. This portrait of him was painted by Charles Jervas.

tenderest friendship, he seems to have been utterly incapable of real love. There is a veil of mystery, however, about this side of his life which makes it uncertain how much blame should attach to him. Vanessa died of a broken heart in 1723, followed five years later by Stella. Swift had always been of a gloomy cast of mind, and now his remorse undermined his health of body and mind. A malady from which he had suffered almost all his life overcame him, bringing insanity and, on October 19, 1745, death. He was buried in St. Patrick's Cathedral, Dublin. Yet during the interval between the deaths of Vanessa and Stella he reached the height of his popularity and fame. He was especially liked by the Irish for his rasping criticism of the English misgovernment of Ireland. He crowned his work with Gulliver's Travels, a condensation of which follows this article.

His chief works were Tale of a Tub (1704), Battle of the Books (1704), Drapier's Letters (1724), Gulliver's Travels (1726–27), and Journal to Stella (written 1710 to 1713).

THE STORY OF GULLIVER'S TRAVELS

WHEN the ship Antelope was wrecked by a storm in the South Seas, the only person saved—according to Dean Swift's fascinating story—was Dr. Gulliver, the ship's physician. After swimming for hours he was washed up on the warm sandy beach of an island.

Worn out by his long struggles against the waves he fell asleep, and when he awakened, about nine hours later, he found he could not move an inch. He was tied fast by a network of little cords, attached to tiny pegs driven in the ground. Even his long hair (for men wore their hair long at that time, over two centuries ago) was securely fastened down by the same means.

Before long he felt something moving on his left leg. As it advanced over his breast almost to his chin he saw it to be a human creature, not six inches high, with a bow and arrow in his hands and a quiver on his back. About 40 more of the same kind followed the first. In his great astonishment Gulliver roared so loud that they all ran back in fright, and some of them fell in their haste to jump off his body. When he struggled to free himself they shot tiny arrows at him, which pricked his hands and face like needles.

The Lilliputians—for it was to the land of Lilliput that he had come—were really decent little people. Gulliver could not speak their language, but he made them understand that he was hungry. So a ladder was set up against his shoulder and a hundred of the little people climbed up and down and filed past his mouth. They gave him whole legs of mutton smaller than the wings of a lark, and loaves the size of bullets. They also mixed a potion with his wine, so that he fell asleep again.

It took 900 of their soldiers to lift the Man-Mountain—as they called him—on to a low truck with wheels, drawn by 1,500 Lilliputian horses. Having succeeded in doing this, they drove him to a temple in the city. The Emperor's smith then brought fourscore and eleven chains, and locked them to his left leg with six and thirty padlocks. Over 100,000 people came to stare at him.

Presently the Emperor himself came on horseback with his court and viewed the Man-Mountain with great admiration. He commanded his cooks and butlers to prepare food for Gulliver, and ordered 600 beds to be brought to the temple. Seamstresses and tailors sewed the beds together, using 150 of them for the length and breadth of Gulliver's bed and placing them four beds deep. By the same computation they sewed together sheets, blankets, and coverlets. When the Emperor left he set a guard to protect the Man-Mountain from the impertinence of the rabble. Some of the Lilliputians, indeed, had the boldness to shoot their arrows at Gulliver as he sat on the ground, and he says:

"One arrow very narrowly missed my left eye. But the colonel ordered six of the ringleaders to be seized, and thought no punishment so proper as to deliver them bound into my hands, which some of his soldiers accordingly did, pushing them forward with the butt ends of their pikes into my reach; I took them all in my right hand, put five of them into my coat pocket, and as to the sixth I made a countenance as if I would eat him alive. The poor man squalled terribly, and the colonel and his officers were in much pain, especially when they saw me take out my penknife; but I soon put them out of fear; for looking mildly, and immediately cutting the strings he was bound with, I set him gently on the ground and away he ran. I treated the rest in the same manner, taking them, one by one, out of my pocket, and I observed both the soldiers and people were obliged at this mark of my clemency."

Gulliver soon gained such favour that, after he had sworn a peace with the Emperor and his kingdom, he was allowed to wander at will through the kingdom. In return for his freedom he promised to give the people warning of his approach that they might keep off the highway and not run the risk of being stepped on. He likewise promised never to lie down in a field of grain, and to use the utmost care not to trample upon the inhabitants or their property.

He made rapid progress in learning the language and in acquainting himself with the kingdom's peculiarities. He found that everything was in proportion to the size of the inhabitants. He marvelled at the sharpness of sight which enabled a cook to dress a lark no bigger than a fly, and a young girl to thread an—to him—invisible needle with equally invisible silk. He discovered that in Lilliput, as in other lands, there were political parties, and that some time before his coming the Lilliputian " Big-Endians "—a party whose members insisted upon breaking their eggs at the big end when the court edict commanded that all faithful subjects of the Emperor should break their eggs at the small end—had been exiled from the kingdom. He also learned that there were then in Lilliput two rival parties, named " Tramecksans " and " Slamecksans," from the high and low heels of their shoes. The low-heeled party was in power, though the Crown Prince was thought to have a tendency towards the high heels; it could be easily seen that one of his heels was higher than the other, which made him hobble.

Naturally Gulliver caused a great deal of trouble to the Lilliputians. He ate so much that he nearly brought on a famine. He wanted a boat to go away in, but they never could have built one big enough with the tiny trees in that country. So he had to stay; and he tried, in every way that he could, to make himself useful to the kingdom.

It happened that about 800 yards north-east of Lilliput lay another island ruled by the Emperor of Blefuscu. When the Big-Endians were exiled from Lilliput they found refuge in Blefuscu, and for six and thirty moons there had been war between the two empires. Just at this time the Blefuscudians had prepared a fleet to invade Lilliput, and the Emperor of Lilliput asked Gulliver's assistance.

Single-handed He Towed a Fleet

Gulliver first spied upon the enemy's fleet across the channel through his pocket telescope. Then he made some rope out of cords, and got some iron bolts and stout hooks, and with these he waded and swam across the channel that separated the two islands. The little people of Blefuscu jumped out of their ships and swam ashore when they saw this Man-Mountain walking through the sea. About 30,000 of them gathered on the shore and discharged arrows at him, but Gulliver protected his eyes with a pair of spectacles and came to no harm. Fastening his hooks in the prows of their warships he cut the anchor cables, gathered up his ropes in his hands, and proceeded to splash back again, pulling behind him the whole Blefuscudian fleet.

And so he became the hero of the Lilliputian people, and the Emperor gave him the title of Nardac, which means " grand duke." But really he had only got himself into deeper trouble by his feat. The favour shown him made enemies for him at the court, and the Emperor was displeased because Gulliver would not go back to Blefuscu, conquer the country and make it a province of Lilliput. Moreover, while peace was being negotiated, Gulliver was so indiscreet as to become quite friendly with the ambassadors of Blefuscu, who invited him to pay their country a visit. His greatest enemies wished to put him to death while he slept. But, as a mark of the Emperor's mercy, it was secretly decided that Gulliver should only have his eyes put out and then gradually be starved to death.

Gulliver was warned of this sentence by a friend who came to him at dead of night; and, by acting promptly, he escaped across the channel to Blefuscu, where he was given a welcome. Presently he found a full-sized ship's boat afloat, from a wrecked ship, and with the good will of all the Blefuscudian people he set sail for his own land. After several days he was picked up by an English sailing vessel, and eventually he was landed safely in London.

On his next voyage Gulliver had another adventure quite as strange as his visit to the land of the Lilliputians. This time he was left by some sailors on the island of Brobdingnag, inhabited by a race of giants. These monsters looked as tall as steeples, and they covered about 10 yards at every stride. They had to take Gulliver up between a thumb and finger and hold him about 60 feet from the ground to look at him. Their cats were enormous, about three times the size of an ox. Some of the dogs were equal in bulk to four elephants, and the rats were the size of mastiffs. Everything in the land was in the same proportion.

Dean Swift gives an account of two other voyages made by Gulliver. One of these took him to a floating island called Laputa, inhabited by a queer race with heads all inclined either to the right or left and with one eye turned inward towards the nose and the other upward towards the forehead. Their clothes bore patterns of suns, moons, and stars, for they were always intent on astronomical or other scientific theories. So absent-minded was this race of philosophers that they walked about in the greatest danger; they would often fall into a day-dream in the middle of a meal or a conversation. Those who could afford it, therefore, employed servants called " flappers," whose occupation was to flap the mouth and ears of their master with a balloon on a string to recall him from his absent-minded day-dreamings.

From there Gulliver travelled to Balnibarbi; to Glubbdubdrib, where the spirits of the great men of ancient days were called up for his questioning; to Luggnagg, where there was a class, called " Struldbrugs," who were immortal and went on living in ever uglier and uglier old age; and from there to Japan, whence he returned to England.

On the fourth voyage he found himself in the land of the Houyhnhnms, where a wonderful race of horses lived, and had as servants and slaves a very inferior race of human beings, called " Yahoos." These horrible creatures (in whom Swift was satirizing mankind in general) were entirely unteachable, were cunning, malicious, treacherous and revengeful. They were kept in huts, and in the day would work in the fields, digging up and eating roots, and catching weasels and rats for their food. Gulliver was in danger of being mistaken for a Yahoo, but his clothes saved him, for the real Yahoos wore only rags, if they wore anything at all. Thus he was better treated than these wretched creatures—although he, too, was a slave. His master (one of the noble horses) explained to him their way of life, which presently he found greatly superior to life in England.

Donkeys to Replace Human Beings

The horses he found far superior to Man in their ideas of justice, honour and courtesy. When Gulliver learned their language he told them something of affairs in England. They had never heard of the art of war, and thought only persons of very little reasoning power could be capable of such enormities. They did not know the meaning of a lie, for they argued that the use of speech was given us to make us understand one another and to receive information of facts; so, if anyone said a thing that was not true, these ends were defeated. They knew nothing of the use of money, and when anyone of them was short of supplies his neighbours contributed whatever was needed.

Near the end of Gulliver's stay with them, the Houyhnhnms debated a proposal that the Yahoos should be exterminated. There were no arguments in favour of these wretched creatures, and it was finally decided to allow them to die out and replace them with a breed of donkeys. Soon after this Gulliver was allowed to build a boat and depart for his native land.—*Retold from Gulliver's Travels.*

HOW *to* BECOME 'AT HOME' *in the* WATER

As it uses nearly every muscle in the body swimming is one of the best forms of exercise. Here are described some of the most popular strokes, including racing ones, and types of fancy dives.

Swimming AND DIVING. An important preliminary step in learning to swim is to acquire the right method of breathing. Swimmers breathe in through the mouth, and breathe out through either the mouth or nose or through both mouth and nose. It is advisable to breathe in deeply and quickly, but to breathe out more slowly.

To become accustomed to breathing in this way one should go into the water up to the hips, breathe in deeply through the mouth, put the hands on the knees and bend forward until the face is submerged to the eyes. Holding the breath, count 10, then lift the head and breathe out. This should be repeated until it is possible to stay comfortably under water while one counts 15. Next, practise breathing out under water; and when you breathe in, turn your face to one side.

Leg Strokes. A good way in which to learn the leg strokes is to grip the rail at the side of a swimming bath and turn the elbows down. Then extend the legs, which will take up a position approximating to that in actual swimming.

The Breast Stroke. For the starting position the arms are fully extended in front of the head, palms touching, fingers closed, legs straight, heels together and toes pointing slightly to the sides. The body is kept flat. The arm stroke is made by turning the palms outward and sweeping the arms backwards on a line straight with the shoulders. As the hands are brought together under the chin ready to shoot forward, the legs are drawn up together with the knees bent and open. Then they are kicked out into a V position and brought vigorously together until the heels touch.

A more recent and faster development of this is the butterfly breast stroke. For this the leg action is similar to that of the ordinary breast stroke but the arms move differently. The hands enter the water in front of the shoulders, wide apart. The arms are kept slightly bent at the elbows and are forced downwards and backwards. As soon as the arms are as far back as possible they are rapidly brought to the surface and pushed forward, when the whole movement is repeated.

The Crawl. This fast and useful swimming stroke comes only after practice, and needs ability to breathe out under water. Introduced into England in 1902 it quickly revolutionized speed swimming. You should go into the water such a distance that when you face the shore, or the end of the bath, and put both hands on the bottom, your head will be above the surface. In this position you should start kicking your legs up and down from the hips, with the toes turned inward (pigeon-toed) and the knees almost straight but relaxed. As you get the feel of this movement slowly increase the speed until it is possible to keep up an even, rapid thrashing. Then go out farther into the water and plunge

Keystone

A FLAWLESS DIVE FROM A SPRINGBOARD

Four stages in making a dive from a springboard are shown in these pictures. At the left is the upward spring, with legs close together. Second from left is the 'jack-knife' —hands almost touching feet and the position of the body resembling that of a pocket-knife with one blade half open. The descent (second from right) is made with the body in a straight line from finger-tips to toes, resulting in a perfect and almost splashless entry into the water (right).

FOUR PICTURE-LESSONS IN SWIMMING AND DIVING

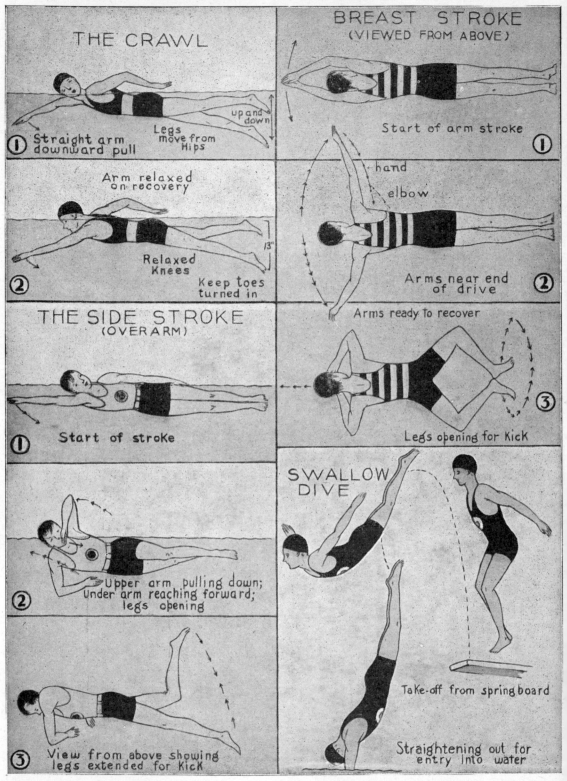

THE CRAWL

① Straight arm downward pull — Legs move from Hips — up and down

② Arm relaxed on recovery — Relaxed Knees — Keep toes turned in — 13"

THE SIDE STROKE (OVERARM)

① Start of stroke

② Upper arm pulling down; Under arm reaching forward; legs opening

③ View from above showing legs extended for Kick

BREAST STROKE (VIEWED FROM ABOVE)

① Start of arm stroke

② hand — elbow — Arms near end of drive

③ Arms ready to recover — Legs opening for Kick

SWALLOW DIVE

Take-off from springboard

Straightening out for entry into water

The crawl stroke—one of the fastest of all—is likewise one of the most popular, though all who wish to become good swimmers should also learn one or more of the other strokes, such as the side stroke and the breast stroke.

The diagrams will help the beginner to master all these strokes, and will also be of considerable help in demonstrating the art of the graceful swan, or swallow, dive, which demands much practice, and is a feature of competitions.

towards the shore, with arms extended, while the legs keep up the thrashing movement. Repeat this until you can keep afloat for a few yards.

The arm movement is an alternate " windmill " stroke, somewhat like half of the butterfly breast stroke. It can be practised standing up by extending the right arm directly in front of the shoulder, then bringing the hand straight down to the hip ; the palm is turned outward, the hand raised upward and forward with the elbow bent until it is at shoulder height; the swimmer should reach forward to the first position. This motion should then be practised a few times with the left arm; later the two may be combined, one arm going forward as the other goes back.

After this the beginner should go out into the water up to the waist, and plunge towards the shore while keeping up the arm movement. As soon as this becomes natural and easy the leg movement may be added. The kick should be started as soon as the feet are off the bottom, and the arm stroke combined with it. There should preferably be six kicks to each complete arm stroke, counting one-two-three to the down pull and four-five-six to the recovery. Most fast swimmers use this crawl.

When the learner can do this in perfect rhythm for as long as the breath can be comfortably held, the face should be turned to one side, breath being drawn in through the mouth during the recovery of the top arm. The arm should be kept relaxed during its forward movement, and the elbow held higher than the hand so that the hand points slightly downward and enters the water first at the beginning of the pull. The back should be arched and the head held high with the eyes at about the surface water line.

The Trudgeon. This differs from the straight crawl only in leg action. A wider kick is taken at the beginning of each cycle, followed by three or five smaller kicks. In the double trudgeon there are two of the wider kicks, one at the end of each arm drive.

The Side Stroke. This stroke is performed while lying on either side. The arms are pulled back alternately without leaving the water. The leg motion is a scissors kick, made by drawing the legs up slightly, keeping the knees and ankles touching, then extending the upper leg forward and the lower leg backward and bringing them together vigorously.

The " single overarm " is the same stroke, except that the upper arm reaches forward above the water while the body makes a quarter roll. In the " double overarm " the body is turned completely on the front with the face under water, to allow the under arm to reach forward above the surface of the water for the next stroke.

Swimming championships are over various distances, and are usually for free style (using any kind of stroke which the swimmer prefers), breast stroke, and back stroke. The last-named is in its primary movements the breast stroke performed on the back. The ambition of the long-distance swimmer is, of course, to swim the English Channel. The first man to do this was Capt. Webb in 1875. During the years 1926–28 there were eleven successful attempts at this feat. E. H. Temme is the only swimmer who has swum the channel in both directions—from France to England in 1927, from England to France in 1934.

Diving. This is an art which can be acquired only by constant practice. " Sloppy " diving is usually caused by drawing up the knees or allowing the feet to flop over as the body enters the water. Or, perhaps, out of an instinctive fear of falling head first, the diver strikes the water flat, perhaps with painful consequences. For plain diving, the body should follow the line of such a curve as would be made by a stone tossed out a similar distance into the water. The hands should be held over the head with thumbs together and palms down, never with palms together. As the body enters the water it should be straight, toes pointed backward. When the body is half-way in, the hands should be bent upward; this will tend to bring the head quickly to the surface and enable the diver soon to breathe. The two main types of diving are springboard diving (including the " running header ") and high diving from firm boards.

Of the various kinds of fancy dive, the swallow dive is best known. For this the arms are flung outwards at right angles to the body and brought together again just before the diver enters the water. The so-called " jack-knife " dive is even more spectacular. Here the diver, when in mid-air, doubles up to touch the toes with the finger-tips. This position is held until just before entering the water, when an upward fling of the legs gives the usual angle for entry.

Life Saving. All swimmers should learn how to save persons from drowning. To avoid being seized and pulled down by the victim, who may be panic-stricken, the rescuer should if possible approach from the rear, thrust the crook of one of his elbows under the chin of the drowning person and tow him backward to safety, doing the back stroke with the legs and the free arm. (For Artificial Respiration *see* pages 1294–95).

Swinburne, ALGERNON CHARLES (1837–1909).

Seldom has a writer been so filled with melody, or allowed himself to be carried away on so inexhaustible a torrent of burning words, as this remarkable man with the small body, over-sized weak-chinned head, greenish eyes and flaming hair.

ALGERNON CHARLES SWINBURNE
In all English poetry there is no finer master of the music of the language than Swinburne. His verses possess enduring beauty of form. His criticism was enthusiastic but unbalanced.

Born in London on April 5, 1837, Swinburne left Oxford in 1859 without taking a degree. The following year, when he was 23 years old, he published two poetic plays: The Queen Mother, and Rosamond. In 1865 he reached the front rank of poets with his tragedy, Atalanta in Calydon. This was followed in 1866 by a volume of Poems and Ballads, and then by a long series of other poems and poetic plays, and several volumes of impassioned prose, of which his much-read studies of Elizabethan literature are noteworthy examples. His volume on William Blake (1868) is possibly his best book of literary criticism, and Songs before Sunrise (1871) his best book of lyrical verse, though some would put the second series of Poems and Ballads (1878) as first among his works.

Swinburne lived a hectic life in London, where he made friends with many of the leading literary figures, such as Dante Gabriel Rossetti (1828–82) and William Morris (1834–96). His health was undermined by excessive drinking. But he found a faithful and devoted friend in the critic Theodore Watts-Dunton (1832–1919), who took him away from his excesses. Swinburne lived with Watts-Dunton for 30 years, though during that time he wrote little that was comparable to the work that

had gone before. He died of pneumonia on April 10, 1909, and, as was fitting for one to whom, as an admiral's son, the sea had made so strong an appeal, he was buried within earshot of the waves at Bonchurch in the Isle of Wight.

He had a marvellous gift of making music with words, and his best lyrics have a matchless quality. He was a passionate devotee of the house of Stuart, and in particular of Mary Queen of Scots, as witness his trilogy of plays, Chastelard (1865), Bothwell (1874), and Mary Stuart (1881). In spite of some splendid enthusiasms and an enormous range of reading in five languages he was not a good critic —always a touch of personal pique was sufficient to turn almost extravagant praise into vehement abuse. All his life he was the victim of his own words, which carried some of his poems and essays to intolerable length and left them lost in sheer wordiness. His influence was wide, and by his daring and masterly use of old metres he enlarged the field of metrical expression. That the bulk of his work will last is improbable, but his finest lyrics will endure as long as anything in English poetry.

In EUROPE'S MOUNTAIN PLAYGROUND

The Swiss are so skilled in such industries as engineering and horology that their products have won world-wide fame for efficiency and accuracy. Catering for the needs of foreign tourists is another important industry.

Switzerland. Among the few entirely inland countries of the world, Switzerland is surrounded by Austria, France, Italy and Germany, being a so-called " buffer " State, 15,900 square miles in area, between those four countries. It includes within its boundaries some of the most noted mountains of Europe, but is not entirely Alpine in its scenery. The north-western half is composed mainly of the valleys of the Rivers Aar and Thun, tributaries of the Rhine, and it is only the south-eastern portion that is pre-eminently mountainous. About a quarter of the country is unproductive, including mountain peaks, glaciers, lakes and rivers. Little of the productive area is suitable for agriculture, and Switzerland is largely dependent upon other countries for its supplies of grain, devoting its own land mainly to pastures. Owing to the demand for wider areas of agricultural land, only about 22 per cent of the area of the country is still under timber.

In the highest Alps, which make up or are near the south-western boundary, are the northern slopes of Mont Blanc (15,782 feet), the snow-crowned heights of which rise from French soil about eight miles over the border; the Matterhorn (14,782 feet), a towering pyramid the precipitous heights of which would seem to defy the boldest Alpine climber, but which has many times been scaled; Monte Rosa (15,217 feet), with

a far-spreading mass of snow and ice, set on the Italian frontier; and a score of other peaks the awe-inspiring grandeur of which prints memories never to be forgotten on the mind of the beholder. Some 20 miles beyond Monte Rosa is the Simplon tunnel, $12\frac{1}{4}$ miles long—longest of the Alpine tunnels—affording one of several routes by which trains pass from Italy into Switzerland.

For outstanding mountain loveliness one must turn northward, cross the valley trough—occupied by the upper courses of the Rhône on the west and the Rhine on the east—and enter the second chain of the Alps, running parallel to the main range from south-west to north-east. Here, in the Bernese Oberland, the crystal spires of the Jungfrau (13,671 feet) and the shining peaks of the Mönch, Eiger, Aletschhorn, and Finsteraarhorn —to name but a few—stand above green valleys. Their thick clustered snow-tops almost equal in height the giants of the main range, and the glory of the panorama which they form is unequalled in Europe. (*See* illustrations in pages 129–32).

Four rivers, flowing into four distant seas, either rise in Switzerland or receive important tributaries from within its boundaries. The Rhine, the source of which in central Switzerland lies at the foot of Mount St. Gothard (famous for its railway tunnel, nearly 10 miles long), after cutting across the eastern face of Switzerland,

Extent.—15,900 square miles. Population 4,543,000.

Physical Features.—The Alps—the Bernese Oberland, Pennine, Lepontine, and Rhaetian Alps, etc.—occupying the greater part of the interior, with great massifs on southern and eastern boundaries. Highest points, Monte Rosa (15,217 feet) and the Matterhorn (14,782) on the Italian border. In the north-west are the Jura Mts. Rivers: Rhône, Rhine, Inn, Reuss and Aar. Lakes: Lucerne, Neuchatel and Zürich, and parts of Geneva, Constance, Maggiore, and Lugano. More than one-fifth of the country is forested.

Principal Products.—Wheat, rye, barley; vegetables, fruit, wine; milk, cheese, chocolate; watches, clocks; silk, embroidery; machinery; chemicals; salt, iron.

Chief Towns.—Zürich (336,000), Basle (162,100), Geneva (124,430), Berne (capital, 130,000), Lausanne (92,000).

M. O. Henchoz

The majestic beauty of the Swiss Alps is breathtaking. It is impossible to gaze upon them without a feeling of awe. Throughout the world the scenery of these heights is renowned and annually attracts thousands of tourists. Here we see the eastern peak of the twin summits of Piz Palu in the Bernina Alps of central Switzerland. In the distance and on the right-hand slope of the snowclad ridge are the figures of four climbers. No corner of this mountain region now remains unexplored, and guides take tourists to places once deemed inaccessible. (*See also* pages 129–132).

M. O. Henchoz

IN THE UPPER ENGADINE

On Alpine meadows which, as in the case of the Engadine valley, may be as much as 7,000 feet above sea level, Swiss farmers grow crops of hay for their livestock. When cut, it is carried down the mountain (as above) to the farmstead.

down a valley to Lake Geneva, and thence through France to the Mediterranean—on the other side of Europe from the Rhine's mouth.

From the southern slopes of the St. Gothard the Ticino runs into Lake Maggiore, thence through Italian soil into the Po, and so into the Adriatic. The Danube receives from the Engadine valley of eastern Switzerland the waters of the River Inn, to discharge them, a thousand miles away, into the Black Sea.

The Swiss mountain ranges are of comparatively recent formation. They lie in four zones, running roughly from south-west to north-east. The northernmost is the Jura region, of folded limestone. Then comes a sandstone plain. The third zone contains a confused mass of mountains, chiefly of limestone. The fourth and southernmost zone consists of the granite and gneiss masses of the Southern Alps. The mineral contents are few, asphalt, salt, iron and anthracite being found but not in very large quantities. Asphalt and iron are worked in the Juras, however, and coal is mined in the canton of Valais. Most of Switzerland's coal is imported from the Saar and Ruhr areas of France and Germany respectively.

Switzerland has 14 lakes, the smallest being more than four square miles in area. The largest two are Constance (or Bodensee), area about 205 sq. m., and Geneva (or Lac Léman), area 223 sq. m., and these are on the frontiers of Germany and France respectively and are not wholly Swiss. On the Italian border are Lakes Maggiore and Lugano, of which only small parts are in Switzerland. Lakes Neuchâtel and Bienne are smaller, as are also the mountain-rimmed lakes of the centre—Zürich, Zug, Lucerne, Thun, and Brienz.

The three "forest cantons"—the word canton means a geographical division—of Uri, Schwyz and

forms part of both the eastern and northern boundaries before turning at Basle on its journey to the North Sea. Its main tributary, the Aar, is also the chief stream of western Switzerland. On the opposite side of the St. Gothard lies the glacier whence issues the River Rhône, flowing westward

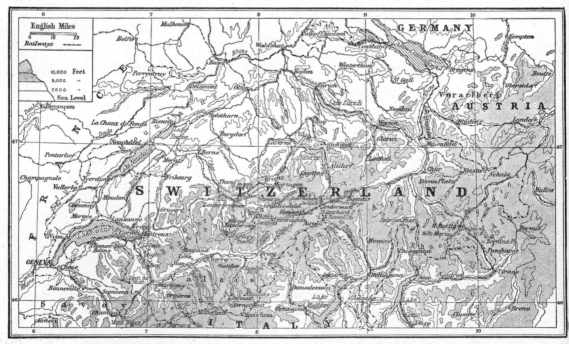

SWITZERLAND : MOUNTAIN REPUBLIC OF CENTRAL EUROPE

Donald McLeish

...wiss-Italian borderland is marked by an Alpine ridge containing some of the highest peaks in Europe.   Here is the Glacier ...rbassière, which leads southward to the jagged Grand Combin, reaching to a height of over 14,000 feet.   Mountaineers have ...ve the dangers not only of the rocky heights but of ice and snow, for a glacier may prove to be treacherous in the extreme.

...e page 3140

Hermann Stauder

FAIR-HAIRED MAIDENS OF SWITZERLAND

Garbed in the pleasing local costume of Hallau, Canton Schaffhausen, these two sisters make an altogether charming picture as the sun lends sheen to their fair hair and additional lustre to their blue eyes. Schaffhausen is one of the most prosperous of the Swiss cantons, and is a German-speaking region.

To face page 3141

Unterwalden, to the north of Mount St. Gothard, were the first to throw off their subjection to the neighbouring counts of Hapsburg, who claimed overlordship in these districts, and bind themselves in an Everlasting League, in 1291. The stories of William Tell in these events are picturesque but largely mythical. In the Battle of Morgarten (1315) the confederated peasants, armed with lances made by tying their scythe-blades to alpenstocks, not only withstood the armoured knights of the Hapsburgs but laid the foundations of a military system which made the Swiss pikemen for 200 years Europe's finest foot-soldiers.

Subsequent victories confirmed their freedom— at Sempach in 1386, when Arnold von Winkelried gathered the lances of the enemy into his own bosom to save his comrades; and on that winter day of 1477 when haughty Charles the Bold of Burgundy was left slaughtered, despoiled and frozen in the marsh at Nancy.

The independence of the Swiss cantons—there were 13 of them by that time—was formally confirmed in the Treaty of Westphalia at the end of the Thirty Years' War (q.v.) in 1648, but the Helvetic Republic, largely under the control of France, was established in 1798. In 1815, when Napoleon fell, the Congress of Vienna guaranteed Switzerland perpetual neutrality. At the same time the number of the cantons was increased to 22 by the formal accession of Geneva, Neuchâtel and other districts.

In most of the cantons, including all those which joined the federation in its early stages, German is the language of the people. But in five western cantons French is the common language, and in one canton in the south (Ticino) the people speak Italian. In one canton (the Grisons) the old dialect called "Romansch"—derived from the ancient Latin of the people—is still in everyday use, and in 1938 it became a fourth official language.

M. O. Henchoz

SWISS MULETEER POSTMAN

In parts of Switzerland where the villages are difficult of access mules are still used as a means of transport, and teams of them carry letters and parcels to villagers living high up in the mountains.

The cities of Zürich (under Zwingli, who lived 1484–1531), and Geneva (under Calvin, who lived 1509–64) were centres of the Reformation, but nearly half the population today are Roman Catholics.

The rural Swiss are very thrifty, forcing out a livelihood from the slimmest strip of valley soil and living in trim and picturesque "châlets." Grapes for wine are raised on the sunny slopes of the Jura and the Alps, and quantities of fruit are grown. Grazing and dairying, however, form the chief agricultural activity.

In summer the people make a village holiday of moving their cattle from the lower to the higher pastures for the sake of the sweeter, fresher grass, and in winter the famous Swiss cheeses ripen in the cellars during Alpine storms. The rivers and streams, which are controlled to prevent floods, at the same time irrigate the Swiss meadows, which in spring are bright with such flowers as the

M. O. Henchoz

LOCARNO ON LAKE MAGGIORE

At the northern end of Lake Maggiore and close to the Italo-Swiss frontier, Locarno is more Italian than Swiss in architecture and the inhabitants speak an Italian dialect. The beauty of its setting has made the town a popular holiday resort.

edelweiss. The women make beautiful embroideries to swell the family savings, and the men often work as guides during the holiday seasons.

There are 27 cities with more than 10,000 population, Zürich, Basle, Geneva, Berne (the capital)—these four are the subjects of separate articles—and Lausanne being the largest. Their clean streets and well-kept walks and parks are attractive to foreigners, and tourists are seen everywhere. Switzerland's splendid roads, leading over the mountain passes into many picturesque valleys, make the land a paradise for motoring; and the efficient government-owned railways, in which electrification plays a large part, and the rack-and-pinion mountain lines, which include that which runs almost to the summit of the Jungfrau, make sightseeing easy. Ski-ing, skating, sleighing, and other winter sports attract nearly as large crowds as the warm summer season (*see* Alps). Several of the towns, like St. Moritz, in the Engadine valley, are entirely tourist centres.

The Swiss cities are rich in historical associations: Geneva, for instance, with its memories of Calvin, Rousseau, and Voltaire. In more recent times historical figures have played out their drama here, for it was the headquarters of the League of Nations (*q.v.*). Switzerland has long been a home for refugees from many lands, including after the two World Wars (1914–18 and 1939–45) deposed kings, outcast nobles and unsuccessful revolutionaries.

Switzerland has manufactures of many kinds. At Geneva, Berne, Neuchâtel, Chaux-de-Fonds, and Locle world-famed watches and clocks are made and jewelry and musical-boxes. Zürich, Basle, St. Gall, Glarus and Appenzell are the centres of a textile industry. Emmenthal and Gruyère make cheese, and chocolate and condensed milk come chiefly from Vevey. In numerous Swiss mountain hamlets exquisite and elaborate wood-carving attracts the money of the tourist.

Technical schools and intelligent development of water-power for furnishing electricity are the two strong arms of Swiss industry. Higher education is given by seven universities, of which the one at Zürich (founded in 1460) is the oldest.

Berne, the capital of the Federal Government, is famous as the seat of various international conferences and associations. Since the adoption of the present constitution in 1848 the Swiss Confederation has had a Government somewhat like that of the United States, with a Supreme Court, a Parliament made up of a House of Representatives and a Senate, President, and Federal Council. The President, however, is elected annually by the two houses of Parliament (the same man cannot be elected for two years in

IN SWITZERLAND'S VALLEY OF WATERFALLS

In a rocky valley of the Bernese Oberland, Lauterbrunnen (German, meaning 'nothing but springs') is noted for the number of waterfalls and cascades in the neighbourhood. The waterfall on the right, named the Staubbach (Dust Brook), is so called because its spray, fine as dust, fills the air. From the village a cable railway runs to Mürren, a winter sports centre. In the distance between the walls of the pass at the end of the valley can be seen the Jungfrau (13,671 feet), which was first climbed in 1811 and can now be ascended almost to the summit by mountain railway.

THE SWORDFISH, BULLY OF THE SEAS
Growing to about 15 feet in length and weighing sometimes as much as 800 pounds, the sword-fish is one of the most pugnacious monsters of the deep. The sharply-pointed ' sword,' formed from the prolonged bone of the upper jaw, may be three feet long.

They are much sought as food, especially in the Mediterranean and off the Atlantic coast of the United States; in the latter area, as off New Zealand, they provide exciting sport. Men catch them with rod and line, using as bait a large fish drawn through the water behind a motor-launch. Swordfish are usually harpooned from small boats, when caught commercially.

succession), and his powers make him little more than chairman of the Federal Council.

Each canton has its own legislature, executive and judiciary. Three of the older and less densely populated cantons have preserved their ancient democratic assemblies, in which each citizen of the canton may appear in person. Usually they meet once a year and always (weather permitting) in the open air. These assemblies elect a sort of standing committee and also the chief magistrate of the canton as well as the judiciary. Elsewhere the system of the referendum, by which the people vote on single controversial issues, is in general use.

Switzerland's policy of permanent neutrality kept her from becoming involved in either of the two World Wars (1914–18 and 1939–45), though she continued her system of universal military training by which every able-bodied man must serve in the armed forces or militia. The population of Switzerland is 4,543,000.

Swordfish. A bully of the open seas is the large swordfish (*Xiphias gladius*), whose weapon, projecting from the end of its nose, is always ready for attack or defence. It is plentiful in the Mediterranean and is widely distributed in the Atlantic and the Pacific oceans. Shaped very much like an enormous mackerel, the swordfish grows from four to 15 feet long and weighs from 150 to 800 lb.

The "sword," sometimes three feet long, is formed by the prolonged and toughened bone of the upper jaw, which is somewhat flattened and has an exceedingly sharp point. The bearers of these weapons dash into schools of mackerel, cod or herring, using the "swords" to cut up the fish, which they then proceed to eat. Occasionally they attack boats and ships, perhaps mistaking them for whales. They shoot through the water at such speed that they have been known to drive their keen, strong weapons through copper sheathing, oak planks and timbers of a ship to a depth of 10 inches.

Sycamore. Although this tree (*Acer pseudoplatanus*) is now common in Britain, it is a native of continental Europe and western Asia and was introduced into England about 1551. It reaches its full growth of from 60 to 80 feet in height in about 50 years, though it is said to live for some 200 years.

The leaves are large and cut into five lobes, which have roughly serrated edges; and as they

H. Bastin
LEAF-LOADED SYCAMORE
Native to Europe and western Asia, the sycamore tree sometimes attains a height of 80 feet. On the left are its winged fruit. Each ' wing ' encloses one seed, which when ripe is carried far by the wind.

WHERE SYDNEY'S FOUNDERS LANDED
Close to the heart of the city, Circular Quay is the chief terminus of the harbour ferries and from it radiate several of the main thoroughfares. It was at this spot that the first settlers in Australia landed in 1788.

Australian Travel Association

are opposite, in pairs, this helps to distinguish them from those of the plane tree (*q.v.*). The flowers, which appear in long, drooping spikes, and are greenish or yellowish in colour and very numerous, are succeeded by the winged fruits, or " keys," which spiral down to the ground in the autumn winds.

The yellowish-pink, fine-grained wood is used in the making of furniture, especially as veneer; it takes a good polish, like most members of the maple family, to which the sycamore belongs.

Sydney. Capital of New South Wales and oldest city in Australia, Sydney is on the shores of Port Jackson, one of the finest natural harbours in the world. The city is laid out in rectangles, rather on the North American plan, and its modern buildings invite comparison with any in Europe. Among the finest are the University, built in 15th-century Gothic style, and the Cathedral of St. Andrew, in 14th-century Gothic. There are a number of parks and public gardens ; the National Park and Kuringgai Chase are remarkable for their natural beauty.

Sydney harbour has an area of about 21 square miles, and the coast is so indented that a number of the wharves are close to the heart of the city. There are several graving docks, including the Captain Cook, opened in 1945, which can take the largest vessels. The bridge across the harbour, opened in 1932, is two and three-quarter miles long, with a central span of 1,650 feet (*see illustration in page 567*).

Manufactures include clothing, boots and shoes, **pottery**, glass, furniture, tobacco, and vehicles;

there are also breweries, distilleries and machine shops. The chief exports are wheat, flour, meat, wool, hides and food products. Coal is obtained from mines less than 100 miles distant. The city is a shipping centre for the South Pacific, and an international airport. It is also a favourite tourist resort, for its harbour provides a delightful picnic-ground for holiday-makers; bays and bathing beaches mark its wooded foreshores, and glorious views can be obtained from the rugged headlands.

Founded on January 26, 1788, six days after he had landed at Botany Bay, by Captain A. Phillip, first Governor of New South Wales, it was named after Viscount Sydney (1733-1800), who suggested the colonisation of New South Wales and was Colonial Secretary when the territory became a British possession. The site of the old town, five miles from the harbour entrance, at the head of Sydney Cove, was chosen because it was near a stream. Gradually the settlement developed, until now Sydney is among the most important commercial centres of the British Commonwealth. The population is 1,484,000.

Syria and Lebanon. Though now two separate States, Syria and Lebanon are linked by the fact that they occupy territory which once was part of ancient Syria. In olden times the entire land between Asia Minor and the Sinai Peninsula and from the Mediterranean to southern Mesopotamia (now part of Iraq) was known as Syria; but the modern republic of that name is a country bordered on the north by Turkey, on the east and south-east by Iraq, on the south by Transjordan (*q.v.*), on the west by Palestine, Lebanon and the Mediterranean, with an area of 66,046 square miles.

The western half of Syria is mountainous, the heights being a continuation of the Amanus range ; near the coast there are forests of pines and evergreen oaks ; olives, vines and fruit trees

---

═══ SYRIA ═══

Extent.—66,046 square miles. Population 3,006,000.

Physical Features.—Plateau in the west formed by continuations of the Lebanon and Anti-Lebanon Mountains and sloping to the Syrian Desert in the east. Rivers : Euphrates, Orontes.

Principal Products.—Wheat, barley, maize, fruit, silk, tobacco.

Chief Cities.—Damascus (capital, 286,300), Aleppo (population 320,200), Homs (population 100,100), Hama (population 71,400), Latakia (population 36,700).

grow in the valleys. The eastern portion is largely desert, except for cultivated strips along the banks of the Euphrates. The only river of importance is the Orontes. The bulk of the population lives on the soil, growing wheat, millet, barley, maize and vegetables. Other crops include mulberries, oranges, lemons, figs, grapes, tobacco and olives. What little industry there is takes the form of handicrafts; but silk and embroideries are made in Damascus, some textiles in Aleppo, and silk in Latakia. The capital is the ancient town of Damascus (q.v.). Other towns are Aleppo (population 320,200), Homs (population 100,100), Hama (population 71,400) and Latakia (population 36,700).

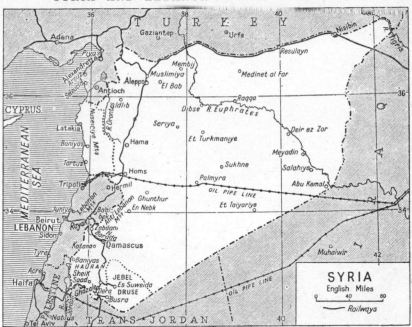

ARAB STATES OF SYRIA AND LEBANON

There are 450 miles of railway, linking Aleppo with the Baghdad railway to the north, and with Damascus and Transjordan (q.v.) to the south. Beirut, in Lebanon (see illustration in next page), is the chief port for Syria and is connected by a narrow gauge line with Damascus. There are some 5,000 miles of roads, usable by motor traffic, and several airports, one of which serves the French Marseilles-Saigon (Cochin China) air line.

The population is a mixture of various ancient peoples—Sumerians, Phoenicians, Hebrews, Druses and Arabs. There are Kurds, Armenians and Turks in the north, and Arabs on the east. Most of the people are Mahomedans, though there is a considerable Christian element.

After having been possessed in turn by the Assyrians, Babylonians and Persians, by the Macedonians under Alexander the Great (356–323 B.C.), and by the Romans, Syria was conquered in the 7th century of the Christian era by the Arabs. The Crusaders established several small States in the country, but were eventually driven out by the Sultans of Egypt, of whom Saladin (1138–93) was outstanding. In 1516 Syria was conquered by the Turks, who remained in possession until driven out by British troops in October 1918, during the course of the First World War (1914–18). After that war the country was detached from the tottering Turkish Empire and was placed under French mandate in 1920.

On June 8, 1941, during the Second World War (1939–45), British and Free (anti-German) French forces invaded Syria to counteract German influence, which was increasing under the Vichy (pro-German) French Government of the country. Damascus was occupied by the Allies; and on September 27, 1941, Syria was proclaimed an independent State, though a Syrian Government was not es-

American Colony, Jerusalem

ALEPPO : CITY OF NORTHERN SYRIA

After Damascus the largest town in Syria, Aleppo is an important commercial centre trading in silk, cotton, wool, leather goods, rugs, cereals and fruit. In the heart of the city and situated on an artificial mound is the citadel, seen here in the background.

BEIRUT : CAPITAL OF THE LEBANESE REPUBLIC
On the Mediterranean Sea, Beirut is the chief seaport for Syria. A busy commercial town, it exports silk, wool, oil, gums and fruit. It is also an educational centre, with French and American universities. It is connected by railway with Damascus in Syria, and with Haifa in Palestine and thence with Egypt.

Ewing Galloway

Syria and on the south by Palestine. It has an area of 3,475 square miles. The mountains, which are pierced by deep gorges, are for the most part barren, and little remains of the once-famous cedar forests. The white colour of the rocks gives its name to Lebanon (Semitic *laban*, "to be white"). The only rivers of importance are the Orontes and Litani.

The principal products are silk, olive oil, wheat and wine; iron, brown coal and gypsum are mined. Most of the towns and villages are built on high ground, for the coastal belt is very hot ; there, however, are the seaports of Beirut (the capital, 234,000) and Tripoli (population 71,500), also the ancient towns of Tyre and Sidon, now of little importance. Beirut has French and American universities, and there are 320 schools organized by Europeans. Roads and railways are good ; Beirut is linked with Haifa in Palestine and thence with Egypt. The inhabitants are mainly Arabs, though there are many foreigners —Turks, Circassians and Armenians. The majority are Mahomedans, but there are also a number of Christians.

The history of Lebanon closely follows that of Syria. After the First World War (1914–18) it was separated from Turkey and placed under French mandate. It was occupied by Allied forces in June 1941, during the Second World War (1939–45), and was proclaimed an independent State in November 1941, though British and French troops remained in occupation until December 1946. As a member of the Arab League, Lebanon joined in an attack on the Jewish State of Israel in May 1948, but concluded a truce in January 1949. The population is 1,186,845.

tablished until January 1944. The evacuation of the country by French and British troops was completed in April 1946. In 1945 Syria joined the Arab League, an association of Egypt, Transjordan, Iraq, Saudi Arabia, Syria, Lebanon and Yemen for furthering the political, cultural and economic interests of the Arab States.

When in May 1948 the Jews proclaimed the State of Israel, ignoring the claims of the Arabs to form a separate self-governing Arab State, Syrian troops invaded Palestine in support of the Arabs. After some inconclusive fighting, the Syrians withdrew behind their own frontier at the end of 1948. The population of Syria is 3,006,000.

The Republic of Lebanon, comprising a 20-mile-wide coastal strip, the two mountain ranges of the Lebanon and Anti-Lebanon and the Bukata valley between them, is bounded on the west by the Mediterranean, on the north and east by

---
LEBANON

Extent.—3,475 square miles. Population 1,186,845.

Physical Features.—Coastal plain backed by the Lebanon and Anti-Lebanon Mountains. Rivers : Orontes and Litani.

Principal Products.—Silk, olive oil, wheat and wine, iron, brown coal and gypsum.

Chief Cities.—Beirut (capital, 234,000), Tripoli (population 71,500).

T

Table Tennis. An indoor game, based on lawn tennis, table tennis was formerly known as ping-pong. In the latter half of the 19th century several kinds of indoor tennis were played on tables. In 1891 cork balls, a net with posts that clamped to a table, and wooden rectangular rackets covered with cloth to enable the player to impart spin to the ball were introduced. The game played with this equipment was completed by the scoring of 21 points by one player.

When the celluloid ball was first used, the sound made when it was hit to and fro over the net led to the game being called ping-pong. From about 1899 to 1904 ping-pong was popular in Britain, then it suddenly died out. Very little was heard of it until 1921, when it was revived and given its present name of table tennis. In 1922 the Table Tennis Association came into being and in 1926 the International Table Tennis Federation was formed. The game is now played on a table nine feet long and five feet wide, with a net six inches high. The celluloid ball must be not less than four and a half inches nor more than four and three-quarter inches in circumference.

The expert player usually stands well back from the table, and hits the ball in much the same manner and with a number of the same strokes as does the lawn tennis player. The racket, which may be of any weight, size, or material (normally it is of wood faced with rubber), is often held with the thumb up the back, though there are several variations of grip.

A game consists of 21 points. Each player has the service five times in succession. Should 20-all be reached, the service changes after every point, the first player to get two points ahead being the winner. The players change ends at the termination of each game, or (in single-game matches) when one has 10 points. The server must stand behind the end of the table, and is not allowed to impart spin with the fingers to the ball. There is no volleying: the ball must bounce both in the server's court and in the receiver's before being returned.

In playing a doubles game, a line or tape is drawn down the centre of the table on either side of the net, and each player defends a quarter of the playing court. The server and his partner change places after each point.

Taj Mahal. (Pron. tahzh ma-hahl'). At Agra, in the republic of India, the Taj Mahal is one of the most beautiful buildings in the world.

It was erected by the Mogul emperor Shah Jehan (1614–66) as a tomb for his favourite wife Mumtaz Mahal. When the Moguls arrived in India early in the 16th century they brought Persian civilization with them; thus it was natural that the Hindu architects and artisans should build in the Persian style, characterised by great splendour.

A story from a Persian manuscript gives an account of how the plans were drawn from a dream which the empress had, and which she described to her husband. He searched India for an architect who could draw plans from her description, but in vain. One day an old man came to the emperor and said, " I can help you to obtain what you seek." To one of the architects at the court the old man offered a drug, saying, " Drink! " Before the architect's bewildered eyes the monument was revealed in all its glory; feverishly he worked, under the spell of the drug, until the plan was finished to its last detail. Then the architect fell back exhausted.

Whether or not this story is true, the Taj Mahal is a monument of wondrous beauty. It is eight-sided, of white marble, 130 feet long and wide, and nearly 200 feet high to the top of the huge dome. It is flanked on each side by two slender minarets, the whole fabric, which is inlaid with precious stones, standing on a vast marble terrace overlooking the River Jumna and surrounded by Persian gardens. (*See* illustration overleaf).

Inside, under the dome, are the marble cenotaphs (literally, empty tombs) of Shah Jehan and his em-

Sport & General

TABLE TENNIS IN PROGRESS

Though the table is not marked out in the same way as a court, table tennis resembles lawn tennis in a number of respects. There is, however, no volleying, and the ball must bounce both in the server's court and the receiver's before being returned. These players are not engaged in a serious contest ; otherwise they would stand farther back from the table.

MIRRORED SPLENDOUR OF THE TAJ MAHAL

On the banks of the Jumna, east of Agra city in the republic of India, stands this 'dream in marble' the Taj Mahal, which was built by the Mogul Emperor Shah Jehan about 1630–50 as a tomb for his beloved wife, Mumtaz Mahal, and in which he himself is buried. It is a perfect example of the Persian style, and numerous people consider it the most beautiful building in the world. The structure, surmounted by a dome, is of white marble, and is set upon a terrace from the four corners of which rise minarets. Round about it is a lovely garden, enclosed by a red sandstone wall. All the important architectural details are inlaid with semi-precious stones, adding colour to the exquisite designs. The name Taj Mahal means 'Crown of the Palace,' one of the titles of the Empress Mumtaz.

press. The sunlight filters into this chamber through marble screens intricately wrought and as delicate as lace. The walls of the interior are covered with floral designs picked out in onyx, jasper, cornelian, and other semi-precious stones cunningly let into the white marble. Inscriptions from the Koran, the sacred book of the Mahomedans, are ornately carved in Arabic characters. The tombs actually containing the bodies of the royal pair stand side by side in the vaulted chamber below, and are devoid of ornament.

Talleyrand-Périgord, PRINCE

CHARLES MAURICE DE (1754–1838). To retain the position of foreign minister of France under three widely different governments— the Directory (the committee who governed France during 1795–99), the Napoleonic Empire, and, after Napoleon's fall, the restored Bourbon monarchs—called for tact and diplomacy of an amazing kind. Usually known as Talleyrand (tal'-ā-rahn), this prince possessed these qualities and others which made him one of the foremost diplomats of Europe. His friendship with Mirabeau (1749–91) taught him the foundations of statesmanship, and visits to England (1792–94) and the United States (1794–95) widened his political vision.

Talleyrand was the second son of a French nobleman, and was born in Paris on February 13, 1754. After the death of his elder brother he had been disinherited on account of lameness caused by a fall when he was four years old. Debarred by this permanent defect from the army, he prepared for the Church, becoming a priest in 1778. He was too independent to stand well with the authorities, and it was not until 1789 that his undoubted ability received recognition and brought to him the appointment of Bishop of Autun.

At this time all France was astir over the approaching meeting, after 175 years' disuse, of the Estates-General (see French Revolution, page 1393). Shortly after his appointment he was chosen by the clergy of his district as their representative in that body, where he joined the liberal clergy in working for reforms, but supporting the Revolution in its conflict with the Church he resigned his clerical position and was excommunicated by the Pope.

Talleyrand was far too able a statesman to approve of the excesses committed by the radical leaders of the Revolution. To avoid danger to himself, he took refuge first in England and later in America. When the Terror was at an end and order once more restored under the Directory, he returned to France (in 1796) and became in the following year Minister for Foreign Affairs. Realizing, however, that Bonaparte was master of the

PRINCE TALLEYRAND
Associated with Napoleon Bonaparte for a number of years as his Foreign Minister, Talleyrand, was an extremely able diplomat. This portrait is by F. Gérard (1770–1837).

situation, he aided him in overthrowing the Directory and in establishing his own power. In return Talleyrand was reappointed Foreign Minister.

But his imperial master decided to keep the control of relations with other nations largely in his own hands, and Talleyrand, perceiving that Napoleon's ambition would eventually overreach itself and fearing for the welfare of France, resigned his position in 1807 and began plotting for the emperor's downfall.

When Napoleon was overthrown by the Allies in 1814, Talleyrand urged the restoration of the Bourbons to the French throne, and when this was done he again became Foreign Minister under Louis XVIII. The most difficult task of his life was now before him—to revive the power and influence of defeated France in the Congress of Vienna. The Allies were determined to impose harsh terms on France, but Talleyrand skilfully took advantage of quarrels among them, and by the close of the Congress, in 1815, France again occupied an important place in the concert of Europe.

As soon as he had accomplished this, Talleyrand resigned his position. After the Revolution of 1830, the new king brought in by that movement, Louis Philippe, offered to appoint him Minister for Foreign Affairs, but Talleyrand preferred the position of Ambassador in London, in which he rendered the last of his great services to his country. He retired from politics in 1834, and died on May 17, 1838.

The embodiment of intrigue and secret diplomacy, his career was marked by many acts of treachery to those who trusted him. But through it all ran two consistent principles— love of France and support of constitutional liberty. No Frenchman of that time did more to repair the damage wrought by reckless fanatics and extreme autocrats.

Tamarisk.

One of the 64 known species of this name, *Tamarisk gallica* is an evergreen shrub common by the seaside in Great Britain, where it grows wild though it is not a native of the country, having been introduced from south-western Europe or western Asia. It grows well near the sea, and is as valuable for holding the sand-hills together and preventing them from being swept away by the wind as for providing shelter along the cliffs. Small leaves cover the long, slender, whip-like shoots, which in summer bear masses of pinkish flowers. It occasionally reaches 20 feet, but is usually not more than half that height.

Another species of special interest is *T. mannifera*, which exudes a sweet, edible juice sometimes called manna: this, according to the Old Testament, was the food of the Israelites in the desert.

Tanager. (Pron. tan'-a-jer). The bird world has nothing more brilliant than the plumage of the male tanagers, and no greater sex contrast than that furnished in some species by the plumage of the female, who in dull olive-green is quite inconspicuous among the foliage that forms a background for her handsome mate.

The tanagers are found chiefly in the tropical forests of Central and South America, though some few species are summer migrants to the United States and Canada. In Great Britain they are seen only in aviaries, for they will not survive the climate without protection in winter. The different species do not vary greatly in size, being about six or seven inches long; nor in habit, for they all feed on insects and fruits, build a saucer-shaped nest on a horizontal tree branch, and lay from three to five eggs, the colour of which varies with the different species. The song is often musical. In these several points they show their relationship to the less spectacular finches, their nearest relatives among British birds.

Perhaps the loveliest of the group is the white-capped tanager (*Stephanophorus leucocephalus*). The body feathers of this exquisite bird are of a deep cornflower blue and the crested head is silvery white, ornamented with a blood-red spot on the forehead. Both the sexes are marked alike in this species.

The best known of the tanagers that venture far from the recesses of their native tropical forests is the scarlet *Pyranga erythomelas* often seen in the United States. The male is dressed in the most brilliant scarlet imaginable, with wings and tail of glossy black. The colours of the female are more sober: olive-green above and greenish-yellow below, with tail and wings dusky, shot with green.

British Museum (Natural History)
SCARLET TANAGER OF AMERICA
Though tanagers are found chiefly in the forests of Central and South America, the scarlet species is among the summer migrants to the United States. Contrasting with its scarlet plumage are wings and tail of glossy black.

Tanganyika, LAKE. (Pron. tan-gan-yē'-ka). This lake of east central Africa, between Tanganyika Territory and the Belgian Congo, is the longest fresh-water lake in the world, measuring nearly 450 miles; its width is 40 to 50 miles. The lake's name signifies " the meeting-place of waters." It lies south of Lakes Albert Edward and Victoria and north-west of Lake Nyasa, and is about 2,700 feet above sea-level. It is very deep—2,000 feet in places. It was first discovered by Burton and Speke in 1858. Ujiji is the principal town on the lake; Kigoma is the terminus of a railway from the port of Dar-es-Salaam, capital of Tanganyika Territory. On the Belgian side is Albertville.

The scenery is varied and beautiful. Here the typical vegetation of East Africa mingles with the flora of the great central forests. The slopes of the surrounding mountains are richly wooded, the principal tree being the *mvule*, from which the natives make dug-out canoes. In the clearings along the shore stand the huts of these natives, who cultivate rice, yams, and sugar-cane, which thrive in the fertile soil. The people are mostly of the Bantu Negro type.

The waters of the lake abound in animal life. The crocodile and the hippopotamus frequent the many inlets. The earliest traders in this district were Arabs from the east coast, but they left little impression upon the virgin wilderness. Today, however, the wooded Tanganyika hills look down on steamers which provide links with the African railway service and carry products for commerce.

American Colony, Jerusalem
DAR-ES-SALAAM : TANGANYIKA'S CAPITAL
With a small, well-sheltered harbour, Dar-es-Salaam besides being the capital is also the chief port of Tanganyika. Its exports include sisal, coffee, cotton, hides and ground-nuts. With a population of 74,000, the town is well laid out and has a number of modern buildings.

Tanganyika Territory, with an area of about 360,000 square miles, and which lies between the lake and the Indian Ocean, was, together with certain parts now belonging to Portuguese East Africa and the Belgian Congo, known as German East Africa until the end of 1917. It was then that the British under the command of General Smuts (*q.v.*) gained possession of the whole colony. The foundation of German power in East Africa was laid by the explorer Dr. Karl Peters, who in the closing years of the 19th century concluded a number of treaties with native chiefs. Subsequently there were revolts by the natives against German rule. The Territory was governed from 1920 by Great Britain under mandate from the League of Nations until the mandate was ended in 1946 and the Territory placed under United Nations trusteeship.

In 1947 the British Government embarked on a scheme of mechanical land-clearing which aimed at bringing under cultivation some 5,000 square miles of country, mainly in Tanganyika, previously covered by scrub. This scheme was intended to produce large quantities of fat-containing ground-nuts. (*See* Ground-nut).

Tangier. At the north-western tip of Africa, about 36 miles south-west of Gibraltar, stands the city of Tangier, international port and gateway to Morocco. It shares with Gibraltar the command of the western entrance to the Mediterranean Sea, and is of such military importance that the European nations will not allow any one country to gain control of it. So they have made it and the surrounding area of 225 square miles an International Zone, without forts or army, guaranteeing it to be neutral in case of war.

The Zone was, until the Second World War (1939–45), governed jointly by France, Spain, Great Britain and Italy, under the Tangier Statute of 1923, amended in 1928. The Sultan of Morocco retained some control of the native population.

In June 1940 Spain took over control, stating that this was necessary in order to maintain the neutrality of the area. In 1945 a conference of representatives of France, Great Britain, Russia and the United States held in Paris called upon Spain to move her troops out of the Zone, and the new International regime was set up.

Believed to be the oldest city in North Africa, Tangier was built by Moroccan Arabs with narrow streets twisting up terraced cliffs, bordered by small shops, Moorish houses, and brightly coloured mosques and minarets. Mahomedans form about 60 per cent of the population of 100,000. There are approximately 12,000 Jews and 11,000 Europeans, chiefly Spanish and French. The port is a centre of trade in leather, eggs and canned fish; foodstuffs and textiles are imported.

Tanks. On September 15, 1916, during the First World War (1914–18), German troops in France were mystified by the sudden appearance of steel monsters moving towards them from the British positions. These were the first tanks, intended to clear the way for the British infantry. The somewhat strange name had been given in December 1915, in order to befog enemy spies. The tank was an armed bullet-proof vehicle fitted with caterpillar tracks and secretly constructed in Britain ; and the name continued to be used after the machine had appeared on the field of battle.

The coming of the tank rendered cavalry and horse-drawn equipment obsolete in the armies of the world, though this was not at first fully realized. It meant that the armies of the future would have to travel on motor vehicles, and that the speed at which battles could be fought would be greatly increased. Between the two World Wars the British Army adopted a small lightly armoured tank weighing five tons and carrying a machine-gun, which was intended to fight in co-operation with mechanised artillery and with infantry carried in lorries.

Germany also favoured light tanks and equipped large numbers of armoured divisions with them. They were, however, supported by " medium " tanks having thicker armour and armed with a 37-mm. (about one and a third inches) gun. After a series of manoeuvres the British Army decided that, apart from light tanks for use as cavalry, a more powerful but slower tank would be needed to assist the infantry in close and heavy fighting, especially to destroy enemy strongpoints. The result was the infantry tank called the Matilda, which had armour up to 90 mm. (about three and a half inches) thick and was equipped with a 2-pdr. gun and one machine-gun. As the anti-tank weapons grew more powerful during the Second World War (1939–45) it became evident that the light tank was far too vulnerable and the infantry tank much too slow, so a tank that would incorporate the best features of both types was evolved. This became known as

J. Bushby

ARAB MARKET IN TANGIER
Close to the Bab-el-Souk, or Gate of the Market, in Tangier, is the native bazaar (above). The town, which shares with Gibraltar the command of the western entrance to the Mediterranean, is an international port in Morocco governed by representatives of Great Britain, the United States, Russia, France, Italy and Spain.

the cruiser tank, and it formed the bulk of the armoured forces of the belligerent armies.

The first British cruiser tank was the Crusader, with a 2-pdr. gun which was later replaced by a 6-pdr. The Cromwell, incorporating the best features of the Crusader, was one of the most successful; it mounted a 75-mm. (nearly three inches) gun. The Churchill, the later models of which were armed with a 95-mm. (nearly four inches) gun, was superior to the United States Sherman in close warfare. The Sherman was the most widely used of the American tanks, and large numbers were employed by others of the Allies. It weighed 35 tons and had a speed of 35 miles per hour. It was armed with a 76-mm. gun or with a 105-mm. howitzer. Against this and the British tanks mentioned, the Germans pitted their Panther (45 tons) and Tiger (50¼ tons). The biggest Russian tank was the KV (47 tons).

The rôle of tanks is seldom to fight each other, except in static defence—when they are usually dug into the ground, with only the turret showing—but rather to pierce or outflank the enemy's position and cut his lines of communication, destroying the motor transport which maintains an army in the field. The rocket-propelled ammunition of the anti-tank weapons with which infantry are now equipped enable determined men to beat off tank attacks and to inflict heavy casualties. A tank with the hatch closed and the driver looking through the narrow slit in the visor is very "blind," and unable to defend itself against attacks from close quarters—because its weapons cannot be brought to bear upon a target inside a range of about 15 yards. Tanks are, normally, formed into regiments of 28, consisting of four squadrons of six, and four with Regimental headquarters. They may operate as a regiment, in squadrons (two troops) or in troops, but normally they fight in squadrons. Communication between the tanks themselves and between them and their headquarters is maintained by wireless telephony. The normal crew is three, consisting of the tank commander, who is nearly always a non-commissioned officer, the gunner-wireless operator, and the driver.

The distance tanks can travel without refuelling their petrol engines is governed by their type, the speed at which they are driven, and the country over which they are operating ; the normal radius of action is about 100 miles. The caterpillar tracks on either side not only carry a tank over most obstacles but are also used for steering—the track on the right being slowed down for a right-hand turn, and vice versa. (*See also* Armour).

Tantalum. The metal tantalum occurs with the similar element niobium widely distributed over the surface of the earth, but in only a few places are the minerals sufficiently rich for the metal to be extracted. The minerals containing tantalum are columbite and tantalite, and occur principally in Australia and the United States.

The extraction of tantalum is a difficult operation. Tantalum powder obtained by an electrolytic method is fused in an electric arc, and rolled into sheet or drawn into wire in an electric vacuum furnace. It is a tough white metal which is ductile and can be drawn into wires. Its atomic weight is 180·88 and its atomic number 73. The chemical symbol is Ta. The relative density of the metal is 16·6, and the melting point 2850° C.

The first metal filaments for electric lamps contained tantalum, although it was replaced in 1911 by tungsten. Tantalum rectifiers (*see* Rectifier) were used extensively in early wireless sets. The metal is employed for making spinnerets for rayon spinning (*see* Rayon). Alloys with other metals are used for tools, and the metal is also alloyed in steel. As it is resistant to acids it can be used, like platinum, for making acid-resisting chemical apparatus. It is unaffected by body fluids, and being completely non-irritant has many uses in surgery for various bone and tissue repairs. Tantalum carbide is very hard and is used for the tips of cutting tools.

Tantalus. Do you know what the word "tantalise" means ? It comes from the name of a king noted in a Greek legend for the punishment that he received after death.

Tantalus was the son of Zeus, and for making known the secrets of his divine father or for other reasons—the stories differ—he had to stand up to the chin in a lake, the waters of which escaped him whenever he tried to drink. Clusters of luscious fruit hung over his head but eluded his grasp whenever he reached for them. In another version a huge rock hung over his head, ever threatening to fall and crush him.

It is from these stories that we get the word "tantalise," meaning to tease, or hold out hopes that cannot be realized. The name "tantalus" is given to a kind of box containing wines and spirits and kept on a sideboard. It has glass doors, but can be locked, so that it truly tantalises any thirsty person who has no key. The metal tantalum (*q.v.*) is also named after him, because when placed in acids it will not take them into combination.

Tapestry. Interior walls of the castles of the Middle Ages were usually unfinished surfaces of rough stone. To relieve their gloominess they were sometimes covered with pictures painted directly on the walls themselves, and sometimes hung with various materials, of which the most prized were tapestries—heavy fabrics in which elaborate designs or pictures were woven.

The stone walls of churches and palaces were completely covered with such tapestries, often hanging loosely from hooks. Beautiful pieces were hung from balconies and windows to decorate the streets on festive days, tournament fields were gay with them, and even on the battlefields they were used—to enrich the tents of great warriors.

The weaving of these beautiful fabrics requires much skill. The heavy undyed warp threads, usually of hemp, are attached to two long poles and stretched tight—22 or 26 threads to an inch. Then they are wound round one of the poles until only a few inches remain open between them. As the weft threads are added the finished fabric is wound on the other pole.

The pattern is usually made with coloured wool threads, although gold or silver threads are sometimes used to give richness. Silk is used in China. With a *broche*, an implement something like a shuttle or bobbin, the worker weaves the coloured weft threads over and under the warp threads so closely that the latter are completely hidden, being marked only by horizontal ribs. Since each broche carries only one colour, and since several different colours are used for nearly every square inch of a com-

TAPESTRY PICTURE WOVEN FOR THE WALLS OF A MEDIEVAL MANSION

Five tapestries of the 15th century, representing the five senses, hang on the walls of the Cluny Museum in Paris, their deep red backgrounds sprinkled with flowers, in what is called *Millefleur* (thousand flowers) style. The tapestry above, with the two ladies carrying a dish of food, depicts the sense of taste. The white lion and the unicorn hold medieval banners, and the background, quite indifferent to perspective, is full of little animals among the flowers.

plicated design, you can realize how lengthy and tedious the process of weaving tapestry is.

Sometimes the pattern or cartoon which the tapestry-maker is following hangs on the wall before him ; then his loom stands upright, and the finished work is known as *haute-lisse* (" upright warp "). Sometimes the loom lies horizontally over the cartoon itself, and the worker follows the pattern beneath ; then the tapestry is known as *basse-lisse* (" horizontal warp "). The work in both cases is done entirely on the reverse side, and in horizontal looms the weaver does not see his design from the front till the whole is finished.

The art of tapestry-weaving dates from the beginning of civilization. The oldest existing tapestries are believed to be those that have been found in Egypt, which may have been woven 1,400 years before the Christian era. Some of these are in the Cairo Museum. The oldest existing mural tapestries were woven in the 11th or 12th centuries A.D. The so-called Bayeux Tapestry, preserved at Bayeux (*q.v.*), in Normandy, is not tapestry at all but fine embroidery (*q.v.*).

In course of time tapestries came to be notable achievements from the standpoint of pure art. The industry became a very large one, hundreds of thousands of workmen being employed, and the greatest artists of the day supplying the cartoons.

Flanders, under the dukes of Normandy, surpassed all other countries. Arras, Brussels, Middelburg, and Delft were the leading centres. During the 14th century many weavers from Arras arrived in England, where " arras " became the general term for tapestry. You may remember how Hamlet, in Shakespeare's play, kills Polonius by stabbing him through the arras.

Almost every country still produces some tapestry. Among the most important works are the celebrated Gobelin looms in France, established about 1601. In France there were also established national factories at Beauvais and Aubusson. The high-warp looms at Merton, Surrey, established by William Morris, have produced beautiful tapestries from designs by Morris, Burne-Jones, Walter Crane and other noted artists. The tapestries of Mortlake, Surrey, first made early in the 17th century, were long famous. Imitation tapestries have been in modern times extensively produced by machine.

Tapioca. The hard and white tapioca grains that swell up and become soft and translucent when cooked for puddings come from the roots of the cassava, or manioc, a plant native to tropical South America. Most of the world's supply of tapioca comes from Java and Malaya ; but the cassava is now grown for local use throughout the tropics, where flour made from the roots is a staple food of the people.

The cassava is a bushy shrub from five to nine feet high, with broad and shining hand-shaped leaves. Its thick fleshy roots, which may be three feet long and weigh 30 pounds apiece, are filled with a milky juice. Two species, the sweet and the bitter cassava, are used for food, but the latter is the important species commercially. Its root contains a poison (prussic acid) under the skin, which must be thoroughly washed out.

The roots, which contain about 20 per cent starch, are pulped and washed through a sieve with a stream of water which carries with it the starch particles. After the starch has settled into a cake of wet flour in tanks, it is further washed and ground. To form tapioca, this cassava flour is moistened and dried on hot disks or plates. Pearl tapioca is formed by dropping the flour through perforated sheets before drying. The starch is also made into glue, gums, and other substances which are useful in industry. The milk, with the poison expelled by heating, is made into a delicious sauce called cassareep. The roots are ground into meal to form a cattle food.

The cassava belongs to the family *Euphorbiaceae*, which includes the castor bean. Scientific name of the bitter cassava is *Manihot utilissima* ; of the sweet cassava, *M. aipi*.

Tapir. (Pron. tā´-pêr). This animal is especially interesting on account of its distribution, for tapirs are found both in the Malay region of Asia (including the islands of Java and Sumatra) and in Central and South America. The Old World tapirs are larger than those of the New World, the Malay form (*Tapirus indicus*) being eight feet long and 39 inches high at the shoulders. In appearance the tapir is rather like a miniature rhinoceros, without the horn and with a nose like an abbreviated elephant's trunk.

W. S. Berridge

TAPIR TRANSFORMATION
The legs and front of the body of the adult Malayan tapir are black or dark brown, whereas the young are striped and spotted all over. Nose and lip are prolonged to form a short trunk with which these animals strip trees of young leaves, shoots and fruits.

In the Asiatic species the legs and front of the body are black or dark brown, but the sides and back are greyish white. Those of the New World are uniformly brown or blackish when full grown. In both species the young are striped or spotted with white. The Brazilian form (*T. terrestris*) inhabits thickly wooded districts, but in the Andes it is replaced by a mountain variety living at altitudes of 7,000 and 8,000 feet. There also are two little-known species in Central America. Tapirs feed on young leaves, shoots, and fruits.

These creatures are very ancient, as their distribution shows, for they once lived all over the northern hemisphere. Then they were driven down into the extremities of America and Malaya millions of years after these areas had been separated by the Pacific Ocean.

Tar. Wood, coal, bones and other organic substances yield the heavy, oily, dark-coloured liquid called tar when they are subjected to intense heat in retorts closed to the air. Commercially there are two chief kinds, wood-tar and coal-tar, the latter being the source of many dye-stuffs and other important products (*see* Coal-Tar). The most familiar uses of tar are as a dust-preventer in road-making, and as a protective coat for woodwork.

Much wood-tar is produced in the pine forests of northern Europe, known, according to the source, as Stockholm tar or Archangel tar, and in the south-eastern United States, especially North Carolina. Because of the large amount of creosote that it contains, wood-tar is largely used for preserving wood, rope and felt.

Pitch, which has been used from the earliest times for waterproofing the seams of boats, is the black resinous substance obtained from wood-tar or the non-resinous residue from coal-tar after the volatile parts have been driven off by heat. Pitch is also obtained from petroleum, bone-tar, and stearine residues. The last two are valued by varnish and turpentine makers. Wood-tar pitch is used to protect timber from insects and the weather; coal-tar pitch is used in the manufacture of black varnishes, for coating iron, and for making lamp-black. Burgundy pitch, produced in Finland from the sap exuded by spruce trees, is a drug much used as a medicine, especially for making plasters.

Tarantula. A large hairy spider, the tarantula is much dreaded by natives of the warm countries where it is found. Its bite is fatal to insects and small animals, and is popularly supposed to be dangerous to Man. From the 13th to the 17th century, epidemics of dancing mania, known as tarantism, were common in Europe, and these were attributed to the bite of the tarantula, though they were really forms of hysteria.

It was believed that the only cure for tarantism was lively music, which inspired the victim to dance until he fell exhausted and bathed in perspiration. From this came the name tarantella, applied to a lively Italian dance.

The true tarantula (*Lycosa tarantula*), which gets its name from Taranto, in Italy, is found only in southern Europe and has a body about three-quarters of an inch long. The term, however, has been applied to large spiders in various parts of the world—for instance to the enormous bird-eating spiders of South America, which may have a leg-span of seven inches.

Tarantulas dig deep burrows, which they line with soft silk. They do not spin webs in which to catch their prey but wait for it to come within pouncing range as they lie concealed among leaves, or rubbish, or hiding within their burrows; they are, therefore, classed among the hunting and trap-door spiders. (*See* Spiders).

Tartaric Acid.

This organic acid is interesting not only on account of its natural occurrence and its many applications but also because the phenomenon of "optical activity" was first discovered in its solutions. The acid, as we have said, is an organic one, and contains carbon, hydrogen and oxygen ($C_4H_6O_6$). It occurs in many fruits, and grapes are particularly rich in it. In wine-making the sugar in the grape juice is converted into alcohol. The tartaric acid present in the grape is precipitated as potassium hydrogen tartrate, which is less soluble in the alcohol solution (the wine) than in the original grape juice. The potassium acid tartrate is deposited on the sides of the vats as "argol" and also in the "lees" or sediment. The argol, a reddish earthy-looking substance, is purified to give the white "cream of tartar."

Cream of tartar is used with bicarbonate of soda in baking powders. Tartaric acid, made from cream of tartar by the action of sulphuric acid, forms large transparent crystals. It is used in calico-printing, dyeing, photography, medicine and in effervescent drinks. Sodium potassium tartrate ("Rochelle salt") is important in sugar analysis; and potassium antimony tartrate ("tartar emetic") is used in medicine and as a mordant in dyeing.

Tartaric acid contains two hydrogen atoms which can be replaced by metals to form salts. In the acid-salt potassium hydrogen tartrate, only one atom is replaced; while in Rochelle salt both are replaced by metal atoms.

In 1844 Eilhard Mitscherlich (1794–1863) showed that although tartaric acid and racemic acid, also obtained from the lees of wine, were identical in chemical properties, a solution of tartaric acid possessed the power of rotating the plane of polarised light (*see* Light); while a solution of racemic acid was "optically inactive," and did not have this power. Then in 1848 Pasteur (*q.v.*) crystallised sodium ammonium racemate and obtained two kinds of crystals. On separating these, a solution of one kind was found to rotate polarised light to the right, in the same way as the tartaric acid from argol; while the other solution rotated it to the same extent but in the opposite direction—to the left. The two corresponding acids were called dextro- and laevo-tartaric acids respectively (*see*

Hugh Main

A TARANTULA SPIDER

Spiders as a class are not popular : this species has not even a skilfully constructed web to its credit. The tarantulas spend their 'off-time' below ground, when hungry hunting on the surface and pouncing on their living prey.

Sugar), the former being the ordinary tartaric acid obtained from argol. On mixing equal quantities of the two acids Pasteur obtained racemic acid again. Racemic acid, a compound of the dextro- and laevo-acids, has no effect on polarised light, because the dextro- and laevo-parts neutralise one another. Pasteur later obtained a fourth form, meso-tartaric acid, which had no effect on polarised light, but could not be separated into the two optically active forms.

There are thus four forms of tartaric acid: dextro- and laevo-, having equal and opposite effects on polarised light; racemic acid, optically inactive but separable into the dextro- and laevo- forms; and meso-tartaric acid, optically inactive and not separable into the two active forms. It was found later that the molecules of the dextro- and laevo-acids contain the same atoms arranged in the same way. They differ as the right hand differs from the left; that is, the one is identical with the "mirror image" of the other.

This property of "optical activity," first discovered by Pasteur in the tartaric acids, is possessed by a large number of naturally occurring organic compounds such as lactic acid, camphor, quinine, and the sugars (*see* Sugar). Optical activity is very important in chemistry and in life processes. Live organisms are very "touchy" about optical activity. Pasteur found that if the mould Penicillium attacked racemic acid, only the dextro-part was affected, and the laevo-part was left unscathed. This is an important way of getting the laevo-acid from racemic acid ; but, of course, the other component is used up by the mould.

Tartars.

"Well may they be called Tartars, for their deeds are those of fiends from Tartarus" (a region of Hell). Such, it is said, was the exclamation of the pious king St. Louis (Louis IX) of France (1214–70), on hearing of the havoc wrought by the Mongol hordes that seethed up out of Asia in the 13th century.

The name really comes from that of the Ta-ta Mongols who originally inhabited the north-eastern Gobi area on the frontiers of China, and came to be applied to the whole group of tribes that formed the hordes of Genghis Khan and other Mongol invaders of later times (*see* Mongols), as well as to the kindred peoples that they subdued. The region from which they came, now loosely known as Turkistan, with the neighbouring regions they overran, was called Tartary.

The name Tartar (more correctly Tatar) today is usually reserved for a group of tribes in Russia and Siberia, numbering about 2,000,000, mostly of Turkish origin and of the Mahomedan religion. Those in Russia are remnants of the Mongol invasion of the 13th century, though they have only slight traces of Mongolian blood. An autonomous republic of the Soviet Union is still known as the Tatar Republic.

Tasmania. The "back of the beyond" —that was what people used to call the island of Tasmania, tucked away below the south-east corner of Australia, from which it is separated by the Bass Strait, about 140 miles across. When the Dutch navigator Abel Tasman discovered the island in 1642 he found it a wildly beautiful spot with a rugged coast-line and high, rough hills, inhabited by a strange black race. But there was little to attract settlers, and no nation attempted to colonize the island until 1803, when Great Britain sent out 400 convicts. The following year Tasmania's capital, Hobart, was founded.

For the next 50 years thousands of "undesirables" from all parts of the British Empire were shipped to Van Diemen's Land, as the island was then called, after Tasman's patron, then governor of the Dutch East Indies. The convicts were compelled to work for the few free settlers, and many evils arose. The native race, then some 5,000 in number, was rapidly exterminated.

In 1853 the importation of convicts was stopped, the name of the island was changed to Tasmania, and the population was granted representative government. But at this period the discovery of gold in Australia lured away virtually all the younger people from the island. It was not until the '60s that Tasmania entered upon a period of prosperity. In 1901 it became a State and the eighth division of the Australian Commonwealth.

Tasmania has a temperate and healthy climate. With lovely lakes, many rivers, abundant rainfall, and a fertile soil, the island is well adapted to agriculture. Wheat is the chief crop, but fruits (especially apples) are also largely exported. On the heavily forested mountain slopes (highest peak, Ben Lomond, 5,160 feet) the principal tree is the "blue gum" eucalyptus, one of the strongest, densest, and most valuable woods in the world. Great logs are hauled along Tasmania's railways to the coast, bound for the far ends of the earth. The peaks and ridges which dot the plateau are rich in minerals—tin, silver, lead, copper, tungsten, and gold deposits are found—and mining is the leading industry. There is a big electrolytic zinc works at Risdon, near Hobart, and important hydro-electric works at the Great Lake. The population of 257,117 largely centres about the capital, Hobart.

The animal life is much like that of Australia, but the island has two beasts of prey found nowhere

> **Extent.**—Including smaller islands, Tasmania contains 26,215 square miles. Population 257,117.
>
> **Physical Features.**—Mountainous, with central lake plateau and several rivers.
>
> **Principal Products.**—Wheat and other crops; fruit, jams and jellies; timber; wool; wood-pulp for paper-making; copper, silver, coal, zinc, and other minerals.
>
> **Chief Towns.**—Hobart (capital) population 76,567; Launceston (40,450).

Beattie's Studio, Hobart

HOBART, TASMANIA'S CAPITAL, ON ITS SHELTERED HARBOUR

On the River Derwent about twelve miles from its mouth on the south-east coast of Tasmania, Hobart has a splendid harbour which can accommodate the largest ships. The town has a climate comparable with that of southern England, and owing to the extensive use of electricity for domestic and industrial purposes is exceptionally clean. Exports include fruit, jam, zinc, copper, wood-pulp and timber. In the background of this photograph is Mount Wellington.

A TASMANIAN DEVIL

About 28 inches long, the Tasmanian devil is a fierce carnivorous animal which, owing to the havoc it causes amongst poultry, has been hunted until it is almost extinct. It lives in a burrow, and carries its young in a pouch.

W. S. Berridge

else. One of these, the Tasmanian wolf (*Thylacinus cynocephalus*), a striped creature very like an ordinary wolf in shape, but having a pouch like a kangaroo for carrying its young, is destructive to sheep. The other, the Tasmanian devil (*Sarcophilus ursinus*), somewhat like a little bear in appearance, is smaller but very savage. It also carries its young in a pouch. It lives in a burrow, and is nocturnal. (For maps, etc., *see* Australia).

Tasso, TORQUATO (1544–95). The story of this Italian poet reads like a romantic tragedy. He was born at Sorrento on March 11, 1544, in that period of Italian history when the wealth and power of the country was in the hands of a number of princes and dukes, whose courts were centres not only of luxury but of art and learning. It was customary for poets, artists and scholars to attach themselves to the Courts of those nobles. The father of Torquato Tasso was himself a poet, but he had suffered so many ups and downs that he decided that his son should follow a more certain profession, and so the father sent him to Padua to study law.

Torquato, however, gave more attention to philosophy and poetry, and in 1562 completed his narrative poem Rinaldo, dealing with the stories of Charlemagne. Given a post in the retinue of Cardinal Luigi d'Este at Ferrara in 1565, he soon became the central figure at that Court. His pastoral drama Aminta was completed in 1573, and in the following year he finished his masterpiece, Jerusalem Delivered, a religious epic based on the First Crusade. Instead of publishing it at once, he sent it to a number of

scholars for their opinion. They criticized the poem so severely that the sensitive Tasso was driven almost to madness. The jealous courtiers at Ferrara added considerably to his sufferings by slanders and insults, and the poet became a prey to melancholy and irritability.

At last Tasso became so violent that the Duke of Ferrara, whose service he had entered in 1571, sent him to an asylum, where he was kept in confinement for seven years. During his imprisonment the Jerusalem Delivered was published without his permission, and he gained no reward for the work. He was released in 1586. After several more unhappy years, fortune at last seemed to smile on the feeble and broken man. He was invited to Rome to receive at the hands of the Pope the poetic crown of laurel—the same honour which had been conferred on Petrarch in the 14th century. But the appreciation for which he had hungered all his life came too late. Before the ceremony was performed he fell ill and died, in the Convent of St. Onofrio, Rome, on April 25, 1595.

Taste. The sense of taste is closely linked with that of smell. It depends on certain little projections, called " taste buds," on the top, sides and back of the tongue. The taste buds contain a special kind of nerve-ending, from which nerve fibres extend as conductors of sensation back to the brain. Sweet things are tasted more acutely at the tip of the tongue and bitter things more acutely at the back. A good many substances have a " combination " taste. Epsom salts are bitter and salt at the same time. Many others have little or no taste, but possess an odour, which is chiefly recognized when in the mouth. Hence smell and taste are linked and confused.

When any substance in solution, or any substance which is capable of dissolving, is taken into the mouth and comes in contact with the nerve-endings, these endings are stimulated and send a message back to the brain. Thus the substance is " tasted." An insoluble substance has no taste, but its presence may be felt in the mouth through the nerves of touch.

There are four kinds of true taste—sweet, bitter, salt and sour. Each of these has its own nerve-endings, its own nerve fibres, and presumably its own centre in the brain. All other so-called tastes are really smells. Thus, if some dry, ground coffee is taken into the mouth while holding the nose it has but little taste; breathe in and out through the nose, and the flavour is instantly recognized. This simple experiment explains why

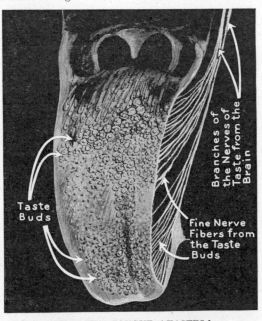

Taste Buds

Branches of the Nerves of Taste from the Brain

Fine Nerve Fibers from the Taste Buds

HOW THE TONGUE 'TASTES'

In some of the small lumps which cover most of the tongue are 'taste buds.' Nerve centres from these join the nerves of taste to the brain ; when the buds come in contact with food the nerves carry the sensation to the brain and the substance is tasted.

many things lose their taste when a cold attacks its victim. It is not the sense of taste but the sense of smell that has gone, by reason of the resulting congestion of the nose.

The delicacy of taste varies for different substances. One part of sugar in 200 of water can just be detected, while one part of quinine in 200,000 of water can be distinctly tasted. Taste, merged as it is into smell, is useful in making a choice of foods; and among animals it is the best guide. But Man lives under artificial conditions, and this is not always true of him.

Tate Gallery. Sir Henry Tate (1819–99) was a prosperous sugar merchant who collected pictures by contemporary British artists. Towards the end of his life he offered 65 pictures to the British nation, together with £80,000 to cover the cost of building a new art gallery. The offer was accepted by the Government in 1892, and in 1897 the handsome Tate Gallery was opened on a site overlooking the Thames at Millbank, London.

Not only Tate's pictures were hung there but several other collections of British paintings and sculptures, so that the gallery at once became, and was soon called, the National Gallery of British Art. There have been several further extensions since then. Works by modern foreign artists were first added in 1915, and by 1950 the whole collection had grown to over 3,500 works, some 3,000 of them British.

When all the works are on view, the Tate Gallery is the best place to learn something at first hand about the wonderful achievements of British artists from the 18th century to the present day. Thanks to the progressive policy of the director and trustees, lively works by the so-called " modern " artists have become increasingly prominent there in recent years.

Taxation. You may have heard people complaining about the rates and taxes they have to pay. It is a very old form of complaint, for from the earliest times people have been taxed and have grumbled about it.

Rates are merely local taxes, payable to the district or borough council towards the cost of the upkeep of schools, parks, roads, refuse-collection, and other services.

Every government needs much money to run the country. The Army, Navy and Air Force alone cost many millions of pounds. In addition, in the United Kingdom there are costly services provided either directly by government departments or indirectly through district and county councils : public education, free medical services, old age pensions, and so on. The amount to be taken in taxes each year is set out in the Budget presented annually (sometimes more often) to the House of Commons by the Chancellor of the Exchequer.

Taxes may be direct or indirect. A good example of an indirect tax is the Customs duty on goods such as wine and tobacco when these are imported. The importer does not bear the burden of the tax; he passes it on by including it in the price he charges. A direct tax is one that cannot be so easily " shifted," e.g., the income tax.

Since taxes have always been more or less unpopular, attempts have been made to show clearly why people should pay taxes, and how the amount of tax should be calculated. Adam Smith, the famous British economist, stated in 1776 the re-

quirements of a good tax. In addition to being levied in proportion to the ability to pay, he said that the tax must be certain and not arbitrary in amount, that it must be payable in the manner most convenient to the people, and that it must be inexpensive to collect. A French minister of finance a century earlier had stated his idea of a good tax somewhat differently : " So pluck the goose (the people) as to produce the largest amount of feathers (money or revenue) with the least amount of squawking."

The income tax is now one of the principal forms of taxation in many countries. Principally because of the two world wars the rate in Britain has been increased from 1s. 2d. in the £ in 1913–14 to 9s. in 1948–49; but only companies and very rich persons pay at the full rate. A certain part of a person's income is not taxed at all; no tax is deducted on a further part if one has a wife or children or other dependants; and the rate charged on what remains after these reliefs will vary according to the total amount of the income. For those with an income exceeding £2,000 a year a second income tax, known as sur-tax, is imposed. This is also graduated from 2s. in the £ to 10s. 6d. on incomes above £20,000, so that a person with an income of, say, £50,000, would be left with only about £6,000.

In 1944 a " Pay-as-you-earn " (PAYE) method of collecting income tax on wages and salaries was introduced into Britain. Every employed person is given a " code number " according to the size of his income, and to the personal allowances or reliefs he is entitled to have for wife, children, etc. Employers are supplied with tables corresponding to the code numbers, and are obliged to deduct tax as shown in the appropriate table from each payment of wages or salary. They are thus tax collectors for the government.

Estate or death duties are a tax levied on the estate of a person after death and before it is divided among the heirs. As with income tax, the rate is steeply graduated, so that the rate of tax increases as the value of the estate becomes larger. Another important kind of tax is stamp duties, which are paid by means of stamps stuck on or embossed on documents such as cheques, receipts for amounts of £2 and more, agreements, and so on.

Besides the taxes already mentioned there are those on special occupations and businesses and activities, and what are called Excise duties on commodities produced within the country. For example, auctioneers, tobacconists and motorists are " licensed "; motor vehicles are also licensed; entertainment duty is included in the cost of a theatre or cinema ticket ; a licence has to be purchased before one can have a gun or keep a dog. The principal Excise duties are those on beer, spirits, licences to sell liquor, saccharin, and matches.

Tchaikovsky, PIOTR ILYITCH (1840–93). Savage gaiety and profound melancholy, varied rhythms and a delight in strong colour—all these national traits of the Russian people are represented in the music of the composer Tchaikovsky (pron. chĭ-kof'-ski).

The son of a mining engineer, he was born on May 7, 1840, in the iron-mining town of Votkinsk in the Ural Mountains. He was always an enchusiastic lover of music, and at 21 began serious study in the Conservatoire of music in St. Petersburg (Leningrad); in 1886 he became professor of harmony in the Moscow Conservatoire. He visited Britain as a conductor on several occasions.

Tchaikovsky's fame as a composer came late in life. His symphonies, particularly the Fifth and Sixth (the " Pathétique ") are very fine examples of symphonic music, and his ballet music, e.g. the Nutcracker Suite, The Swan Lake and The Sleeping Beauty, is popular.

His other compositions include the noisy 1812 Overture, the delicate Serenade for Strings, much chamber music, and the opera Eugene Onegin. Tchaikovsky died on November 6, 1893, only 10 days after the 6th Symphony had been acclaimed on its first performance.

Tchekhov, ANTON PAVLOVICH (1860– 1904). During the early years of the 20th century the plays of Tchekhov (pron. chek'-of) became popular on the English stage, in spite of the fact that they are the very reverse of the usual English conception of a theatrical " hit."

Tchekhov's plays rely neither on " stars " nor on stage effects: they have no exciting plots or thrilling climaxes. What they do portray, in marvellous fashion, is the reactions of one person to another under the influence of external events. Though it is often difficult for English people to sympathize with Tchekhov's characters, since the mind of the Russian is so different, yet so alive are they that even the most insignificant rôle is invested with a stirring and emotional human interest. Each of his plays is a complete and highly individual work of art. The best are The Three Sisters, The Seagull, Uncle Vanya, and The Cherry Orchard.

He also wrote a number of short stories, which influenced writers in almost all countries. Most deal with the tragedy of a sensitive mind brought into sharp contact with the hard realities of life.

Born on January 17, 1860, at Taganrog, in South Russia, Tchekhov was the son of a tradesman and the grandson of serfs. He entered Moscow University, and took his degree as a doctor of medicine in 1884, but his life was mainly devoted to literature. He died on July 2, 1904. Another common transliteration of his name into English is Chekhov.

TEA from PLANTATION to the CUP

Yielding the principal ingredient of one of the world's most popular drinks, the tea plant is cultivated in the Orient. Much labour is expended in the fields and after the picking of the leaves before the liquid is available.

Tea. The story of the discovery of tea is lost in Chinese legend, but it is sometimes attributed to the Emperor Shennung, about 2737 before Christ. It is certainly a commodity of very ancient usage, and may have been used in China for medicine as early as the 3rd or 4th century B.C. Tea-drinking was first introduced into England in the 16th century, but did not become popular until the middle of the 17th century, since the price of tea was at first as much as £3 a pound. Tea-caddies, in those early days, were locked cases in which the valuable commodity was kept. Towards the end of the 19th century tea-drinking became general among all classes in Great Britain, and in the 1890s tea-shops were becoming popular.

The tea of commerce is the dried and prepared leaf of several varieties of evergreen shrubs or small trees of the family *Theaceae*, chiefly *Camellia thea* ; to this family also belongs the Camellia

of our gardens. At the beginning of trading in tea, China held first place as a producing and exporting country. About 1840 British India began to export tea grown mainly from Chinese seeds, and because of improved methods of cultivation and preparation the growers of India became the largest producers in the world. Ceylon began to market tea in about 1876, and the industry is now the most important in the island. Java and Japan also produce a considerable amount. In the 1920s tea-growing became a prosperous industry in British Africa— Kenya, Tanganyika, Uganda and Nyasaland.

A plantation of Ceylon or of the countries of India and Pakistan may cover hundreds of acres, the low bushes, set in rows four feet apart each way, having such widespread branches that the hills are covered with grey-green foliage. In the wild state the plants often grow to 50 feet high, but under cultivation they are kept pruned to a

Empire Tea Marketing Expansion Bureau
PATIENT PICKERS IN A TEA FIELD
Unhurriedly, for the day is hot, skilled women workers gather leaves from the bushes, making careful selection. They are part of a team working under supervision on a big plantation.

height of from three to five feet. All the leaves are thus within easy reach of women and children who do most of the picking. The pruning also encourages the growth of leaves rather than wood.

The plant produces a profusion of scented white or pinkish blossoms, which somewhat resemble small wild roses, their petals (which are thick and waxy) encircling a cluster of yellow, hair-like stamens. The leaves are leathery and lancet-shaped, with saw-like edges ; those of the Chinese plant when full-grown are seldom more than three inches long, but those grown in the sub-continent of India, Ceylon, and Java may reach nine inches in length. In China layers of jasmine leaves are spread on top of the tea for a few hours during the process of manufacture. This gives the distinctive, somewhat smoky, flavour to China tea.

Plants are ready for the first picking when they are about three years old and are sending out an abundance of young leaf shoots. As new shoots grow from the broken tips another crop is gathered. In the tropical plantations of Ceylon, Formosa and the sub-continent of India they may be ready for picking every two or three weeks throughout the year, but in the colder parts of China and Japan there are only three pickings a year.

With big baskets or bags hanging from their heads or shoulders the pickers single out the tender young shoots and deftly break off the tops of these and toss them into their baskets. Using both hands experts can pluck 30,000 shoots a day ;

3,200 of them go to a pound of tea. Only the buds and the first few leaves are gathered ; for the finest teas, only the buds and the first two leaves. The younger and smaller the leaf, the more delicate and expensive is the tea.

The stimulating and refreshing qualities of tea come from the small percentage of caffeine (formerly called theine) which it contains. Caffeine or closely related substances are also found in coffee, cocoa, Paraguay tea or maté, and the kola nut. Chemically, caffeine is an alkaloid, which acts as a heart and brain stimulant and is dangerous when taken in considerable quantities. A small percentage of tannin gives tea its colour, and an essential oil adds its distinctive flavour. Japanese scientists claim to have found in tea some quantity of Vitamin C, a valuable food auxiliary.

Green tea and black tea are made from the leaves of the same plant by different processes of manufacture. The first step in curing black tea is withering, which takes place in large lofts of the factory. The leaves are spread out on racks exposed to the outside air, where they stay for about 24 hours, in which time they become quite soft.

The next step is rolling, which may be done either by hand or by machine. The purpose of rolling is so to twist and crush the leaves that their juices come to the surface. Then the leaves are ready for fermenting. The temperature in the fermenting room is much lower than in the rest of the factory; the air is moist, and sunlight is

Empire Tea Marketing Expansion Bureau

READY WITH THEIR BASKETS FOR A LONG DAY'S WORK

They are big baskets to fill with small leaves, but these nimble-fingered Indian women will work methodically and the task for the day will be accomplished. So that all parts of the bushes are within convenient reach they are kept pruned to a height of from three to five feet ; and in the sub-continent of India, in Ceylon and Formosa, the same bushes may be picked-over every two or three weeks throughout the year. The bushes are never stripped at one operation.

Empire Tea Marketing Expansion Bureau

One of the machines used for 'firing' tea is seen in the upper photograph. After the leaves have been fermented, during which process they turn a bright copper colour, they pass on moving trays through hot-air chambers, in which the temperature varies from 220 to 250 degrees Fahrenheit. This process of 'firing' extracts all the moisture, and the leaves become black. They are then ready for grading, the various qualities of tea being determined by the size of the leaf. The grading is done by a machine which shakes the leaves through screens of varying mesh. As shown in the lower photograph graded tea for export is weighed and packed in wooden tea-chests, which are lined with lead foil to protect the contents from sea air which would spoil the flavour.

excluded. The leaves are spread on the floor or on tables and remain there for four or five hours. By that time they have changed in colour to a golden brown, and give out a pleasant aroma somewhat like that of ripe apples.

After fermenting, the leaves go to the firing room, where hot air (220° to 250° Fahrenheit) passes through and over them for half an hour to prevent further fermentation. Eventually they are sorted and graded by a machine consisting of a series of sieves of varying mesh.

Green tea is not fermented, and comes mainly from Japan and China. It is steamed immediately after picking, to seal the pores of the leaf and prevent the sap fermenting. Next, it is lightly rolled and twisted, and then is fired. Modern machinery is rare in China, and in Japan its use is still limited, so green tea is usually rolled and twisted by hand, and fired in tall baskets or copper pans over a charcoal fire. It is sometimes described as "basket fired" or "pan fired" according to the method used. Oolong, a species of green tea, comes from the Chinese island of Formosa, and is only slightly fermented. The name Pekoe, given to various species, means "white down," and denotes the delicate tips of the young shoots.

The Chinese and Japanese prefer the lightly fermented teas, which produce a straw-coloured drink, and their most delicate varieties are rarely exported. The British usually prefer black teas, which make a dark, full-flavoured drink.

Brick or tablet tea, used extensively in Tibet, Mongolia and Russia, consists of small, broken leaves and dust pressed into hard, compact blocks. In Tibet another kind of brick tea is used, made of very coarse leaf and sometimes even containing twigs and stalks.

Different countries prepare tea differently. In Japan the dried leaves are reduced to a fine powder and water is then added to form a thin paste. Sometimes the liquid is strained, but frequently the Japanese drink powdered leaves and all. In that country the "tea ceremony" has long been an important ritual, connected with the Zen sect of Buddhism. It is partly a beauty-worship ritual, partly a way of entertaining guests. It often takes place in a special tea-house or tearoom, in accordance with the strict convention of old-time Japan.

Cream tea is the favourite form in Turkestan, Central Asia, very strong black tea being used.

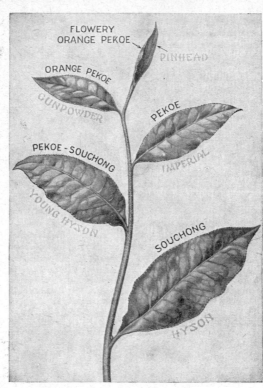

DIFFERENT KINDS OF TEA
Various teas get their trade names not from different kinds of tea plants but from the position of the leaves on the stem—the nearer the tip the better the grade. Names in bold type in this illustration are used for black teas, those printed lightly for green or China teas. Variations in quality may be due also to the character of the plants and the districts where they grow.

The leaves are boiled until the liquid is nearly black; cream is added; bread is then soaked in the liquid and eaten. The Persians boil the leaves in a pot until the water becomes blackish and very bitter, after which they add fennel, aniseed, cloves and sugar. The Russians seldom use milk but sometimes add a spoonful of jam or hold a lump of sugar in the mouth while drinking.

Tea is packed for export in boxes lined with lead or aluminium to protect it from the sea air, which spoils the flavour.

Teak. One of the most important timber trees of the world is teak; for general use in tropical countries its wood has no equal, and for some purposes in temperate climates it is preferred to all others. Because of its extreme durability it is largely used in building in shipbuilding and in the manufacture of furniture. In the sub-continent of India and Burma teak beams are said to have lasted more than a thousand years. The so-called white ants, or termites (q.v.), eat the outer sapwood but rarely attack the heart wood, and almost no other kind of timber is safe from their attacks. It is often used for laboratory benches for the strongest acid has little effect on it. Once seasoned, the timber does not split, crack, shrink, or alter its shape; yet it is not very hard, is easily worked and takes a fine polish. It has much elasticity and strength and it floats when seasoned.

The teak tree (*Tectona grandis*) is a native of the sub-continent of India, Burma, the Philippines, Java, and parts of the Malay Archipelago, and has been planted elsewhere in tropical Asia. Its cultivation is one of the largest and steadily growing industries of India and Pakistan, where the forests are conserved. The forestry department designate which trees are to be cut. They are then girdled (that is, a cut is made right through the bark and sapwood into the heartwood) and left standing to season for two years. Then they are cut, hauled out of the jungle by elephants, and floated down a river to the sawmill. (*See* illus., page 1142).

It is a large deciduous tree with a tall straight trunk and spreading crown. In 15 years it attains an average height of 60 feet. Specimens as high as 150 feet are known. The rough green oval leaves, which vary from one to three feet in length, yield a red dye, and are used in Burma for wrapping packages and for thatching the native huts.

During the rainy season teak trees can be picked out at a great distance by the whitish flower sprays which overtop the foliage, and during the dry season the feathery seed containers distinguish it from other trees.

Teasel. Native to Europe, western Asia and the Canary Islands, the teasel is represented in Britain by two wild species—the purple-flowered Common Teasel (*Dipsacus sylvestris*), whose stout spiny stems reach five to six feet in height, and the shorter and more slender, white-flowered Small Teasel (*D. pilosus*). Both are biennial (flowering in the second season, then dying), and the flower-heads are seen in August and September.

The taller species, with its prickly heads of flowers, is specially striking in appearance. Furthermore, the long and pointed stem-leaves are without stalks, and opposite ones are joined together by their bases so that each pair forms a " cup " in which dew and rain collect and into which insects attempting to climb the stems fall and are drowned. In due course their remains dissolve and are absorbed by the plant.

The Fuller's Teasel (*D. fullonum*), believed to be a cultivated variety of *D. sylvestris*, is so-called because the hooked scales of the flower-heads were used by the " fuller "—a worker who thickened and cleansed cloth with the aluminium silicate we still call " fuller's earth." The fuller used teasel heads to tease or comb wool ; the plant is cultivated today in Britain, but only for raising the nap on cloth. The dried flower heads are fixed on the rim of a wheel which is made to revolve against the surface of the cloth.

Teeth. These are bony outcrops from the jaws—weapons for defence and attack in many animals, from the dog to beasts of prey; and in many fish, such as sharks and whales. The poison fang of a snake is a specialized tooth, as is the tusk of an elephant.

In Man, teeth bite and grind food and also help in speech. Like most mammals he has two sets: a " milk " set in early life, followed by the permanent set. These are present as rudimentary structures in the embryo, so that the nature of the tooth-shaped substance is largely decided before birth. In Man the adult teeth consist of the following groups: four chisel-shaped *incisors* in either jaw, designed for cutting food. These occupy the middle position. They are flanked on either side by the *canine* teeth adapted for tearing. Running back are the *premolars* and *molars*, built for crushing, which make up 32. The child has no molars, and so only has 20 milk teeth, all told.

H. Bastin

PRICKLY TEASEL HEADS

Handsome plants are these teasels, up to six feet in height, with their conical, prickly, purple-coloured flower-heads at their best in August and September.

A tooth is made of four materials — ivory, enamel, cement and pulp. Ivory forms the greater part of the tooth; in the crown it is covered by a layer of *enamel*, the hardest substance in the body. In the fang under the gum is a layer of *cement* (tooth-bone). The *pulp*, in the inside of the structure, is most important to its life, containing as it does the cells for its renewal, the nerves, and blood-vessels. Few of us are left unaware that here, in fact, lies the sensitivity of the tooth.

Very great care should be taken of so precious a possession as our teeth. The beauty of a face depends necessarily on good teeth; and adequate biting and grinding surfaces are essential to smooth digestion and to health. Unlike the common hen or the lowly earthworm, Man has no gizzard in which to grind up his food; and food badly prepared in the mouth sets up many ills. Moreover, one type of tooth cannot really do the work of another; an incisor cannot grind, and a molar cannot cut. When a tooth is absent, therefore, the help of a dentist must be sought to replace it. Indeed, any gaps in a jaw should be filled, for teeth exercise themselves by rocking against their fellows

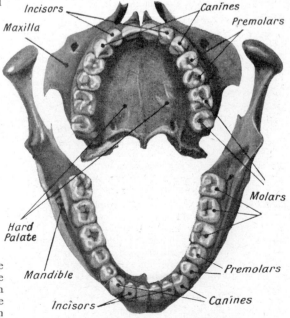

ARRANGEMENT OF THE TEETH

In the upper jaw, or maxilla, the third molars, or wisdom teeth, have not yet appeared. The lower molars are larger than those in the upper jaw, but the lower incisors are smaller.

in the opposing jaw; and want of this rocking always lessens their vitality.

Teeth should be carefully brushed several times daily after meals. This is especially important last thing at night, because at night food particles lodging in the interspaces are not disturbed as by day. As a result, these particles decay, and bacteria multiply and attack the enamel and the gums, causing unhealthy, painful tissue. Such decay, taken in hand early, can be stopped and the tender gum restored to firm health. Herein lies the necessity for a three-monthly visit to the dentist, a visit which loses its terrors if made as a routine.

The back molars, or "wisdom" teeth, "erupt" or come through between 20 and 30 years of age. Sometimes they do not erupt, but cause mechanical obstruction in the jaw and become infected. Any such un-erupted molars, shown by the X-ray, must always be removed (a painless procedure of modern dental methods), since the harm they can do, and the far-reaching upset they can cause, is

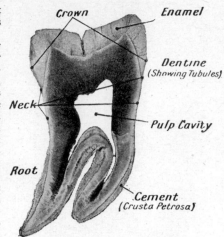

STRUCTURE OF A TOOTH

Below the crown of a tooth is a narrower portion called the neck, and underneath this are the roots or fangs. The framework of a tooth consists of a bony substance known as dentine ; around the roots is a kind of cement.

almost incredible. In a lesser degree, perhaps, the same is true of *all* decayed and infected teeth. They drain their toxic (poisoning) material back into the tonsils, spoiling the structure and function of these germ-stopping "filters"; they prevent infected mucous membranes lining the sinuses from becoming healthy. Even distant organs like the gall bladder harbour their poison. Modern dentistry removes such infected teeth and with them their septic sockets, to the well-being of the patient and the satisfaction of his doctor.

Like Man, all animals have two sets of teeth during their lifetime. The temporary teeth are smaller than the permanent and have a distinct neck between crown and root. Owing to the fact that in domestic animals the teeth appear at more or less fixed ages, it is possible to discover the approximate age of an animal by examining them. The teeth of the horse continue to grow throughout life. Cattle have no incisors in the upper jaw, their place being taken by a hard dental pad.

CODED SIGNALS *that* GIRDLE *the* EARTH

*Y*ou may type out a message on a keyboard in London, and simultaneously that message, letter by letter, will be printed by a similar machine in New York. This is the marvel of modern telegraphy.

Telegraphy. Swift communication over distances was for ages the goal of inventive minds. Beacon fires lighted on lofty hills sent a signal, but men had to arrange beforehand what this signal was to mean. Much later, windmill vanes were used to convey a coded message. Then the semaphore, with its movable arms, came into use; and the army signaller used two painted disks which he held with his hands and placed in different prearranged positions according to a code. But until Samuel Morse (*q.v.*) invented his simple and convenient code of dots and dashes, or longs and shorts, even the electric telegraph did not make very rapid progress, though it proved a boon in railway signalling from station to station.

Morse's code was applicable to aural and visual signals. You could watch the deflections of a needle, or listen to the beats of a sounder. Then Morse adapted his sounder mechanism to work a pen, and mark dots and dashes on a moving tape. Other inventors had used the chemical action of the electric current to imprint marks on a prepared paper tape, and there were various attempts to secure a record of a coded message. But Morse's basic principle had come to stay, and it set the pattern for many years. It proved cumbersome when men tried to render the entire process automatic, and to make a printing telegraph which would spell out a message in plain language.

The modern printing telegraph utilises a special code quite different from that of Morse, as you can read in this story. But the world's debt to Morse should be remembered none the less.

Oersted's work (*see* Electricity) demonstrated that a magnetised compass needle can be deflected by an electric current, either one way or the other, according to the direction of the current. If, then, we have a magnetised needle in one place, and a battery and a reversing switch in another, and we connect them up with two wires (or even with a single wire and an "earth" return) we can, by reversing the current, make the needle at the distant end deflect one way or the other. If we arrange a code of so many deflections each way to mean a certain letter, we are able to send messages by this means.

The first practical telegraph, constructed in 1837 by Cooke and Wheatstone between Euston and Chalk Farm (London) on this method, operated on slightly different principles, however. It had five needles and five connecting wires. The letters of the alphabet were arranged in diamond formation on a dial, and the reversing switches operated so that two of the needles pointed to the required letter, so that messages could be spelled out.

In the United States Samuel Morse was working on different lines, and he developed the Morse Code, a system of short and long impulses (or dots and

'TELEGRAPHING' MESSAGES THROUGH THE AGES

In early times signals were made by fire and smoke; later, disks, flags, mirrors, sirens and even the arms of windmills were used. These methods were rendered obsolete by the electric telegraph which, with wireless, can flash information across oceans and continents. People on land are able to talk to others on ships at sea or in distant aircraft.

THE MORSE ALPHABET

A ·—	H ····	O ———	U ··—
B —···	I ··	P ·——·	V ···—
C —·—·	J ·———	Q ——·—	W ·——
D —··	K —·—	R ·—·	X —··—
E ·	L ·—··	S ···	Y —·——
F ··—·	M ——	T —	Z ——··
G ——·	N —·		

Note.—On the needle instrument the dot of the above alphabet is represented by a beat to the left, and the dash by a beat to the right.

Numerals

1 ·————	4 ····—	7 ——···	0 —————
2 ··———	5 ·····	8 ———··	
3 ···——	6 —····	9 ————·	

Abbreviated Numerals

(For use only in the repetition of figures which immediately follows the signalling of the message).

1 ·—	4 ····—	7 ——·	0 ———
2 ··—	5 ·····	8 ——·	
3 ···—	6 —····	9 ——·	

Bar of division (/)	—··—·
Fractional bar (—)	———··
Signal to be used between whole numbers and fractions	—··—

Full Stop · — · — · —		* Underline · · — — · —	
Break signal (between the address and text, and between text and signature of sender, if any, and for fresh line),	· — · — ·	* Parenthesis ( )	— · — — · —
		* Inverted ""	· — · · — ·
		commas	
		Understand or completion of telegram	· · · — ·
Apostrophe (')	· — — — — ·	Rub out	— · · · · · · · ·
Hyphen (-)	— · · · · —	Go on	— · —
Interrogation (?)	· · — — · ·	Wait	· — · · ·
Exclamation (!)	— — · · — —	Acknowledgment	· — ·
		Clear of work	— · · —

Note.—The signals marked * are sent *before and after* words so treated, and are counted as one additional word.

Courtesy of Postmaster-General

SIGNALS OF THE MORSE CODE

Although it is not now used by the British Post Office inland telegraph service, having been superseded by the five-unit code (*see* illustration below, *and* text in facing page), Morse is still employed by small coastal stations when signalling to ships at sea.

dashes) which could be sent over a single wire. Morse used the " sounder " system, in which the current is not reversed but merely " keyed " or interrupted by a hand-operated " Morse Key." At the other end of the line an electro-magnet pulls down an iron " armature," which when released is pulled back again by a spring. As it moves up and down, it strikes against stops, giving a clicking sound which can be read by ear. If a pen is attached to the armature it can be made to bear on a moving paper tape, so that an actual record of the short and long impulses can be made. Morse code can also be adapted to the magnetic-needle type of instrument, a movement of the needle in one direction being called a dash, and in the other a dot.

Although both sounder and needle telegraphs were used for many years, it soon became obvious that they were by no means fast enough. A telegraph circuit, whether consisting of miles of underground cables, or miles of overhead wires, is a very expensive item. It can only be set up, and messages sent over it at a reasonable price, if it is made to work as hard as it can, carrying as many messages as possible in a given time. If, for example, a line from London to Manchester could carry only thirty words per minute (about the limit for a first-class operator) one of two things would happen. Either we should have to

lay extra lines—thus making telegraphs more expensive—or, in a single day, the offices at both London and Manchester would be so choked with telegrams awaiting their turn for the line that it would be quicker to send a letter by a man on horseback. Either a faster method than 30 w.p.m. must be found, or the line must be made to carry several messages at a time. In fact both these speeding-up devices are necessary.

We can shorten the actual sending time for a message, and thus get more messages on the line in a given time, by using automatic transmission. We can for example punch holes, corresponding to dots and dashes, in a paper tape, and draw this tape between two electrical contacts, so that they are separated by the insulating paper, and only touch where a hole occurs. By this method the speed at which we feed the dots and dashes into the line depends not upon the flexibility of the operator's wrist, but upon the speed at which we move the tape. If we use a Morse inker at the receiving end, the message will be written down faster than an operator could read it, and can be read later.

If, now, we put ten men at the transmitting end to punch message tapes, at 30 words per minute each, we can feed it to the line at 300 words per minute, and use ten men to decode it at the other end. We have increased the capacity of our line tenfold. Wheatstone Automatic Morse, based on these principles, has been very largely used, and speeds of up to 400 words per minute have been claimed for it.

But the speed of telegraphy cannot be increased indefinitely by making the machines run faster and faster. A telegraph line or cable has both inductance and capacity (*see* Electricity), and there is a limit to speed of response which can be obtained from it. It is no use feeding high-speed signals into one end of a line if they are to emerge at the receiving end blurred and unrecognizable.

Very few telegraph lines are short enough for the sounder or printer to be connected directly to them—the currents are too feeble, because of the resistance of the line. " Relays " are used to overcome this. A relay is a delicate electro-magnet which, in response to the feeble signal currents, closes very light contacts which are connected to the sounder or printer and to a " local " battery. Now, in effect, the relay " repeats " the feeble message, using the power of the local battery to do the heavy work. By utilising special balanced cir-

Letters	Figures	1	2	3	4	5	Letters	Figures	1	2	3	4	5
A	—	●	●				Q	1	●	●	●		●
B	?	●			●	●	R	4		●		●	
C	:		●	●	●		S	,	●		●		
D	Ans. back	●			●		T	5					●
E	3	●					U	7	●	●	●		
F	%	●		●	●		V	=		●	●	●	●
G	@		●		●	●	W	2	●	●			●
H	£			●		●	X	/	●		●	●	●
I	8		●	●			Y	6	●		●		●
J	Bell	●	●		●		Z	+	●				●
K	(	●	●	●	●		Letters		●	●	●	●	●
L	)		●			●	Figures		●	●		●	●
M	.			●	●	●	Space				●		
N	,			●	●		Carriage Return					●	
O	9				●	●	Line Feed			●			
P	0		●	●		●							

Fig. 1. The Five-Unit code which has largely replaced the Morse code.

uits in these relays, it is possible to send messages in both directions simultaneously without interference, each relay being sensitive only to the signals from the *other* end, and ignoring *its own* transmitter. This is known as "duplex" working; and by an extension of these principles it is possible to obtain "quadruplex" working.

The next move in speeding up is to get rid of the decoding of Morse code into plain language by human operators, and to use printing telegraphs which, in response to code impulses, produce not merely a record of dots and dashes but a message spelled out in ordinary characters. Many ingenious instruments have been devised for this purpose, and the most famous and widely-used up to recent times is the Baudot Multiplex. This, in addition to speedy transmission and direct printing of the message in ordinary characters, could be worked with up to six instruments operating on a single line.

It is almost impossible to design a printing telegraph to operate on Morse code, owing to the unequal lengths of its characters; i.e. "E" is only one dot, while "H" is four dots, and numeral "0" is five dashes long. In the "five-unit code" used by the Baudot machine (and by the modern teleprinter) each character is composed of five elements which are either "marks" or "spaces." For example, E is mark - space - space - space - space; Z is mark- space- space- space - mark . . . and so on (*see* Fig. 1). Since with five elements only thirty-two combinations are possible, the number is doubled by using a "shift" mechanism (like that employed for the letters and figures on a typewriter), and using a special signal to operate the shift mechanism from small letters to capitals, and of course back again.

Transmission on the Baudot system was by means of a tiny "piano" keyboard containing five keys, one for each element of the five-unit code. To send "E," for example, only No. 1 key was depressed; while for Z Nos. 1 and 5 would be chosen. Spaces were automatically sent for the keys which were not depressed. At the receiving end, five electro-magnets (one for each element) were either energised or not, according to whether a mark or a space had been received for their element. Thus these magnets operated a system of selector levers, and rotated a type-wheel to the correct position for the combination received, the type-wheel then marking a paper tape with the character selected.

At both transmitting and receiving ends was a rotary switch or "distributor" consisting of a number of contacts arranged in a circle, and continuously traversed by motor-driven brushes, so that each segment or contact was connected to the line once per revolution. Both switches were arranged to run in synchronism, so that at any given instant corresponding contacts were connected to the line. Each set of five contacts was connected to a

Baudot machine, so that, as the brushes traversed the five contacts of one machine, it "told it" which of the five keys were depressed at the other end of the telegraph line, and then passed on to the next set. Using 30 contacts, six machines could be operated over one line.

Since about 1928 multiplex systems have been dying out in favour of "voice-frequency telegraphy." This has nothing to do with the human voice, and the name is given to a system of transmission which uses alternating current at frequencies which we usually associate with the audible range (about 300–3,000 cycles per second). This frequency range is divided into eighteen "channels," of 420, 540, 660, etc., cycles per second; and each machine works on a different frequency, all being connected to one line through filters. A filter is a particular arrangement of inductance and capacity which will allow current to pass at one frequency, and shuts out those frequencies above or below (remember how you "tune" your wireless set to admit only the frequency of the station which you wish to hear). Thus 18 separate messages can be carried by one line, being "sorted out" at the receiving end, and passing to their correct instrument. The use of voice-frequency transmission, with the consequent tremendous increase in the number of simultaneous messages on one line, enables medium high speed transmitters to be used, and for this function the British Post Office uses the Teleprinter.

This remarkable machine requires no knowledge of any telegraphic code for its use, since it both transmits and receives in "plain language." Teleprinter communication is, in fact, rather like being able,

Courtesy of Postmaster-General

SPEEDING TELEGRAPHY
Electrically-operated, the teleprinter has greatly accelerated the transmission of telegraphic messages. This machine links the Central Telegraph Office, London, with Buckingham Palace.

by tapping the keys on your own typewriter, to type out messages on someone else's typewriter a long way away. There are two main models in use—one which prints on a sheet, line after line, returning the carriage and feeding the paper up after every line, like a typewriter. The other prints the message word after word, on a continuous paper tape which is afterwards cut into lengths and gummed on to a telegraph form. The reason for this method having been preferred by the General Post Office is that, if a word is sent wrongly (or "corrupt" as it is called), and repeated, it is easy to cut out the wrong word and produce a "clean" message.

The teleprinter uses the Baudot five-unit code, but operates on what is known as the "start-stop" principle. One of the chief troubles with the Baudot—or with any other synchronised system—is to keep the revolving brushes at each end of the line moving in exact synchronism. The start-stop system gets over this trouble by running the *receiving* distributor slightly faster than the transmitter, and by stopping it once every revolution. The starting and stopping is done by means of code impulses from the transmitter—a "space"

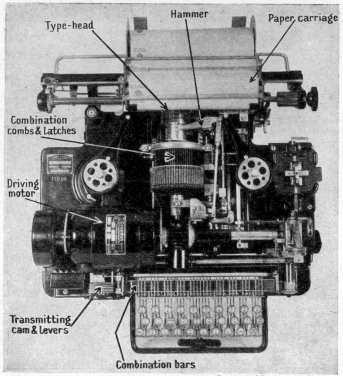

Type-head   Hammer   Paper carriage

Combination combs & Latches

Driving motor

Transmitting cam & Levers

Combination bars

Courtesy of Postmaster-General

MECHANISM OF A TELEPRINTER

A complex piece of machinery, this teleprinter is of the type used by the British Post Office. It transmits and receives messages in plain language.

for start, and a "mark" for stop, so that every letter requires not five, but seven signals. By this means, since the sending and receiving ends are "checked" at every letter, they cannot get badly out of step.

The action of a teleprinter is as follows. At the transmitting keyboard a key is pressed. Let us suppose that it is letter Y, whose five-unit code is mark-space-mark-space-mark (*see* Fig. 1 from which you will note that this coding also stands for the figure 6 in the alternative series of characters brought into use by pressing a shift key). A small electric motor, which is already running, rotates, by means of a ratchet-clutch, a drum-shaped portion known as the "transmitting cam sleeve"; this has six grooves running round it, in each of which rides the end of one of six levers which press on the sleeve. Each of the six grooves has a slot cut in it, so that, as the drum rotates, the end of the lever falls into the slot, and the lever falls. The slots are cut in different positions around the outside of the drum, so that, as the drum rotates, the levers fall one by one, rising again afterwards (Fig. 2).

The other ends of the levers move a pair of contacts to give either

"marking" or "spacing" impulses. When the levers are all in the up position, the contacts remain in the spacing position; but, as the drum revolves, the levers drop, one by one, into the marking position, unless they are held up by something else and prevented from doing so.

If the drum were revolved with all levers free, each would drop in turn, and five "marks" (the "case-shift" signal) would be sent. If, however, we hold the levers up in some other way, a "space" is sent for that particular element. The sixth lever, the start-stop one, is actually in its slot at the beginning of the revolution of the drum.

When the key for "Y" is depressed, the drum starts to revolve and the start-stop lever is raised, thus putting the contacts in the "space" position, and sending a space signal to start the receiver. The first of the five code element levers now drops into its slot, and sends a "mark." The second would follow it, but other levers (known as the "combination bars") which are part of the keyboard mechanism, restrain it, and a "space" is sent. The third lever is free to drop, and sends another "mark," the fourth is restrained ("space"), and the fifth drops ("mark"). The start-stop lever now drops again, sending another mark signal ("stop") and the cycle is complete. The ratchet-clutch is then released, and the drum stops revolving, until the next letter key is pressed. This repeats the cycle, according to the key which is pressed.

At the receiving end of the teleprinter line (Fig. 3) there is a revolving "type head," a wheel containing type bars which can slide forwards and strike the paper when tapped by a small type hammer. This wheel revolves so that any letter can be brought opposite the type hammer, and the problem is, of course, to stop the wheel when the correct letter is in position. To do this, the wheel

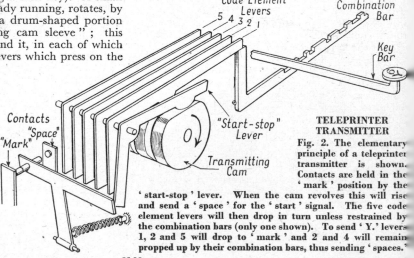

Code Element Levers
5 4 3 2 1

Combination Bar

Key Bar

Contacts
"Space"
"Mark"

"Start-stop" Lever

Transmitting Cam

TELEPRINTER TRANSMITTER

Fig. 2. The elementary principle of a teleprinter transmitter is shown. Contacts are held in the 'mark' position by the 'start-stop' lever. When the cam revolves this will rise and send a 'space' for the 'start' signal. The five code element levers will then drop in turn unless restrained by the combination bars (only one shown). To send 'Y,' levers 1, 3 and 5 will drop to 'mark' and 2 and 4 will remain propped up by their combination bars, thus sending 'spaces.'

TELECOMMUNICATION : WRITING AND SPEECH

H.M. Postmaster-General

High-speed automatic systems of transmission are in use today for the dispatch of messages by the British Post Office. The upper photograph, taken at the Birmingham Head Post Office, shows teleprinters in operation. The message is tapped out on a typewriter keyboard, and is received at the destination on a strip of paper which is pasted on to the telegraph form (bottom left) for delivery. Then it is not long before a motor-cyclist (right) has rushed it to its destination. To expedite delivery still further, especially in country districts, you can telephone a telegram to a post office and address it so that it can be telephoned from the receiving office to the recipient.

H.M. Postmaster-General

To enable telephone conversations to take place over the British Post Office system, the caller and the distant subscriber have to be 'connected' to form an electric circuit. To the central office switchboard each subscriber is linked by a pair of wires, terminating in a jack. In the case of a manual exchange, such as the one seen above, the circuit is completed by the operator inserting a pair of plugs joined by a flexible cord into the jacks of the respective subscribers. At the same time she presses a button, causing a bell to ring on the telephone of the person being called. If there is no reply, the operator will inform the person making the call to that effect and remove the plugs.

TOLL AND INTERNATIONAL EXCHANGES

H.M. Postmaster-General

'Toll' exchanges are in operation for telephone calls to the country districts surrounding the large cities; one is shown in the upper photograph. For longer distances 'trunk' calls must be made. The lower photograph is of a small section of the London International Telephone Exchange, which is a channel of communication to almost all countries. If a man on a liner in mid-Atlantic wishes to speak to a friend in Australia, a girl pushes home two plugs with connecting wires and the thing is done. With the help of this international exchange it is possible for a British telephone subscriber to speak to almost any one of millions of other subscribers in a number of countries.

UNCANNY MECHANISM OF THE 'DIAL' SYSTEM

H.M. Postmaster-General

Few of us realize how complex and ingenious is the mechanism we set in motion the moment we dial a telephone number. A prominent feature in a British automatic exchange is the vertical racks of ' selectors,' clearly seen in the upper photograph. These selectors, which automatically ' find ' the number required, are the heart of the marvellous system which connects the two subscribers, rings the distant subscriber's bell, registers the call, and, when the conversation has finished, returns the apparatus to normal. The lower photograph shows the intricate maze of wiring in the apparatus room, and, on the left, the control desk which is used by the supervising operator.

driven by an electric motor (through a clutch which will slip when the wheel is stopped), is fitted with a projection known as the "stop arm," which can catch against any one of a number of latches. These latches are arranged in a circle about the same size as the wheel itself, and there are sixty-two of them. They are normally held clear of the stop arm, but if any one of them is allowed to fall, it collides with the stop arm, thus arresting the type wheel in the correct position to print the character corresponding to that particular latch.

The latches are prevented from falling by a series of "combination combs" (Fig. 3). These are steel disks which have notches cut in their outer edge, so that they look a little like toothed gear-wheels. Five combs, each corresponding to an element of the five-unit code, are arranged in a row, inside the circle of latches. They are connected to the mechanism of the receiver so that each one can be rocked through a very small angle when a mark is received for its particular element of the signal. When a space is received, the particular comb does not rotate, but remains in what we will call the "space" position, to which they all return at the end of each letter.

The latches can fall only when the notches between the teeth of the combs are all in line, forming a continuous slot; and the teeth are ingeniously arranged so that only one slot is ever free for any given position of the combs. Each slot will allow two latches, side by side, to drop into it. In our imaginary transmission of the letter " Y " we sent mark-space-mark-space-mark. This means that combs 1, 3, 5 will move, and combs 2 and 4 will not. The teeth on the combs are now lined up so that the latches for either " Y " or " 6 " can fall. The final selection is done by a sixth comb, known as the " shift comb," which, being in the " letters " position, locks out " 6 " and allows " Y " latch to

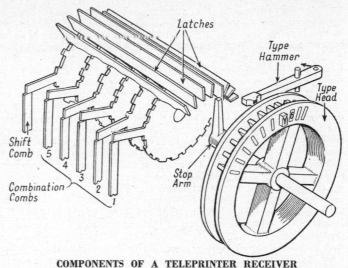

COMPONENTS OF A TELEPRINTER RECEIVER
Fig. 3. The working of a teleprinter receiver is shown. The combination combs, 1, 3 and 5 have rotated in response to ' mark ' signals, allowing a latch to fall which catches the stop arm attached to the revolving type head and halts it with the character ' Y ' under the type hammer.

fall, thus stopping the type head with " Y " in the printing position. The hammer strikes, prints the letter, and moves the paper on while the combs are rearranging themselves for the next letter.

All this takes place in a fraction of a second—in fact these uncanny machines will transmit as fast as one can work the keys. They are automatically prevented from jamming (i.e., running two signals together by striking another key too soon), since the depression of a key locks the keyboard, so that only one key can be depressed at a time.

In addition to the normal use of teleprinters by the Post Office for their own public services, it is possible to rent teleprinter service (known as " Telex ") for private firms to use over telephone lines, working with other firms similarly equipped. An ordinary telephone call is made, and then both subscribers switch to teleprinter, and continue with their "conversation" in typewriting.

TEACHING ELECTRICITY *to* TALK

When Alexander Graham Bell invented the first practicable telephone he gave us world-wide speech transmission and the germ from which in due course should develop modern broadcasting and all its wonderful offspring.

Telephone. The first time that electricity was used to transmit intelligible speech was on March 11, 1876, when Alexander Graham Bell, a naturalised American born in Edinburgh, called to his assistant in an adjoining room, " Mr. Watson! Come here, I want you!" Three days later he filed his application for a patent.

The principle established by Bell, of causing an electric current to vary in response to sound waves acting on a flexible diaphragm, and then causing this current to move a second diaphragm at the receiving end, thus reproducing the original sounds, is dealt with in this book under the headings Microphone and Sound Recording. Although

telephone apparatus has changed in detail and appearance, and telephone transmission and traffic principles have altered beyond recognition, the fundamentals of the telephone and the principles underlying them remain surprisingly little changed.

Both Bell and Watson were comparatively young men at the time of the great discovery and, unlike many pioneers, they lived to see their invention flourish. In January 1915 the historic sentence was repeated by Bell into a replica of his original instrument. This time, however, Watson, instead of running in from the next room, replied " It would take me a week, now, Mr. Bell." For Bell was in Boston, and Watson was in San Francisco, and the occasion was the opening of the first transcontinental telephone line.

Two hours after Dr. Bell filed his application for a patent in Washington, Elisha Gray, an American who had been working along similar lines, filed an application covering some of the same principles (*see* Bell, Alexander Graham). Since that time the telephone has been greatly improved, but most of these improvements are merely expansions of Bell's original idea.

In 1837 Charles G. Page, an American, had conceived the idea that electric current might carry sound, but he did not develop it. In 1860 Johann Philipp Reis, a German, actually constructed an electrical telephone, but did not follow up the work, owing to what seemed to him to be insurmountable obstacles. So it was left to Bell to produce the first telephone that really worked. It was exhibited at Philadelphia in 1876, and caused great excitement.

A public telephone service was first provided in England in 1879, with an exchange with eight subscribers. The number of subscribers and exchanges rapidly grew and now there are over 5,800 exchanges and over 4,000,000 telephones. Since 1912 practically the whole telephone system of the country has been conducted by the General Post Office.

Like other great inventions, the telephone was the product of many minds. Some inventors contributed ideas which other men developed; some followed unproductive by-paths which seemed to lead nowhere, but it is not unknown for an idea to remain "buried" and forgotten for half a century and then to serve a later inventor as foundation for an astounding new device. Something of the telephone's story is told under Microphone, and David Edward Hughes (1831-1900) was a notable pioneer whose principles are still utilised in the telephone transmitter.

Distance has always been the telephone engineer's biggest problem. Once a workable transmitter and receiver had been devised there was little difficulty in extending the range from a few yards to a few miles; but beyond this, the problem of "attenuation" begins to give trouble. Attenuation means, literally, "making thin" and this is a very good description of what actually happens on a long telephone line—the losses are so large that, beyond a certain distance, it is not possible to put enough power into the transmitting end to ensure that the few milliwatts (thousandths of a watt) necessary to operate the receiver will arrive at the distant end at all.

The problem was not solved satisfactorily until the arrival of the valve amplifier (*see* Electronic

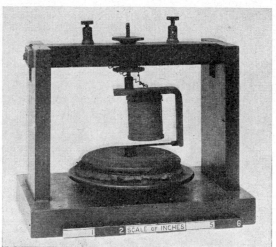

Science Museum, London
AN EARLY TELEPHONE
One of the earliest instruments with which speech transmission was obtained, this apparatus is very similar to the transmitter exhibited by Alexander Graham Bell in 1876. A battery of several cells was placed in the circuit.

Devices), after which it no longer presented any difficulty. "Repeater stations," consisting of valve amplifiers, are now inserted in the circuit every few miles to combat the attenuation of the line and to restore the signal to its full strength. By this means, speech can now be received over several thousand miles with the same loudness and quality as over a few hundred yards. It is not, however, possible to lump all the amplification in one spot. The repeaters must be distributed evenly along the length of the line, so that transatlantic telephony by submarine cable is not yet possible. The difficulty of designing an amplifier which can be buried at the bottom of the ocean and forgotten can be realized. Today we can, it is true, telephone to America; but that is done by inserting a "radio link"—i.e., by transmitting part of the way by wireless (*q.v.*).

For ordinary land-line telephony, both overhead wires and underground cables are used, although the tendency nowadays is more towards the use of cables; overhead lines are used for country areas where subscribers are thinly scattered, and the cost of cables would be prohibitive. Cables must be used in towns, of course—imagine what London's sky-line would be like if overhead wires were used for her hundreds of thousands of telephones! But a cable containing 542 "pairs" of wires is only a few inches in diameter. Cables used for main "trunk" lines have a further advantage in being free from troubles due to the weather; whereas overhead lines collapse under ice, and are blown down in storms.

If you have a telephone in your house you can talk almost immediately to any other telephone subscriber—from the grocer round the corner to your cousin in Australia—although the latter will cost you a great deal more. The methods used for the interconnexion of one telephone with another form one of the most interesting parts of telephone work.

Each subscriber's line leads directly to his local telephone exchange, which is situated as nearly as possible in the centre of the district which it serves. A large town or city will have more than one exchange—for flexibility, and to avoid excessive cable lengths. Let us for the moment consider a purely local call—one between two subscribers on the same exchange. Suppose that you are calling, for instance, a friend who lives a few streets away, whose number is 2368. (We will imagine that your number is 2237.)

If your exchange is of the "manual" type, your pair of telephone wires, after being sorted out on a "distribution frame," will be taken with other pairs to a switchboard, where they will end on one of hundreds of small sockets or jacks, which are arranged in numbered rows on the vertical surface of the switchboard where the operator sits. On the desk portion of the board are " ringing and speaking keys," and a number of plugs which fit into the jacks; these are connected together in pairs by flexible cords which are pulled out of sight, when not in use, by weights hanging under the desk.

When you lift your telephone from its hook or its rest, a switch bar, hitherto held down by the weight of the telephone, rises and completes a circuit, lighting a tiny lamp by " your " jack on the switchboard. The operator, seeing that No. 2237 wishes to make a call, chooses a disengaged pair of plugs; she inserts one of them into your jack, presses a speaking key which connects the telephone which she wears on her head into your circuit, and says " Number please." When you answer " 2368 " (the number of the subscriber you wish to call), she takes the other plug of the pair and inserts it into another jack, bearing this number. Your line is now connected with your friend's line. She then moves the key into the ringing position, and your friend's bell begins to ring. When he answers, she switches herself out of circuit, and proceeds to answer the next caller.

When you have finished your conversation, and both hang up your telephones, your indicator lamps (which were extinguished when the operator first answered you) light up again as a sign that the line can be " cleared." This is done by pulling out the plugs after the operator has pressed another key to register the call on a meter, so that you will be charged for it. If you make a call from a public box, you will, of course, have paid for your call beforehand.

Telephone switchboards are arranged in long rows, with an operator to each section. Each number appears in several sections (there will be several jacks marked " 2368 ") so that this number can be connected at any portion of the board. Otherwise, the operators would have to walk up and down the exchange, trailing long cords behind them. There is, then, a possibility that your friend may already be connected to someone else, through one of the other jacks. In that case, the operator, when she touches the edge of the jack with the plug, will hear a sharp click, known as the " busy " signal, and will inform you that the number is already engaged.

An automatic exchange is quite different in action from the manual exchange. Here, instead of rows of plug-boards with girl operators ceaselessly engaged in connecting subscribers, we find rack after rack of clicking

relays and " selector switches." The Strowger selector (named after one of the pioneers of automatic telephony) is the heart of the automatic telephone system, and Fig. 1 shows the principles upon which it operates. The selector shown has 100 contacts, arranged in semi-circular formation in ten levels. The wipers or contact arms are controlled by three magnets. One *raises* the wipers, step by step, as impulses are applied to the magnet; after which the second magnet *rotates* it around the row of contacts, advancing one contact for each impulse applied to the magnet. The third magnet is a " release," which disconnects the ratchet mechanisms of the other two, and allows the wiper to return to its normal position. The selectors now used by the British Post Office do not have a

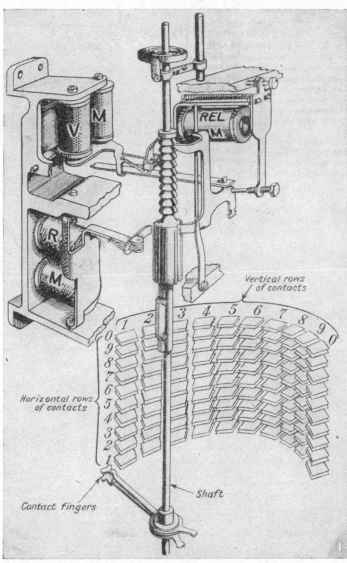

HOW THE AUTOMATIC ' SELECTOR ' WORKS

Fig. 1. When a subscriber ' dials ' a number he sends current through the electro-magnets V M and R M which move the shaft carrying the contact fingers first vertically and then horizontally, until they rest on the particular contact required. When the conversation is finished, the electro-magnet REL M releases the shaft and a coiled spring returns it to its original position.

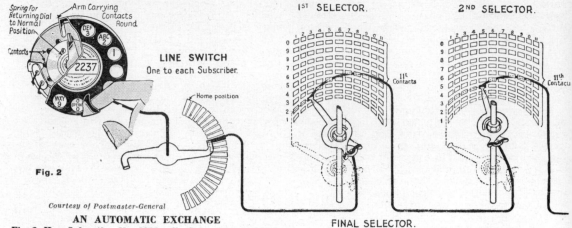

1ST SELECTOR.   2ND SELECTOR.

LINE SWITCH
One to each Subscriber.

Courtesy of Postmaster-General

AN AUTOMATIC EXCHANGE

Fig. 2. How Subscriber No. 2237 calls Subscriber No. 2368 on the same exchange without human help is shown in these diagrams. When the receiver is lifted the subscriber is automatically connected to a disengaged ' first selector.' The dialling of the first number (2) transmits two electric impulses, which raise the contact fingers to the second line of contacts, where they automatically sweep along until they find a disengaged contact connected with a ' second selector.' The figure ' 3 ' next being dialled, the fingers of the second selector find a contact in its third line and automatically make a connexion with a disengaged ' final selector.' There vertical and horizontal movements of the selector find the sixth line and the eighth contact in that line—the number required, 2368.

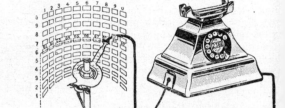

FINAL SELECTOR.

release magnet, but return to their normal position by completing their travel and dropping down at the end of the row.

To select number 68, for example, six impulses would be given to the vertical magnet, thus raising it to the " 60 level "; then eight impulses to the rotating magnet would revolve the wipers to the 8th contact on this level, thus giving contact 68.

The other chief apparatus of an automatic exchange are rotary switches which have contacts arranged in semi-circular banks like the selectors but have no vertical movement. The wipers (one set to each bank) are stepped round with a rotary motion only. Plain relays, opening and closing contacts when energised, are also largely used.

Now, let us see how these are applied to the working of a completely automatic system. We will take the same numbers as before—your number being 2237, and your friend's 2368.

When you lift your receiver, a rotary switch (called a line-switch) which is connected to your line rapidly steps itself round from one contact to another hunting for a disengaged " first selector." When it finds one, it stops and you are connected to it; until you have finished, no one can take it from you. At the same time the apparatus applies the dialling tone, a low-pitched burring sound, showing you that your line-switch has found you a selector, and that you can begin to dial the number you want. Putting your finger in a numbered hole, revolving the dial to the stop and then releasing it, causes the mechanism of the dial to send out that number of impulses. You dial 2..3.. 6......8.......

The first two impulses step up the first selector to level 2 (i.e., the 2000 group). The selector then automatically hunts along that level until it finds a disengaged " second selector " in the 2000 group. Your " 3 " impulses then step up this selector to the third level (i.e. the 300 group). The wipers of this selector automatically hunt along the row until they find a disengaged " final selector." You have now got as far as the 2300 group. The final selector gets the last two sets of impulses, the " 6 " stepping up the wipers to the 6th level (i.e., the 60 group), while the " 8 " impulses rotate them to No. 8 contact in that level.

You have now picked out your friend's number from 10,000 lines; and, if it is not already engaged, current is automatically applied to ring *his* bell while, at the same time, the " ringing tone " (a low-pitched burr-burr) is switched on to *your* line, to let you know that his bell is being rung. When you have finished your conversation and replace the receiver, all the selectors and line-switches are released, and return to their " homing positions " ready to take another call.

If, when you dialled his number, your friend was already engaged, the " busy " tone (a high-pitched interrupted buzz) would have been switched on to your line to warn you that he was engaged, and that you must try again later. Should you in error dial five figures (when the proper number has only four), or dial a number which is not in use or out of order, the same mechanisms will give you the " number unobtainable " tone (a high-pitched continuous note). In some rural districts a subscriber can dial the number of an exchange by using two figures in front of the subscriber's number with which he desires to get into touch.

So far we have only thought about making calls to numbers on the same exchange. If, as in the London area, there are many exchanges and we wish to dial from any one to any other, the problem becomes more complicated. If every exchange had trunk lines connecting it directly with every other exchange the problem would still be fairly simple—we could add more figures to the code to select the exchange first. If we put letters on the dial as well as figures, we could arrange a three-figure code for each exchange so that the figures (when read as letters on the dial) spelled the first three letters of the exchange name. Thus, if your friend's number, instead of being 2368 was " Central 2368," we can see from Fig. 2 that dialling CEN 2368 actually gives us " 236–2368 " of which 236 is the exchange code corresponding to CEN.

For reasons of first cost, and of operating efficiency, however, it is not possible to connect each exchange with every other one, and most are laid out for " tandem trunking," which means that to reach one exchange from another a call may have to go through several other exchanges. It is still possible to arrange automatic switching in each exchange to route the call through to the desired one; but *the same code cannot be used throughout the system.* This is easily understandable if you think of two extreme cases—one where the call is to an adjoining exchange; and one where it has to go through six others, where we should need at least six sets of " exchange code " figures (one for each exchange through which the call has to pass).

This Does the Thinking for You

We must have universal numbering, for it would not be practicable to expect a caller to remember that if he rings the same number from six different places he must dial six different exchange codes. So we call to our aid a remarkable device known as the " director." Clever telephone engineers have assembled the director from relays and selectors, and have almost endowed it with an intelligence — and have certainly given it a " memory." It takes upon itself the task of selecting the different codes which you could not remember, and does the thinking for you.

Let us suppose that you are calling your " CENtral 2368 " from a number on exchange " A " which must route the call (owing to the run of the cables) through " B," " C," and " D " exchanges. Immediately you begin to dial you are connected with a disengaging director which listens to the code you feed into it and " remembers " it. Then the director re-transmits not the code you fed into it, but the correct code for the route required. It first of all sends out a code number to cause a selector to switch it through to exchange " B." To " B " it gives another code number to connect it with exchange " C "; to " C " it gives yet a third code to route the call through to " D "; and to " D " it passes a fourth code to route it through to Central. Once it is through to Central it repeats the number unchanged, and this number is dealt with by the selector there in the ordinary manner.

Other codes are dealt with by the automatic mechanism in the same way. In the London area, O by itself will give you the attention of a human operator; TRU will give you Trunks, for long-distance calls; TOL gives you the Toll exchange for calls outside the London area, but not considered " trunk " calls; TEL gives you the Telegram service; ENG the Post Office Engineering Department; TIM the Speaking Clock, which tells you the exact time (*see* Photo-Electric Devices); and " 999 " gives an emergency call for police, ambulance, or fire services.

Carrier Telephony and the Scrambler

In our story of Telegraphy we explain about the method of cramming 16 messages on one cable by the use of different frequencies, each message being " sorted out " at the receiving end by the use of filters which allow certain frequency bands to pass through, and cut out others. The same principles are applied to telephony, except that the frequencies used are much higher. This is because, instead of having to carry impulses at telegraph speed, they have to carry currents at speech frequencies (*see* Sound). The process is, in fact, more like " wired wireless " if we may use such a contradiction in terms; each transmitter and receiver are " tuned " to the appropriate frequency, and a copper conductor is used instead of electro-magnetic waves in the transmission through space (*see* Wireless). By the use of co-axial cables (*see* Cables) it is possible to transmit 600 messages on one cable.

Although, with the use of high-frequency transmission, the " tapping " of a telephone line is no longer a simple matter of climbing a pole and connecting a telephone to the wires, it is not impossible for clever persons to tap lines and overhear conversations. But where there is an urgent need for absolute secrecy (as, for example, at operational headquarters in wartime) it is possible to make speech completely unintelligible to anyone who listens in. This is done by a device called a " scrambler," which consists of two elaborate sets of filters and transformers, one for each end of the line. These are devised so that certain frequencies of the voice are " coded "— i.e., a different frequency is actually transmitted— and are then " decoded " at the other end, the original frequency being there reproduced.

By this means, although the persons actually using the two instruments can hear intelligible speech, anyone listening on the line would hear only an incomprehensible jumble of sounds. An extension of this idea of " coding " speech frequencies, called the Vocoder (short for " voice coder "), has been invented, based on the idea that to make speech intelligible, it is not necessary to transmit all the frequencies produced by the voice; and that the information could be divided into " packets " and be coded. This greatly reduces the band of frequencies required for each conversation, and enables more conversations to be transmitted over a line. Its chief disadvantage is that the actual inflections of the voice are lost, and the speech sounds inhuman or mechanical. It is probable, however, that some arrangement of this sort will be used for more economical working of very long-distance lines.

COLLECTING LIGHT *from* REMOTE SPACE

Without the telescope to gather in more light from distant stars than our unaided eyes can receive, we might know little more of the awe-inspiring wonders of the universe than did the astronomers of ancient Egypt.

Telescope. When the Italian astronomer Galileo, with the aid of the telescope which he had constructed (1609), scanned the heavens for the first time it was "an adventure comparable to a voyage across an unknown sea, and the discoveries made with it were as marvellous as the new lands which Columbus and his followers found by sailing westwards from Europe." Within a short time Galileo (*q.v.*) discovered with his telescope four of the moons which circle about Jupiter, the rings of Saturn, mountains and plains on the moon, spots on the sun, and the rotation of that mighty body on its axis.

The telescope comprises essentially (1) a convex lens (the "objective") or a concave mirror (the reflector or "speculum") set in one end of a tube to focus the light from a distant object, producing a bright image; and (2) a lens called the "eyepiece," to magnify this image and bring it to the eye. If the telescope has a convex lens (objective) it is a "refracting" telescope; if it has a speculum it is a "reflecting" telescope. The refracting telescope is the older type. (*See* Lens; Mirror).

Although Roger Bacon (*q.v.*) had sound ideas about the theory of the telescope, and although some few people before the early years of the 17th century may have used such an instrument for magical or other similar purposes, the credit of the invention of the first practical astronomical telescope is now generally given to Hans Lippershey, a Dutch spectacle-maker, who constructed one about the year 1608.

It was not until after Lippershey's success that Galileo made his first telescope, although, because of the great improvements that it received under his hands, and the wonderful discoveries that he made with it, the

refracting telescope came to be known as the Galilean, and he is sometimes regarded as the inventor.

When the telescope is pointed at a star, the light rays entering the telescope are practically parallel. They thus form an image at the focal point of the objective and it is then magnified by the eyepiece, which is really nothing more than a simple magnifying glass. The large cylinder of rays which enters through the objective is condensed to a smaller pencil by the time it emerges from the eyepiece. Consequently, many more rays of light enter the eye than would enter without the telescope, and this greatly increases the apparent brightness of the star.

Early refracting telescopes were subject to two serious drawbacks. The images they produced were distorted: first, because the rays passing through the margin of the lens were brought to a focus before the others (spherical aberration); and, second, because the blue rays were brought to a focus before the red (chromatic aberration).

It was almost 150 years before an English optician discovered that these defects could be overcome by making the objective of *two* pieces of glass, the outer piece convex and made of crown glass, the inner concave and made of flint glass.

Meanwhile the reflecting telescope, invented in 1666–69 by Sir Isaac Newton (*q.v.*), had come into use. In the Newtonian reflecting telescope the light passes along the entire length of the tube to a curved mirror, called the "speculum," which reflects the rays back in the shape of a cone to a prism or a diagonal reflector. The prism diverts the rays at right angles to an eyepiece at the side of the tube. Such a telescope is free from chromatic aberration, but the position of the eyepiece makes it awkward to use. In another form of reflecting telescope, the Cassegrainian, the cone of rays reflected from the speculum is intercepted by another curved mirror placed near the upper end, and is reflected back through a hole in the centre of the speculum to the eyepiece. Both reflecting and refracting telescopes are used in astronomical observatories. The advantages of the reflector are its cheapness and its perfect "achromatism" (lack of chromatic aberration); while the main advantage of a refractor is its permanence and freedom from trouble after once it has been well adjusted. The largest of all telescopes are

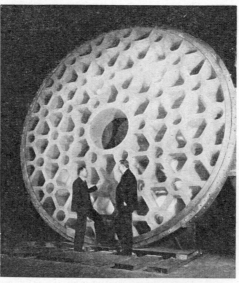

'EYE' OF THE TELESCOPE
The telescope mirror disk made for the 200-inch telescope on Mount Palomar, California, weighs 20 tons. Of hardened glass, it was cast in one piece and honeycombed at the back (above) to save weight.

The Astronomer Royal, Sir H. Spencer Jones, at the guiding eyepiece of the 26-inch refracting telescope of the Royal Observatory.

THE GIANT EYE OF MOUNT PALOMAR

Press Association

Under the mammoth dome of the observatory on Mount Palomar near San Diego, California, in the United States, the world's largest telescope is shown here as it was being assembled in 1945. Its mirror, 200 inches in diameter, is twice the size of the Mount Wilson mirror, which was previously the largest. The towering structure of steel, supporting the mirror, weighs about 140 tons. The total weight of the moving parts is 450 tons, yet a 1/12 horse-power motor is sufficient to keep it in motion. Its range is 300 million light years. *See also* illustration in opposite page.

reflectors. Metallic mirrors are no longer used, because when they tarnish they must be polished by a skilled optician. Glass mirrors can be ground and polished once for all, and then covered with a thin renewable film of silver or aluminium.

The magnifying power of a telescope is expressed in diameters. The focal length (*see* Lens) of the objective or speculum, divided by the focal length of the eyepiece, gives the magnifying power, and every telescope has eyepieces giving various powers. Why not use always the highest power possible? Because imperfections are magnified with the image, and the image loses in brilliancy as it gains in size. Consequently, a faint object can only be magnified up to a certain degree, because further magnification would make it too dim to be seen well. The Yerkes 40-inch refractor, for example, can be used advantageously to give 1,000 diameters, and still higher powers are possible.

The most important part of a telescope is "the man at the small end." Next in importance is the objective lens or the mirror, which must be made with the greatest possible precision. The surface must be accurate to a fifty-thousandth part of an inch; and months or even years of labour are often required to cast and polish a single objective. So sensitive to changes of temperature is the great 10,000-lb. 100-inch mirror at Mount Wilson, California, U.S.A. (*see* illustration in page 2412), that it is kept in a water-jacket in the daytime, and the dome is insulated to keep out the heat. The mounting and controlling mechanisms of telescopes are also marvels of human ingenuity (*see* Observatory). Many modern telescopes are so constructed that they take direct photographs at the focus. Thus

A TOWER TELESCOPE

Among the auxiliary buildings of the Mount Wilson Observatory, California, are two tower telescopes, the one shown above being 150 feet high. At the top of the structure is a special mirror which reflects the sun's image down the tube.

the photographs can be examined at leisure afterwards with a microscope.

In all astronomical telescopes the image seen at the eyepiece is inverted. In other telescopes an additional lens or system of lenses has to be introduced to re-invert the image. The opera glass is a pair of small Galilean telescopes which are fitted with concave lenses for eyepieces.

The most efficient and modern instrument of this type, called the prism field-glass or " binocular," has two reflecting prisms in each tube. This gives it as much magnifying power as could be obtained with an ordinary field-glass three times as long, besides permitting the use of a better type of eyepiece, which gives the observer a much larger field of view with superior definition.

Telescopes of various kinds are incorporated in a large number of instruments, such as surveyors' levels and theodolites, range finders, telescopic rifle sights, and even in delicate precision laboratory balances, where all readings and manipulation must be made from a distance to avoid disturbances due to heat radiated by the worker's body.

While the Hooker reflector at Mount Wilson was for a long while the largest telescope of any kind, it is now surpassed in size by a 200-inch giant reflector erected in 1948 at Mount Palomar for the California Institute of Technology. This mirror is mounted in a tube more than 20 feet in diameter, and is 16 feet 8 inches wide and weighs about 20 tons. The total weight of the telescope and mounting amounts to over 450 tons. Nevertheless, it is so perfectly balanced that it can be driven to follow the stars with only a 1-12 horse-power motor. Some idea of the vast size of the glass disk forming the mirror can be gained from the fact that the

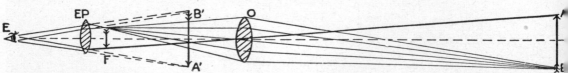

HOW THE ASTRONOMICAL TELESCOPE WORKS

Let us suppose we are viewing the moon or one of the planets, represented by the arrow (AB). The object glass (O) brings the image AB to an inverted focus at F, where it is viewed by the enlarging eyepiece (EP), which presents it to the eye (E) as though it were a large near object (B'A'). The radiating lines from B indicate how light rays are focused by the object glass. Viewed with the naked eye, comparatively few of the rays from B would be seen, but with the lens (O) in the way, virtually all the light from B which strikes the surface of that lens is brought together again at the upper end of F. Similarly rays from A are brought to F. The larger the lens, of course, the more light it collects.

central hole, 40 inches across, left to allow the light to reach the Cassegrain focus, would just accommodate the biggest lens in the world.

The grinding and polishing, or "figuring," of such mirrors imposes a terrific strain on the workers. It is not unusual, in figuring a large mirror, to polish for three minutes, and then wait for an hour while the glass cools from the heat given it by the delicate polishing operation. Much more time is spent in cooling and testing such surfaces than is devoted to the actual operation of polishing.

The largest telescopes must be of the reflecting type, since the practical limit of casting a large refractor seems to have been reached in the 40-inch lens of the Yerkes telescope in the observatory of the University of Chicago, U.S.A. These lenses are made of several pieces of glass, of different refractive indices, and their weight mounts enormously when their size is increased. Apart from the great difficulty experienced in grinding and polishing large lenses of this type, their own weight would cause serious distortion when they were mounted, so that they would be useless.

The 200-inch telescope can penetrate twice as far into space as the 100-inch instrument, and permits the exploration of a sphere having 8 times the volume of that previously known to astronomers. It is expected that photographs taken with it will enable the structure and composition of the nearer stars to be studied in much more detail than has hitherto been possible. Perhaps more important, though, is the fact that it will also be used to explore the farthermost recesses of the universe; it may tell us whether the universe is expanding or not, and perhaps even whether space itself is bounded or, as some scientists suppose, is infinite in extent.

Paul Popper

IN LONDON'S OBSERVATORY

Here are two photographs of the telescope in the London University observatory at Mill Hill, London. In the foreground of the upper picture are the counterweights which balance the instrument so delicately that it responds to the slightest adjustment. In the lower photograph the telescope is seen in position for observation, with the floor lowered to a more convenient level.

Television. The chief difference between the wireless transmission of a picture and the transmission of speech or music is that the ear hears a piece of music *as it happens*—a note at a time—whereas the eye sees a picture *all at once*. If we could break a picture down into small elements, like the notes of a piece of music, and " play " it back to the eye, note by note, the actual details of transmission would be on the lines of ordinary wireless, with the carrier wave (*see* Wireless) " modulated " by the tones in light and shade of the picture instead of by the notes of the music.

This in fact is what we do in television. The eye has a quality known as " persistence of vision." If we show it a picture for a fraction of a second, and rapidly take the picture away, the eye will continue to " see " it for another 1/25 of a second after. We make use of this principle in the cinema, and we can do the same with television. If we can " play all the notes " of our picture to the eye inside 1/25 second, the eye will not distinguish the separate " notes," but will see the complete picture ; if, then, we show it a new picture every 1/25 second, we can televise events which are actually happening.

To transmit a picture, then, we cut it into a number of thin slices or lines, and each line is " scanned " in succession. A stream of signals is sent out by wireless, telling whether each little spot scanned along the length of the line is black, white, or an intermediate grey. At the receiving end, we build up the slices again, reproducing each in rapidly varying tones of black, white or grey as the transmitter tells us.

In actual practice, the method is a little more complicated than just a series of simple slices. The Marconi-E.M.I. system, as used by the British Broadcasting Corporation, employs 405 lines to scan a picture, and first scans lines 1, 3, 5, and so on, up to 202½ lines. Then it flies back again to the top of the picture and fills in lines 2, 4, 6, and so on, thus forming a pair of " interlacing frames." The complete pattern is known as a " raster " (*see* Fig. 1). The complete raster is repeated 25 times per second, so that the total speed of scanning is more than 10,000 lines per second—not counting the " fly-back " portion as the scanning beam returns from the end of one line to the beginning of the next. There are no mechanical devices which will travel at this great speed; a stream of electrons is the only method which we can use for scanning in this manner.

In our story of Electronic Devices we describe the cathode ray tube, in which an " electron gun " shoots out a high-speed beam of electrons which can be deflected or bent in any direction, like a pointer, by deflector coils or plates. In the television

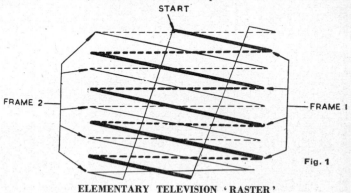

ELEMENTARY TELEVISION 'RASTER'

Fig. 1. From the 'start' point the moving spot of light moves from left to right and traces out the 'odd' lines making up Frame 1 (heavy lines). It then flies upwards and fills in the 'even' lines of Frame 2 (light lines).

camera there is a device known as the Emitron, of which an elementary diagram is shown in Fig. 2. The scene to be televised is focused by the camera lens on to a " mosaic screen " made up of a thin sheet of mica coated with silver on one side, and having on the other side thousands of little tiny " islands " or elements which are photo-sensitive (*see* Photo-Electric Devices). We can regard the mosaic as being made up of thousands of tiny photo-electric cells, which behave at the same time as thousands of tiny condensers, holding electric charges. (*See* Electricity).

As the picture is focused on the mosaic, each tiny cell takes up a charge of electricity corresponding to the amount of light which falls on it. The electron beam from the " gun " then moves rapidly backwards and forwards, scanning the picture in the appropriate pattern or raster, and discharges the cells. This results in a continuous variation in the current flowing, which is fed to an amplifier, and caused to modulate the wireless wave sent out. The variation is something like that represented in Fig. 3, where a high current indicates " white," and a low current stands for " black." Intermediate currents represent greys of various intensities; and zero current is a " synchronising pulse " to warn the receiver that the transmitter has finished scanning the line, and is about to fly back and start another. Unless we have had perfect synchronism between

PRINCIPLE OF THE EMITRON

Fig. 2. Light rays from the camera lens are focused on the 'mosaic,' which is continually 'scanned' by the moving beam of electrons from the cathode of the electron gun.

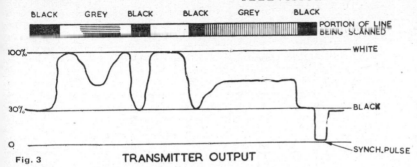

BLACK   GREY   BLACK   BLACK   GREY   BLACK

PORTION OF LINE BEING SCANNED

100%   WHITE

30%   BLACK

O   SYNCH. PULSE

Fig. 3   TRANSMITTER OUTPUT

HOW THE TELEVISION SIGNAL IS SENT OUT

Fig. 3. Above is shown how the transmitter output (determining the strength of the wireless wave) varies with the blacks and whites of the picture as seen by the Emitron at any one instant. Black is represented by about one-third (30 per cent) of output strength, white by 100 per cent. Various tones of grey are represented by strengths in between 30 and 100 per cent of the output current. Zero current represents a 'synchronising pulse' to inform the receiver that the transmitter has finished the line.

ray tube. In the story of Radar we learn how these signals can be used to present a map of the echoes received; and we apply similar principles here, but the tube must have no "afterglow" and the bright spot "painted" by the electron beam must go out instantaneously. Our "time base," too, is arranged not to move the beam round and round from the centre, but to deflect it backwards and forwards to follow the raster pattern which the transmitter is using.

Each time the beam sweeps across the tube to trace a line of the picture its intensity is varied in accordance with the incoming signal, so that it causes the tube to glow brightly for a white spot, not-so-brightly for a grey spot, and not at all for a black spot. The beam also registers black (i.e.,

the transmitter and the receiver we should not get a picture, but a mere jumble of blacks and whites.

At the receiving end, our aerial picks up the wireless signal and, after suitably amplifying it, passes the signal to the electron gun of a cathode

Dominion Press

TELEVISION IN ACTION IN THE STUDIO

A general view of a rehearsal for a television broadcast, from a studio at a Radiolympia exhibition, London, is seen here. The cameras on their 'dollies' are both focused on the man behind the bar—in the background can be seen the 'sound' man, with his microphone on a long balanced microphone boom which can follow the player yet be kept out of camera range. The director in a glassed-in control room above can see the output from each camera, on a 'monitor screen,' and can select (from these versions at different viewpoints) which one he considers best to put on the air no glow at all) for each time it flies back to begin another line or another frame. It thus traces out, line by line, the picture seen by the camera lens. Although there is really at any given instant only one tiny spot of light on the screen of the television receiver, this spot moves so rapidly that the eye is convinced that it is seeing the whole picture at once. The "sound" portion of the programme is simple wireless transmission, sent out on a slightly different wavelength so that it does not interfere with the picture transmission.

Since the range of frequencies used for picture transmission is very much larger than that for simple sound broadcasting, this means that a very high frequency wireless wave is required, which in turn means that it must be one of a very short wavelength. Such very short wireless waves travel in almost "line-of-sight" paths, so that the range is very limited, and it is not possible to cover the whole of England by even two or three stations. In the original British television service only one station was put in operation (at Alexandra Palace in North London), so that normal reception was limited to a region of about thirty miles or so around London. In the U.S.A. it is proposed to relay television by means of aeroplanes flying at heights very much greater than that at which any aerial tower could be built, so covering very much larger areas.

Normal television is in black and white (or rather, the colour of the tube glow, a faint, light blue). Experimentally, television has been carried out in colour by the use of the same principles as employed in three-colour printing or in natural-colour photography. This involves the presenta-

tion of three images, in red, blue and green. It is done either by combining the separate images from three cathode ray tubes, or by the use of a colour wheel carrying red, blue and green filters travelling rapidly across a single tube which presents the three images in turn, leaving the eye to combine them. Either system is at present too complicated and expensive to be adopted commercially, but there is every probability that colour television will come eventually into general use.

Early Work in Television

Television became practicable only when the two electronic devices we call the photo-electric cell and the thermionic valve had been invented and improved (*see* Photo-electric Devices). The idea of utilising the persistence of vision was exploited by early experimenters with motion pictures, long before the days of the cinema. Paul Nipkow, a German, seems to have introduced the idea of scanning a picture and thus breaking it up into many tiny elements of light and darkness, or graduations of brightness. His scanner was a disk having a row of holes in a spiral about its periphery. It was set in front of a selenium cell, and the light reflected from the illuminated picture to be scanned passed through the holes in the disk and reached the selenium cell (which was the only practicable photo-electric cell of those days of the 1880s).

John Logie Baird (1885–1946), a Scotsman, worked at a system of television and gave successful demonstrations from 1926 onwards. He used a mechanical scanning device not unlike Nipkow's disk, but had the enormous advantage of a thermionic valve (*q.v.*) to amplify the current variations, and was able to use improved photo-cells. The British Broadcasting Corporation supported Baird's system, and gave facilities for transmissions from their London station.

As explained earlier in our story, mechanical scanning is far too slow to enable fine results, and the pictures produced were coarse in texture. After about 1925 inventors were getting better results by employing a form of cathode ray tube to generate an electron stream, and using this stream to scan the picture. One of the leading men in this field was Vladimir Zworykin (b. 1889). The new scanning methods superseded Baird's original system; though this inventor adopted electronic scanning, competitors were more speedy in bringing the process to a commercial stage. So it was that when Baird died, in 1946, his invaluable work had been lost sight of by many, though due honour was paid to him by the few who realized the debt that the new art owed to him.

British Broadcasting Corporation
TELEVISION CAMERA IN ACTION
To get pleasing results the television cameras must be able to move swiftly and silently. The 'dolly' shown enables the camera, complete with its operator, to be trained, raised and lowered exactly as required. Headphones are worn by the entire crew of a television studio, thus enabling the director from his control room to convey instructions instantly without making any sound which would interfere with the broadcast.

Telford, THOMAS (1757–1834). A herd lad who was born in Dumfriesshire, Scotland, on August 9, 1757, and turned journeyman mason at eighteenpence a day, lived to build the Caledonian Canal between Moray Firth and Loch Linnhe in Scotland. He also made locks and aqueducts, and roads like the Carlisle–Glasgow and Shrewsbury–Holyhead. Even so the tale of his achievements is not told, for he constructed harbour works, the Menai Suspension Bridge between Anglesey and Caernarvonshire in Wales, and the St. Katherine Docks in London. Yet success did not turn his head, and so genial was Thomas Telford, who carried out these great projects and many more, that a new landlord of the London coffee-house which he frequented confessed to having paid a premium of £750 to the owner because Telford attracted so many customers.

The son of a poor shepherd, " Laughing Tam," as he was called by his early associates, could not attend school regularly because he had to help to keep the humble little home going. But, having learned to read, he borrowed books and learned to love what he read, and whatever he did he did supremely well, which was one of the secrets of his genius. How he started as a master builder is not known; it was in 1784 that he obtained his first commission—to superintend the building of a house for the commissioner of Portsmouth Dockyard. Telford helped to found, and was the first President of, the Institute of Civil Engineers. He died on September 2, 1834, and was buried in London's Westminster Abbey.

Tell, WILLIAM.
According to legend, the Swiss village of Altdorf was ruled early in the 14th century by a tyrannical Governor named Gessler. One day Gessler erected a pole upon which he placed a hat to represent the Duke of Austria, the ruler of the country, and he ordered that everyone who passed the pole must pay homage to the hat. One of the villagers, a skilled crossbowman named William Tell, refused to salute the hat, and was arrested and taken before the Governor.

Gessler heard the charge against Tell and said, " I am told you can shoot an apple from a twig at 100 paces, and I want to see you do it. We will place the apple on your son's head, and you shall shoot at that mark, or you and the boy shall both die ! " The boy was bound to a tree, and Tell took an arrow from his quiver, examined it carefully and slipped it under his belt. Then he fitted another to his crossbow. The shaft sped through the air and pierced the apple. " A good shot ! " exclaimed Gessler. " But for what was the other arrow ? " " To slay you, tyrant, had I killed my son ! " was the reply.

In a rage, Gessler commanded his soldiers to seize and bind Tell and take him to prison on the other side of the lake. A storm arose and Tell escaped, and soon after he shot and killed Gessler from an ambush. The story was long accepted as historically true, but it is now known to be a legend. It was probably written about 1470.

Tellurium.
Although one of the rarer elements, tellurium occurs widely in the free state, and combined with gold, silver, copper, lead and other metals in ores. In the late 18th century ores containing tellurium were suspected to contain a new metal. Fifty years later Berzelius showed it resembled sulphur and selenium. These conclusions were both right. Tellurium belongs to the oxygen, sulphur and selenium group in the Periodic Table (*see* page 768) and its chemical properties are those of a non-metal ; but it also shows metallic properties. In its crystalline form it is silvery-white and in appearance just like a metal.

The chemical symbol of tellurium is Te, its atomic weight is 127·6 and its atomic number 52. The crystalline form has a relative density of 6·25, and the amorphous variety one of 5·85. It melts at 453° C., and the liquid boils at 1,400° C. Tellurium is obtained in the sludges from the electrolytic refining of copper and lead ores, and in the flue dusts from the smelting of tellurium gold ores. The compounds of tellurium are evil-smelling, and are unpleasant substances to handle.

Tellurium has not many uses. It was at first used in crystals in wireless sets; and a tellurium compound was one of the first anti-knock agents used in petrol (*see* Petrol). A very small amount of tellurium, one part in a thousand, added to lead greatly increases the strength of the latter. Tellurium is coming into use in the rubber industry and is also employed in photography.

Tempest, THE.
On an island in the Mediterranean Sea, according to this romantic play by Shakespeare, lives an exiled Duke of Milan, by name Prospero, with no companions save his lovely daughter Miranda, and his books of philosophy and magic. By the magic power which he possesses he brings into his service an ugly, half-human creature called Caliban, and the fairy spirit Ariel.

One day Prospero discerns a ship blown towards the island, and, knowing by his magic that the King and the Prince of Naples, as well as his false brother, who had usurped his dukedom, are on board, he sends Ariel to wash them into the sea and land them safely on widely-separated parts of the island.

It is Prospero's hope to bring about a marriage between Miranda and the young Prince of Naples. To his great joy not only do the pair fall in love, but the King himself is delighted and restores the dukedom to Prospero. At the end of the play Prospero breaks his wand, and sets free Ariel, who is sometimes held to represent imagination. Some people think that Prospero expressed the feelings of Shakespeare who, with this play (written in 1610–11), laid down his pen for ever.

Tennessee.
An inland State of the United States, Tennessee extends 448 miles eastward from the Mississippi river to the Appalachian Mountains and has an area of 42,246 square miles. It is bounded on the north by Kentucky and Virginia, on the east by North Carolina, on the south by Georgia, Alabama and Mississippi, on the west by Arkansas and Missouri.

On the eastern border are the Great Smoky Mountains—part of the Appalachian system—the highest point being Clingman's Dome (6,643 feet), but most of the State is undulating country. The chief rivers are the Mississippi, Tennessee and Cumberland. In the Tennessee valley are the works of the Tennessee Valley Authority, an organization established in 1933 to develop this area. Dams have been constructed on the Tennessee, and power-houses built to provide electric light and power over a wide area. Factories also were erected for the production of fertilizers and aluminium.

Tennessee is essentially an agricultural State; the staple crops are maize, cotton, hay, wheat and tobacco. Cattle, sheep and horses are bred. Fruit-growing is an important industry. Coal is the most valuable of the State's mineral resources, which include copper, zinc and iron, marble and limestone. The forests yield oak, chestnut, hickory, walnut, ash and maple.

The capital of the State is Nashville (population 167,000). Other large towns include Memphis (population 293,000), Chattanooga (population 128,200) and Knoxville (population 112,000). At Oak Ridge is the huge works where the first atomic bomb was made during the Second World War (1939–45). The population of the State of Tennessee is 2,916,000.

Tennis.

Even those who have no desire to play " real " tennis—so called to distinguish it from lawn tennis (q.v.)—may at least be interested by three things about it. These are its ancient origin, the strange expressions connected with the game and the complicated rules.

The word " real " is derived from the Old French *réal*, meaning royal, and the game was enormously popular with the Kings of France and England during the 16th and 17th centuries. Henry VII played it, and Henry VIII built the court at Hampton Court Palace, Middlesex.

A tennis court, for which there is no standard size, may be from 90 to 96 feet in length, some 30 feet high, and about 38½ feet wide. Round three sides is a kind of covered corridor (the pent-house), formed by a wall with a sloping roof. In this wall on either side of net are a number of openings known as galleries. At one end of the court—the service side—is an opening called the dedans from which spectators (suitably protected by a net) can watch the play. In the right-hand corner at the other end—the hazard side—is a much smaller opening, the grille. A point is scored should the ball be struck into either of these. On the hazard side there is a buttress, projecting from the wall opposite the pent-house, called the tambour—another word of French origin.

A net is stretched across the centre of the court, and the main object of the game, as in lawn tennis, is to return the ball over the net. The server must strike the ball from the service side so as to hit the pent-house on the hazard side and then to fall beyond the service line. Scoring is also similar to lawn tennis, though the best of 11 games is usually played, and there are numerous rules and scoring variations.

Real tennis is played today to a limited extent in France, England and the United States. In the latter country it is known as Court Tennis. The chief British competition is the championship meeting held annually at Queen's Club, London, by the English Amateur Tennis Association.

Tennyson,

ALFRED, 1ST BARON (1809–92). Eminent Poet Laureate of the Victorian Age, Tennyson was born at Somersby, Lincolnshire, on August 6, 1809, and was educated at Louth Grammar School and Trinity College, Cambridge. He began to write verse in childhood and, with his brother Charles, produced a collection of poems before going to Cambridge, where he won the Chancellor's prize for poetry with his Timbuctoo, written in blank verse. A volume published in 1833 contained several of his finest minor poems, such as The Lotus Eaters, The Lady of Shalott, A Dream of Fair Women, and The Miller's Daughter.

Sport & General

WHERE ' REAL ' TENNIS HAS BEEN PLAYED SINCE TUDOR TIMES

At Hampton Court Palace, Middlesex, is the oldest 'real' tennis court in existence (above). It was built for Henry VIII in 1530, and he and a number of other English and French kings were players of this game, which began to lose popularity in the 17th and 18th centuries. The above view shows part of the pent-house, which is a kind of covered corridor running round three sides of the court. There is no standard size for the court, which has a stone or composition floor, but it is usually from 90 to 96 feet long and 38½ feet wide ; the net is five feet high at the sides.

When his In Memoriam appeared in 1850, inspired by the death of his friend Arthur Hallam in 1833, Tennyson had already won his place as the first poet of Britain and had been granted an annual pension of £200 by the Government. The sale of his poems had gradually increased to such an extent that it was possible for him to settle down, and on June 13, 1850, he was married to Emily Sellwood, who was the sister of his brother Charles's wife.

Less than six months later he succeeded William Wordsworth (1770–1850) as Poet Laureate. In 1854 he wrote The Charge of the Light Brigade, commemorating the charge of the British Light Cavalry at Balaclava during the Crimean War (1854–56), and in 1859 appeared the first volume of the Idylls of the King. Raised to the peerage in 1884, the poet assumed the title of Baron Tennyson of Aldworth and Farringford; Aldworth was the name of his house at Haslemere, Surrey, and Farringford that of his home near Freshwater Bay in the Isle of Wight.

All Tennyson's work is marked by rhythm and by intimate feeling for the beauties of land and sea. The narrative poems of the Idylls of the King have as their hero the legendary Arthur, the ideal king (see Arthur, King). The poet traces the establishment of the Order of the Round Table (q.v.) and the building of the kingdom, various events in the lives of Arthur and his knights, including the quest for the Holy Grail (cup used by Christ at the Last Supper), and the decay of the kingdom through the sin and treachery of those whom the king had trusted. In The Passing of Arthur he pictures that "last, dim, weird battle " in which Arthur receives a mortal wound and is borne away to "the island-valley of Avalon." Underlying this story a deeper allegorical meaning is suggested, that of "sense at war with soul," the struggle of the human soul as it passes through life to death and immortality.

Tennyson stole his way into the hearts of English-speaking peoples everywhere with his matchless lyrics and narrative poems and little bursts of song that almost set themselves to music. There is little doubt that his verse is among the most perfect, technically speaking, in the English tongue.

From the epic Tennyson turned to drama, and as a dramatist his chief disappointment was the failure of his persistent attempts to write historical pieces that could be acted. Neither Queen Mary (1875) nor Harold (1876) was an enduring work, and in 1884, after publishing the tragedy of Becket, he gave up all attempts at writing for the stage. Curiously enough, it was this very play that proved, after his death, a striking success, with Sir Henry Irving in the name part. Tennyson died at Aldworth on October 6, 1892, and was buried in Westminster Abbey, London.

Apart from those already mentioned, his other chief works include: Poems, chiefly Lyrical (1830); Maud (1855); Enoch Arden and Other Poems (1864); various poetic dramas from 1875 to 1884; Ballads (1880); and Locksley Hall—Sixty Years After (1886).

Terbium. This is one of the middle members of a group of elements known as the rare-earth metals. If you look at the Periodic Table (see page 768) you will see that the space after Barium (No. 56) is occupied not by one element but fifteen. These fifteen elements, with atomic numbers from 57 to 71, are the rare earths, and they are put into one space in the table because they resemble one another very closely, far more closely than do any other group of chemical elements.

In 1794 the Finnish chemist Gadolin discovered what he thought was a new element in a mineral from Sweden. Actually his element was a mixture of over a dozen resembling one another so closely that they appeared to be one. Gradually new elements were isolated from the mixture by a number of chemists whose work was spread over a hundred years. In 1926 the fourteenth element out of the fifteen known to be possible was discovered. The fifteenth element (atomic number 61) was never discovered in rare-earth minerals, but has recently been found among the elements produced in the fission of Uranium. (See Uranium).

ALFRED LORD TENNYSON
Appointed Poet Laureate in 1850 (succeeding William Wordsworth in that office) Lord Tennyson reflected the greatness and the limitations of the Victorian Age.

The rare earths are not all " rare," but are really widely distributed and together form as high a proportion of the earth's crust as does lead. The rare-earth minerals usually contain many other elements, including the radio-active Thorium. These minerals are found in Scandinavia, Russia, India, America and Australia. The chief source of cerium is the monazite sands (see Sand), found mainly at Travancore in southern India.

In isolating individual rare earths the whole group is first separated from the other elements present in the mineral. Then begins the laborious separation of the rare-earth elements from one another. Since they resemble one another so closely this separation has to make use of the very slight differences in solubility of certain salts of the elements, and thousands of crystallisations have to be done before compounds of the individual elements are obtained. In order to separate the less common elements from the minerals many pounds of ore have to be used at the start, while at the end of the process crystallisations are being carried out on very small quantities. The earths are separated into three fractions : (1) Cerium earths ; (2) Terbium earths ; (3) Ytterbium earths ;

each fraction consists of several elements and each is then separated into the compounds of the individual elements.

The rare-earth elements are metals, white or yellowish in colour, with a metallic lustre. They somewhat resemble calcium in properties; they tarnish in air, and react slowly with water, giving off hydrogen. Many give coloured compounds, and have magnetic properties like iron and cobalt.

Not many uses have been found for the rare earths. Cerium, the most abundant of them, is used in gas mantles, and its compounds in dyeing. Rare earths are used in carbon arcs, as they give a bright white light for film projection. An alloy of iron with a mixture of rare-earth metals, called " misch metal," is used in cigarette lighter " flints."

Terbium is one of the less common of these elements. It is a metal, although it has not been prepared in the free state. Its atomic number is 65 and its atomic weight 159·2. The symbol is Tb. Terbium compounds are colourless, unlike those of some of the other rare earths. The name terbium derives from Ytterby, the Swedish village from which rare-earth ores were first obtained.

Termites. These creatures, the so-called " white ants," which are neither white nor ants, belong to an order of their own, the *Isoptera*. Even in their social life they differ very widely from the bees, ants, and wasps, all of which have a good deal in common with one another. The termites' social organization is a good deal more intricate and remarkable than that of their most highly-developed rivals.

Termites are typical especially of tropical lands, and they form one of the oldest orders of insects, their fossil remains being found in many places. Today they occur in Africa, Asia, America and Australia, wherever it is very hot, whether in the forest or the bare, dry desert. They have always attracted Man's attention because of their enormous nests, or termitaries, which may tower 20 feet above ground. In such nests there is a population running into hundreds of thousands.

In inhabited parts of the tropics termites are important to Man, for they do a tremendous amount of damage. They eat everything except metal, and in many places wooden structures cannot be erected for fear of their damage. More-

INSIDE THE TERMITES' GIGANTIC NEST

In Africa, Australia and South America certain insects, called termites, build mounds as high as 20 feet. The outer walls consist of earth particles held together by moisture and baked as hard as concrete by the sun. Inside, the termites fashion chambers and passage-ways with provisions for ventilation and drainage. For clearness, the divisions in this cross-section drawing are made more precise than they are in reality ; in the 'servants' quarters' the 'workers' live.

over, they always start in a small way, out of sight, and work at once inwards, eating all the insides out of a tree, a beam, or wooden floor. They leave the outside whole, so that one day it suddenly gives way, crumbling into dust and showing that all but a very thin film has been eaten.

To help the termites in coping with their diet of wood, they have in their stomachs a host of tiny protozoa whose job it is to reduce the cellulose of the wood to a state fit for termite digestion. Often the protozoa themselves are digested by the termites. It has been shown that termites which have been deprived of their friends inside will starve, although they still eat as much actual wood as ever.

Not all termites work their feeding arrangements in this way, for some species eat humus—decayed vegetable matter—and others live on minute fungi which they grow in " gardens " actually inside their nests. These gardens are only one of the wonderful features of the termitary.

There are nurseries, which in some instances are kept warm by the heat given off from fermenting vegetation; there are ventilation shafts; there are deep tunnels, going down as much as 50 feet, by which water may be brought up during the droughts of tropical desert regions ; and there is the " royal cell," in which lies the enormous queen of the nest, a vast insect that may be four inches long, a living egg factory (*see* illustration in page 1733). The queen of some forms

Australian National Travel Association

EARTHEN SKYSCRAPER BUILT BY TERMITES

This is a truly enormous example of termite architecture, as you can see by comparing it with the man who is sitting on the top. When you consider that it is built entirely by the efforts of termites individually only half-an-inch or so in length, you can realize what labours these tiny creatures are capable of. Compare with diagram in the facing page.

may continue to lay eggs at the rate of 30,000 a day for years, so that although she never moves about, and is constantly attended by hundreds of workers and guards, she is a very hard-working monarch. There are also males in the termite community, which, like the queens, may be either winged or wingless; the wings are discarded after mating. The male termite who is the " king " of the colony lives in a cell with the queen.

As in the other social insects, the termite community consists largely of workers of various sorts, but an important feature is the large range of castes. There are small workers, which do the ordinary jobs

in the nest—tending the developing young, cleaning up and carrying on routine jobs. There are larger workers, with more powerful jaws, which do the harder tasks, often outside the nest. And there are " soldiers," forms in which the jaws are developed out of all proportion to the rest of the insect; these defend the community against the attacks of their great enemies the ants, and they wage war against other termite cities. In some soldier types the mouth-parts are modified into a syringe-like object by means of which a liquid may be squirted at their enemies. These forms have to be fed by the workers, and almost all the termites secrete various substances which are greedily licked off their bodies by other members of the community. The queen gives off more secretions than anyone else, and is consequently being licked continually by her subjects.

One difference between termites and other social insects is that, whereas in the other forms the workers are all sterile females, those of the termite city may belong originally to either sex. But differences in feeding from their emergence from the egg ensure that they *shall* be workers, remaining sterile, while only the chosen few are fed up so as to make them into active males and females which will carry on the race. Moreover, only the winged males and females are really capable of producing all types of the community; and, should they die, the wingless royalties continue to reproduce their own kind and workers, but no winged royalties.

BREAKING UP A VAST TERMITARY

The size of the termites' nest is one of the most marvellous things about these extraordinary insects ; and in this photograph you see a particularly large nest being overturned by the united efforts of a crowd of African natives. Nests such as this often continue for as far beneath the surface of the ground as they rise above it.

These insects provide science with many problems that still baffle it, and which have prompted modern writers of all nations to try to see some ruling principle behind the termites' amazing organization. Yet none has been discovered, and there still remains as the only generally accepted explanation the word " instinct," coupled with what science calls " tropisms " (*see* Animals, Behaviour of). Yet how does even that account for the habit, for example, of the " compass " termite (*Hamitermes meridionalis*) of Australia, whose huge nests are built along a line from north to south and flattened so that they expose their flat sides to the sun on the east and west?

Teutons. Those peoples who speak any one of the various Teutonic languages—English, German, Dutch, Flemish, and the various Scandinavian tongues—are broadly grouped together as " Teutons." The name is occasionally more narrowly applied to the people of Germany.

The name " Teutonic invasions " is often applied to the wandering of Germanic peoples, from the 4th to the 9th centuries inclusive, which resulted in the overturning of the Roman Empire in the West and the establishment of the nations of Western Europe in more or less their present positions. Their culture was by no means uniform, as the early Teutons included tribes of different types. The name Teutoni or Teutones was originally that of a tribe of northern Europe which first appeared in history in the 2nd century B.C. (*See* Europe; Goths; Northmen; Roman History).

Texas. Southernmost and by far the largest of all the United States, Texas (its area is 263,644 square miles, equal to the total area of France, Belgium, Holland and Denmark) is separated from Mexico by the picturesque Rio Grande and from Oklahoma for 400 miles by the Red river. It is mountainous in the west, the highest point being Guadalupe Peak, 8,751 feet. Fertile prairie land is in the centre, and it has a sandy coastal plain bordering on the Gulf of Mexico.

Across the centre of the State flows the Colorado river (which should not be confused with the river of the same name emptying into the Gulf of California), on which is the capital, Austin (population 87,000). Texas is the largest cotton-producing and live-stock-raising State, and is also noted for its oilfields, which produce nearly half of the petroleum of the United States. In the east are forests which yield valuable timber, and on the coast of the Gulf of Mexico are grown citrus fruits. The greater part of the population is engaged in agriculture, and the State is noteworthy for breeding goats, mules, and turkeys.

Texas has had an eventful history. Since the establishment there of a French colony in the late 17th century it has flown the flags of Spain, Mexico, an independent Texan Republic, the United States, and (during the American Civil War, 1861–65) the Confederacy of Southern States. Texas joined the Union of the United States in 1845, and almost immediately a dispute arose between the United States and Mexico concerning the boundary of the new State with Mexico. The Mexicans were defeated in the ensuing war of 1845–48, and the Rio Grande was established as the international boundary as far west as El Paso.

Principal towns are Houston (population 384,000) Dallas (294,000), San Antonio (253,000), Fort Worth (177,000), and El Paso (96,000). Houston and Galveston (60,000) are the principal ports through which cotton and other products are shipped. The population of the State is 6,787,000

HISTORY WOVEN into FINE FABRICS

The history of our civilization can be traced in the tapestries and cloths produced through the centuries by inventive mankind with appliances and machines that range from the primitive distaff to the modern power-loom.

Textiles. Some 2,500 years before the Christian era, the Egyptians knew how to weave, making fine fabrics from the linen they had long since discovered. Their favourite motif was the lotus. Waves were represented by a zigzag, and the sacred beetle or scarabaeus was usually included somewhere. In Greece, in the 3rd, 4th, and 5th centuries before Christ, costumes were made apparently of linen or cotton or wool. A design across the bottom of the tunics, in geometric fretwork, or zigzag patterns, was either woven or embroidered.

Fox

Heavy fabrics with inwrought designs, tapestries were used as wall-hangings. Here an old work is being repaired.

Silk was not in general use until early in the Christian era. We read of gorgeously arrayed Roman Emperors, though probably very few of their beautiful fabrics were made in Rome, but were brought from the textile centres of the East. The Chinese, who made the first usable silk thread about 2600 B.C., were the only people in the world who knew how to twist silk and weave it into rich and lovely fabrics, including brocades and a cloth-like damask. They combined colours to make beautifully-woven fabrics and embroideries.

In the 5th century the Copts of Egypt wore a plain, coarse linen for their garments, embellished with a kind of woven decoration resembling tapestry. About this time (A.D. 500), the natives of Peru were using the same methods of textile making, and employing the same characteristics of pattern and colour. This does not necessarily indicate that workmen from one country travelled to the other, but it does show that if primitive people start with the same equipment at about the same time, they may produce the same results.

We find great progress in Persia under the powerful Sassanid kings. Until the 7th century the Persians brought the raw silk from China. Of it were woven fine damasks (named after Damascus), a cloth on which a pattern appears in a satin weave against a plain ground; and brocades, similar to damasks except that the pattern was also made to stand out in relief, by tensing the threads. As the demand grew, entirely new designs were created. Large circles called roundels usually enclosed representations of birds, beasts, or warriors. These Persian silks went travelling, especially to Constantinople (then called Byzantium). Some textiles were made there, but most came from Persia or China.

The great Mahomedan conquests revolutionized art design. The artists, forbidden to picture any living thing, filled the roundels with inscriptions from the Koran, piling the picturesque Arabic script letters one on another. When these conquering Arabs reached Spain they mingled their designs with the native art. Interlacing lines, geometric patterns, flowing arabesques, and above all a pseudo-Arabic script, united with the earlier Spanish motifs. But, since the Spaniards were not Mahomedan, their designs included men and animals.

The conquering Mahomedans visited Sicily. The weavers of Palermo were famous for their beautiful silks with big, flowing designs. Wide, waving bands developed into elongated ovals with pointed ends. The flowers were more realistic. When in the 13th century a new government drove the weavers out to various towns in Italy, the greatest number settled in Lucca. There we find the beginnings of the famous Italian Renaissance silks.

From the looms of Florence came rich crimson damasks, brocaded silks of many colours, gold brocade, and blue satins. The patterns were bold, beautiful, and graceful. To Venice sped the first traders from the East with their shiploads of silk. Venetian style was a combination of eastern and western motifs in reds, blues, gold, some exquisitely embroidered with gold threads. Many weavers settled in Genoa and worked on a special kind of velvet of silky pile and gay colours. Bold, sweeping designs combining cut and uncut velvet stood out vividly against rich satin or brocaded backgrounds of white. Small, all-over patterns were also popular.

Tapestries, made by the Egyptians as early as 1400 B.C., are heavy woollen fabrics with inwrought

Victoria & Albert Museum, London

WOVEN SILK A THOUSAND YEARS OLD
Dating from the 8th or 9th century A.D., the above Byzantine square of red silk was intended for a tunic. The pattern in the 'roundel' represents two horsemen, back to back; beneath each of them are a wounded lion and a hound.

designs. The 13th, 14th and 15th centuries provided the best of the Gothic tapestries, made mostly in France and Flanders. Primarily for use in churches, they were woven with large pictorial patterns of religious significance. By the beginning of the 16th century the designs were bold and full of life and movement. Many illustrated an old tale. Under Louis XIV of France in the early 17th century the Gobelin factory was set up. It turned out large wall coverings full of light and colour and skilfully giving the illusion of reality.

Most of the fine fabrics we have been considering were made of silk, and the tapestries of wool. Now we come to cotton. The Egyptians used it, and the Greeks and Romans, too. Then as a medium for beautiful textiles it went out of fashion. India, however, had used cotton for hundreds of years and printed it with a distinctive pattern. The best-known design is called "The Tree of Life." A small, all-over pattern with tiny flowers or leaves or a conventionalized pattern scattered over a white ground was called a "chint." The merchants of the East India Company in the early 17th century began to import "chints" in great quantity. To day we call them chintzes.

Louis XIV (1643–1715) built Versailles and had brocades and damasks woven specially for it. Fine tapestries were made at Beauvais and by the Gobelin factory. The early Louis XIV patterns developed from the Renaissance, and the later period added scrolls and curving conventionalized floral decoration. Then came the revocation of the Edict of Nantes in 1685, when hundreds of families of weavers were driven from France to Flanders and England.

In the early 18th century brocades became even more gorgeous, but in a lighter way. Taffetas embroidered with bright nosegays became the vogue. A court favourite interested in the East India Company introduced the fashion of decorative cotton prints, and many a court lady wore a bright-flowered print that exactly matched the decorations of her boudoir. Near the end of the century stripes were seen everywhere, with small bouquets placed here and there with great precision. Decorative details included gardening tools, and medallions with classically draped figures. Cloth, too, was very important at this time. Tapestries grew smaller and patterns were finer and daintier.

England began to grow as a weaving centre. From 1725 to 1750 French refugees made brocades and damasks. But England kept her place in the textile world mainly by her decorative linens and chintzes. When imports were forbidden, native factories boomed. Small designs characterized taffetas, brocades, and damasks.

The modern trend in art is being widely applied in both woven and printed designs in cloth, rugs, and laces, with very striking and beautiful new effects. Many of these designs are geometrical, with triangles, rectangles, or straight lines boldly employed. Others show highly stylized scenes, bits of city life, or common, everyday objects imaginatively treated.

Economic conditions have led to the introduction by chemists of "synthetic" textiles—rayon, nylon; and many other strange materials. (*See also* Cloth, Rayon; Silk; Weaving).

POPULAR TEXTILE DESIGN

In the sub-continent of India, cotton is frequently printed (stamped) with a distinctive design known as the ' Tree of Life ' (lower). Carried out in crewel (a kind of worsted) embroidery on a bedspread (upper) is a British variant of that pattern ; the stitches, in soft shades of blue, green, brown and red, stand out against the white background.

Thackeray.

WILLIAM MAKEPEACE (1811–63). Of all the outstanding British novelists of the 19th century there is none who gives so strong a sense of real people living in a real world as does Thackeray. He writes of men and women in action, against a background of English society—men and women loving, hating, pretending, gossiping, sinning and suffering.

Thackeray was born at Calcutta, India, on July 18, 1811, and was sent to England at the age of six. His education at Charterhouse School, and at Trinity College, Cambridge; his travels about Europe; his experience as a fashionable young man; all these gave him familiarity and ease in dealing with the characters of Vanity Fair. He knew real gentlemen—Henry Esmond and The Newcomes could never have been written otherwise.

He first became known as a contributor to magazines of all kinds of literature, much of it satirical in vein. In 1842 he began to write for Punch, to which he contributed nearly 400 sketches. Vanity Fair was his first novel, published in 1847-48. Next appeared Pendennis (1848–50), and then Henry Esmond—a tale of the days of James Stuart, the Old Pretender to the British throne which its author regarded as his best novel. This is often said to be the finest historical novel in the English language. Henry Esmond, the hero, although he tells the story himself, contrives to impress the reader as chivalrous, brave and self-sacrificing. The Virginians (1857–59) was a sequel to Henry Esmond, and was followed by Lovel the Widower (1860) and Philip (1861–62).

Apart from his novels Thackeray will probably always occupy a high position in English literature for his brilliant satirical essays, which, indeed, many consider more readable than his more ambitious works. These include The Yellowplush Papers, Jeames's Diary, and The Book of Snobs. The Roundabout Papers are other delightful essays. In English Humorists—like The Four Georges originally delivered as lectures—we can meet Goldsmith, Sterne, Gay, and several more of the notable writers of the 18th century. Thackeray also wrote light verse of merit. He died on December 24, 1863.

Thallium.

One of the most interesting of the metallic elements, thallium was discovered by Sir William Crookes in 1861. He was examining flue dust from a sulphuric acid works for selenium and tellurium, and found with the spectroscope a bright green line which he recognized as belonging to a new element. He called the element thallium from the Greek "a young twig," on account of the bright green spectral line. A year later Lamy also discovered it in flue dust, prepared the element, and investigated its compounds.

Thallium is found in a number of minerals occurring in Sweden and Macedonia; and also in small amounts in a wide variety of other minerals—including pyrites from which, in producing sulphur dioxide, it finds its way into the flue dusts.

Thallium is placed in Group III in the Periodic Table (see page 768). Its atomic number is 81 and its atomic weight 204·4. The symbol is Tl. It is a greyish-white soft metal resembling lead, with a relative density of 11·85 (lead 11·38), and a melting point 303° C. (lead 327° C). The metal is oxidised in air but can be kept untarnished under air-free water. It forms two series of salts, thallous and thallic, which are interesting because of the resemblances they bear to a number of salts of other elements. Thallous chloride is like silver chloride, and like the latter is darkened by light. Thallous iodide is like lead iodide. Thallous hydroxide absorbs carbon dioxide as caustic potash does, while thallic hydroxide is like ferric hydroxide.

Thallium compounds are used in making highly refracting optical glasses. They are very poisonous, like those of lead, and the sulphate is used as a rat poison. An oxysulphide of thallium has a photo-electric effect like that of selenium, and is used in " thalofide " cells to measure light intensity.

National Portrait Gallery

WILLIAM MAKEPEACE THACKERAY

As a novelist and as a moral influence through the medium of his kindly satire, Thackeray was one of the outstanding literary figures of the 19th century. Above is a reproduction of the portrait by Samuel Laurence (1811–84).

Thames.

(Pron. temz). The longest river flowing entirely in England, the Thames is also the most important, probably having as great a traffic as any river in the world. It rises in the Cotswold Hills in Gloucestershire, and flows in an easterly direction to the North Sea. About 210 miles long, it is navigable for large vessels as far as London, and for barges as far as Lechlade in Gloucestershire.

It is 750 feet wide at London Bridge, 2,100 feet at Gravesend (Kent), and expands between Shoeburyness (Essex) and Sheerness (Kent) to a width of five and a half miles. At several points in the lower reaches of the river its natural course has been artificially altered. Waterworks have in places necessitated weirs; and traffic requirements and the danger of floods at high tide have caused the building of locks and embankments.

The extensive dock system comprises on the northern bank the London, George V. Millwall, Tilbury, and other docks ; and on the southern side the Surrey Commercial Docks. Opposite Tilbury is Gravesend, where incoming ships take on pilots. Between London Bridge and the Tower Bridge the river is known as the Pool, and (to commemorate King George V's Silver Jubilee) the section between Westminster Bridge and London Bridge has been known since 1935 as King's Reach.

About two miles below London Bridge is the Thames Tunnel, connecting Wapping with Rotherhithe ; this tunnel is traversed by the Underground Railway. There are other deep tunnels for railway traffic, and the road tunnels include the Blackwall Tunnel, Greenwich Tunnel, and Rotherhithe Tunnel. The construction of a new tunnel from Dartford (Kent) to Purfleet (Essex) was begun in 1936, but work on this was suspended during the Second World War and was not resumed until 1947.

The Thames and Severn Canal joins the Thames at Inglesham, just above Lechlade; the Grand Union Canal joins the river at Brentford, Middlesex, the Regent's Canal at Limehouse, the Grand Surrey Canal at Rotherhithe and the Oxford Canal at Oxford. All matters concerning traffic, locks, ferries, etc., are controlled from the estuary to the

end of the tidal portion by the Port of London Authority; and between Teddington Lock and Lechlade by the Thames Conservancy Board.

The river is noted for its beautiful scenery and above Richmond is much resorted to for boating. Regattas are held at Henley, Kingston, Molesey, Staines and other places ; and the Oxford and Cambridge boat-race is rowed each year from Putney to Mortlake. At and about Oxford the river is often called the Isis.

Tributaries include the Windrush, Cherwell, Thame and Colne on the left bank, and the Kennet, Mole and Wey on the right. At Sheerness the Thames is joined by the Medway, the important estuary of which extends to Rochester.

Together with its tributaries the Lea and the Colne, the Thames is a valuable source of domestic water. The Metropolitan Water Board, drawing mainly on the Thames and the Lea, supplies water to 6,500,000 people, its King George VI reservoir at Staines, Middlesex, opened in 1947, having a storage capacity of nearly 4,500 million gallons. The Colne Valley Water Company supplies water over a large area of Hertfordshire.

30 CENTURIES of THEATRE HISTORY

The story of the plays that are performed in the theatre has been told in an earlier entry under the heading Drama. In the present article we learn of the invention and development of the actual playhouse building.

Theatre. Close to the Acropolis, the citadel of Athens, are the ruins of the theatre of Dionysus, in which were presented the plays of the " Golden Age " of Greece (*see* Drama). In the earliest period of Greek drama the theatre was merely an open space in which the altar of Dionysus (patron god of the theatre) was set up and round which the chorus revolved, while being addressed by a solitary actor from his place upon a wagon. The first theatre built in Athens was that of Dionysus. Constructed of stone, it was begun in 500 B.C. and seated 30,000. As the ancient Greek dramas remain one of the loftiest expressions of human genius, so the nobly proportioned Greek theatre is one of the most impressive memorials of ancient architectural design.

The seats of the ancient Greek theatre were usually built on the side of a hill. Thus all the spectators on the rising slope had a clear view of the " orchestra," the circle where, in the beginning, Dionysus was worshipped with choric dances. At the back of the orchestra was a platform about 10 feet high, which in time developed into the stage. Across the rear of the stage extended the decorated front of the stage buildings, which took the place of a back drop and contained dressing-rooms for the actors. (*See* illustration in page 1540.)

The words used by the Greeks for the principal divisions of the theatre are the same words that are used in Britain, slightly modified through the centuries. " Orchestra " is the Greek word meaning " dancing-place," and is still used to denote the part of the theatre immediately in front of the stage. The word " scenery " comes from the Greek *skene* meaning a booth, and used to denote the stage buildings which served the Greeks as scenery. " Proscenium," the term applied to the part of the

modern stage in front of the curtain, is derived from the Greek *proskenion*, which denoted the stage-front.

The theatres of the Greeks were all roofless, and the performances were given by daylight; hence there was no need for artificial lighting. Changes of scene were very rare, and only the most rudimentary stage machinery was employed, such as a " thunder-machine " and a crane for suspending in mid-air actors who represented gods. In order that the actors might be heard well in all parts of the vast theatre they wore masks, which increased the carrying power of their voices and also showed the appropriate facial expression. Tragic actors wore in addition a thick-soled boot or " buskin " to increase their height.

Drama was first performed at Rome as early as 240 B.C., but it was not until 61 B.C. that the first stone theatre was built. The theatres of the Romans were copied from the Greek structures, with certain variations and improvements. By the use of supporting arches they were able to build sloping theatres, instead of using hillsides as the Greeks did (*see* illus., page 1038). The orchestra was no longer used for the performance of dances, and persons of note were seated there. At the same time the stage was lowered and enlarged. The chariot races, gladiatorial fights, and combats with wild animals took place in such structures as the Circus Maximus of Rome and amphitheatres (like the Colosseum) which sprang up all over the Roman Empire.

As dramatic art grew more corrupt and debased and the circus more brutal, the power of the Christian Church was exerted against them, until, eventually, all theatrical and kindred performances were forbidden. In the course of the Middle Ages the arenas and the amphitheatres were filled with buildings used for shops and dwelling-houses.

DE SCHOUBURGH van binnen
op 't Tooneel aen te sien

Top left is a reproduction from a copper engraving of 1673 showing the stage setting for the production Empress of Morocco at the Duke of York's Theatre in Lincoln's Inn Fields, London. Top right, a décor by the great Italian scenic artist Ferdinando Galli-Bibiena (1657–1743), for Il favore degli Dei (The Favour of the Gods), Parma, 1690.

The designs of the Bibiena family are noted for their spacious proportions and bold perspective. In the lower picture is a setting by the Dutch designer Nicolaas van Kampen, for a theatre in Amsterdam in 1638. This is in the rigid, architectural style, which was at this time beginning to be discarded in favour of a stage adapted to changing scenery.

CONTROLS FOR THEATRE LIGHTS

Associated Press

The lighting equipment of a large modern theatre is varied and complex. Above is a switchboard from which the stage lighting of an Opera House is controlled ; spot lights, which play directly on the actors, are usually operated from the back of the auditorium.

the body of the house. Favoured spectators sat on the stage or in the three-storeyed covered balconies that extended all the way round the building, even behind the stage. The " groundlings," as Shakespeare called the people in the " pit," stood during the performance and were unprotected from the weather. Flags were flown above the buildings in order to show that a play was being acted. (*See* picture of the Globe Theatre in page 1039).

At the back of the stage were dressing-rooms and a curtained recess used for such scenes as the play within the play in Hamlet, and Desdemona's chamber in Othello. The performance was always given by day, so that there was no lighting. Scenery was very simple and there was no curtain.

The public theatres during the reigns of Queen Elizabeth (1558–1603) and James I (1603–25) were not patronized by women. If the court wished to see a performance, the company was " commanded " to appear at the palace. The form of entertainment which the higher classes preferred was the masque, which resembled the modern pageant. Painted scenery was used and the entire production became very elaborate, thus foreshadowing the opera.

The tendency throughout the 17th and 18th centuries was toward extreme elaboration. In Italy the scenic effects in opera became more and more resplendent. In the 19th century such well-known Italian opera-houses as La Scala at Milan and San Carlo at Naples (two of the largest playhouses in the world) were built on a still grander scale. France, Germany, England and America followed the example.

Scenery and stage apparatus were enormously improved, resulting in such finely equipped theatres as the Royal Opera House, Covent Garden, in London. There the stage is divided into six sections,

During the Middle Ages there were no theatres in the proper sense. The chief form of drama consisted of miracle plays and mysteries, which at first took place inside the churches, and then, when they came to attract more spectators, among the grassy mounds in the churchyards or in temporary booths. Gradually the religious drama came to be replaced by the secular, but for a long time plays were performed only by strolling players in barns, tents, or the courtyards of inns. Not until late in the 16th century were permanent buildings used.

The theatres of Shakespeare's time (1564–1616) were built in imitation of an inn courtyard. They were eight-sided, for the most part, with a raised stage built across one of the sides and extending into

HOW SCENES ARE SWIFTLY CHANGED

Hana

The revolving stage, which was traditional in the Japanese popular theatre, came to Great Britain by way of Germany. It takes the form of a turn-table, set level with the floor of the stage, and operated by machinery from below. This picture was taken under the revolving stage in a London theatre.

HOW THE THEBANS BROKE THE POWER OF SPARTA

At the battle of Leuctra, in 371 B.C., the Theban leader, Epaminondas, devised a military manoeuvre which routed the dreaded Spartan phalanx. The Spartans as usual drew up their forces in three masses, with the strongest on the right (as in the foreground of this picture). To oppose the right Epaminondas consolidated the bulk of his army, 50 shields deep, while his weaker centre and right he withdrew slightly, so that they would not come into contact with the Spartans until after his powerful left had crushed the Spartan right. The plan worked out as he had expected.

which may be raised or lowered by electrical power. Overhead is a maze of pulleys, cables and wires, controlling scenery and lighting. In some theatres there is a revolving stage, which enables one portion to be used while the remainder is being set.

Through the latter half of the 19th century performances grew more and more spectacular, and settings and costumes became still more elaborate. At the end of the 19th and the beginning of the 20th centuries a tendency to simplification arose. Gordon Craig (born 1872) in Britain, Max Reinhardt (1873–1943) in Germany, and Constantin Stanislavsky (1863–1938) in Russia influenced later producers such as Michel St. Denis (born 1897) and Tyrone Guthrie (born 1900).

A 20th-century development in the United States and Britain has been the increasing popularity of the open-air theatre ; performances of Shakespeare have been given regularly in summer in Regent's Park, London. This celebrated open-air theatre was established by Sydney Carroll (born 1877) in 1933. In the United States the Hollywood Bowl in California forms a 60-acre natural amphitheatre with seating for 20,000 people and standing room for a further 10,000.

Thebes. (Pron. thēbz). An insignificant little country town of about 5,000 inhabitants, 44 miles north-west of Athens in Greece, stands today on the spot which was once the seat of one of the oldest and greatest powers of Greece, the " seven-gated city of Thebes." Only a few ruins are to be seen today on the Cadmea, the acropolis (hill citadel) of ancient Thebes, so called after Cadmus, its mythical founder.

Thebes lies in the central part of Boeotia, in eastern Greece, a region of fertile and well-watered soil but fog-laden atmosphere. The Boeotians were said by their Athenian neighbours to be as dull as their native air, and their stupidity passed into a proverb. Nevertheless, they produced such writers as the poet Pindar and the biographer Plutarch, and warriors who achieved glory in battle.

Her historic past—about which grew up a group of legends scarcely less interesting than the stories of Troy—her central situation, and her strong fortifications made Thebes chief among the cities of Boeotia. As such she frequently came in conflict with Athens, and when rivalry between Athens and Sparta culminated in the Peloponnesian War (431–404 B.C.) Thebes sided with Sparta.

After the war was ended, however, Thebes became Sparta's bitter foe, because of the variable and tyrannical policies of her former ally. After numerous conflicts the people of Thebes expelled the garrison which the Spartans had by treachery put in possession of the Cadmea, killed the leaders of the pro-Spartan party, and formed a combination of Greek states against Sparta. The Spartans, after some military reverses, made peace with all their foes except Thebes, which was left unaided to bear the onslaught of the dreaded Spartan phalanx. This tactical device consisted in drawing the heavy-armed infantry up in a solid mass, eight or twelve men deep, so that the onrush flowed through the hostile lines.

But the Theban commander, Epaminondas, returned an effective answer to this Spartan device. When he met the foe in 371 B.C. on the plain of Leuctra, about eight miles from Thebes, Epaminondas arrayed his finest troops on the left, 50 shields deep, directly opposite the right wing of the Spartans, where they had massed as usual their heaviest force, 12 deep. His shallower and weaker centre and right wings he kept drawn up so that the one was ranked to the right and rear of the other, and thus held them in reserve while the massive Theban left drove against the Spartan right and crushed it. Then the Theban centre and right came into action and completed the rout. Over half the Spartans engaged were slain, and the Spartan power was ended.

For nine years Thebes held the supremacy of all Greece, but its power was based on the genius of Epaminondas and collapsed with his death at the battle of Mantinea (362 B.C.). Here he once more saw his troops break the Spartan phalanx but as he pursued the retreating foe he was pierced in the breast by a javelin. He was told by his physician that he would die as soon as the weapon was extracted. When news came that the victory was secure, he drew out the javelin with his own hand, saying, " I have lived long enough! "

When Philip of Macedon (382–336 B.C.) invaded Greece a few years later, Thebes joined forces with Athens, influenced by the eloquence of the orator Demosthenes, and made a brave but unsuccessful stand in the decisive battle of Chaeronea (338 B.C.), bearing the brunt of the attack. At the accession of Alexander the Great (356–323 B.C.) to the Macedonian throne, Thebes attempted to recover its liberty, and, by way of punishment, was razed to the ground in 336 B.C. Though later rebuilt, it was never again an important city. The Greek Thebes should not be confused with the Egyptian city of the same name, 450 miles up the Nile, which was for hundreds of years the capital of the Pharaohs.

Thermionic Valve.
With the exception of the dynamo and the transformer the thermionic valve is possibly the most important piece of electrical apparatus ever developed. Without it radio, radar, television, long-distance telephony and a host of other things which we take for granted, would be quite impossible.

As is the case with so many important inventions, the effects of the thermionic valve were discovered long before any explanation could be provided for those effects. In 1883, Thomas Alva Edison discovered that if an ordinary incandescent electric lamp had another electrode sealed into the bulb, a current could apparently pass between this electrode and the hot filament. Yet the word " electron " had not yet been coined, J. J. Thomson had not discovered the properties of what he called " particles," and it was not until 1905 that Ambrose Fleming built the first practical rectifying valve. (See Rectifier).

From our story of the Electron you can learn that certain metals when heated tend towards " thermionic emission "—i.e., the release of free electrons.

If, then, we seal up in a vacuum a filament capable of being heated, and another electrode (variously called the " anode " or " plate ") we shall have a two-electrode thermionic valve, or *diode*.

Heating of the filament (also known as the " cathode ") releases electrons from the material, and a few of them travel through space inside the bulb to reach the anode, which up to this time was negatively charged (*opposite* polarity to the cathode). As the electrons settle on the anode, it becomes *negatively* charged with electricity, and (as you may read in Electricity) " like " charges always repel one another. Once the anode is thus charged, all the rest of the electrons cannot reach it, and they hang about between cathode and anode in a sort of cloud called the " space charge " (Fig. 1). These space-charge electrons cannot themselves

THE WORKING OF A THERMIONIC VALVE
Figs. 1 and 2. At the left (Fig. 1) is an elementary two-electrode valve, or diode, showing a 'space charge' of electrons crowding round the cathode (C) but not travelling to the anode (A). The anode here is negative (—). In Fig. 2 (right) a positive charge (+) has been applied to the anode (A). The electrons stream from the cathode (C) to the anode, since the 'space charge' has been dissipated.

reach the anode, and they repel any other electrons which would otherwise stream out from the cathode, so that the cathode cannot send out any more. If, now, we connect into the valve circuit another source of electricity, such as a battery, so that its *positive* pole is connected to the anode, we shall charge the anode *positively*, and the electrons in the space charge will be attracted to it. Instantly the space charge is dispersed, and electrons will flow from cathode to anode in a steady stream (Fig. 2). If, then, the positive charge is removed from the anode, the stream will cease and the space charge will re-form—as it will if the battery is reversed so that the anode is made negative.

Since a stream of electrons in one direction is equivalent to an electric current flowing in the other direction, this means that we have a true " valve " device. It will conduct electricity in one direction only, and has, therefore, a rectifying action on alternating currents.

In 1907, Lee de Forest added a third electrode to the simple diode, thus forming a three-electrode valve or *triode*. The third electrode is usually called the " grid," and takes the form of a wire spiral, a wire mesh, or similar open-type lattice-structure ; it is placed between the anode and the cathode.

When the grid is made negative with respect to the cathode, the space charge will form between the cathode and the grid; and, no matter how large a positive charge is applied to the anode, only a few electrons will slip through the meshes of the grid to reach the anode (Fig. 3), the remainder being "throttled" or repelled by the negative charge on the grid. When the grid is made less strongly negative (Fig. 4), by applying less "bias" voltage, the throttling effect is reduced, and a steady stream of electrons can flow from cathode to anode.

A variation in the *charge* on the grid of a three-electrode valve has very much more effect on the *current* flowing from the anode than has the same variation in anode voltage; and by suitably arranging the "characteristics" of the valve quite tiny variations in grid voltage can have quite large effects. The triode can, therefore, be used as an amplifier of tiny variations. By connecting up two or three valves (or more) in "cascade," so that the output from the anode of the first triode is fed to the grid of the second, and so on, it is possible to amplify very tiny variations up to thousands (or even millions) of times.

In addition to the properties of rectification and amplification, the thermionic valve has another exceedingly useful function—as a generator of high-frequency oscillations. The action is rather difficult to follow, but a simple analogy will help us. If you can imagine a simple telephone circuit with a receiver and a microphone at each end, "A" and "B," each receiver being held in front of its own microphone, you will get some idea of an oscillatory circuit. A very small sound in the microphone at A will be transmitted along the wire to the receiver at B, which repeats it to the microphone at B and thus to the receiver at A again, which once more repeats it to A's own microphone. In a very short time a high-pitched whistle will occur, the effect travelling round and round the circuit, and continuing until one of the wires is disconnected or one of the receivers is moved far enough away from its microphone to stop the sound waves "feeding-back."

In an oscillatory circuit (shown in the usual manner in Fig. 5), the anode circuit has inductance and capacity (*see* Electricity) to form a tuned or resonant circuit.

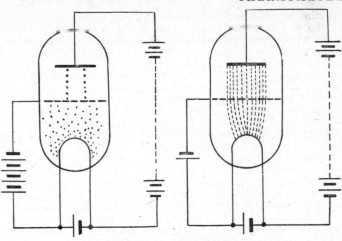

VALVE WITH A THIRD ELECTRODE

Figs. 3 and 4.   At the left (Fig. 3) is a triode valve, which has a third electrode —known as the 'grid'—interposed between the cathode and the anode. The diagram shows how a strongly negative 'grid' almost prevents the electron stream flowing from cathode to anode. In Fig. 4 (right), the grid is now less negative and allows the electron stream to reach the anode.

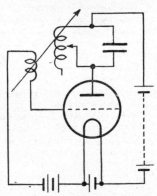

Fig. 5. A typical circuit for causing a valve to act as a generator of high frequency oscillations. The resonant circuit in the anode circuit is magnetically coupled to the coil in the 'grid' circuit; thus energy is fed back to the 'grid.' (*See* text).

A coil in the grid circuit is magnetically coupled to the anode coil, so that there is a certain amount of feed-back of the energy in the resonant anode circuit. This feed-back reinforces the change in the grid potential, and the change is passed on, magnified to the anode circuit once more—and so on, as with our telephone example. The valve will thus generate high-frequency alternating current, the actual frequency depending upon the design of the valve, and the "constants" (i.e., the amount of inductance and capacity in the circuit).

The thermionic valve is made in thousands of different forms. There are valves with two, three, four or even five grids; and there are valves with two or more anodes. They are made in glass envelopes, in metal envelopes, and in quartz envelopes. There are valves so large that they take two or three men to lift them; and there are valves so small that two or three can be put into a teaspoon. All operate on the same fundamental principles, although each one is specially designed to do one particular job better than others.

We have here dealt only with valves which operate in a vacuum. Gas-filled valves, which conduct by means of "ionisation" (*see* Ions) and have totally different characteristics, are briefly described in our story of Electronic Devices.

Thermometer AND THERMOSTAT. The first thermometer or temperature-measuring instrument was made shortly before the close of the 16th century by Galileo, the famous Italian astronomer (*see* Galileo). It was an air thermometer, quite different from the thermometers now in use, and, indeed, only a rough and ready instrument. A few years later Galileo improved this by using alcohol instead of air.

Galileo's air thermometer, constructed in 1592, was not only the very first, but was the earliest "gas thermometer," utilising a principle employed in our own time for standard instruments from which others are calibrated. Galileo used a vertical tube standing in a shallow bowl of water, and having at its top end an air-filled glass bulb attached and sealed at the joint. When he warmed the bulb, the water which had risen in the vertical tube began to descend; when, on the contrary, he cooled the air-bulb, the water column in the tube began to rise. All the water did was to register the differences in pressure of the air in the bulb under varying temperature. The principle was the same as that used in most thermometers of today—that liquids or gases when heated or cooled expand or contract faster than glass. When coloured alcohol, for example, is confined in a slender glass tube, the difference of expansion, indicated by the height of the column, is a measure of temperature.

Mercury is used in most thermometers, because it has a rather high boiling-point (675° F.), a low freezing-point (− 38° F.), and a uniform expansion when warmed. For temperatures lower than −38° F. alcohol is used, because its freezing-point is far below any cold encountered in Nature. For exceedingly high temperatures, gas and electrical thermometers, usually called " pyrometers " (*q.v.*) are employed.

Ordinary thermometers are made by filling with mercury or coloured alcohol a glass bulb provided with a slender glass tube. Heat is applied until the mercury overflows, when the top of the tube is sealed by melting the glass. As it cools the mercury contracts, leaving an almost perfect vacuum in the upper part of the tube. When the thermometer has become normal after the heating and cooling process, a scale for reading the changes in temperature is marked either on a strip of metal or porcelain or on the glass itself.

There are two temperatures that are easy to determine—the freezing-point and the boiling-point of water at sea-level. The thermometer is packed in melting ice to determine the height of the mercury at the freezing-point of water; and to determine the boiling-point it is suspended in steam arising from boiling water. The vertical distance

between these two points is divided into uniform spaces called degrees, and the scale of degrees is extended the full length of the mercury column.

In the Centigrade (" hundred-step ") scale, which is almost universally employed in science, the freezing-point is marked zero (o) and the boiling-point 100. This scale was introduced by a Swedish scientist, Anders Celsius (1701–44), and is sometimes called the " Celsius " instead of the Centigrade. In the Fahrenheit scale, which is in ordinary use in the English-speaking countries, the freezing-point is marked 32 and the boiling-point 212. This scale was devised early in the 18th century by Gabriel Daniel Fahrenheit (1689–1736), a German scientist, who found that a mixture of salt, water, and ice gave a temperature far below the freezing-point. This point he marked as zero. In the scale named after Réne A. F. de Réaumur (1683–1757), formerly much used on the European continent, the freezing-point is zero and the boiling-point 80.

Usually temperatures are given only in one scale, so that it is well to know how to compare readings on both the Fahrenheit and Centigrade scales. To change readings on the Centigrade scale to the Fahrenheit scale, multiply by $\frac{9}{5}$ and add 32. For example : 20 times $\frac{9}{5}$ plus 32 equals 68. Thus 20° Centigrade is the same as 68° Fahrenheit. To change 68° Fahrenheit back to Centigrade, subtract 32 and multiply by $\frac{5}{9}$, which gives 20.

Thermometers play an important part in modern life. The doctor has a special kind, called the " clinical thermometer," which he puts under your tongue when you are ill to see whether you have an abnormal temperature. The normal temperature of the body is 98·4° Fahrenheit, and the clinical thermometer reads from about 93° Fahrenheit to 110° Fahrenheit.

Besides the pyrometers, described under their own heading, there are other thermometers which do not use alcohol or mercury as the registering fluid. The hydrogen thermometer utilises a bulb filled with hydrogen gas, and connected with a column of mercury in a vertical tube. The space above the mercury in the registering tube is exhausted of air as far as is possible. When the gas bulb is warmed or cooled, the pressure exerted by the hydrogen increases or lessens, as the case may be, and the mercury level changes correspondingly. The hydrogen thermometer was selected by an international committee as the standard instrument for temperature measurement.

The success of many manufacturing processes depends upon exact temperature control, and for these thermometers and pyrometers are essential.

Many automatic devices called " thermographs " have been invented for making a permanent record of temperature changes. In the simplest type a needle is attached to a spiral coil of metal, which winds or unwinds as the temperature changes. This needle records its movements on a long roll of paper revolved by clockwork. A similar device (or else a " compound bar ") is used in some of the dial types of household thermometers which are now so common.

If you have ever looked through a magnifying glass at the balance wheel of a good watch you may have noticed that the rim of the wheel was made of two layers of different metal " sandwiched " together ; and also that the rim was not

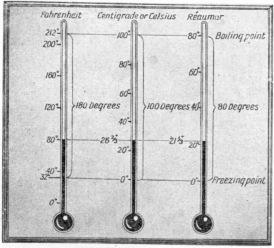

THERMOMETER SCALES
The scales on Fahrenheit (left), Centigrade (centre) and Réaumur (right) thermometers differ. On the three instruments shown are indicated their respective boiling and freezing points, and the corresponding temperatures on the C. and R. scales when the F. reading is 80 degrees.

continuous, but was cut through at two points. Such a balance wheel is said to be compensated against temperature changes. The inner strip of the sandwich is of a metal having a lower coefficient of expansion than that of the outer strip. In warm weather the outer strip expands and lengthens; in an uncompensated rim this would increase the diameter of the wheel and cause the watch to beat slower, and to lose time. But in the sandwiched rim the outer strip may expand, but since the inner strip expands less, the effect is to bend the rim inwards at the gaps. Do you see what this means?

It means that the diameter of the rim is *reduced* in proportion as the *increased* temperature has made the outer strip grow longer; this action is thus a compensating one. The compound bar, or bi-metal strip, can be employed to work an indicator, as in the thermograph or the dial thermometer. A more robust arrangement of a bi-metal rod can be utilised to turn on or shut off gas to the burners of a gas-cooker; or to regulate the temperature of an electric oven. Yet another application of this harnessing of unequal expansion is to turn on more oil fuel to the furnace of a water-heating boiler.

In furnaces burning solid fuel, the regulating device will open or close dampers controlling the air supply to the furnace, and so regulate the heat output indirectly. Indeed, we can have a room "thermostat"—all these devices are called thermostats—in our sitting-rooms, and can set the regulator beforehand to that temperature point at which we desire the warmth of the room to be "held." Then the thermostat will open or close water or steam valves, or govern other control devices, without human interference. These are only a few examples of what the "big brother" of our simple thermometer can do.

Thermopylae. (Pron. thêr-mop'-i-lē).

In this pass, leading from northern to central Greece, Leonidas, king of Sparta, made his famous stand against the mighty army of Xerxes, king of Persia, in 480 B.C. With 300 Spartans and some Thespians and Thebans (less than 1,000 men in all) he held the pass until the treacherous Ephialtes showed the Persians an unguarded path over the mountains and allowed them to attack the Spartans in the rear, when every man of the defenders was killed (*see* Persian Wars). Here again, in 279 B.C., the Greeks held at bay an army of Gauls until these, too, found a way over the mountains. In 191 B.C. Antiochus III of Syria was defeated here by the Romans.

Thermopylae means "hot doors," and takes its name from some remarkable hot springs, which still exist. Besides one large spring, used as a bath, there are four smaller ones. The water is said to be beneficial in cases of rheumatism and other affections. The pass, which lies between Mount Oeta and the sea, is not as narrow as in ancient times, for the wash of neighbouring streams has built up the seaward side into a broad plain.

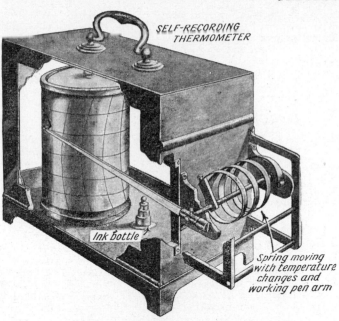

SELF-RECORDING THERMOMETER

Ink bottle

Spring moving with temperature changes and working pen arm

HOW THE THERMOGRAPH WORKS

Fluctuations in temperature are recorded automatically by this instrument. The spring, a bi-metal sandwich (made of two metals, welded together), bends as the temperature changes, causing the pen to mark the paper on the moving drum, which is driven by clockwork.

When the Germans invaded Greece in 1941, during the Second World War, a division of New Zealand troops took up their positions on April 20 on the Thermopylae line, from the sea to the summit of the mountains, covering the coast road, and held it for about a week until they were ordered to retire.

Theseus. (Pron. thē'-sūs).

The best remembered legendary hero of Attica (a district of ancient Greece) and Athens was Theseus, who was said to have been the son of Aegeus, king of Athens. He was born in a far-distant land, and his mother did not send him to Athens until he had reached young manhood and was able to lift a stone under which his father had put a sword and a pair of sandals.

After varied adventures Theseus arrived at Athens, and found the city in deep mourning, because it was time to send to Minos, king of Crete, the yearly tribute of seven youths and seven maidens to be devoured by the Minotaur, a terrible monster —half man, half bull. Theseus offered himself as one of the victims, hoping that he would be able to slay the monster. When he reached Crete, Ariadne, the beautiful daughter of the king, fell in love with him, and gave him a sword, with which he killed the Minotaur, and a ball of thread, by which he was able to find his way out of the winding labyrinth or maze where the monster was kept.

But Theseus forgot that if he succeeded in his undertaking he was to hoist white sails on his ship instead of the black ones with which the vessel had set out. Aegeus, seeing the dark sails returning, and thinking that his son was dead, cast himself into the sea, which is still called, after his name, the Aegean. Theseus now became king of the Athenians.

Other brave deeds were ascribed to him. He was also said to have been one of the Argonauts (*q.v.*), who went in search of the Golden Fleece, and to have conquered the Amazons. He was once about to engage in a contest of arms with Pirithoüs, king of the Lapithae, but the two heroes were so filled with admiration for each other that they swore eternal friendship. Theseus came to the aid of Pirithoüs in his struggle against the Centaurs (*q.v.*). The hero was eventually killed by treachery during a revolt of the Athenians.

In later times his memory was held in the greatest reverence, and at the battle of Marathon (490 B.C.) many of the Athenians fancied that they saw his spirit, clad in armour, charging at their head against the Persians. After the Persian Wars the oracle at Delphi ordered the Athenians to find the grave of Theseus on the island of Scyros, where he had been killed, and to bring back his bones to Attic soil. The oracle's instructions were obeyed, and the bones placed in a temple built to receive them in Athens.

Thessaloniki. (Pron. thes-*a*-lon'-ik-i).

Known as Salonica until 1937 when the Greeks revived its ancient name, Thessaloniki is situated at the head of the gulf of the same name and is one of the largest ports in south-east Europe. Largely rebuilt after a destructive fire in 1917, the city is mainly modern and has an imposing appearance as it rises from the shores of the harbour in a series of terraces to the turreted citadel, built on a hilltop overlooking the town. In normal times the chief exports are cotton, wool, wine, tobacco and fruit.

Founded by Greeks from the city of Corinth in 315 B.C., the city became the capital of the kingdom of Macedonia. Saint Paul knew it as Thessalonica and addressed the two Epistles to the Thessalonians to its Christian inhabitants. The Saracens captured it in A.D. 904, and it became a Turkish possession in 1430 for a period of nearly 500 years. The Treaty of Bucharest which terminated the Balkan War of 1912 awarded Thessaloniki to Greece. It was a base of the western Allies in the First World War (1914–18).

Bombed by the Italians after their invasion of Greece on October 28. 1940, during the Second World War (1939–45), the city was occupied by Germans on April 9, 1941. It remained in German occupation until they withdrew—after destroying the port installations before British troops arrived on November 1, 1944. The population is 236,500.

Thirty Years' War (1618–48).

Primarily a contest between the forces of Roman Catholicism and Protestantism, this civil war raged over almost all Germany. The quarrels between the religious bodies were very bitter, and led to the formation of a Catholic League and a Protestant Union in 1608. The religious question was complicated by political differences, and also by the fact that non-German States joined in the war.

The war began in Bohemia (now in Czechoslovakia), when the Protestants of that country revolted against their Catholic king, Matthias. On May 23 1618, his representatives were thrown out of a window in Prague, and in 1619 Frederick, the Count Palatine of the Rhine, the leading Protestant prince in Germany, was elected king of Bohemia. Thus in its first phase the war was a struggle for the throne of Bohemia, Spain supporting the Catholic Ferdinand II, nephew of Matthias. The Bohemian struggle was short; Frederick was defeated at White Mountain near Prague on November 8–18, 1620. The troubles of the empire furnished the opportunity for its neighbours to interfere, and the war developed into a European conflict.

After the Bohemian campaign (1618–24) the struggle may be divided into three main periods. In the first, 1625–29, King Christian of Denmark appeared as the champion of the German Protestants. He was no match, however, for the army of the Catholic League, under Marshal Tilly or for the able Imperial General Wallenstein, who crushed all Protestant resistance.

The hero of the second period was the Swedish king Gustavus Adolphus (*q.v.*), also a Protestant champion. His brilliant victories over Tilly forced the Emperor Ferdinand II to recall Wallenstein, who had been dismissed at the demand of the Catholic princes. This period may be said to have ended with the death of the military genius, Gustavus Adolphus, at the battle of Lützen on November 16, 1632. His death changed the character of the war. From a religious contest it became outwardly a gladiatorial encounter, the prize being the aggrandisement of the individual generals; inwardly it became a struggle between France and Spain. The Protestants in 1633 formed the League of Heilbronn, and sought the aid of France.

The last phase covered the years 1635–48, when the French statesmen Richelieu and Mazarin used the French armies

WATERFRONT OF THESSALONIKI, PORT OF GREECE
E.N.A.
On a gulf of the Aegean Sea, the seaport of Thessaloniki has a magnificent harbour close to which is the White Tower (above), part of the old fortifications. The town was known as Salonica until 1937, when the Greeks revived its ancient name.

THE INCIDENT THAT PRECIPITATED THE THIRTY YEARS' WAR

War between Protestant Bohemia and the Holy Roman Emperor Matthias, who was also ruler of Bohemia, was started in 1618 by the event depicted in this almost contemporary engraving. Indignant at the treatment meted out to the Protestants by the Emperor's Regents, the Protestant leaders hurled the Emperor's councillors out of the windows of the Hradčany Palace at Prague. Subsequent hostilities developed into the Thirty Years' War (1618–48.)

under Turenne to secure the dominance of their country on the Continent by supporting the Protestants. That a Catholic country should interfere on behalf of the German Protestants shows that the war had long ceased to be a merely religious conflict. By this time the people of Germany were thoroughly exhausted. For 17 years armies had been marching over the country, and all except that of Gustavus Adolphus had lived on the territory through which they passed, until by the close of the war the land was in a state of desolation and the people starving.

In 1641 peace was seriously discussed, but the questions involved were so complicated that it was not until 1648 that the Treaty of Westphalia was signed. According to the terms of the treaty affecting religion, the princes of Germany might choose the faith of their lands. The political questions were more difficult to settle, but France and Sweden really desired the division of Germany. In the end, Sweden received territory on the German coasts of the Baltic and North Sea; France obtained Alsace; the Protestant states of Saxony and Brandenburg (Prussia) in Germany were enlarged; Spain acknowledged the independence of the United Netherlands, and Swiss independence was confirmed.

Thistle.

When King Alexander III was ruler of Scotland (1241–85), King Haakon of Norway landed an army on the shores of that kingdom and attempted to conquer it. In a night attack on the Scottish camp at Largs, Ayrshire, a barefoot man trod on a thistle and cried out in pain. The Scots, warned by the noise, beat off the attack, and soon afterwards King Haakon had to withdraw his army and surrender the Hebrides, which then were part of his kingdom, to Scotland.

In remembrance of this battle of Largs the Scots adopted the spear thistle as their national emblem. In 1687 the order of Knighthood called the Order of the Thistle, dedicated to St. Andrew, was established by King James II.

The spear thistle (*Cnicus lanceolatus*) grows to about five feet in height, the lance-shaped leaves are often a foot long, and the purple

Van Dyck, Pinakothek, Munich

WALLENSTEIN

One of the ablest commanders of the forces of the Holy Roman Empire during the Thirty Years' War was Albrecht von Wallenstein.

STURDY SPEAR THISTLE

Harold Bastin

The thistle is the national emblem of Scotland, and of the several species the spear thistle is a notable example. It grows to about five feet, and the lance-shaped leaves are sometimes twelve inches long. The purple flowers, in massive heads, appear from July to October.

flowers appear from July to October. There are several other British species of *Cnicus*. Thistles of the genus *Carduus* include the unbranched musk thistle (*Carduus nutans*), whose crimson flowerheads are the largest of the British species; height varies from two to five feet.

Thistle flower-heads, which each contain a large number of blooms—for thistles belong to the order *Compositae*—form large downy seedballs, which the wind scatters far and wide.

Thor. Ages ago, according to myths of North Europe, there lived a powerful god named Thor. It was he who chased away the frost and called gentle winds and warm spring rains to release the earth from ice and snow. The lightning's flash was his mighty hammer Mjölnir, hurled in battle with the frost giants, and the rolling thunder was the rumble of his fiery goat-drawn chariot.

Thor was a good-natured, careless god, always ready for adventure, and never tired of displaying his enormous strength. He could shoulder giant oaks with the greatest ease and slay bulls with his bare hands. For sport he sometimes rode among the mountains, hurling his hammer at their peaks and splitting them in two. This adventurous god once visited Jotunheim, the land of his enemies, the frost giants. The king of the giants looked at him scornfully and said: " Is this stripling the mighty god Thor? Perhaps you are mightier than you appear. In what do you deem yourself skilled? "

" I will test my prowess in a drinking bout with anyone," said Thor. The king thereupon bade the cupbearer bring a drinking horn, and said: " Whosoever is a good drinker is able to drain this horn at a single draught." Thor placed the horn to his lips and drank long and deep, but when he removed it the liquid had scarcely diminished. Three times he tried to empty the horn and failed. Next he attempted to lift the king's cat from the ground, but only succeeded in raising one of its paws. The giants jeered, saying, " Is this the mighty god whom we have been taught to fear? "

Thor then offered to wrestle with anyone who would stand against him, and a toothless old woman accepted the challenge. Desperately he attempted to throw her, but he could not succeed. In shame he left the palace.

When Thor was outside its gates the king of the giants came to him and said: " Mighty Thor, when you attempted to empty the drinking horn you performed a feat so marvellous that, had I not seen it myself, I should never have believed it. The sea itself lay at the end of that horn, and when you come to the shore you will see how much of the waters have fallen away. Terror overcame me when you lifted the cat's paw from the floor, for that cat is the serpent which encircles the earth, and the whole world shuddered when its hold was loosened. To fight the old woman for so long was marvellous, for it was Old Age with whom you wrestled, and no man may conquer her. Magic, and not the prowess of the frost giants, has overcome you! "

That is but one of the stories told of the powerful Thor. In his honour the fifth day of the week is still called " Thor's day," or Thursday. (*See* illustration in page 980).

Thoreau, HENRY DAVID (1817–62). American author and naturalist, Thoreau (pron. thōr'-ō) was born at Concord, Massachusetts, on July 12, 1817, and was educated at Harvard University. He worked for a time as a surveyor, maker of lead pencils, and schoolteacher, but his tastes were those of a naturalist and a recluse. Deciding in 1845 that the various forms of employment at which he had tried his hand all took more of his time than he was willing to exchange for earning his living, he went to live in a hut on the shores of Walden Pond, near the town of Concord

There Thoreau cleared a patch of ground on which he grew vegetables. By selling his surplus produce and by working at one of his trades for six weeks of the year, he was able to pass the remaining 46 as he wished. Most of his time was spent in studying bird and animal life, as told in his book entitled Walden or Life in the Woods (1854). Later Thoreau returned to Concord, where he wrote, lectured or made pencils for a living. For some time he lived with the poet and philosopher Ralph Waldo Emerson (*q.v.*). He died in Concord on May 6, 1862

Henry David Thoreau, American author and naturalist, tried his hand at several trades before he found his niche in life.

Thorwaldsen, BERTEL (1770–1844).

The son of a carver of ships' figureheads, the sculptor Thorwaldsen was born in Copenhagen, Denmark, on November 19, 1770, and studied at that city's art school. In 1793 he won a scholarship, which enabled him to live abroad for three years. Settling in Rome in 1796, he worked there until 1819, during which period his sculptures won him fame, especially a statue of Jason completed in

Thorwaldsen Museum, Copenhagen

GRACEFUL SCULPTURE BY THORWALDSEN

Much of the best work of the Danish sculptor Bertel Thorwaldsen is statuary of figures taken from the mythology of ancient Greece and Rome. This sculpture is of Ganymede, who was cup-bearer to Zeus, the supreme god of the Greeks.

1809. After a visit to Denmark, Thorwaldsen returned to Italy where he remained until 1838. He died at Copenhagen on March 24, 1844.

He excelled in mythological statuary, wherein he reproduced most successfully the style and spirit of ancient Greek sculpture. Colossal figures of Christ and the apostles in Copenhagen Cathedral are the best-known of his religious pieces. A collection of his work is exhibited in the Thorwaldsen Museum, Copenhagen.

Thread.

About a century and a half ago the convenient reel of cotton thread, so indispensable today to the housewife and the garment manufacturer, was unknown. The only thread used was hand-twisted linen thread sold in hanks, just as knitting yarn is today. The idea of using machinery for making cotton fibre into thread began to be developed towards the end of the 18th century. Today many great factories, employing thousands of people, are manufacturing the world's thread. Manchester is the centre of thread-making in England and Paisley in Scotland. Linen thread is made chiefly in Northern Ireland.

The best grades are made from the long-fibred Egyptian cotton. It is spun in the same manner as is yarn for weaving (*see* Cotton; Spinning; Weaving). But these threads are very fine, and a number of them must be twisted together before a thread strong enough for sewing can be made. Ordinary sewing cotton consists of six separate strands twisted together. The fineness is denoted by the number on the label of the reel. Thus No.

24 is a strong, coarse thread for sewing on buttons; Nos. 40 and 50 are for hand seaming. Thread for use in sewing machines is finer, up to Nos. 60 or 80.

Linen thread is useful for carpet sewing, rug-backing and such tasks. Silk sewing thread is used for good tailoring work. Threads are specially made also for crochet, embroidery and knitting.

The winding machine for filling the reels has a number of revolving spindles, on each of which a reel is held while the thread is wound, a guide travelling to and fro and spreading the thread evenly.

When the proper amount has been wound, the spindle stops, and a metal finger moves across the reel, catching the loose thread. At the same time a knife comes up and cuts a notch in the flange. The first finger carries the thread over the notch, and a second finger catches it and pulls it firmly down. As the thread is cut free the filled reel is pushed off, an empty one taking its place.

Thrush.

Representative of a family which boasts some of the finest musical artistes in bird-land, the song-thrush (*Turdus ericetorum*) is one of Britain's cheeriest songsters. Thrushes are widely distributed throughout temperate and even cold regions. There are numerous species, which vary considerably in size and coloration; but whatever the colour of the parent birds may be all young thrushes, until their first autumn moult, have spotted breasts. The song-thrush is spotted all its life and so is the larger mistle—ormissel—thrush (*T. viscivorus*). Both these are resident in Great Britain, whose migratory thrushes include the fieldfare (*T. pilaris*) and redwing (*T. musicus*), which are winter visitants from Scandinavia and Russia.

Thrushes build untidy nests, usually of mud mixed with grass, straw or twigs. The eggs of the song-thrush are bright blue with black spots (*see*

Topical

HANDSOME SONG-THRUSH

Upraised, expectant beaks in the nest demand this thrush's close attention—but not to the complete exclusion of happenings, or likely happenings, in the immediate neighbourhood. Hence the hen bird's expression of alertness.

C. W. Teager

A MIGRATORY THRUSH : THE FIELDFARE
A winter visitor to Britain, the fieldfare spends the summer in Russia and Scandinavia. In plumage it resembles the common thrush but has not that bird's vocal powers.

colour plate facing page 440). The food consists of insects, worms and berries. The song-thrush is also fond of snails, which it " shells " by striking them on a stone. When a large stone is found surrounded by broken snail shells, it is often referred to as a " thrush's breakfast table." The name of the missel-thrush, which is sometimes also called the stormcock from its habit of singing during the worst weather, is derived from its fondness for mistletoe berries. The eggs are whitish, with brown speckles.

Thucydides (c. 464–c. 404 B.C.). Before Thucydides (pron. thū-sid′-i-dēz) men recorded past events either in long epic poems in which mythology was more important than accuracy, or else in the form of mere chronicles. Thucydides was the first philosophical historian; that is to say, he was not content merely to give an accurate narrative, but he endeavoured to show the causes that underlay the events which he described.

Thucydides came of a wealthy Athenian family, and during the eighth year of the Peloponnesian War (424 B.C.) was in command of an Athenian fleet detailed to protect the coast of Thrace, where he owned some gold mines. His failure to prevent Amphipolis from falling into the hands of the Spartans, which was attributed to his anxiety to save his own property, led to his being exiled for 20 years.

At the beginning of hostilities he had begun to write the history of the war, " believing that it would be great and memorable above any previous

war." Events justified his judgement, for the Peloponnesian War proved to be a 27 years' fight to a finish between Athens and Sparta for the leadership of the Greek world. Thucydides' history, in eight books, gives an account of the struggle down to 411 B.C.; the war did not end until the surrender of Athens to Lysander in 404.

The history is characterized throughout by the most scrupulous accuracy. Thucydides took the utmost pains to verify his facts. Furthermore, the tone of the work is absolutely impartial. Thucydides' love and admiration for his native city as the intellectual centre of the Greek world did not blind him to her defects and mistakes, and he holds the balance equally between Athens and her enemies.

A notable feature of the history is to be found in the speeches which Thucydides puts into the mouths of prominent men on both sides, such as the magnificent funeral oration delivered by Pericles on the Athenians who had fallen in the first year of the war. Some of these speeches were undoubtedly the substance of what the speakers actually said; others are no more than a convenient means of giving expression to sentiments proper to the occasion and to the character of the speaker. Though his style is often harsh and difficult to understand, Thucydides' history as a whole takes a very high place as a work of literary art. His account of the Athenian expedition to Sicily was regarded by the British historian Macaulay (1800–59) as the finest prose composition in the world, and its author as the greatest historian.

Thyme. Carpeting the ground in summer with tiny purple flowers, the fragrant wild thyme plant (*Thymus serpyllum*) grows no more than three or four inches high. Native to Great Britain and most parts of northern Europe and Asia, it is a shrubby perennial and, like most other aromatic herbs, such as mint (*q.v.*) it is a member of the order *Labiatae*, or "lipped flowers," one of the petals of each flower being prolonged to form a sort of lip. This makes a convenient alighting place for bees and other insects which visit all these flowers in large numbers for the sake of the nectar. The leaves of the wild thyme are small and dark green, oval in shape, and as in other members of the family they are borne all the way up the stems in opposite pairs. The tight-bunched flowers cling close to the ground. The garden thyme (*T. vulgaris*) is of taller growth, from six to 10 inches in height, is a native of the Mediterranean region, has been cultivated in England since 1548, and is the species which is used in cookery for flavouring

Among common wild herbs of the same order is the marjoram (*Origanum vulgare*), a stiff upright

THUCYDIDES
As an historian Thucydides not only gave an accurate narrative but also endeavoured to show the causes of the events he described. His account of the Peloponnesian War (431–404 B.C.) is absolutely impartial.

plant with purple stems three feet high. It bears flat masses of reddish-purple flowers, very similar to those of the wild thyme. Then there are the clary, or wild sage (*Salvia verbenaca*), a hairy plant, two feet high, with bluish-purple flowers and four-angled stems; and the wood sage or germander (*Teucrium scorodonia*), with yellowish flowers, stiff wiry stems, two feet in height, and narrow serrated leaves. The cultivated sage and the garden salvias are related to the wild sage. The order contains also the so-called "dead" (stingless) nettles (*see* page 2335); and the foot-high bugle (*Ajuga reptans*), a common plant of moist woodlands, which has bluish flowers produced in long, leafy spikes.

A. W. Dennis

SWEET-SCENTED WILD THYME

This diminutive plant grows in Britain on the chalk downs and heath-lands, especially where rabbits or sheep have left the grass close-cropped. Bees and other insects flock to the small spikes of rosy-purple flowers for the nectar therein.

Tiber, RIVER. The swift-flowing stream on which ancient Rome was built is laden with historic memories and associations. The Romans fondly called it " Father Tiber," for they loved the stream which watered their land, joined the city with the sea, and helped to protect them from invasion. Yet sometimes the river god appeared to be angry, for the swelling waters rushed over the land in disastrous floods, as, indeed, they have done even in recent times, though massive embankments have lessened this danger.

Beginning as a mountain brook on the western slopes of the Apennines, over 4,000 feet above sea-level, the Tiber is joined by other small streams as it flows southward and westward to the Mediterranean. As it gains in force and volume it gathers great quantities of tawny clay, which gives it its yellow colour and the name of Yellow Tiber, sometimes used. So much sediment has been deposited at its mouth that Ostia, ancient port of Rome, is now four miles inland.

The Tiber is the most important stream of Italy south of the valley of the Po. Along its winding course of 245 miles are important cities, chief of them Perugia. The Tiber is navigable for small steamers to Rome, 26 miles from the sea, and for lighter vessels for about 60 miles farther up.

An account follows of a legendary feat of arms performed by a Roman against the Etruscans in defence of a bridge over the Tiber.

HOW HORATIUS KEPT THE BRIDGE

IN the brave days of old—according to an ancient legend told by the Romans and retold by Lord Macaulay in his stirring Lays of Ancient Rome—the city of Rome was threatened once by an invasion from the neighbouring state of Etruria. A line of Etruscan kings had formerly ruled over Rome, but the last of the Tarquins, as this line was called, had been expelled, and Rome had become a republic. In order to re-establish their power, the Etruscan leader, Lars Porsena of Clusium, with his army was marching toward Rome.

News came that the Etruscans had taken the Janiculum, the outpost on the Tiber's farther shore, and would cross the bridge into Rome. "The bridge must straight go down," ordered the consul, but hardly had he spoken when he realized that the vanguard of the enemy would be upon them before this could be done.

Then up rose a brave Roman named Horatius, who offered at the risk of his life to hold the Etruscans at bay while the Romans cut the bridge down. Two of his friends took their places by his side, while their countrymen seized their axes and attacked the timbers which supported the bridge.

Against that great host these three men stood their ground and smote one after another of the famed Etruscan leaders. Horatius himself received a blow from the boldest of them all, but "like a wild cat mad with wounds" he turned upon his assailant and slew him, striking terror into the hearts of the foe.

And now the bridge hung tottering over the foaming tide. "Back ere the ruin fall!" cried the Fathers of the city. The two companions of Horatius darted back, and Horatius stood alone on the other side until the bridge fell crashing into the foaming Tiber. Then the hero turned towards the river with (to quote Macaulay again) these words:

> O Tiber! Father Tiber!
>   To whom the Romans pray,
> A Roman's life, a Roman's arms,
>   Take thou in charge this day!

and plunged into the stream. The current was swift, for the river was swollen with months of rain. But bravely did Horatius struggle, in spite of his wound and his heavy armour, and Father Tiber bore him safe to the other shore. He was received with shouts of joy, and rewarded with a gift of land—

> As much as two strong oxen
> Could plough from morn till night.

A statue was erected to his honour in the public square, and ever afterwards his countrymen loved to tell the story of his heroism. In another version of the legend Horatius defended the bridge unaided and was drowned in the Tiber.

HIDDEN LAND *among* ASIA'S HEIGHTS

Guarded by deserts and by the world's highest mountains, Tibet remains largely a land of mystery. Few travellers have visited it; none has thoroughly explored it. It is still a land to which few foreigners are admitted.

Tibet. Called The Roof of the World because it contains the largest and highest mass of mountains anywhere to be found. Tibet is bounded on the north by Chinese Turkistan, on the east by China, on the south by the Himalaya Mountains, on the west by Kashmir. The average altitude of much of the surface is 15,600 feet, even the valleys being higher than the loftiest peaks of numerous other lands. Large areas of Tibet are barren and rocky, and what little soil there is at the higher altitudes is frozen solid for eight months of the year; there is scarcely any vegetation and few signs of life. On the lower central plateau yaks feed upon scanty pastures, but agriculture is almost impossible.

In the south a huge valley stretches across the country. Here are the headwaters of the Brahmaputra river, which flows through a gorge at the eastern end of the Himalayas to join the Ganges. The Indus rises not far from the source of the Brahmaputra, but flows round the western extremity

> **Extent.**—About 470,000 square miles. Population is estimated at 3,722,000.
>
> **Physical Features.**—Contains the highest mountain mass in the world, with the Himalayas bordering the fertile region in the south. In the lofty plateaux of the north are several lakes, and in the east are dense forests. The rivers Brahmaputra, Indus, Yangtze, Hwangho, and Mekong are among those that have their source in the country.
>
> **Principal Products.**—Cereal crops, fruit, live-stock, woollen goods, minerals.
>
> **Chief Towns.**—Lhasa (capital, 50,000), Gyantse (5,000), Chamdo (2,000).

of the Himalayas to the Arabian Sea. In the Brahmaputra valley the mountain sides are covered with forests, and the soil is fertile. Among other rivers rising in Tibet are the Sutlej, Mekong, Yangtze and Hwangho.

Rice and barley are the main cereal crops; sheep and yaks are bred, the latter used as beasts of burden. Water buffaloes, camels and pigs are also reared. Though there are scarcely any manufactures beyond local handicrafts, Tibet is rich in mineral resources, which are as yet largely undeveloped; gold is found in the river beds in the north and north-east, and turquoise mines are worked. There are no railways, but a number of trade routes connect Tibet with China and the sub-continent of India. The capital is Lhasa (population 50,000) situated in the south-east and for long known as The Forbidden City, owing to the fact that foreigners are not allowed to visit it.

The religion of the Tibetans is Lamaism—a strange combination of Buddhism, sorcery and certain ancient Hindu beliefs. The wildest superstitions flourish, as the people are completely uneducated. There are numerous monasteries throughout the country in which dwell enormous numbers of Buddhist monks or Lamas. The Dalai Lama, whose palace is near Lhasa, is the ruler of the country, though his authority does not extend very far beyond central Tibet. Spiritual affairs are in the hands of the Tashi Lama, the head of a famous monastery at Tashilunpo.

The Tibetans are short in stature and not unlike the Chinese in appearance, except that their eyes are less almond-shaped and their skins are reddish rather than yellow. Neither men nor

W. F. Taylor

COURTYARD OF A TIBETAN MONASTERY

In southern Tibet, not far from the border of the independent Himalayan State of Bhutan, is the town of Gyantse. The most imposing building is the large Buddhist monastery, whither the townsfolk go to attend services in the temple, of which the entrance is half-hidden by long strips of cloth (above). Gyantse is a trading centre for merchants from the sub-continent of India.

TIBETAN LAMA GARBED FOR THE DEVIL DANCE

Tibet, shut off from the outer world by barriers both physical and political, is a land of superstition and legend. The lamas, or priests, pass a strange life of meditation and holy teaching, broken occasionally by the weird ritual of the Devil Dance, a religious performance in which the priests wear fantastic masks.

E.N.A.

THE RED-WALLED CLIFF-LIKE PALACE OF TIBET'S PRIEST-KING AT LHASA

By whatever road the traveller comes to Lhasa, the golden roof of the Potala, the home of the Dalai Lama, or priest-king of Tibet, is the first sight to meet his eyes. This vast .... From a base of some 900 feet of dead wall, it rises by tiers of numerous windowed floors to a height women, except those of the highest rank, take much care of their persons; they wash rarely, and they have a habit of covering their face and hands with rancid butter as a protection against the bitter winds.

Tibet was a powerful kingdom in the 7th century of the Christian era, and remained independent until the 17th century when it came under Chinese domination. In the 18th century friendly relations were established between Tibet and the British East India Company, but these were terminated in 1792 when a British General assisted Nepalese troops to invade the country. The Tibetans closed their frontiers against foreigners for more than a century, but in 1904 a British expedition penetrated to Lhasa and contact with the Government of India was restored. Foreigners, however, are only allowed into the country by official permission.

After the Chinese revolution of 1912 Tibet was proclaimed an independent State, and attempts by the Chinese Republic to reassert Chinese

W. F. Taylor

TIBETAN SCHOOLBOYS AT THEIR STUDIES

Education, such as it is, in Tibet is entirely in the hands of the monks, who give their pupils instruction in reading, writing, very elementary arithmetic and religion. Few children attend these schools, because most of the people are too poor to pay even the small fees asked by the monks, most of whom are very ignorant judged by Western standards.

authority by force were vigorously resisted by the Tibetans; but since 1939 a representative of China has been permitted to reside at Lhasa. The estimated population is 3,722,000.

Tides. Everyone who has lived by the sea has noticed how the waters creep slowly up the beach for about six hours, and then for six hours slip steadily down again. The connexion of this movement with the moon was noted very early, but until Sir Isaac Newton's discovery of the law of gravitation the cause could not be satisfactorily explained.

It is now known to be due to the pull of the moon on the earth, sometimes helped and sometimes hindered by the sun, according to whether these two bodies are in a straight line and pull on the earth together or pull in different directions. The moon is so much nearer to the earth than the sun that, although its mass is far less, its tide-raising force is more than twice that of the sun.

Whenever the moon rises over the sea, it heaps

Mount Everest Committee

EVEREST SEEN FROM TIBET'S RONGBUK MONASTERY

The world's highest mountain (29,141 feet), Mount Everest is here seen (centre background) from the walls of the Rongbuk monastery. The tall, strangely-shaped structure on the right is a chorten, a receptacle for religious offerings often built over the relics of some Buddhist saint. Chortens are found in the precincts of every Tibetan monastery and also by the wayside.

up the water that is just under it into a peak pointing directly from the earth's centre to the centre of the moon. So a great wave is started travelling across the wide sea, making a high tide. Then by reason of the earth's movement the peak passes on, and the water goes back to its own level.

This is called the " direct " tide. There is also the " opposite " tides which occurs at the same time on the opposite side of the earth, and explains why we have two high tides in every 24 hours (or, more exactly, in 24 hours and 49 minutes). While the moon lifts the water on the side nearest to it, there is also a tendency for water to pile up on the line connecting the centres of the moon and the earth, on the earth's opposite side, since the water there is, so to speak, left behind.

Twice in the course of every month, when the moon is new or full, it comes into line with the sun and the earth. At these times both sun and moon pull together, and the higher tides which are produced are called " spring " tides. These have nothing to do with the season of the year. " Neap " (possibly meaning " nipped ") tides, which occur near the first and last quarters of the moon, are low, because the " pulls " of the sun and moon are then opposed.

In the mouths of some rivers, and sometimes in sharply narrowing ocean inlets, the rising of the spring tide occasionally has a curious effect. The tides overcome the current of the river, and a single high wave, moving onward like a wall of water, rushes with great violence and a roaring noise up the river bed. This phenomenon, notable in the Rivers Severn and Trent, is called a " bore " (q.v.).

The extent of the rise and fall of the tide varies considerably in different places. In mid-ocean the difference between high and low water is noticeable only in the neighbourhood of islands, and is then seen to be two or three feet. On the shores of the continents, especially in gradually narrowing bays, the height may be large. In England, at Newport and Chepstow, on the Bristol Channel, the spring tide may rise as much as 38 feet. Lake tides are too small to be noticeable, and in land-locked seas like the Mediterranean the tides are also slight. The varying depth of the ocean, and the irregular shape of the land masses of the earth, cause considerable differences in tides in widely separated parts of the world.

A knowledge of tides is important to the navigator, as a difference of a foot or two in depth on a dangerous shoal may involve the lives and property of the ship. Governments therefore furnish tables showing the fluctuations at the principal ports for every hour and every day for as much as a year ahead.

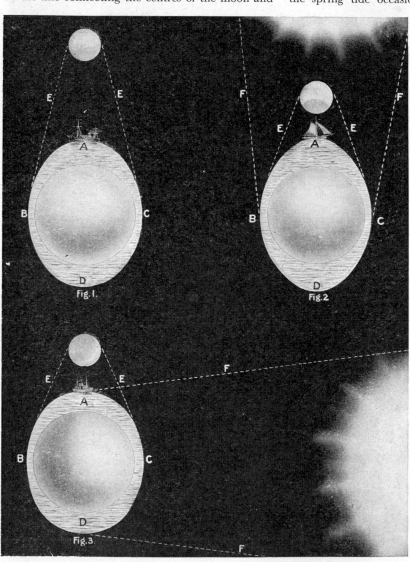

WHAT MAKES THE TIDES RISE AND FALL?

Tides are caused mainly by the moon, as shown in Fig. 1. The moon, acting along lines of attraction EE, heaps up the waters of the sea at A, causing high tides at this point and low tides at B and C ; at the same time the waters at D, being farther away, feel the pull of the moon less, and so tend to be ' left behind,' so to speak. Fig. 2 explains the higher or ' spring ' tide, when the sun and moon reinforce each other ; FF are the lines of attraction of the sun and EE of the moon. The ' neap ' tide, when sun and moon are pulling at right angles, thus somewhat counteracting each other, is shown in Fig. 3.

There have been numerous attempts to find a way to make use of the tides to work machines, usually by causing the water to lift large floats. Much energy is present, but to make this available involves considerable engineering difficulties, which have not yet been successfully overcome.

Tientsin. (Pron. tē-ent-sin′).

Next to Shanghai, Tientsin is the chief port of China. It is the trade centre of the province of Hopei, situated at the junction of the Pei Ho, which connects it with the former capital, Peking (or Peiping), 70 miles to the north-west, and the Yuho or Grand Canal, which gives it water communication with Hangchow and the Yangtze river. Taku, about 45 miles south-east, at the mouth of the Hai To (the estuary of the Pei Ho), serves as the port for large ocean vessels. In winter time when the rivers are frozen the ice-free harbour of Chinwangtao to the east serves as an auxiliary port.

Tientsin carries on an enormous trade with the interior by waterways and railways. There are manufactures under both native and European management. Cotton yarn and cloth, soap, candles, bricks, tiles, cement, cigars, cigarettes, and leather are the chief products. Wool, cotton, hides, and skins, bristles, straw braid, ground-nuts, and vegetable oils are the most important items among the exports.

In 1860 Tientsin was opened to foreign trade as a treaty port, and the principal European Powers and Japan later established concessions in the foreign settlement. After the Boxer Rebellion of 1900, during which the foreign residents in the city were besieged for 27 days, the old city walls were pulled down, the streets were widened, and many radical improvements were undertaken. Between 1874 and 1894 Tientsin was the headquarters of the famous diplomat Li Hung-Chang, then viceroy of Chihli, and there he negotiated important treaties with foreign representatives. In July 1937 the Japanese bombed the city from the air, destroying the university—one of the first big incidents in the war between Japan and China which had broken out that year. In August 1937 Tientsin was occupied by the Japanese, and did not return into Chinese hands until 1945, after the end of the second World War. The population of Tientsin is about 1,718,000.

E.N.A.

PICTURESQUE BUSINESS THOROUGHFARE IN TIENTSIN
In Northern China at the junction of the Pei Ho river and the Grand Canal, about 45 miles from the Gulf of Chihli, Tientsin is a thriving port and trading centre. The entrances of some of the business streets are spanned by a brightly painted arch, as above, and outside the shops hang the merchants' colourful signs.

Tiger.

On the African continent the lion reigns supreme, but in Asia his place is taken by the tiger (*Felis tigris*). The tiger is the most perfect and beautiful of the cat tribe, owing to the bright colouring of his coat, his litheness, and graceful proportions. Next to the lion he is the largest of the cats, a fully grown male being six feet from the nose to the root of the tail, which is itself about three feet long. The female is usually a foot shorter. The Bengal tiger is the best-known type, other varieties being the Siberian or Manchurian, Caucasian and Malayan. The coat of the Bengal tiger has a ground colour of tawny yellow, with black stripes on the body and limbs, the tail also being ringed with black. This colouring makes it very difficult to see in a thicket or even in long grass, for it resembles closely the play of the deep shadow and strong sunlight of the tropics. The hair is short in the Bengal variety, longer and more woolly in the Siberian type. The Malayan tiger is smaller, and so heavily striped as to appear considerably darker in colour.

Tigers are good swimmers, which is unusual in the cat family, and if hard pressed will occasionally climb trees. They prefer to hunt at night by stalking their prey, but also prowl about in the daylight, preying upon both wild and domestic

Sport & General

A TIGRESS AND HER CUBS IN CAPTIVITY

At Whipsnade, the Zoological Society's country garden in Bedfordshire, many wild
animals lead almost natural lives.   These tiger cubs, seen with their mother, were born there.
Born with plain coats, tiger cubs early develop their characteristic stripes.

Time. For most
purposes the world gets
its time from the sun,
reckoning a day as the
average interval of
time from noon to
noon ; that is, from
the moment the sun
reaches the meridian
to the moment when
the revolution of the
earth brings the sun
again into the same
position. This is called
"mean solar time."
The time indicated by
a sundial, called "ap-
parent solar time,"
does not as a rule
agree with this mean
solar time, because the
actual solar day is
constantly changing in
length owing to the
shifting of the earth's
position as it revolves.

animals. They do not normally care to attack
Man, but once a tiger has taken to man-eating it
becomes a confirmed man-eater, preferring human
flesh to all other.   Those who hunt tigers usually
do so from elephants, or by lying in wait at night,
perched up a tree, at a spot where
a tiger has made a "kill," or at a
beast tethered as bait.

In its search for prey and its
effort to avoid hunters, the tiger
is cunning and bold.   In its
native wild state it is the most
bloodthirsty of beasts, and when
in captivity is treacherous.   Tiger
kittens number from two to five
in a litter. The young remain
with the mother till the third year,
while she teaches them to hunt.

Tigris. (Pron. tī'-gris). This
river of western Asia rises in the
mountains of Turkish Armenia,
south and west of Lake Van.   It
is joined at Til by the Bitlis, unites
with its sister stream the Euphrates
at Korna, and from this point to
the Persian Gulf is known as the
Shatt-el-Arab.   Its whole course
is some 1,150 miles long.   In its upper part it is a
swift stream, and because of the tributaries which it
receives from the east its volume is greater than that
of its companion stream the Euphrates.

In ancient times the Tigris was the main river
of Assyria and Babylonia; it is the river called the
Hiddekel in the Old Testament.   Nineveh, Seleucia,
and Ctesiphon stood on its banks.   Its chief cities
now are Basra, Baghdad, Mosul and Diarbekr.   It
is navigable for steamers at all seasons below Mosul.
Germany's plans to control the fertile lands of
Mesopotamia ("the land between the rivers"),
which under irrigation could again be made
enormously productive, were one cause of the First
World War (1914–18). (*See* Euphrates; Iraq).

Mean solar time, when determined by local
observation, is obviously the same only for places
on the same meridian or north to south line, because
the sun travels 15 degrees of longitude every hour.
If every place went by its "local" time a railway
traveller in the latitude of
London might have to alter his
watch one minute for every 11
miles or so.   In order to

A. F. Kersting; Paul Popper

TIME SIGNALS, OLD AND NEW

The 17th century sandglass (above) from Ivinghoe Church
Buckinghamshire, was used to time the length of sermons
Lower, checking the clock at Mill Hill Observatory, London
by wireless signals from Greenwich, recorded electrically
on a strip of paper with the time registered by the clock

ny ways the tiger is more like our domestic cat than is the
nd the resemblance is clear if we study the detailed features
h a specimen as the magnificent lord of the jungle whose
it you see here. The square 'face,' short nose, deep-set
nd small ears are all features we can see faithfully repro

duced in the most domesticated of tabbies, for the members of the
whole cat tribe have a remarkable uniformity of detail and
general appearance. Although it is not always stronger than the
lion, the tiger is a good deal more active in confined spaces—the
circumstances of its home in the jungle make this necessary

e page 3212

ASLEEP AND ON THE PROWL

FOR all their size and ferocity in the wild, tigers take quite kindly to the comparatively restricted life of the Zoo, as the animal above shows by the way in which it is contentedly sleeping in the afternoon sun. On the right, in a wonderful photograph from a wild-life film, you see the way in which the strong sunlight and shadows of the Indian jungle bring out the protective value of the tiger's stripes. These stripes, too, are remarkably symmetrical, and most wild tigers have a regularity of pattern which would do credit to the most pure-bred members of the domesticated cat family. The largest of all cats in actual length, tigers are sometimes considered the strongest, though, as a matter of fact, there is little to choose in this respect between this great beast and its noble cousin the lion.

To face page 3?

HOW TIME VARIES IN DIFFERENT PARTS OF THE WORLD

Passing around the world are imaginary lines (drawn in this picture) which mark out the standard zones of time. All standard time is based on the time at such meridians drawn 15 degrees apart, beginning at Greenwich Observatory, London. The picture, therefore, shows the standard time at points all over the world when it is noon at Greenwich.

do away with such possibilities of confusion most civilized countries have established time zones, approximately 15° wide, throughout each of which the same time—known as "standard time"—is observed, so that the time of each belt will vary by an even hour from those on either side. These belts are measured east and west from one centred on Greenwich Observatory, London, and stretching $7\frac{1}{2}°$ each way, so that the regions between $7\frac{1}{2}°$ and $22\frac{1}{2}°$ east of Greenwich set their clocks one hour ahead of G.M.T. or Greenwich time ("Central European Time"), and those between $22\frac{1}{2}°$ and $37\frac{1}{2}°$ east are set two hours in advance ("Eastern European Time"). A "Greenwich time signal" is broadcast daily. By setting clocks at noon when it is really only 11 a.m. by standard time, sunrise and sunset can be made to come one hour later

by the clock. This is known as "daylight saving" (q.v.) or "summer time," which first came into operation in Britain in 1916 and has been adopted by many countries for the summer.

Now suppose we follow the "time zone" system round the earth. When it is noon in Greenwich—Greenwich is used because it is the centre of world-wide time—of, say, April 15, it is only 7 a.m. in Washington, U.S.A.; and in the time zone in which the Samoan Islands lie it is midnight. That is, April 15 has only just begun in Samoa. If we go east from Greenwich, when it is noon in the British Isles it is already 2 p.m. in Leningrad, 5.30 p.m. in Madras, India, and so on, until in the time zone marked by the Fiji Islands, just west of Samoa, the 15th would be within an hour of changing to the 16th. Thus,

By courtesy of Royal Observatory

FOR CHECKING SIDEREAL TIME

This instrument, known as Airy's Transit Circle, is situated on the Greenwich meridian. It is used, among other purposes, for observing the transit of certain stars with a view to the accurate determination of sidereal time. The steps on both sides give easy access to the instrument in all positions.

when it is noon at Greenwich there is a "line" between Samoa and the Fiji Islands on one side of which April 15 would be just beginning and on the other side it would be just ending.

That is why ships gain or lose a day when they sail round the world. Suppose a ship is approaching Samoa from the Fiji Islands at 11.59 p.m. on the night of the 15th. Ten minutes later it "crosses the line"—and its time is now nine minutes after midnight on the *morning* of the 15th ! That is, it has spent the 15th in sailing east towards Samoa—and now it has the 15th to use again !

If it were going west, it would lose a day. Just before crossing the line it would be at the beginning of the 15th, while a few minutes later, after crossing the line, it would be in the early morning of the 16th.

This imaginary line where the date changes in this way is called the "international date line." It was put in the Pacific Ocean, the other side of the world from Greenwich, where the change of date causes the least possible trouble. It deviates from the 180th meridian in various places, in order to avoid cutting through the land groups that the meridian encounters.

The usual division of the day into "a.m." (Latin, *ante meridiem*, before midday) and "p.m." (*post meridiem*, after midday) groups of 12 hours each, has given way for some purposes to the "24-hour" day in various countries. On the "24-hour" clock the hours begin with zero at midnight and run to 23; thus 1.30 p.m. is called 13.30 o'clock, and so on. This method of time-recording is in general use on the railway and air-line systems of the Continent. It is also used in the Services and by astronomers.

On board ship, "Greenwich time," or time corresponding to that at Greenwich, London, is kept by an accurate chronometer for use in determining the ship's position (*see* Latitude and Longitude). "Clock time" is also kept on passenger liners and corrected every noon to allow for the ship's position. In the navies of most European nations time is kept on the basis of standard-time zones, like those used on land.

The ship's routine, however, is governed by "watches" and "bells." The day is divided into seven "watches"—from 8 p.m. to midnight, first watch; midnight to 4 a.m., middle watch; 4 to 8 a.m., morning watch; 8 a.m. to noon, forenoon watch; noon to 4 p.m., afternoon watch; 4 to 6 p.m., first dog watch; 6 to 8 p.m., second dog watch.

Half an hour after the beginning of a watch "one bell" is struck. A half-hour later, or one hour after the beginning of the watch, "two bells" strike, and so on. In the second dog watch, although only three half-hours have elapsed since "one bell" the end is denoted by "eight bells," for the reason that 8 o'clock is always "eight bells." Under this system, noon, 4 p.m., 8 p.m., midnight, and 4 a.m. are "eight bells," with the other hours and half-hours corresponding.

Another method used by astronomers of calculating time is "sidereal time." The day of sidereal time is the period of one complete revolution of the earth upon its axis, and is determined by measuring the transit of fixed stars. The sidereal day contains 23 hours, 56 minutes, and 4 seconds of mean solar time.

In music, time means the division of a measure into the fractional parts of a whole note. It is usually indicated by a fraction, as $\frac{2}{4}$, $\frac{3}{4}$, placed immediately after the clef at the beginning of a piece or a movement. Common time ($\frac{4}{4}$) is sometimes indicated by C. In such fractions the lower number indicates the kind of notes to be used as time standards, while the upper figure shows how many make up a single bar.

Time Switch. Any switch which automatically operates to open or close a circuit under the influence of time is known as a time switch. The simplest example is probably the electric alarm clock which closes a pair of contacts at a given time each morning, to operate an electric bell or a buzzer. Another very simple type is used on the landings in blocks of flats to control staircase lighting—we switch on the lights before we mount the stairs, and a clockwork escapement switches them off again after a certain period— say, after half a minute, when we have had time to reach our landing.

More elaborate forms of automatic device switch "on" for a certain time *at* a certain time. A "programme clock" can be arranged to ring bells at a school, say, every three-quarters of an hour for five seconds; to wait a whole hour at lunchtime, and not to operate at all on Saturdays and Sundays. Other forms of switch can be arranged to turn the wireless set on and off at certain times, so that we hear only the programmes that we prefer to hear. Yet others switch street lights, or shop window lights, on and off at the correct times. Another class of automatic switch measures short intervals of time, for the exposure of photographs, and other similar uses.

Time switches can be roughly divided into three classes—mechanical, synchronous, and electronic. In the mechanical types the operation is by clockwork; and the mechanism for operating the switch is worked directly by means of levers which are moved by pins on a rotating disk driven by the clockwork. Similar operating principles are used in the synchronous type, the main difference being that the driving mechanism is not clockwork, but is a synchronous motor as used in electric clocks (*q.v.*). Both types have their advantages and disadvantages : the synchronous motor, for example, falls " out of step " if there is a long interruption of the current supply. If this should occur on, say, a street lighting circuit, it would be necessary to send a man round to every lamp-post to advance the clocks again. On the other hand, clockwork time switches require regular winding every week, or fortnight, or so.

When used for controlling street lighting, both types of time switch are usually arranged to switch on the lights half an hour after sunset, and switch off half an hour before sunrise. To do this, they are fitted with a device known as a " solar dial," which changes the position of the contacts by a small amount each day; thus, winter and summer, the time of switching on and off changes with the sun's variation in time of rising and setting.

When very short intervals of time are required, the accuracy of a mechanically operated switch may not be sufficient for the purpose; and accurate timing devices have been built utilising electronic methods. In these the time taken to discharge a condenser is used to " fire " a thyratron (*see* Electronic Devices), for example. Such devices are used in the accurate timing of welding processes.

Tin. The largest use of this metal is in coating steel to protect it. The millions of tin cans we use every year are made of tinplate because tin resists food acids. A coat of tin less than one-half of one-thousandth of an inch thick is enough for this purpose. Steel for cans is plated by dipping sheets of it in molten tin or by passing continuous strips on high-speed rubber rollers through an electrolytic tinning bath. Kitchen utensils are electroplated with a thicker coat of tin.

Tin enters into many alloys, such as bronze, Babbitt and other bearing metals, type, solder, pewter, and the low melting-point alloys of which fuses are made (*see* Alloys). Alloys of tin are used to make collapsible tubes such as those for tooth paste. Tin chloride is used in dyeing and weighting silk. Pure tin is bluish-white. With a specific gravity of 7·3, it is heavier than zinc. In hardness it is between lead and gold. The melting point is 449° F.; boiling point, 4,100° ; chemical symbol, Sn (from Latin, *stannum*); atomic number, 50; atomic weight, 118·70; valence, 2 and 4.

The chief ore is cassiterite or tinstone, a dioxide of tin. Before smelting it is crushed to a powder and roasted to remove arsenic and sulphur. At the smelter it is heated with carbon to separate the tin from the zinc, copper, bismuth, and iron that it

contains. Tin is also refined by electrolysis. The refined product is called " block tin."

The Malay States lead in tin-ore production, followed by Bolivia and the Netherlands Indies. Siam (Thailand), Nigeria, China, Belgian Congo, Australia, Burma, and England yield commercial quantities. Although the United States is the world's largest user of tin, it has no important deposits. Alaska, the chief domestic source, produces but little. Most of its imports of refined tin come from smelters in Singapore, England, and Indonesia.

The use of tin in the form of bronze, an alloy of tin and copper, began thousands of years ago (*see* Bronze). Since deposits of this metal were hard to find, it became an important factor in early commerce. To get it, the Phoenicians sailed from the Mediterranean as far as Cornwall in Britain.

Tipperary. An inland county of the province of Munster, Eire, Tipperary has an area of 1,643 square miles. Much of the surface is level and fertile, though there are hills on the borders. The highest point is Galtee More (3,015 feet) in the Galtee Mountains. The chief river is the Suir. The Shannon flows along the north-west boundary. In the west is the fertile Golden Vale.

Dairy farming is the most important industry. Coal, copper and slate are worked. The county town is Clonmel (population 10,000), where brewing, flour-milling and the making of footwear are carried on. Other towns are Cashel, Tipperary, Thurles, Carrick-on-Suir and Roscrea. The population of the county is 136,000.

Tirol. (Pron. tir'-ol). A beautiful mountainous region, with fertile valleys and quaint villages, the Tirol is divided between Austria and Italy, though the Italian portion is usually referred to as the Trentino. The Tirol lies between Bavaria, Germany, on the north; Switzerland and the northern plain of Italy on the south; with the Austrian provinces of Salzburg and Vorarlberg on the east and west respectively.

The Austrian province of Tirol comprises a series of Alpine ranges intersected by valleys, one of the longest being the valley of the Inn, which rises in Switzerland and flows through Austria into Germany. The western and southern boundaries are very mountainous; almost the only way into Italy is by the Brenner Pass. Main occupations are lumbering in the extensive forests; cattle grazing and dairy-farming on the Alpine pastures; and mining for lead near Landeck and for salt in the neighbourhood of Hall. The capital of Tirol is Innsbruck (*q.v.*).

The region is much visited by tourists in normal times, the principal attraction being the magnificent scenery. The traditional costume of the Tirolese peasants is still sometimes seen: the women in wide velvet hats, embroidered bodices and aprons with snow-white linen sleeves; the men in green velvet waistcoats, black velvet knee-breeches and coloured stockings. The population is 422,000.

The Trentino or Italian Tirol is part of the department of Venezia Tridentina and contains the Dolomites, with their pointed, beautifully-shaped peaks. Owing to the peculiar crystalline composition of the rocks these mountains shimmer in the sunlight with the colours of the rainbow. The southern part of the Italian Tirol is much less mountainous

than the north; and in the warmer climate citrus fruits, olive trees and vines are cultivated. There are also silkworm farms. Chief towns are Bolzano (population 41,000) and Merano (population 12,000).

The people living in the northern part of the Italian Tirol are mostly of German origin, because by the Treaty of St. Germain, signed in 1919 after the First World War (1914–18), Italy was given all former Austrian territory south of the Brenner Pass, including Upper Adige.

Titanium. This silvery metal is almost as strong as steel, but weighs only half as much as that alloy. It was discovered as long ago as 1791 by William Gregor, in the form of compounds, while investigating the black sands found in Cornwall. The German chemist M. H. Klaproth (1743–1817) soon after this isolated the element from the ore rutile, a titanium oxide (TiO_2). It

Dorien Leigh; Paul Popper

'MIDST MOUNTAINS OF THE ITALIAN TIROL

Partly in Austria and partly in Italy, most of the Tirol is mountainous and renowned for its magnificent scenery. In Italian Tirol are the Dolomites, a branch of the Alps, which contain several peaks of over 9,000 feet, such as Le Tre Cime, or Three Peaks (upper). Also in Italian Tirol, in a district noted for its orchards and vineyards, is the health resort of Merano, with its 14th-century church (lower). From the 12th century to about 1420 Merano was the capital of Tirol.

was Klaproth who named it Titanium, after the Titans of Greek mythology, rebellious giant offspring of Uranus.

The chemical symbol for Titanium is Ti; its atomic weight is 47.9, and its atomic number is 22. Its density is 3.5; the metal melts at a temperature of 3,140° F. Ilmenite, named from the Ilmen mountains in south Russia, is the principal ore; followed by rutile (found in Scandinavia, Switzerland, the Urals and the U.S.A.); and by arizonite. Hitherto titanium has been used mainly for making white pigments; but it promises to become important as an alloying agent in light but strong metals for aircraft parts and such uses. An oxide is used to " load " thin paper for books, in order to render the leaves opaque; also it has applications in the processing of rayon. Today, as in the time of its discoverer William Gregor, the black sands of certain beaches afford much of the raw material for this metal.

Titian (c. 1477-1576). The old artist laid down his brush and gazed at the masterpiece before him, a painting in which he had marvellously revealed the splendour of 16th-century Venice. " I think," he said, "I am beginning to learn something about painting."

It was Titian (pron. tish'-an) who spoke — Titian, the Venetian painter, who, during his long life of industry, success, and honour, produced more than 600 pictures, glowing miracles of colour, many of which are today numbered among the greatest masterpieces.

Titian, whose name in Italian was Tiziano Vecelli, was born at Pieve di Cadore in northern Italy. He spent the first 10 years of his life amid magnificent scenery, and was always attracted to the landscapes of his childhood. In his early pictures it is possible to recognize the places which were familiar to him, and of which he made many pen-and-ink sketches.

He arrived in Venice with his elder

brother, also a painter, early in the 16th century. After a short time in the studio of a mosaic worker he became a pupil of Gentile Bellini (about 1430–1516), one of the most eminent Venetian painters, and about 1507 came under the influence of Giorgione (1477–1511).

Titian's pictures soon brought him fame, riches, friends and honours. In 1513 he became superintendent of paintings to the Venetian Government, which office brought him a considerable income. Among his duties were the completion of certain works begun by Bellini and the painting of the portraits of the Venetian doges or rulers, as they succeeded one another in their office. Between 1510 and 1518 he painted some of his finest compositions. The masterpiece of his youthful period is Sacred and Profane Love, in the Borghese Gallery, Rome. His portraits of celebrated men are among his outstanding works, and include The Man with a Glove, and Unknown Man—both

Anderson

GLORIOUS PORTRAIT BY TITIAN

Titian ranks as one of the greatest of all portrait painters, and his work is unrivalled for grandeur of style and sumptuousness of colouring. The portrait above, in the Pitti Gallery, Florence, is typical of his manner. The identity of the sitter is unknown ; by some it is stated to be a Duke of Norfolk, but others consider it more likely to be a certain Ippolito Riminaldi.

in the Louvre, Paris. His first portrait of Charles V of Spain so delighted that monarch, who was also ruler of the Holy Roman Empire, that Titian was made a Count and Knight of the Golden Spur and his children were raised to the rank of nobles of the Holy Roman Empire.

In 1518 the Assumption—Titian's first notable religious painting—was unveiled in the church of Santa Maria dei Frari in Venice. Other works included The Assumption of the Madonna, Christ and the Pharisee, Bacchus and Ariadne, The

Fletcher, Teager and Markham
THREE SPECIES OF BRITISH TITS
Active hunters of insects, the tits or titmice are welcome visitors to the garden for they are not only extremely decorative but they eat enormous quantities of harmful pests. For this latter reason these birds are welcomed also by the wise farmer and the fruit-grower. Above, the two lively little beak-to-beak creatures are blue tits or tomtits. Top right, a great tit. Lower right, a coal or cole tit.

dresseri) has a black head, grey wings and back, and white cheeks, throat and breast. Much more rare is the crested tit (*P. cristatus scoticus*) found in the pine forests of some parts of Scotland; it has a pointed crest of black and white feathers, the rest of its plumage being reddish-brown. The red-brown bearded tit (*Panurus biarmicus*) is found only in the Norfolk Broads. The long-tailed tit (*Aegithalos caudatus roseus*) has a black back mixed with

Entombment of Christ, and the Virgin with a Rabbit. In 1537 he painted the Battle of Cadore (destroyed by fire in 1577), regarded by his contemporaries as his finest work. His wonderful Venuses include the Dresden Venus (begun by Giorgione) and the celebrated Venus and Adonis (of which several copies were made). Titian died of plague on August 27, 1576.

Tits. Members of the tit or titmouse family (*Paridae*) are widely distributed throughout the world, most abundantly in the northern hemisphere. One very familiar species in Britain is the lively little blue tit (*Parus caeruleus obscurus*), about four and a half inches in length, with blue head, white cheeks, yellowish-green back, black throat, blue wings and tail, and sulphur-yellow underparts.

Other British species include the great tit (*P. major newtoni*), which is about six inches long and the largest of them all. It has a glossy black head and throat, a white patch under each eye, and greenish-yellow underparts. The coal or cole tit (*P. ater britannicus*) can be recognized by its black head, a white patch on the nape of the neck, and general bluish-grey plumage. The marsh tit (*P. palustris*

rose, the wings and tail are black edged with white, and the tail is very long. It builds a wonderful domed nest, with an entrance hole in one side near the top (*see* illustration in page 443). All the other tits nest in holes in trees, old posts and similar positions. The eggs though small are astonishingly numerous, those of the long-tailed tit sometimes numbering as many as fifteen.

These are extremely useful birds to the farmer and gardener, for though they sometimes peck holes in fruit their food consists chiefly of insect pests. The tits have astonishingly keen sight and they diligently hunt for and pounce upon insects' eggs deposited in cracks in the bark of trees.

Toad. Of the 100 or so species of toads, two—the common toad (*Bufo vulgaris*) and the natterjack (*B. calamita*)—are native to Great Britain. The common toad is about three and a half inches long when fully grown, brownish in colour, with some darker spots or marblings, and with the underside whitish, speckled with black. The natterjack is smaller than the common toad—about three inches in length—and is distinguished by a yellow line down the back. Its general colour is greenish.

Unlike that of the frog (*q.v.*), the skin of the toad is dry and warty, and contains glands from which a milky fluid may be exuded if the animal is roughly handled. The eggs are laid in yard-long strings—not in masses as is the case with frog's spawn. The tadpoles hatch out in about three weeks. Toads

hide from their enemies during the day under loose stones, rubbish, or an old log, and come out at night for food—insects, slugs and small worms. During the winter they hibernate (sleep) for months at a stretch.

The South American toad (*B. marinus*), six inches long, is the largest of all the species. The Surinam toad (*Pipa americana*), native to the Guianas and Brazil, has its back studded with spine-bearing pimples; the eggs stick to the back of the mother, and the soft skin rises between and around them so

A. B. Thompson; J. Clegg

TWO KINDS OF TOAD

They may not be considered handsome, but they live upon slugs, caterpillars and other small vermin of the garden and the farm. At the top is seen the common toad, in colour brownish above and whitish below. The lower species is the natterjack toad, greenish in colour with a yellow streak down the back.

that they become entirely embedded in it. They develop in this position until the tadpole stage is ended (about 12 weeks), when the perfectly formed toads emerge and the mother sheds the pitted skin.

From ancient times superstitions about the toad have been generally believed. It was once thought that it carried a jewel hidden in its head. And its long and deep winter sleep may have given rise to the belief that a toad could live for hundreds of years entombed in a hole in a tree or rock.

Tobacco. According to an old story, a servant of Sir Walter Raleigh (1552–1618) one day saw clouds of smoke rising around his master's head. Startled at the sight, the servant dashed the con-

tents of a tankard over Raleigh and ran shouting for help. This was the first time he had seen anyone smoking, for the use of tobacco was unknown in European countries until the discovery of the New World. The plant was first brought to Europe in 1558. It owes its generic name *Nicotiana* to Jean Nicot (1530–1600), who was the French ambassador to Portugal and did much to spread its popularity.

The earliest explorers of America found the natives using the tobacco leaf for smoking and chewing and as snuff; and pipes have been found in burial mounds dating back to A.D. 700. The name tobacco comes, indeed, from the native word (*tobago*) for a stick used as a pipe by the ancient inhabitants of what is now the Dominican Republic in the West Indies. Often, as with the pipe of peace of the North American Indians, its use was a sacred tribal custom. This strange Indian practice of " drinking smoke " appealed to the Europeans as one of the marvels of the New World. Tobacco was first used in Europe as a medicine, then as a luxury, and the fashion of smoking was set by Sir Walter Raleigh.

From the time of its earliest use in Europe there was much outcry against tobacco. James I (1566–1625) of England and Scotland published a pamphlet against its use. In the face of all opposition its popularity increased until now there is scarcely a people or tribe which does not use it in some form.

There are more than 50 varieties of the tobacco plant, but only three are in commercial use. *Nicotiana tabacum*, native to central America and the West Indies, grows to six feet or more and bears pink or rose-coloured flowers, and is the basis of the tobacco industry of the United States. *N. rustica* is a smaller plant (four feet) with yellow flowers, which originated in Mexico and is now the main source of Turkish and Egyptian tobacco. The third species is *N. persica*, which has white flowers. It is scarcely known in the western world, for it is grown only in Persia and is smoked in the hookah of that country. All *Nicotianas* are annuals; that is, they do not live on from year to year.

There are considerable variations in size, thickness and colour of the leaf, when tobacco is grown in varying soils and climates. The plant is generally coarse and rank, with drooping leaves on a thick central stem, gummy and clammy to the touch owing to the sticky secretion of short hairs. The buds of the showy, trumpet-shaped blossoms of plantation plants are usually cut off before they open; and the black seeds are so small that 60,000 of them would just about fill a tablespoon.

The leaf is green when harvested and does not acquire the characteristic colour and flavour until

GROWING AND SHIPPING RHODESIAN TOBACCO

By courtesy of the Rhodesian Government and the Port of London Authority

Some of the British Colonies and Dominions cultivate tobacco with marked success; from Rhodesia alone there now comes a crop of about 47 million pounds a year. The photographs show: 1. A field of tobacco plants in Southern Rhodesia. 2. Sorting tobacco leaf into grades. 3. Tobacco barns, where the leaves are 'cured,' the process involving drying and fermenting. 4. Hogsheads of tobacco in a bonded warehouse (under supervision of Customs officials) in London, from which they may be drawn only upon payment of duty. 5. Unloading hogsheads at the Port of London. The production of tobacco in Rhodesia and other parts of the British Commonwealth has been stimulated by the fact that in Great Britain the duty paid is less than on leaf imported from the United States.

it is cured, which includes drying, fermentation and ageing. There are three methods of drying. Sometimes the leaves are sun-dried, which results in a sweet chewing tobacco. Cigar tobaccos are usually air-dried in barns so constructed that ventilation can be carefully controlled. The third method is by artificial heat, either from open fires or flues. Open fires tend to give the tobacco a smoky odour. In flue-curing the fires are outside the drying-sheds, and the heat is brought in by iron pipes. This is the process which produces the bright yellow leaf used for light cigarette and pipe tobacco. The black Latakia tobacco is grown in Syria, its distinctive flavour and colour being produced by subjecting the leaves to the smoke of green boughs of the evergreen oak.

With all kinds of tobacco, after drying, the leaf is brittle and cannot be handled without crushing it to a powder, so it is left hanging in a damp atmosphere for the leaves to absorb moisture and become soft and pliable. They are then stripped from the stem, sorted, made up into small bunches, and fermented by piling in stacks five or six feet high and leaving for three or four weeks at a temperature of 130° Fahrenheit. When fermentation is complete the tobacco is graded and packed. It is sometimes aged in a warehouse for a period of years to make it more mellow. For the manufacture of cigarettes and pipe tobacco very careful blending of different grades of leaf is necessary.

The tobacco industry is of vast economic importance, the world's crop being well over two million tons a year. Various regions are specially suitable for growing particular types of tobacco. The leaf from Cuba, for instance, is most suitable in making cigars, and that of Turkey and the Balkans for making the best quality "Turkish" cigarettes. Canada, Rhodesia and South Africa each produces thousands of tons a year. The climate of Great Britain is not as suitable as that of hotter countries to ripen the leaf.

For pipe and cigarette smoking tobacco is often flavoured and given an artificial aroma with "sauces" made from essential oils and spices, though in Great Britain there are strict government regulations as to what may be added.

Tobacco owes its sedative and habit-forming powers to the drug nicotine, a deadly poison, though most of this is burnt during the process of smoking. Nicotine itself may be dissolved out of the tobacco leaf by treating it with a solution of lime or caustic soda; the nicotine goes into solution and may then be distilled off. It

has a use as an insecticide; for killing insect pests in plants it is either sprayed over the plants in the form of a dilute solution, or is mixed with some harmless powder and then dusted on.

In most countries a government tax on tobacco, whether home grown or imported, is a valuable source of revenue.

Tokyo. (Pron. tō'-ki-ō). At the head of Tokyo Bay on the east coast of Honshu Island is the city of Tokyo, the capital of Japan. Twice the city was devastated in the first half of the 20th century: in 1923 earthquake and fire destroyed nearly half of it; and in 1944 and 1945 incendiary and high explosive bombs dropped by United States airmen during the Second World War (1939–45) wiped out more than three-quarters of what was then the centre of the Japanese Empire.

Between 1923 and 1930 a new Tokyo rose from the ruins of the old. To reduce the risk from fire, the main streets were widened and several areas were cleared of buildings and converted into parks. Wooden bridges over the numerous canals were replaced by concrete spans. New structures in the business section, which extended from the waterfront to the centre of the city, were designed to withstand earthquakes, with frames of concrete and steel. Schools and factories were modernized, with balconies and roofs to serve as outdoor gymnasia. Then came the Second World War (1939–45), during which most of this new city was destroyed.

Nearly one-fifth of Japan's industrial products came from the capital's factories; Japan's network of railways started from the central station close to the harbour; and the business life of the country centred in the Ginza, Tokyo's main thoroughfare,

Sport & General

BOMB HAVOC IN TOKYO, CAPITAL OF JAPAN
Devastated by earthquake and fire in 1923, Tokyo suffered still more severely from high explosive and incendiary bombs dropped by United States airmen during the Second World War (1939–45). The business section was almost wiped out (above), only a few steel and concrete buildings surviving. (*See also* illustration in page 3222).

TOKYO'S MODERN COMMERCIAL QUARTER
The business life of Tokyo centres on the Ginza (above) and neighbouring streets, where only a few buildings escaped destruction in the Second World War. The circular structure is the Nippon Theatre, over which float balloons carrying advertisements. (*See also* illustration in page 3221).

Tolstoy. Count Leo (1828–1910). Few men of modern times have had greater effect on the world's thought than Tolstoy. His novels are models of power and realism, and his social ideas had world-wide influence. He was born on the family estate of Yasnaya Polyana in the Russian province of Tula, on September 9, 1828, the fourth child of a noble family. He was educated at home and at Kazan University, and in his book Childhood he writes of his life in the country, of learning to ride a horse, and of trying to fly by jumping out of a second-storey window.

After a visit to the Caucasus, in southern Russia, he seems to have become more serious-minded, and in 1852 he joined the Russian army. With little to occupy his spare time he began writing, Childhood being the first of a series of stories which appeared within the next two years. His experiences as an officer in the Crimean War (1854–56) provided him with plenty of material for what was then his hobby. The Sevastopol Stories expose the horror of war. His campaigns gave him the basis for his story of Napoleon Bonaparte's invasion of Russia, which is entitled War and Peace (1864) and is regarded by some critics as the best novel ever written. At intervals appeared various other works, the most outstanding of which are, perhaps, the novels Anna Karénina (1875) and Resurrection (1899).

Although Tolstoy was acclaimed as a superb novelist, fame as a writer did not satisfy him. Even as a youth he had tried to relieve the dreadful poverty of the peasants on the family estate, and in

and the neighbouring streets. The city had three large universities—the Imperial, Waseda and Keiogijuku—naval and military colleges, and numerous technical schools.

On a low hill in the centre of Tokyo stands the Imperial Palace, a collection of buildings surrounded by a double line of moats. It is a modern building erected in 1888, and it suffered some damage during the air raids of the Second World War. Near the palace is the Nihonbashi (Bridge of Japan), from which for years all distances in the country were measured.

For centuries merely a fishing village called Yedo or Jeddo, Tokyo received its present name in 1868 when it was made the capital of Japan. During the Second World War it was first raided by United States aircraft in April 1942, but it was not attacked again until November 1944. Thereafter the bombing became more frequent and intense, and when the Allies entered the city in September 1945 they found 80 per cent had been laid waste. The headquarters of the Allied occupation forces in Japan was in Tokyo. The population in 1940 was 6,779,000, making it the largest city in the world after London and New York,

TOLSTOY : NOVELIST AND REFORMER
Tolstoy was born and lived much of his life at Yasnaya Polyana (' bright glade '), about 130 miles south of Moscow. This painting, by Repin, shows him clad in peasant dress working in his scantily-furnished study. The illustrious novelist renounced his artistic work to become the prophet of a new creed.

later life he was led by his religious beliefs to a stern conception of his duty towards the peasants.

In 1891 he declared his beliefs: To be perfectly pure; to be free (not to take oaths of allegiance); never to use violence for the protection of oneself or of others, even against an animal; to do good to one's enemies. To carry out such a programme of life seems impossible as society is constituted now ; but Tolstoy, with his accustomed fervour, tried hard to put his beliefs into practice He was as simple in his habits as a peasant, and he divided his wealth among his family. Even so he could not gain happiness, for his eccentric ways angered his relatives; so in the last year of his life he determined to leave his home and to live among the peasants. He left his estate on October 28, 1910, but fell ill and died at a railway station on the following November 7.

The Kingdom of God is Within You, one of the works containing his religious views, was banned in Russia for its revolutionary ideas and was sent to England and the United States, where it was published in 1892. His home at Yasnaya Polyana became a Tolstoy Museum, but was almost destroyed by the Germans during the Second World War (1939-45).

Tomato. It seems strange that this annual plant, whose fruit (red or yellow when ripe) is so widely enjoyed, is a relative of the poisonous deadly nightshade. A native of South America, it was first introduced into Britain in 1596 and was grown originally as an ornamental greenhouse plant. The early name of the fruit was " love-apple." It was not until well into the 19th century that the idea that tomatoes were poisonous was proved false, and the plant began to be cultivated for its produce.

Grown from seed, the tomato plant (*Lycopersicum esculentum*) is naturally bushy, with yellow, bell-like flowers. It is cultivated in all temperate regions of the world, and there are a number of varieties. The fruit, which is produced in bunches of six or more on a strong stem, is eaten raw or cooked, and is also made into soups, sauces and relishes. The juice is drunk, and numerous tinned food products are flavoured with tomatoes.

In Britain the plant is too tender to allow of a long season of growth outdoors, so for open-air crops seed is sown under glass early in the year and the resulting plants set out in the open ground in early June, for the fruit to be produced and to ripen in the few weeks of summer.

Tongue. This specialized muscular structure has a fixed hind part or " root " and a mobile front part or " tip." It is very richly supplied with blood vessels and nerves, and is covered with a complicated mucous membrane which forms little projections, called papillae, on its upper surface. These register the sense of taste (*q.v.*). The tip of

the tongue tastes sweet things best; the edges taste acid, and the back bitter and salt—the four main divisions of taste. Taste and smell (*q.v.*) really run in a coupled team.

The tongue plays a part in the first process of digestion, which takes place in the mouth. It pushes the food mass around and under the teeth, mixing it with saliva and helping it on its way down the gullet. But it is in speech that the tongue has its supreme function. Just as the opposable thumb gave Man the lead over the monkey, enabling him to grasp tools and to undertake delicate and subtle work, so the tongue is indispensable to speech, the great distinguishing mark between Man and the lower animals. In speech it works in unison with the speech centre (not present in " dumb " animals) of the brain, the teeth, and the larynx which houses the vocal cords. (*See* Voice).

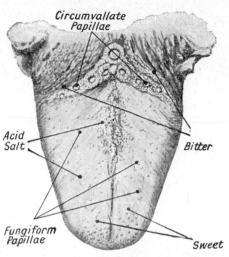

THE TONGUE'S TASTING AREAS
Little projections called papillae register the sense of taste. The circumvallate (walled in) ones are surrounded by a raised ring of membrane ; the fungiform type resemble fungi.

The under surface of the tongue is covered by thin mucous membrane in which large blood vessels are very close to the surface. A drug placed under the tongue is absorbed almost as quickly as if it were injected by a hypodermic syringe. Sometimes the strand of mucous membrane which attaches the tongue to the floor of the mouth is too tight, and the condition is known as " tongue-tied." A skilful snip by the surgeon cures it. In health the tongue is moist and clean; in disease it is generally dry and coated.

Toronto. On the north-west shore of Lake Ontario, Toronto is the capital and chief city of the Province of Ontario, Canada, and is the second town in size and importance in the Dominion, ranking next to Montreal. It occupies a plateau which rises gradually from the lake to a height of about 300 feet. Two rivers, the Don and Humber, and a number of wooded ravines make the residential areas very attractive.

There is a frontage of about 10 miles on the lake, and from there steamers go regularly to Canadian and United States ports, fetching chiefly iron ore, grain and coal. On the lake front also are the grounds and permanent buildings of the annual Canadian National Exhibition. Cheap electricity is obtained from the Niagara Falls and the Gatineau river power plants and is utilised by hundreds of industries. The products of Toronto include aeroplanes, motor-vehicles, agricultural implements, electrical equipment, metal goods, tinned fruits and vegetables, and flour. It is also the printing and publishing centre of Canada. A number of United States firms have established factories in the city.

In the centre of the city is Queen's Park, in which stand the provincial Parliament buildings and the University of Toronto. Founded in 1827, the university is one of the largest in the British Commonwealth. The Royal Ontario Museum and the

MEMORIAL TO TORONTO'S FOUNDER

Canadian National Film Board

This statue of John Graves Simcoe, founder of the city of Toronto and
first Lieutenant-Governor of Upper Canada, stands in Queen's Park,
Toronto, close to the Ontario Provincial Parliament building.

Art Gallery, the last-named opened in 1926, are
prominent in the educational life of the city. There
is also a flourishing Conservatoire of Music.

First named York, Toronto was founded in 1794
on the site of a fort erected by the French in 1749.
In the war of 1812–14 between Britain and the
United States, it was twice taken and damaged by
the Americans. It became a city in 1834, when it
was named Toronto, a Huron Indian word meaning
"place of meeting." The population is 667,500.

Torpedoes. This name was originally
applied to any explosive weapon which could attack
a ship under water, whether in the form of a mine
(*q.v.*), an explosive charge on the end of a long spar
over the bow of a boat or, at a rather later date, the
automotive torpedo. Nowadays the mine is regarded as quite a separate weapon; the spar
torpedo is quite out of date, with quick-firing guns
able to keep any vessel at a distance; and the
automotive torpedo has improved out of all recognition. The germ of that idea came from an Austrian
naval officer who took his plans to Robert Whitehead (1823-1905), an English engineer, who had
settled in Fiume, to make a working model.

This proved quite impractical, but
it started Whitehead thinking, and by
1866 he had invented a cigar-shaped
torpedo which not only propelled
itself, without the help of ropes connected with the shore, but had also a
means of making it maintain a set depth
below the water in order to hit the target
where it was most vulnerable. This
last all-important invention took advantage of the fact that the pressure
of water increases with the depth. By
connecting horizontal rudders to a
hinged flap, open to water pressure on
one side and having a very delicately
adjusted spring on the other, Whitehead
contrived exactly what was wanted.

When the torpedo got too deep, the
pressure of the water overcame the
spring, the flap would press down, and
the rudder turned up so that the torpedo immediately came towards the
surface until the spring got the better
of the pressure, when the missile went
down again until after a few preliminary wobbles the torpedo kept a
steady depth. It was perfect in theory,
but the early mechanism was too crude;
some of the torpedoes hit the bottom,
others jumped right out of the water;
some went round in a circle and hit
the boat which had fired them. There
was also a tendency for them to get out
of their course after they had been
fired, but that was rectified later by
the installation of a powerful gyroscope
(*q.v.*), which kept them heading straight
for the target.

In spite of early imperfections the
principles of Whitehead's torpedoes in
the 'sixties are still in use. Projecting
out of the nose of the torpedo is a
"firing pistol" which, when it hits the
side of a ship, is driven back on to a
detonator made of a composition which goes off
when struck (like the cap in a toy pistol). This sets
off the main charge of explosive carried in the
warhead, which can be taken off in peacetime and
replaced by a dummy for practice purposes.

Astern of the warhead is a "flask" of highly
compressed air; this air is released when the
torpedo is fired, driving two beautiful little engines
at tremendous speed. If the torpedo were fitted
with a single screw it would go round in circles;
and there is no room to fit twin screws side by side,
as they are in a ship. So the shaft of the after
screw is made hollow, and another shaft, for the
second screw, passes through it. With the screws
revolving in opposite directions the torpedo keeps a
straight course. It is only the principles which have
continued unchanged; in matters of detail any
number of improvements have been contrived and
are still to be devised. When the British Navy
bought the right to use Whitehead's patent in 1871
the torpedoes were 16 inches in diameter, with a
very sharp nose. Their shape is to be seen on the
arm badges of torpedo ratings in the Navy; but it was
soon discovered that a blunt nose was far better in

every respect. The first torpedoes could maintain 9½ knots for 250 yards, and 6 knots for 800, giving the average man-of-war plenty of time to dodge them. But speed was soon improved. The 16-inch torpedo was abandoned for a 14-inch type with much better speed; and the original launching trough, which tipped the torpedo into the sea off a ship's deck and left it to proceed entirely on its own power, was replaced by a tube which gave it a start by shooting it a considerable distance by a charge of gunpowder or compressed air.

The first torpedo tubes were all fitted on deck, shooting the torpedo into the water with a mighty splash; and these are still in use in destroyers, motor torpedo-boats, and other types. Before very long, however, the submerged torpedo tube was introduced. The unfired torpedo was not nearly as likely to be exploded by a chance bullet or small shell, but the aim was not usually so accurate as with the deck-fired weapon, and measures had to be taken to prevent the pressure of water breaking the torpedo in two before it got clear of the ship.

Through the 'seventies and 'eighties constant improvements were being effected. The explosive was made far more powerful; the torpedo was made faster and given a longer range; above all it was made more reliable. The reliability of the torpedo depended on it being kept in first-class condition on board ship, and the highly trained Torpedo Branch of the Royal Navy

saw to that. Torpedoes are still like ships, in that no two behave in precisely the same way; but the men soon became accustomed to them and put them right.

Naturally the designers of ships liable to be attacked built them with greater protection, and a more powerful torpedo became necessary. The biggest explosive charge in a 14-inch torpedo was 79 lb. but in 1891 the 18-inch torpedo was introduced, with a charge of 199 lb. which was of course much more dangerous. In later types the charge was reduced a little to secure a better shape, but for many years it was sufficient to sink a battleship of ordinary type or a large cruiser. But protection was improving rapidly, as well as the speed and handiness of ships, and the power of the quick-firing guns which were mounted as a protection against

Admiralty Official

BEFORE AND AFTER THE DISCHARGE OF A TORPEDO

On the deck of a British warship torpedoes are seen (upper) in position in their tubes for discharging. These are 21-inch weapons, with an extreme range of about 25,000 yards. When the target is struck the explosive charge carried is fired by a rod fixed in the torpedo's nose. Lower, a torpedo just after it has been projected from its tube. A gyroscope keeps it on a straight course; and the depth of submersion is regulated by mechanism adjusted before firing.

torpedo craft. As a result, more attention was paid to increasing the speed and range of torpedoes. Ships were fitted with steel nets hanging from long booms clear of their sides when they were at anchor or steaming very slowly, the idea being that they would detonate an enemy torpedo well clear of the ship, where its explosion could do little harm. As a

reply, net-cutters were fitted in the noses of torpedoes, and they were soon able to go right through the nets to their target.

The torpedo-boats which were built to fire torpedoes in the 1870s developed into the destroyers, capable of destroying torpedo-boats and of torpedoing big ships themselves. In the 'nineties and at the beginning of the 20th century the submarine (q.v.) was made practical, at first relying entirely on the torpedoes she carried as her weapon of offence.

The submarine, of course, always fired from a submerged tube, aiming with the periscope, and seemed to be a more dangerous enemy to the big ship than any of her predecessors. So the warship designers had to spare more and more weight as protection against torpedoes, giving the ships an internal wall of armour some distance from the ship's side which, combined with numerous water-tight bulkheads, limited the amount of water which a single explosion was likely to admit into the vessel.

Torpedoes were next made 21 inches in diameter, with high speed and a range up to 11,000 yards; they carried an explosive charge so powerful that it would often fracture the internal armour as well as the side of the ship. These were the torpedoes which were generally used during the First World War (1914–18), in submarines as well as in all the up-to-date surface vessels; and they were responsible for sinking a large proportion of the ships destroyed on both sides. Accuracy had been greatly improved, but there was still a large proportion of misses. As practically all nations used torpedoes of the same sizes, and as they were very expensive weapons which took a long time to manufacture with the necessary precision, they were fitted so that they filled with water and sank when they had reached the end of their run. This was in order that the enemy should not pick them up and be able to use them.

Fox; Charles E. Brown

TORPEDO AND TUBES IN A SUBMARINE
Lowering a torpedo into a submarine (upper) is a tricky business, because the weight is about one and a half tons and the length 22 feet. In the lower photograph the rear ends of four torpedo tubes in a submarine are visible; the torpedoes are discharged by compressed air, their own motors being automatically started as they leave the tubes.

TORPEDOES

After the First World War the British battleships Nelson and Rodney were fitted with torpedoes 23 inches in diameter, but although these gave a tremendous explosion they were not considered as satisfactory as the 21-inch type. A little later the Japanese went in for still bigger torpedoes—up to 27 inches—but they, again, had many disadvantages to set against their increased explosive power. In the meantime the dropping of torpedoes by aircraft was developing rapidly. In the earlier types the aircraft could not manage to lift anything bigger than an 18-inch without sacrificing other qualities ; but long before the end of the Second World War (1939–45) improved aircraft carried 21-inch torpedoes, and did an immense amount of damage.

In the early part of the Second World War there had been an enormous wastage of torpedoes dropped by aircraft ; but as the war progressed, and training improved, this trouble was overcome and torpedoes dropped from the air came to be regarded as the best means of pulling down the speed of a fleeing enemy warship by tearing a hole in her side and so giving the heavy ships the chance of coming up and destroying her by gunfire. Battleships, and even cruisers, were shown to possess a considerable resistance to torpedo explosion ; they were more easily sunk by salvoes of heavy, high explosive shells.

The Germans, Italians, and Japanese were all enthusiasts on torpedo warfare, and had spent large sums on experiments before 1939. The main object was to overcome the great disadvantage of the torpedo ; when its compressed air had done its work in the engines, the spent air had to escape, which meant that it left a line of bubbles which showed the torpedo's path and, what was more serious, the position of the submarine which had fired it. While the British had been improving the speed and range, the Germans worked on evolving a torpedo which did not leave any track, and the Japanese tried to overcome the handicaps of very large size. The Japanese torpedoes, as much as 27 inches in diameter, when they hit the target would blow away the ship's side for a length of 75 feet. The Italians were far behind, but were given most of the results of their allies' research.

The Germans' efforts were the most interesting and scientific. At the end of the Second World War they had solved the difficulties of the trackless

Central Press; Charles E. Brown

TORPEDOES CARRIED BY AIRCRAFT

Naval aircraft, as well as submarines, launch torpedoes against enemy vessels. Top, a torpedo is being fitted to the special launching mechanism underneath the fuselage of an aeroplane. Lower, a torpedo is seen at the moment of release : the pilot has brought his aircraft almost to the surface of the water before letting the torpedo go. The launching gear starts up the engine of the torpedo, which is aimed by the pilot pointing his machine at the target.

British Official

A 'HUMAN' TORPEDO IN ACTION

First used by the Royal Navy in 1943, this form of torpedo was manned by a crew of two, who wore waterproof suits and oxygen helmets to enable them to breathe under water. In front of the craft was a detachable explosive charge (with a time-fuse) which could be attached to an enemy vessel, the crew then leaving the danger zone on the hull of the torpedo.

torpedo, but it was not yet in full production. Various means had been tried. One was not to drive the engines on ordinary air but to compress two gases which, when they combined after doing their work, formed a liquid which mixed with the sea instead of coming to the surface in bubbles. A prominent scientist was experimenting with the use of a new chemical fuel that would give a torpedo a range of many miles, and by radio waves could bring it home again at the end of its run. Electric torpedoes did away with the track, but after trying them British naval officers preferred the extra range and speed given by the old method. Torpedoes were fitted to steer a corkscrew course under the water, and this, when they were fired into a convoy, greatly increased the chances of a hit. Others were fitted with acoustic and magnetic firing apparatus so that they were discharged by the noise or magnetism of a ship as they passed close to her. Such a " near miss " would not do much harm to a big man-of-war, but it was enough to sink a merchantman. Another type was the " spider torpedo," connected to the firing point by very thin wire which was paid out as it travelled and which carried electrical impulses by which it could be steered towards the target.

The Japanese used pure oxygen, ordinary air, and electricity for propulsion, and in spite of the huge sizes that were fitted in some ships their navy preferred the 21-inch electric type, with a range of 7,500 yards at 30 knots, to any others.

Then what came to be known as the " human torpedo " was developed by all the navies. It took various forms. In some it was an ordinary torpedo taken close to its objective by one or two men riding

astride ; it could then be aimed at short range, the mechanism was started and the men left it and attempted to escape by swimming. The Japanese type carried the pilot inside, and he was naturally blown up by the explosion. In another type the engine made very little noise to betray its position to listening gear, and the warhead was detachable and could be fixed to the hull of the enemy ship to be set off by a time fuse.

After their victory the Allies took possession of enormous stocks of torpedoes and all the notes made by enemy scientists on the work that they had been doing. These are still being studied by the victorious navies and, with experiments to test their quality, will keep Allied experts busy for years.

Torpedo-fish. A living electric battery, the torpedo-fish (*Torpedo marmorata*) belongs, as its alternative name of electric ray implies, to the ray family. It gets its electricity from a group of prism-shaped compartments of muscular fibre running perpendicularly through the body near the head. The upper side of the fish is the positive pole of the battery, the lower side the negative. When it is out of water, the torpedo-fish must be touched at two distinct points before the circuit is complete and the shock received. But in water, which is an excellent conductor of electricity, only one point of contact is necessary.

W. S. Berridge

'ELECTRIC' TORPEDO-FISH

Belonging to the family of skates and rays, the torpedo-fish has a system of electric storage cells. It uses this ' shocking ' apparatus not only to defend itself but also to kill its prey. A large specimen may weigh nearly 200 pounds.

This " shocking " apparatus is used not only for defence but to stun and kill prey. Without this the fish would probably starve, for it cannot swim very fast, and the teeth and small mouth are not suited for catching other fish. So it lies on the bottom of the sea until some creature comes close enough to be electrocuted. Human swimmers occasionally touch one of these creatures with their feet, and mysterious cases of drowning may be attributed to the crippling effect of such electric shocks.

Like other fish of the ray family the torpedo-fish is flat, with its mouth on the underside. It is rarely found in British waters, but frequents the Mediterranean and the waters off the Atlantic coast of North America. It attains a length of four feet.

Other fish that have the faculty of generating electricity are the electric eel (*Electrophorus electricus*) of Brazil and Guiana and the electric catfish (*Malapterusus electricus*) of the waters of tropical Africa.

do not expect beauty from a member of the tortoise family, the species of water-tortoise, or terrapin, seen here is a some creature. This picture was made as the reptile tried mb up the sides of the aquarium, in which it was kept as a pet, and thus displayed its underside to full advantage. The strange arrangement of the markings has earned it the name geographic terrapin, since the underside looks like a sort of map; and on the side of the head there is a brilliant scarlet stripe.

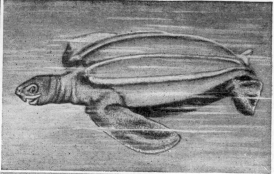

THREE KINDS OF AMERICAN TURTLE

At the top left is the green turtle, source of turtle soup ; this one ventures ashore to deposit its eggs. Top right, the huge leather-back, whose jacket is leathery and ridged with seven keels, swims solemnly along in search of cuttlefish. The snapping turtle (lower) is unable to withdraw into its small shell, but its enormous head and strong jaws are, on most occasions, protection enough.

turtle (*Dermochelidae coriacea*) occurs in tropical waters, but is occasionally seen off the coast of Britain. Its "shell" is a leather-like case somewhat resembling crocodile skin in texture. Most turtles are flesh-eaters; the huge leatherback is especially fond of cuttlefish.

The hawksbill turtle (*Eretmochelys imbricata*) is valuable on account of the fact that it yields the finest tortoiseshell of commerce; the shields from its bony shell, when polished, are a mottled brown and almost transparent. It takes its name from its long hooked snout, and grows to about 30 inches in length. The snapping turtle (*Chelydra serpentina*) of North and Central America grows to a length of three feet, is very fierce, and protects itself with its powerful jaws.

The name terrapin is loosely applied in the United States to a number of edible turtles, found mainly in brackish water. One of these is the geographic terrapin, its markings resembling a map

HE MAY HAVE SEEN NAPOLEON !

When Napoleon's empire crumbled and the emperor was taken to St. Helena in 1815, this giant tortoise already lived there. He was still crawling about the island walks when Napoleon died ; he was still crawling in his ancient way when Napoleon III rose and fell ; and, unless some accident has overtaken him, he is still around there today.

flesh, which float about like weeds in the water and lure small water creatures to the turtle's ready jaws.

In prehistoric times tortoises and turtles reached even larger dimensions than the modern species. Some were six feet in length and three or more feet high. Like other monsters of bygone ages these eventually became extinct.

(*see* colour plate facing page 3228). The diamond-back species is popular in the United States as a table delicacy, and is specially bred for the markets.

In rivers of South America, New Guinea and Australia live "side-necked" turtles, which bend the neck sideways instead of retracting it into the shell. The matamata of the Guianas and northern Brazil, sometimes over a yard in length, has the neck fringed with filaments of

Toucan. A freak of the bird world, the toucan has an enormous bill, far too big for its head, which gives it a completely unbalanced look. It reminds one of the beak of a hornbill (*q.v.*), and, as in the case of that other huge bill, no satisfactory explanation has ever been given for this extraordinary feature. The toucan's tongue is also unusual, for it has side notches and is flat and feather-like; the tail is joined to the body with a ball and socket joint, and can be raised above the back with a jerk. In so far as the beak and tongue are concerned, these are possibly adaptations enabling the bird to hold the heavy fruits on which it feeds, and to reach forward among the branches without falling over; for though large and strong the beak is honeycombed with air spaces and is very light in weight.

The plumage is black and green, usually marked with white, orange, red, or blue. The eye, with a double iris of green and yellow, has a broad blue orbit and is surrounded by a patch of bare orange-coloured skin. There are 50 to 60 species of this bird. The common toucan (*Rhamphastos toco*) is about two feet long, including its eight-inch beak. It is most abundant in the Amazon valley; some species are found in Central America and Mexico, and indeed they are the New World's equivalent of the Old World hornbills. They feed on insects and reptiles, as well as fruit, often doing great damage to orange orchards. The nest of this curious bird is built in a hollow tree; the eggs are white and glossy.

Touch. The sense of touch is manifested in various ways and is one of several senses localized in the skin. True touch is aroused by light contact of any object with the skin. The sensation of cold is imparted by objects of a lower temperature than the skin and does not require contact. If there is a cold object near, we know it. The feeling of warmth is quite distinct from both touch and cold, and is felt when the temperature of the skin is raised. Pain is caused by excessive stimulation or by injury. Any sensation of any of the kinds mentioned may become painful if its intensity becomes too great.

It can be shown by going carefully over a small area of skin with a light hair or wooden point that the touch sensation can be aroused only in certain places. This is because there are special nerve-endings for touch, and these vary in number in different parts of the body. So, too, with the other senses; each has its own nerve fibres, its own

F. W. Bond

WHAT A TOUCAN CAN DO

The beak of the toucan is enormous compared with the size of its head, and why it should need so huge a pair of mandibles is still a mystery. This red-billed toucan is holding an egg in its beak.

pathways in the spinal cord, and its own centre in the brain.

Touch is important in giving us information in regard to contact, shape, smoothness or roughness, and so on. You can deceive the sense of touch if you get the nerve-endings out of their usual relation. For example, cross your fingers and feel for a marble or the end of a pencil. On touching it, it will feel like two objects.

In addition to the four sensations named there is also one of pressure, connected with the muscles and joints and the skin. By this we judge weights. By the so-called "muscle sense" it is possible to tell the position of any limb pretty accurately. If you are blindfolded and somebody bends your arm, you can tell at what angle it has been set. In the blind the sense of touch becomes very important and can be cultivated to a high degree. (*See* Blind).

Tower of London. Except for some scattered Roman remains the Tower is the building that can take you farthest back into London's early history. This ancient fortress, palace and prison is enclosed by high massive stone walls—the best part of a mile in total length. They were built when men still fought with bow and arrow. They antedated gunpowder, and the heaviest battering ram would be powerless against them.

Bastion towers are placed at each corner of the wall, and there is a moat (now used as a parade-ground) with a drawbridge across it. Indeed, the Tower is a magnificent example of a medieval castle with moat and wall, outer and inner wards, "donjon" or keep, and the usual arrangement of battlements and towers.

Let us suppose we have arrived at the Tower by way of the Thames. To the right is Tower Bridge, to the left London Bridge. Coming down Tower Hill to the Lion Gate, on the western side, you proceed through the Middle Tower, cross the moat by means of a drawbridge, and enter the outer ward The warders of the Tower are popularly called Beefeaters (*q.v.*); their uniform dates from Tudor days. (*See* colour plate facing page 396).

In the centre of that side of the Tower facing the river is Traitors' Gate, through which State prisoners were brought by water. Passing down the outer ward until you are opposite this entrance, you turn

Fox

FORBIDDING PORTAL OF TRAITORS' GATE

At the foot of St. Thomas's Tower, which lies at the Thames' edge in front of the Tower of London, is the wide archway of the Traitors' Gate. Through this water-gate State prisoners used to enter the Tower, among them Lady Jane Grey and Sir Thomas More. In the old days the water came right up to the Gate.

workers formed for the purpose of maintaining wages and salaries, regulating hours of work, and dealing with the general working conditions of the members. A number of these unions are very powerful organizations, and their weapons of collective bargaining (joining together for a common purpose), and of striking if their demands are not met, are effective as a rule, unless their objects fail to obtain the general support of the public.

In Britain the Ministry of Labour and National Service has the power to intervene in trade disputes with a view to settling them by arbitration. During the Second World War (1939–45) a National Arbitration Tribunal was established, which dealt with all industrial quarrels between workers and their employers. This was the first measure of compulsory arbitration to which the trade unions gave their assent.

Combinations of workmen, with some of the characteristics of trade unions, existed long before the Industrial Revolution (q.v.) in the latter part of the 18th century, though it was a criminal offence for two or more workmen to combine to secure an increase of wages or any change in the terms of their employment until the repeal of the Combination Acts in 1824. This marked the beginning of the modern trade union movement.

Unions grew stronger and more numerous, and gradually smaller ones began to consolidate into national amalgamations. In 1868 the Trades Union Congress was established as a voluntary association of British trade unions for safeguarding their interests in Parliament and to initiate legislation for the benefit of labour as a whole.

Apart from their political work in conjunction with the British Labour Party, trade unions have a number of other activities. They negotiate with associations of employers and with the government; they make cash allowances to their members during periods of unemployment and sickness, collect contributions, and undertake educational work through week-end and summer schools and lectures.

Trafalgar, BATTLE OF. October 21, 1805, was the greatest day in the annals of British naval history. By 1804 Napoleon Bonaparte (q.v.) had made himself master of continental Europe, and only the sea power of Britain remained as an obstacle to his ambition of conquering the British Isles and regaining lost French possessions in North America and India. Nelson (q.v.), had joined forces with Lord Collingwood off the Spanish port of Cadiz, where the French and Spanish fleets had sought shelter.

Nelson then disposed his fleet in such a way as to tempt the enemy to come out, which they did on October 19. In the early morning two days later the two fleets came in sight of each other. Having given his signal "England expects that every man will do his duty," Nelson closed with the enemy off Cape Trafalgar, between Cadiz and Gibraltar.

Collingwood in the Royal Sovereign actually led the first attack on the rear of the enemy with the stronger of the two units into which the English fleet was divided. The latter consisted in all of 27 ships-of-the-line and four frigates, and was opposed to a Franco-Spanish fleet of 33 vessels, commanded by Admiral Villeneuve. The most remarkable part of the battle was probably the close fighting between the Victory, Nelson's flagship, and the Téméraire on the one side, and the French Redoutable and Fougeux. A shot from the Redoutable mortally wounded Nelson at the height of the action.

Fifteen enemy ships were captured or destroyed, and 12,000 prisoners were taken. The English losses in personnel were only 449 killed and 1,242 wounded, and not one ship lost. Napoleon's hopes of invading England were thus finally shattered.

NELSON'S BRILLIANT VICTORY AT TRAFALGAR

The defeat of the combined French and Spanish fleets off Trafalgar, on October 21, 1805, established British maritime supremacy. The above illustration is after the painting by Clarkson Stanfield in the Royal United Service Institution.

Bearing down upon the enemy in two parallel lines, Nelson and Lord Collingwood broke the French line at two points, and half the enemy ships were either captured or destroyed. Not a single British ship was lost, but Nelson was killed.

About the TRAMCAR and its RIVALS

Steam trams came into use long ago to transport workers to and from their homes, but generally the horse-drawn tram served towns until the electric car replaced it—to be challenged, in turn, by the trolley-bus.

Trams and Trolley-Buses.

The word " tramway " at one time meant a " way " (i.e. road, which might even be of rough stones) over which " trams " or tubs of coal were drawn. Rails came later, and the first tramways thus formed inspired the first railways. The more modern idea of tramways in cities for passenger hauling came much later. Horse-drawn trams were running in London between Paddington and the Marble Arch in 1851, and the horse-drawn tram did not, in fact, disappear until after the First World War (1914–18). Steam trams were popular at one time—as were " cable cars," pulled along by clamping themselves to an endless rope laid over pulleys in an underground conduit. But the tram as most of us know it—or rather, knew it, for it is fast disappearing in Britain—is the electric tram.

This appeared at a time when there was no such thing as a reliable petrol engine, and the motor-bus was a thing unknown. The idea of a tramway system, clean and smokeless, run by electricity generated at a central power station, must have seemed very attractive, particularly as public transport was becoming a vital necessity. The first overhead-wire tramway system in Britain was operated in Leeds, from Roundhay to Sheepscar, in 1891. By 1925 there were more than 14,000 trams in Great Britain.

Unlike electric railways, tramways are laid in public streets, and it is not possible to use an exposed third rail to carry the current. Many systems of current collection, some ingenious and some frankly foolish, have been designed; but only two have survived: the overhead wire to which contact is made by a grooved wheel or a carbon block supported on a " trolley-pole " (or boom); and the conduit system, in which a third rail runs in a small tunnel or conduit between the lines, and connexion is made through a " plough " attached to the tram. The plough passes along in a slot at the top of the conduit. Certain sections of the London tramways used both systems; and where the conduit system ends the trolley-boom is raised to the overhead lines and the plough is removed—to be transferred to a car going in the opposite direction. The overhead system is more commonly met with, since its cost per mile is about half that of a conduit system.

Direct current is universal for tramway work, and the voltage used is in the neighbourhood of 500 to 600 volts. The running rails are used for a return conductor.

Widely Varying Design of Trams

There is a vast difference in appearance, speed, and power—to say nothing of passenger comfort—between the trams of 1900 and those of today. The early cars had two $7\frac{1}{2}$ horse-power motors (modern motors are at least ten times as powerful for the same weight), open upper decks and driver's platform, and hard bench seats. The " Feltham " tram of today has complete enclosure, comfortable seats, and pneumatically operated doors, yet the fundamentals of operation are very much the same as with the trams of almost half a century ago.

From the trolley-boom, which bears on the overhead wire, the current is taken through a " circuit breaker " (an automatic switch which opens if the current rises past a safe value) to the " controller." This last is a switching device having a number of contacts inside which open or close in a certain sequence, as the driver moves the handle, to regulate the speed of the vehicle.

Trams almost invariably operate on " series-parallel " control (*see* page 1129), there being two motors per tram. When the driver moves the handle of the controller from the " off " position to the first " notch " (so called because there are actual notches in a " star wheel " inside, into which a spring-loaded roller falls, thus giving movement in definite steps, and preventing the contacts being left in a half-and-half state), both motors are connected to the line, in series with each other and with a resistance.

" Notching-up," or further movement of the handle, cuts out the resistance in several steps, until the " full series " notch is reached, and the motors are connected to the line without any resistance. But at this stage they are *in series* with each other, so that each one receives only *half* the full voltage applied. The next notch re-inserts all the resistance once more, but connects the two motors *in parallel*; and further notches cut out the resistance once more, until the full-speed notch is reached, and both motors have *full* voltage applied. The speed of the tram then depends on the car weight (i.e. number of passengers), the gradient of the track, and, to some extent, on the wind.

The Different Methods of Braking

The earliest means of checking the speed of a tramcar was by a hand brake operated by a revolving handle; most trams are still so fitted, although other types of brake are now provided in addition. Air brakes, like those fitted on trains, are often used; and there are two principal types of electric braking—" rheostatic " and track-shoe braking. In the latter, steel " shoes " are mounted just above the track, and are fitted with electro-magnet coils. When these coils are energized, the shoe is attracted to the rail and bears down hard upon it. In order that an interruption of supply (such as the trolley jumping off the line) will not render the brake useless, the electro-magnet is usually energized from the motors themselves; and the motors, when switched off and driven by the momentum of the still moving car, act as dynamos.

This principle of running motors as dynamos is used in rheostatic braking—the motors are switched off the supply line and are connected across the resistance, the latter being cut out step by step. This results in a heavy current flowing, generated by the moving car itself; and since no dynamo will give electrical power without our first putting in mechanical power, the momentum of the car is.

British Thomson-Houston Co., Ltd.; Metropolitan Vickers Electricity Co., Ltd.

OVERHEAD-TROLLEY TRAMS: OLD AND NEW

Early in the 20th century tramways were put into operation in densely-populated areas in Britain ; the first trams (left) had an open top deck and were unsightly compared with the latest all-enclosed models (right). Both these vehicles, running on rails, are operated by the overhead system: a trolley attached to a pole makes contact with a conductor wire.

rapidly absorbed—at a rate depending on the amount of resistance across the motor terminals. Either type of electric brake is exceedingly powerful at high speeds, but the braking effect gets weaker as the speed drops, so that it will not bring the car to a dead stop, or hold it on hills. For this reason the hand brake or air brake is used to supplement the braking power of the electric brakes.

Electric braking is usually applied by the controller, the motorman moving the main handle in one direction for the power notches; and in the reverse direction for the braking notches. The controller has another one (or sometimes two) small handles upon it. The first is the reversing switch and the second (when fitted), is a " hospital " switch, which can cut out of circuit either one of the motors. Thus, in the event of the breakdown of one motor, the tram can at least " limp home " on the other.

The Trolley Vehicle Which Needs No Rails

Although experimental trolley-buses (first called trackless trams or trackless trolley-cars) were built as early as 1909, it was not until the early 1920s that the trolley-bus emerged as a serious rival to both trams and motor-buses. The relative advantages of the systems are roughly as follows. Motor-buses can go " anywhere," and require no track or overhead wires, thus being cheaper in the first place. On the other hand, they are expensive in running costs and repairs; they carry relatively few passengers as compared with a tram; and they require petrol or Diesel fuel oil which must be imported.

Trams use electricity generated at a central station, and are cheap to run (particularly when they are required to move large numbers of passengers). Their machinery is much simpler and stouter than that of the motor-bus. They have a very long life and cost little in repairs. On the other hand, the cost of track laying is enormous; and the track needs re-laying every 5 to 10 years. Trolley-buses, like trams, use electricity from a

central supply, and are simpler than motor-buses. They carry more passengers than do motor-buses (but not so many as trams). They do not require a track, but do need overhead supply lines, and cannot run about " anywhere." They are much more silent and comfortable than either trams or buses; they cost more to run than trams, although not so much as buses.

The trolley-bus is a sort of hybrid between bus and tram. Like the bus, it is steerable, and rubber-tired. Like the tram, it has an electric motor (usually only one), and obtains its power from overhead lines. Since it has no steel track to act as a return conductor, it needs double wires, and two trolley booms. These are longer than those fitted to trams, to allow the vehicle to move some distance sideways without the booms coming off the wire. When a tram breaks down, the track is blocked and there may be a traffic " jam " which will last for hours. But when a trolley-bus breaks down the conductor merely pulls down its trollies, and other vehicles steer past it. Most trolley-buses are fitted with batteries so that they can manoeuvre at a slow speed for short distances independently of the supply.

Compared with trams, the differences in control are that the controller of a trolley-bus is operated by pedal; and very often " regenerative braking " is used. Instead of the plain series motor (see Electricity; Motor) a compound-wound motor (i.e. one having both shunt and series fields) is used. When braking is required, an adjustment of the field strength enables the motor to be loaded up like a dynamo; but the power, instead of being expended uselessly in resistances (where its energy is dissipated as heat), is returned to the supply line.

In Great Britain, the tram is on the decline. Of more than 14,000 trams in service in 1925, there were little more than half left twenty-five years later. The route mileage of tramways had dropped from 2,700 in 1920 to a little over 1,000 miles.

Trolley-buses had taken over some 800 miles, the remainder being replaced by motor-buses.

In other countries the tram still flourishes, being operated more on the lines of a " light railway." This means that instead of ending at the town or city boundaries, they often link up adjoining towns, with limited stops, high-speed operation, and a track separate from (but not fenced in from) the roads. In America, for example, there have been great strides made in the last few years in the design of trams (or "street cars," as they are called there) in the matter of passenger comfort, smooth acceleration, and high-speed operation. A recent design, known as the "P.C.C." (President's Conference Car), contained many revolutionary

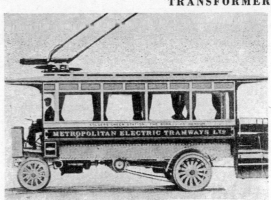

British Thomson-Houston Co., Ltd.

TROLLEY-BUSES OR TRACKLESS TRAMS

In 1909 the first experimental trolley-bus (upper) ran in England. This type of vehicle did not become a serious rival to the trams and the motor-buses until the 1920s. A modern trolley-bus is seen in the lower photograph (its trolley-boom here being in the lowered position).

features, which have been still further developed. It seems probable that the future of the tram lies along the lines of light-railway procedure rather than that of a system confined to crowded city streets.

Transformer. When Michael Faraday built his famous iron ring, with two separate coils of wire wound upon it, and demonstrated that a momentary electric current in one coil would cause a similar momentary current in the other one, he little knew that he had, in fact, made the first transformer. This is a device so important to the electrical industry that modern power systems would be impossible without its aid.

The principles of electro-magnetic induction are explained elsewhere in our volumes (*see* Electricity; Induction Coil), and it is sufficient here to remind ourselves that the rise or fall of a " magnetic field of force," when interlinked with a conductor, sets up an electromotive force in the conductor, in exactly the same way as if the magnetic field were stationary and the conductor moved.

A transformer is the simplest possible piece of electrical machinery, possessing no moving parts. It consists in its simplest form of two coils of insulated wire, known as the primary and secondary windings, magnetically linked by means of an iron

core. The primary winding is supplied with alternating current, thus setting up an alternating magnetic flux in the core, and inducing an alternating current in the secondary winding. If the two windings have equal numbers of turns, the secondary voltage will be *equal* to the primary voltage; if the number of turns are not the same, the voltages will be *proportional* to the number of turns in each winding. Thus a transformer with 1,000 turns on the primary, and 10,000 turns on the secondary, having 100 volts applied to the primary, will give 1,000 volts on the secondary. In the transformer we have the simplest possible method of converting alternating current from one voltage to another for any purpose. Transformers used for power work (i.e. at the mains frequency of 50 cycles) vary in size— from the tiny " pocket-size " transformer used for ringing door-bells off the electric mains (having an output of about 5 volt-amperes), to the giants of the Grid (*q.v.*), which deliver 100 MVA (100,000 kVA or kilovolt-amperes) at 132,000 volts. Even higher voltages are encountered and some transformers for high-voltage testing step up current from 3,000 volts to 1,000,000.

The core which provides the magnetic circuit for linking the coils is " laminated "—built up out of thin sheets of special quality steel. Unlike the induction coil, which has a short core, the transformer core forms a continuous path. In the case of ring cores, there are no joints at all, and these cores are the best from the magnetic point of view. On the other hand, it is difficult to wind coils on to a ring, and it is impossible to use machine-wound coils for this purpose; so that for convenience in manufacture the core must have joints. But it is usual to arrange that these joints are " staggered," i.e., overlapped so that they do not come opposite. When the coils surround the core, the transformer is called a core-type one; when the iron surrounds the coils, the apparatus is a shell-type transformer.

Large transformers are almost invariably of the core type. If, as is usually the case, they are intended for three-phase work (*see* Electricity), they have three (or sometimes five) " legs " to the core; for single-phase work they have only two legs. It is usual to put half the primary and half the secondary

British Thomson-Houston Co., Ltd.

A TRANSFORMER IN A POWER STATION

An electrical device for changing alternating current from one voltage to another, transformers are essential pieces of machinery in electric power systems. The one above delivers current at 132,000 volts.

on each leg, and not to wind the primary on one leg and the secondary on the other. This is to keep down to a minimum "magnetic leakage" (i.e., flux which does not pass through both coils).

High-frequency transformers, such as are used in wireless work, are usually made without iron cores on account of the losses which would occur. Another type of core is known as the dust core, where the coils are embedded in a container filled with dust of highly magnetic alloys.

Although the transformer is highly efficient, even losses of only 1 or 2 per cent on a large transformer represent a great deal of power which must be dissipated as heat. It is usual to immerse transformers of above about 5 to 10 kVA in a tank of oil, which also helps to insulate the windings. Cooling is carried out by fins or circulating tubes on the tanks, but very large transformers have separate oil radiators, and fans to provide an air blast.

"Auto-transformers" are a class in which the primary and secondary are not electrically separate, but are joined on to one another so that the low-voltage winding is tapped across a portion of the high-voltage winding. This results in a considerable saving in copper in many cases.

For high-voltage work it is not convenient to connect ammeters or voltmeters direct to the supply, and therefore voltage transformers and current transformers are used. The voltage transformer or potential transformer has its primary wound for the supply voltage (say 11,000), and the secondary for 110 volts. Since the ratio between primary and secondary is fixed, the voltmeter can be calibrated to read 11,000 volts, although the actual voltage applied is only 110. In the same way current transformers are connected in series with the load; their primary is frequently a single turn, or a straight bar pushed through a ring core

on which is wound the secondary. The latter is connected to the ammeter which has a 5-ampere winding even if the primary current is one of several thousand amperes.

Transjordan. An Arab kingdom of south-west Asia, which lay wholly east of the Jordan river, Transjordan (the name means "across Jordan") in June 1949 proclaimed itself the Hashimite Kingdom of the Jordan (see Jordan), having extended its territory to the west of the river. It is bounded on the north by Syria ; on the east by Iraq ; on the south by Saudi Arabia. Much of the country is desert, except in the west, where wheat, millet, date palms, barley, maize, tobacco, and vines are grown. Many of the people keep herds of sheep, horses, and goats, moving continuously to fresh pastures. Potash is found in the Dead Sea, and there are deposits of phosphate. There are 372 miles of motor roads, affording communication with Baghdad in Iraq, and Jerusalem and Haifa in the State of Israel. The capital is Amman (population 55,000), where there is an aerodrome. Other centres are Es Salt (50,000), Irbid, Ma'an, and Mafrak.

Under Turkish rule from the 13th century to the end of the First World War (1914–18), Transjordan was established as a State controlled by Great Britain under a mandate of the League of Nations in 1923, and it became an independent Kingdom in 1946. During fighting that broke out in Palestine between Arabs and Jews after the withdrawal of British troops in 1948, Transjordan forces played a leading part on the Arab side with a view to establishing an Arab State in Palestine. After some inconclusive fighting, hostilities ceased in April 1949. The population is about 400,000.

Transport, MINISTRY OF. Established in 1919, this British Government Department took over various responsibilities in connexion with transport which had formerly been dealt with by the Board of Trade and by other branches of the Government. The new Ministry was made responsible for measures ensuring safety on the roads and the railways, and while it had nothing to do with the management of the transport systems of the country it gave advice on various matters connected with them.

In the Second World War (1939–45) the Merchant Navy, which played such an important part in keeping up the food supplies of Great Britain, was at first controlled by the Ministry of Shipping, but this latter was combined with the Ministry of Transport in 1941. The new Ministry took the title of Ministry of War Transport, and controlled all shipping, railways, ports, road transport and highway maintenance. In 1946, however, the shipping responsibilities were handed over to the Board of Trade, and the Ministry of Transport resumed its old title. In that year, too, it became the authority for the control and maintenance of 7,500 miles of major roads in Great Britain, which had formerly been looked after by Local Authorities.

The Minister of Transport appointed the members of the British Transport Commission established by the Transport Act of 1947 to direct all forms of public transport (excluding air transport), which were nationalised by the Labour Government on January 1, 1948. The administration of these transport services for passengers and goods is the responsibility of six public bodies, known as the Railway Executive, the London Transport Executive, the Road Haulage Executive, the Road Passenger Executive, the Docks and Inland Waterways Executive, and the Hotels Executive.

Transvaal. (Pron. tranz′-vahl). One of the four Provinces of the Union of South Africa, the Transvaal is separated by the Limpopo river from Southern Rhodesia on the north, from the Indian Ocean by the Portuguese Colony of Mozambique on the east, by the Vaal river from the Orange Free State in the south, by the Limpopo from the Bechuanaland Protectorate in the west. Its area is 110,450 square miles; much of it is a continuation of the South African plateau, with an elevation varying between 3,000 and 5,000 feet.

Extent.—Area of the Transvaal 110,450 sq. m. Population 4,183,800, of whom about a quarter are Europeans.

Physical Features.—Bush-covered veld between rivers Limpopo and Vaal, with isolated hills, including the Witwatersrand ridge, and (in the south-east) the Drakensberg Mts. (highest point in Transvaal, Mt. Anderson, 7,490 feet).

Principal Products.—Maize, tobacco ; live-stock ; gold, silver, diamonds ; coal, copper, iron, lead ; machinery ; bricks and pottery ; soap and candles.

Chief Towns.—Johannesburg (762,910), Pretoria (capital of province and administrative centre of the Union, 167,649), Germiston (133,880).

The climate is dry and healthy, rain falling chiefly in summer. The main rivers are the Vaal and Limpopo, which with their tributaries drain most of the Province. In the south-east is a range of the Drakensberg Mountains, of which Mount Anderson (7,490 feet) is the highest point.

The mineral resources of the Transvaal include gold (the main source of wealth), diamonds, copper, coal, iron, silver, tin and lead. Stock-raising is the leading agricultural industry; cattle, sheep and goats are reared. There are also ostrich farms. The principal crops are maize, tobacco, potatoes, barley, oats, coffee, cotton, tea and grapes. In the cities are iron and brass foundries, brick, tile and pottery works, and soap and candle factories.

The largest city is Johannesburg (q.v.), the centre of the gold-mining industry. Pretoria (q.v.) is the capital of the Province and the administrative centre of the Union, though the South African Houses of Parliament are at Cape Town.

On the eastern border of the Transvaal is the Kruger National Park, nearly 8,000 square miles in extent, one of the world's largest game preserves (see illustration in page 3014), where there are

Courtesy of South African Railways

NATIVES CROSSING A FORD IN THE TRANSVAAL

here is much wild and hilly country in the Transvaal, a province of the Union of South Africa, and generally roads cross the rivers at a drift or ford. Natives are seen fording the 'Njelele river in northern Transvaal. Though the water is only knee-high a storm in the hills at its source would soon change the slowly-flowing stream into a torrent, which might hold up all traffic for several hours and cause severe damage to the native villages on its banks.

representatives of nearly all the animals known in Africa, from elephants to the smallest deer.

The Transvaal was settled by Boers (descendants of the early Dutch colonists) who trekked northward from Cape Colony after the British had freed their slaves in 1834. Great Britain recognized the Transvaal as an independent Boer Republic in 1852, but annexed it in 1877, this action leading to a Boer rebellion. In the ensuing war the British were defeated at Majuba Hill in 1881, and the independence of the Transvaal was restored, though Britain retained control of foreign policy. Fresh difficulties arose when gold was discovered on the Witwatersrand (the Rand) in 1884, and thousands of non-Boers flocked to the goldfield. These immigrants soon outnumbered the Boers, who denied them any say in the government of the country. The British Government endeavoured to intercede on behalf of the newcomers, but negotiations proved fruitless and the Boer War (1899-1902) broke out.

The conflict was ended by the Peace of Vereeniging, under the terms of which the Transvaal became a British Crown Colony; but it was granted self-government in 1906. In 1910 it was incorporated into the Union of South Africa. The population is 4,183,800, of whom 1,042,000 are Europeans.

Treasury. A Government Department in Whitehall, London, the function of the Treasury is to control the management, collection and expenditure of the national revenue. Its nominal head is the First Lord of the Treasury, an office usually held nowadays by the Prime Minister. The other Lords Commissioners of the Treasury, who are all members of the Government of the day, are the Chancellor of the Exchequer, three or four Junior Lords and a Parliamentary and a Financial Secretary (who are Government " Whips," i.e., persons responsible for seeing that the members of their party vote when required). The Chancellor of the Exchequer holds a most responsible post, among his duties being the presentation to Parliament of the Budget, or " balance sheet " of the nation's expenditure, usually once, but sometimes twice a year. The Permanent Secretary of the Treasury ranks as the chief official of the British Civil Service.

Treaties. Compacts or agreements between two or more States are known as treaties, and are much like contracts between individuals. They can be made only by sovereign (independent) countries. The constitution and laws of every government determine in whom the power of negotiating treaties resides. In the greater number of European countries the treaty-making power nominally resides in the sovereign or the head of the State.

The most important class of treaties is political. Nations are created or destroyed, or their boundaries changed, by the treaties of peace by which countries settle their differences at the end of wars, as in the case of the Treaties of Versailles, St. Germain, and Sèvres, which ended the First World War (1914–18).

Another class of treaties which have been important in making history are those forming alliances or leagues. Usually such alliances are defensive, the nations agreeing to aid one another only in case of attack, as in the Triple Alliance of Germany, Austria and Italy, made before the First World War; and the North Atlantic Treaty agreed upon in 1949 by the United States, Canada, Great Britain, France, Belgium, the Netherlands, Luxemburg, Norway, Italy, Portugal and Iceland.

Treaties of arbitration have become increasingly important—some for the settlement of particular disputes, others providing for the peaceful settlement of any " justiciable " (suitable for examination in a Court of Justice) dispute which may arise (see Arbitration). Other political treaties determine boundaries, or guarantee the maintenance of certain conditions, as the neutrality of Belgium and Switzerland or of the Suez and Panama canals.

The increasing interdependence of nations has resulted in the growth of an enormous body of treaties relating to many subjects which are not political—Customs duties, fisheries, the extradition of criminals, postal regulations, telegraphs, submarine cables, weights and measures, monetary standards, and so on. These agreements are often distinguished from political treaties by the name " convention." Several of these have resulted in permanent international organizations such as the Universal Postal Union (see page 2662). International conferences in connexion with such subjects paved the way for the Charter of the United Nations, which has taken over the regulation of many of these world concerns (see United Nations). The United Nations also provides for doing away with the evils of secret treaties, by a provision requiring the registration with it of all treaties among its members.

Treaties become valid only when they have been ratified (approved by the Governments of the contracting parties), and States may refuse ratification if their representatives exceed their authority. With few exceptions the negotiation and the ratification of treaties in European countries are conducted by the same officials, and ratification follows as a matter of course. In the United States, however, though the President makes treaties, these have to be ratified by the Senate to become effective.

Refusal to abide by a treaty is a cause of war, unless it has been cancelled by mutual consent or otherwise annulled. If either party refuses to perform a single stipulation of a treaty the other party is released from his obligations, and the entire agreement ceases to be binding; or the injured party may insist upon compliance and demand indemnities for damages caused by the breach. Usually the period of its duration is stated in the treaty.

Many important treaties and conventions are framed by international bodies known as " congresses " or " conferences," such as the Congress of Vienna (1815) and the Congress of Berlin (1878). The determinations of such bodies may be expressed in statements known as " declarations," such as the Declaration of Paris (1856). " Concordat " is the name applied to an agreement between the Pope and a secular power for the regulation of ecclesiastical affairs. The earliest concordats were associated with the so-called " Investiture Contest," concerning the appointment of candidates to ecclesiastical offices and the conditions under which they were to hold Church and lay property, which disturbed Europe in the 11th and 12th centuries and was eventually settled by the Concordat of Worms in 1122.

Eric J. Hosking

trees have taken so kindly to British soil—in the south at —as the Wellingtonia, and here is a magnificent group of of these trees in an English park. In their native Californian haunts they are the largest trees in the world, but they will scarcely reach such dimensions with us. Even so, many individuals have already exceeded 100 feet in height, though introduced only in mid-Victorian days. Its conical shape and buttressed bole make this tree easy to recognize even from afar.

lecay while the tree continues to flourish, with little danger to its chances of long life except through its slightly diminished powers of resistance to the wind and its increased liability to retain moisture, which may lead to disease. " Tree surgery "—a modern profession—repairs such damages by cleaning out the cavity and applying a waterproof filling.

In the case of palms, which have no heartwood, sapwood, cambium, or true bark, the woody tissue runs in a complex network of fibres scattered throughout the pithy trunk. (*See* Palm).

Trees perform indispensable services to the land itself. They rank with grasses as defenders of the soil against the encroachment of the sea and floods. Willows in cold and temperate regions, and mangroves in the tropics, are among the most efficient soil-makers and soil-binders. In wooded regions the temperature is more equable and the atmosphere moister than in treeless regions, other conditions being the same. The long roots of trees enable them to tap underground water sources inaccessible to types of vegetation with roots near the surface, and the foliage of a large tree gives out an enormous amount of moisture.

Again, trees have an immense influence on the fertility of the soil—not merely that underlying the forest itself, but that of the whole watershed which drains it. The leaf-mould (decayed fallen leaves) of centuries produces one of the richest soils, which absorbs and retains moisture well. Thus the forests act as reservoirs of rain water, from which it drains slowly. Furthermore, in hilly regions trees prevent the rain from washing away the soil, by holding it with their roots, and make life possible where otherwise there would be nothing but bare rock.

Deforested regions, visited by infrequent torrential rains, are subject to destructive floods and droughts, and tend to become desert, as in parts of China. The institution of forest reserves, and the increasing interest in the science of forestry, indicate an awakening appreciation of the invaluable service of trees.

Among the strangest trees are the tropical mangrove and banyan, which send down from their extended branches roots that grow into supporting trunks, so that the tree in time becomes a grove (*see* Banyan Tree). Then there is the baobab or monkey-bread tree, which grows immensely broad without becoming proportionately tall, so that its trunk may measure 20 to 30 feet in diameter with a height of only 60 to 70 feet; and its branches, 50 to 60 feet long and each as thick as a good-sized tree, sweep the ground with their foliage. The melon-like fruit, eaten by monkeys, is known as monkey-bread. Another arboreal oddity is the

Australian bottle-tree, which is shaped somewhat like a soda-water bottle (*see* page 533). In South American forests are several different " cow-trees," which yield a creamy, pleasant-tasting juice, said to form a substitute for milk; these are generally related to the trees from which rubber is obtained. The " deadly upas-tree," whose poisonous breath was once believed to be fatal to every living creature within 10 miles, has been proved a traveller's fable; the real upas, however, does have a poisonous juice.

There are only three portions of the solid earth in which trees do not grow; near the Poles, on mountain tops above the timber line (which of course varies in height according to the latitude), and in deserts.

Willow and birch, so stunted as to be the size of shrubs, grow farther north than any other woody plants; farther south are conifers, which usually form also the highest forest belt in the mountains of northern latitudes, and extend into the temperate lowlands and beyond.

From the north temperate zone southward we find the broad-leaved deciduous trees, and breadth of leaf or density of finer leaf growth becomes more and more characteristic of tree foliage as we go from latitudes where oak and ash, elm and willow flourish into those in which palm and rubber and banana trees grow (*see also* Forests). Certain families of the conifer tribe occur in the tropics, and are found here and there in the Southern Hemisphere, but they nowhere dominate as do conifers in the far north.

From the present distribution of trees it is possible to learn something of the world's history, as we can from the study of animal distribution. The magnolias (*q.v.*), for example, are found in North America, Japan and China. How did closely related species come to be so widely separated ? Vast cosmic changes swept their intervening relatives out of existence millions of years ago, leaving two groups on opposite sides of the earth. But the magnolias and other broad-leaved groups are young compared with the conifers and their allies. The giant sequoias and redwoods of the Pacific Coast are the sole survivors of an ancient and formerly widely distributed conifer group ; the scattered araucarias or monkey-puzzles of the Southern Hemisphere are remnants of another formerly powerful clan. The cycads and the gingko or maidenhair (*see* Gingko) have a lineage that goes back to the Coal Age—for, when we burn coal, we are consuming wood and vegetable debris of a far-distant past when the prevailing forest tree combined a number of the characteristics now found in the fern, cycad and conifer. (*See* Coal).

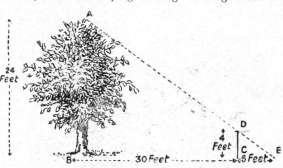

CALCULATING THE HEIGHT OF A TREE
To calculate the height of a tree, AB, walk a known distance, BC, from its base. At C, place upright in the ground a stick, CD, whose length you also know. Then move onwards along CE, a continuation of BC, until, lying down with the eye as nearly as possible on ground level, you see the top of the tree coincide with the top of the stick. Measure carefully distance CE. Then you have a sum to do : CD divided by CE equals BA divided by BE. You know all the dimensions except BA, the height of the tree, which you can then calculate.

The tree ferns of the tropics are the only members of the lower plant groups to reach tree size. All other trees are included in the two main divisions of seed-bearing plants, the *Gymnosperms* or naked-seeded plants, and the *Angiosperms*, plants which hide their seeds in various fruits or seed-cases (*see* Plant Life). The gymnosperms include the conifers ; the small group of the tropical cycads, which are often mistaken for tree-ferns or palms when seen in greenhouses ; and a group represented among living plants only by the gingko.

Of the two principal divisions of the angiosperms, the most primitive, *monocotyledons* (having only one seed lobe), is represented among the trees chiefly by the palms—unless we reckon that giant grass, bamboo, as a tree. The monocotyledonous lily tribe, too, has some tree-like members—branched yuccas which grow 40 feet or so tall. All the other trees belong to the division with two-lobed seeds, or *dicotyledons*.

Among them, the most important tree group, including as it does numbers of the finest timber trees, is found the catkin-bearing, apetalous (having no petals) group, whose inconspicuous flowers lack the corolla and sometimes also the calyx (*see* Flower). They include walnuts, hickories, willows, poplars, birches, alders, beeches, chestnuts, oaks, elms and mulberries. Another group has flowers of normal type, often very beautiful. These are more noted for their blooms and fruits than for their timber, although the maple, the teak and mahogany are valuable timber trees. It includes the very extensive rose family, in which are found the most valuable of our fruits, as well as such trees as mountain ashes and hawthorns. This group also includes the magnolias, the tulip-tree, the horse-chestnut, hollies, and the pea family.

The principle trees native to Great Britain include the oak, elm, ash, Scots pine, beech, birch, lime, poplar, holly, yew ; introduced species include spruce, larch, and several other conifers, the chestnuts, walnut and sycamore.

Trevithick, RICHARD (1771–1833).

This young Cornishman, born at Illogan, was the son of a mine manager, and before he was out of his 'teens held a responsible position as a mining engineer. At Camborne he built a steam road carriage, utilising a high-pressure engine far in advance of the practice of his day. After several tests this carriage came to grief, so the story goes, because Trevithick and his friends went into an inn to get refreshment, and forgot to ensure that enough water had been left in the boiler, which ran dry, got red-hot, and ruined the engine! This was in 1801. Later he built a road carriage which

Science Museum, London

A TREVITHICK ENGINE

In 1801 Richard Trevithick built a steam road carriage, and later turned his attention to stationary engines. The high-pressure engine and boiler here seen were built about 1812 and were in service until 1879.

was taken to London and made trips between Holborn and Paddington (1803).

While in Wales installing his high-pressure engines at ironworks, he built a locomotive to run on the iron tramway connecting an ironworks at Penydarran with the Glamorganshire Canal, a distance of nearly ten miles (February 21, 1804). In 1808 he was again in London, where he opened a miniature public railway running on a circular track near the present Euston Station. After this Trevithick turned his attention again to stationary engines, and it was thus left to George Stephenson (*q.v.*) to take the locomotive the further steps needed to make it a practical means of haulage.

Trevithick's work with the high-pressure engine is his chief title to fame. Boulton and Watt (*see* Watt, James) were building low-pressure engines, and Trevithick was their chief rival. Of course, the making of a boiler to withstand a pressure of 40 to 50 lb. per square inch was very difficult in those days, and some of his boilers blew up—one because the man tending it tied down the safety valve while he went away for food ! Trevithick's competitors made the most of these accidents, but the inventor then fitted two safety valves, with other protective devices. One such was a fusible plug in the top of the furnace above the boiler; if the heat became too fierce, owing to insufficient water, this plug melted and the water "drowned" the fire. A similar plug became a recognized protection for boilers.

The boiler which Trevithick originated was a cast-iron one, cylindrical in shape, and had a " return flue " of horseshoe shape bolted to the inside of the front end. The furnace was in one " leg " of the horseshoe, and the hot gases, after circulating around the bend, came out to the front again to enter a smoke-stack there. He licensed other engineers to build machines on his patented system, and they were used to drive rolling mills, to pump water, to grind corn and to furnish power for thrashing machines. In the London Science Museum is a Trevithick engine which was built about 1812 and gave service until, in 1879, it was presented to the museum.

Trevithick became famous outside Britain also, and he was invited to Peru to improve the steam engines used in the mines. After six years in Peru he lost all his savings in the War of Independence there, and then went to Costa Rica (1822). Returning to England in 1827, he found that though his engines had revolutionised more than one industry, his name, alas, had been forgotten. Robert Stephenson gave him employment for a time, but he died in poverty at Dartford, Kent, on April 22, 1833.

Trigonometry. It often happens in surveying that it is possible to measure one side of a triangle and two of its angles, but because there is a river or some other natural feature in the way the other two sides or the third angle cannot be measured. By the use of trigonometrical rules these facts about the triangle can be calculated without crossing the river, etc., for trigonometry (from the Greek words *trigonon*, " triangle," and *metron*, " measure ") relates the measurement of angles in degrees to the measurement of the sides of triangles in units of length. The main purposes of trigonometry are to determine the area and shape of triangles, the lengths of their sides, and the sizes of their angles.

When, say, we study the sides and angles of a " three, four, five " right-angle triangle, then the side opposite the right angle (the hypotenuse) is five units long, the angle between this and the side three units long is 53 degrees, and the remaining angle is 37 degrees. Thus, we know all the properties of this triangle. Considering the 37-degree angle, the side opposite this angle—three units long—is termed the *opposite* side, while the four-units side is the *adjacent* side.

The ratio of the opposite to the hypotenuse is known as the *sine* of this angle (from the Latin *sinus*, " curve "). The value of this ratio is $\frac{3}{5}$ or 0·6. The ratio of the adjacent to the hypotenuse is termed the *cosine* (complement to the sine) and is here $\frac{4}{5}$ or 0·8. The ratio of the opposite to the adjacent, however, is known as the *tangent* (from the Latin *tangens*, touching). Its value for an angle of 37 degrees is $\frac{3}{4}$ or 0·75. These three terms are usually abbreviated to " sin " (pron. sĭn), " cos," and " tan " respectively. The reciprocals of these ratios are also given special names, as follows :

$$\frac{1}{\sin} = \text{cosec}, \frac{1}{\cos} = \text{sec}, \frac{1}{\tan} = \text{cot}$$

which are abbreviations of *cosecant*, *secant*, and *cotangent* respectively.

It is not necessary to work out the values of every trigonometrical ratio, for they have been determined for every angle and fraction of an angle, and assembled in the form of tables. Sometimes we have to multiply or divide the values of, say, certain sines or cosines, and to make this as simple as possible tables of the logarithms of all the trigonometrical ratios have been made. (*See* Logarithms).

If we want to find the height of a tree we can mark off a distance of, say, 100 feet from its bole and there set up some simple " theodolite " for measuring the angle that an imaginary line drawn from the top of the tree would make with the ground at the point where the instrument has been placed. If this is, say, 31°, then, looking up the value of its tangent in a table of tangents, we find it to be 0·600. This figure is really the ratio of the height of the tree to our distance from its bole. So, multiplying 0·600 by 100 gives us the height of the tree, which is 60 feet. (*See* Geometry; Mathematics).

Trinidad. Most southerly of the islands of the British West Indies, Trinidad is a land of fertile plains, wooded hills and occasional mountains. Tucuche Peak (3,100 feet) is the highest point. The island is seven miles off the coast of Venezuela, close to the mouth of the Orinoco river, and has an area of 1,864 square miles. The climate is tropical, but Trinidad does not suffer from hurricanes that sometimes devastate other West Indian islands.

Agriculture is one of the main occupations. Sugar, cocoa, coconuts and citrus fruits (oranges, lemons and grape fruit) are the chief products. Trinidad is one of the most important sources of oil in the British Commonwealth. Another leading industry is the production of asphalt, which is used for surfacing roads. This is obtained from the Pitch Lake, a mile across and three miles in circumference. (*See* illustration in page 272).

Port of Spain (population 107,000) is the capital, as well as the chief port. The white inhabitants are mostly English, French, Spanish or Portuguese; the large coloured population is of African or East Indian origin. The East Indians, descended from labourers brought to the island in the 19th century to work in the sugar plantations, remain a distinct community with their own costumes and language.

Trinidad was discovered by Christopher Columbus in 1498 and remained a Spanish possession until 1797, when it was captured by British forces. It was eventually awarded to Great Britain under the terms of the Treaty of Amiens (1802). A crown colony, it includes administratively the island of Tobago to the north-east. During the Second World War (1939–45) air and naval bases on the island were leased to the United States for a period of 99 years. The population is 500,000.

Trinity House. On Tower Hill, London, is the headquarters of Trinity House, the corporation which supervises pilotage round the coasts of Britain and is responsible for the lighthouses, lightships and beacons on the coasts of England, Wales and the Channel Islands. Its approval is needed for changes to be made in the lighthouses of Scotland or Northern Ireland. An additional duty is that of marking and removing dangerous wrecks.

It was already a guild of mariners when King Henry VIII granted it its first charter in 1514. It is controlled by a Master, Deputy Master and a Board of Elder Brethren. The latter are chosen from among members of the Royal Family, retired naval officers of high rank, prominent officers of the Merchant Navy, and statesmen. A number are appointed as an honour and perform no duties; the active members have at times to sit with the judges of the Admiralty Division of the High Court of Justice and assist them in trying special cases connected with shipping.

Trinity House supervises some 60 lighthouses and 40 lightships, and maintains a fleet of nine steam or motor vessels. It owns considerable property, maintains almshouses, and gives pensions to distressed British mariners or their widows. (*See also* Buoys; Lighthouses).

Trojan War. It was because of a quarrel among three goddesses, so a Greek legend states, that the war arose which resulted in the destruction of the mighty city of Troy (*q.v.*)—the war which inspired the immortal epics of the Greek Homer and the Roman Virgil which are known as the Iliad and the Aeneid respectively.

The gods and goddesses were feasting together to celebrate the marriage of Peleus and Thetis, when Eris, the goddess of discord, who alone of the immortals had not been invited, came and threw among the guests a golden apple, on which was inscribed " For the fairest." It was claimed by Hera (Juno), the wife of Zeus (Jupiter) and the queen of heaven, by Athena (Minerva), the goddess of wisdom, and by Aphrodite (Venus), the goddess of love.

As the strife became bitter, Paris, the son of King Priam of Troy, was called upon to award the prize of beauty. Hera promised him power and riches if he would decide in her favour, and Athena offered him glory and renown in war. But when Aphrodite whispered to him that, if she were awarded the prize, she would give him the love of the most beautiful woman in the world, Paris gave her the golden apple. From that time the goddesses Hera and Athena were the bitterest enemies of Paris and Troy.

The fairest of all women on earth was Helen, who was already the wife of King Menelaus of Sparta, in Greece. Under the protection of Aphrodite, Paris sailed to Greece and, while being entertained in the palace of Menelaus, won the love of Helen. Then he carried her away with him across the sea to his home on the Hellespont (the ancient name for the strait which is now called the Dardanelles).

Menelaus called upon all the kings and princes of Greece to help him to avenge this great wrong. Among those who joined the expedition were the swift-footed Achilles, who was to win the greatest

Anderson

DEATH OF A TROJAN PROPHET
Depicting the crushing of the mythical Laocoön and his two sons by serpents this piece of sculpture was discovered in Rome in 1506 and is now in the Vatican Museum, Rome. Laocoön warned the Trojans not to admit the wooden horse of the Greeks into Troy and foretold the fall of that city.

renown for strength and bravery; mighty Ajax, the gallant Diomedes, the crafty Odysseus (Ulysses), and the aged Nestor who was no longer able to engage in battle but to whom the younger Greeks looked for wise counsel. Agamemnon, king of Mycenae (one of the small Greek kingdoms) and brother of Menelaus, was chosen commander-in-chief of the Greek forces.

After two years' preparation the Greek fleet set sail for Troy. The Trojans were well prepared for the conflict. King Priam, though too old to take an active part in battle, had gathered immense supplies of provisions and formed alliances with the neighbouring princes and chieftains. The city was protected by mighty walls, and the Greek warriors were matched by such men as Priam's son Hector, Aeneas, Sarpedon, and other valiant leaders.

For more than nine years the Greeks besieged Troy, with varying fortune. Then Achilles, the bravest and ablest of the Greeks, quarrelled with Agamemnon and refused to take further part in the conflict, until the death of his friend Patroclus caused him to go forth once more to seek vengeance. But after slaying Hector, Achilles himself was killed, and the Greeks were in despair. Then Odysseus advised that, since they could not take the city by force, they should take it by craft. He devised the stratagem of the wooden horse, by which the Greeks succeeded in taking and destroying the city. How this was done is told in the story that follows. (*See also* Troy).

HOW THE WOODEN HORSE CAME TO TROY

"FOR 10 years we have laid siege to Troy," said Odysseus (Ulysses), thinking of his dear island-kingdom of Ithaca (one of the Ionian Islands in the Mediterranean). " The bravest of the Greeks are dead. Still the city is not ours, and Menelaus is not revenged upon the Trojans for stealing Helen."

" Odysseus, wilt thou not devise some plan by which we can take the city? Our wives and children will grow weary with too long waiting. Surely it was given to thee to save us with thy great wisdom!" Thus spoke Agamemnon, the leader of the Greeks.

Then Odysseus, aided by the goddess Athena (Minerva), devised the famous Wooden Horse. He got a Greek sculptor to build a colossal hollow horse of wood, large enough to contain 100 armed

warriors. Into it crept Odysseus, Menelaus, and others of the Greek heroes. The opening in its side was closed with strong bolts. Then the Greeks broke up their camp and set sail, leaving the Horse.

When the Trojans saw the ships, which had so long been drawn up on the sands of their harbour, sail away toward the island of Tenedos and disappear in the mist, there was great rejoicing, for they thought that the Greeks were returning to their homes. Had not they left an image of a horse as a peace-offering to Athena, who was angered because the Greeks had stolen her statue from Troy? Others, as they ran through the gates to gather about the great Horse, said that it was a trick.

" Put no trust in the Horse, men of Troy!" cried the priest Laocoön. " Whatever it is, I fear the

EMERGING FROM THE WOODEN HORSE
While the city slept, the bolts of the door in the side of the Wooden Horse were drawn and out clambered the hidden Greeks.

Without more ado, the Horse was brought within the walls. That night there was rejoicing in the long-besieged city. All the Trojan warriors went to sleep, secure in the belief that the gods would be favourable to them now that they had the Horse.

While they slept, Sinon drew the bolts and out came the hidden Greeks, who lighted a fire as a signal to their ships, which had turned back towards land. A fair wind and a bright moon guided the galleys and soon thousands of Greek warriors swarmed in the streets of Troy, shouting aloud in their joy.

It was a rude awakening for the Trojans. When they saw the enemy, they recalled the words of Laocoön and the hollow sound made by his spear against the Horse's ribs. All night the slaughter continued, and by morning only smouldering ruins marked the place where had stood the city. And old King Priam's headless body lay on the seashore.

Helen, for whose sake the dreadful war had been waged, was again in the arms of her husband, Menelaus, and the war-weary Greeks made ready to return to the wives and children whom they had not seen for 10 years.—*Retold from Virgil's Aeneid; Book* ii.

Trollope, ANTHONY (1815–82). Barchester and Barsetshire will not be found on the map of England, yet they are so well known that no one would be blamed for looking for them there. In fact, they are a county and town created by the imagination of a 19th-century novelist, Anthony Trollope, who was born on April 24, 1815, in London. During Trollope's early childhood the circumstances of his family were straitened and his poverty-stricken life at Winchester and Harrow made him shy, miserable and backward. He was luckily helped into a clerical position in the General Post Office in London in 1834, but remained poor. When he was transferred to Ireland in 1841 he took on a position of greater responsibility and from that time his circumstances improved. His official duties took him all over the country, and later all over the world.

When at home Trollope led an extremely active life, fulfilling his duties with meticulous care, but finding time to hunt three times a week, to play whist every day, and to write. More than 50 novels came from his pen, besides a large amount of journalistic work. This was made possible only by the most careful apportionment of his time. Today he is remembered almost entirely for the Barchester series: The Warden (1855) ; Barchester Towers (1857) ; Dr. Thorne (1858) ; Framley Parsonage (1864), and The Last Chronicle of Barset (1867). This series is rightly regarded a memorable achievement. In it Trollope's great gift of character drawing is revealed at its best. Few novelists have better captured the atmosphere of mid-Victorian England or been more successful in their treatment of the commonplace and the usual.

Greeks, even bearing gifts." As he departed to offer sacrifice, he hurled his spear against the sides of the Horse, and there came back a hollow sound.

His warning was drowned in the shouts of the people as they watched the approach of some shepherds, who were bringing along a captured Greek with hands fettered. This was a soldier, Sinon by name, who had been left behind to persuade the Trojans by a guileful tale to take the Horse within the gates of the city.

"Have pity on me!" he begged. "I escaped from the hands of the Greeks when they were about to sacrifice me to the gods. The Wooden Horse was built as a peace-offering to the offended Athena. It was made of such immense size to prevent you from taking it within your gates. For then the favour of Athena would be transferred to the Trojans."

Some still doubted, when suddenly a strange thing happened which seemed an omen from the gods. Two huge serpents rose from the water and, entwining themselves about Laocoön and his two sons, crushed the hapless ones to death.

"Surely this is a punishment for Laocoön's sacrilege against the sacred gift!" cried the Trojans.

Trollope died on December 6, 1882, and the following year his autobiography, edited by his son, was published.

Trotsky, LEON (1879–1940). For more than 10 years before the Russian Tsar was overthrown in the revolution of 1917, Leon Trotsky had been a "man without a country." His real name was Lev Davidovitch Bronstein, and he was born on October 26, 1879, at Yanovka, in the Ukraine, son of a Jewish farmer. In 1900 and again in 1905 he was imprisoned for taking part in revolutionary activities. Shortly after the latter date he fled from his native land. Paris, Vienna, Switzerland and the Balkan states knew him as an agitator who preached extreme doctrines and lived from hand to mouth on the slender earnings of his pen.

The spring of 1917 found him in New York, where for a few weeks he had been one of the editors of the Russian Socialist paper *Novyi Mir* (The New World). News of the Tsar's overthrow sent him hurrying to Russia. Interned for a month in England, he arrived in Petrograd (later Leningrad) at the moment when Kerensky was just rising to the head of a provisional Russian government.

Trotsky at once associated himself with Nikolai Lenin, leader of the Bolshevist faction. The newcomer's fiery oratory, tireless energy and relentless preaching of the most extreme measures soon brought him to the fore. When Kerensky was overthrown by the Bolsheviks in November 1917 it was Trotsky who walked into the Smolny Institute (the party's headquarters) with Lenin, to take over the government in the name of Bolshevism (*q.v.*).

First he was Minister of Foreign Affairs and then Minister of War. Under his guidance were formed the famous "Red Armies," which defeated so many military attempts to overturn the Bolshevist Government. He was the chief man of action of Soviet Russia, as Lenin was its prophet and theorist. After the death of LENIN in 1924, Trotsky's influence waned. A fierce personal rivalry developed between him and Stalin, who at that time had moderated his ideas of world revolution. Trotsky, on the contrary, continued to the end his advocacy of a world-wide assault upon capitalism. His enemies in the Communist Party stripped him of power, dismissed him from the Party in 1927, and in 1929 he was exiled from Russia. But he continued to write and, it was said, to plot against the Stalinist Government and its conception of Communism; and in the many trials of high officials in Russia almost all confessed to being Trotskyite plotters, spies and wreckers. Trotsky was expelled from several European countries, before settling in Mexico, where he died following a murderous assault by an unknown assassin, on August 21, 1940.

Associated Press

LEON TROTSKY

Though he fell into disgrace with the Russian Government in 1927, Trotsky had played an important part in the history of the development of the Soviet Union, his organizing ability having proved of assistance to Lenin in the formation of the Red Army.

Trout. Authorities have long disagreed as to whether there are different varieties of trout or not, owing to the fact that these fish show considerable differences in various localities. Names have been given to as many as 20 species, but it is now thought these are either local types or variations due to poor feeding. The common trout (*Salmo fario*), sometimes known as the brown or river trout, is greenish brown above, dirty white below and has black spots on the head, sides and back. The average length is a foot, and the weight varies up to two pounds, though specimens of 30 pounds have been caught. Found in Britain and throughout Europe, it lives in clear, swift-flowing streams or in the lakes from which such streams originate, feeding on insects, snails, worms, small fishes and the eggs of salmon and other fish. Like salmon (*q.v.*) trout seek the shallow upper waters of the rivers for spawning, and in their journey to the breeding-ground they will leap out of the water to pass over weirs and small waterfalls.

A variety called the sea trout (*S. trutta*) migrates to the sea and returns to fresh water at the breeding season in the same way as the salmon ; but it is doubtful whether even this is a distinct species. The beautiful, brightly-coloured rainbow trout (*S. irideus*) comes from the rivers of the Pacific coast of North America, and has been bred to a limited extent in fish hatcheries in Britain for stocking rivers and lakes.

Newtonian Press

TROUT DISGUISE

When in the presence of danger trout assume a blotchy appearance, matching so closely the stony bottom of the stream that they are almost invisible. (1) Trout showing his protective camouflage and (2) normal appearance of the fish.

Troy. The traveller today may still see the ruins on the site of " the topless towers of Ilium," as Troy was also called. Near the coast of Asiatic Turkey, looking across the narrows of the Dardanelles at the spot where they open into the Aegean Sea, are, in part, the ruins of the city whose siege and destruction was the theme o Homer's Iliad. Looking toward he south-east we can still see snow-capped Mount Ida, on whose lofty height, so the poet tells us, Zeus, king of the gods, sat and watched the conflict. Half-way between the shore and the mountains is a long mound about 100 feet in height, crowned by heaps of debris. This is the so-called Hill of Hissarlik, where for centuries ancient Troy lay buried.

In 1870 Heinrich Schliemann (*q.v.*) began to dig into this mound, and it was eventually discovered that this was the very spot where the Trojan War was waged. The excavations of Schliemann further revealed the fact hat several walled cities had stood upon the spot long before Homeric Troy. Schliemann and his successors found between 1870 and 1893 the ruins of nine towns built one upon another during a period of 3,500 years. The first was built by men of the late Stone Age (about 3,000 B.C.), and the last in Roman times, when Julius Caesar visited the place.

Homer's Troy was first thought to be the sixth city. Further excavations were carried out in 1932 and these revealed the existence of yet another city, making 10 in all. The sixth city was destroyed by an earthquake about 1300 B.C., and the Troy of Homer was the seventh, which came to a violent end about 100 years later. Numerous copper, bronze, gold, and silver objects were found here and placed in museums. (*See also* Achilles ; Ajax ; Hector ; Homer ; Trojan War ; etc.).

Truman, HARRY SHIPPE (born 1884). To follow in the steps of Franklin Delano Roosevelt (*q.v.*) as President of the United States of America, while his country was still at war with Germany and Japan, was the destiny of this farmer's son who was born near Lamar, Missouri, on May 8, 1884. He was educated at the High School in Independence, Missouri, whither his family had moved shortly after his birth ; and he served in France with the United States Army during the First World War (1914–18).

After working as a road overseer, tax collector and postmaster, Truman was appointed a County Court judge in 1922. He studied at Kansas City Law School from 1923 to 1925, and in 1926 was elected to the post of Presiding Judge of Jackson County Court.

HARRY S. TRUMAN
Succeeding Franklin D. Roosevelt as President of the United States in April 1945, Mr. Truman was elected for a further term in 1948.

In 1934 he was elected to the Senate, and was re-elected in 1940. In 1941 Truman was made Chairman of a special committee examining national expenditure, which after the United States entered the Second World War in December 1941 exercised a powerful check upon waste and corruption.

Becoming Vice-President in 1944 (a post which made him next in succession should the President die during a term of office), Truman was sworn in as President on April 12, 1945, a few hours after the death of Franklin Roosevelt. After the surrender of Germany, in May 1945, he represented the United States at the Potsdam Conference in the following July and August, which was also attended by the Russian leader Joseph Stalin, and by Mr. Winston Churchill and Mr. Clement Attlee as British representatives. To Truman's lot fell the giving of the order which resulted in the dropping of the first atomic bomb on the city of Hiroshima, Japan, on August 6, 1945. After his term had expired, the election of November 1948 sent Truman again to the White House as President.

Tsetse Fly. One of the greatest scourges of Man and animals in the tropical regions of Africa, this blood-sucking fly, which is little larger than Britain's common house-fly, causes incalculable harm every year and makes many parts of that continent almost uninhabitable. By its bite tiny parasites are introduced into the blood, one species of the fly (*Glossina palpalis*) producing the dreaded sleeping sickness in Man; and another species (*G. morsitans*) causing the disease known as *nagana* in cattle, horses, dogs and other domestic animals, as well as another form of sleeping sickness—so called because the victim in the last stages falls into a coma.

Not until early in the 20th century was it discovered that these diseases were caused by the tsetse. Now, since the fly breeds chiefly in the undergrowth on the banks of lakes and rivers, its ravages have been greatly lessened by cutting the bush for some distance from settlements. In 1949 a new drug, "Antrycide," was discovered by Dr. D. G. Davy and Dr. F. H. Curd, and it was claimed that cattle injected with this would be immune from the tsetse pest for about six months.

The female tsetse, instead of laying eggs, deposits single full-grown larvae at intervals of about two weeks, and although this obviously limits the number which can be produced in a single season it also " hurries up " the life history of the fly. The adult fly is brownish, banded with darker brown, and is distinguished by its habit of resting with the wings folded longitudinally down the back.

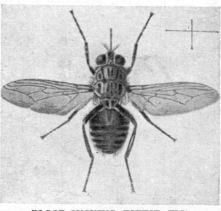

BLOOD-SUCKING TSETSE FLY
Sleeping sickness is contracted through the bite of an infected tsetse fly, the species carrying the West African type of parasite being the one here. Its actual size is shown in the top right corner.

Tudor This family numbered among its members Henry VII, who came to the throne of England in 1485, and his descendants, Henry VIII (reigned 1509–47), Edward VI (1547–53), Mary I (1553–58), and Elizabeth (1558–1603). The family traced its descent on the male side from the Welsh border lord Owen Tudor, who appeared in the court circle in 1429 and later married Queen Catherine, widow of Henry V.

Its claim to the throne was based on the marriage of Owen's son, Edmund, to a Lancastrian princess of the Beaufort line. The future Henry VII (known as the Earl of Richmond) was the son of this union, and the only remaining claimant of the Lancastrian line. He made two attempts to win the throne, in the second of which the last Yorkist king, Richard III, was defeated and slain at Bosworth (1485).

Henry VII was crowned with the fallen monarch's crown, picked up on the battlefield. After his coronation he ended the Wars of the Roses by his marriage with Elizabeth of York, the daughter of Edward IV, so uniting the houses of York and Lancaster. The Tudor rose, which typifies this union, is a red rose superimposed upon a white. From Henry VII's daughter Margaret, who married James IV of Scotland, James I of England was descended.

Tulip. There is nothing bashful or timid about tulip flowers, rising majestically on stems up to 18 inches in height, especially when the plants are gorgeously massed in garden beds or borders. They are, indeed, probably unequalled in brilliance, variety of form and colour and extensive range of flowering time.

Tulips in their wild state are native to north and west Asia, and one species, the yellow-flowered *Tulipa sylvestris*, is indigenous to Great Britain but is now rare. Cultivated species of this hardy bulbous plant of the family *Liliaceae* were introduced into Europe via Turkey and the Balkans about three centuries ago, and by cross-breeding florists have produced the present great number of varieties ranging in colour from white, through red and yellow, to dusky purple, or with petals beautifully splashed with contrasting shades.

As early as the year 1600 Holland became the centre of its production, and in 1634 began a " tulip mania," an astonishing craze for speculation in the bulbs, which were sold by weight

Malby

CONTRAST IN TULIPS
The feathery-edged petals of the colour-splashed tulips of the parrot class (upper) distinguish them at once from the plainer but equally attractive type in the lower photograph.

like diamonds. Admiration for the flower and the interest in its culture took second place to this wild gambling, which lasted for four years. Now millions of bulbs are grown in Holland each year for export. In Britain the centre of the industry is in Lincolnshire.

Tungsten. Although known to science since the 18th century, tungsten was long considered useless. Then, in the early 1900s it suddenly became so valuable that for a time its ores commanded as high a price as gold ores. Its name comes from the Swedish *tung* meaning heavy, and *sten* meaning stone. It is, indeed, one of the heaviest of substances, weighing almost twice as much as lead. It has the highest melting point among metals (6,100° F.) and its general resistance to the effects of heat chiefly accounts for its value.

The targets in X-ray tubes, which must withstand enormous temperatures, are made of tungsten (*see* X-rays). It is also a very useful material for filaments in electric lamps and radio valves, because it can be kept at white heat for a long time without undue softening. For the current they consume, tungsten filaments give from two to five times as much light as the old carbon lamp filaments.

The difficulty of drawing this extremely hard and brittle metal into fine wires delayed for years its adoption for lamp filaments (*see* Wire). The solution of this problem by W. D. Coolidge of the General Electric Company's research laboratories at Schenectady, U.S.A., revolutionized the lighting industry in 1912. He moulded tungsten powder into rods and beat them with mechanical hammers in the fierce heat of the electric furnace until they were small and tough enough to be drawn through finishing dies. Now we have tungsten wires so fine that six of them would hardly equal the diameter of a human hair, yet equal in strength to copper wire ten times their size. In general, the tensile strength of tungsten treated by the method described exceeds that of any other known substance, since a rod one inch square can support more than *half a million pounds*.

Important as is this use of tungsten in radio valves and electric lamps, it requires only a small part of the annual production. More than nine-tenths of the output is used in making high-speed tool alloys for machining metals. Among these are the alloys of tungsten carbide with cobalt, which are the hardest compounds known to science. (*See* Alloys).

Tungsten resists the action of most acids and

other corrosives at ordinary temperatures, and the consequent difficulty of extracting it from its ores is in part responsible for its cost. Most of these ores (chiefly wolframite, hübnerite, scheelite, and ferberite) are mined in China, Burma, in the Malay States, Bolivia, Nevada, Colorado, California, and Arizona. They are often found with tin ores. Tungsten (chemical symbol W, from the German *wolfram*, an alternative name of the element) was first isolated in 1783, several years after its original discovery by K. W. Scheele in the form of tungstic acid. Its atomic weight is 184; atomic number, 76; and density, 18·8. Sodium tungstate impregnated in cloth makes the cloth fire-resistant. Lead tungstate makes a good white paint.

Tunisia. A French protectorate in North Africa, Tunisia is bounded on the north by the Mediterranean Sea, on the east by Tripolitania and the Mediterranean, on the south by the Sahara Desert, on the west by Algeria. Much of its area of 48,300 square miles is mountainous; the deserts of the south and east are barren; but the numerous elevated valleys in the interior are extensively cultivated, especially in the north, producing cereals, oranges, figs, grapes, almonds, dates and olives. The most important river, the Medjerda, flows from Algeria and empties into the Gulf of Tunis near Porto Farina. There are lakes, but those in the south dry up during the hot summer.

The chief industry is agriculture; others include wool-spinning, carpet-making, and the manufacture of leather goods, pottery and copper ware. Phosphate rock is exported. Other mineral resources include lead, zinc, iron and manganese.

Sponge fishing is carried on. There are 1,327 miles of railway connecting the main centres with the Algerian system, and 5,350 miles of roads. The capital is the city of Tunis (population 220,000). Among other places of importance are Sfax (population 43,000); Bizerta (28,500), and Susa (28,500). Inland from Susa is Kairwan, the holy city of African Mahomedans.

The population of Tunisia is very mixed and includes Arabs, Kabyles, Italians, Jews, Maltese and French. The Arabs are divided into two classes: the town-dwellers and those who still lead the wandering life of their ancestors. The wanderers are found mostly on the borders of the Sahara desert, where they irrigate large tracts and cultivate date palms. The Kabyles, the original inhabitants of the country, live in the uplands of the interior, where they practise agriculture and raise herds of sheep and goats. Never completely conquered by the French, they retain their racial purity.

In the earliest times a possession of Egypt, Tunisia was later occupied by the Phoenicians, who in the 7th century B.C. founded the celebrated city of Carthage (*q.v.*) not far from where Tunis stands today. The power of Carthage was broken in 146 B.C. by the Romans, who called the region Africa and made it the granary of the Roman Empire. There are still a number of Roman remains in Tunisia, including the aqueduct, west of the site of Carthage, which brought water from the mountains 56 miles away. Subsequently passing under the domination of the Arabs in the middle of the 7th century, and in 1575 being seized by the Turks, the country remained a part of the Turkish Empire, though virtually independent, until the French invasion of 1881. Tunisia was officially placed under the protection of France in 1883 and is under the control of a French Minister Resident-General.

During the Second World War (1939–45) Tunisia proclaimed its allegiance to the pro-German Vichy-French Government after the surrender of France to Germany in June 1940. It was not occupied by the Germans until November 1942, when Allied landings in Morocco and Algeria led the Germans to fly in troops from Italy and Sicily and to occupy the city of Tunis and the surrounding country. The British, French and United States forces advancing eastward from Algeria linked up in Tunisia in April 1943, with the British 8th Army, which had swept back the Italians and Germans from the Egyptian frontier. Allied forces entered Tunis and Bizerta on May 7, 1943; the German and Italian commanders surrendered on May 12 and 13 respectively. Some 250,000 of the enemy laid down their arms, and the Allied campaign in North Africa was brought to a triumphant conclusion. The population of Tunisia is 2,608,000.

W. F. Taylor

A SHOP IN TUNIS, CAPITAL OF TUNISIA

On a small lagoon close to the Mediterranean Sea, Tunis is the seat of Government of the French Protectorate of Tunisia and an important trading centre. It is an ancient city with a large Arab quarter, in which is the above shop in the Souk el Attarine or Street of Perfumes.

MAN-MADE BURROWS *for* ROAD *and* RAIL

Mountains and rivers are the obstacles which tunnellers usually burrow under; but in crowded cities our railways run in deep tunnels which can follow a direct course to their destination, almost regardless of surface contours.

Tunnels. Men burrow into the earth and construct ways for roads or railways or water channels. Generally there is an obstacle to be circumvented; or costly property above ground to be avoided. When the first underground railways of London were constructed, many of the tunnels were made on the " cut-and-cover " principle, often following the line of the highroads above. A deep and wide trench was dug, lined with brickwork and roofed over with a continuous brick vaulting. Often the tunnel was so close to the surface that ventilating shafts could be carried up to the roadway and covered with a grating to let out the smoke and steam which the steam locomotives then in use belched forth in profuse quantity.

A half-century later, when the " tube " railways began to be constructed in London, the deep tunnels enabled these lines to go whither their engineers desired, without having to consider surface obstacles. From the stations, vertical shafts took passengers down to the trains. North and south London were connected by under-river tunnels which, like those beneath the ground elsewhere, were lined with iron or steel segmental curved plates bolted together through flanges. Twin tunnels accommodated the " up " and " down " tracks, and were expanded into wider ones at the stations to allow for platforms.

Tunnels to take canals under high ground were built early in the 19th century. These were narrow, and to propel the barges the men had to lie on the deck and urge the craft forward by thrusting the feet against the tunnel side. The horse which normally towed the barge had to make a circuit and take up its load again at the far end of the tunnel. Contrast these dark and noisome passages with the modern canal tunnels such as that connecting the Rhône canal system with Marseilles—4¼ miles long, 70 feet broad, having a navigable width of 50 feet.

Another kind of tunnel is that which enables vehicles to pass beneath the Mersey between Liverpool and Birkenhead. It is more than two miles in length. There are many tunnels beneath the Thames, not counting the " tube " ones. Isambard Kingdom Brunel (*q.v.*) and his father built the first, between Rotherhithe and Wapping; they used a circular cast-iron shield to hold back the ground while the tunnel was lined with brickwork.

This tunnel was begun in 1825, completed in 1843, and closed in 1866. It was intended to provide a double roadway between the opposite sides of the river; but the approach roads were never made, owing to engineering difficulties, and the tunnel was used only by pedestrians, who had to descend to it through shafts. After its closing to the

FIVE-MILE TUNNEL FOR SEA-GOING BARGES

In the south of France is the Rove tunnel (above), which connects the Rhône canal system with the port of Marseilles and which pierces the hills to the north-west of the city. Begun in 1911, it was completed in 1925 and permits the passage of sea-going barges of 1,200 tons. Over four miles long, the tunnel is 70 feet wide and has a navigable channel 50 feet broad. The man (right) is standing on one of the towing paths which run along the tops of the arches.

PURFLEET

PURFLEET BY-PASS

BRIDGE BUILT OVER L.M.S. RLY.

NORTH ENTRANCE

HIGH WATER

LOW WATER

DARTFORD

BRIDGE BUILT OVER SOUTHERN RLY

OUT TO DARTFORD SOUTHERN BY-PASS

TUNNELLED BY-PASS THAT LINKS KENT AND ESSEX BELOW THE RIVER THAMES

How the tunnel under the Thames between Dartford and Purfleet was constructed. Upper inset, method of boring by a circular shield. 1. Sliding platforms to excavate in front of cutting edge. 2. Erector to hoist segments. 3. "Trams" removing excavated material. 4. Cementing holes. 5. Finished tunnel. 6. Pavements with for men. 10. Concrete raft. 11. Air pipes. 12. Air lock for materials. 13. Cages. 14. Hydraulic rams. 15, 16. Chambers where shield for pilot tunnel and main tunnel were built. 17. Working shafts. 18. Southern entrance. Section of tunnel: 19. Working shaft. 20. Peat and Thames mud. 21. Sand and ballast. 22. Depth public, in 1866, the East London Railway bought the tunnel and used it to take a double line of railway through. From the dates given it will be realized that the engineers encountered many difficulties. Twice the river broke through, and bags of clay were used to stop the leaks. The tunnel was advanced by about two feet in 24 hours of work.

The shield used to build the Rotherhithe-Wapping tunnel was a cast-iron one moved forward by many screws (working like screw-jacks) which took a bearing against the brickwork already built behind it. When the road tunnel beneath the Thames at Blackwall was constructed (1892–97) the middle part, about 3,200 feet long, was made with the aid of a compressed-air shield of steel, driven forward by hydraulic rams. Air-locks enabled a pressure to be kept up sufficient to hold back the water in the soil. This tunnel was lined with segmental cast-iron members which formed a ring.

In 1908 a railway tunnel between Rotherhithe and Ratcliff was built on a similar system. The shield used for the first Thames tunnel had no cutting edge; workmen in twelve compartments at its face had to dig out the soil in front of it before it could be forced onward by screws. The shields used later had a cutting edge, and hydraulic rams drove them into the tunnel face; the soil was removed inside the shield, and then the cast-iron lining was fixed.

London Transport Executive

TUNNELLING FOR A RAILWAY UNDER LONDON'S STREETS
The inside of an underground railway boring is lined (as the tunnelling progresses) with cast-iron segments bolted together to form a continuous tube. Here segments are being placed in position, and secured by bolts through the flanges.

These methods are of use only when and where the soil is soft enough to be cut through. In rocky strata, although a shield may be used, and compressed air is employed to hold back water, the cutting away is done by pneumatic rock-drills. As an example let us take the Simplon tunnel through the Alps, begun in 1898, opened in 1906, and nearly $12\frac{1}{2}$ miles in length. Only the use of air-driven drills enabled this task to be undertaken. Holes were bored to take charges of explosives; masses of rock were blasted away and the débris cleared; slowly the tunnels (there were two) advanced.

Air for ventilation and cooling was forced in through smaller tunnels known as "headings," and these headings were later enlarged to full size. Water was piped in to cool the working face after the blasting, and to carry the shattered rock back out of the way. The average rate of forward progress in the Simplon tunnels was a little under six yards per 24 hours.

Tunnellers in the 20th century had, of course, many advantages over the earlier builders. Power was freely available to work cutting and boring tools; lighter and stronger steels were ready to hand for tunnel linings; the shields could be built with vast improvements over the earlier ones; electric light turned the tunnel gloom into perpetual daylight. One of our pictures explains the methods used to dig the road tunnel between Dartford, in Kent,

Courtesy of Swiss Federal Railways

TUNNELLERS MEET BELOW THE ALPS
When the nine-miles long Loetschberg double-track railway tunnel was driven through the Swiss Alps the work was carried out simultaneously from both ends. Engineers and contractors of the two sections are seen meeting as the last portion of rock was pierced.

and Purfleet, in Essex, under the Thames. You will notice that a pilot tunnel (corresponding to the heading tunnels used for the Simplon) was bored first, and afterwards enlarged.

Another photograph shows the working face for a " tube " railway tunnel. Either a cutting shield or a rotary excavator is used today; this picture shows a shield of the type originated by James Henry Greathead (1844–96). Greathead used his shield to cut the subway tunnel under the Thames near the Tower of London, in 1869; the same system was used to dig the tunnel of the City & South London Railway—first of the " tubes "—and other deep tunnels.

A word must now be said about a project, first conceived in the days of the great Napoleon, and actually begun in 1876—for a tunnel beneath the English Channel, to connect England and France. Experimental tunnels were driven on each side, from a shaft near the Shakespeare Cliff, Dover, on the English side; and from Sangatte, near Calais, on the French side. Work was stopped in 1882 by order of the British Board of Trade. Since then, every few years, there have been attempts to revive the scheme, but the political and financial problems involved have hitherto hindered any resumption.

A FEW OF THE WORLD'S TUNNELS		
Ben Nevis	Hydro-electric pipe-line	15 miles
Simplon	Railway	12½ miles
Apennines	Railway	11½ miles
St. Gothard	Railway	9¼ miles
Mont Cenis	Railway	7¾ miles
Rove	Rhône-Marseilles Canal	4¼ miles
Severn	Railway	4 m. 624 yds.
Totley	Railway	3 m. 950 yds.
Mersey	Vehicular Roadway	2 m. 13 yds.
Blackwall	Roadway	1¼ miles
Rotherhithe-Stepney	Roadway	1¼ miles

accomplished fact. Engineering difficulties which in the 1880s loomed large would today prove less fearsome; and many engineers consider that a success could be made of a tunnel allowing through running of trains from Dover to the Continent.

Tunny. If an artist were asked to paint a picture of an ideal fish, for beauty, strength and speed, the picture would probably resemble closely the great leaping tunny, the king of all ocean game. This fish, also called the " tuna," the " giant mackerel," and the " giant albacore," is the largest member of the mackerel family; it has a record length of more than 10 feet and a weight of 1,500 pounds.

From its sharp nose to the slender base of its tail the tunny (*Thunnus thynnus*) swells out and tapers again in almost perfect curves. Its body, indeed, has provided a natural model for the builders of the fastest racing yachts. Driven by powerful tail fins, it flashes through the waves with the speed of an arrow, frequently hurling itself out of the water and seizing the swift flying-fish—its favourite food.

Tunny are found in the Mediterranean and off the Pacific and Atlantic coasts of North America, and very occasionally off the Yorkshire shore of England. In the Mediterranean, where tunny fisheries have been carried on from very early times, they are caught in funnel-shaped nets; the fish enter the mouth, and when they reach the narrow end they are killed with harpoons. The flesh, which looks very much like beef, is eaten either fresh or preserved in oil and is very popular in southern Europe. On the Pacific coast of the United States tunny fishing provides thrilling sport, the great fish being caught from motor-launches on lines baited with flying-fish.

During the Second World War (1939–45) there were fears that the Germans, then in control of the Calais area and much of France, might secretly drive a tunnel from the existing heading, and might surprise us with a passage through which their giant tanks could cross to Britain. But these fears proved groundless. Perhaps in the future the Channel Tunnel may become an

A TUNNY GOES ABOARD   *Fox*

Though for a considerable time tunny fishing has been a favourite sport in the United States it is only of recent years that the pastime has become popular in English waters. Above we see a fine tunny, caught after an exciting tussle, being hauled aboard a yacht off the Dogger Bank.

Turbine, STEAM. No doubt you have seen at some time or other the piston of a stationary steam engine moving to and fro. The power is delivered in a series of pulses, which only the heavy flywheel is able to smooth out. Contrast this action with that of a rotary engine, such as an electric motor, where the power is delivered smoothly in a continuous rotation of the armature shaft. For many years inventors tried to make a practical steam engine in which the steam should drive a wheel *directly*. No changing direction of a piston at each stroke, with its waste of energy in bringing the piston to a stop, and then moving it again in the opposite direction !

There are two main types of turbine : the *impulse* type and the *reaction* turbine. In our story of Hydro-

Electric Installations a good deal has been said about the turbine as a means of harnessing water power; much of the information there given about design and principles applies to the steam turbine also. In page 1670 is a picture of a Pelton wheel, which illustrates the principle of the impulse turbine : a jet of water at high speed is directed upon scoop-shaped buckets fixed to the wheel, and the impulse causes the wheel (and the shaft to which it is fixed) to revolve. In the steam turbine the vanes are very much smaller and there are many more of them. The De Laval turbine, invented by C. G. P. De Laval in 1885, is an

ONE OF THE FIRST PARSONS STEAM TURBINES
In 1884 the British engineer and inventor Sir Charles Algernon Parsons (1854–1931) built this 10 horse-power steam turbine engine, seen above coupled to a dynamo on the right. It is to be seen at the Science Museum, South Kensington, London.

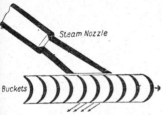

Fig. 1. The arrangement of the steam nozzle and buckets in a De Laval turbine is shown in this diagram.

When steam issues from a nozzle of the shape seen in Fig. 1, widening towards the mouth of the

example. It is a single disk in the simplest form, having many curved vanes set about its edge (see Fig. 1). The steam nozzles are at the side of the wheel, and they send the steam through the vanes from one side to the other, as shown in Fig. 2, below.

nozzle, the steam expands, and gains enormously in velocity at the expense of pressure. If the outlet of the turbine is connected to a chamber in which a vacuum is maintained, the velocity increase is greater still. The effect of the expanding nozzle is something like what happens in a " Venturi " (see Meters). It is the velocity of the jet which impels the vaned wheel around. Since it proved difficult to use up all the velocity of the steam in a turbine having a single wheel, De Laval turbines were later made with several wheels, which the steam fed in succession, expanding at each " stage."

The reaction turbine works on a different principle. See Fig. 3, which shows a section through

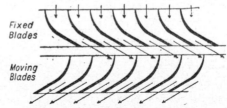

REACTION TURBINE'S BLADES
Fig. 3. The fixed blades on the casing of a reaction turbine (above) guide the steam to the moving ones on the turbine shaft. The course of the steam is indicated by the arrows.

the " fixed " blades, into which the steam is first directed; and through the " moving " blades, which are attached to the turbine shaft. The fixed blades guide the steam to the moving ones, and are attached to the turbine casing. Follow the course of the steam, shown by the arrows, and you will see that it changes direction completely in passing through the turbine. The bladed wheel, in the diagram, will rotate towards the right, urged round by the pressure difference between the steam at the inlet (to the fixed blades) and at the outlet (escaping from the moving blades).

The name " reaction turbine " is given to this type because the steam leaves the moving blades with a " push-off " effect, and drives the bladed wheel around in the opposite direction to that taken finally by the steam. The De Laval turbine wheel (see Fig. 1 again) is impelled around by the steam in the same direction in which the jet

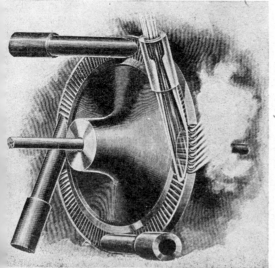

The De Laval Steam Turbine Co.
DE LAVAL TURBINE
Fig. 2. The steam nozzles in the De Laval turbine are set at the side of the wheel and send steam through the buckets or curved vanes around its edge from one side to the other.

among the most important being the Rateau, the Curtis and the Zoelly. Today, in addition to the monsters used for ship propulsion and for electric generators, there are simpler turbines having a single wheel and made in quite small horse-power to drive pumps, air blowers and similar machines. (*See* Gas Turbine ; Hydro-Electric Installations ; Ships).

Turgeniev, IVAN SERGEIEVICH (1818–83). The Western world first became acquainted with Russian literature through the novelist Turgeniev (pron. toor-gen'-yef), who was born at Orel, Russia, on November 9, 1818. The son of an ancient noble family, he studied at the universities of Moscow, St. Petersburg (now Leningrad) and Berlin. His mother wanted him to enter Government service, but the young man was determined to devote himself to a literary career.

For the democratic ideas expressed in his writings, notably in a Letter to Gogol (1852), Turgeniev was exiled to his country estate for two years, and in 1855 he left Russia, never to return except as a visitor. The rest of his life he spent mostly in Baden-Baden (Germany), and Paris.

On the family estate he saw numerous examples of the ill-treatment of the peasants, who were little better than the slaves of the land-owning nobility. The conditions under which they lived are described in his first book, A Sportsman's Sketches (1852). This work, which was translated into English in 1895, helped Russian society to realize in some measure the evils of their social system and was of considerable influence in hastening the emancipation of the peasants in 1861. By a number of critics it is thought to be Turgeniev's masterpiece. Other short novels include A House of Gentlefolk (1859), and On the Eve (1860).

His novel of Russian society entitled Fathers and Sons deals with the conflict between the fathers, who symbolize the old-fashioned conservative party in politics and believe in the rights of the nobility, and the children who represent the democratic faction with revolutionary ideas. The hero, a young doctor, is a " nihilist," a term first used in this novel. As there described, a nihilist is " a man who bows before no authority and accepts no principle unproved."

In all his novels Turgeniev pictures the Russian people, especially the gentry and the various intellectual types of his own time. He is both a realist and an idealist, and the outstanding prose writer in 19th-century Russian literature. Turgeniev died at Bougival near Paris, on September 3 1883, and was buried at St. Petersburg.

Turin. (Pron. tūr-in'). With broad, straight partly arcaded streets, beautiful buildings, fine summer climate, and magnificent view of the Alps Turin (Italian *Torino*) is situated on the River Po upon the site of the ancient Roman town of Augusta Taurinorum.

From its position near the French border directly opposite Mont Cenis Pass and Mont Cenis tunnel, Turin has gained considerable commercial importance. It is the fifth largest city in Italy, and is the centre of the motor-car industry in that country.

Since the earliest days, when the Romans took the city from the Taurini, Turin has been

A WHEEL TURBINE IN ACTION
Leaving the nozzle at high velocity the steam strikes the side of a bucket (above), setting the wheel in motion ; but as only a portion of the available energy is expended, the steam is caught in a chamber and returned to the wheel.

The Terry Steam Turbine Co.

enters the buckets; thus the wheel in both this diagram and in Fig. 3 will be moving to the right.

The common revolving lawn sprinkler gives us an example of reaction; the jets point one way, horizontally, but the sprinkler head travels around in the opposite direction, driven by the " push-off effect " of the water escaping from the nozzles. Hero or Hiero of Alexandria (?282–221 B.C.) is said to have made a tiny reaction steam engine. Giovanni Branca, of Padua, is credited with the invention of an impulse turbine (probably in 1616) in which a steam jet drove a bladed wheel something like a De Laval one set horizontally.

In 1884 Sir Charles A. Parsons (1854–1931) introduced his compound reaction turbine, which thereafter came into use for propelling ships, driving electric generators, and supplying power for many other purposes where its high speed was not a drawback. One of his earliest turbines is shown in page 3259, coupled to a dynamo.

The story of his ship Turbinia is told in page 2949, and of the sensation it caused when it appeared unofficially at the naval review held in 1897 at Spithead to celebrate the Diamond Jubilee of Queen Victoria. In the Science Museum, London, is the after part (45 feet long) of this historic vessel, with her Parsons turbine engines. Other inventors, of course, developed turbines, of great strategic importance. The Romans built a 21-foot wall round it, portions of which still remain. The Gothic Cathedral, built during 1492–98, contains interesting frescoes. In the north-east of the city is the Piazza Castello, where are the huge and rather ugly Palazzo Madama, which was damaged during the Second World War (1939–45), and a 13th-century fortress. North of the Piazza is the plain, red-brick royal palace, which dates from 1660 and also suffered damage during the war. Several important thoroughfares radiate from the Piazza, one of them being the Via di Po, which leads to one of the city's four bridges spanning the River Po.

As capital of the principality of Piedmont and later of the kingdom of Sardinia, Turin was the nucleus round which grew the present Italian kingdom. It was the capital of united Italy from the union in 1860 until 1865. After Italy signed an armistice with the Allies, in 1943, during the Second World War, Turin was occupied by German troops. On April 27, 1945, the people of the city rose against the Germans, and three days later American troops entered.

The museums contain many interesting relics of the early history of the region, and the art galleries possess important works by Van Dyck and sketches by Raphael, Michelangelo and Leonardo da Vinci. The University of Turin was founded in 1400. It was, however, damaged by the bombing of the Allies during the Second World War, when part of its fine library was destroyed. Altogether 31 churches and 67 palaces were more or less badly bombed late in 1942.

Besides motor-cars, aeroplanes, and other engineering products, Turin manufactures chiefly cotton, silk, ribbons and velvet, leather and chemicals. The power for its industrial plants is mostly derived from electricity generated by mountain torrents. The population of the city is 712,000.

Turkey.

Christmas festivities in Great Britain are traditionally associated with roast turkey, a bird which belongs to the pheasant family. There are several varieties, all derived from the wild turkey (*Meleagris gallopavo*), which is a native of North America. It was introduced into Europe early in the 16th century, when Spanish explorers brought it from Mexico. The bird's name may have arisen from a mistaken notion that it came from Turkey, or it may have originated in the call-note—*turk, turk, turk*.

E.N.I.T.

TURIN'S COMMEMORATIVE CHURCH
In memory of the liberation of Turin from the French in 1706 the church of La Superga (above) was erected in 1717–31, on the summit of the Hill of Superga (2,300 feet) not far from the city.

Distinguishing features of the turkey are the head and neck bare of feathers, and the long red wattle hanging from the forehead. The tail of the domestic turkey is broad and round, with 14 to 18 blunt buff-tipped feathers. These the male bird spreads fanwise and raises about his back when he is courting the female. The dark plumage has metallic green, copper and bronze reflexions, and the male has a beardlike growth of black bristles, nine inches long, hanging from the centre of the breast. The birds when full grown are about four feet high and may weigh up to 30 pounds. The eggs are whitish with brown spots, and from nine to 15 are laid. The chief domesticated breeds are the mammoth bronze, the Cambridge bronze and the Norfolk black. In Europe turkeys are bred for market in England, Ireland, Hungary and Poland.

Keystone

A DOMESTICATED TURKEY
A native of North America, the turkey has long been domesticated in Britain. The male (above) spreads its tail feathers fanwise in the mating season.

TURKEY: *An Asiatic* NATION REBORN

With a chequered history dating back to the 13th century, losing prestige and possessions under 'Abdul the Damned' and his successors, Turkey was raised to prosperity again by that soldier of fortune Kemal Ataturk.

Turkey. The peninsula of Asia Minor, or Anatolia, which constitutes the main part of Turkey, is a historic land, which has been from the earliest times a great centre of migration and a battle-ground of warring nations (*see* Asia Minor). It consists for the most part of a high plateau sloping towards the sea on three sides, its surface divided by mountains, which break up the country into many more or less isolated districts. Turkey is bounded on the south by the Mediterranean Sea, on the north by the Black Sea and on the west by the Aegean Sea. Its land frontiers (east and south-east) touch Syria, Iraq, Persia and Russia.

The peasants on the Aegean side are able, aided by the fertile soil, warm sunshine and plentiful moisture, to produce an abundance for their needs of wheat, oats, and barley, as well as tobacco and cotton, grapes, olives, and figs for export. The coast of the Black Sea is much colder, and on account of the narrowness of the valleys there is comparatively little arable land; but so fertile is the soil that not only corn but also many fruits are produced, while the mountains abound in forests of walnut, oak, fir, box, beech, plane and other woods. The southern coast below the Taurus Mountains is almost tropical in climate, and there olives, mulberries, pomegranates, figs, oranges, lemons and sugar-cane are grown. There are large swamps and marshes and, in the centre of the country, salt lakes.

In the interior much of the land is suitable only for cattle and sheep raising, and part of it is almost a desert. There are valuable mineral resources that have never been fully developed, and about 4,600 miles of railways (mostly State-owned). A sector of the famous railway known as the Berlin-Baghdad line runs through Turkey.

The Turks are frequently fine-looking people, well-proportioned, and of medium stature, with aquiline noses and bright dark eyes and dark or chestnut hair. In war their courage and capacity for enduring hardship and privation make them excellent soldiers when properly led.

The ancestors of the "Osmanli" or Ottoman Turks (their name came from their early leader Othman or Osman, who lived from 1259 to 1326) were barbaric pagan herdsmen when they first wandered from central Asia into western Asia in the 13th century. They belong to the Ural-Altaic branch of the Mongolian race. Embracing Mahomedanism with fanatical zeal, they settled on good pasture lands in north-western Asia Minor, and, largely as a result of their military ability, the whole of that peninsula was soon under their sway.

It was under Orkhan (who reigned during 1326-59), the son and successor of Othman, that the Turks wrested from the Byzantine Empire most of its Asiatic provinces and gained a foothold in Europe by the capture of Gallipoli. It was probably Orkhan also who started the practice of levying the tribute of Christian boys, causing them to be educated as Mahomedans and trained under rigid military discipline for the famous military corps known as the Janissaries, or "new soldiers," who later formed the backbone of the army. As the centuries passed this force became so powerful and enjoyed so many privileges that leading Moslem families were eager to enlist their sons in its ranks. But in times of peace the Janissaries mutinied often and turned upon their masters. It was not until 1826 that the whole of this force was abolished by the Sultan Mahmud II

> **Extent.**—Total area, 296,000 square miles, and population, 18,860,000. Area of Turkey-in-Europe, 9,250 sq. miles.
>
> **Physical Features.**—Anatolian plain, with mountainous borderlands, including the Taurus Mts. in the south. Rivers include the upper Euphrates and Tigris.
>
> **Principal Products.**—Cereals, tobacco, opium, figs; silk, cotton, carpets; olives; fish.
>
> **Chief Cities.**—Istanbul (Constantinople; pop., 845,000), Izmir (Smyrna, 200,000), Ankara (Angora, capital, 227,000), Seyhan, Bursa, Konia, Gaziantep.

THE TURKISH REPUBLIC IN EUROPE AND ASIA MINOR

SOME SCENES IN THE REPUBLIC OF TURKEY

Dorien Leigh

Proclaimed a republic in 1923, under the leadership of Kemal Ataturk, who was elected the first President the same year, Turkey was almost completely modernized within the next 25 years. The dam at Çubuk (top left) near Ankara, the capital, supplies electric light and power over a wide area. In Station Avenue at Ankara in Asia Minor is the monument of the Republic (top right). Connecting the Black Sea and the Sea of Marmora is the Bosporus (lower) on which stands Istanbul, the Turkish capital until 1922. On the western shore of the strait Turkey still possesses a fragment of her former European Empire, much of which she lost in the Balkan wars of 1912–13.

THE TURKS CAPTURE SZIGETVAR IN HUNGARY

After the battle of Mohács in 1526 almost the whole of the kingdom of Hungary was overrun by the Turks, but the remnants of the Hungarian nation continued to fight the invaders for two centuries. One incident of the struggle was the capture of Szigetvar by the Turks in 1566, which is depicted above in a contemporary woodcut.

the head of magnificent armies. Mosques, hospitals, and schools were built.

But few sultans after Solyman the Magnificent were great warriors or statesmen. Most of them were dissolute idlers. Indeed, by the 17th century, heirs to the throne were secluded in the "cage," or seraglio, ignorant of the ways of government. The heir was not the sultan's eldest son, but the oldest male member of the imperial family; this rule was the direct cause of much tangled intrigue and many murders.

Only five years after Solyman's death the Turks were defeated in the naval battle of Lepanto, (see illustration, page 2294), at the hands of Spain, Venice, and the Papal forces. Dissensions within the Ottoman Empire were added to disasters without. Then for a time there was a revival of power, and in 1683 the Turks made another formidable attempt to take Vienna; but King John Sobieski of Poland led an army of Polish knights to the relief of the city, and the Turkish hosts were put to flight.

After that the Turkish power ebbed steadily. By 1718 Hungary was lost; and about 1783 Russia

(1808–39). Under Orkhan's successors the empire grew steadily. Adrianople was captured in 1361. Vast Christian armies were overthrown in the Balkans at Kossovo (1389) and Nicopolis (1396); and even the defeat and capture at Angora (now Ankara) of Sultan Bajazet I in 1402 by the mighty Timur Leng (Tamerlane), the Mongol, administered only a temporary check. Bajazet's son, Mohammed I, who ruled during 1413–21, recovered all the lands which the Mongols had overrun, and consolidated Turkish power in Asia Minor. Under his successors, Murad II (1421–51) and Mohammed II (the Conqueror, ruled 1451–81), the Turks extended their conquests in Europe, although they were held back by the heroic efforts of the "white knight," Janos Hunyady (1387–1456), Prince of Transylvania, and of Scanderbeg, the hero of Albania. At last Constantinople fell in 1453 to Mohammed II. Selim I the Grim (reigned 1512–20) took over the holy cities of Arabia—Mecca and Medina—and the title of Caliph, spiritual head of all Moslems, in 1517.

Under Solyman the Magnificent (1520–66) Turkey attained the zenith of its power and glory. This "Grand Turk" crushed the forces of Hungary at Mohács (1526) and led his army to the gates of Vienna. Although Vienna was saved by its Austrian defenders, almost the whole of the kingdom of Hungary was converted into a Turkish province. From the Carpathian Mountains the Turkish power extended to the frontiers of Persia and around the Mediterranean to Morocco. The Black Sea was practically a Turkish lake, and Turkish corsairs reinforced by pirates of other nations ruled the Mediterranean. Solyman was lord over 50 million Moslems and Christians.

When the Turkish Empire was at its height, agriculture and trade prospered. Sultans rode at

Dorien Leigh

TURKISH PORT OF MERSIN

On the shore of the Mediterranean Sea, Mersin is the port for Adana, 40 miles inland. The old town, which has largely escaped modernization, includes amongst its exports wool, cotton, grain, timber and fruit.

C. Uchter Knox

GREAT MOSQUE OF A TURKISH TOWN

On the shores of the Bosporus, opposite the former Turkish capital of Istanbul, stands the thriving town of Uskudar, or Scutari, formerly the terminus of the caravan route across Asia Minor. There are eight mosques in the town, of which the most notable is the 16th century Valideh Jami, or Great Mosque, above.

To face page 3264

TURKISH SCENES IN TOWN AND COUNTRYSIDE

On a hill overlooking the Sea of Marmora the road to the quays of Scutari leads through the Biyuk Mezaristan, the largest of the Moslem cemeteries, seen in the upper photograph. Some of the headstones are most curiously carved. The lower photo-graph shows, at the end of the street, the tall Galata Tower, Istanbul. This structure, which affords a magnificent v over the city, was built by the Genoese, and marks the in section of the east and west walls of Galata in the 15th cent gained control of the Crimea and the regions north of the Black Sea. The 19th century saw the gradual redemption of the Christian provinces of the Balkans.

There was no force within the outworn Turkish Empire strong enough to hold together so many peoples of different race, language, and religion in the face of the rising power of Russia and Austria. Turkey was "the sick man of Europe," as Tsar Nicholas I of Russia (1796–1855) called it, and the only question was who should at last fall heir to Turkey's European territory. What should be done with these coveted lands— especially Constantinople— that formed the gateway to the East? This was "The Eastern Question." When Russia took matters into her own hands in the Crimean War of 1853–56, fear of

REVOLUTIONARIES IN ISTANBUL
After Turkey's defeat in the Balkan War of 1912–13 the Turkish Government was preparing to hand over the town of Adrianople to Bulgaria, when the Opposition party, known as the Young Turks, raided the Government offices, compelled the Cabinet to resign and replaced them with members of their own faction. Above is seen the crowd outside the Government offices in Istanbul during the revolution.

Russian aggrandisement led England and France to aid Turkey, and save the country from breaking up. Again, following the Russo-Turkish War of 1877–78, brought on by Turkish cruelties in Bulgaria, Great Britain and Austria intervened and demanded that the peace terms of San Stefano, which Russia had dictated to Turkey, should be revised by a congress of the powers at Berlin (1878). It agreed that Bulgaria should be autonomous, that Rumania, Serbia and Montenegro should be independent principalities, and henceforth the Powers jointly should decide the status of Turkey.

Under Sultan Abdul-Hamid II (1876–1909) the people suffered from extortion. Because of his cruel and oppressive measures he was sometimes called "Abdul the Damned." Then came the "Young Turk" revolution of 1908–09, under the leadership of European Turks educated abroad and organized into a far-reaching secret society. Having gained the support of the army, the Young Turks seized the government in July 1908 and proclaimed the restoration of the greater freedom which Abdul-Hamid had granted in theory in 1876 and then had disregarded. When in 1909 the Sultan tried to suppress the revolt, they deposed him and placed on the throne his younger brother Mohammed V, who was succeeded on his death in 1918 by another brother, Mohammed VI.

Turkey's difficulties were not over, however, Austria took the provinces of Bosnia and Herzegovina, and Bulgaria declared its complete independence. There were party quarrels and political assassinations. Then Italy fought a successful war to gain Libya (1912); and the next year the Balkan allies (Greece, Serbia, Bulgaria and Montenegro) fought a war which took from Turkey almost all of her European possessions. The Young Turks' ill-advised alliance with Germany in the First World War (1914–18) completed the ruin of the

empire, but Turkey rendered great assistance to Germany and Austria in the course of that war.

Russia was cut off from the Mediterranean by the closing of the Dardanelles in 1914. Turkish warships attacked Odessa in October of that year. Russia declared war on the Turks on November 3, and France and Great Britain did likewise on November 5. Failure of the Allies to combine their land and sea forces enabled Turkey to hold the Dardanelles against a strong attack in 1915; on April 25 Allied armies attempting to take Gallipoli were repulsed with the loss of 55,000 men. Not until 1917 did Turkey weaken before the Allied drive, chiefly British; the British overran Mesopotamia (Iraq), took Palestine, and forced Turkey to sue for an armistice on October 30, 1918.

By the treaty of Sèvres, which was never ratified by the Turkish Government, Turkey was to be stripped of all territory in Europe, save for a small area around Constantinople. She was also to give up practically all her possessions in Asia outside Asia Minor, thus being reduced to an area of about 175,000 square miles, against a former area of 613,000 square miles.

Turkish resentment flamed high at these terms, and a revolutionary (Nationalist) government was set up at Ankara under the leadership of Mustafa Kemal. In 1922, after Kemal had routed the Greek armies of occupation in Asia Minor and had retaken Smyrna, the Nationalists deposed the Sultan and forced the European Powers, by the Treaty of Lausanne, to allow them to reoccupy Eastern Thrace up to the boundary of 1914.

The new Turkey discarded her outgrown institutions. The Caliphate, which had given sultans a shadowy but powerful religious leadership over all Islam, was abolished in 1924. Four years later Mahomedanism ceased to be the State religion. A new civil code, based on that of Switzerland, was

Dorien Leigh

AIR MEMBERS OF THE TURKISH BOY SCOUTS

While he was the leader of the country Kemal Ataturk (1882–1938) encouraged all movements which he considered would be of benefit to the youth of the nation. In this photograph members of the air branch of the Turkish Boy Scouts are taking part in a parade, dressed in airmen's overalls and some of them carrying model aeroplanes.

Similar improvements have been made at Turkey's ports, Constantinople (renamed Istanbul, *q.v.*), Samsun, and Izmir (or Smyrna, *q.v.*). These ports clear incoming cotton and woollen goods, metals, machinery, sugar, and chemicals, and ship tobacco, fruits, vegetables, animal products, and cotton, and are important trade centres, as they have been for centuries. Great industrial plans were launched, and the railway and road systems improved and extended. In 1939 the first blast furnace in Turkey started operations.

During the Second World War (1939–45) Turkey observed an armed neutrality, declaring war on Germany and Japan only on March 1, 1945, probably in order to qualify for admission to the United Nations. Turkey's strong political resistance, and the fact that she might be of military value to the Allies, caused the Germans to act with care in the eastern Mediterranean area, and kept the Dardanelles secure. After the war Russia exerted considerable pressure on Turkey. In 1946 there was a Russian demand to alter that clause in the Montreux Convention of 1936, signed by the Great Powers of Europe, which gave Turkey the right to re-militarise the Dardanelles; but the other nations disagreed with Russia on this.

In the Turkish Republic, first proclaimed in 1923, all power is vested in the Grand National Assembly, whose members are elected every four years. The President has a Cabinet of advisers. Kemal Ataturk (who died in 1938) was the first to hold this office. He was succeeded by his close friend and associate Ismet Inönü (born 1884). For local government Turkey is divided into "Vilayets." Each has a "Vali," or Governor, and an elected council.

adopted in 1926. The Gregorian (western) calendar replaced the Mahomedan; the religious orders were abolished, and monasteries closed. A law of 1925 required every man to wear a hat instead of a fez. The use of Arabic letters was displaced by that of the Latin alphabet ; and in 1934 the metric system of weights and measures became obligatory.

Women in the old Turkey had almost no rights. Today women vote and polygamy is prohibited. Unveiled women and girls in European clothing work with men and boys in classrooms and offices. Many women are now doctors, dentists, lawyers, and journalists. Primary education is compulsory.

All this modernization owes its inspiration to the Turkish dictator, Kemal Ataturk, who, as Ghazi Mustafa Kemal, was elected first President of the new Turkish Republic in 1923. His title " pasha " was won by his fighting in the First World War, and " ghazi " (the victorious) was added in 1921 when he defeated Greek armies of occupation. He was already a national hero when he rallied his countrymen to save Turkey from partition under the Treaty of Sèvres, and dethroned the Sultan in 1922. He assumed the name of Ataturk, or Chief Turk, in 1934. (*See* Kemal Ataturk).

Kemal laboured hard to introduce 20th-century machinery and farming methods to peasants plodding in the ways of 2,000 years ago. He moved the capital from Istanbul (Constantinople) on the Bosporus, to Ankara (*q.v.*), in the heart of the Anatolian plain, and converted it from a simple country town to a city of modern appearance.

Turkistan. In the heart of Asia, between the Kazak Soviet Socialist Republic on the north, the Gobi Desert on the east, Tibet, Afghanistan and Iran (Persia) on the south, and the Caspian Sea on the west, lies a vast region which has an interesting history. Known as Turkistan, a name originally meant to apply to all territory inhabited by Turks, it now has neither racial, geographical nor political unity.

Divided between China and the Soviet Union, the population of Turkistan includes Chinese, Russians, Turkomans, Kirghiz, Uzbeks, and representatives of a number of other races. A land of mountains, barren plateaux, deserts, a few grassy steppes (plains) and some fertile river valleys, it is divided into two parts by the Tien Shan Mountains: to the east of the range lies Chinese or Eastern Turkistan, and to the west Russian or Western Turkistan.

Eastern Turkistan forms part of the Chinese province of Sin-kiang and is an isolated region, hemmed in by mountains on three sides. To the east is the Gobi Desert, which extends into Sin-kiang. Agriculture is possible only at the foot of the mountains or where the soil is irrigated, as in the valleys of the Kashgar and Yarkand rivers. Most of the inhabitants are Mahomedans and are more akin to their neighbours in Russian Turkistan than to the Chinese. Agriculture is the main occupation; fruit, rice, cereals, vegetables and cotton are cultivated. Jade is worked, and a little gold is mined. Yarkand, Khotan and Kashgar are among the most important towns.

Western Turkistan, conquered by the Russians between 1860 and 1870, has under the Soviet Government been divided into four Soviet Republics. Once one of the most backward parts of the former Russian Empire, it is being rapidly industrialized. Trains and motor-vehicles are replacing the bullock-cart, camel and donkey; mineral resources are being developed; and irrigation systems have reclaimed enormous tracts. Most of the cotton produced in the Soviet Union is grown there.

The Kirghiz Soviet Socialist Republic, established in 1924, is in the extreme east of Western Turkistan and has an area of 76,900 square miles. The State is noted for its live-stock, and numbers of horses, cattle and sheep are pastured on the upland meadows of the Tien Shan Mountains. Sugar-beet, hemp and cotton are the main crops. Coal, oil, gold, silver, lead, mercury and antimony are found. There are sugar-refineries, tanneries, flour-mills and metal works. The capital is Frunze (population 93,000). The population of the republic is 1,460,000.

Formed in 1929, the Tajik Soviet Socialist Republic is mainly in the Pamirs. A number of the valleys are more than 10,000 feet above sea level, and the area is 55,700 square miles. The northern part is exceptionally fertile, much of it being irrigated. Cattle and sheep are bred. Cereals, fruit, cotton and sugar-cane are grown. Coal, lead, oil and mica are worked. Since 1930 a number of motor roads have been constructed, and there is a railway from Stalinabad to Termez, a distance of 124 miles. The capital is Stalinabad (population 83,000). Three-quarters of the population are Tajiks, who speak a language very similar to Persian and are considered to be the descendants of the original Aryan inhabitants of Turkistan. The population of the Republic is 1,485,000.

To the east of Tajikistan is the Uzbek Soviet Socialist Republic, which was created in 1924 and contains most of the fertile valley of Fergana—an area 180 miles long and 100 miles wide, covered by a network of canals fed by the Syr Daria river. With an area of 143,000 square miles, it is the chief cotton-growing region of the Soviet Union, and it produces also lucerne, rice, grapes and apricots. Minerals include coal, oil and gold. Tashkent, the capital (population 585,000), is also the chief industrial city of the region and manufactures cotton goods and agricultural implements. Ancient

Samarkand (population 154,000) was rebuilt in the 13th century by the Mongol Emperor Jenghiz Khan on the site of the city destroyed by Alexander the Great (356–323 B.C.). It was made the capital of the Mongol Empire by Timur Leng (Tamerlane), and Timur's splendid tomb still stands there. Bokhara, an ancient seat of learning once known to the Western world for its beautiful rugs, is now a thriving manufacturing centre. The population of the State is 6,283,000.

Extending westward from Uzbekistan to the Caspian Sea is the Turkoman Soviet Socialist Republic, or Turkmenistan, formed in 1925. The area of the state is 189,000 square miles, of which the northern portion is occupied by the Kara Kum Desert. The main occupation is agriculture based on irrigation, and even large areas of the Kara Kum Desert have been rendered productive by tapping underground water supplies. The region is noted for fiery horses, fat-tailed sheep, Astrakhan fur and rugs. Soda, sulphur, and other minerals are extracted from the waters of the Caspian Sea. In the desert there are deposits of magnesium and coal. The capital is Ashkabad (population 127,000). The inhabitants of Turkmenistan number 1,254,000.

Turner, JOSEPH MALLORD WILLIAM (1775–1851). Acclaimed by a number of critics as the world's outstanding landscape and seascape painter, Turner was born near Covent Garden, London, on April 23, 1775, and was educated at small schools in London and Margate. By the time he was six years old he had convinced his father, a barber, that he was going to be an artist, and his drawings were

M. O. Williams

FROM THE LOOMS OF TURKISTAN
Specimen carpets from the looms of Merv and Bokhara are commonly displayed for sale in the markets of Turkistan, spread over the shoulder of some Turkoman vendor and contrasting strikingly with his coloured coat and sheepskin hat.

hung in the shop for sale. In 1789 he entered the Royal Academy school of painting, and to help meet the expenses of his education, he coloured prints for engravers, washed in backgrounds for architects, and made drawings in the evenings.

His somewhat dreary boyhood may have given rise to the irresistible longing to picture " the light that never was on sea or land " which became the passion of his later years. For always Turner painted light—light as he found it in the transparent air of noonday, in the afterglow of the evening, in the passing cloud, or reflected in water, until at last he was able to catch the very sunshine and put it on his canvas. He may be said to have been the first of the Impressionists (q.v.), because he developed that technique by the use of which the Impressionists of the 1870s founded a new school of painting in France.

While still in his teens he received a commission to make drawings for a magazine, and in the next few years tramped over most of England, Wales, and Scotland, and visited France and Italy. In 1799 he was elected an Associate of the Royal Academy and in 1802 a Royal Academician. He was gradually developing his mastery of vivid and moving colour effects, and in 1829 came Ulysses Deriding Polyphemis, with a riotous exuberance of rich colour new to English painting. In 1838–39 appeared The Fighting Téméraire, and Modern Italy, in which a classic composition is blended with romantic colour treatment. From about 1840 came a marked change in Turner's style. More and more he concentrated on the suggestive effects of colour, whether glowing and brilliant, as in the

Burial at Sea (1842), or the cold greys of the much-discussed Snowstorm, a seascape of the same year.

Turner never married, and he kept aloof from Society. He lived for a time under the assumed name of Booth, in Chelsea, London, where he died on December 19, 1851. He was buried in St. Paul's Cathedral, London, where he lies beside Sir Joshua Reynolds (1723–92).

His oil paintings are supreme, but as a water-colour artist also Turner has never been excelled. His earliest success was won by his engraved plates of landscapes, a number of them engraved by himself. This work was so much in advance of former landscape engraving that it might almost be reckoned a new development of art. Most of his paintings and drawings are in the Tate Gallery, London, though there are a few in the National Gallery, London. His pictures and drawings, the latter numbering nearly 20,000, were bequeathed to the nation, a fitting memorial to one of the world's masters of landscape and Britain's most eminent painter. Turner must also be accounted as one of the most original of the artists who freed art from the principles of the Renaissance.

Turpentine. Crude turpentine resins or gums come from many varieties of trees, growing about the Mediterranean and in the southern United States. The finest turpentine is made by distilling the clear colourless gum, chiefly of the yellow pine. The gum exudes from cuts made in the bark, usually from April to October. If the sap-wood is not cut through, this does not seriously injure the tree. The gum is a pale, straw-coloured,

VENICE THROUGH THE EYES OF TURNER

Tate Gallery, London

The first of Turner's series of Venetian pictures, this painting was exhibited at the Royal Academy, London, in 1833. His portrayals of the Italian city are remarkable for their splendour of colour, for to him, to quote his own words, Venice appeared as ' a city of rose and white, rising out of an emerald sea against a sky of sapphire blue.' The British author John Ruskin (1819–1900), who wrote an essay on Turner, placed him among ' the seven supreme colourists of the world.' Equally with his oil paintings, his water-colours have never been excelled.

oily, inflammable liquid. Turpentine is also obtained by distilling the wood itself. About 85 per cent of the supply goes into paints and varnishes, since turpentine absorbs oxygen and assists the action of the drying oils. It is used also in medicine; in making synthetic camphor, in dyes, inks, insecticides, and leather; and as a solvent for waxes, sulphur, phosphorus, resins, and so on. Oil of turpentine is the crude product freed of resin and refined by distillation.

Twain, MARK (1835–1910). In the early days of steamboats on the river Mississippi, in the United States, the most exciting event in the port of Hannibal was the arrival of a steamer. When the whistle blew, the small boys raced to the village wharf to see the boat arrive, while the look-out took soundings of the water and the pilot shouted his orders. It was actually from the call of " mark twain " (by the two fathoms mark or 12 feet) to denote the depth of water under the boat that this celebrated North American humorist and novelist took his pen-name. Mark Twain, whose real name was Samuel Langhorne Clemens, was born in the town of Florida, Missouri, on November 30, 1835, but his parents moved to Hannibal soon after his birth. There he was educated, learned the printing trade, and later became a river pilot.

After earning his living in mining camps and as a reporter and editor, Clemens went in 1866 on a trip to the Sandwich or Hawaiian Islands in the North Pacific, and soon after started his long and successful career as a lecturer and popular author. His first story, the Celebrated Jumping Frog of Calaveras County, appeared in 1867, and as the result of a tour in the Mediterranean he wrote Innocents Abroad (1869), a book which gained him a world-wide reputation.

Mark Twain's humour was recognized at once as being characteristically North American—clean, shrewd, good-natured and independent in opinion. It is frequently exaggerated to the point of burlesque; but there is no sting in it. Not content with his role of humorist, he wrote a beautiful idyll, The Prince and the Pauper (1882) ; A Connecticut Yankee at the Court of King Arthur, a satire on the romances of chivalry ; and an historical novel, Personal Recollections of Joan of Arc (1896). He drew upon the experiences of his boyhood for material for his boys' classics : The Adventures of Tom Sawyer (1876) and its sequel The Adventures of Huckleberry Finn. These books give an account of the escapades of boys in the Mississippi valley, and glimpses of a vanished way of life.

In 1895 the failure of a New York publishing house in which he had invested almost all his money left him a poor man, but he was a universal celebrity and by making a lecture tour round the world he soon overcame his financial difficulties. Later works include Captain Stormfield's Visit to Heaven (1909), and Is Shakespeare Dead? (1909). Mark Twain died at Redding, Connecticut, on April 21, 1910.

H. J. Barratt
MARK TWAIN
Samuel L. Clemens, better known under his pen-name of Mark Twain, was an artist in shrewd humour which had a wide appeal.

Tyler, WAT. As the principal leader of the first great revolt of the common people in England, Wat (or Walter) Tyler flashed into the light of history only to come to a violent end. This revolt, which took place in 1381, was known as the " Peasants' Revolt," or " Wat Tyler's Rebellion."

The peasants and artisans all over England were discontented. The peasants wanted to be freed from serfdom and to pay a reasonable rent for their farms, and both town and country labourers were weary of being forced by law to work at wages that were no longer sufficient.

The Hundred Years' War (1338–1453) between England and France, too, was going badly, and many people felt that the counsellors of the young King Richard II were responsible for its failure and for the heavy taxes that oppressed them. A priest named John Ball went about preaching against social and economic injustices, demanding that the distinction between lord and serf should be wiped out, and taking as his text the popular rhyme :

When Adam delved and Eve
    span,
Who was then the gentleman?

When the government passed a law enacting that everybody, rich and poor, should pay a poll tax (so much per head) revolt broke out. Under Wat Tyler (who was apparently a tiler of Dartford, Kent) the men of Kent marched toward London, destroying tax rolls and title deeds, and burning houses of officials, lawyers, and unpopular landlords. When they reached London they were joined by crowds of dissidents coming from other directions.

When King Richard came to them, Wat Tyler presented their demands. Richard granted everything, and the great mass of the rebels began turning homeward. Tyler himself remained till the next day, for another interview with the King. At this interview he was stabbed by the Lord Mayor, because Tyler was alleged to have insulted the King. With their leader slain, the rebels were easily crushed. Thus the revolt did not have any immediate results, but changes in methods of farming and other developments led to a gradual abandonment of the serfdom against which Tyler's rebellion had been largely directed. (*See* illustration in page 1400).

Tyndale, WILLIAM (?1492–1536). Mankind owes a considerable debt to this learned Englishman, for it was upon his wonderful translations that the Authorized Version of the English Bible was based. Unlike most previous scholars, he translated straight from the original texts. He followed the originals very closely, using simple language that anyone could understand.

Tyndale was born probably in Gloucestershire, and was educated at both Oxford and Cambridge. His work exposed him to many dangers. Finding it impossible to finish his translation in London on account of the persecution of the clergy, he was forced to leave England in 1524, and, after continuing his labours in various towns on the Continent, was arrested for heresy and imprisoned. On October 6, 1536, he was strangled and burned at the stake at Vilvorde, near Brussels. Though long an exile, Tyndale was one of the greatest forces of the English Reformation; his translation had an important influence on the development of English prose. (*See* illustration in page 426).

Tyndall, JOHN (1820–93). This brilliant thinker and popular teacher of science was one of the first to show the English-speaking world that science is as entrancing as a novel.

He was born at Leighlin Bridge, Carlow, Ireland, on August 2, 1820. Largely self-trained and in early life a surveyor, he devoted himself to physics. He was greatly influenced by early association with Faraday (*q.v.*), whom he succeeded as professor of natural philosophy and superintendent at the Royal Institution, London. Tyndall made original investigations on many subjects, including the motion of glaciers, the action of radiant heat on gases and vapours, and sound. Among his most popular works are Glaciers of the Alps, and Forms of Water. In 1887 he resigned his professorship at the Royal Institution (an organization for the encouragement of scientific research), and he died on December 4, 1893.

Type AND TYPOGRAPHY. The piece of metal or wood bearing a raised letter or figure used in printing is called a type. There are many different styles of type face—such as roman, italic, gothic, script, etc.—and the sizes range from the tiny types of the "thumb" editions of the Bible to the enormous letters of the hoardings. All except poster type are usually made of type metal, the large letters being carved from hard fine-grained woods.

No matter how the printer's letters may differ as to style and size, the type body must be alike in one particular—height—so that when thousands of them are wedged tightly together to make a page, the printing surface will be perfectly even. As cast by English and American type foundries, the height is ·92 of an inch.

The letter itself, known as the face, is on the upper end of the type body. The body has a shallow groove — sometimes several—on one surface, so that the printer, when setting up type, can tell by a touch or a glance which is the front. In English and American types the front of the body is "nicked," and in French type the back. The bottom end of the type body is also is often hollowed out, so that the type has two "feet" on which to stand. (*See* illus. on left).

Face
Shoulder
Serifs
Pin Mark
Body or Shank
Groove
Nick
Feet

TYPE BODY
Typefounders have a special name for each portion of a single type body, as in the above diagram. The height is ·92 of an inch.

Type metal is an alloy of lead, antimony, and tin, and sometimes copper. It fills the mould and shrinks little in cooling, less than any other useful alloy. Although exposed constantly to air, water, oils, inks, and alkaline solutions, type is little affected.

Great Primer .... 18 pt.
English .... 14 pt.
Pica .... 12 pt.
Long Primer .... 10 pt.
Bourgeois .... 9 pt.
Brevier .... 8 pt.
Minion .... 7 pt.
Nonpareil .... 6 pt.
Ruby .... 5¼ pt.
Pearl ... 5 pt.

TYPE NAMES AND POINT SIZES
Sizes of type were distinguished by the names given above, but they are now identified by points (72 to the inch).

The first printers cast their types by pouring the hot melted metal into hand-moulds. Soon type foundries were established, and the cutting of the punches and the making of types became a business separate from the printing trade. Type-casting machines were introduced about 1845, and in 1890 the Barth automatic type-casting machine came into use which was capable of casting 150 completed types a minute.

The use of hand-set type has been greatly reduced by the introduction of the Linotype, which casts solid lines of reading matter, and the " Monotype," which casts separate types as set for printing. Both are operated by keyboards (*see* Linotype ; " Monotype "). Many large printing establishments now have machines on which type for hand setting is cast in the office. A "fount" of matrices of the desired type is purchased or rented from the type foundry and an indefinite number of replicas made from it. The " Monotype " caster can be used in this way for casting type to be used in hand-setting.

A fount of type includes all the characters in sufficient numbers for ordinary composition. In almost any combination of English words the letter *e* is used most frequently, so a fount of type contains more of *e* than any other letter, and very few of *z*, which is seldom needed. A pair of printer's type " cases " consists of an upper and a lower case. These are arranged at an angle on a frame, the lower case nearest, and the upper one above it. In the upper case the capital letters, small capitals, figures, and certain special characters are kept; in the lower case are the small letters, punctuation marks and spaces. Capitals are called " upper case " letters, and small letters " lower case." In a " double " case (used when large quantities of type are not needed) there are sections for upper and lower case letters, but the old names remain.

Formerly sizes of type were indicated by special names, many of great age ; but now the more accurate " point system " is used in designating type faces, a point being $\frac{1}{72}$ of an inch.

So far we have considered the type merely as a piece of metal or of wood having a raised letter on its top end. " Typography " is the art of choosing types of suitable face for a particular piece of printing ; of arranging them so that the text can be read clearly; and, further, of securing a result which pleases the aesthetic sense of the reader. Seven out of ten—perhaps nine out of ten—readers do not knowingly consider the aesthetic quality; but if our

WHERE TYPE IS ARRANGED IN THE COMPOSING ROOM

Taken in the Amalgamated Press printing works, where this book was printed, the above photograph gives some idea of what happens to the type after it comes from the type-setting machines. First the lines are arranged on a 'galley,' a metal tray to hold a column, and then they are made up into pages. 'Making up' includes the insertion of illustrations and headings, and is done by hand at the frames. The pages are 'proofed' on a press (right centre) and finally imposed, as seen on the tables, i.e., so placed that when a sheet, on which are several pages, is printed and folded the pages come in correct sequence and the proper margins are left to allow for folding, stitching and trimming.

present pages, for example, were printed in the same way as that of some newspapers, you would know at once that the result was unpleasant—though you might not know why.

When the present edition of the New Book of Knowledge was being planned, certain changes were made in the types and faces in order to improve the typography of the book. As you look through, you notice that the titles of the stories are set in a bold type which catches the eye easily when you are seeking a particular entry; but observe that these bold and black letters are not set close together. That would have produced an ugly effect; and so a very thin white space separates each letter from its neighbour. Again, the types chosen for the explanations under the pictures were selected with an eye to their contrast with the darker masses of the photographic blocks above them; and to their blending, in the page, with the type matter around.

Typography must take great notice of the white spaces around the types. You can see a good example of this in the title page to a volume, where the effect is due as much to the " whites " as to the types. Look at some of the advertisements in magazines and newspapers: these show another aspect of the typographer's art. Advertisers have their own ideas about the types they would use; but the typographer and the printer must consider also the effect of any single advertisement when it is put with others in the same publication.

If you study advertisements you will notice that a " fashion " of typography seems to influence a great many people every now and then; from very light and plain type faces the tendency may swing over to darker, ornate and even grotesque letters.

Type founders must cater for all tastes, and it is left to the typographer to produce an artistic result along with legibility and, in the case of advertisements, with a lay-out which arrests the reader's attention.

Every good printer is of necessity a typographer; but business concerns which spend a good deal of money on advertising, or on printed matter for other purposes, often employ a man solely in this capacity—to supervise their printed matter, select the types to be used, and to draw up rough sketches called " visuals," which show the department heads what the printed matter will look like if set in a certain manner. (*See* Book; Printing).

Typewriter. The first typewriter—a crude, unwieldy affair—invented by an English engineer named Mills, was patented in 1714. An early machine, intended primarily for the use of the blind, and printing embossed letters, was devised by A. E. Beach in 1856. It was not until 1874 that the first practical typewriter was placed on the market. It was made by E. Remington and Sons, gun manufacturers, and was based on a design by C. L. Sholes, a United States journalist.

In the early years of its development the type-writer usually worked on one of two general principles. The first Remington, a type-bar machine, carried type letters on the end of steel bars. These bars, about 38 in number, were pivoted about a horizontal ring, making an almost complete circle. When the operator depressed the keys, the type arms rose sharply to a common centre on a hard rubber cylinder carrying the letter paper. In front of the cylinder and between it and the head of the hammer-like type bar an inked ribbon was passed, this producing the inked

Left, the Science Museum, South Kensington; right, courtesy of Imperial Typewriter Co

TYPEWRITERS OF YESTERDAY AND TODAY

The early typewriters were heavy and clumsy compared with the efficient instruments in use today. The machine on the left is a Sholes & Glidden typewriter of 1875, manufactured by the gunmakers E. Remington & Son, at Ilion, New York. Though awkward in size and appearance, and limited to capital letters only, it embodied the right idea, and from it most modern typewriters have been developed. On the right is a British-made Imperial typewriter.

impression of the letters on the paper. At first there was only one letter on each type bar, and the machine typed capital letters only; by 1878, however, there were two letters on each type bar, and, in conjunction with a shift-key, it became possible to produce both capital and small letters.

The second kind of typewriter was the shuttle machine, now much less used than that with the type bar. On the shuttle machine the letters and signs were cast on a curved plate, called the shuttle. When a key was depressed the shuttle was brought into position, and the paper forced against it to make the impression. One advantage was that the shuttles were interchangeable, making it possible to produce different styles of type on the same machine.

Most modern typewriters follow the conventional type-bar model modified so that, instead of the old horizontal ring, the frame holding the type bars is an arc of a circle, with the type bars striking the common centre on the front of the rubber cylinder instead of the lower side. By this arrangement the work is visible at all times.

The arrangement of the keys which have to be depressed to mark the paper is now almost everywhere the same, though there are certain variations in use in different countries, because the frequency with which some letters are used varies with different languages. The principle of the so-called " universal " keyboard is that the letters in most frequent use are most readily available to the typist's fingers. Each type bar now carries two or more characters, including small letters, capitals, figures and various other signs in general use. The " touch typist " is taught to use all her fingers, and she can keep her eye on what she is copying without watching what is being typed.

The typewriter now plays an increasingly important part in the conduct of the world's business. Tabulating and adding mechanisms, added to ordinary typewriters, have made it possible to do commercial book-keeping and accounts on the same machine as is used for correspondence. Machines have also been devised for writing on stiff cardboard, on the pages of a bound book, etc. A recent development is an electrically operated machine, which types automatically from a stencil pattern and can produce 20 sheets of average length in an hour.

Portable typewriters, which can be easily carried about, produce work equal in appearance to that of a full-size machine. The so-called noiseless typewriters, which actually do make a little noise, are worked by what is termed pressure-printing, the printed impression on the paper being produced by the overthrow of a weighted cam. The increasing use of typewriters in offices has had considerable influence on the entry of women into business. It was found that women could manipulate the typewriter as well as, if not better than, men. The average typist can produce 60 words a minute—about three times as much as the average writer with the pen. Experts can keep up a rate of over 100 words a minute.

Tyrone. The largest county of Northern Ireland, Tyrone has an area of 1,280 square miles. It is bounded on the north by Londonderry, on the east by Lough Neagh and Armagh, on the south by Fermanagh, on the west by Donegal— the latter a county of the Irish Republic. Tyrone is mainly hilly, with the picturesque Sperrin Mountains and other ranges; but in the east there is a level tract. Rivers include the Derg and Blackwater, and the Foyle divides the county from Londonderry. Agriculture is mainly confined to the east, where oats, potatoes and flax are grown; cattle and poultry are reared. Manufactures include textiles, earthenware, whiskey, chemicals and soap. The county town is Omagh (population 6,000). Other centres are Strabane, Dungannon and Newtown Stewart. The population of Tyrone is 127,000.

U

Uganda. In British East Africa, between the Anglo-Egyptian Sudan, Tanganyika Territory, the Belgian Congo and Kenya, is the Protectorate of Uganda, described under East Africa.

Ukraine. (Pron. ū-krān′). In the south-west of the Soviet Union, on both sides of the lower course of the River Dnieper and bordering on the Black Sea, is the region called Little Russia or the Ukraine. The Ukrainian Soviet Socialist Republic has an area of about 225,000 square miles and contains some of the most fertile land in Europe, producing huge crops of wheat, rye, barley, oats, sugar-beet, potatoes, cotton and flax.

The coalfields of the Donetz basin are immensely valuable, and this coal combined with iron ore from around Krivoi Rog has given rise to a vast iron and steel industry, which in normal times is the largest in European Russia. Other mineral deposits include manganese, aluminium, oil, salt and gypsum. Hydro-electric installations on the Dnieper serve thousands of communities. The capital is Kiev (*q.v.*) on the Dnieper. Odessa (*q.v.*) and Kharkov (*q.v.*) are other large cities.

The name Ukraine, which means " border-land," was given to this region when it was a stretch of more-or-less neutral territory situated between the Slavonic countries to the west and the Tartars and Turks to the east. There in the 16th century gathered bands of restless and lawless men from Lithuania, Poland, Russia and even Turkey, who became known as Cossacks (*q.v.*). In the 18th century most of the Ukraine was annexed by Russia, but the western part was taken by Austria, where the Ukrainians became known as Ruthenians.

When the Imperial Russian Government was overthrown by the Bolsheviks in 1917, an independent Ukrainian People's Republic was set up. After a period of confused fighting, in which the Bolsheviks, Tsarist Russians, Poles and Germans were involved, a Soviet republic was proclaimed in 1920. In 1923 the Union of Soviet Socialist Republics was formed and the Ukrainian Republic was incorporated in it. A part of the Ukraine which had been annexed by Poland in 1919–20 was regained in 1939 after Poland had been divided between Germany and Russia. In 1940 Rumanian Bessarabia and Northern Bukowina became part of the Ukraine, and that part of Ruthenia belonging to Czechoslovakia was added in 1945.

During the Second World War (1939–45) the Ukraine was devastated as the Russian and German armies alternately advanced and retreated across it.

Most of the large cities were badly damaged and numerous industrial installations destroyed, but the work of reconstruction was begun as soon as the Germans had been driven out of the country in 1944. The population is nearly 40 million. (*See* Russia).

Underground Railways. One of the chief problems of life in a large city is that of transporting large numbers of persons rapidly from one place to another. If (on a hot afternoon) you have ever sat in a motor-bus which crawled slowly along a crowded street, you will have realized that there is a very definite limit to the amount of traffic which a street can carry. This problem is a very big one in all large cities, but particularly so in those, such as London, where the streets have not been scientifically planned, but have merely grown from the days when the population was very much smaller.

The transport problem can be approached in two ways—by widening the roads, or by taking some of the traffic away from the roads. In many cases, the first method is not possible—the land is not available for widening the roads, and it is necessary to carry the people in other ways. Railways must take the place of road traffic. Now, to find room for a surface railway is as difficult as to find room for wider roads. Therefore, we must go either overhead (as in the New York Elevated Railway) or underground. Overhead construction has several disadvantages (such railways are generally being demolished) and our solution is, then, to burrow underground.

London is by no means the only city to put its urban railways underground. New York

E.N.A.

SUMMER LANDSCAPE IN THE FERTILE UKRAINE
Most of the Ukraine, or Little Russia, is very fertile, and the country about Poltava, of which we have a glimpse above, is especially so, producing wheat, barley, oats, sugar-beet, rye and flax. The region was devastated during the Second World War (1939–45), but work of reconstruction was begun at once after its liberation from the Germans in 1944.

1 & 38. Steel tunnel sections erected in segments.
2. Sliding doors.
3 & 25. Specially-prepared glass for windows and interior panels.
4 & 31. Steel panel plates.
5. Car frame.
6. Electric batteries.
7, 8, & 36. Chairs, rails and sleepers.
9 & 10. Air compressors and ducts.
11. Ventilating plant.
12. Compressed air gear for operating doors.
13. Car heaters.
14. Springs.
15. Axle roller bearings.
16. Steel wheels.
17. Motor traction gears.
18. Electric traction motor.
19. Air brakes.
20. Steel flooring.
21 & 22. Seat springs and seats.
23. Door frame.
24. Advertisement panels.
26. Electric drop lights.
27. Fire extinguishers.
28 & 29. Windscreen wiper.
30. Driver's loud-speaker outfit.
32. Controller.
33. Automatic couplings.
34. Electric cables.
35. Porcelain insulators.
37. Concrete foundation on which track is laid.

LONDON'S UNDERGROUND—DETAILS OF THE 'TUBE' TRAINS AND THE TUNNELS IN WHICH THEY RUN (with the biggest network in the world), Paris, Moscow, Naples, Barcelona, Glasgow and many other cities have their undeground lines. Most of them are in comparatively shallow tunnels, like the original urban lines in London, the Metropolitan (which was first opened on January 10, 1863, from Paddington to Farringdon Street), and the Metropolitan District, which followed five years later, and originally ran from Westminster to Kensington High Street. Both lines were originally worked by steam and, in spite of the fact that the line contained some surface sections, and the tunnels were ventilated by gratings in a number of places, travelling was a very uncomfortable affair. Electrification of both these lines, since then considerably extended and interconnected, was completed in 1905.

Electric traction, with its absence of smoke and fumes, made it possible to contruct the deep level " tube " railways which are peculiar to London. The first of these, the City & South London, from Stockwell to the City, was opened in 1895 and reconstructed in 1922–24. The Central London, from the Bank of England to Shepherds Bush, followed in 1900; and between this time and 1907 the Bakerloo, the Piccadilly and the Hampstead lines were built. Surface extensions of these railways, running in the open out to London's suburbs, are of more recent construction. Under an Act of 1933 the entire network of Underground railways, together with London's buses, trams, and trolley-buses was transferred to be operated by the London Passenger Transport Board. In 1948 this became known as the London Transport Executive, as a group of the nationalised " British Railways."

Although semi-surface or shallow railways are more convenient from the passenger's point of view, in that time is saved getting from street level to the trains and *vice versa*, there are sound reasons for London's deep Tubes. In the first place, it is necessary to go deep to ensure suitable ground for tunnelling (the " London clay "). Some remarkable engineering feats have been accomplished in their building—for example the station at Tooting Broadway, with escalator tunnels, platforms, subways, tracks, and cross-over, was built in what was practically an underground lake.

Some idea of the immense help given by underground railways in transporting large numbers of people can be obtained from an American survey in which it was stated that to carry the same number of people by motor vehicles as could be dealt with by a four-track underground railway would require 20 express highways of the same width. Some of the worst congestion in the world occurs in New York, where certain of the lofty office buildings contain more people than can be dealt with by ten

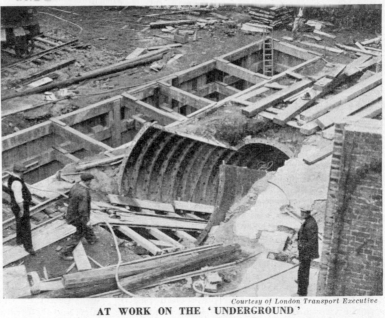

Courtesy of London Transport Executive

AT WORK ON THE ' UNDERGROUND '

Remarkable engineering feats have been accomplished in building London's underground railways. Above, work is in progress on the escalators (moving stairways) of a new station ; in the right foreground is the entrance to a pilot tunnel—a small boring which is later expanded to full dimensions.

tightly-packed ten-car underground trains; the Eighth Avenue subway is reputed to handle 90,000 persons an hour in the rush period.

To handle dense crowds at a high speed, it is essential that every possible means of eliminating delays—if only of fractions of a second—is used, and one has only to look at London's Underground to see the methods in use. The old-fashioned booking-offices have been replaced by booths equipped with automatic ticket-printing machines and change-giving machines. Approaches from the booking-hall to the platform have been kept as short as possible, and escalators run in twos and threes at crowded stations. Many trains have air-operated doors, and the signalling system (*see* Railways) is designed to allow the very shortest possible " headway "—distance between one train and others in front and behind—consistent with safety. On certain sections 48 trains per hour are worked.

As we explain in our story of Tunnels, the primary reason for putting railways in tunnels was to avoid obstacles, such as buildings or roads, on the surface. The earliest of London's underground lines were intended to link up the terminal stations of the big north-south and east-west main lines. These tunnels, shallow ones on the "cut-and-cover" principle, often followed the course of the roads above. Electrification, with its elimination of smoke and steam, allowed greater use of tunnels and, of course, of deeper ones.

It also permitted better and automatic systems of signalling. The general adoption of motor vehicles for public and private transport, with the crowding of the highways that resulted in city approaches, was another big inducement to put the passenger lines deep below the surface. It yet remains to apply this principle to special lines which will take merchandise from one point to another.

LATEST CHAPTER *of* BRITAIN'S STORY

Earlier divisions of the history of the British Isles will be found under the headings Britain, England, Scotland, and Ireland. This outline deals with 'our island story' from 1707 to the present day.

United Kingdom, HISTORY OF THE, FROM 1707. The Act of Union between England and Scotland was, in effect, an Act for the weakening of England's ancient enemy. Only the Lowlands were united in heart and mind to England in 1707. Scottish national unity, which had been largely maintained by antagonism to England, broke down with the union of the two countries; and France, in her future wars with England, could look for help only to a diminishing section of the Scottish people instead of to a national Scottish Government.

The crowns of England and Scotland in 1714 passed to the Elector of Hanover in Germany, who was elected King of the United Kingdom by the Whig (Liberal) Parliament. A new era in the British Constitution had begun: the King was no more than a figure-head, and power had passed from the Crown into the hands of Parliament. No longer did the King attend Cabinet meetings; his place was taken by a first, or Prime, Minister.

From 1721 to 1742 the Prime Minister, Sir Robert Walpole, guided the destinies of the country, and left a permanent mark on English history by his non-intervention in European wars, his development of commercial activity, his tolerant administration, and his constitutional reconstruction. But Walpole's tolerance did not extend to his rival colleagues in Parliament, for he was intensely fond of power. Many discontented Whigs joined hands with the reviving Tory party and formed a strong opposition.

War broke out in 1739 over commercial disputes with Spain, but this soon merged into the general European war of the Austrian Succession, which followed on the death, in 1740, of the Emperor Charles VI without male issue. Walpole tried to limit England's participation in the war, but, finding the opposition too strong for him, he resigned in 1742.

Meanwhile, abroad the French had overrun the Austrian Netherlands, penetrated into Holland, and in India had captured Madras. But British sea-power was sufficient to rob France of all the fruits of her victories, and the Treaty of Aix-la-Chapelle in 1748 despoiled France of her gains.

ENGLAND'S FIRST PRIME MINISTER
Sir Robert Walpole, head of the government from 1721 to 1742, is generally regarded as the first ' Prime Minister.' This engraving by A. Fogg, after a painting by William Hogarth (1697–1764) and Sir James Thornhill, shows Walpole conversing with Mr. Speaker Onslow (seated).

This proved, however, to be merely a truce, and in 1756 the Seven Years' War (*q.v.*) began.

During this conflict William Pitt the Eldei became Minister for War, and Britain established the beginnings of her empire in India, as well as securing possession of Canada. Quebec fell to the British in 1759, and French dominion in India was shattered by British victories at Plassey in 1757 and at Wandiwash in 1760.

George III came to the throne in 1760, and the Tories, whose allegiance to the exiled Pretender had weakened, now rallied round the throne in an effort to break the long Whig supremacy which was at last on the wane. The early part of the reign was a struggle between the King and the Whigs, Pitt being replaced as Prime Minister by the King's tutor, Lord Bute. The King wanted to be a personal ruler, and by forming his own party in the House of Commons and by placing his own confidants in the Cabinet, he succeeded in undermining one ministry after another until at length he secured in Lord North a Prime Minister who was more or less his personal agent.

To meet the costs of the Seven Years' War, Parliament thought of taxing the British North American Colonies, but the colonists felt that, whatever their share in the common expense, it must be granted by Colonial governments. From the first the King regarded the colonists' attitude towards taxation as rebellious, and though some in England felt sympathy with the colonists, forces hostile to them were now in power. The Stamp Act of 1765 met with strenuous opposition from the colonists, who adopted the principle of " no taxation without representation," meaning that they wished to be represented in the British Parliament. Ten years later agitation broke out into open warfare at Lexington, Massachusetts, and on July 4, 1776, the 13 colonies in North America adopted their Declaration of Independence. (*See* American Independence).

By 1778 the war was extended, for France and other countries intervened to wipe off the scores of the Seven Years' War, until Britain found herself pitted against almost the rest of Europe. In America she

THE ENGLISH FLEET RAISES THE SIEGE OF GIBRALTAR

Disastrous to Great Britain was the outcome of the American War of Independence (1776–82) with the North American colonists, yet towards the end of that struggle some memorable victories restored her naval prestige. This quaint illustration, which appeared in the European Magazine in 1782, depicts the relief of Gibraltar by the English fleet under Admiral Darby on April 12, 1781. Stores for the starving garrison were landed under fire.

was defeated when the colonists compelled a British army to surrender at Yorktown, Virginia, in 1781, but against France and Spain she was more successful, thanks to her naval supremacy and the failure of the Spaniards to recover Gibraltar. The loss of the American colonies was a check to the personal power of the King.

William Pitt (*q.v.*) the Younger, second son of the Earl of Chatham, was not yet 25 when he became prime minister in 1784. He began his career as an independent Whig, but the French Revolution, which broke out in 1789, made him a Tory or Conservative. For over four years the revolution was disregarded by Britain, but after the execution of Louis XVI in 1793 she played a leading part in the war with France which lasted until 1815. Britain was compelled, however, to confine her energies to war by sea, for her small and inefficient forces were soon swept out of the Low Countries (Belgium and Holland), and she did not intervene in the Spanish Peninsula until a popular rising had prepared the way.

Her sea-power was her salvation. Admiral Lord Howe (1726–99) destroyed the French Atlantic fleet on June 1, 1794; the Spanish fleet, which the French had compelled to fight with them, was annihilated at Cape St. Vincent in February 1794, and the Dutch off Camperdown, the Netherlands, in October 1797; Nelson sank the French Mediterranean fleet at the battle of the Nile in 1798, and destroyed the Danish navy at Copenhagen in 1801; at Trafalgar in 1805 he disposed of the French and Spanish fleets which Napoleon had re-created, and in 1807 a new Danish fleet was seized at Copenhagen.

Only command of the sea saved Ireland for the British Empire and prevented the French from aiding the Irish rebellion of 1798 in the same way as they had assisted the American insurgents in

1778–81. The victory of America had helped to precipitate Great Britain's tardy recognition of the independence of the Irish Parliament in 1782.

The Irish rebellion which followed 16 years later was the outcome of one of the worst governments in Europe, and Pitt thought that the union of Ireland and Britain, coupled with the granting of the right to vote to the Roman Catholics, would at least be an improvement. George III's religious scruples foiled his hopes of emancipation for the Catholics, and he had to purchase the consent of a corrupt Irish Parliament to the Union of 1800.

Although Pitt entered into alliances with a number of Continental powers to counteract the threat of Napoleonic domination, the Continental allies wearied sooner than the British of a struggle which brought them relatively little advantage political or commercial. Pitt resigned in 1801, and the Peace of Amiens was signed. This proved, however, to be nothing more than a truce, and when in 1803 war broke out again Pitt once more became Prime Minister. His brief term of office was darkened by Napoleon's crowning victory over the Austrians and Russians at Austerlitz in December 1805, was glorified by the British naval victory at Trafalgar in 1805, and ended by his death on January 23, 1806. (*See* Pitt, William).

In 1808 the war took a fresh turn, with the Spanish insurrection against Napoleon and the British expedition to the Peninsula. But progress was slow. Napoleon had little difficulty in crushing Austria in 1809, but in 1811 his relations with the Tsar of Russia, who had been his ally since 1807, grew strained ; and in 1812 the disaster following upon the French invasion of Russia and subsequent retreat from Moscow made Spain a secondary sphere of operations. First Prussia and then Austria threw in their lot with Russia, and at Leipzig, in October 1813, Napoleon's armies in

Germany were annihilated. In March 1814 Napoleon abdicated and was exiled to Elba, an island in the Mediterranean. He returned to France a year later to take advantage of the fact that the Allies had quarrelled amongst themselves, but they hastily settled their differences, and the British, Germans and Dutch, under the Duke of Wellington, defeated Napoleon at the battle of Waterloo, Belgium, on June 18, 1815.

During the reign of George III England began to change from an agricultural to an industrial country, and the period which followed the war was a time of great distress. The poor obtained no part in the profits produced by the Industrial Revolution (q.v.), and high prices were maintained by legislation like the Corn Laws, which, in the landowners' interests, forbade foreign corn to be imported into Great Britain until the home price of wheat had reached 80s. a quarter (640 lb.). In 1819 great riots broke out, and at Manchester the mob was charged by soldiers, and a number of rioters were killed in the event known as the " Peterloo Massacre."

George III died, an imbecile and blind, in 1820. During the reign of George IV government became more tolerant, Acts against Nonconformists were repealed, and Roman Catholics in Britain were given the right to vote. In 1830 George IV died and was succeeded by his brother, William IV. The Reform Bill, which extended the franchise (right to vote) and abolished the " rotten boroughs " (districts which, though the population had decreased to a mere handful, still had the right to be represented in Parliament), was passed in 1832.

The first reformed Parliament, which met in 1833, disappointed expectations. Slavery was, indeed, abolished in British Dominions by an Act and certain minor reforms carried out, but these did not satisfy the Radicals (extreme Liberals) and

in 1838 the Chartist movement (so called from its charter of reforms) was founded. In 1841 Richard Cobden (q.v.) started the Anti-Corn Law agitation, and Free Trade (abolition of the taxation of imports) became the main issue in politics. The Prime Minister, Sir Robert Peel, was reluctantly convinced, partly by famine in Ireland, of the need for repeal of the Corn Laws. which he carried in 1846, thereby breaking up his party and putting an end to his own political career. Lord John Russell became Prime Minister and passed a succession of bills to free imports from duties.

The first half of the 19th century had been a period of Imperial expansion, and the growth of the overseas dominions involved Britain in the obligation of maintaining their communications. Britain's naval supremacy was enough to protect the sea routes, but it could not relieve her of anxiety with regard to the land approaches to India, for here British expansion was matched by a Russian advance across Siberia and in Central Asia.

Britain's fear for the safety of her eastern possessions led to the Crimean War (1854–56), in which she was supported against Russia by France and Turkey. The conduct of the war reflected little credit on the Allies, and peace was made in 1856.

The following year the Indian Mutiny broke out, and after the harrowing sieges of Delhi, Lucknow, and Cawnpore it was suppressed in 1858. It was clear, however, that a change in the government of India was essential. The East India Company, originally a trading concern, had now become the owner of an empire. Pitt's India Bill of 1784 had given the Crown joint control with the Company, and an Act of 1833 had vested the supreme direction of the government in a Governor-General and Council. Now, in 1858, a new India Act transferred all the territories and powers of the East India Company to the Crown.

From 1855 to 1865 Lord Palmerston's keen interest in foreign affairs led to stagnation in domestic politics. After the death of Palmerston in 1865, Lord John Russell resumed the work of reform. Disraeli (q.v.) became Prime Minister in February 1868, but was defeated in the elections of the autumn and W. E. Gladstone (q.v.) formed his first Liberal government Its reforming activity far surpassed that of its predecessors. The Irish Church was disestablished (separated from the State) in 1869 In 1870 the first of the Irish Land Acts, easing the position of the Irish peasants and tenant farmers, was passed and Forster's Ac

PEOPLE AND MILITARY IN BLOODY CONFLICT
On August 16, 1819, a mass meeting took place in St. Peter's Field, Manchester, in favour of parliamentary reform. The magistrates ordered out the military to break up the meeting, and 11 people were killed and many wounded. This incident was known, from the spot where it took place, and in imitation of Waterloo, as the Peterloo Massacre.

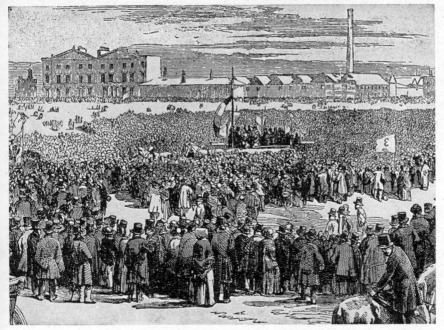

A MASS MEETING OF THE CHARTISTS
In April 1848, Feargus O'Connor, a leader of the Chartists (supporters of a charter for Parliamentary reforms) arranged for a petition to be presented to Parliament by Chartists marching from Kennington Common, south London. Fearing a revolution, the Government posted troops, and the procession was abandoned. The meeting at Kennington is seen in this old engraving.

an even more serious rebellion broke out in the Sudan under a Mahomedan fanatic called the Mahdi. General Gordon, who had gone out there to try to persuade the Mahdi to make peace, was killed at Khartum in January 1885, while an expedition was coming to his relief.

The chief domestic measure of the government was the Franchise and Redistribution Act of 1884–85, which gave the right to vote to some two million agricultural labourers. Town artisans had received it in 1867. In 1885 Gladstone's government was defeated on the Budget, but after a short interim government led by Lord Salisbury Gladstone formed a third ministry in 1886, pledged to some form of Home Rule for Ireland. This led to grave dissensions in his own party; the Home Rule Bill was defeated in July 1886, and Salisbury again came into power. With but a short break, the Conservatives held office until 1906.

Lord Salisbury's six years' administration saw the establishment of free education, and county councils were instituted. In 1890 large parts of Africa were divided between Britain and Germany.

Gladstone returned to office after the elections of 1892, but when his second Home Rule Bill was thrown out by the House of Lords he definitely retired and was succeeded in the premiership by Lord Rosebery. Lord Salisbury resumed office in 1895. In South Africa the Jameson Raid of December 1895 (*see* South Africa) was an ill-advised indication of the government's policy of Imperial expansion; but the reconquest of the Sudan was brilliantly carried out by Kitchener (*q.v.*) in 1896–98.

The disputes with the Boers in the Transvaal arising out of the Jameson Raid were not well handled, and the Boer War broke out in 1899 which lasted three years and ended with the annexation of the Transvaal and Orange River Free State. With the conclusion of peace in 1902 a reaction against the Conservatives set in which was accentuated by Balfour's Education Act (leading to the passive resistance movement of Nonconformists in protest against the obligation to contribute as ratepayers to Church of England schools), and by the introduction of cheap Chinese labour into South Africa.

The general election of January 1906 brought the Liberals into power, under Sir Henry Campbell-Bannerman (1836–1908). The army was reorganized and old age pensions introduced, but repeated attempts to solve the education, Irish,

establishing public compulsory education by means of popularly elected school boards. In 1872 the Ballot Act established secret voting at parliamentary (other than university) elections, and the judicial system was remodelled by the Judicature Act of 1873. And the army was completely reorganized.

In 1874 Disraeli came for the second time into office as Prime Minister, and diverted public attention from domestic problems to foreign and Imperial policy. Disraeli's administration saw the first outburst of modern British imperialism. His initial achievement was the purchase, in November 1875, of shares in the Suez Canal (*q.v.*).

The construction of that waterway in 1869 had profoundly altered the strategic situation of the British Empire by providing a sea route to India very much shorter than round the Cape. The purchase of these shares led to an increasing amount of British intervention in Egypt, until the whole of that country and a good deal more passed under British control. Similarly, attempts to counter the advance of Russia involved the government in Afghan wars, and encouraged a pro-Turkish policy which hampered the liberation of south-eastern Europe from Turkish domination, and brought Britain to the verge of war with Russia in 1877–78.

But Disraeli's indifference to Turkish atrocities estranged a large section of British opinion, and in 1880 the Liberals were returned to power with a large majority. Gladstone's second administration, which lasted for five years, had to deal with the revolt of the Transvaal Boers, who were re-granted their independence after they had defeated the British at the battle of Majuba Hill in 1881.

In Egypt, Britain had to deal with a formidable native revolt in 1882, and when this was crushed and licensing problems failed; and in 1910 the government, to whose leadership H. H. Asquith had succeeded in 1908 on the death of Campbell-Bannerman, made up its mind that no progress could be made until the power of the House of Lords to refuse to pass Bills which had already received the assent of the House of Commons was to some extent curtailed. A beginning was made by means of Lloyd George's land-tax budget of 1909, which the Lords were successfully tempted to reject. The general election in January 1910 gave the government a reduced majority of 118.

The budget was then passed, and the government took up the question of the Lords' powers. A conference between the two parties having failed to reach an agreement, a second general election in December 1910, slightly increased the government's majority, and King George V, who had succeeded his father King Edward VII in 1910, agreed to create enough peers to secure the passing of the Parliament Act of 1911. The threat was sufficient, and the Lords lost the power of rejecting a measure which had been thrice passed in successive sessions by the House of Commons. The first use to be made of the Parliament Act was to pass Home Rule and Welsh Church Disestablishment; but the passage of the Home Rule Bill was marked by increasing trouble with Ulster (today part of "Northern Ireland"), which threatened armed resistance if Irish Home Rule was introduced. Much political excitement was caused by the National Insurance Act of 1912, which made insurance against ill-health and unemployment compulsory

for certain classes of workers; and by the "Votes for Women" campaign (women over 30 gained the right to vote in 1918). However, in 1914, these domestic broils were lost sight of in the greater crisis of the First World War. (See World Wars).

Great Britain's entry into the war called a temporary truce to party political differences. In 1915 a Coalition government was formed under Asquith to enable the war to be prosecuted with the utmost efficiency, and in 1916 the Conscription Bill was passed. But winter brought a feeling of discontent, and in December Lloyd George (q.v.) succeeded Asquith as premier.

The change of government was ushered in with a feeling of optimism as ill-balanced as the preceding depression. The Germans' defence in the West held fast, while their submarine offensive came perilously near success. When at last the war was ended by the Armistice of November 11, 1918, in England, alone of the Allies, the moment was seized for a general election; and Lloyd George was returned to power. Irish affairs now came to the fore once again. The 73 Sinn Feiners (Irish Nationalists) returned to the British Parliament refused to take their seats, and formed a Dáil Eireann, or assembly of Ireland. Bloodshed in Ireland was rife; there was, in effect, a guerrilla civil war raging until the treaty with Britain of 1922 established the Irish Free State. Thenceforward the "United Kingdom" was no longer the United Kingdom of Great Britain and Ireland, but only of Great Britain and Northern Ireland; and Northern Ireland had her own Parliament, at Belfast.

Topical

'VOTES FOR WOMEN' DEMONSTRATION BY SUFFRAGETTES IN LONDON

At the beginning of the 20th century an active movement was started to compel the Government to grant women the right to vote at Parliamentary elections. Supporters of the campaign to obtain the suffrage (right to vote) for women were known as suffragettes, and they endeavoured to draw attention to their demands by various means, such as staging demonstrations (above). The vote was accorded to women over 30 in 1918, and in 1928 on the same terms as to men.

DÁIL EIREANN, THE PARLIAMENT OF SOUTHERN IRELAND, IN SESSION

Though it was not recognized by the British Government, the Dáil Eireann was formed in January 1919. At a session held in the Mansion House at Dublin (above) on August 23, 1921, the members rejected the offer of the British Government to set up two Parliaments—one for Southern and one for Northern Ireland—and demanded one Parliament for the whole country. Seated in the high-backed chair behind the table (left) is Eamon de Valera.

After the First World War there was a brief period of prosperity; but a general trade depression then set in, accompanied by a steady increase in unemployment. To encourage trade and commerce successive Governments eased taxation. Income tax was reduced from six shillings in the pound to five shillings in 1922, to four and sixpence in 1923 and to four shillings in 1925. Other measures introduced had little effect upon the general depression, which aroused deep dissatisfaction. This feeling found expression in increasing support for the Labour movement. The Coalition government of 1918 had been succeeded in 1922 by a Conservative government, headed first by Bonar Law and, after his death, by Stanley Baldwin.

In 1923 the Labour Party was returned to Parliament as the largest single party and assumed office for the first time, under the leadership of J. Ramsay MacDonald (q.v.). They found themselves unable to cope with the gigantic unemployment problem; and the publication in the London press of what was known as the Zinoviev Letter, purporting to come from Russian Communists and inciting British Communists to rebellion, helped to defeat Labour at the general election of 1924, when the Conservatives, under Stanley Baldwin, were once more returned to Parliament with a majority.

Baldwin's second ministry was marked by the granting of the franchise to women on the same terms as men, and by the general strike of May 4–12,

1926. The strike had a disastrous effect on trade and industry, but things seemed to be once more on the up-grade until, in 1929, a world-wide trade depression raised unemployment to alarming heights.

By 1931 the economic situation of the country had become desperate. The budget was unbalanced and the pound sterling dropped steadily in purchasing power both at home and abroad. On August 23 the Labour Government, which had been in power since 1929, came to an end owing to a majority of the Cabinet refusing to agree to drastic economies that were advocated by the Prime Minister Ramsay MacDonald.

The next day MacDonald, at the invitation of King George V, formed a National Government, composed of some of his Labour supporters, Conservatives, and Liberals. The new Government immediately proceeded to enforce the economy measures and to increase taxation. In October Parliament was dissolved and MacDonald asked the electors to give him a free hand in implementing measures to restore national prosperity.

Ramsay MacDonald was returned to power, and the Government proceeded to deal with the position arising out of Britain buying more from abroad than she was selling. As a result of various enactments, Britain's traditional policy of Free Trade was abandoned, and duties were imposed on imports.

One highly important event in Imperial affairs was the passing in 1931 of the Statute of Westminster, which confirmed the practically independent status of the Dominions (Australia, Canada, New Zealand, South Africa, Irish Free State, and Newfoundland) which had been agreed upon at the Imperial Conference of 1926.

In the years that followed, Great Britain's domestic policy was overshadowed by the predominance of foreign affairs due to momentous political events abroad. Of these the most notable were the Japanese invasion of Manchuria in 1931, and the Italian annexation of Abyssinia in 1936, both of which the League of Nations proved powerless to stop. Then came Italian, German and Russian intervention in the Spanish Civil War which broke out in 1936 and lasted for nearly three years; Japan's undeclared war on China, which started in July 1937; Germany's series of invasions of the neutralised Rhine, of Austria, the Sudetenlands, Czechoslovakia itself, and Memel; and Italy's conquest of Albania. In face of this continued expansionist policy, Great Britain was compelled to increase her armed forces. In the decade 1929–38 the British national expenditure devoted to defence and armaments was estimated at 14 per cent of the national income; in 1939 it rose to some 47 per cent.

Meanwhile King George V had died on January 20, 1936, and had been succeeded by his eldest son, the Prince of Wales, as Edward VIII. The new sovereign was immensely popular, but towards the end of the year his resolve to marry a divorced American lady brought about a crisis. The King abdicated on December 11, 1936, and his brother, the Duke of York, was proclaimed King as George VI. The new King and his consort, Queen Elizabeth, were crowned in Westminster Abbey, London, on May 12, 1937.

Outbreak of the Second World War

On September 3, 1939, despite efforts at appeasement, Great Britain was again at war with Germany. After the overrunning of Poland by Germany in September 1939 the first few months of the Second World War were quiet ; but the apparent inactivity of the Government and the shock of the Allied defeat in the Norwegian campaign of April-May 1940 roused the entire nation to angry resentment. In May 1940, as a result, the Prime Minister Mr. Neville Chamberlain resigned and was succeeded in that office by Mr. Winston Churchill.

In May and June 1940 the Germans conquered the Netherlands, Belgium and France. On June 11, 1940, Italy declared war on Great Britain, and on June 22 France signed an armistice with Germany. Under the inspiring leadership of Mr. Winston Churchill the United Kingdom set herself determinedly to wage the war, with the full support of the members of the British Commonwealth. In August and September 1940 the German Air Force was defeated in the Battle of Britain (q.v.) by the Royal Air Force, and the German plan for the invasion of Britain was frustrated.

Meanwhile, the United Kingdom acquired a new importance as the rallying ground for the fighting forces and Governments in exile of those countries which had been overrun by the Germans. After December 1941, when Japan entered the war on the side of Germany and Italy, and the United States allied herself with Britain, the Czechs, Poles, Norwegians, Dutch, Belgian, Free French and British Dominion and Colonial forces in Britain were joined by United States contingents. An air bombardment of German industry and communications, growing ever more intense, was carried out from various bases in the United Kingdom.

The German submarine menace was overcome by the Allied air forces and navies in the Battle of the Atlantic (q.v.) In the United Kingdom was assembled that vast army of liberation which set forth from its shores in June 1944 to free north-west Europe from the Germans and to achieve complete victory by May 1945.

At the General Election of July 1945 Mr. Winston Churchill's Government was defeated and a Labour administration under Mr. Clement Attlee was returned to power. The Labour Government embarked upon a programme for the nationalisation of the United Kingdom's chief assets and industries. The Bank of England, the coal industry, the supply of electricity and gas, and the railways were all nationalised within the next three years, and in 1948 a Bill was introduced into Parliament for similar treatment of the iron and steel industry. The power of the House of Lords was curtailed by a new Parliament Act, which reduced the period for which the House of Lords could delay the passing of any bill. In addition a comprehensive scheme of

L.N.A.

SILVER JUBILEE OF KING GEORGE V

In May 1935 was celebrated the 25th anniversary of King George V's accession, marked by a Thanksgiving Service in St. Paul's Cathedral. Above, King George and Queen Mary are seen at Temple Bar; the King is touching the City Sword which he has been offered by the Lord Mayor of London as a symbol of the City's submission to the Crown.

Photographic News Agency

BRITAIN'S ROYAL FAMILY AND PRIME MINISTER ON VICTORY-IN-EUROPE DAY
In the Second World War (1939–45) victory in Europe was achieved on May 8, 1945, when the unconditional surrender of Germany was announced, and in the early afternoon huge crowds gathered outside Buckingham Palace. Their Majesties King George VI and Queen Elizabeth appeared on the balcony, accompanied by Princess Elizabeth (left), Princess Margaret (right), and Mr. Winston Churchill (centre), who had been British Prime Minister since May 1940.

social insurance was put into operation, including a national health service for all. At the General Election of March 1950 the Labour Party was returned with just a sufficient majority over the other parties to enable them to form a new Government.

The Second World War left the United Kingdom nearly bankrupt, and to enable the country to pay for imports and raw materials necessary for the revival of her export trade and industry a huge loan was granted by the United States. This loan was calculated to last till 1951, but it was almost spent by mid-1947, and the United Kingdom was saved from financial disaster by the granting of further sums by the United States under the European Recovery Programme, designed to assist in the industrial revival of most of the States of Western Europe.

By the end of 1950 the economic balance was thought to be sufficiently restored to allow such help to the United Kingdom to be suspended. Meanwhile the attitude of the Soviet Union to the European Recovery Programme and other measures had been hostile. Most of eastern Europe had fallen under Russian influence since the end of the war, and the menace of Communism to western Europe led to the signing of the Atlantic Treaty in March 1949. The original signatories were the United States, United Kingdom, Canada, Luxembourg, France, the Netherlands, Belgium and Norway, who were pledged to assist one another against any aggressor nation.

In 1947 the Indian Empire was divided into the Dominions of India and Pakistan, India becoming a republic in 1950. In 1948 Ceylon became a Dominion and Burma left the Commonwealth as an independent republic. In April 1949 Eire severed her last link with the United Kingdom and the Crown, when the Republic of Ireland Act came into force.

United Nations. Created in April 1945, the United Nations (U.N. for short) is the organization of States which replaced the League of Nations (*q.v.*). The first step towards its formation was taken on August 14, 1941, when President Roosevelt of the United States and Mr. Winston

Churchill, Prime Minister of Great Britain, after a conference aboard a British warship in mid-Atlantic issued a joint statement of principles and policies which came to be known as the Atlantic Charter. It outlined a scheme affording all nations a guarantee against aggression and for the establishment of a permanent system of general security. Four nations —China, the United Kingdom, the United States, and the Soviet Union—assumed responsibility for the planning of this new international authority.

Representatives of the four powers conferred at Dumbarton Oaks in the United States during August and September 1944 to work out detailed plans, and in due course invitations were sent out to attend a conference on the international organization held at San Francisco, United States, in April-June 1945. At this meeting the charter of the United Nations was drawn up and signed by the delegates of the 50 nations taking part. Later admissions to the organization, during 1946–50, raised the membership to 60 nations.

The charter, the obligations of which are accepted by all members of the United Nations, consists of an introduction and 111 articles relating to the aims and sections of the organization. The six main bodies established under the charter are: The General Assembly, the Security Council, the Economic and Social Council, the Trusteeship Council, the International Court of Justice, and the Secretariat. The General Assembly is a body in which all the members, big and small, meet on equal terms. A regular session is held each year, but special ones may be convened. It may discuss, and make recommendations on, any international question, unless it is already being dealt with by the Security Council.

The Security Council is responsible for maintaining peace and security and consists of 11 members, of which China, France, Russia, the United Kingdom and the United States are permanent. The remaining six are elected by the General Assembly and sit for two years. It is hampered in the carrying out of its duties by the fact that decisions requiring action must be approved by all five permanent members. This means that any one Great Power can exercise a veto on action and so prevent the Council from exercising its proper functions.

The Economic and Social Council carries out the directions of the United Nations with regard to international economic, social, cultural, educational, health and related matters. The Trusteeship Council considers reports from the controlling authorities of territories placed under the supervision of the United Nations, and members of the Council make periodic inspections, checking social, economic and educational conditions.

The International Court of Justice is the principal judicial body of the United Nations, and it delivers judgements on matters of international law submitted to it by members or departments of the United Nations. The Secretariat is composed of the Secretary-General, who is the principal administrative officer of the organization, and an international staff appointed by him under regulations established by the General Assembly.

The headquarters of the United Nations are at New York. But much of the work is decentralised, and the buildings at Geneva, Switzerland, taken over from the League of Nations are used as a European centre. *See* Korea.

United Provinces. In the northwest of the republic of India, this State (in 1950 renamed Uttar Pradesh) is composed of the former divisions of Agra and Oudh. Surrounding Indian States are Nepal, Bihar, Orissa, Vindhya Pradesh, Rajasthan, and Punjab (Eastern). Tibet lies on the northern frontier. With an area of 106,247 square miles, it contains the plains of the upper Ganges and the Jumna rivers and their tributaries. In the northern mountainous region are the Siwalik Hills and the Garhwal section of the Himalayas, where are Nanda Devi, Kamet and Badrinath, all over 25,000 feet.

The Great Doab, a well-irrigated and fertile plain between the Ganges and the Jumna, is intensively cultivated and produces wheat, barley, sugar-cane, cotton, millet, indigo and opium. There are several important cities in the United Provinces, the largest being Lucknow (*q.v.*), capital of Oudh ; Cawnpore (population 487,300), a manufacturing centre ; Agra (*q.v.*) ; the Hindus' holy city of Benares (*q.v.*) ; Allahabad (population 284,000), which is situated at the junction of the Ganges and the Jumna ; and Bareilly (population 193,000). In this densely populated province five-sixths of the inhabitants are Hindus ; most of them speak Hindi, which in 1947 replaced English as the official language.

In 1833 part of the Presidency of Bengal became the Presidency of Agra, but two years later the name was changed to North-Western Provinces. In 1856 Oudh was added, and the title of the combined territory was altered in 1901 to the United Provinces. When the British left India in 1947 the United Provinces became part of the newly-established Dominion of India and were placed under the Governorship of Mrs. Sarojini Naidu, who was the first woman to hold such a post. The population is 55 million.

Topical

UNITED NATIONS : FIRST SESSION OF THE GENERAL ASSEMBLY

Delegates to the first meeting of the General Assembly of the United Nations in the Central Hall at Westminster, London, on January 10, 1946, were welcomed by Mr. Clement Attlee, the British Prime Minister, who is here seen addressing the members from the speakers' rostrum. The central figure seated on the platform is Dr. Eduardo Zuleta Angel (Colombia), acting chairman of the Assembly. In Arab dress in the front row are delegates of Saudi Arabia.

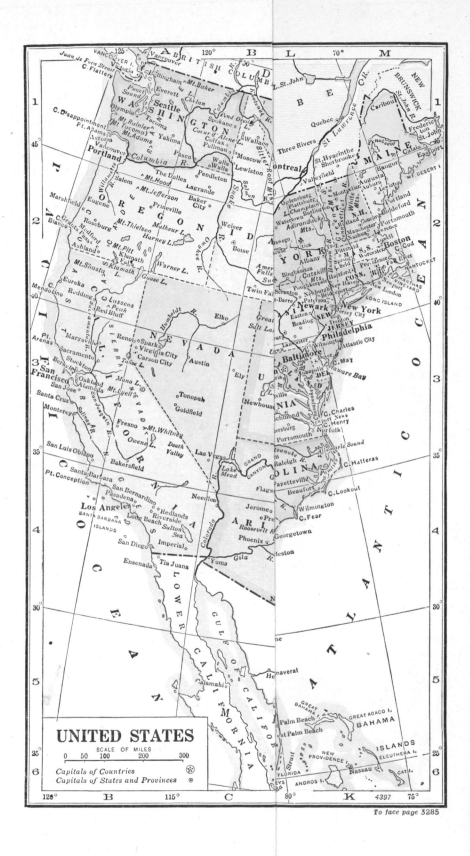

UNITED STATES

SCALE OF MILES

0   50   100   200   300

Capitals of Countries
Capitals of States and Provinces

MIGHTY WONDERLAND of the WEST

In population the United States ranks fourth among the nations, but it is the richest and most highly industrialised country of all. Here is a glimpse of its geography, its amazing diversity of peoples and their occupations.

United States of America.

The population of the United States is made up of nearly every race under the sun. The sprinkling of Red Indians has long been almost lost to sight under the flood of immigrants from other lands. Puritans from England, driven out by religious persecution, landed on Plymouth Rock; the Dutch, seeking trade, came to New York; Swedes and English settled in New Jersey; Quakers and German religious refugees founded Pennsylvania; proud English Cavaliers settled in Virginia; Spaniards seeking gold, established themselves in Florida, Texas, and California; and Germans, Austrians, Poles, and Irish, for economic or political reasons, made their homes chiefly in the Mississippi valley.

On the Pacific slope and in the islands beyond is a medley of races—Malays, Japanese and Chinese from the Orient; Spaniards, recalling the days of the old Spanish empire; a sprinkling of descendants of Russians in Alaska; and Italians, Jews, Slavs, Armenians and Syrians are found in every considerable city. No other land shows such a diversity of races and peoples. The population of the country (1940 census) is nearly 132 million.

Possessing the most favoured regions of the New World, the continental United States lies wholly within the temperate latitudes. Its vast area—about equal to that of Europe—the fertility of its soil and its well-nigh inexhaustible mineral wealth have made it into one of the foremost Powers of the world. It is the world's largest producer of both food and raw materials for manufactures.

From West Quoddy Head in Maine (the easternmost point), due west to the Pacific Ocean, the distance is 2,807 miles; and from the southernmost point of Texas, due north to the Canadian border (the 49th parallel), it is 1,598 miles. The total coastline is nearly 12,000 miles long—5,560 miles on the Atlantic, 2,730 miles on the Pacific, and 3,640 miles on the Gulf of Mexico.

The chief mountains consist of two ridges running north and south, one near the Atlantic, the other close to the Pacific. The eastern ranges make up the Appalachian system, and the western the Cordilleran. Each system is broken up into parallel ridges and cut across by lower levels called "passes" and "gaps," through which rivers flow. The rugged Cordilleran system abounds in scenes of marvellous beauty and grandeur. Notable among these natural beauties are the Grand Canyon of the Colorado, the valley and falls of the Yosemite, the snow-clad peaks and rivers of ice in Glacier National Park, and the geysers of Yellowstone Park. The principal ranges in the west, the Rocky Mountains (6,000–14,000 feet), extend mainly through northern Idaho, western Montana and Wyoming, and central Colorado. Also, there are the Coast Ranges (3,000–5,000 feet) extending along the Pacific coast.

The Rocky Mountains are separated from the Cascade Range (6,000–14,000 feet) of east central Washington and Oregon by the Columbia Plateau, from the Sierra Nevada (10,000–14,000 feet) of west and central California by the Great Basin, and from the Western Sierra Madre (5,000–8,000 feet) by the Colorado Plateau in central Arizona.

The high ranges between the Pacific coast and the plateaux hold back most of the moisture-laden atmosphere blowing in from the Pacific, and so these plateaux were miscalled by the earliest explorers the "Great American Desert." These upland valleys and table-lands can produce abundant crops when irrigated.

The Columbia Plateau, covering most of south-east Washington, eastern Oregon, and southern Idaho, forms a large part of the Columbia river drainage basin, and represents mainly an ancient and enormous lava field. The Colorado Plateau of south-west Colorado, north-west New Mexico, south-east Utah, and northern Arizona is noted chiefly for the Grand Canyon (q.v.). In the Great Basin, which covers most of Nevada, the western part of Utah, and south-eastern California, the small rivers either disappear underground or unite to empty into some interior salt sea or lake, such as the Great Salt Lake in the state of Utah.

Between the heights of the Cordilleran and Appalachian systems lies an area of plains and plateaux 1,000 miles wide. From the foothills of the Rockies the Great Plains slope gently to the Mississippi valley, being continued eastward to the

---

Extent.—North to south 1,598 miles; east to west 2,807 miles. Area 3,022,387 square miles (with U.S. Great Lakes area, 3,082,809 square miles). Population (1940 census) 131,669,275; with territories and possessions (except Philippines) 134,265,231.

Physical Features.—Atlantic Coastal Plain rising to Appalachians; Central Plains with Great Lakes Basin to the north and Gulf Coastal Plain to the south; Great Plains; Cordilleran system of mountain ranges running north and south (highest point, Mt. Whitney, 14,495 feet) and dropping abruptly to the Pacific. Rivers and lakes: Hudson, Delaware, Susquehanna, James, and Great Lakes-St. Lawrence system flowing into Atlantic; Ohio-Mississippi-Missouri and Rio Grande, into the Gulf of Mexico; Colorado, into Gulf of California; San Joaquin-Sacramento and Columbia, into Pacific.

Products.—Maize, wheat, oats, cotton, hay and forage, fruits and vegetables; cattle and dairy products, pigs, sheep and wool, horses; coal, petroleum, natural gas, clay products, cement, iron, copper, lead, zinc, gold, silver, - aluminium; timber; fish products; meat packing, textiles, steam and electric rolling stock, iron and steel products (including machinery, foundry and machine-shop products), aircraft, motor vehicles, clothing, flour and meal, petroleum products, boats and ships, bread and bakery goods, shoes, leather and rubber goods, electrical machinery, chemicals.

Chief Cities (1940 census).—New York (7,454,995), Chicago (3,396,808), Philadelphia (1,931,000); Detroit, Los Angeles (over 1,500,000); Cleveland, Baltimore St. Louis (over 800,000); Boston, Pittsburgh, San Francisco (over 600,000); Washington (capital, 663,091)

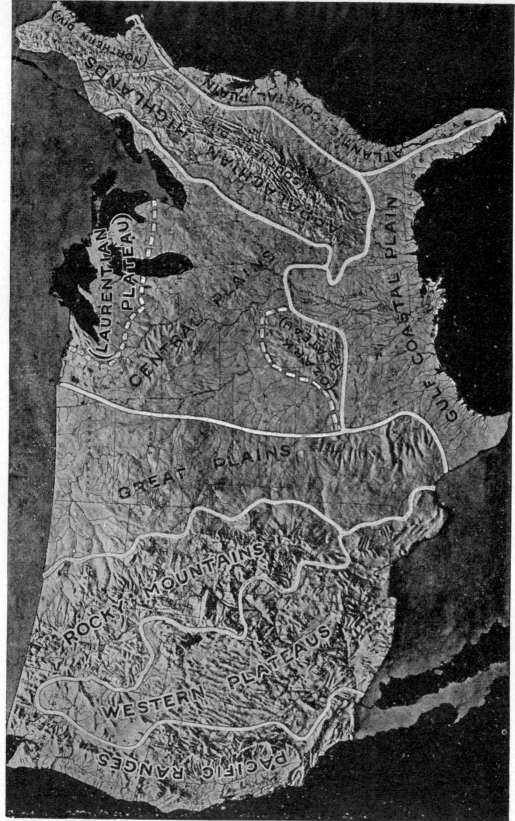

THE GREAT NATURAL REGIONS OF THE UNITED STATES OF AMERICA

Here we see the eight great natural regions of the United States, with three sub-divisions. Mastery of this regional grouping is important to the student of geography, because not only does it determine physical features such as the flow of rivers, but to a great extent indicates the activities pursued by the people within the regions. As we might expect, agriculture rules the plains regions. The Gulf Plain raises products suited to a warm climate. The Central Plains produce crops typical of a temperate climate, and the Atlantic Plain shades from one to the other. The Great Plains are more suited to cattle-raising owing to their comparative lack of water—the mountains farther west blocking the rains from the Pacific. In similar ways, the physiography of other regions exercises a profound influence upon the lives of their people.

3286

Appalachian Plateau by the Central Plains, mostly prairie. In the south these divisions merge into the Gulf Coastal Plain, which comprises most of the area of the States bordering on the Gulf of Mexico.

The mountains were an important factor in keeping the early pioneers in close communities. In the New England States they crowded the settlers into the narrow Coastal Plain, in an area only 70 to 100 miles wide. In the South Atlantic States the mountains recede 250 miles from the sea, and so the settlers here spread out from towns into big tobacco and cotton plantations along the river banks. This is one reason why in the early days there were fewer cities in the South than in the North.

But if the mountains confined the first settlers to the Atlantic seaboard, the rivers that broke through the mountain passes guided the pioneers of later generations through the gaps and across the plains from the Atlantic to the Pacific. As for the Great Lakes, the early pioneers could hardly believe that they were not a sea. Lake Superior is almost 400 miles long. From the head of Lake Michigan to the foot of Lake Erie is a distance of 1,000 miles, while from the Mississippi east and west run rivers for 14,000 miles, with arable parklike lands covering 1,240,000 square miles.

The Mississippi (*q.v.*) and Missouri (*q.v.*) together rank with the longest rivers in the world. From source to the Head of Passes in the delta the combined lengths of the two rivers is 3,988 miles; the so-called

A SNOW-CAPPED PEAK OF THE CASCADE RANGE
In the far north-west of the United States, near the Canadian border, is some of the finest scenery in North America. The Rocky Mountains, there known as the Cascade Range, include several mighty peaks, of which Mount Rainier (above), with a height of 14,363 feet, is the third highest in the country if the Alaskan mountains are excluded.

"passes," which empty into the Gulf of Mexico, and old meanders, now cut off, made the length about 4,200 miles. The Rio Grande, rising in the mountains of Utah and Colorado and flowing into the Gulf of Mexico, and the Yukon, threading the whole length of Alaska and part of Canada, are both some 2,000 miles long, as are the Colorado, Green and Columbia rivers, which empty into the Pacific. Although the Hudson and Potomac are only a little over 300 and 280 miles long respectively, they were of importance to the early settlers, because they led inland from the Atlantic seaboard. The fur in greatest demand in Europe at the time of the early explorations and settlements was the beaver, then used for hats. And so it came about that the beaver first led the settlers across the continent from Atlantic to Pacific. When they reached the Mississippi Basin, they learned from the Indians the uses of tobacco and Indian corn or maize. The Mississippi valley would grow not only these, but also cotton, grains and vegetables. And the grasses that grow so abundantly on these plains would sustain cattle by the million. So the frontiersmen stayed on the plains and became settlers. Only the more venturesome pushed on across the Rockies, or ventured on to trade with the Spaniards of New Mexico.

The settlers found coal in plenty in Pennsylvania, West Virginia, Alabama, Indiana, Illinois and Ohio; iron at the head of the Great Lakes, and copper in the Upper Michigan peninsula; and gold, silver and copper in the Rockies. Thereafter the hitherto slow movement of the population westwards became a mad stampede for rich metal deposits. After the discovery of gold in California in 1848 settlement went forward faster west of the Mississippi in 50 years than it had gone east of the Mississippi in 250 years.

When the settlers entered the forests of the Alleghenies, the Adirondacks and the Cumberlands and even Wisconsin and Michigan, they found them an obstruction to settlement because the forests hid their Red Indian foes, hindered the planting of crops and fostered a damp atmosphere. But when they poured into the Great Basin of the Mississippi they found no forests except in park-like clumps on the uplands or round the lakes. Whole forests in other parts were burned to clear the land for cultivation during the 19th century, and by the beginning of the 20th century timber had become scarce. With increasing need for timber the forests of the Rocky Mountains and the Pacific slope became tremendously valuable.

For some time cotton had been grown in the southern States and had proved so profitable that the settlers carried it with them across the Mississippi to Texas and Arizona. In the second half of the 18th century the invention in England of cotton-spinning and weaving machinery had created a wide demand in Europe for raw cotton. As the cities of Massachusetts grew, the people began to see that it would pay them to manufacture the cotton on their side of the ocean and ship it in the form of cloth; and the same with leather, timber, and iron and steel. The result was that numbers of textile and other factories sprang up.

At first wooden water-wheels were used to drive machinery, then steam was employed in bigger factories with heavier machines. Soon came another change—electricity. Later it was discovered that waterfalls could be used to generate electricity, and so where there were waterfalls or at places where they could be created by damming rivers, still larger factories were built.

Then oil was discovered; "gushers" were found in Pennsylvania, West Virginia, Kansas, Oklahoma, Texas, Louisiana, and southern California, that spouted from 25,000 to 100,000 barrels a day.

Today almost every known industry is practised somewhere in the United States. In Massachusetts the workers make shoes and woollen and cotton goods. In New York and New Jersey they manufacture clothing, shoes, leather, silks, sugar and chemicals, and build ships. From Delaware, Rhode Island and Pennsylvania come leather, woollen and cotton goods, steel, machinery and chemicals. In the southern States the industries include production of cotton cloth, tobacco, sugar, cotton-seed oil, cattle food, fertilizers and steel.

In the Middle West are tanneries and factories making farm implements; pork and beef are canned, flour is ground and petroleum refined. On the Pacific coast the leading occupations are lumbering, preserving fruit and fish, and building ships. The most valuable industries are those producing food and clothes, and these are followed by those engaged in manufacturing railway rolling stock, motor vehicles and aircraft, machinery, metals and various chemicals.

The well-watered central plains and those along the Atlantic seaboard and the warm coast of the Gulf of Mexico are the chief centres of the agricultural industry. Maize (known as corn in the United States) is the main crop in the central plains. Other crops include wheat, oats and hay, and dairy farming is engaged in on an enormous scale. Cotton is the most important crop of the Black Belt (so called from the colour of the soil), which extends from southeastern Virginia through North and South Carolina, Tennessee, Louisiana, Texas, Oklahoma and south-east Missouri. Other products of this region, which has plenty of rain and a moderately warm climate, are rice, sugar, maize, tobacco and cattle.

CENTRE OF THE U.S. MOTOR INDUSTRY
This aerial view shows the General Motors Building at Detroit, an enormous building containing 700 separate offices, an exhibition hall, an auditorium, and numerous showrooms. The maximum of light is provided by 5,000 large windows. The manufactures of Detroit are to a very large extent connected with transport—motor vehicles, aeroplanes, and ships being constructed on a large scale.

VEHICULAR AND RAILWAY BRIDGES SPANNING NEW YORK'S EAST RIVER

To provide adequate means of communication between Manhattan and the suburbs of New York on the opposite sides of the East river and the Hudson river has been a constant problem to the civic authorities. Completed in 1936, the Triborough Bridge (left), which accommodates vehicles only, rises from the Astoria section of the borough of Queens and curves to the right over Randalls Island, in the middle of the East river. Near the farther bank the bridge forks, one portion leading to the Bronx suburb, the other turning left and crossing the narrow Harlem river to the crowded island of Manhattan. Railway traffic crosses by the bridge and viaduct on the right.

On the Great Plains, between the Mississippi valley and the Rocky Mountains, wheat is the premier crop. Throughout the mountainous western States, with the exception of the Pacific coast, livestock—mostly cattle and sheep—are bred. Much land, however, on which formerly cattle grazed has been turned into farms and orchards by irrigation. On the Pacific coast fruit is grown, chiefly apples, oranges, lemons and grapes. Other fruit-producing areas are Florida, western Michigan, the south shore of Lake Erie, New England (Maine, New Hampshire, Vermont, Massachusetts, Rhode Island and Connecticut) and parts of Arkansas.

The forests of the United States occupy more than 600 million acres. The chief supply of timber comes from the southern States, where enormous quantities of yellow pine are cut each year. Next comes the north-west, with its forests of Douglas firs. Other important woods, which yield timber mainly for building purposes, are white pine and hemlock. Most of the valuable hardwoods have become scarce, and to protect the remaining timber a number of huge national forest reserves have been established.

In mineral resources the United States is extremely rich. Coal is mined in 30 States. The principal coal fields are in Pennsylvania, the Southern Appalachian Highlands, the central plains, the Rockies, and in eastern Montana and western North Dakota. Next to coal in importance is oil. The country produces about three-fifths of the world's output. There are numerous rich deposits of iron ore; the best is that around Lake Superior in northern Michigan and Minnesota. A number of the iron ore mines are close to important coal fields. Three States—Arizona, Mon-

tana and Utah—yield about a quarter of the world's supply of copper; gold and silver are also extensively mined. The Ozark Mountains of Arkansas and Missouri are rich in lead. Oklahoma, New Jersey and Kansas are the main sources of zinc. Clay for bricks and pottery is found in every State. Limestone and granite come chiefly from the Appalachian Mountains, slate from Pennsylvania and New York; and marble from Vermont.

The fisheries are very valuable. The chief fishing grounds are north of the Carolinas in the Atlantic (haddock, cod, mackerel and herring), north of San Francisco in the Pacific (salmon and halibut), and in the Great Lakes (lake herring and lake trout). Oysters, the most valuable fisheries product after salmon, come chiefly from the Chesapeake and Delaware bays and Long Island Sound. The best lobster fisheries are off the coast of the State of Maine.

Hand in hand with the industrial expansion of the nation has gone the development of its railways and waterways. In railway mileage (240,000 miles) the United States leads the world, and it has 30,000 miles of navigable waterways. There are over 5,000 airports in use.

Much of the foreign trade is with Canada, Mexico, the West Indies, as well as Central and South America. Nickel, printing paper, wood pulp and pulp wood, and wheat are imported from Canada; bananas and copper from Mexico; sugar and molasses from Cuba; tropical fruits, coffee, and cocoa from Central America; coffee and crude rubber from Brazil; wool and hides from the Argentine; and copper from Peru and Chile. From the Orient are imported silks, rice, tea, tin, gums, fibres and vegetable oils; the European countries send chiefly manufactured articles.

In return for these the United States exports a wide variety of products—cotton, meat and dairy products, iron and iron goods, petroleum, timber and wood products, copper, tobacco, motor vehicles and leather.

In population the United States ranks fourth among the nations. Only China, the Soviet Union and the Dominion of India have larger populations. Of the urban population about half are grouped in a comparatively few enormous metropolitan areas. First of all comes the New York City district, composed of New York City proper, with three other New York State cities, three in Connecticut and 25 in New Jersey. It has nearly 12 million inhabitants, making practically a single economic unit (*see* New York). Chicago and her neighbours, with nearly 4,500,000 people, ranks next to New York. At the head of Delaware Bay is the Philadelphia urban district of over 2,000,000 persons.

The Constitution of the United States, which was first put on paper in 1787, provides for three departments of government: a Congress to make laws, a President to enforce them, and a Judiciary (Supreme Court) to interpret them. In theory the three branches are co-ordinate; but each one has powers which neither of the others can take away, and each acts independently of the others, subject to certain limitations.

Congress consists of two chambers, the Senate and the House of Representatives. The House of Representatives represents the people, and is therefore composed of members chosen by the people of each State, the number of representatives depending on the population. Members serve for two years. The Senate represents the 48 States which form the United States and is composed of two members from each. A Senator serves for six years and is elected by the governing body of his own State.

Congress can pass laws only in connexion with certain matters which are enumerated in the Constitution, such as levying taxes and customs dues, coining and borrowing money, regulating foreign and interstate commerce, and so forth. Congress also governs the possessions of the United States and admits new States into the Union. Its powers have been increased by amendments and broad interpretations of the terms of the Constitution.

The duties of the President are in general to execute and administer the laws made by Congress. In addition, the President makes treaties with foreign powers, appoints ambassadors and justices of the Supreme Court, and other officers of the United States whose appointment is not otherwise provided for in the Constitution. Treaties and appointments thus made must be approved by the Senate, and this approval is rarely withheld.

The Constitution provides for a Federal judiciary, the chief duty of which is to try " all cases in law or equity arising under the Constitution, the laws of the United States, and treaties made . . . under their authority."

Amendments to the written Constitution may be proposed by a two-thirds vote of both the Senate and House of Representatives, or by a constitutional convention when requested by two-thirds of the State governments. In either case such proposed amendments become parts of the Constitution when ratified by the legislatures or by conventions in three-fourths of the States. There are 21 amendments to the Constitution at present.

The two main political parties in the United States are the Democrats and the Republicans. The former, whose traditional stronghold is the Southern States, stand in the main for State and individual rights as opposed to the preference of the Republicans (descendants of the " Yankees " of the North) for a strong central government. In detail, there is very little difference between the two parties. There are also a weak Socialist Party and a strong Trade Union movement.

The GROWTH of the AMERICAN NATION

A British colony which became the world's greatest republic : such is a swift summing-up of the United States. The chronicle of its astonishing development in global influence is crowded with events of far-reaching importance.

United States of America:
HISTORY. The story of the U.S.A. falls naturally into four parts: the colonial period (to 1783), the formation and growth of the Union (1783–1829), the division of the North and South over slavery and the ultimate reunion (1829–77), and the era of industrial expansion and increasing world influence (1877 onwards).

One by one, over a period of more than a century, the 13 original colonies which formed the nucleus of the United States were settled. After several unsuccessful attempts directed by Gilbert and Raleigh (*see* Raleigh, Sir Walter) the English in 1607 founded their first permanent settlement at Jamestown, Virginia. In 1732 the last English colony, Georgia, was settled by James Oglethorpe, largely as a refuge for prisoners for debt. The others of the 13 colonies arose as follows : Massachusetts (1620), Maryland (1634), Connecticut

(1635), Rhode Island (1636), North and South Carolina (1663), New York and New Jersey (1664), Delaware (1666), New Hampshire (1680), and Pennsylvania (1682).

Though the colonies were separated by wide stretches of wilderness, and though they differed somewhat in government, in institutions, and in manner of life, movements towards union were made even before the date when the last colony was settled.

First, the colonies of New England formed a confederation (1643) for defence against the Indians, French and Dutch, and this lasted until 1684. After France had been defeated by Great Britain in 1763, the colonists began to combine against the Mother Country. In 1765 representatives of the colonies met to protest against British methods of taxation. A similar meeting of protest was the First Continental Congress in 1774; but it was the Second Continental Congress in Philadelphia which began to direct the united revolt of the colonies in 1775.

The Declaration of Independence in 1776 marked the beginning of a separate existence for the colonies, but it was two years before the United States was recognized—by France—as an independent country. After several years of fighting Britain in 1783 agreed to a peace, which gave the new government all land east of the Mississippi which she herself had held—except Florida, which went to Spain.

Though the land was now independent it could not yet be called a full-grown nation. The government had been somewhat strengthened by the Articles of Confederation— the first Constitution of the United States (drawn up in 1777, adopted 1781)—but only slowly was a national spirit created, ending in the present Constitution of 1787.

George Washington (q.v.) used his influence in favour of a strong union, and his name and fame were a rallying point for the new central government. Much credit, too, belongs to the Federalist party, which also believed in a strong central government.

The control of the government, however, soon passed into the hands of the party of Thomas Jefferson— then called "Democratic-Republicans." But though, in theory, this party believed in the supremacy of the individual States, in practice the nation grew under their leadership both in territory and in spirit. In 1803 the vast territory known as Louisiana, extending from the Mississippi to the Rocky Mountains, was purchased from France, and Florida was secured from Spain in 1819.

By then, the war of 1812 with Britain had welded together the young nation, though it brought no additional territory and settled no disputes. The close of the war saw the country with infant industries to protect and in possession of a self-consciousness that began to shape a national foreign policy in the Monroe Doctrine. First expressed by President Monroe in 1823, this was to the effect that no European power should be allowed to acquire territory on the American Continent.

Texas, after winning its independence from Mexico, was admitted to the Union in 1845. A boundary war followed with Mexico (1846-48), which added territory now included in the states of California, Nevada, Utah, and most of New Mexico and Arizona. A treaty with Great Britain gave the Oregon country, up to the 49th parallel, to the United States (1846). Then, in 1853, an area of 45,535 square miles south of the Gila River, in southern Arizona and New Mexico, was bought from Mexico for £2,000,000. This gain in territory did not prove an unmixed blessing, for it gave

BELL THAT RANG FOR LIBERTY
In the State House, or Independence Hall, in Philadelphia is the famous Liberty Bell (above), which is said to have been rung to summon the people of Philadelphia to the reading of the Declaration of Independence.

increased importance to the question of slavery. For over 30 years this source of disagreement between the North and the South overshadowed other political issues. During these years of political strife within the nation men tried to settle the slavery question by compromise and negotiation, but all proved in vain, and in 1861-65 the quarrel was fought out on the battle-field. In the end, contrary to many people's expectations, the northern States won the war.

Later, there was a prolonged and extremely bitter quarrel between President Andrew Johnson and Congress, but Congress in the main had its way, amending the Constitution. The 13th Amendment (1865) prohibited slavery, and the 14th and 15th amendments (1868 and 1870) protected the former slaves and gave them the right to vote.

About this time the United States began to be drawn into world affairs. In 1867 she had, by the purchase of Alaska from Russia, acquired territory separated from the rest of the States. While Benjamin Harrison was president (1889-93), a revolution occurred in Hawaii in the North Pacific, the native monarchy was overthrown, and the new government at once applied for annexation to the United States. A treaty granting this was negotiated, and the islands finally became a part of the United States (1898). In the same year the United States engaged in war with Spain, as a result of which she gained the West Indian island of Puerto Rico, Guam and the Philippines, and freed Cuba from Spanish rule.

When President McKinley was assassinated by an anarchist in 1901, the Vice-President, Theodore Roosevelt (q.v.), took office, and he was elected for a second term in 1904. His Presidency was marked by a much more vigorous participation of the country in foreign affairs, and he was also responsible in large measure for the construction of the Panama Canal (q.v.).

In 1913, for the first time for 16 years the nominee of the Democratic Party—Woodrow Wilson (q.v.)— was elected President. A high-minded idealist, Wilson strove for the betterment of the great mass of the people, but his plans for social reform were interrupted by the First World War (1914-18), into which, despite all the President's efforts for conciliation, the country at last entered (1917). The entry of America proved the determining factor in winning the war for the Allies, and their cause was immensely strengthened by the declarations of Wilson in favour of a just peace. After the conclusion of the Armistice in 1918 he went to Paris at the head of his country's Peace delegation, and though he proved no match for the representatives of the other nations he had the immense satisfaction

HOW THE U.S.A. HELPED TO LIBERATE EUROPE AND ASIA

Outstanding events in the story of the United States in the Second World War are here briefly listed. *See also* text, this page; Eisenhower, Gen.; Hiroshima; Japan; MacArthur, Gen.; Marshall, Gen.; New Guinea; Normandy Invasion; Pacific Ocean; Pearl Harbour; Philippine Islands ; Roosevelt, F. D. ; World War of 1939–45 (Two Wars That Shattered the World).

1941

Dec. 8   Declaration (with Britain) of war on Japan.
Dec. 11   U.S. declared war on Germany and Italy.

1942

Jan. 26   First American Expeditionary Force landed in Northern Ireland.
Mar. 17   Gen. MacArthur assumed command of United Nations' forces in South-West Pacific.
Apr. 25   American troops landed in New Caledonia.
May 4–8   U.S. Navy defeated Japanese invasion fleet in battle of Coral Sea.
June 3–6   U.S. Navy defeated Japanese in battle of Midway.
July 1   First U.S. airmen raided Germany.
Nov. 8   American forces invaded N. Africa.

1943

Feb. 6   Gen. Eisenhower appointed Commander-in-Chief of United Nations' forces in N. Africa.
Apr. 8   British and U.S. forces joined in Tunisia.
Sept. 9   American 5th Army invaded Italy at Salerno.

1944

Mar. 6   First U.S. troops fought in Asia, seizing Walawbum in Burma.

June 4   American 5th Army entered Rome.
June 6   U.S., British and Canadian forces invaded France at Normandy coast.
Aug. 15   U.S. and French landings in south France.
Aug. 25   Americans marched into Paris.
Sept. 2   Gen. Hodges's 1st Army crossed from France into Belgium.
Sept. 11   American 1st Army crossed German border east of Aachen.
Oct. 20   Americans began Philippine campaign with invasion of Leyte.

1945

Mar. 8   U.S. troops crossed the Rhine at Remagen.
Apr. 26   American and Russian armies joined at Torgau.
June 26   With 49 other nations signed charter of United Nations.
July 5   MacArthur announced complete liberation of the Philippines.
Aug. 6   American aeroplane dropped atomic bomb on Hiroshima; and, Aug. 9, on Nagasaki.
Aug. 27   American occupation force entered Japan.
Sept. 2   Japan surrendered formally aboard U.S.S. Missouri in Tokyo Bay.

---

of seeing his long-cherished dream, a League of Nations, come into actual being.

But on his return to America the Senate refused to ratify the Peace Treaty, and the United States never became a member of the League. Worn out by nervous strain Wilson collapsed, and for the rest of his term of office he was an invalid. One of the outstanding features of his administration was the adoption in 1920 of the 18th Amendment to the Constitution, whereby the whole country became " dry," the manufacture of intoxicating liquors as beverages being forbidden. " Prohibition " proved unworkable in practice, and the curse of " boot-legging " (i.e. the illegal preparation and sale of liquor) became so apparent that in 1933 the Amendment was repealed.

More successful was the 19th Amendment, granting equal political rights for men and women. This was ratified in time for women to vote in the presidential election of 1920, when the Republican candidate, Senator Warren G. Harding, of Ohio, was elected. He died suddenly in 1923, and under his successor, Calvin Coolidge, who was elected for a full term in 1924, America was revealed to the world as a land where there seemed to be no limit set to the upward surge of material prosperity.

In 1928 Herbert Hoover became President, and in the following year an economic " slump," or trade depression, came to America. There was a panic on the stock markets; hundreds of banks closed; millions of men and women of all classes walked the streets unemployed, with no form of government relief to alleviate their distress.

Never had the country experienced such a catastrophe, and on every hand it was realized that the age of prosperity had gone—perhaps for ever. The country was crying out for leadership, and it found it in the person of Franklin Delano Roosevelt (*q.v.*),

a distant kinsman of President Theodore Roosevelt, but, unlike him, an ardent Democrat, filled with reforming zeal. In 1932 Franklin Roosevelt put up for the Presidency as the Democrats' nominee, and he was returned in triumph. In March 1933 he took office, and soon restored confidence to the despairing and put new heart into business, instituting National Recovery measures under the title of a " New Deal " for the relief of the poor, economic recovery, reform, and permanent reconstruction.

There was much opposition of one kind and another, and the President had the mortification of seeing a number of his proposals nullified by the Supreme Court, which pronounced them to be " unconstitutional." However, in 1936 he was re-elected President with the greatest majority ever known in American history. In 1940 he was again elected, and though at first he kept the United States out of the Second World War (1939–45), it soon became clear that, without American aid, there was a danger that the Germans would conquer all Europe. Franklin Roosevelt apparently hoped that aid short of actual fighting, if given in sufficient quantity, would be enough, and in 1941 he launched the scheme known as " Lease-Lend," by which war supplies were sent to the Allies without being paid for at the time of delivery, the payment, in the form of a lease, being spread over a long period.

On December 7, 1941, however, the Japanese attacked the United States Pacific Fleet at Pearl Harbour (*q.v.*), and at once the United States was at war with Japan, Germany and Italy. From then on the whole weight of United States industry was thrown into the prosecution of the war. Huge numbers of aeroplanes and ships were built, and a new army, navy and air force were created in a surprisingly short time. Before the war ended in

1945 the armed forces of the United States reached a total of more than 11 million.

Further disasters followed the crippling of the U.S. Pacific Fleet at Pearl Harbour—the strategic islands of Wake and Guam in the North Pacific were lost, and in May 1942 the Japanese completed the capture of the Philippine Islands. Later in 1942 important naval victories were won in the Pacific against the Japanese in the Coral Sea, off the Solomon Islands and near Midway Island. Landings were made on Guadalcanal, one of the Solomon Islands in the south-west Pacific, the first step on the long road back to the Philippines.

United States forces took part in the campaigns in North Africa, Sicily and Italy, and in conjunction with British and Canadian armies drove the Germans from France, Belgium and the Netherlands. Fighting in Europe ceased on May 8, 1945, when the unconditional surrender of the German forces was announced. The end was also in sight in the Pacific. On October 20, 1944, American landings were made on Leyte Island in the Philippines; the liberation of the whole group was completed by July 5, 1945. On the following August 6 the first atomic bomb was dropped on the city of Hiroshima, resulting in the surrender of Japan on August 15, 1945.

President Roosevelt had died suddenly on April 12, 1945, and had been succeeded by the Vice-President, Mr. Harry S. Truman (q.v.), who announced that he would continue the late President's general policy, but when the Second World War ended he at once stopped Lease-Lend aid to the Allies. However, at the instigation of George Marshall, Mr. Truman's Secretary of State (who was Chief of Staff to the U.S. army during the war), a new scheme for helping the economic recovery of the Western European nations came into effect in 1948. In the same year Mr. Truman was re-elected President : the United States, which had hitherto striven not to become involved in the quarrels of the European nations, was now one of the leading factors in world politics and concerned with the fate of nations in Europe and Asia.

In April 1949 the United States signed the Atlantic Treaty, under the terms of which she, the United Kingdom, Belgium, Canada, Denmark, France, Iceland, Italy, Luxembourg, the Netherlands and Norway were pledged to assist one another against aggression. (See World Wars).

POETS and PROSEMEN of the UNITED STATES

Though a comparatively new nation, America has a literature which, marked as it is by virility and originality of outlook, constitutes a major contribution to that of the English-speaking world.

United States, LITERATURE OF. In the American colonies there was for a long time hardly anything worthy of the name of literature. In the homeland the period from Shakespeare to Dr. Johnson was rich in great names—dramatists and poets, historians, essayists and novelists—but the colonists lived lives of hard toil and had little time or inclination for any book except the Bible.

The first colonial writer was that adventurous Englishman Captain John Smith (1580-1631), whose romantic True Relation of Virginia was printed in England in 1608. The poetry of the time consisted mainly of hymns and the Psalms done into queer rhyme. The Bay Psalm-Book (1640) was the first book in English printed in America. Two famous preacher-writers were Cotton Mather (died 1728), who wrote on theology, New England history, and witchcraft ; and Jonathan Edwards (died 1758), author of The Freedom of the Will.

Before, during and just after the Revolution, any American who had a gift for writing put it to hasty but practical use. Pamphlets and speeches abounded, all filled with a growing spirit of citizenship and patriotism. But these writings can scarcely be regarded as literature.

Once the wars with Great Britain were over the country could turn with renewed attention to developing its resources and evolving a

WASHINGTON IRVING
At his best as an essayist, Washington Irving was also a pioneer of the short story, most of his works dealing with the romantic past.

distinct civilization. Authors found both leisure and stimulus to write for the sake of writing. Presently four really great writers appeared whose work had a distinctly national flavour and won prompt fame abroad as well as in their own country.

Washington Irving, " father of American literature," was the first, with his humorous Knickerbocker's History of New York (1809) and his Sketch-Book, which show skill in description and story, and in the use of history and legend. Then came James Fenimore Cooper (1789-1851), who set up a broad New World stage of forest, plain and sea for such thrilling novels as The Spy (1821) and The Pilot, and created a new sort of American romance in The Last of the Mohicans and other Red Indian tales. (See page 902).

The breadth and sweep of Nature in the New World inspired also America's first great poet, William Cullen Bryant (1794-1878), whose Thanatopsis appeared in 1817. Not much later appeared the work of Edgar Allan Poe (1809-49), clever detective tales, thrilling mysteries, vivid tales of horror, symbolic stories, all written with the beauty and wonderful word-music that his poetry possesses, whether it be the sombre Raven or Ulalume, or The Bells. (See page 2633).

From the war of 1812 to the Civil War, great national questions demanded discussion and settlement. This was the time of America's big orators: Henry Clay, John C. Calhoun, Daniel Webster, Wendell Phillips and Edward Everett.

About the year 1840 began the great creative period—that of the poets, essayists and other writers who made the middle 19th century America's golden age of literature.

The loftiest writer in this group was Ralph Waldo Emerson (1803–82) who did more than any other American writer of his time to make people think. Associated with him in life and ideas was Henry David Thoreau (1807–62), a poet and the first American writer on Nature. At Cambridge, Massachusetts, Henry Wadsworth Longfellow (1807–82) put his literary knowledge and his gift for making melodious verse into writing the poetry that has made him the best loved and the most widely read of all American poets. (*See* page 2022).

John Greenleaf Whittier (1807–92) wrote calm Quaker hymns and stirring war poems, and pictured the simple life on a New England farm. The charming physician, Oliver Wendell Holmes, in his delightful Autocrat of the Breakfast Table showed American readers the value of culture and entertained them with wise thought and clever fun. James Russell Lowell (1819–91) author of Biglow Papers, and a host of other poems, was an ardent anti-slavery poet and also a fine critic.

A very different sort of poet was Walt Whitman (1819–92), the child of the New York metropolis.

AN INCIDENT FROM MOBY DICK

Herman Melville served for four years on a whaling vessel, and his Moby Dick, a tale of the whaling industry, is now considered his masterpiece. The above incident shows the boat containing Captain Ahab, the commander of a whaler, being hurled into the air by the tail of Moby Dick, the great white whale he was determined to kill.

From Moby Dick (Herman Melville); illus. by Rockwell Kent; by courtesy of Random House Inc.

He wrote with entire freedom from the usual rhyme and rhythm and with equal freedom of thought. His noblest poem is his tribute to Lincoln entitled My Captain.

Novels appeared at a somewhat later period in America, but the time of the early American poets and essayists brought to light the gifts of Nathaniel Hawthorne (1804–64). Born and bred in old Salem, he put into his romances, The Scarlet Letter and The House of the Seven Gables, an atmosphere that was Puritan New England itself.

Equally romantic, although in the realm of adventure rather than of subtle mood, was Hawthorne's friend and neighbour Herman Melville (1819–91), whose Moby Dick, regarded as merely a " tall yarn " when it appeared, has of late years been revalued highly. Harriet Beecher Stowe's Uncle Tom's Cabin (1852), for all its sprawling construction and stock characters, contains elements of sincerity which make it live.

During the Civil War period (1861–65) appeared a famous short story, The Man Without a Country, by Edward Everett Hale. Of the historians of the pre-Civil War era we may admire the courage as well as the vivid narrative style of William Hickling Prescott (1796–1859). Blinded by an accident at Harvard College, he wrote with fingers guided by a mechanical device. He could make little use of notes, and could not easily revise. The result was a rich, concise, well-considered style, which makes his Conquest of Mexico and Conquest of Peru glow with the colour of a great painting. Prescott was fascinated by the brilliance of Spain, but John Lothrop Motley (1814–77) detested its tyranny, and pictured Dutch resistance to Spain in The Rise of the Dutch Republic. The impassioned democrat George Bancroft (1800–91) produced a dozen sound and accurate volumes on the history of the U.S.A. up to the forming of the Constitution, which still serve as a mine of material for historians.

The voice of the Middle and Far West began suddenly to be heard in literature after the Civil War, and it was extremely popular. Men began to write about America and Americans. The story of " local colour " became the fashion, with the West as the favourite field from the time when Bret Harte (1839–1902) started to portray the Californian mining camps and " gold rush " villages.

New England types and characters appeared in the novels of William Dean Howells (1837–1920), who had a great following and a great influence on other writers. The New England background was likewise utilized by Edith Wharton (1862–1937), a disciple of Henry James, and one of America's most distinguished novelists. Vignettes of New York life were sharply cut in the stories of " O. Henry " (Sydney Porter, 1862–1910), who, as a master of the short story, ranks with de Maupassant. The Central States were chosen by Hamlin Garland in A Son of the Middle Border; by Edward Eggleston in The Hoosier Schoolmaster; and by Booth Tarkington (1869–1946), known to boys by Penrod and more widely by his very successful sentimental novel and play Monsieur Beaucaire.

F. Marion Crawford (1854–1909), who spent most of his life in Italy, made Italy the scene of most of his stories. Louisa May Alcott's Little Women (1868) and Little Men (1871) like her other stories of boys and girls, were very popular. Lew Wallace's historical romance Ben Hur (1880) is still a " best seller." Frank R. Stockton's tales had a great vogue.

Two figures which stand out as of first rank among the large group of writers following the Civil War are strangely contrasted men : Henry James (1843–1916) and " Mark Twain " Samuel L. Clemens (1835–1910). Henry James was one of the most important novelists of the late 19th and early 20th centuries. He applied a new technique to the novel, and developed the psychological treatment of character. Many of his novels and stories show the effect of the complex civilization of Europe upon the direct American mind. His art was essentially aristocratic, while that of Mark Twain was "of the people."

HENRY JAMES

Born in the United States, Henry James became a British subject in 1915 and was awarded the Order of Merit in 1916.

Twain's was the humour of the practical man, which destroyed in the acids of common sense a world of sentimental and high-flown nonsense.

Genuine American material is in E. W. Howe's The Story of a Country Town, in Stephen Crane's The Red Badge of Courage, in Frank Norris's McTeague, and The Octopus ; but their workmanship is inferior to that of men of thinner talent. Nevertheless, these writers, Upton Sinclair (born 1878) in The Jungle, and others, did undoubtedly swing public taste away from thin romances, shallowness and childish self-complacence.

Realism was making game of the old type of make-believe, and putting a stronger colour of life into literature at the turn of the century. Like a ponderous dredge, Theodore Dreiser (1871–1945) brought up sombre tales from the deep places of personal and social life in An American Tragedy (1925) and other realistic novels ; these, though devoid of literary style, became standard works. Dreiser's unyielding mass has been one of the great forces in modern American writing, as have the angry satires of Sinclair Lewis (1885–1951), who somewhat acidly depicted the small town in Main Street and the successful provincial business man in Babbitt; and the stark realism of William Faulkner (born 1897).

The hardships, the drama, and the morning sun of romance in American pioneer days were the themes of Willa Cather (1876–1947). Early days in New England supplied the background for many of the tales of Joseph Hergesheimer (born 1880), a writer who gloried in colour. Gertrude Atherton (1857–1948) in stories of old-time California, and Owen Wister (1860–1938) who sent The Virginian out to adventure in the West, drew upon the romance of vanished times.

No one ever depended less upon native soil for fictional settings than James Branch Cabell (born 1879) who, in several novels, dwelt on the tragicomedy of human affairs in the imaginary kingdom of Poictesme. Americans in adventures against a foreign background appeared in A Farewell to Arms, and For Whom the Bell Tolls, by Ernest Hemingway (born 1898), whose manner of writing —direct, telegraphic, with a studied use of the short, adjectiveless sentence—greatly influenced American literature of the 1930s.

The clatter of crowds over pavements, the small doings of humble city workers, attracted the pens of Fannie Hurst (born 1889) and Edna Ferber (born 1887), though the latter, in Show Boat, and Cimarron, later turned to stories of pioneer America. Other notable women writers were Ellen Glasgow (1874–1945), a social satirist of the South ; and Pearl Buck (born 1892), who wrote movingly of the Chinese peasant in The Good Earth.

Thornton Wilder (born 1897) published his first novel, The Cabala, in 1925, and established an international reputation with The Bridge of San Luis Rey (1927). He achieved distinction as a dramatist with Our Town (1938) and The Skin of Our Teeth (1942). William Saroyan (born 1908) scored a success with The Daring Young Man On the Flying Trapeze (1934) and gained some fame as a dramatist. His plays included The Time of Your Life (1939) ; and The Beautiful People (1941).

Just as American novelists have ranged from delicate aestheticism to the harshest and crudest type of what is termed modern realism, so poets of the 20th century have flowered in the widest variety. The fine lyric gift of William Vaughan Moody made itself evident at the beginning of the century. A decade or more later, when "free" verse was still not free from controversy, Edgar Lee Masters (1869–1950), from the tombstones of the village dead, produced poetry of a new form and special flavour in The Spoon River Anthology. Emily Dickinson (1830–86) was a poet whose mysticism few could fully understand. She retired almost completely from public life, and when a selection of her poetry appeared posthumuously in 1892 she was hailed as a great poet.

SINCLAIR LEWIS

Main Street, a novel of American provincial life published in 1920, brought recognition to Sinclair Lewis, who still further enhanced his reputation with Babbitt (1922). He received the Nobel prize for literature in 1930, the first American to do so.

Nicholas Vachel Lindsay (1879–1931) chose themes that were unhackneyed but adhered to traditional rhyme and rhythm, a rhythm like the beat of a tom-tom in Congo and in General Booth Enters Heaven. Perhaps American poetry can scarcely claim Ezra Pound (born 1885), who in 1907 settled in Europe ; yet he was born in Idaho of old American stock, a kinsman of Longfellow. In sponsoring " imagism," he had a profound influence upon poets both in America and abroad. Discerning analysis of character in verse of precision and beauty places Edwin Arlington Robinson among poets of the first rank. Also deeply moving, and far from spectacular, was the work of Robert Lee Frost (born 1875) of intense simplicity, tinged with a quality of mysticism.

A more human and therefore more popular treatment was also applied to writing in other fields. The influence of H. G. Wells's Outline of History was reflected in America by Hendrik Willem Van Loon's The Story of Mankind (1922) and Will Durant's The Story of Philosophy. New trends of thought in sociology and philosophy were indicated in Walter Lippmann's A Preface to Morals.

Among critics, the most formidable and tireless was Henry Louis Mencken (born 1880) who attacked all the humbugs of life and literature, as he saw them. The professional wit has always held a special place and added a special savour in American literature. Among the best known were Damon Runyon (1884–1946), chronicler of the minor gangster of Broadway, Dorothy Parker (born 1893), Alexander Woollcott (1887–1943), and James Thurber (born 1894).

Universities. Although there were schools of rhetoric (art of oratory) and philosophy in ancient Greece and Rome, and although Mahomedanism developed its schools for religious teaching in Egypt, Turkey, and Asia, it is chiefly from institutions fostered by the Christian Church in medieval Europe that the universities of today take their origin.

In Britain the term " university " is applied to institutions for advanced study which are empowered by charter to grant degrees. Of the 12 English universities the oldest and most eminent are those of Oxford and Cambridge. The newer universities are London, Durham, Manchester, Birmingham, Liverpool, Leeds, Sheffield, Bristol, Reading, and Nottingham. Scotland's oldest university is St. Andrews, the others being at Glasgow, Aberdeen, and Edinburgh. There is a University of Wales, with colleges at Aberystwyth, Bangor, Cardiff, and Swansea. The premier university of Eire is Trinity College, Dublin. (See frontispiece to this volume).

One of the oldest universities of Europe was the University of Paris, which dates from the 12th century. The Sorbonne, formerly its theological school, in modern times became the teaching centre for science and literature. Bologna University in Italy was noted for its law school in the 11th century ; and that of Salerno (also in Italy) was renowned in the Middle Ages for its instruction in medicine. Some of the best known universities in Germany prior to the Second World War (1939–45), during which a number were destroyed, were Heidelberg (founded 1385), Leipzig (1409), Jena (1548), Tübingen (1477), and Berlin (1810). In the United States are Harvard, Yale, Princeton, Cornell, Johns Hopkins, and scores of others.

From the time of matriculating—that is, qualifying for entrance—until he takes a degree (becomes a graduate), a student is called an undergraduate. Degrees are of different grades (bachelor, master, and doctor), and are either " honours " (in a single subject) or " general " (in a group of subjects). Many universities now have post-graduate courses, and undertake research into various subjects. Archaeological and exploring expeditions are other features of advanced work. The chief divisions of a university are faculties or schools (as of arts, science, law, theology, medicine). ʻThe nominal head of an English or Welsh university is the Chancellor, and of a Scottish the Rector. The university " session " consists of three terms—six months in all. Women are admitted to most universities on equal terms with men.

U.N.R.R.A. These initials, familiar in the latter days of the Second World War (1939–45) and in the first two years of the subsequent peace, stood for United Nations Relief and Rehabilitation Administration. In 1943 it was suggested by the United States Government that some organization should be formed to help those nations which had suffered most as a result of the war, and 44 nations were represented at its formation. At its first session U.N.R.R.A. recommended that each member government whose territory had not been occupied by the Germans should contribute to it one per cent of the national income, and that other governments contribute whatever they could.

The main function of the organization was to provide food, clothing, medical supplies and materials for restarting agriculture and industry in those countries which had been most badly devastated by the war. It also helped to return to their home countries over seven million people (known as Displaced Persons) who had been forcibly removed by the Germans during the war. Many thousands of people (particularly in Italy, Greece and Yugoslavia) were undoubtedly saved from starvation by U.N.R.R.A., and it did valuable work in all parts of Europe.

The cost of its work was, as had been originally suggested, met by those countries which had escaped the worst effects of the war. The United Kingdom contributed £155 million, Australia £12 million, New Zealand £2,600,000, South Africa £275,000, Canada 77 million dollars, and the United States 2,500 million dollars. Over 22 million tons of material were supplied.

The Director General in charge of the Administration was, from 1943 to 1946, the American Herbert H. Lehman, and he was succeeded by Fiorello LaGuardia, a former Mayor of New York. By the end of 1946 it was considered that the emergency which U.N.R.R.A. had been formed to meet was more or less over, and on December 31 of that year it officially ceased to exist, though it was not finally wound up until the middle of 1947.

Some parts of the work of U.N.R.R.A. continued to be necessary, and it was therefore decided that it should hand over its responsibilities in regard to helping to supply Europe with food to the Food and Agriculture Organization (a section of the United Nations), and its work in resettling refugees and dealing with Displaced Persons to a new international refugee organization, set up under the control of the United Nations (q.v.).

Ur. The birthplace of Abraham (*q.v.*). Ur was founded about 3500 B.C. and was situated on the banks of the Euphrates in Mesopotamia (now called Iraq). For long the site of what is usually regarded as the world's oldest city was marked by nothing more than an unsightly mound of debris. Then, in 1855, the ziggurat, or temple-tower, and other remains were excavated by J. E. Taylor, on behalf of the British Museum, London; and after the First World War (1914–18) a joint expedition of the British Museum and the museum of the University of Pennsylvania in the United States, led by the archaeologist Sir Leonard Woolley, made further discoveries.

The brick ziggurat stands high above the surrounding plain, rectangular in shape, about 195 feet long, 150 feet wide, and 70 feet high. The walls rise in successive stages, and three long staircases lead to the platform on which stood the shrine of the Moon god. An earlier tower, buried under the existing structure, is believed to have been built about 3000 B.C. Streets, houses and shops were uncovered, and numbers of school exercise tablets and official documents were found.

One of the most interesting discoveries was a statue representing a ram caught in a thicket, reminiscent of the animal found in a similar position which Abraham sacrificed instead of his beloved son Isaac, although it should be added that the statue was made nearly 1,500 years before the incident recorded in the Bible.

A royal grave contained 74 bodies of men and women, relics of human sacrifice. Some of them were of soldiers, armed with gold-headed spears, and a helmet of the precious metal had hammered tracery symbolical of the hair of the head. After the overthrow of the Babylonian Empire by the Persians in 538 B.C., Ur lost its importance; the recession of the Persian Gulf also contributed to its economic decay. The population gradually drifted elsewhere and by 300 B.C. the city was a heap of ruins. (*See* Mesopotamia).

Ural Mountains. The longest mountain chain in Europe, the Urals form a part of the geographical boundary between Europe and Asia, separating European Russia from Siberia. They consist mostly of a series of table-lands, extending nearly due north and south from the Arctic Circle almost to the Caspian Sea, a distance of about 1,600 miles, with an average elevation of less than 1,500 feet. The isolated peaks rarely reach 5,000 feet. Much of the lower slopes is covered with forests.

Mining of salt, iron and copper began in the 16th century; extensive gold deposits were found in 1745. Other minerals worked include manganese, platinum, uranium, iron, tellurium, chromium and silver. There are also extensive coalfields. The precious stones of the Urals include topaz, sapphires, emeralds, beryls and amethysts. Under the Soviet regime, many new industrial cities, including Magnitogorsk, Berezniki, and Krasnouralsk have sprung up. When the Germans invaded Russia in 1941 during the Second World War (1939–45), a number of industries were moved into the area of the Urals. Besides heavy engineering plants there are china, glass, cement and brick works, and textile and leather factories.

Uranium. In 1945 uranium became the focus of the world's interest as the element which gave Man the atomic bomb. Before that, it interested scientists as the heaviest of all the elements, and as the parent of the radio-active elements, including radium. It has played small part in

RECONSTRUCTION OF A SHRINE AT UR

Among the remains of the ancient city of Ur excavated in Iraq were the ruins of the ziggurat, or temple-tower, of which a reconstruction by the British archaeologists Sir Leonard Woolley and F. G. Newton is seen above. With a core of mud bricks faced with kiln-fired ones, the tower, with slightly sloping-in sides and receding terraces, was 70 feet high, and upon it was built the shrine dedicated to the Moon god.

industry, but may be used to colour pottery and to make fluorescent glass and luminescent paint.

Most uranium comes from pitchblende mined in the Great Bear Lake region of north-west Canada and in the Belgian Congo; and some from carnotite mined in eastern Utah, western Colorado, Australia; and from Portugal and elsewhere in Europe.

The existence of uranium has been known since 1789, when a German chemist, Martin Klaproth (*see* Titanium), discovered an oxide of this element and named it after the planet Uranus. But a French chemist, Eugène Péligot, in 1841, was the first to isolate pure uranium. It is a white lustrous metal somewhat softer than mild steel. Its melting point is about 3,362° F. The chemical symbol is U; the atomic weight is 238·14; and the atomic number is 92. The density of the metal is 18·7.

There are several natural varieties or isotopes of uranium, each known by its atomic weight. The isotope U-238 makes up nearly 99·3 per cent of the uranium present in Nature; U-235, ·7 per cent; and U-234 only ·006 per cent. U-235 was the basic ingredient of the first atomic bomb. (*See also* Atom ; Electron ; Radiation ; Radium).

Uranus. Far back in the beginning of things, so the ancient Greeks believed, all was chaos. Gradually then things began to take form. First appeared Sky and Earth, whom the Greeks called Uranus and Gaea. Sky, the first ruler of the world, took Earth to wife. Among their many children were 12 huge Titans; three terrible brothers called "Cyclopes" who had only one eye apiece; and Briareus and his two brothers, who were strong and had 100 hands and 50 heads each. Uranus detested his children, and thrust them into Tartarus, the vast abyss below the earth. But Earth called on the Titans to rise against their father, and Cronos, the craftiest, made himself ruler.

The seventh planet from the sun was named after Uranus. It is a huge, unfinished world spinning through space about 1,700 million miles away, 15 times as heavy as the earth, its surface hidden by clouds of marsh gas, a mass more than 30,000 miles across, with a year that lasts as long as 84 of our years. For centuries Uranus had been seen. Thousands of times the old astronomers of Assyria and Chaldea must have looked at it, but it was thought to be a star and no more. It was not till nearly two centuries ago that Uranus was found to be a planet.

It was an organist at Bath, in England, looking through his home-made telescope, who saw Uranus on March 13, 1781, and knew it to be more than a star. His name was William Herschel, and he was the first modern man on earth to discover a planet. It lay far beyond the path of the most distant planet known. The universe beyond the orbit of Saturn was impenetrable darkness to Man, except for the eternal movement of the stars. Saturn was the boundary line of knowledge. We knew there were worlds on *this* side of his path, but no man dreamed of the existence of worlds beyond.

Every day and hour it was watched after William Herschel found it. Every movement was recorded, that a history might be made of the full circle of its 84 years. Astronomers knew where it was on any day since it was found; they knew where it was on any day before it was found; they thought they knew where it would be on any day in ten thousand years to come. But when Uranus was half-way round its circle it was found to have strayed from its calculated path through space. This wobble of the giant planet was thought to be due to the pulling influence of some invisible planet even farther out in space. And this planet was discovered 65 years later and called Neptune (*q.v.*).

Uranus has five small moons circling around it. (*See* Astronomy; Planets).

Urban. Of the eight Popes who have borne this name, URBAN II (Pope 1088–99) was a monk of Cluny, in France, and was called to Rome and made a cardinal by Gregory VII, whom he followed in the papal chair after a three years' interval. He was a reforming Pope, but is chiefly remembered for his part in calling the First Crusade. (*See* Crusades).

URBAN VI (Pope 1378–89) was elected while a Roman mob was howling about the place of conclave, threatening the cardinals if they did not give them "a Roman or at least an Italian Pope." Some of the cardinals, who disliked Urban's zeal for reform, seized upon this pretext to declare the election invalid and elect a French cardinal as antipope, Clement VII, who set up his court at Avignon. Thus began the Great Schism (1378–1417), in which half of western Europe adhered to Urban and his successors at Rome, and the other half to Clement VII and his successors. Urban was on his way to seize the throne of Naples, vacated by the death of Charles, whom he himself had crowned, when he was thrown from his mule and he died from the injuries he received.

Uruguay. (Pron. ōōr-oo-gwā). A fertile soil, a temperate and equable climate, and a fortunate geographical position combine to make the South American republic of Uruguay a land of great possibilities.

Its general outline is almost square, with a seaboard of 120 miles on the Atlantic, 235 miles on the

---

Extent.—Area 72,000 sq. miles.   Population 2,200,000.

Physical Features.—Undulating, with little woodland except bordering the numerous streams. The River Uruguay is the western, and the Rio de la Plata the southern, boundary.

Principal Products.—Animals and animal products ; wheat, maize, and other crops ; grapes, oranges, and other fruit.

Chief Towns.—Montevideo (capital 730,000), Paysandu, Salto, Mercedes, Fray Bentos.

Rio de la Plata, and 270 miles along the eastern bank of the River Uruguay. These two rivers separate it from Argentina. The Brazilian frontier in the north is about 450 miles long. Uruguay is also marked out from its sister states in that it has no stretches of rugged barren mountain territory such as are found in the republics of the Andes, no tangles of jungle and swamp such as Brazil has, no desert tracts like southern Argentina, and no flat monotonous pampas like central Argentina. Apart from its sandy coast and a few barren hill-tops, there is scarcely an acre of useless ground. There are no mountains of more than 2,000 feet. The southern and eastern parts of its surface are undulating grassland, with a few stretches of valuable timber. To the north and west rise swelling downs, intersected here and there by low ranges of hills with fertile valleys. A network of about 500 rivers and streams gives it abundant water.

The climate is one of the most delightful and healthy in the world. Frosts occur only on the

uplands of the interior, and the midsummer temperature rarely exceeds 86°, except near the sub-tropical region bordering on Brazil. The sunny blue skies, fresh sea breezes, and balmy temperature in winter and summer alike, make Montevideo (*q.v.*), the capital, a favourite resort for wealthy Brazilians and Argentineans.

Abundant crops of wheat, linseed, oats, barley, maize, tobacco and grapes can be grown, Uruguayan or "Montevideo" wheat being nowhere surpassed. But so far the development has been chiefly pastoral, Uruguay having some eight million cattle and 18 million sheep. The chief problem of the farmer is excessive drought, which recurs every six or eight years.

Hides, salted beef, wool, and other stock-raising products furnish 85 per cent of the exports. Uruguay has at Fray Bentos one of the largest beef-extract factories in the world. But the country seems destined to remain a land of farms rather than of manufactures, because of its lack of coal. There are, however, gold mines; and silver, copper, iron, and manganese occur to a limited extent. A large proportion of the inland trade is carried on in boats of light draught, the Uruguay being navigable for about 200 miles and the Rio Negro and other streams for shorter distances. The electrification of the country is being carried out by damming the Rio Negro. More than 1,400 miles of railway have been built, chiefly with British capital. The railways were bought by the Uruguay Government in 1948. All the lines radiate from Montevideo, which thus has connexion with the principal cities, and with Brazil and the Argentine. Carrasco, near Montevideo, is an international airport.

Most of the population are of south European descent, chiefly Spanish and Italian. The largest early immigration—in the 18th century—came from the Canary Islands. The present rate of immigration is low, and 70 per cent of the population are of native birth. Education, if better than in most of Latin America, is still backward, though in theory all children should attend school.

Uruguay fought first against Spain to gain her freedom, and then against the Portuguese rulers of Brazil. In 1830 Uruguay was proclaimed an independent republic. From 1843 to 1852 she most resolutely resisted the aggressions of Argentina, and between 1865 and 1870 she was the ally of Brazil and Argentina in a war against Paraguay. Acute political divisions have existed within the country

Dorien Leigh

STREET SCENE IN URUGUAY'S CAPITAL
At the mouth of the Rio de la Plata, Montevideo, the capital of Uruguay, has claims to be regarded as the pleasantest city in South America, with its wide streets, imposing public buildings and temperate climate. Manufactures are few owing to lack of coal ; and exports consist mainly of livestock, canned meat and meat extracts.

ever since Generals Oribe and Rivera strove for the mastery three-quarters of a century ago.

Because General Oribe rode a white horse and his followers carried white banners, while General Rivera's horse was bay and his banners red, the Uruguayans were for long divided into *Blancos* and *Colorados* (Whites and Reds), and revolutions and assassinations have been frequent. As Clemenceau, the great French statesman, said, "When a boy is born in Uruguay he is given a white or a red ribbon, which he is enjoined to defend and hand down to his children." Generally speaking, the *Blancos* were Conservatives and the *Colorados* the Radicals. Notwithstanding this almost incessant political warfare, Uruguay became after the beginning of the 20th century one of the most peaceful and progressive countries of South America. Then an economic depression in 1929 brought on a period of political unrest, and in 1934 a new Constitution was adopted. This was later approved by popular vote ; it gives the President wide powers, and contains progressive social and labour provisions. The population of Uruguay is 2,200,000.

Utah. An inland western State of the United States, Utah is bounded on the north by Idaho, on the north-east by Wyoming, on the east by Colorado, on the south by Arizona, and on the west by Nevada. Its area is 84,916 square miles. The Wasatch Mountains extend south from the northern boundary, and in the north-east is the Uinta range. The principal rivers are the Colorado, and the Weber, Bear and Jordan, which empty into the Great Salt Lake. About 70 miles long and from 20 miles to 50 miles wide, the Great Salt Lake is an important source of salt and is crossed by a railway bridge. To the west of the lake is the Great Salt Lake Desert.

Owing to lack of water only about one-tenth of the State is under cultivation, but irrigation has rendered thousands of acres fruitful. The principal crops include wheat, hay, sugar-beet, vegetables and fruit; cattle and sheep are bred in the un-irrigated districts. The most important industry is mining, which provides employment for half the working population. Copper, silver, lead, gold and zinc are the leading sources of mineral wealth; others include bismuth, antimony, manganese, tungsten, salt and gypsum. The capital is Salt Lake City (population 150,000). The only other town of any size is Ogden (population 44,000). The majority of the inhabitants of Utah are Mormons (*q.v.*); members of this religious sect, led by Brigham Young, settled in the State in 1847. The population is 550,000.

Utrecht. (Pron. ū'-trekht). A quaint old Dutch city, Utrecht stands at the point where the Rhine divides into two branches, the Old Rhine and the Vecht. The Romans called it *Trajectum ad Rhenum*, or " ford of the Rhine," and its present name *Oude Trecht* or Utrecht means " old ford." In the centre of the town stands the Gothic Cathedral of Saint Martin, begun in the 13th century on the side of older buildings and finished in the 15th century. In 1674 a storm blew down the nave, which was never rebuilt, and so today an open space separates the western tower from the choir and transept. Graceful Gothic cloisters connect the cathedral with the University, one of the most famous in the Netherlands. Among other buildings of historic interest is the " Pope's house," built in 1517 by the future Pope Adrian VI.

Utrecht is traversed by two canals, spanned by over 90 bridges. The roadways lie above the level of the canals, which are reached by steps, and a number of people live in cellars beneath the road-ways, their doors opening on the canals. The old ramparts have been converted into promenades, bounded by the Buiten Gracht (outer canal). Good water communications and railways make Utrecht an important centre of trade, and there are manu-factures of woollens, chemicals, carpets, pottery, cigars, and machinery. During the Second World War (1939–45) Utrecht was under German occupa-tion from May 1940 until May 5, 1945, but it suffered little damage. The population is 187,000.

Courtesy of the Netherlands Information Bureau

UTRECHT : A PICTURESQUE CITY OF THE NETHERLANDS

In the heart of Utrecht, fourth largest city of the Nether-lands, is the Cathedral of St. Martin, which was begun in 1254 and completed in the 15th century. The tower (centre), 338 feet high, is isolated from the rest of the edifice, because the nave was blown down by a storm in 1674 and never rebuilt. Good communications by water and rail have made the city an important commercial centre, manufacturing woollens, chemicals, pottery and machinery.

V

Vaccination. The name of this method of inoculation derives from *vacca*, Latin for " cow," and describes a protective inoculation against small-pox. In the late 18th century this disease was raging in England, so widely so that if a woman was not scarred by it she ranked as a beauty for this reason alone. At this time it so happened that Dr. Edward Jenner (1749–1823), a country doctor in the West of England, heard a remark by a pretty dairy maid, who had been congratulated upon not being pock-marked: " But you see, sir, I have had cow-pox," she explained, cow-pox being a mild common eruption of blisters caught from the udders of cattle.

Jenner (*q.v.*) was intrigued by this explanation, and investigation proved it to be true. Though the one disease is so virulent, and the other so mild, the nature of the virus which causes them both is the same; and an attack of cow-pox does, in fact, protect against small-pox for some six years. Jenner began by deliberately giving cow-pox to a boy in his practice by introducing under his skin this lymph from a cow-pox blister. Some time later he deliberately inoculated him with lymph from a small-pox pustule. The boy did not develop small-pox. Though Jenner, like many pioneers, was laughed to scorn by his colleagues, the results confirmed his theories. Vaccination became general, and banished small-pox from England except for cases that arrive unrecognized from abroad.

From 1853 infants in Britain had to be vaccinated unless parents lodged a conscientious objection. The National Health Service Act of 1946 abolished compulsory vaccination, but local authorities were required to make free vaccination available. Special calves are kept for the purpose of preparing the vaccine, and from these the lymph is collected. Anyone who has been in contact with small-pox, which is extremely contagious and dust-borne, should be vaccinated at once. Cow-pox takes four days to develop, and small-pox 12, so there is a fortunate margin of time in which to render the disease less deadly, if not to prevent it altogether.

One result of the success of vaccination in wiping out small-pox is that people seldom see the results of this dread disease, and do not realize its dangerous nature. Consequently, many perhaps avoid vaccination who would otherwise see that their children were given protection by this method.

Vacuum. One of the hardest things in the world to get is an airless space—one containing " nothing." Scientists have been trying for many years to produce a perfect vacuum, that is, an enclosed space with absolutely nothing in it, but so far they have failed. The reason is plain. Take a bottle and attach an air pump to it. With the first stroke you remove part of the air. But the remainder immediately expands and fills the bottle again (*see* Gas). Keep on pumping as long as you like, yet the slight quantity of air left behind will always spread out and occupy the entire bottle. The pressure from the air remaining inside gets smaller and smaller but never quite disappears.

Perhaps you question that word " pressure" when we are talking about a vacuum. Is not a vacuum something that produces suction—the very reverse of pressure? This seeming contradiction clears up when we recall that the so-called " force of suction " is not really due to the " pull " of the vacuum but to the " push " of the air outside (*see* Air). One way to measure the vacuum in our bottle is to find the difference between this larger outside push and the smaller push inside. Atmospheric pressure at sea level is about 14·7 pounds per square inch. This is about equal to the pressure exerted by a column of mercury 30 inches high. Let us, therefore, fasten one end of a long U-shaped mercury tube called a " manometer " to our bottle, leaving the other end open to the pressure of the atmosphere. If there were no counteracting pressure in the bottle, the mercury would, of course, be forced up on that side a full 30 inches. But if it falls short of this by two inches, this indicates a remaining pressure equal to two inches of mercury —about one pound to the square inch.

Why cannot we produce a perfect vacuum by withdrawing a liquid such as mercury from a space which it previously filled? Because all substances, including solids, exude their own vapours or other gases (which are ordinarily imprisoned near their surface) as soon as the surrounding pressure is greatly lowered.

After as much air or gas as possible has been removed by mechanical pumps, the vacuum can be further perfected by the use of mercury vapour pumps of the Gaede or Langmuir type. Vapour rising from heated mercury shoots past the opening of the vessel which is being evacuated. There it entangles many of the gas molecules remaining in the vacuum, and carries them away. By this method, a vacuum can be produced so nearly perfect that the pressure left is less than one ten-thousand-millionth of the atmosphere pressure. Yet this still contains *more than a thousand million molecules of gas per cubic inch.*

Scientific interest in vacuum centres largely upon the behaviour of the small quantities of remaining gases when electric currents are passed through them. Experiments of this kind led to the discovery of X-rays (*q.v.*) and electrons, and to many basic inventions, such as thermionic valves (*q.v.*). The commonest use of vacuum is in electric lamps, from which air is removed to prevent the filament from burning up. In the manufacture of these lamps and other types of vacuum tubes, chemicals known as " getters " are often placed inside them which tend to absorb the remaining gases or turn them into solid compounds as soon as the getters are heated.

The air pumps used in so-called vacuum cleaners are not effective enough to produce a vacuum; but they do lower the pressure inside the blower casing enough to cause the air outside—and with it the dust and dirt—to rush in and so get carried to the bag or cylinder. In large buildings the suction is often produced by a central pump with hose attachments on each floor. Because vacuum speeds up evaporation and lowers the boiling points of liquids, it plays an important part in industrial chemistry, food and paint manufacture, oil and sugar refining, refrigeration, ice making, and many other processes. The vessels used for boiling liquids at low pressure are called vacuum pans.

The vacuum flask is truly named, for it is a double-walled vessel in the sealed wall-cavity of which a state of vacuum has been produced. This comparatively airless space acts as a heat- or cold-insulator; the walls of the double part are coated with a metallic layer to reflect away any heat rays.

Valencia. Every morning at daybreak the dwellers in the fertile plain in which lies Valencia, one of Spain's two leading Mediterranean ports and her third largest city, listen for the great bell of the cathedral. Its ringing hour by hour is the sign of each man's turn to release the waters into the channels that make his dry land fertile. And every Thursday is held the oldest tribunal in Spain, the "court of the waters"—a meeting of the peasants to decide whether any have used the water contrary to regulation. Such careful irrigation has turned the plain, which yields four or five crops a year, into a great orchard (or *huerta*), with groves of citron, orange and mulberry trees.

Set in this garden region, which the Moors trained to fertility many centuries ago, Valencia is one of the most Moorish-looking of Spanish

RIVER GUADALAVIAR AT VALENCIA
Capital of the province of the same name, Valencia is also a Mediterranean port. Among the remains of its medieval fortifications is the Torres de Serranos (above) overlooking the bridge across the Guadalaviar, at the mouth of which is one of the best harbours on the east coast of Spain.

cities. The city lies two and a half miles from the mouth of the River Guadalaviar, and its harbour (El Grao) is one of the safest on the Mediterranean.

Valencia exports rice, melons, oranges and other fruits, wine, silk, and olive oil. Silk spinning is one of the leading industries, and the Silk Exchange, a beautiful Gothic building erected on the site of the Moorish Alcázar (palace), is one of the best surviving examples of civil architecture in the Middle Ages. Other industries are hemp and linen weaving, tobacco manufacture, and the making of the bright-coloured glazed bricks known as *azulejos*. The city is the seat of one of the foremost universities of Spain, founded in 1411.

Soon after the beginning of the Civil War in 1936 the Government moved their capital to Valencia, but in 1937 moved again to Barcelona. Valencia underwent intensive bombardment from Nationalist aircraft. Its population is 520,213.

Valley. Like most land forms, river valleys are constantly changing in shape. While the river is deepening its bed, other forces—rain, frost, wind, and the atmosphere—are loosening the material of the valley walls, so that it falls into the stream and is carried away by the rush of water.

At first the deepening will proceed rapidly. When, however, the stream approaches the level of the lake or sea into which it empties, it grows more sluggish and deepening is slowed down ; but the stream then aids the process of widening by swinging from side to side when confronted by obstacles in the channel. In arid regions the deepening forces far outstrip the weathering process, and thus deep gorges are made.

Valleys are classified as young, mature, and old. A young valley is narrow with steep sides, and carries a vigorous stream which has recently worn away the soil. A mature valley is deep and open, having widening sides and gentle upper slopes; and an old one is very wide, with a broad bed and extremely low slope. A river working on soft material may bring its valley to old age in less time than that required by a stream opposed by hard rocks, and because of this one river valley may be both "young" and "old" in different parts of its length.

The word "valley" does not necessarily indicate the presence of a river. The term is applied to depressions made in other ways, and to long narrow "structural valleys" created by movements of the earth's surface, sometimes called faults. The best example of these is perhaps the "rift valley" of Abyssinia and East Africa.

The sea may encroach on the lower reaches of a river. The result of this is what is called a "drowned valley." Some important harbours in different parts of the world are drowned valleys—for example, Plymouth, Hong Kong and Sydney.

Valparaiso. (Pron. val-pa-rī'-zo). Ships from all over the world may be seen in the broad bay of Valparaiso, a city of Chile and the principal seaport on the Pacific coast of South America. The bay is semicircular, its entrance on the north. Here a breakwater one-half mile long protects the harbour from the "northers" that used to blow ships up on the shore. To build the breakwater engineers sank 2,000-ton concrete blocks 190 feet to the sea bottom, cut down a hill near by, and dumped its earth over the blocks.

"Paradise Valley"—for that is the meaning of "Valparaiso"—is a singularly inappropriate name for this crowded commercial and manufacturing city, set in a semi-circle of rugged barren hills. From the bay, one sees first the business district on the narrow strip of shore; then, farther back, the residential section, rising sharply from the bases to the very tops of the hills and cliffs. Lifts and cable railways carry passengers to the various levels. On one of the highest of these stands Chile's naval academy, looking out toward Viña del Mar. This resort, six miles from the city, is noted for attractive residences and fine beaches. Buildings of steel-framed concrete have been the rule since an earthquake of 1906, one of several which have severely damaged the city.

Dorien Leigh

VALPARAISO : CHILE'S PORT AND NAVAL BASE
On the bay of the same name, which is sheltered on three sides but open on the north, Valparaiso is the principal port on the west coast of South America. Chile's main naval base, the city is also an industrial centre, its products including textiles, sugar, leather goods, paints and chemicals.

Valparaiso is the western terminus of the Transandine railway, which connects it with Mendoza in Argentina. Important manufactures include textiles, sugar, foundry products, paints, varnishes and enamels, cotton seed oil, shoes, tannery products, drugs, cosmetics and chemicals. The population of Valparaiso proper is about 215,000; of its suburb Viña del Mar, about 70,000.

Vanadium. This metallic element was discovered by Del Rio in 1801. It is not found free in Nature, and occurs only in combination in certain minerals, of which the chief is vanadinite, found in Spain and South America. The chemical symbol is V; the atomic weight is 50·95; and the atomic number is 23. Vanadium is a light grey or white metal, with a density of 5·5 and a melting point of 3,092° to 3,272° F.

The metal is extracted from its ores by treatment with strong hydrochloric acid; from the solution which results, the compound ammonium vanadate is precipitated by evaporation with an excess of ammonium chloride. Next the vanadate is roasted to yield vanadium oxide. For steel alloying a compound of vanadium and iron is used, prepared from the mixed oxides in an electric furnace. A very small amount of the vanadium compound added to the steel removes non-metallic impurities.

Vancouver. When one sees the wonderful harbour of Vancouver, the metropolis of British Columbia, Canada, filled with ships from China, Japan, Australia and India, it is hard to realize that in 1880 the site of the present city was covered by a trackless forest. The city was laid

G.P.A.

VANCOUVER : CANADA'S PORT ON THE PACIFIC COAST
Possessing a magnificent harbour on the southern side of Burrard Inlet, on the mainland of British Columbia, Vancouver has 98 miles of water frontage and spacious docks. The chief industry is shipping. Grain, timber and minerals are exported all over the world. The city is modern, because most of the buildings have been erected since a disastrous fire in 1886. The skyscraper on the left is the Marine Building, 349 feet high. Vancouver is the terminus of the Canadian Pacific Railway and is also served by Canadian National Railways and Trans-Canada air lines.

out as the western terminus of the Canadian Pacific Railway, which now extends 3,300 miles to St. John, New Brunswick. Fire destroyed the new town of Vancouver in 1886, but a more substantial city of stone and brick rose on its ruins.

Built on a peninsula projecting into a spacious arm of the ocean, the city has 98 miles of water frontage. It has unlimited electric power, which is made available by harnessing the torrents of the mountains that surround the city. Lumbering, mining, fishing, the manufacture of paper and pulp, shipbuilding, iron and steel manufactures, sugar refining, and meat and fruit packing are some of the leading industries of the district. It is the centre of the Canadian salmon tinning industry and is one of the world's great wheat markets.

Situated on one of the best harbours on the Pacific coast, and with good railway communica-

A PORTRAIT GEM BY VAN DYCK
Painted in 1638, this picture of Lord John and Lord Bernard Stuart is in Lord Darnley's collection at Cobham Hall, Kent. Primarily a portraitist, Van Dyck influenced British art considerably, Sir Joshua Reynolds in particular owing much to him.

tions, Vancouver ranks third among the cities of Canada, with a population of more than 275,000.

The Panama Canal, which enables goods to be shipped from Vancouver for various Atlantic ports, has increased the trade of the port. Across the Strait of Georgia from the city lies the island of Vancouver, named, like the city, after the British navigator George Vancouver (1758–98), who sailed round it in 1792. It has an area of 12,400 square miles, and is the largest of the many islands which fringe the coast of British Columbia. It has rich deposits of iron and copper ores, and its coal-mines supply the whole Pacific coast. Dense forests of magnificent timber, abounding in big game, cover most of its surface, and its rivers yield gold and are a potential source of incalculable water-power. Where the land has been cleared it produces cereals and fruits abundantly, as well as providing excellent pasturage. The chief city is Victoria, the capital of British Columbia. (*See* Victoria, Canada).

Vandals. Looted churches, wrecked buildings and shattered statuary marked the path of these German barbarians of the early Middle Ages. So thoroughly did they plunder the countries through which they passed that the word " vandal " has come to mean one who recklessly destroys property.

At the beginning of the 15th century A.D. the Vandals left their home on the Baltic Sea and migrated westward. Crossing the Rhine, they invaded Gaul (now France), and in 409 made their way into Spain. There they remained for about 20 years, until Genseric or Gaiseric (*c.* 395–477) succeeded his brother as king in 428. Some of the Vandals had already settled in North Africa, and in 429 Genseric led the rest of his people to join them. He conquered the African possessions of the West Roman Empire and established his capital at Carthage, which the Vandals held for nearly a century.

In 455 Genseric assembled a large fleet to transport an army for the capture of Rome, which was accomplished without much difficulty. For 14 days the Vandals systematically plundered the city, removing their spoil to Carthage. Genseric seized Sicily, Sardinia and Corsica, and his power remained unshaken until his death on January 25, 477. The pirate fleets of the Vandals spread terror over the whole Mediterranean for a number of years, but in 533 the Byzantine Emperor Justinian (483–565) sent his very able general, Belisarius, against them and the Vandals were defeated near Carthage, which was taken by Belisarius. Their king, Gelimer, was captured and the power of the Vandals was shattered.

Van Dyck, SIR ANTHONY (1599–1641). Few foreign painters have had such an influence on British art as this Flemish master, the chief note of whose portraits is distinction. A mysterious grace and delicacy and charm pervade them all. His figures are tall and stately, with heads proudly poised and long tapering fingers. Gleaming jewels sparkle on their hands and breasts, and they are clothed in lustrous satins and rich brocades. Dogs and horses he often brought into his portraits, and gorgeous backgrounds of splendid gardens and marble terraces and balustrades.

The genius of Van Dyck (pron. van-dīk) matured early. He was born in Antwerp on March 22, 1599, and began to study painting at the age of 10, and about 10 years later entered the studio of Rubens. Soon his skill in portraiture rivalled his employer's. His fame spread to England, and he was taken to King James's court. This first visit to England was brief, and the young painter soon went to Italy, where he spent four years studying the great masters, especially Titian, and rapidly producing scores of magnificent religious and mythological canvases. During these years he also painted the wonderful series of portraits of the patricians of Genoa.

He returned to his native city in 1626 as a famous and fashionable painter. For six years he remained there, painting princes and nobles and rich burghers, with occasional visits to other cities to execute commissions. Then came an invitation to the court of Charles I. He was knighted, given a pension, and had the King and Queen for his first sitters. So great did his vogue become that he set up a studio, like Rubens, with assistants to block in the painting from his preliminary sketches. To this practice is due the poor quality of many of his later portraits. The sitters have a " wooden " look, their faces lack character and their poses seem unnatural. He died in London on December 9, 1641. An important influence on portraiture throughout Western Europe, Van Dyck was also an etcher of great skill, and had much influence on the art of engraving.

Van Gogh, VINCENT (1853–90). Among all the strange tales of the lives of artists there can be few quite so moving as that of this tortured genius, the greatest of all modern Dutch painters. Van Gogh (pron. van-gokh') was born at Zundert in Holland, on March 3, 1853, the son of a Calvinist preacher, and at 16 he became an assistant in The Hague branch of the Goupil Galleries, which were under the management of his uncle. When he was 20 he was sent to the London branch of that firm. He later decided to be a pastor, living among the Belgian miners of La Borinage as an idealistic Communist.

After studying painting at The Hague under Anton Mauve (1838–88) he settled at his father's old home in the country, living as a peasant; again he left home to study art and in 1886 he went to Paris and there lived with his devoted brother Theodore. The work of the Impressionists produced a profound effect upon him; his pictures became full of brilliant colour and light, and he was strongly influenced by the method of Seurat (1859–91). In 1888 he went with the painter Paul Gauguin (1848–1903) to Arles, in Provence. There, for the first time, he found contentment. He painted orchards and meadows, flowers and portraits—works which were to become world famous. But as a result of sunstroke and the privations of his life his mind began to give way.

Gauguin's violent temperament and destructive criticism drove the highly nervous painter to madness. He spent most of the last two years of his life in an asylum, and finally shot himself, dying on July 29, 1890.

As an artist he was unappreciated except by his brother, who helped him throughout his life, but during the early years of the 20th century his pictures became known to a wide public and today he is regarded as one of the most courageous as well as one of the most original artists of his time. His trees and clouds seem twisted in the torment of their creator's mind. Even in the famous self-portrait, done when he had cut off his own ear in remorse after a quarrel with Gauguin, there is the same air of tragedy, though the colours are subdued and the composition restrained. (*See* illustration in page 1687).

Vanilla. When the Spaniards first landed in Mexico, they found the Aztecs flavouring a strange substance, chocolate, with an equally strange sweet-smelling extract obtained from the fermented pods of a plant native to the country. This new flavour was vanilla, today the commonest of all flavouring extracts used in baking and confectionery. It is also used largely in making perfumes.

The vanilla plant most used is *Vanilla planifolia*, a climbing orchid with bright green fleshy leaves and fragrant, greenish-white flowers. It is extensively cultivated in Mexico, Central America, the West Indies, Ceylon, Tahiti, East Africa and elsewhere. The seedlings sprout in the ground and send up slender twining stems which climb the trees on which they live, to a height of 20 to 30 feet, clinging by fibrous roots. The species from which the most valuable vanilla of commerce is obtained has slender pods from six to 10 inches long. These pods, picked before they are fully ripe, are filled with oily pulp surrounding the seeds. The aroma, due to the presence of vanillin, develops during the slow curing and fermentation of the pod. When the vanilla pod or " bean " is ready for the market it is chocolate-coloured, wrinkled, slender and pliable, and in the best qualities, known as " frosted," the pods are covered with tiny crystals of the vanillin. Vanilla extract is prepared by dissolving the vanillin in alcohol, but modern vanilla is largely made synthetically by chemical processes from other substances, including oil of cloves and coal-tar. (*See* illustration in page 3061).

Varnish. Solutions of certain gums or resins in alcohol, linseed oil, or a similar solvent, used to produce a shining transparent hard coat or surface, are called varnishes. They are named according to the solvent used, e.g. spirit varnish, where the solvent is alcohol, acetone, etc.; turpentine varnish; and oil varnish, where drying oils such as linseed, poppyseed, etc., are used. They are also named from the gum used, such as amber varnish, lac varnish, copal varnish, etc. The resins commonly used for spirit varnishes are shellac, produced by the lac, a scale insect of the Orient; mastic, from a small evergreen tree of the Mediterranean region; sandarach, the resin of the tear tree of North Africa and Australia; and dammar, the product of several coniferous trees of the Molucca Islands. For other varnishes amber and copal, resinous fossil substances, are used. (*See* Gums; Lacquer; Paints).

Vasco da Gama (1460? - 1524).

In their efforts to find a new route to the East Indies the Portuguese spent more than 60 years, slowly but steadily sailing farther and farther south down the west coast of Africa. The Cape of Good Hope was reached by Bartholomew Diaz (d. 1500) in 1488, but for nearly 10 years nothing further was achieved, and in the meantime . Portugal's neighbour Spain entered the race for a route to the East by sending out Christopher Columbus. Spain had, it seemed, already won the contest when Vasco da Gama (pron. gah′ma) sailed from Lisbon in July 1497 in a final attempt to reach India by the route round Africa. The son of a noble family, he had first gone to sea as a lad, and he was selected for the command of the fleet of four small vessels—not unlike those of Columbus—because he was " a discreet man, of good understanding, and with great courage for

VASCO DA GAMA

The route to the East round the Cape of Good Hope was found by the Portuguese navigator Vasco da Gama during his voyage to India, 1497–'99.

any great deed." After reaching Cape Verde on the west coast of Africa Gama steered for the Cape of Good Hope, called by his men the Cape of Storms. It required all his resolution to persuade his crews to continue the voyage after they had passed that point. On the east coast of Africa Gama met Indian traders, who gave him a pilot for the rest of the voyage. In May 1498 he landed at Calicut on the west coast of India. His reception by the ruler of the city was unfriendly, and, after seeing enough to convince himself of the wealth of the country, he returned home.

When the few survivors—55 out of about 170—arrived in Lisbon in September 1499 they were given a splendid reception. Vasco da Gama was granted the coveted title *Dom* (approximating to a British knighthood), and his pension and facilities for trade with the Indies made him one of the richest men in the kingdom.

In February 1502 Dom Vasco da Gama set sail a second time for India, and returned in September 1503 with gold from the East. In spite of the part he had played in gaining a foothold for Portugal in the Orient it was not until 1524, when he was more than 60 years old, that he was appointed governor or viceroy of India. He began energetically to reform abuses in the government, but soon after taking office he died at Cochin in south-west India, on December 24, 1524.

Vatican, CITY AND STATE.

Almost continuously throughout hundreds of years His Holiness the Pope, Holy Father of the Roman Catholic

E.N.I.T.

THE CITY OF THE VATICAN IN THE MIDDLE OF ROME

In 1929 the Italian Government recognized the independent sovereignty of the Pope in the Vatican City, which has an area of 108 acres and about 1,000 inhabitants. Amongst other buildings it includes the huge palace of the Vatican, St. Peter's Cathedral, of which the massive dome is seen above, the Vatican Museum and Library, and the Governor's Palace (centre). The city has its own railway station, postal service, coinage, newspaper and wireless station.

Church, was the ruler of territory in central Italy stretching from the Tyrrhenian Sea to the Adriatic Sea. In 1870 the Papal States, as the territory was called, were incorporated in the newly-founded Kingdom of Italy. Bad feeling between Church and State was the result, and the Popes made a resolve never to leave the walls of their palace, the Vatican.

In 1929 the Italian Government, however, recognized the full and independent sovereignty of the Pope over the Vatican and some adjacent territory, and signed three treaties, under the terms of which the Pope's political and spiritual spheres of influence were recognized and compensation was paid for the loss of the Papal possessions in 1870.

The Vatican, the city of the Holy See, lies in Rome on the west bank of the Tiber and covers 108 acres. It includes not only the huge palace of the Vatican but also St. Peter's Cathedral, St. Peter's Square (*Piazza di San Pietro*), the Sistine Chapel, decorated by Michelangelo and other eminent Italian artists, and the wonderful Vatican Library and art collections. It has its own railway station, postal service, coinage, newspaper, and wireless station; its population is just over 1,000. (*See also* Papacy; Rome).

Velazquez, Diego Rodriguez de Silva y (1599–1660).

Spain's most notable painter and one of the supreme artists of all time. Velazquez (pron. ve-las'-kez; Spanish, vā-lahth'-keth) was born in Seville, on June 6, 1599, the son of a lawyer. In his early teens the boy, already well educated, began to study art under noted painters.

In 1623 Velazquez went to Madrid, where his work attracted the attention of King Philip IV, whose portrait he painted the same year. The artist made two visits to Italy—the first one in 1629, when he especially studied the works of Tintoretto, Raphael, and Michelangelo; and the second in 1649, when he bought a number of the paintings of Titian, Tintoretto, and Veronese and 300 pieces of statuary for the Royal Gallery of Spain. Except for these journeys his life was spent at Madrid as Court painter, for Philip, of whom he painted a series of portraits, had become his friend and patron.

The works of Velazquez include landscapes, mythological and religious subjects, and scenes from common, everyday life (*genre*); but most of them are magnificent portraits of royalty and Court

Anderson

VELAZQUEZ PAINTED BY HIMSELF
Appointed Court painter to Philip IV of Spain at the age of 24, Velazquez, Spain's most distinguished artist, was unsurpassed in the ability to recognize the essential details of a subject and to place them on canvas with a few sure strokes, as he has done in this self-portrait. He was an impressionist in the general meaning of the word, for he painted exactly what he saw at a given moment.

notables. Duties connected with the Court occupied much of his time, and these provided him with opportunities for studying its notabilities. In 1660 Velazquez had charge of his last and most important ceremony—the wedding of the Infanta Maria Theresa with Louis XIV of France. Worn out with his labours, the artist contracted a fever from which he died on August 6, 1660.

Velazquez was above all else a realist. Truth was his ruling passion, and no painter has surpassed him in the ability to seize the essential facts and place them on canvas with a few broad, sure strokes. By reason of his consummate craftsmanship he is called " the Painter's Painter," while his treatment of light and colour led him to be hailed by the French Impressionists of the 19th century as their forerunner. In the National Gallery, London, are several of his works, notably the Venus and Cupid. (*See* illustration page 3045).

Venezuela. (Pron. ven-e-zwē'-la). The geographical position of Venezuela, at the north of the continent of South America, and its rich oilfields combine to give the country considerable commercial advantages. It has 800 miles of coast on the Caribbean Sea and Atlantic Ocean, the gateway to the Panama Canal, and possesses several good harbours. Besides oil, it has other valuable natural resources which have only begun to be developed. Lying just north of the Equator, Venezuela, which has an area of 352,143 square miles, is a land of dense tropical forests, low grassy plains and mountains, and on the coast and in the interior lowlands it is intensely hot, except where moderated by trade winds.

Grassy llanos or plains, which cover more than one-fourth of the total area, extend along the River Orinoco almost from its delta to the Andes in the north-east. In the east and south are the Guiana highlands, comprising nearly half of the total area—forest-covered plateaux, broken by chains of mountains and hills and inhabited solely by scattered tribes of Indians. The remaining fourth consists of the mountain districts of the north and the west. The Sierra Nevada de Mérida, a branch of the Andes, extends north-east

---

Extent.—Estimated area 352,143 square miles. Population 3,851,000.

Physical Features.—Main chain of the Andes, with an eastward extension along the Caribbean. River Orinoco and vast basin. Lake Maracaibo.

Principal Products.—Coffee, cacao (cocoa beans), wheat, maize, cotton, beans, sugar-cane, tobacco; live-stock; rubber, gums; petroleum, asphalt, gold, silver, copper and coal.

Chief Cities.—Carácas (capital, 269,000), Maracaibo (112,500), Nirgua, Valencia.

---

from Colombia into Venezuela and continues as the Maritime Andes or Caribbean Hills.

In the north-west corner of the country, between the Sierra de Mérida and the northern coast, is the Lake Maracaibo basin, one of the richest parts of the republic. Several short rivers and streams from the mountains empty into this shallow lake, which is the centre of one of the world's most productive oil regions. Thriving towns have sprung up on its shores, taking the place of the Indian fishing villages, built on piles, which gave the country its name, for the literal meaning of Venezuela is "Little Venice."

The Orinoco river, 1,600 miles long, and its numerous tributaries, drain four-fifths of Venezuela. It is the third greatest river system in South America, being surpassed only by the Amazon and the La Plata. Through a fan-shaped delta of about 50 mouths the Orinoco empties into the Atlantic. In flood time the tributaries flowing through the llanos overflow and drown thousands of cattle; while in dry seasons the rivers often disappear, so that vegetation withers and cattle perish of thirst. It is thought that with proper storage of water the llanos would rival the plains of Argentina as a cattle-raising region.

CARÁCAS : HIGH-PERCHED CAPITAL OF VENEZUELA

Although it is only six miles from the sea, the approach to Carácas is so steep that the valley in which it lies is 3,000 feet above sea level. One of the oldest American cities, it was founded by the Spaniards in 1560–67 under the name of Santiago de Leon de Carácas. But it contains few old buildings, because it was almost completely destroyed by an earthquake in 1812, when 12,000 people were killed. A beautiful city, it was the birthplace of Simon Bolivar, the liberator of Venezuela and other South American republics from Spanish rule; his house is preserved as a museum

Coffee is the chief export crop; other agricultural products are cacao (cocoa beans), sugar-cane, cotton, maize, beans, tobacco, and wheat. Rubber and other valuable trees are found in the forests. Since the 1920s oil has been the republic's main source of wealth; other minerals include gold, silver, iron, coal, copper and asphalt. Poor communications have hindered the development of mining and agriculture. There are fewer than 700 miles of railway, and some 6,000 miles of good roads. The Orinoco system affords about 6,500 miles of navigable waterways. An air service operates to and from the United States.

The capital and largest city is Carácas (population 269,000), situated in a valley of the Maritime Andes, 3,000 feet above sea level, and connected by railway with its port of La Guaira. Its climate, described as that of perpetual spring, is free alike from the cold of the Andean heights and the sweltering heat of the tropic lowlands. Maracaibo, on the shores of Lake Maracaibo, is the chief port. Other centres are Nirgua and Valencia. Venezuela is believed to have a larger proportion of *mestizos*, of mixed, white, Negro and Indian descent, than any other South American country. Whites comprise only about 10 per cent of the whole population; the mestizos are estimated at 70 per cent. The rest are Indians or Negroes. Though elementary education is compulsory, comparatively few people can read and write. Spanish is the official language. The State religion is Roman Catholic. The country is a Federal Republic, each of

VENEZUELA'S MILE-HIGH WATERFALL
In 1937 an American airman, who crashed in the remote Caroni region of eastern Venezuela, discovered this waterfall. It is estimated to be a mile high, which would make it the highest known. The waters of the Niagara Falls make a leap of only 175 feet, but have a larger volume.

VENEZUELA ON THE CARIBBEAN SEA
From the Merida Mountains of western Venezuela the land slopes to the plains of the Orinoco basin and then rises in the south-east.

the States being self-governing. But the Constitution of 1947 introduced a number of changes. Amongst other provisions, it gave Congress wide powers in the development of the national economy; granted pensions, paid holidays and the right to strike to the working classes; and empowered the President to arrest anyone suspected of plotting against the Government.

The history of Venezuela begins in 1498 when its coast was first sighted by Christopher Columbus. Spanish settlements were established early in the 16th century, and the country remained under Spanish rule for three centuries. A republic was declared in 1811; but the rebellion was soon crushed, and it was not until 1823 that Spanish domination came to an end. For a few years Venezuela was part of the Republic of Colombia, but in 1830 it became an independent State. From 1870 to 1935 the country was ruled by Dictators, a fact that did much to impede development of its natural resources. In 1936 constitutional rule was established. Venezuela was neutral in the Second World War until February 16, 1945, when she declared war on Germany and Japan. The population is 3,851,000.

The Lovely 'MISTRESS of the ADRIATIC'

One of the most beautiful and remarkable cities in the world, Venice abounds in historical interest, for it differs little, even today, from what it was at the height of its glory and power.

Venice. When the hordes of barbarian invaders swept over Italy in the 5th century, a number of the inhabitants along the north-western coast of the Adriatic Sea sought refuge on the low mud islands some miles off the shore between the mouths of the Rivers Piave and Adige. There they laid the foundations of Venice, whose rulers from the 12th to 18th centuries each year threw a ring into the Adriatic (called the wedding of the sea), in token of their claim to dominion over that sea. Hence, Venice became known as the " Mistress of the Adriatic."

No roar of traffic disturbs the quiet of the city, which is broken only by the sound of water lapping at the foundations of ancient palaces or the songs and cries of the gondoliers steering their black craft through the city's canals. Almost the sole intrusion of the noise of the outer world is the distant whistle of trains as they cross the bridge, two and a half miles long, from the mainland, or the chug of a motor-boat.

Venice (Italian *Venezia*) is built on wooden piles driven into the mud of the Venetian Lagoon, and on numerous islands. There are some 150 canals, crossed by nearly 400 bridges. Two of these bridges are world-famous—the Rialto and the " Bridge of Sighs." The former, which is mentioned in Shakespeare's Merchant of Venice, crosses the Grand Canal and is lined with shops. The Bridge of Sighs, which is referred to in Byron's poem Childe Harold, leads from the upper storey

of the Doge's (doge, or duke, was the title of the rulers of Venice) Palace to the state prison. Over it many political prisoners of the Venetian Republic passed to torture and death—hence its name.

There are many churches and old palaces, each a delight to the artist and architect. In some respects the city is more Greek than Italian in architecture, the result of its long connexion with the Byzantine Empire. Its libraries contain numerous rare manuscripts, including the early records of the city. There are almost no large factories to mar its beauty ; the glassware, for which it has been famed since the Middle Ages, is made on Murano Island.

The harbour is separated from the sea by a long sand-bank called the Lido, which is protected from the waves by a sea-wall and has become a fashionable bathing beach. Connecting Venice to the mainland is a railway bridge and a fine modern roadway, the Littorio Bridge, opened in 1933. From the railway station the Grand Canal winds its way to the Doge's Palace on the Piazza of St. Mark. This palace, where the rulers of Venice formerly held their court, was begun in 1301 and took two centuries to complete. The result is a magnificent example of Italian architecture.

Overshadowing all else on the piazza is the Cathedral of St. Mark (San Marco), the patron saint of the city, just north of the Doge's Palace. No other building can be compared to it for amazing architectural design, ornamentation and wealth of colour. In general it is Byzantine in style, with its five Oriental domes, and resembles the former church (now a museum) of Santa Sophia at Istanbul, Turkey. Near St. Mark's is the bell-tower or campanile, built in the style of the original one, which collapsed in 1902. Over the main entrance stand four bronze horses, which once ornamented Nero's arch in Rome. Carried to Constantinople by Constantine (A.D 288–337), they were brought to Venice in 1204, removed by Napoleon, and restored to Venice after his final defeat. (*See* illus., page 1773).

For centuries Venice was considered part of the Byzantine or Eastern Roman Empire, but in reality she early became a self-governing republic, under her own doge.

During the Crusades Venice developed an extensive trade in spices, perfumes, sugar, silks and other goods coming from the Orient, and for

WHERE THE MERCHANTS OF VENICE TRADED
Mentioned by Shakespeare in his play The Merchant of Venice, the Rialto bridge crosses the Grand Canal in what was formerly the business quarter of Venice. It has a single marble arch with a span of 90 feet, and was built in 1588–92. In the right foreground are mooring-posts for gondolas and motor-launches.

WHERE VENETIAN HISTORY IS WRIT IN STONE

Dr. Gebhard Rossmanith; Donald McLeish

Connecting the judgement halls of the Doge's palace with the State prison is the so-called Bridge of Sighs (top left) completed in 1605 and over which many a prisoner of the Venetian Republic passed to torture and death—hence its name. The heart of Venice is the Piazza of St. Mark (lower, foreground) on which is the Cathedral of St. Mark (background). Formerly the private chapel of the Doges, it is Byzantine in style and unique in richness of material and decoration, for by law every Venetian merchant trading with the East had to bring back something with which to adorn the church. Right, the bell-tower or campanile, built in the style of the original one that collapsed in 1902.

several centuries Venice and Genoa controlled the sea routes of the eastern Mediterranean.

By the persuasion of the Venetians, under their blind doge Dandolo, the Fourth Crusade was directed against Constantinople instead of against the Holy Land. Its fall in 1204 gave the Crusaders rich loot, and Venice received as her share the Greek islands in the Aegean and Ionian Seas, a portion of Constantinople, and land commanding the entrance to the Black Sea.

A series of wars with Genoa over trade rights ended in 1380, when the Venetians trapped the Genoese fleet inside the Chioggia lagoons, south of the city, and compelled it to surrender. This victory made Venice the supreme naval power in the Mediterranean. Conquests on the Italian mainland followed, which extended Venetian territory to the north and west.

The city of the doges was now at the height of her power, but a decline speedily set in. First the Turks, who had captured Constantinople in 1453, began to strip Venice little by little of her Greek possessions. In 1488 the discovery by the Portuguese navigator Vasco da Gama of the sea route to the East Indies round the Cape of Good Hope destroyed the value of the Mediterranean routes, and brought the riches of the Orient to the Portuguese, the Dutch and the British. Eventually the European Powers banded together in the League of Cambrai and wrested from Venice almost all her territory on the mainland of Italy (1508). During this period, however, Venice reached her highest point of artistic development, and her artists, headed by Titian (q.v.), founded the Venetian school of painting.

The last doge abdicated in 1797, when the republic was conquered by Napoleon Bonaparte. After Napoleon's defeat in 1815 Venice passed into the possession of Austria. She took a leading part in the unsuccessful revolution of 1848 against Austrian rule in Italy, and was finally given up by Austria to the new kingdom of Italy in 1866.

The city's treasures escaped almost uninjured in the Second World War (1939–45). British troops entered Venice on April 29, 1945. The population is 303,000.

Venturi. In several of the stories of scientific mechanisms throughout these volumes you will find a reference to a "venturi tube," and in pursuing physics further you are sure to come across other references to this narrowing of a tube, with wider portions at either side. The principle is explained in page 2154, with a diagram. Imagine a subway which is parallel for some distance; then it slopes in until it is narrower, after which the passage slopes out wider until it is its original size again.

A throng of people is walking steadily at the wider part of the subway; the flow of people through the entire passage *must remain the same*, despite the narrowing at the " venturi throat." So when they come to the throat they must step out more quickly, though they can slow down to the original pace once they have passed the " bottle-neck," as we call such a narrowing of a traffic lane.

In dealing with the passage of fluids under pressure through a venturi we must remember that when they *gain* velocity in traversing the narrowed converging part, they *lose* pressure. When later on they come to the diverging part (where the tube widens again) the state of affairs is reversed, and they gain *pressure* and lose *velocity*. Our analogy of a crowd in a subway cannot, of course, help us in this: under pressure they would be killed at the narrow part of the tube!

Venus. Originally a goddess of gardens, the Roman goddess Venus became identified later with Aphrodite (q.v.), the Greek goddess of love. She was represented as the highest ideal of feminine

E.N.I.T.

VENICE'S MAIN WATERWAY: THE GRAND CANAL

Life in Venice, which is situated at the head of the Adriatic, centres about the Grand Canal, lined with palaces once owned by the city's most noted and wealthiest families. The waterway winds in the shape of an enormous S and divides the town into two almost equal parts. Above, the buildings and boats are decorated for a regatta. Venice is built on wooden piles driven into the mud of a lagoon and on numerous islands; the 'thoroughfares' are mostly canals, of which there are about 150. It is connected to the mainland by a railway viaduct, two and a half miles long.

HOW VENUS'S FLY-TRAP CATCHES ITS PREY
A fly (left) approaches the reddish-tinged leaf-tip, alights on the surface—and the lobes close up (centre) around it. The spines along the edges interlock (right), and the fly can find no way out. A fluid from the leaf-glands dissolves the victim's tissues, and when the leaf has digested its meal the lobes open, and the plant is ready for the next comer.

beauty. The goddess was especially honoured at Rome, as Romulus, the legendary founder of the city, was believed to have been descended from her son, the hero Aeneas (*q.v.*).

The planet Venus, which often shines so spectacularly in the early morning twilight and also in the dusk, is named after the goddess. It is the second planet in order of distance from the sun, being nearly twice as far from the sun as Mercury. Both the mass and diameter of Venus are only slightly less than those of the earth. Owing to difficulty in observing any markings on the planet, it has been very hard to find out how long it takes to turn on its axis, if indeed it does rotate at all. Ultra-violet photographs taken of the planet seem to show that it is surrounded by dense clouds. Like the moon and Mercury, Venus has phases, being at times a thin crescent, at others a perfect disk. So brilliant is the planet at certain times that it will cast a shadow on moonless nights. (*See* Astronomy; Planets).

Venus's Fly-trap.
Of Nature's strange insect-eating plants, the Venus's fly-trap (*Dionaea muscipula*) is perhaps the most remarkable. At the end of each leaf it carries a pair of jaws that catch the insects on which it dines.

A small plant, found only in moist sandy areas of North and South Carolina, in the United States, it bears white flowers on a central stalk and spreads its long hungry leaves over the ground like a rosette. Each leaf ends in two lobes that are hinged at the midrib and edged with spines. On the surface of each lobe three highly sensitive jointed hairs are set up in triangles. Crimson glands give the lobes a reddish tinge to attract insects. If grown in shade, however, the glands are green.

The moment an insect alights and touches one of the irritable hairs the lobes close up around it and the spines along the edges interlock to hold the captive fast. The glands then secrete an acid digestive fluid that dissolves the victim's tissues. From them the plant absorbs the nitrogenous matter which is lacking in the swampy soil where it grows. Then the lobes open up and the un-digested portions drop out. It takes several days to digest one insect, and a leaf rarely enjoys more than two or three meals in its lifetime. (*See* illustrations facing page 2621, and illustration in page 2624; *also* Sundew).

Vera Cruz.
(Pron. vār-*a* krōōz.) The principal port of Mexico, Vera Cruz is situated on the Gulf of Mexico to the east of the capital, Mexico City. The Spaniards named it *La Villa Rica de la Vera Cruz*—" The Rich Town of the True Cross "—but it was long known as the " City of the Dead," because of the prevalence of yellow fever and malaria. Now the draining of swamps in which the disease-carrying mosquitoes bred has made it a healthy city.

The harbour is spacious and well-protected, and the bulk of the sea-borne trade of the country passes through it. Coffee, sugar and rubber are the leading exports, and iron and steel goods are the principal imports. Cigars and furniture are manufactured. Four railways and a motor road give access to the interior of Mexico. The population of Vera Cruz is 76,000.

Verb.
As the noun is the important element of the subject of a sentence, so the verb is the important element of the predicate (*see* Sentence). The noun names the thing or person referred to; the verb asserts or predicates something about the subject. The verb is the most vigorous and vital part of the sentence, and the early grammarians called it *verbum*, which is Latin for " word." It is *the* word, without which no grouping of the other parts of speech would make a sentence. *Dogs* and *fast* by themselves tell us nothing. Put in the verb *run*, and you get a complete statement.

There is one very important verb that merely expresses existence and links the subject with the rest of the predicate. This is the verb *be*. Consider the sentence " The orange *is* yellow." Here *is* merely links the subject with the predicate adjective *yellow*. For this reason *be* and other verbs which perform a similar duty, like *become*, *seem* and *remain*, are called *copulative* or *linking* verbs.

A verb that expresses an act involving something besides the actor is said to be *transitive*. One that does not express an act involving something besides the actor is called an *intransitive* verb. In the sentence " She *stood* still," the verb *stood* expresses the act of standing, which does not involve anything besides the actor, the girl, and is therefore intransitive. In the sentence, " She *tore* the letter," the verb *tore* expresses an action which involves the letter as well as the actor, the girl, and is transitive. The word or group of words which denote the other things involved in the act besides the actor is called the *object*. In the sentence, " She tore the letter," the word *letter* is the *object*.

By various changes in form, and by the help of certain other *auxiliary* (" helping ") ones, verbs are able to convey a number of ideas in addition to their own meaning. For example, the form *am* tells us that the speaker is talking about himself ; *buys* tells us that the subject is in the third person (for persons, *see* Pronouns) ; *will go* tells us that the action is to take place in the future ; *jumped* tells us that the action has already taken place. Such changes or *inflexions* in the form of verbs are called *conjugation*, and to conjugate a verb is to name in order all its forms.

The various ideas which may be expressed by merely changing the form of a verb or using an auxiliary with it are five: person, number, tense, mood, and voice. By *person*, it tells us whether the subject is speaking, spoken to, or spoken of. By *number*, it tells us whether the subject represents one or more. *Tense* tells us the time of the action. *Mood* is the manner of assertion, that is, whether the action is asserted as an actual fact, as doubtful, as desired, or as commanded, etc. *Voice* denotes whether the subject is acting or is acted upon.

A verb is said to agree in person and number with its subject. In most English verbs there is only one change in form made to show change in person and number, namely, the addition of *s* to the root or simplest form of the verb to make the third person singular of the present indicative. Examples are *take, takes ; find, finds*. The verb *to be* is the only one that makes more than this change to show person and number. Its present tense is as follows:

	SINGULAR	PLURAL
First person:	*I am*	*We are*
Second person:	*You are*	*You are*
Third person:	*He, she,* or *it is*	*They are*

In the past tense this verb has two forms: *was*, singular, and *were*, plural. But *you were* is used for both singular and plural.

In English the verb has six tenses: *present*, denoting action going on in the present (I *write* or *am writing*) ; *past*, denoting action in the past (I *wrote* or *was writing*) ; *future*, denoting action that is going to take place (I *shall go*) ; *present perfect*, denoting action completed just before the present (I *have spoken*) ; *past perfect* or *pluperfect*, denoting action completed in the past (I *had gone*) ; *future perfect*, denoting action that will have been completed at some future time (I *shall have gone*).

To show the attitude of the speaker towards his assertion there are three moods. The *indicative* mood is used to state something as a fact; the *imperative* is used to express a command or an entreaty; the *subjunctive* is used to express something

as wished, possible, or merely thought of. In English the indicative, imperative, and subjunctive forms are for the most part alike. The subjunctive mood omits the ending *s*, " Long *live* the king ! " The verb *to be*, however, has the subjunctive form *be* for all persons and numbers in the present tense, and the form *were* for all persons and numbers in the past tense. Familiar examples are: " if it *be* I " and " if I *were* you." The subjunctive mood is little used in spoken English today. Instead, we commonly use phrases formed with certain auxiliary verbs, e.g. " if it *should rain*."

A verb that represents its subject as acting is said to be in the active voice, as " I *tore* the letter." One that represents its subject as being acted upon is said to be in the passive voice, as " The letter *was torn*." The passive forms are made by combining the six tenses of the verb *to be* with the past participle of the verb conjugated.

There are two other forms of the verb—the *infinitive* and the *participle*. They both may take an object, and the infinitive may take a subject as well, but they resemble nouns, adjectives, and adverbs, in that they cannot of themselves form a predicate. In general, they are equivalent to condensed clauses and may be used like clauses, with the functions of an adjective, an adverb, or a noun. For example: *To err* is human (infinitive used as a noun) ; He came to *see* me (infinitive used as an adverb) ; *Seeing* is *believing* (participle used as a noun) ; *Fearing* detection, he fled (participle used as an adverb) ; the *blushing* rose (participle used as an adjective). Both infinitives and participles have voice and tense, but neither person nor number. The participle occurs in the present, past, and perfect tenses; the infinitive in only the present and perfect.

A verb that forms its past tense and past participle by the addition of *ed*, *d*, or *t* is called a *regular* verb or a verb of the regular conjugation. This conjugation includes by far the greater number of English verbs. Examples are: *lay, laid, laid ; keep, kept, kept ; walk, walked, walked*. To the regular conjugation also belong all verbs whose forms are alike throughout, as *set, set, set*. Verbs that do not add a *d* or *t* sound to form the past tense and past participle are generally irregular, as *see, saw, seen ; do, did, done ; fight, fought, fought*. Strong verbs generally change the root vowel in the past tense, but many weak verbs also change. The verb *to be* is irregular, formed from three different roots ; its forms are *be, am, is, are, was, were, being, been*. A few verbs used as auxiliaries are defective, which means that they are used in only one or two forms, as *ought, must, will*.

Some of the commonest errors in the use of verbs are illustrated in the following sentences:

Lack of agreement between subject and verb—" We *was* there " instead of " We *were* there."

Misuse of the present for the past—" I *come* here a year ago " for " I *came* here a year ago."

Confusion between the participle and the past tense—" I *seen* it " for " I *saw* it "; " I was *took* " for " I was *taken* "; " I have *wrote* " for " I have *written*."

Incorrect formation of tense—" I *knowed* the lesson " for " I *knew* the lesson."

Confusion between verbs similar in meaning—" We *laid* down on the beach " for " We *lay* down on the beach "; " *Lay* down, Fido ! " for " *Lie* down ! "

Verdi, GIUSEPPE (1813–1901). A popular operatic melody is the Anvil Chorus from the opera Il Trovatore. Verdi (pron. ver′-dē), who composed this and numerous other splendid tunes,

VERDI AT THE PIANO

Composer of popular operas, the Italian Giuseppe Verdi studied music at Milan and his first work appeared in 1839. Rigoletto, Il Trovatore and La Traviata brought him world-wide fame, but greater works are Aïda, Otello and Falstaff—his last opera, composed when he was 80.

was born at Roncole, near Parma, Italy, on October 9, 1813, and received his first lessons in music from the village organist, whose place young Verdi took at the age of 10. He attended school at Busseto and was given a grant by that town to study music in Milan, where he went to live in 1838.

His first opera, Oberto, appeared in 1839, and was followed three years later by Nebucco. With the production of I Lombardi in 1843, Verdi's reputation as the leading Italian composer was established, and his fame became world-wide with the appearance of Rigoletto (1851), and Il Trovatore and La Traviata, both in 1852. In Aïda (1871) he wrote both musically and dramatically a masterpiece, which some critics consider his best work. Others place even higher his two works on Shakespearean themes: Otello (1887) and Falstaff (1893). With this last, his sole attempt at comedy, Verdi closed his active career as the most popular Italian operatic composer of the 19th century. Of

his sacred music the Manzoni Requiem (1874) and Stabat Mater express considerable imaginative power. He died at Milan on January 27, 1901.

Vermeer, JAN (1632–75). Acknowledged during his lifetime as one of his country's finest painters, Vermeer (pron. ver-mār′) was completely forgotten within a few years of his death. It was not until the middle of the 19th century that his paintings were once again fully appreciated. He was born at Delft, in the Netherlands, and christened on October 13, 1632.

He is believed to have been employed in one of the china factories in Delft, and it is clear that he showed remarkable ability as a painter at an early age, for in the records of the guild of which he was a member his name is entered as a master-painter in the year 1653.

Vermeer worked slowly and deliberately and produced few pictures. He made little money and sometimes was compelled to pay tradespeople with his paintings. He produced chiefly portraits and interiors of houses in Delft. The beauty of his work lies in his treatment of light, his warm colours, perfect design and restrained sense of balance. Each one is in itself a little masterpiece. Among the best-known are: Head of a Girl, View of Delft, Lady at the Virginals, The Music Lesson, Girl with Pearl Necklace, and The Artist in his Studio. Only 41 of his paintings are believed to be in existence. He died at Delft on December 13, 1675.

Vermont. An inland State in the north-east of the United States, with an area of 9,609 square miles, Vermont is bounded on the north by Canada; the Connecticut river separates it from New Hampshire to the east; Massachusetts lies to the south; and Lake Champlain forms more than half of the western boundary with New York State. The Connecticut is the only river of importance. The Green Mountains extend throughout the State

W. F. Mansell

VIEW OF DELFT BY JAN VERMEER

During his lifetime the Dutch artist Jan Vermeer (1632–75) of Delft was recognized by critics as one of the finest painters of his day. His View of Delft bathed in late afternoon sunshine is matchless in its crystalline purity of light and in the beauty of its soft-toned colours. (See also illustration in page 2325.)

from north to south and contain several peaks over 3,500 feet high.

Though much of Vermont is rocky and unproductive, the land in the vicinity of Lake Champlain is very fertile. Hay, potatoes and fruit are the leading crops; dairy farming is of considerable importance; and the State is noted for its maple sugar and syrup. Marble and granite are quarried in the Green Mountains; other mineral products include slate, asbestos, talc and china clay. The main manufactures are machinery, textiles and paper. The capital is Montpelier (8,000). Other towns are Burlington (28,000), Rutland (17,000) and Barre (11,000).

. The first English settlements were established about 1700, and for some time possession of the region was disputed between New Hampshire and New York. Vermont was declared an independent State in 1777, and remained so until it joined the 13 original States of the Union in 1791. The population is 359,000.

Verne, JULES (1828–1905). Vast numbers of grown-ups as well as boys and girls have been entranced by the stories written by this French author.

JULES VERNE
Creator and successful exponent of scientific romance, the French author Jules Verne had most of his works translated into English.

Twenty Thousand Leagues under the Sea, From the Earth to the Moon, Five Weeks in a Balloon, Around the World in Eighty Days, The Mysterious Island—the very titles thrill.

All Jules Verne's stories are based on scientific knowledge, carried usually to lengths of achievement that seemed impossible at the date they were written. But it is astonishing how often his wildest fancies have in a measure come true. The Nautilus (in his book Twenty Thousand Leagues Under the Sea), for instance, is an anticipation of the modern submarine, which, although it cannot travel so long or so deep under water and cannot ram enemy ships—as Captain Nemo loved to do —can at any rate stay beneath the surface for a good long time and at a considerable depth.

Born at Nantes, Jules Verne published a play when he was 22. He soon found his true vein, and from 1862 (when Five Weeks in a Balloon was published) until his death he poured forth stories that have made his name famous the world over. Most of his books have been translated into English. A condensation of his Twenty Thousand Leagues Under the Sea follows.

TWENTY THOUSAND LEAGUES UNDER THE SEA

IN the summer of the year 1867 the American frigate Abraham Lincoln was steaming in the Pacific, hunting, on behalf of the whole civilized world, for a monster that had terrified all who sailed there. What this monster was no one knew, but the general opinion inclined to the view that it was a gigantic narwhal—a vast, cigar-shaped creature; at any rate, it was the enemy of shipping in all the Seven Seas. Among those on board the Abraham Lincoln were Professor Aronnax, of the Paris Museum, an expert on marine life; his servant, a Dutchman named Conseil; and Ned Land, a Canadian, generally admitted to be the greatest of living harpooners.

After thousands of miles of travel, the Abraham Lincoln, having chased the monster at nearly 20 knots without catching it, was as last approaching it as it lay apparently asleep on the surface of the ocean. Shells from a powerful gun had failed to make any impression on it, and now came the moment when Ned Land was hurling his harpoon at it from close quarters. The harpoon hit it—and rebounded with a clang ! The monster spouted water at the ship, and in another moment the professor, Conseil, and Land were in the sea.

But they were not lost, for they soon found themselves clinging to the hull of the monster itself— its hull, and not its skin, for it was covered with steel plates ! For the rest of the night the unfortunate three were dragged through the water at great speed; then, as daylight came, the monster slowed down; a door opened, figures appeared, and the three were seized and dragged inside the hull.

Inspection of their prison showed the men that they were inside a steel chamber, roughly furnished and lighted by electricity. Two men came in and inspected them; they were brought strange food. They spoke to one of the men, explaining who they were in as many languages as they could, but without obtaining any reply; then, dead tired, they went to sleep. When they awoke, their chief captor reappeared. Land and Conseil he sent away, but M. Aronnax he entertained as his own guest. To him he explained the situation. They were his prisoners, in the marvellous electric submarine, the Nautilus, of his own creation. He called himself Captain Nemo (nemo in Latin means " no one "), and he was the sworn enemy of all civilized mankind. So long as they were in his ship they were free and could do as they pleased, except that when he ordered them, as might happen sometimes, to their own rooms, they must promise to obey.

To all this they had perforce, to agree. Although Land found it irksome and was continually giving way to his natural temper, the professor in particular was soon enchanted with his new life. For Captain Nemo, who confessed to having been a man of immense riches in his former life—as he always considered it—had furnished the interior of the Nautilus in the most sumptuous manner. A magnificent museum of art and science and a library of 12,000 volumes were collected there and at the disposal of the prisoners.

And as they sailed round the seas of the world, all the mysteries of the deep were unfolded before them. From behind the Nautilus's windows, as well as on their excursions in diving suits, they saw fishes and corals and squids, and the forests and pastures of the submarine world. They fought a duel with a giant shark; they saw pearls without price, and they fed on the rare delicacies of the Oriental seas. They visited the South Pole, and they found the lost continent of Atlantis. Only once did Captain Nemo remind them of their one promise; and the day after they had been thus shut in, he buried one of his crew in his submarine cemetery. One other sailor was lost in a fight with giant squids, and on each occasion Captain Nemo was moved by profound sorrow.

All this time Ned Land was planning escape. The idea was to take to the small steel boat which was fitted flush with the Nautilus's hull on the top deck. In this they would escape when within reach of civilized land.

The Nautilus was driven northwards, until Captain Nemo found the wreck of a French Republican ship, the Vengeur, and there, the next day, he attacked and sank a man-of-war that had fired at the Nautilus as it lay on the surface. He sank it by driving straight through its hull; and then, suddenly, the Nautilus was whirled northwards, as fast as she could travel. The prisoners had provisioned the boat, had prepared their escape; and when the time came they let themselves out into the boat, clad in their diving suits.

But the prisoners' plan never came to fruition; for the Nautilus was caught in the Maelstrom, the dread whirlpool off the Norwegian coast, and even as they prepared to free their boat it was torn off in the whirlpool, and they were hurled into the sea. When they recovered the three men found themselves in a hut on the far-off Lofoten Isles. There the Professor set himself to write of that incredible journey of Twenty Thousand Leagues under the Sea.

Versailles. (Pron. văr-sī'). On January 18, 1871, the throne-room of the beautiful palace at Versailles, about 10 miles south-west of Paris, was the scene of an historic ceremony. The Prussians, who had defeated France in the war of 1870–71, were proclaiming there, in the heart of the vanquished nation, that King William of Prussia was henceforth to be emperor of the newly-formed German Empire.

In June 1919 the statesmen of 27 Allied countries sat in this same palace at Versailles. The German Empire had been defeated by the Allies, in the First World War (1914–18), and the Allied representatives were discussing what peace terms should be imposed. There was something singularly appropriate in the choice of the palace at Versailles for this meeting, because it helped to wipe out the memory of France's humiliation in 1871.

The palace of Versailles is one of the most magnificent in the world. In building it Louis XIV (1638–1715) spent money so lavishly that he destroyed the accounts so that his people should never know the extent of his extravagance. It has so many rooms that it takes several hours to walk through them all. The Battle Gallery is lined with paintings of notable French victories.

Near by, Louis XIV built a smaller palace, called the Grand (big) Trianon, and later his great-grandson, Louis XV (1710–74) had a still smaller one, the Petit (little) Trianon, built, in which Marie Antoinette, the wife of Louis XVI (1754–95) lived.

The palace, now a museum, is surrounded by a wonderful park with terraces, beautiful woods, ornamental waters, and numerous fountains.

THE PALACE OF VERSAILLES : SCENE OF AN HISTORIC TREATY
The main block and part of one wing of the huge palace at Versailles, in which the peace treaty between the victorious Allies and Germany was signed in 1919 (after the First World War), are seen above as they appear from the park. Louis XIV built the enormous structure which, begun in 1661, became in 1683 the chief royal residence in France.

Vertebrates.

Animals with backbones, including the most highly developed creatures—fishes, reptiles, birds, and mammals—are called vertebrates. They differ from the invertebrates or " backbone-less " animals in many other ways. The jointed hollow backbone and its upper extension, the bony brain-box or cranium, together form a protecting case for the central nervous system. Typical vertebrates have a head, four limbs, a trunk, and a tail—though snakes have lost all their limbs, whales have lost two, and the higher apes and human beings have lost their tails.

Almost all young vertebrates have " gill-slits," showing racial development from a water-inhabiting ancestry. Fishes and some amphibians breathe through these gill-slits throughout life; but in most amphibians (frogs, for instance) the gill-slits close and disappear during the tadpole stage. In the higher vertebrates the slits disappear before the animals are hatched or born.

Most important of all is the supporting rod in the back. When the animal starts life this rod is just gristle, and is called the notochord. In some primitive forms, such as the amphioxus (lancelet), it never develops further. Sharks and rays may have it sheathed in a cylinder of gristle. In the true vertebrates the notochord develops into a backbone. Some recent schemes of classification group primitive animals having only notochords together with the true vertebrates in the phylum *Chordata.*

Vespucius, AMERICUS (1451–1512).

In a geography book printed in 1507 a German professor, Martin Waldseemüller, wrote: " Another fourth part of the globe has been discovered by Americus Vespucius. So I do not see why anyone should rightly object to calling it ' America,' after its discoverer, Americus." This suggestion resulted in the naming of the New World after a Florentine merchant and navigator, who accompanied several expeditions to South America and wrote about them, instead of after its real discoverer, Christopher Columbus.

Americus Vespucius (or Amerigo Vespucci, as the name is spelt in Italian) was born in Florence, Italy, and was educated in that city. For some years he was employed by a firm of merchant bankers, and in 1492 he set up in business for himself at Seville, Spain. In a letter, printed in 1504, he claimed to have made four voyages to the New World, on the first of which (1497) he explored the South American coast. This would make him the discoverer of the American continent, for at that time Columbus had only reached the outlying islands. He certainly did make several voyages to South America in Spanish and Portuguese ships, and after his last voyage in 1503 he spent much of his time drawing maps and charts of the regions he had visited. He died at Seville, on February 22, 1512.

Vesta.

The hearth in ancient times was the centre of family life. It was the place where meals were prepared and round which the family gathered. The ancient Romans worshipped Vesta as the goddess of the hearth, and the guardian of the family life, and a temple in the Forum was dedicated to her service. Here the ever-burning sacred fire was guarded by priestesses called Vestal Virgins, at first four but afterwards six in number.

These maidens were between six and 10 years old when chosen to serve the goddess, and they spent 30 years in the temple—the first 10 in learning their duties, the second 10 in performing their services as priestesses, and the last 10 in teaching their duties to the 10 newly chosen maidens.

They were bound by vows to remain chaste and pure, and to protect the sacred fire, even in time of danger ; for to allow it to be extinguished would, it was believed, bring disaster upon Rome. If a Vestal violated her vow she was stoned to death or buried alive. On the first of March the sacred fire was renewed. The chief festival in honour of Vesta was celebrated in June.

In much the same way the Greeks worshipped the goddess Hestia, and in her honour a sacred fire was also kept constantly burning.

Vesuvius, MOUNT.

Across the Bay of Naples, Italy, less than 10 miles from the city, stands this volcano, a cloud of steam and ashes

Fox

EVER-ACTIVE CONE OF VESUVIUS
Above the summit of Vesuvius hangs a perpetual cloud of dust and steam, for the volcano never slumbers. In the centre is the active cone, surrounded by a huge crater. During a violent eruption a black column of dust, ashes and rocks is hurled thousands of feet into the air, while streams of molten lava flow down the mountain side.

wreathing its summit, for Vesuvius never slumbers. The dwellers at its foot cast many an anxious glance at its menacing bulk whenever the cloud seems blacker and denser than usual.

Mount Vesuvius is about 30 miles in circumference at the base. The height varies according to the effects of successive eruptions, but it averages 4,000 feet above sea-level. The mountain has two summits; the lower, called Somma, half encircles Vesuvius proper, the present active cone. The crater at the summit is about 2,000 feet across. A cable railway ascends the mountain and an observatory is maintained near the cone, whence warnings are issued if the volcano shows signs of erupting. The region about the volcano has been densely populated for over 20 centuries, despite the fact that there have been several disasters.

An eruption on August 24, A.D. 79, blew off the top of the mountain and destroyed Pompeii and Herculaneum (*see* Pompeii); another in 1631 killed 18,000 people.

One of the most destructive eruptions of modern times took place in April 1906. For a week Vesuvius had been ominously quiet, then masses of red-hot rocks and ashes were shot up to the height of a mile or more. The eruption increased in violence spasmodically. Suddenly heavy explosions tore open the mountain side and made new outlets for the streams of lava which covered the volcano from base to summit in a bright red glow. Terrific explosions followed in rapid succession, and soon portions of the rim were blown away. The crater was considerably widened; and the height of the mountain reduced by 300 yards on the north-east side. Thousands of tons of cinders and small stones descended on the villages below. For a week this deadly shower was almost constant, and caused widespread destruction, with heavy loss of life. An eruption in 1944 increased the height of Vesuvius by about 500 feet.

Victor Emmanuel II, King of Italy (1820–78).
The first monarch of united Italy, Victor Emmanuel, the son of Charles Albert, King of Piedmont-Sardinia, was born at Turin, Italy, on March 14, 1820, and received a strict military and religious training, but little intellectual education. He commanded a brigade during the disastrous war against Austria in 1848–49, and his father abdicated in his favour after he had been defeated by the Austrians at Novara on March 23, 1849. Refusing to be intimidated by the Austrians, the young king maintained the newly-adopted Constitution of his kingdom and appointed the Italian statesman Count Cavour (*q.v.*) to the post of Prime Minister.

VICTOR EMMANUEL II
King of Piedmont-Sardinia from 1849 to 1861, Victor Emmanuel II refused to submit to Austria after the defeat at Novara in 1849 and struggled to create a united kingdom of Italy, of which he became the first sovereign in 1861.

With France, Great Britain and Turkey, Victor Emmanuel participated in the Crimean War (1854–56) against Russia. He gave France the province of Savoy and the town of Nice in order to form an alliance with that country which enabled him to wage war on Austria in 1859 and to liberate Lombardy, which was added to his kingdom. In the following year the petty States of Tuscany Parma and Modena revolted against Austrian rule and united themselves to Piedmont. Garibaldi's (*q.v.*) conquest of Naples and Sicily in 1860 incorporated further territory in Victor Emmanuel's dominion, and on February 26, 1861, he was proclaimed the king of united Italy. The inclusion of Venice in 1866 and Rome in 1870 completed his realm. On July 2, 1871, Victor Emmanuel made his state entry into Rome, which then became the capital of Italy. He died on January 9, 1878.

Victor Emmanuel III (1869–1947), the son of King Humbert I (1844–1900), was born at Naples on November 11, 1869. Entering the Army in 1887, he devoted himself to the study of military science until he succeeded to the throne on the assassination of his father on July 29, 1900. In the First World War (1914–18) Italy fought with France and Great Britain against Austria-Hungary and Germany, and the King took an active part in the direction of the campaign against the Austro-Hungarian and German forces in north-east Italy.

His relations with Benito Mussolini (*q.v.*), the Fascist leader who became Italian Prime Minister in 1922, were at first cool, but he eventually allowed himself to be used as the spokesman and figurehead of the Fascist movement. After the Italian conquest of Abyssinia in 1936, the King was proclaimed Emperor of that country.

Victor Emmanuel III was opposed to Italy's entry into the Second World War (1939–45), but he did nothing to prevent Mussolini declaring war on France and Great Britain in June 1940. Italy signed an armistice with the Allies in September 1943; and on June 4, 1944, the King retired from public life, abdicating in favour of his son (Humbert II) on May 9, 1946. Victor Emmanuel died at Alexandria, Egypt, on December 28, 1947.

Victoria, Queen of Great Britain and Ireland (1819–1901).
The daughter of Edward, Duke of Kent, who was brother of William IV, Queen Victoria was born at Kensington Palace, London, on May 24, 1819. She received a sound education in languages, history, and in the British political system, and at the age of 13 she began a series of tours throughout the country with a view to obtaining knowledge of social and industrial con-

ditions. She proved a very charming girl, simple-hearted, lively, fond of music and dancing.

When she was 18 (in 1837), her uncle, William IV, died and she, as his heir, succeeded to the British throne. Being a woman, she could not also claim the throne of Hanover, which had been occupied by British sovereigns since the accession of George I in 1714, and this passed to the nearest male heir. Of her bearing at her first Privy Council the Duke of Wellington said: "She not only filled the chair, she filled the room." Of her speech dissolving Parliament, an American orator, Charles Sumner, said: "Her voice was sweet and finely modulated. I think I have never heard anything better read in my life."

The young Queen had been strictly brought up, and she established at once something new in Court life, for a high standard of morals and behaviour was expected from everyone connected with the Court. She had a great deal to do with inculcating in the nation that spirit of reticence and sober morality which has come to be called "Victorian."

It was fortunate for her that her first Prime Minister was the Whig (Liberal) leader, Lord Melbourne, for he took great pains with her political education, and played the part of Prime Minister, father, and private secretary to the young Queen.

Nearly three years after her accession she married her first cousin, Prince Albert of Saxe-Coburg-Gotha (*see* Albert, Prince Consort). It proved a marriage of love on both sides. He was a man of the highest character and culture, devoted to art, music and literature. She looked up to him, and made him her chief adviser and private secretary. In 1857 she conferred on him the title of "Prince Consort." After his death in 1861 the Queen lived much in seclusion. But she gave time every day to affairs of State, and demanded that all dispatches should be laid before her.

In her earlier years as ruler she was a strong Whig, but later she was a staunch supporter of Disraeli, the Tory or Conservative leader. In 1876 he obtained the passage of a bill through Parliament conferring on her the title "Empress of India." His fall from power in 1880 was a hard blow to the Queen; she never concealed her dislike of Gladstone, the Liberal Prime Minister who succeeded Disraeli, and kept up a secret correspondence on State affairs with the fallen minister. In her later years, too, she pressed her foreign policy in support of the Turks against Russia even to the

verge of war, and she was anxious to see Britain, then the foremost naval Power, take a more active part in world affairs.

Queen Victoria took great pleasure in her visits to Balmoral Castle, in Aberdeenshire, Scotland, and spent much time there and at Osborne, in the Isle of Wight, and at the royal palace at Windsor. After the Prince Consort's death she was seldom in London more than a day or two at a time, but at her Golden Jubilee (fiftieth anniversary of her accession to the throne) in 1887 and at the Diamond Jubilee 10 years later there was a spontaneous exhibition of loyalty from all the peoples of the Empire. Victoria reigned longer than any other sovereign in English history. She was 81 years old when she died at Osborne on January 22, 1901, and had ruled 63 years. She had nine children, of whom the second-born succeeded her as Edward VII. She was buried at Frogmore in Windsor Park, Berkshire, where is also the grave of the Prince Consort

National Portrait Gallery; W. & D. Downey
QUEEN VICTORIA
The portrait of Queen Victoria (upper) by Sir George Hayter (1792–1871) shows her in the robes she wore at her coronation on June 28, 1838. The photograph (lower) was taken on the occasion of her Diamond Jubilee in 1897.

Victoria, AUSTRALIA.

Though it is the smallest of the States of the Australian Commonwealth, with the exception of Tasmania, Victoria has the second largest population and is the most important agricultural area of Australia. Victoria has five times as much land under cultivation as Queensland, which is nearly eight times as large.

Wheat and hay are the chief crops. The production of wine from Victorian grapes is an industry of increasing value. As in the rest of Australia, sheep and cattle raising are leading industries. Gold mining was formerly the greatest source of wealth, but the production declined during the Second World War (1939–45). Coal is mined in increasingly large quantities. Millions of acres are covered by the forest-clad Dividing Range and its foothills, 50 to 60 miles from the coast. The highest peaks are always snow-clad.

VICTORIA, AUSTRALIA

Extent.—Area 87,884 square miles. Population 2,031,000.

Physical Features.—Low-lying coastal belt. Great Dividing Range, the eastern portion of which is known as the Australian Alps. Beyond, the Murray river basin.

Principal Products.—Wool, gold, coal, grain, flour, butter, hides and skins, meat, live-stock.

Chief Cities.—Melbourne (capital, population 1,226,920), Geelong (44,561), Ballarat (40,181), Bendigo (30,779).

The climate is pleasantly bracing and is the nearest approach to that of England to be found in Australia. The chief cities are Melbourne (q.v.), the capital, which contains over half the population of the State, Geelong, Ballarat, the centre of one of the gold-yielding regions, and Bendigo. The University of Melbourne is the leading institution for higher education.

Captain Cook was the first white man to sight Victoria ; this was while he was en route for Botany Bay in 1770. Port Phillip, on which stands Melbourne, was first entered in 1802, but the first permanent settlement was not established until 1834. Responsible self-government came in 1836, and 15 years later Victoria was separated from New South Wales. In 1901 it was one of the colonies, renamed States, formed into the Commonwealth of Australia. The administration today is in the hands of a Governor, who is advised by a State cabinet, and a Parliament of two Chambers.

Victoria, CANADA.

Lying at the south-east end of Vancouver Island (see Vancouver), Victoria is the Pacific gateway to Canada. There is scarcely an hour of the day or night that some ocean liner from a distant port, or some coasting steamer, does not enter the fine harbour. Three miles away is Esquimault, the Pacific Coast head-quarters of the Canadian Navy.

Victoria's prosperity is chiefly due to its position as the capital of British Columbia, though it also ranks as one of Canada's main commercial centres by reason of its shipping and the lumber, mining, salmon-canning, and fishing industries which are centred here. Its chief industries are shipbuilding and the manufacture of hardware, furniture, machinery, and biscuits. It has the largest dry dock in North America. The Parliament buildings are an architectural feature. Victoria leaped into prominence with the gold rush of 1858. It became the capital of British Columbia 10 years later, in 1868. The population is about 44,000.

Victoria, LAKE.

In 1858 the English explorer J. H. Speke, seeking for the sources of the Nile, discovered this huge expanse of fresh water, and named it Victoria Nyanza, or Lake Victoria, in honour of the Queen of England. By further exploration he was able to prove that this was indeed the long-sought " birthplace " of the Nile. In 1875 and 1889 H. M. Stanley (q.v.) sailed round it. It is over 255 miles long; its average breadth is 155 miles, and its area about 26,000 square miles. It is situated at a height of 3,700 feet.

Victoria Nyanza lies midway between Kenya Colony and Tanganyika Territory. Numerous steamships ply on its waters, connecting Entebbe and other ports on the western shore with those on the east—Kisumu in Kenya, and Mwanza in Tanganyika, termini of the railways which run to the coast. Flying-boats on the Empire airway to South Africa also alight at Kisumu. There are many islands, most of them densely forested. The Kagera, Katonga and Bukora are the chief feeders. In 1948 a hydro-electric scheme was devised which would raise the level of the lake by some three feet, and would provide two and a half million kilowatts a year.

Victoria Falls.

This mighty waterfall is in Southern Rhodesia, Africa, at a point where the Zambezi passes from the central African plateau to lower levels. Its roar is like continuous thunder, and the vapour from the falling waters rises in a column that can be seen for miles. The native name for the falls is " Thundering Smoke " (Musi-oa-tunya). We can imagine the sensations of awe and exultation with which Livingstone (q.v.), the first white man to view it, gazed in 1855 upon this mighty spectacle.

The height of the Falls is nearly 360 feet, over twice that of Niagara, and they are over a mile wide. They are divided by islands into four separate cataracts, of which the middle two, Main Fall and Rainbow Fall, are the widest. The river pours perpendicularly into a deep chasm, set squarely across the current. The railway from the Cape to the Congo, which since 1905 has enabled visitors to reach the spot, crosses the canyon on a single-span bridge, so close to the Falls that passengers are wetted with the spray. A hydro-electric station, developing 2,000 kilowatts, was started here in 1938. (See colour plate facing page 3016).

Victory, H.M.S.

Lord Nelson's renowned flagship was laid down in dry dock at Chatham, Kent, in 1759 and floated out in 1765, a first-rate line-of-battle ship of 2,162 tons, 226½ feet over all by 52 feet by 21½ feet depth of hold. Built of the finest oak, her frames so close together that there was no space for a round-shot to pass between them if it penetrated her thick planking, she proved unusually handy for a three-decked line-of-battle ship and was always in demand as flagship, flying the flags of a long series of distinguished admirals.

She carried 100 guns: 42-pounders on the lower deck, 24-pounders on the main deck and 12-pounders above them when she was new, although several changes were made during her career, and she cost just over £100,000, ready for sea.

Starting her fighting career in action against the French off Brest in July 1778, a few weeks after she

H.M.S. VICTORY : NELSON'S FLAGSHIP
Exactly as she was in 1805, Nelson's flagship H.M.S. Victory is kept in dry dock at Portsmouth, Hampshire, and on the anniversary of Trafalgar (October 21) she is dressed with flags and laurel wreaths in honour of the great admiral.

was commissioned, she was constantly in action until the end of the war with the revolting North American Colonies and France in 1785, and again when war with France broke out afresh in 1793. Always leading the line as flagship she naturally suffered a great deal of damage, as the enemy's fire was always concentrated on her. In 1789 she was paid off for large repairs, and again in 1801, being ready for service, once more against the French, in 1803 when Nelson as Commander-in-Chief of the Mediterranean Station chose her as his flagship. She served as such in the long blockade of Toulon, the pursuit of the French fleet to the West Indies and back, and then at Trafalgar on October 21, 1805. There again she was seriously damaged and sustained many casualties. Repaired in time to see more active service before the end of the naval war in 1814, she was then rebuilt, the beak and bulkhead being done away with and the bow brought right up to deck level. Some years later the Admiralty suggested selling her to the shipbreakers, but there was a public outcry and she became the harbour flagship of

the Commander-in-Chief at Portsmouth. After that the Victory was a popular show-ship for nearly a century. In 1922 it was realized that she was almost falling to pieces, and by the generosity of James Caird, a shipowner, and of members of the public, a large sum was raised to save her by replacing the faulty timbers, restoring her to her exact appearance as at Trafalgar, and putting her into a steel cradle which was cemented into a dry dock at Portsmouth, where she may still be seen. (*See also* Nelson; Trafalgar).

Vienna. Contrary to general belief, Vienna (German *Wien*), the capital of Austria, is not situated actually on the banks of the Danube; for the city's oldest districts are several miles from the river, and the newer parts are farther still. A branch of the Danube, however—the so-called Danube Canal—flows through Vienna.

The *Innere Stadt* (Inner Town) is the old, historic quarter round which there were fortifications until 1858–60, when the walls and moat were removed to make way for the magnificent *Ringstrasse*, with its splendid wide roadways and promenades. Along this street are most of the buildings for which Vienna is so noted. The stately Grecian houses of Parliament look out upon the lavishly decorated Gothic rathaus (city hall), while near by is the university, a magnificent specimen of Renaissance style. Farther round this two-mile circular thoroughfare are the opera house, luxurious shops, the Academy of Art, and the Hofburg. Formerly the residence of the Austrian emperors, this palace comprises a number of buildings of various epochs and styles. It contains a valuable library and national museum. The Schoenbrunn palace is on the south-western outskirts of the city.

In the narrow, crooked streets of the inner city still lingers something of the spirit of the Middle

VIENNA STREET SCENE
St. Joseph's Fountain in Vienna's Hoher Markt was designed in 1705 by Johann Bernhard Fischer von Erlach in the Baroque style for which he was so noted. It depicts the betrothal of St. Joseph to the Virgin Mary, and there are Biblical scenes in the panels above the base.

Ages, some of the old buildings dating back to the 13th and 14th centuries. Chief among them is St Stephen's Cathedral (the Stefansdom), which was badly damaged during the Second World War (1939–45). Only a step away is the street called the Graben, with its smart modern shops, banks and cafés; and leading down to the Ringstrasse is the equally well-known Kärntnerstrasse.

In Vienna the café is still the centre of social life. Each one has its own particular group of patrons; one is favoured by merchants who come to discuss prices and transport; at another you will find leading actors and musicians immersed in the small talk of their profession. Perhaps the part the cafés play is so important because the Viennese live mostly in flats; and the cafés serve as a second home, club, and reading-room.

Certainly it was the street life that gave Vienna a distinctive charm before the First World War (1914–18), when she was still the capital of Austria-Hungary and a city of gaiety, of life, of music, and of dancing. While the aristocracy rode leisurely up and down the Ringstrasse, the rest of Vienna promenaded along the pavements. In the people's playground, the Hofgarten near the Hofburg, the benches were filled all day with Viennese seemingly always happy.

A favourite resort of both yesterday and today is the Prater, a beautiful 2,000-acre park to the east of the Danube Canal. Once an imperial deer-park, it contains a large fun fair and a number of restaurants. There are several other parks and beautiful private gardens. Vienna itself now extends beyond the Gürtel (the outer ring) and covers an area of 469 square miles.

It is the cultural as well as the political capital of Austria. The university (established in 1365) is particularly noted for its medical school. Viennese influence in music, the theatre and literature has been world-wide. In normal times Vienna produces leather goods, jewelry, scientific instruments, furniture, machinery, railway engines and carriages, textiles and chemicals.

Bulwark of Western Europe

The history of Vienna goes back to the early years of the Christian era, when Roman legions captured the Celtic village of Vindomina, changed its name to Vindobona, and built a fortified camp. The town was overrun with the barbarian hordes that poured into the Roman Empire in the 5th century A.D., Attila (c. 400–453) and his Huns staying there for a time on their way to the West. After remaining in obscurity for several centuries Vienna, as it had come to be called by then, was made the capital of the Ostmark, territory belonging to the Dukes of Babenberg. During the Crusades the city prospered greatly from the traffic that flowed down the Danube, and grew to the size of the present inner city, but it was not until 1276 that he became the capital first of the German and then of the Austrian Empire.

For several centuries Vienna was the bulwark of western Europe against the Turk, and twice, in 1529 and 1683, she withstood Turkish sieges. In 1814 the city was the scene of the Congress of Vienna, which reorganized Europe and reshaped its map after the defeat of Napoleon Bonaparte. In grim contrast was the position of Vienna at the end of the First World War (1914–18), for the great Empire of which she had formerly been the capital had now vanished, and Austria and Hungary had become separate States. The Treaty of St. Germain which terminated the war for Austria left the small, newly-formed Republic of Austria which was only a fraction of the size of the Austria of 1914, with a huge capital city in Vienna. There was no home market for the products of her factories, and for several years thousands of the inhabitants lived on the verge of starvation.

In July 1934 fighting broke out in the city between the supporters of the Government and the Socialists and Austrian Nazis (pro-Germans), and on July 7 the Austrian Chancellor, Engelbert Dollfuss, was murdered by Nazis, though the Government managed to suppress the rising. Austria ceased to be an independent State on March 11, 1938, when German troops invaded the republic and its union with Germany was announced. Under the Germans Vienna was lowered to the status of the chief city of Ostmark, as Austria was once more called.

During the course of the Second World War (1939–45) the city was bombed a number of times by the Allied Air Forces before its capture by Russian forces on April 13, 1945, after more than a week's street fighting during which the eastern districts suffered severely. After the war Vienna, though lying in the Russian zone of occupation in Austria, was divided into British, United States, French and Russian sectors; but at the same time it became once again the seat of a republican Austrian Government. The population is 1,548,000.

Viet-Nam. This independent State within the framework of the French Union consists of the former protectorates of Annam, Tonking, and Cochin-China (see Indo-China). During the Second World War when the Japanese invaded Indo-China and ejected the French from this part of the French Colonial Empire the Japanese allowed the natives to set up a republic.

When the French returned to Indo-China in 1946 they found in power a Communist organization, known as Viet-Minh, and fighting broke out.

In March 1946 negotiations were held between the French and Dr. Ho Chi Minh, leader of the Viét-Minh party, to frame a treaty recognizing the Republic of Viet-Nam as a free State within the French Union. Dr. Ho wanted to combine all French Indo-China in the State of Viet-Nam, but the French would not agree to this. The negotiations broke down, and fighting continued.

In September 1947 Bao Dai, former Emperor of Annam (1926–45), called Viet-Namese leaders together to negotiate with the French. An agreement was reached in March 1949 by which France recognized Bao Dai's leadership, and in June he was invested as the new head of the State of Viet-Nam. But Dr. Ho Chi Minh refused to give in, and in January 1950 Viet-Minh proclaimed itself the government of Viet-Nam, and was recognized as such, with Ho Chi Minh as president, by Russia, the Chinese Communist Government, Albania, and Yugoslavia. Bai Dai was supported by the French and recognized by the United Kingdom, the U.S.A., Australia, Belgium, and the Netherlands, and he continued the fight against Viet-Minh forces.

Vinegar.

"Sour" or "keen" wine is the meaning of the word vinegar, and sour wine is really what one variety of vinegar is. Wine vinegar is made by exposing a mixture of wine and strong vinegar to the air until the alcohol has been changed into acetic acid. In the U.S.A. much vinegar is made similarly from fermented apple juice, or cider.

"Malt" vinegar is prepared by fermenting with yeast a "wort" or infusion of malt and grain so that a weak solution of alcohol is produced. So-called "wood" vinegar is mainly acetic acid which has been flavoured and coloured. (One method of preparing acetic acid is by the distillation of wood.)

The process of fermentation is usually hastened in the commercial manufacture by pouring the alcoholic liquid into a cask or vat filled with purified beech-wood shavings, which have been soaked in strong vinegar. As the liquid soaks down through the shavings it is rapidly fermented, since large surfaces are thus exposed to the air. The liquor that filters through is poured in at the top again and again, until practically all the alcohol has been changed into acetic acid.

The characteristic sharp taste is given by the acetic acid, which is usually present in the proportion of four to eight per cent. (*See* Fermentation).

Violet.

This lovely little flower has always been the symbol of modesty, because of the way in which it hides its beauties beneath the herbage of the wayside, so that it is often unnoticed. Only one of the wild violets found in Britain is really fragrant, that being the sweet violet (*Viola odorata*), which is also the parent of the many cultivated varieties. The flowers are used to obtain the oil of violets employed in perfumery, confectionery, and other trades.

The wild sweet violet has dark purple flowers, and large, bright green leaves. Those of the dog violet (*V. canina*) and the wood violet (*V. sylvestris*) are smaller and of a paler, less brilliant hue. Other species native to Britain are the marsh violet (*V. palustris*), whose flowers are lilac or white ; the hairy violet (*V. hira*) ; and the very rare sand violet (*V. arenaria*). They are all hardy perennials.

A. W. Dennis

SCENTLESS DOG VIOLET
One of the wild violets of Britain, the flowers of this species are, unfortunately, without scent, and they are smaller and less brilliant than the dark purple blossoms of the wild sweet violet. They are lovely, nevertheless.

Violin.

For sweetness and richness of tone the violin has no rival among musical instruments. In the hands of a master, like Fritz Kreisler (born 1875), Yehudi Menuhin (born 1916) or Jascha Heifetz (born 1901), a violin can be made to "sing" as can nothing else but the human voice. Age and use mellow the instrument and bring it to perfection. New violins, however perfectly made, seldom if ever produce as rich and full a tone.

The violin is a shell of wood. Across a bridge on its upper side are stretched four strings made of gut. At either side of the strings are soundholes, which permit the air inside the sound-box to vibrate.

The tone is produced by the vibrations of these strings when they are set in motion by the friction of the bow. The beauty of the tone is due not only to the strings but also to the delicate shell-body against which the air vibrates.

The forerunners of the violin came from the East. According to tradition the first stringed instrument played with a bow was invented by a king of Ceylon about 5000 B.C. The Arabs had a one-stringed fiddle, called the "rebek," which found its way to Europe some time before the 10th century of our era. Later drawings and sculptures of the Middle Ages show similar instruments with variously shaped bodies and two, three, or more strings. From this crude instrument developed the violin and its larger cousins. The violin was perfected in Italy, where in the latter half of the 16th century it took approximately the form it has today.

Its chief home was Cremona, a little town near Venice. Here lived the celebrated Andrea Amati (*c.* 1520–*c.* 1580). The violins made by Andrea from 1554 to 1580, and by his grandson, Nicolo (1596–1684), are now almost priceless treasures.

Of all the masters of that old Cremona school the name which stands highest is that of Antonio Stradivari (*c.* 1644–1737), who was first a pupil and then a master there. His special contribution was to make all the curves and arches of the violin body very delicate, yet strong and resonant. He then experimented until he created a varnish that gave the body the rich colour of amber. The secret of this perfect varnish seems to have been lost. Several violins, violas, and 'cellos still exist bearing his name, most of them made between 1690 and 1730. Of the other masters who wrought at Cremona the greatest was Giuseppe Guarneri, known as Guarneri del Gesù (1666–*c.* 1739), a member of another celebrated family of violin-makers. Among Italian composers whose works developed the technique and scope of the violin were Arcangelo Corelli (1653-1713); Antonio Vivaldi (17th century); Giuseppe Tartini (1692-1770) ; Giovanni Battista Viotti (1753-1824); and Nicolo Paganini (1784-1840).

About 70 pieces of wood go to the making of a violin. The wood must be chosen, seasoned, and shaped with the greatest care, so that it will not warp. It is held together only by glue. For the top of the sounding-box pine and silver fir are used because of their elasticity.

Maple or sycamore is generally used for the back, sides, bridge, and neck. The richness of tone depends on the exactness with which the proportions are distributed, and on the size and positions of the sound-holes. Horsehair is used for the bow, because each hair has many minute bristles which give the bow its "bite."

In the same family as the violin are the *viola*, which is about one-fifth larger than the violin ; the much larger *violoncello*, and the *double bass*, whose deep voice is the bass of the whole orchestra. The instruments of this group are often referred to as " the strings," and they are really the backbone of the orchestra, for they outnumber all the other instruments together.

Vipers. These are the most dangerous of all the poisonous snakes. The cobras and a few other snakes possess a more powerful poison, but the fangs of the vipers are longer, and, instead of the deep groove on the front side, as in the cobra, a tube or canal leads from the poison glands through the tooth itself to a spot near the sharp tip. Unlike other poisonous snakes also, the vipers are able to erect that part of their upper jaw which holds the fangs, thus bringing these weapons into more dangerous prominence.

Among the best-known of the " true vipers " are the common viper or adder (*Vipera berus*), the only British poisonous snake; the sand viper (*V. ammodytes*) of Europe, which bears a fleshy horn upon its nose; the puff-adder (*Bitis arietans*) of Africa, which inflates its body and hisses loudly when approached; the Egyptian and the Sahara horned vipers (*Cerastes*), with a horny spike over each eye; and the Russell's viper (*V. russelli*) of Asia, which is the largest and most poisonous of the whole group. Nearly all vipers bring forth their young alive, and this has led to the tale that they swallow their young when danger threatens.

The " pit " vipers have a deep depression on the head, in front of the eyes. The rattlesnake (*q.v.*) is a member of this group. (*See* Snakes).

Virgil or Vergil (70–19 B.C.). The greatest Roman poet, Publius Vergilius Maro, was not a Roman by birth, for he was born on his father's farm in the village of Andes, near Mantua (in the province of Cisalpine Gaul). He was sent to school at the neighbouring town of Cremona and then to Milan, and at Rome he studied rhetoric and philosophy under the best masters of the day.

After the battle of Philippi, Virgil's farm was among the estates confiscated. An estate, however, was procured for him, and he was introduced into the intimate circle about Octavian, who was soon to become the Emperor Augustus. Chief of his friends and patrons was Maecenas, the great minister of Augustus, and through his liberality, Virgil was enabled to devote himself entirely to literature.

In the quiet years that he spent in the country he read and studied the Greek poets. Following Theocritus as a model, he wrote his

G. Hearn

HANDSOME MALE VIPER

The only British poisonous snake is the common viper or adder, usually from 20 to 25 inches long. Along the back is a dark zig-zag line and on each side is a row of dark patches, which make the reptile easy to recognize. The male (above) is more clearly marked than the female, which is a duller brown and a dirty white.

Eclogues or Bucolics, pastoral poems in which he gave expression to his tender feelings for the beauty of Italian scenes. The Georgics, on the art of farming and the charms of country life, established his fame.

The year after they were published he began his epic, the Aeneid, taking as his hero the Trojan, Aeneas (*q.v.*), reputed founder of the Latin nation, and thus celebrating the glory of Rome and the imperial family. He had devoted more than 10 years to this work when he contracted a fever, which proved fatal. On his deathbed he begged that the Aeneid should be destroyed, saying that it still wanted three years' revision on the rough draft to bring the work to perfection, but Augustus prevented the carrying out of this request, and thus saved a masterpiece for the enjoyment of future generations.

Virgil's works exercised a tremendous influence, being widely consulted in the Middle Ages as oracles (*sortes Vergilianae*). The Christian Church at one time regarded him as divinely inspired, and his influence continued through the Middle Ages into modern times. Dante (*q.v.*) revered him as his master and represented him as his guide in the Divine Comedy. His tomb at Naples came to be regarded with religious veneration, and a body of legend arose which represented Virgil as a powerful magician.

Anderson

VIRGIL : ROMAN POET

A perfect literary artist, Virgil's craftsmanship and his deep understanding of humanity have compelled admiration in numerous countries. Perhaps his finest work is the Aeneid, an epic poem in 12 books.

From a bust in the Capitoline Museum, Rome

Virginia. One of the original States of the American Union, Virginia has an area of 42,620 square miles. It is situated on the eastern seaboard of the United States, and is bounded on the south by North Carolina, on the west by West Virginia and Kentucky, on the north by Maryland. Its greatest extent from north to south is about 200 miles, and from east to west 440 miles. The capital is Richmond (population 193,000). Other important cities are Norfolk (144,000), Roanoke (69,000), and Portsmouth (50,000).

The first English charter for settlement in America was that granted in 1606 by James I for colonizing in Virginia, and in the following year Jamestown was founded. The colony was named Virginia in honour of Queen Elizabeth.

In the east the surface is low, and sometimes swampy. There are several good harbours. The coast plain rises gently into spurs and broken ranges of the Blue Ridge Mountains. Between these and the Alleghenies (the western boundary) lies the fertile Great Valley of Virginia, the limestone region of which abounds in caves, natural bridges, and underground rivers. Chief rivers are the Potomac, Rappahannock, York, Roanoke, and James.

Originally tobacco-growing was the chief occupation. Now maize and wheat are more important

Wide World Photos

VIRGINIA'S STATE CAPITOL AT RICHMOND
The Congress and Senate of Virginia in the United States meet in the Capitol (above) at Richmond, the capital of the State. The building was constructed in 1785–92 from a plaster model of a Roman temple at Nimes, France. Richmond, on the James river, has tobacco and chemical factories, iron works, and publishing houses.

crops. Much fruit, too, is raised. Coal and iron are abundant in the west. The oyster and crab fisheries are valuable. Among important manufactures are tobacco products, iron and steel, leather, boots and shoes, rayon, chemicals, and cotton goods. The population is 2,677,000.

In the American Civil War, Virginia, after much hesitation, seceded from the Union and joined the Southern States. Many Virginians, especially in the west, disapproved of this decision, and in 1863 there was born the State of West Virginia, the area of which is 24,000 square miles, and the population 1,901,000. The chief cities are Huntington (78,000), Wheeling (61,000), and Charleston (67,000), the capital. Much mineral treasure is contained in the heart of the Alleghenies, and the production of petroleum and natural gas is also important.

Vistula. This river of central Europe winds its course of 650 miles from the northern slope of the Carpathian Mountains through Poland to the sea, emptying through several arms into the Frisches Haff and Baltic Sea. Good-sized craft can pass up to the Galician boundary, and smaller boats to Cracow.

The river has considerable traffic in grain, lumber, and other products, and forms the most important commercial highway of Poland. The Treaty of Versailles (1919) made Danzig, at its mouth, a free city, and established a " corridor " across East Prussia to give Poland its needed outlet to the Baltic. After the Second World War (1939–45) Danzig became Polish, and East Prussia (formerly German) was also added to Poland, so that the Vistula became a Polish river.

The Vistula has a drainage area of about 74,000 square miles. Breaking up into almost parallel arms in its lower course, the river encloses beautiful wooded islands. Because these arms keep changing their channels, and owing to the amount of their discharge, they have to be carefully regulated to safeguard navigation as well as to protect the delta regions from floods. The chief tributaries are the San, Bug, and Pilica. A canal connects the Vistula with the River Oder, the boundary between Poland and Germany.

Vitamins. Within the last decades scientists became aware that, scattered among the three great food groups— protein, starch, fat—were tiny quantities of some mysterious chemicals, difficult to pin down, but determining the health and growth of an animal. Sir Frederick Gowland Hopkins (1861–1947) observed that young rats fed on pure protein, starch, fat, salt and water did not thrive or grow until a teaspoonful of fresh milk was added daily. Then it was noted that men of the East, eating polished rice from which the husk and embryo had been removed by milling, fell ill with nervous or general symptoms of the disease called beri-beri, as did pigeons similarly fed. Given unpolished rice they recovered in due course. Something necessary to health was obviously present in the rice-husk. But what was this " something "?

It had long been known that sailors making far sea voyages, and deprived of green vegetables and fresh fruit got the spongy bleeding gums, loose teeth, and painful joints characteristic of the ailment called " scurvy "; but that when they touched land and were fed on fresh food and vegetables they recovered. Moreover, it was found that if vegetables were kept germinating on board for their use, and the juice of lemons was issued to the seamen, they did not get scurvy.

Another puzzle was the disease known as rickets. Why should a child's bones develop ill-formed and crooked ? One single observation led far in solving this. Starving children from the slums of Hull were in the habit of going to the docks when the fishing trawlers came in ; and as the cod were cleaned on deck the cod-liver oil ran down and the children dipped their bread in it. Their rickety bones grew strong again. Why was this ? The answers to all these problems are now known, but were obtained only after much research. Vitamins in fresh food, in vegetables, in fruit juices and in fish oils made all the difference.

The five main vitamins are called A B C D and E, though there are many subdivisions of these, and many others have been isolated. Vitamin A is found in most animal fats, in fish-liver oil, and in green vegetables. Tomatoes, bananas and dates have a quota. Its absence causes eye-disease, with destruction of tissue resulting in blindness. In the First World War (1914–18) many barrels of cod-liver oil were sent to Central Europe to save the eyes of the children there. A shortage of this vitamin also causes " night-blindness," by interfering with the mechanism for seeing in partial light. It has great influence on the mucous membranes.

Vitamin D most often " hunts in a couple " with vitamin A, and is present in milk, butter, eggs. Cod-liver oil and halibut oil are extremely rich in it. The action of sunlight on the skin can " manufacture " vitamin D, and herein lies the explanation why cod-liver oil is so loaded with it. Small seaweeds float on the surface of the mid-Pacific ocean basking in the sun and absorbing its rays. Tiny fish eat the sea plants, and they in turn are gulped down by larger fish, until the greedy cod engulfs the lot. The stored sunlight is lodged in his liver as vitamin D. Deficiency of this vitamin causes rickets, for without it calcium and phosphorus cannot be absorbed from the gut to build firm bone. Cod-liver oil is the essential cure of rickets, but is given in doses of not more than one teaspoonful. Larger doses check the flow of digestive juices and, interfering with the absorption of food, defeat their own purpose.

Vitamin B is divided into some six fractions and is present in yeast, liver, milk, green vegetables and in the germ of cereals. Lack of B causes beri-beri, the disease of the East to which reference has been made. Lack of B_2 causes pellagra, an ailment which is characterized by intestinal distress and by mental deterioration. Vitamin C is found in fresh vegetables, in oranges, tomatoes, in germinating wheat and, especially, in lemons ; it is not present in limes, as is popularly but wrongly believed. The vitamin is destroyed by prolonged boiling, and by the alkalis often ignorantly added to vegetables to keep them green while cooking. A person feels well almost in direct proportion to the amount of vitamin C floating around in his tissues. There must be constant intake, for this valuable vitamin cannot be stored in the body for longer than 24 hours. It is the essential cure for scurvy, as has been shown. Vitamin E is found in lettuce, egg yolk, and wheat germ. Without it an animal becomes sterile.

Vladivostok. (Pron. vladi-vos'-tok). As the chief seaport of Asiatic Russia and the outlet for the products of the Amur Valley, Vladivostok (see colour map facing page 2844) is one of the Soviet Union's most important centres for foreign trade. Situated at the southern end of the Muraviev Peninsula, it is Russia's Pacific naval and air base. Daily air service is maintained with Moscow, some 6,000 miles to the west. The Trans-Siberian Railway, from Leningrad to Vladivostok, is the longest transcontinental railway line in the world. It also has regular connexion with Russia proper by two water routes : the northern, through Arctic water and ship canals to the Baltic Sea, and the southern, through the Suez Canal and the Dardanelles to the Black Sea.

Its commercial growth began in 1905 when Dalny (now Dairen) fell to Japan. With the development of Siberia after the First World War (1914–18), and the exploitation of its lumber and mineral resources, trade increased still more. Soya beans, soya-bean oil, lumber and fish are the chief exports ; manufactured goods are imported. The strongly fortified harbour, known as the Golden Horn, is four miles long and a mile wide. Dry docks, shipyards, and every modern shipping facility line its shores. Icebreakers are used to keep open a channel in the bitterly cold winter months.

The city, which was founded in 1860 and whose name means " Ruler of the East," is the seat of the University of the Far East, and it has several technical, industrial and professional schools. The population of Vladivostok is 206,000.

Voice. The lungs drive a current of air through the larynx, a cartilaginous box situated at the top of the windpipe, in the front of the neck. As the " Adam's apple " (as it is called) the larynx can be seen moving up and down. In this " box " are suspended two fibrous bands, the vocal cords, tethered fore and aft. (See diagrams alongside).

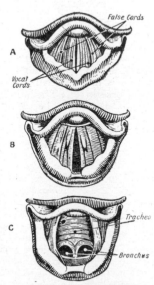

IN THE ' VOICE BOX '
A. Vocal cords almost closed, for a high note. B. Cords open for quiet breathing. C. Cords wide for deep breathing. The false cords are folds of membrane ; bronchi (plural of bronchus) are air passages to the lungs ; the trachea is the windpipe.

In quiet breathing, the air passes noiselessly between the cords as they have relaxed ; but in speaking or singing the cords are tautened by muscular pull, and the air passing through under pressure causes vibration, resulting in sound (q.v.). This sound is modified and reinforced by the cavities of the mouth, nose and throat. The cavities vary in shape with each individual, and lend to each voice its own defining characteristics.

Loudness depends on how hard the air is forced through, pitch depends on the degree of tautness of the cords. In a man the cords are heavier and thicker than in a woman, and for this reason the man's voice is lower pitched. In the young boy the cords are like those of a girl ; hence the pure, high notes of the choir boy's voice. At the brink of that stage of growth and development we call " adolescence," the secretion of the glands gets to work ; the boy's voice " breaks " and is out of control for a time, until he presently acquires the deep voice normal to the grown man.

Singing consists in the production of " musical " notes—of which the vibrations are in a definite mathematical relation to one another. While each person turns for delight and release to the sport or art best suited to his understanding and experience, it seems agreed that in listening to a gifted singer the highest enjoyment is reached.

Speech is peculiar to Man, lifting him above all the other animals and distinguishing him from them. They have no speech centre in the brain, and can only make mating calls, maternal cluckings, or sounds of alarm. A parrot does not really understand the words that it has been taught with such patience; and the sounds made by monkeys are too rudimentary to be called speech. Dumbness is the inability to talk. This may be due to deafness, for a child learns to talk by imitation. By the most amazing patience and skill, however, a deaf and dumb child can be trained to talk by teachers versed in technical methods.

Inflammation of the vocal cords is the cause of hoarseness or loss of voice. In simple cases the inhaling of steam relieves the congestion, and it is the only serviceable remedy for this troublesome condition. A voice should never be used above a whisper at such times, or its quality may be permanently damaged.

Volcanoes. An opening in the earth's crust from which hot rock is ejected is called a volcano; the name comes from Vulcan, the Roman god of fire. In many cases the hot rock has been molten, when it is usually called lava. The lava may flow out quietly, or it may be ejected forcibly. In the latter case much or all of it may be solid. Small fragments of solid lava are called cinders, but if they are as small as particles of fine sand or dust they are called ashes or volcanic dust. They may take more than a year to settle. Volcanic ash does not, however, imply combustion; it is simply powdered lava.

Besides lava, numerous gases or vapours escape from volcanoes. Among the vapours steam is the most abundant; indeed, it is the principal force in the violent expulsion of materials from volcanoes of the explosive type. Chlorine and sulphur and various compounds of these elements are among the commonest fumes escaping from volcanic vents. Carbon dioxide also is one of the common gases. Some of the gases are poisonous. At depth there is great pressure, and the gases often dissolve in the molten rock.

The solid material and the liquid lava which escape from volcanoes accumulate about the vents and build up volcanic cones. In the top of a volcanic cone there is generally a depression, the " crater," in the bottom of which is the vent. When a cone becomes high, the lava may break through its sides.

When a volcano ceases to be active it is said to be extinct; in fact, it is no longer a volcano. When the activity of a volcano is temporarily suspended the volcano is said to be dormant, that is, sleeping. It is often difficult to tell whether a volcano is extinct or only dormant. Vesuvius (*q.v.*) was thought to be extinct until the time of its destructive eruption in A.D. 79. A volcanic vent often continues to give off vapours and gases long after lava ceases to issue

from it. Vapours and gases also escape, sometimes in large quantities, when no lava is being ejected.

When volcanoes cease to be active their craters may be occupied by water, giving rise to crater lakes. Such lakes are found in the Auvergne Mountains in France, and in the Eifel district in Germany; and there is a very large one, known as Crater Lake, in Oregon, United States.

Volcanic cones retain their perfect form for a short time only, since the action of rain and melting snow soon modifies them. Volcanoes are often associated with earthquakes, and the violent eruptions of volcanoes are sometimes the direct cause of earthquakes. In numerous cases, however, it may be true that the two phenomena, the earthquakes and the volcanic eruptions, are to be referred to a common cause rather than either to the other.

In the explosive eruptions of Vesuvius the quakings have been felt for considerable distances from the crater. In some cases of violent eruption the old cones are partly or wholly blown away. Even large parts of islands where they occur may be demolished. Outside the present cone of Vesuvius there is a remnant of an older cone, partially destroyed in a violent eruption subsequent to its formation. A large part of the island of Krakatoa, between Sumatra and Java, was blown away in a volcanic eruption in 1883. The explosion was heard in Australia, 2,000 miles away.

The great destructiveness of volcanic action is more commonly due to the solid material blown out than to the lava which flows out. Lava usually flows slowly, and perhaps only a short distance before it congeals.

Torrents of rain, due to the condensation of the escaping water-vapour, frequently fall with the ashes, converting them into a sort of hot fluid mud, and this is sometimes most destructive in its flow. In the Krakatoan eruption of 1883 it has been estimated that bits of pumice and dust were sent up into the air 20 miles, some of the dust being carried by currents in the upper air several times round the earth. If the vent has become blocked with solid matter, large pieces of lava may be hurled miles from the volcano.

The number of active volcanoes is estimated to be between 300 and 400. About one-third are situated on continents and the rest on islands. Most of the volcanoes on continents are relatively near the coasts, though extinct volcanoes occur at great distances inland. Continental volcanoes are, on the whole, more numerous about the borders of the Pacific Ocean than about those of the Atlantic.

Numerous islands are really little more than the crests of volcanic cones which have been built up above the surface of the water. There are, doubtless, volcanic cones the tops of which are still below sea-level, but of these little is known.

Active volcanoes are much more numerous in regions where the rock formations are relatively young than where they are old. They are thought to occur in regions where the crust of the earth is in movement, that is, where it is either sinking or rising, rather than in regions where it is stable.

No existing volcano seems to have been active for a period of time which would be considered long as geologists reckon time. Some of those now known, however, have been active since the beginning of the historic period. The largest existing volcano is

HOW A VOLCANO BUILDS ITSELF UP TO A PEAK

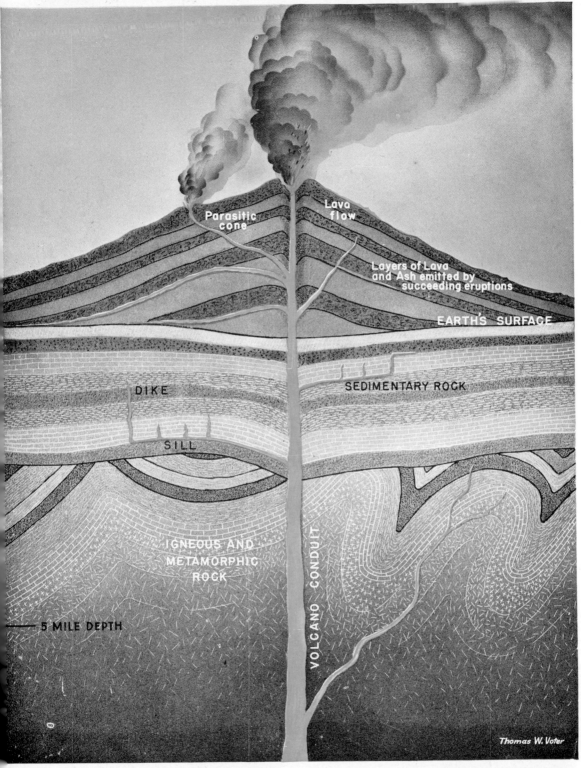

Parasitic cone

Lava flow

Layers of Lava and Ash emitted by succeeding eruptions

EARTH'S SURFACE

DIKE

SEDIMENTARY ROCK

SILL

IGNEOUS AND METAMORPHIC ROCK

VOLCANO CONDUIT

5 MILE DEPTH

Thomas W. Voter

Molten lava reaches the vent at the top of the cone in the manner shown in this sectional diagram. Sometimes another outlet, known as a parasitic cone, may also be formed. Occasionally, too, lava may flow underground along a crack or fissure in the rock ; if this flow is horizontal between the strata, or layers of rock, it is called a 'sill' ; a vertical flow which fills cracks without reaching the surface is known as a 'dike.' The ejected solid material and liquid lava accumulate about the vent and build up a cone, in the top of which there is generally a depression, called the 'crater.'

E.N.I.L.M.: Will F. Taylor

DORMANT VOLCANOES

OVER 10,000 feet high Tjerimai (above) is in Java, an island in the Netherlands East Indies. It still emits steam and ashes but is regarded as harmless, the last serious eruption having occurred more than 100 years ago.

Mont Pelée (left), in the French island of Martinique in the West Indies, was the cause of over 30,000 deaths during two eruptions which took place in 1902. Ruins of the town of St. Pierre, destroyed by the first eruption, are seen at the base of the 4,500-foot mountain.

To face page 3329

Mauna Loa, Hawaii, rising more than 28,000 feet above the ocean floor on which it stands.

Various plans have been proposed for harnessing volcanoes and using their immense energy for industrial purposes, but on anything more than a small scale these plans have proved failures.

Volga.

The longest river of Europe, the Volga rises in the cold marshes of the Valdai Hills, about 200 miles south of Leningrad in European Russia. Sweeping in vast slow curves to the south-east and the south, it is joined by the Oka at Gorki (a town previously called Nijni-Novgorod), and by the Kama below the towered citadel of Kazan. Past Kuibishev, Saratov, Stalingrad and the mosques and minarets of Astrakhan it flows, watering the sandy Caspian steppes before it sinks through some 200 mouths into the inland Caspian Sea, after a journey of over 2,000 miles.

Navigable for nearly the whole of its course, the Volga is not merely the main commercial highway of Russia but a link between Europe and Asia. Down its course go the manufactures and timber of the north; upward travel grain from the Ukraine, hides from the steppes, fish from the river's own mouths, oil from Baku, and cotton from Iran.

The Volga has no natural communication with the ocean, but a system of canals linking its upper courses with the Neva connects it with the Baltic and makes Leningrad the chief port, as it were, of the whole Volga basin. In addition, the river is connected with the Moskva (Moscow) and Don by canals.

Fifty million people—of Slavonic and other races—inhabit the fertile basin of the Volga and its tributaries, and an even more motley human stream—Russians, Cossacks, Georgians, Circassians, Armenians, Persians, Chinese, Turkomans, and gipsies—flows up and down its surface. Five centuries and more—from the 10th to the 16th—were needed to make the Volga Russian from source to mouth, and the Greek cathedrals, Lutheran churches, and Moslem mosques along its banks suggest various periods in Russian history. Barges were formerly dragged up the river by teams of men toiling along the banks. To keep in rhythm they used to sing, one of their plaintive folk-tunes having become world-famous as the " Volga Boat Song." During the Second World War (1939–45) one of the most important battles of the German campaign in Russia took place on the banks of the Volga. This is described in the article on Stalingrad.

Giraudon

VOLTAIRE, SMILING SCEPTIC

In the Louvre, Paris, this bronze head of Voltaire, whose real name was François Marie Arouet, by J. A. Houdon (1740–1828) reveals the true man, the supreme genius in critical mockery.

Voltaire.

(1694–1778). François Marie Arouet, who wrote under the name of Voltaire, hated institutions that had outgrown their usefulness and given rise to abuses and he never hesitated to show fierce anger against them and to attack them with sharp, biting wit. His long life began at Paris, where he was born on November 21, 1694. In his youth he shocked his father by his gay habits, his indifference to the study of law, and his way of writing bold, cutting, witty verses—a dangerous pastime in the days when Louis XV was the ruling monarch of France.

Young Voltaire turned out so many biting and clever verses that one day he was accused of attacking the government, and was thrown into the Bastille, the fortress-prison of Paris. It was after his release that he assumed the pen-name of Voltaire, saying that he hoped to have better luck with his new name than with the old one. Eight years later he again found himself in the Bastille, and on release he departed for England. Here he found freedom, for here men of genius could say and write what they thought without fear. After three years Voltaire returned to France, in 1729, with a new vision of liberty, and with an established literary reputation.

Again Voltaire got into trouble. His book, called Letters on the English, not only sang the praises of England but was a veiled attack on every French institution. He was obliged to beat a hasty retreat from Paris to Lorraine. Having made an ample fortune by various speculations he wrote play after play, and in 1751 was invited by Frederick the Great of Prussia to pay a long visit to his Court. Unwisely he went. There, though Frederick greatly admired his genius, Voltaire learned something about the unreliable favour of princes, and he returned in three years home-sick and angry.

But the French king would not allow him to return to Paris. Voltaire, therefore, bought the estate of Ferney, on French soil, but only three and a half miles from Geneva in Switzerland, so that he could easily cross the border if King Louis sent messengers to arrest him. At Ferney he was to know as much peace as his restless soul could. He built a large house, entertained lavishly, gave a home to needy relatives, lifted the peasants from starvation to comfort, sheltered religious refugees from Geneva, started industries including a prosperous watch factory, a silk-stocking factory, and a lace colony, wrote and produced plays, managed lawsuits, defended persecuted people, and ran a farm.

He returned to Paris when he was a feeble old man of 84. In his native city he was fêted and honoured, but the excitement and exertion killed him. He died on May 30, 1778, just as the first mutterings of the French Revolution could be heard. Thirteen years later, in the midst of this Revolution, his body was carried in state through the streets and placed in triumph on the ruins of the Bastille (destroyed in 1789) where as a youth he had been imprisoned.

Voltaire's publications were vast and various, but his chief works were La Henriade (1728); Siècle de Louis XIV (The Century of Louis XIV) published in 1751; Candide (1759); and Zadig.

Vosges Mountains. (Pron. vōzh).

A range of rather low mountains with rounded summits—in aspect very similar to the mountains of the Black Forest, which lie on the opposite side of the valley of the Rhine, in Germany, the Vosges are situated in eastern France and are rather less than 100 miles in length. The system extends from Belfort north-eastward almost to Saverne, and at its widest point near Colmar is about 30 miles wide. The name Vosges, however, is sometimes also applied to the uplands to the north of the mountains, reaching as far as Mainz.

On the rounded, grassy tops of almost uniform height (about 4,000 feet) sheep and cattle are pastured in summer. The lower slopes are vine-clad, with forests of pine and beech higher up. The range is composed mainly of granite and red sandstone, and contains deposits of iron, lead, coal and copper.

Vote.

"Who shall be allowed to vote?" is one of the questions which must be answered in drawing up the constitution of any self-governing organization, whether it is a company, a unit of local or Parliamentary government, or a group of nations. This privilege of voting is called suffrage or franchise.

Until recent years suffrage was restricted in most countries to males above the age of 21. The agitation for "votes for women" in Britain began at the time of the second Reform Bill (1867), when it was suggested that the word "male" be deleted from legislation concerned with the granting of the right to vote. This amendment was defeated. The first big "protest meeting" was held in 1905, and from that time onward the "suffragettes," as the female members of the "votes for women" movement were called, drew attention to their cause by interrupting meetings, by breaking windows, and by instituting hunger strikes in prison.

After years of effort the right of women to vote at Parliamentary elections was recognized by an Act which became law in February 1918. The minimum age was then 30. Not until the Representation of the People (Equal Franchise) Act was passed in 1928 was the vote given to women at 21 on the same terms as men.

Since the Representation of the People Act of 1948 no person can have more than one vote. Formerly persons could have two votes if they had premises in two constituencies. University representation was abolished and graduates could no longer send a member to Parliament as before. Voting at a Parliamentary or local government election is secret (*see* Ballot). At company meetings and the like, however, voting is sometimes carried out by the people voting in favour of a motion holding up their hands.

Vulture.

Seen at close quarters this great bird of prey is not a very pleasant object. Its feathers have a rough and unkempt appearance and it has an evil look.

The typical Old World vulture is the black or cinereous vulture (*Vultur monachus*), found in wooded districts of the Mediterranean region and as far eastward as India and China. Often over 40 inches long, it has black feathers shot with dark brown, and, like all members of the group, it feeds almost entirely on carrion and other refuse, being thus useful as a scavenger.

The European griffon vulture (*Gyps fulvus*) is a slightly smaller bird, and unlike the black vulture is found in open and rocky regions. It is brownish-grey in colour and has a large white ruff round its neck. The Egyptian vulture (*Neophron percnopterus*) is a still smaller, whitish species, about 25 inches long. It occurs in the Mediterranean region, and generally throughout Africa and as far eastward as Persia and the sub-continent of India.

The New World vultures differ from those of the Old World in having no partition between the nostrils. They include the turkey vulture, king vulture and condor. (*See* Condor).

Berridge

THE GROTESQUE VULTURE

All vultures are ugly to look at, and this American king vulture is no beauty in its class. Note the bare neck, the monstrous wattle overhanging the great bill, and the huge and powerful feet with talons suited to this bird's carnivorous habits. One thing is to be said in the vultures' favour : they feed on carrion and thus are scavengers.

W

Waders. As a group these birds are easy to recognize. The term " wader " is really applied to those with long legs, and usually long beaks, which spend their lives in marshy places or in the shallow waters of estuaries and mud-flats. Their length of leg and of bill enables them to walk about in the shallow water and probe the mud for food without getting their bodies wet— not that they object to a wetting, for they can mostly swim well if occasion arises.

Amongst the common waders of Britain are the snipe (*q.v.*), the curlew, the redshank, and the common sandpiper. The curlew is Britain's largest wader, a biggish bird distinguishable by its very long, curved beak and by the call which is responsible for its name. In winter large flocks of curlew assemble in estuaries, and are often seen flying overhead, their long wings driving them forward at great speed. They nest in marshy, moorland districts. The redshank, a smaller bird, gets its name from its bright red legs: it loves the wet water-meadows in river valleys, and is recognizable when flying by the flashes of white beneath the body and on the wings. In river-valleys of a different type we find the sandpiper, which frequents the shingle beaches and rapid, rocky streams of the north and west. This is one of Britain's smallest waders, a pretty bird with brown and white plumage. It nests, like all its relatives, on the ground, laying its eggs among the shingle and relying on their resemblance to their background for protection.

Most of the waders are pale brown and white in colour, but one exception is the handsome oyster-catcher (*see* illustration in page 456), which is black and white, with an orange bill. Another is the very rare avocet, also black and white, which has extremely long legs, and is distinguished from all other birds on account of its strange bill, which curves upwards, not downwards like that of the curlew and various other species. The waders belong to the same great order (*Charadriiformes*) as the plovers (*q.v.*). Besides the species mentioned, and a few other rarer examples which breed in Britain, vast flocks of other types visit the country in winter, coming from far north, for, as a rule, these are birds of the colder parts of the world. (*See* Birds).

Wagner, WILHELM RICHARD (1813–83). More than any composer of his time, Richard Wagner (pron. vahg´-ner) imposed his genius on every established form of music, though he is usually regarded as an innovator who re-created opera by giving it hitherto unknown power and splendour. The youngest son of a municipal official, Wagner was born at Leipzig, in Germany, on May 22, 1813, and was educated in Dresden. He began to study music in 1820, and his first production, an overture, was performed when he was only 17, at Leipzig, and astonished those who heard it by a continuous use of the drum.

In 1839 he went to Paris, where he hoped to produce his opera Rienzi; but at that time Parisian audiences preferred Italian opera, and Wagner's plans came to nothing. Three years later Rienzi was produced at Dresden, and its success resulted in the composer's appointment as musical director of the Dresden theatre. There he gained some fame as a conductor, especially of Beethoven's symphonies.

His operas, The Flying Dutchman and Tannhäuser, were likewise produced at Dresden, where they provoked open opposition. The stories were realistic dramas, and Wagner, unlike the composers of his day, made his music for both voice and instruments closely follow the meaning of his text. Thus his operas differed radically from accepted works, and while a few masters, notably Liszt and Schumann, saw in them the beginning

Stanley Crook

TWO WADERS COMMON IN GREAT BRITAIN

All members of the wader group have certain outstanding features in common, which include long legs and bills and the habit of living in marshy places. Examples are the curlew (left) and the redshank (right). Britain's largest wader, the curlew is distinguishable by its very long curved beak and the call from which it gets its name. The redshank, which owes its name to its bright red legs, is recognizable in flight by the flashes of white on body and wings.

of a new art, the public found them " tedious " and " eccentric." Lohengrin, Wagner's next opera, was written in 1848 but had to wait for production until 1861.

In 1864 King Ludwig II of Bavaria invited him to come to Munich and continue his musical work. Wagner's operas from this period onwards are known as music-dramas, for in them he worked out his theory that a combination of all arts is necessary to produce a perfect art unit. Thus literature, music, and action have equal part, and considerable attention was given to the scenic effects. But for Wagner's huge spectacles the Munich opera house proved inadequate, so he planned a " festival theatre " designed by himself. King Ludwig enthusiastically supported the idea, and the outcome was the Wagner theatre at Bayreuth, in Bavaria. The first Wagnerian festival was given at this theatre in 1876, the year that the composer removed to Bayreuth, which remained his home till his death at Venice on February 13, 1883.

Wagner developed his greatest powers comparatively late in life ; his most mature work was written after his 40th year. His finest operas include

RICHARD WAGNER

A musical genius of the 19th century, Richard Wagner is famous for his operas and music-dramas, and for the huge spectacles he staged at Munich and at Bayreuth. He died in 1883.

Tristan and Isolde (1857–59), Parsifal (1877–82), and Der Ring des Nibelungen (1853–74). The Mastersingers of Nuremberg (1862–67) is virtually a comic opera. Wagner wrote the words as well as the music of all these works. (For the stories of some of Wagner's operas *see* pages 2438–2442).

Wagtail. All day long this bird lives up to its name. As it walks or runs—never hopping—about the grass one sees its tail wagging up and down, as though its owner were always in a flurry of excitement; and when the bird stops to perch on a wall or roof the tail still goes on wagging. The commonest British species is the pied wagtail (*Motacilla alba yarrelli*). It is fond of water, and is therefore also called the water-wagtail. Its plumage is all black and grey and white, and it often nests in a barn or other outbuilding, or in a pile of faggots, a creeper on the wall, or in old masonry. Including the long tail the bird is between seven and eight inches in length.

Other common British wagtails are the grey and yellow species. Of these the first (*M. cinerea*) is a rich blue-grey on the back, and bright lemon-yellow below. The yellow wagtail (*M. flava rayi*) is a greenish-yellow all over. Other species sometimes found in Britain, especially as migrants, are the white (*M. alba*) and blue-headed (*M. flava*) wagtails, both difficult to distinguish from the pied and grey species respectively. Food of all the species consists mainly of insects, hence the wagtails are of benefit to farmers and gardeners.

Wakefield. On the River Calder, nine miles south of Leeds, is the city and market-town of Wakefield. It is the county town of the Yorkshire West Riding and the seat of a bishop. The Cathedral of All Saints is a 15th-century structure and is noted for its fine spire.

The city's industries include the manufacture of woollens, engineering, boiler-making, and chemical and machine-tool works. The battle of Wakefield, between the Yorkists and Lancastrians, was fought near the city in 1460 during the Wars of the Roses. In this battle Richard of York was defeated and killed by the forces of Margaret, Queen of Henry VI. The population is 58,000.

Wake-Robin. A decidedly curious British wild plant is the wake-robin (*Arum maculatum*), known also as cuckoo-pint, lords-and-ladies, and starchwort. In March one may see its large, arrow-shaped leaves, spotted boldly with purple or black, pushing through the tangled herbage of a hedge-bottom or the dead leaves carpeting a wood, and arising from a tuberous rootstock about a foot below the ground.

Then, in April, appears in the midst of the leaves a flower-stalk carrying a huge, rolled-up pale green

S. Crook

A PIED WAGTAIL AT ITS NEST

Black, grey and white in plumage, the pied wagtail is a native of Britain and usually builds its nest in a hole in a tree, bank or wall. It is also called the water-wagtail, owing to its liking for water-side haunts.

"envelope" or spathe. Gradually this unrolls, and there is revealed within a purplish rod or column which is a part of the flower, the rest of it being hidden inside the base of the spathe. At the base of the rod are various organs representing the male and female parts of the flower. The top series of organs are stamens which never become functional; then comes a perfect series, bearing pollen; then a perfect series of stigmas, the lower ones of which secrete nectar. The whole flower smells of carrion, and this attracts flies, which, once inside the spathe, are unable to escape. These may bring pollen from another wake-robin flower, in which case they fertilize the stigmas; later, the anthers will ripen, dropping their pollen on to the flies below. Then the long, downward pointing hairs which project from the top stamens and have so far prevented the flies from escaping shrivel up and the captives' way out is no longer barred.

So off the captives go, each flying with its load of pollen which was sprinkled upon it. Some of them will explore another wake-robin flower, and become temporarily imprisoned and with the aid of the pollen thus introduced the fertilizing process will there be repeated. The fertilized stigmas produce clustered berries which at first are green and later red. By the time these are red and ripe on the " spike " the spathe has withered and

H. Bastin

WAKE-ROBIN OR CUCKOO-PINT
The flowers of this common British wild plant are not visible in the photograph ; they are clustered at the base of the ' rod ' whose tip can be seen just behind the front edge of each of the large unrolled ' envelopes ' (spathes) which occupy the greater part of this picture.

decayed and the scarlet cluster of fruits stands up stiffly and alone. It is to these brilliant spikes that the popular name " lords-and-ladies " refers.

' *The* LITTLE LAND *behind the* HILLS '

*R*ich *in beautiful scenery, and at the same time scarred by the pits and installations of industry, Wales is a fascinating land ; and its people, though closely linked with England, retain their strong individuality.*

Wales. One of the greatest of modern Welshmen, David Lloyd George, who was Prime Minister of Great Britain during the First World War (1914–18), once affectionately called Wales " the little land behind the hills." Really it is not only *behind* the hills but all over and between the hills to the west of England.

Wales (from the Anglo-Saxon *walas*, meaning " foreign ") is a mountainous peninsula—136 miles from north to south, 96 miles wide at its broadest part. It contains 12 counties, six in North Wales and six in South Wales. Monmouthshire, though in England, is counted as part of Wales for some purposes, such as education. At the north-west corner, cut off by the narrow Menai Strait, is the island of Anglesey, with its port of Holyhead, from which steamers maintain a service to Dun Laoghaire (Kingstown), in the Irish Republic.

Though Wales appears such a confused mass of mountains when seen on a map, there are several distinct ranges. The Berwyn Mountains run from the Shropshire border right across North Wales ; the Snowdon group, rising to 3,560 feet, lies wholly in Carnarvonshire ; the Black Mountains extend westward from Herefordshire into Carmarthenshire ; and almost in the centre of the country is

the Plynlimmon system, covering nearly 500 square miles and having as its highest point the mountain of the same name, about 2,465 feet high.

Of the numerous Welsh rivers and streams the most important are the Dee, which rises in Lake Bala and flows by Chester into the Irish Sea ; the Severn, rising in Plynlimmon and winding through Shropshire to the Bristol Channel ; the Wye, which also has its source in Plynlimmon, and joins the Severn at Chepstow in Monmouthshire ; and the Usk, which traverses Brecon and Monmouth before entering the Bristol Channel at Newport.

The land is one of the richest in minerals in the world, for in addition to wide and deep seams of the best quality coal, including anthracite, there are extensive deposits of iron, copper, zinc, tin, lead and even some gold. One-fifth of all the coal of the British Isles is produced in Wales, and Cardiff (*q.v.*), on the Bristol Channel, is in normal times the most important coal-shipping port in the world. Other industrial centres are Swansea (*q.v.*) and Merthyr Tydfil, both in the same mining district as Cardiff.

The Welsh are of Celtic stock and have a Gaelic language akin to those of Cornwall and Brittany. Like most mountain peoples, they have many legends and traditions. The Anglo-

Extent.—Area 7,466 square miles. Population (including Monmouthshire) 2,553,000.
Physical Features.—In the north the Cambrian Mountains, including Snowdon (3,560 feet). Among the mountains of central Wales are Plynlimmon and Cader Idris. The principal rivers are the Severn, Wye, Usk, Dee, Towy and Teifi. Bala is the largest lake.
Principal Products.—Iron and steel goods ; coal, tin, iron and other minerals ; light engineering and plastic manufactures ; agricultural and dairy produce.
Chief Cities.—Cardiff (population 242,100), Swansea (158,800), Rhondda (111,800), Merthyr Tydfil (59,600).

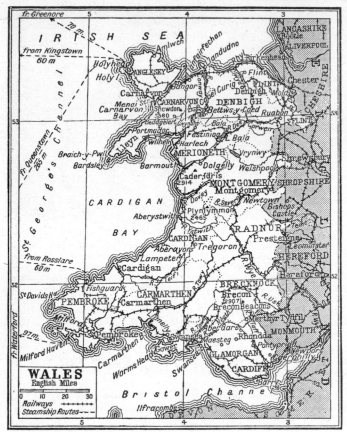

WALES
English Miles

| 0 | 10 | 20 | 30 |

Railways +++++++
Steamship Routes ----

camp by the Calvinistic Methodists, and the Baptists and Congregationalists became important. In 1914 was passed an Act disestablishing (making un-official) the English Church in Wales which, suspended during the First World War (1914–18), eventually came into operation in 1920.

The 19th century saw the rise of modern industry in Wales. Copper and tin had long been mined, but the find-ing of large deposits of the best coal in South Wales changed the whole char-acter of the country, both industrially and politically. Along with the mining industry came modern agriculture. Wales, although much more thinly populated than England, is generally fertile and well farmed.

The latter part of the 19th century saw also the development of parish councils, of district councils, and county councils, revolutionizing the local government of Wales. The influence of the owners of large estates diminished, and local aspirations found a voice in Parliament.

In the 20th century there has been a marked revival of Welsh culture. This movement has been fostered by a rising interest in the Welsh language, in Welsh literature, and in Welsh music. Programmes broadcast by the Welsh Regional station of the B.B.C. are often in Welsh, and are designed to increase interest in and knowledge of the lan-guage. A characteristic and picturesque feature is the annual bardic congress, the Eisteddfod (q.v.).

Movements to introduce Home Rule for Wales have been instituted from time to time but have met with only slight support. In 1947 the British Government rejected a request for the creation of a Welsh Office and a Secretary of State for Wales, which would give Wales the same status as Scotland.

With a view to preventing a return of the un-employment which was so prevalent in South Wales in the years preceding the Second World War the Government encouraged the establishment there of factories that would bring new industries into the area, and also facilitated the enlargement of existing installations concerned with the important steel and tinplating industries. The population of Wales (including Monmouthshire) is 2,553,000.

Wales: LANGUAGE AND LITERATURE. The Welsh tongue is akin to the Breton and Cornish dialects.. It is usually known as *Cymric*, a tongue of the Brythonic branch of the Celtic family. Divided into Early, Middle, and Modern Welsh, in each period it struggled against foreign languages before attaining further development. The first struggle was with Latin, during the Roman occupation; the second was with Norman-French, which affected its art of poetry; the third was the long struggle with English. The language is still spoken extensively; but along the English border, in Radnorshire, South Pembrokeshire, South Glamorgan, and in West Monmouthshire only a minority speaks Welsh. That *Cymric* has survived as a living language may

Saxon conquest of Britain (5th and 6th centuries A.D.) drove the Britons into the fastnesses of the western mountains beyond the " marches," or bor-der districts, and the Welsh are their descendants. The country remained independent, under native princes, until Edward I of England subdued their leaders, Llewellyn (1246–82) and his brother David, and gave to his infant boy the title of Prince of Wales. From 1301 the son and heir of the English sovereign has been created Prince of Wales. King Edward VIII, who was created Prince of Wales by his father King George V in 1910, was the first prince to be actually invested with the title in Wales, the ceremony taking place at Caernarvon Castle in 1911. (*See* illustration in page 3337).

During the reign of the Lancastrian Henry IV, Owen Glendower (1359–1415) carried on a war for Welsh independence, and won his place as the chief of Welsh heroes. The reign of Henry V (1413–22) saw Wales once more subdued. The Tudor sovereigns, being of Welsh descent, took a special interest in Wales, and gave it representation in Parliament and a form of local government similar to that of the English, in place of the old tribal law and organization. By the Act of Union in 1536 the Principality (another name for Wales, because it is nominally under the control of a prince) was peaceably absorbed into the Tudor realm.

Henceforth the history of Wales is mainly con-cerned with religious and educational progress. Puritanism won many converts, and in the 18th century the Methodist movement took fast hold on Wales. In 1811 a split was made in the Methodist

BEAUTIFUL NORTH AND BUSY SOUTH WALES

W. F. Taylor; Western Region British Railways

Wales,' wrote George Borrow (1803–81), 'is a country in which Nature displays herself in her wildest, boldest, and occasionally loveliest forms.' Some of the finest mountain scenery in the country is to be found in Caernarvonshire, and in the upper photograph the Snowdon group is seen from Nant-Gwynant. The industrial regions of Wales are in the south, in the counties of Glamorgan and Carmarthen, where are the extensive coalfields. On the Bristol Channel and about seven miles from Cardiff is Barry, of which the docks are seen in the lower photograph. The port has been in existence since 1889; through it passes a large part of the South Wales export of coal.

W. F. Taylor

GLIMPSES OF NORTH WALES
The valley road from Llangollen to Ruthin passes for miles through unspoilt country (above). Left, workmen are overhauling the suspension cables of the 1,710-foot road bridge over the Menai Strait between the mainland and Anglesey.

be ascribed to three causes—the isolation of the Welsh people behind their mountain wall, their retention of the traditions of bardism and the Eisteddfod (*q.v.*), and (indirectly) the Methodist revival in the 18th century.

After the earliest fragments of written Welsh that can be traced, with a few verses of the 9th and 10th centuries, the true beginnings are found in the Four Ancient Books of Wales. Of these, the Black Book of Carmarthen, so-called from the Black Friars of that town, contains verse dialogues, religious pieces and odes. The Book of Aneurin and the Book of Taliesin contain poetry of equal power. And from the Red Book of Hergest comes the one medieval Welsh prose work that has captured the imagination of the outer world; entitled the Mabinogion, it is a collection of 12 ancient Welsh tales, first translated and published in English in 1838.

The greatest name among Welsh poets is perhaps Dafydd ap Gwilym (*c.* 1340–*c.* 1400), almost a contemporary of Chaucer (*q.v.*). He may be said to have founded the standards of modern Welsh. To him succeeds Iolo Goch (died *c.* 1405) the bard of Owen Glendower (*c.* 1359–1415).

During the 16th and 17th centuries a freer melody came into vogue. Edmwnd Prys (1541–1624) was a popular poet. Huw Morus (1622–1709) was a Royalist who masked his politics in allegory, and excelled in love songs and carols. Of 18th century poets, Goronwy Owen (1722–69) carried on the classic tradition with individuality, and William

A. W. Cutler

WELSH LASSIES IN TRADITIONAL GARB

The national costume of the Welsh women is marked by delightful originality and quaintness, as may be seen from this photograph of three cheerful lassies in a country lane near Llangwm. Skirts and aprons in Wales show many combinations of checks and colours, but the high black hat (now rarely seen) is uniform.

Above, Fox; left, The Times

CUSTOMS OF OLD WALES

THE men of Cenarth, in west Wales, fish for salmon from coracles made of ox-skins, ash struts and pitch, similar to the boats used by their forefathers 2,000 years ago. Above you see the coracle-men off to the river. On the left a Welsh bard is singing " pennillion " with the harp. A pennill is an original topical composition sung to the accompaniment of a harpist, who changes the tune and introduces variations as he or she pleases. The singer takes up the strain at the second, third, or fourth bar, and must end exactly with the music.

Williams of Pantycelyn (1717–91), an inspired hymn writer, became the living voice of the people.

The 19th century produced two lyric poets of genius. Ceiriog (1832–87) wrote love songs; his Alun Mabon is a mountain idyll familiar wherever Welsh is spoken. Islwyn (1832–78), of more religious mould, was a nature poet. The founding in 1893 of the University of Wales gave a new impetus to Welsh literature which owes much to the influence of Sir Owen Edwards (1858–1920). Revival of interest in the Eisteddfod has been a stimulus to poetry, fiction, and folk drama.

The movement to extend the teaching and use of the Welsh language in the schools has been increasingly successful, and over 30 per cent of the population is now bi-lingual.

Within recent times there have been many outstanding Anglo-Welsh writers and poets: among the best-known are Ernest Rhys (1859–1946); W. H. Davies (1870–1940) ; Richard Hughes (born 1900); and Dylan Thomas (born 1914).

Wallace, EDGAR (1875–1932). As a week-old baby—destined to become a writer of thrilling stories—Edgar Wallace was abandoned by his parents, and found in London by a Billingsgate fish porter who later adopted him.

When a boy Wallace knew poverty and want; after going to an elementary school, he sold newspapers on the streets and did other odd jobs. At 21 he joined the Army, and went to South Africa as a private. In his spare time he wrote stories and articles, and on the outbreak of the Boer War in 1899, having left the Army, he was appointed war correspondent of Reuter's. He was South African representative of the Daily News (London) in 1900 and the Daily Mail during 1901–02. He edited a South African daily paper for a time, then returned to England and became a reporter for London newspapers. He rapidly made a name for adventurous " thrillers " of a new type, The Four Just Men (1906) being his first marked success.

Wallace wrote over 150 novels, 14 plays, several film scenarios and innumerable newspaper articles. His most typical novels are mystery stories. Among the best known are The Fellowship of the Frog, The Crimson Circle, and The Joker. He also wrote tales of Africa, introducing such characters as Sanders the Commissioner, and Bosambo the native chief. In his later years Wallace turned to the theatre and scored successes with plays about crime, e.g. The Ringer, The Terror, and On the Spot.

He died in Hollywood, where he had gone to write film scripts, on February 10, 1932. In 1934 a memorial tablet to " Edgar Wallace, Reporter," was erected at Ludgate Circus, London, above the spot where he had once sold newspapers.

WALES GREETS HER PRINCE
The future King Edward VIII, who became Prince of Wales in 1910, was the first Prince actually to be invested in Wales, the ceremony (above) taking place at Caernarvon Castle in 1911. The infant son of Edward I was made the first Prince of Wales in 1301.

Topical

EDGAR WALLACE
Beginning life as a newspaper-boy in London, Edgar Wallace made a name as the author of a number of ' thrillers ' and plays. The long cigarette holder was one of his special fancies.

Wallace, SIR WILLIAM (1270?–1305). Very little is known of the early life of Wallace, one of Scotland's national heroes, until the time when as a young man he killed an Englishman who insulted him, and in consequence was outlawed.

He then collected a small band of men and began a struggle against the English.

Gradually the number of his followers grew, until most of Scotland was in a state of rebellion. As soon as an English army approached, however, the Scottish nobles deserted him. In spite of this, Wallace defeated and almost destroyed the English at Stirling Bridge (September 11, 1297), drove the enemy out of Scotland, and devastated the northern part of England as far south as Newcastle.

As a reward for this success Wallace was elected guardian of Scotland. Soon a new and larger English army, commanded by King Edward I (1239–1307), marched into Scotland against him. Again the Scottish nobles deserted, and on July 22, 1298, Wallace was defeated in the battle of Falkirk. He sought refuge in the mountains, and for several years carried on guerrilla warfare against the English. But at length, on August 5, 1305, he was captured, near Glasgow, and taken to London, where he was tried and condemned as a traitor ; he was executed at Smithfield on August 23, 1305.

Although Wallace had failed to free his country from the yoke of England, his efforts were not in vain. He had inspired others to carry on the struggle, and a few years later Scotland's independence (retained until James I became King of England and Scotland in 1603) was secured under Robert Bruce (1274–1329). A monument near Stirling commemorates Wallace's heroism.

Walnut. The tree (*Juglans regia*) that produces in such great abundance the much-wrinkled, hard-shelled fruit we know as the walnut was introduced into Britain in 1592. Its original home extends from the mountains of Greece to Afghanistan; and it was known to the ancient Romans, who called it *Jovis glans* (Juglans), the " nut of Jove," so highly did they rate it.

The male and female flowers, which precede the nuts and appear in May, are very different from each other in form, for the male (pollen-bearing) flowers are borne in catkins, green and about three inches long, while the female flowers (which when fertilized by the catkins' pollen produce the nuts) are curious little stubby " buds " appearing singly or in groups of two or three.

The nuts are ripe when the thick outer husks turn brown in autumn. When the nuts are required for pickling they are gathered earlier, whilst the shells are still soft and green. From the husks a brown dye is obtained, and the timber of the tree is valued for furniture and cabinet work. It is also used for making gun-stocks.

Walpole, HORACE (1717–97). Though himself of little importance historically, Horace Walpole is interesting as typifying his age and as a recorder of its strange doings. The son of Sir Robert Walpole (*q.v.*) he was born in London on September 24, 1717, and was educated at Eton and King's College, Cambridge. Owing to his father's influence he was given several political posts, entailing no work, and he devoted his time to hobbies—literary, architectural and antiquarian. In 1747 Walpole went to live near Twickenham,

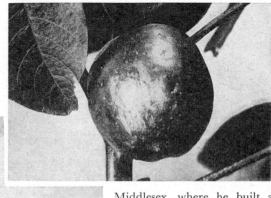

Middlesex, where he built a kind of Gothic castle, collected furniture, pictures and curios, and established a private printing press. His chief original literary work is the novel The Castle of Otranto (1764), an essay in the mysterious and gruesome, which set a fashion for "tales of terror." His most valuable works were his Memoirs and Reminiscences, and his Letters, which give an account of how people lived in 18th century England. He succeeded to the earldom of Orford in 1791, and died in London on March 2, 1797.

Walpole, SIR ROBERT, 1ST EARL OF ORFORD (1676–1745). Remembered as Britain's first Prime Minister, Walpole was a hard headed, hard-riding country gentleman whose financial genius was greater than his political honesty. Son of an M.P., he was born at Houghton, Norfolk, on August 26, 1676, and was educated at Eton and King's College, Cambridge. He soon made

WALNUT TREE AND ITS FRUIT
Above, Natural History Museum; top, S. V. Waters
Remarkable for the spread of its branches, the walnut tree reaches an average height of about fifty feet. It flowers in May, and the nuts are ripe when the thick outer husk turns from green to brown in Autumn. In the top picture the nut is still in its outer husk. (*See also* the illustration in page 2408).

his mark in Parliament as a Whig (Liberal), becoming Secretary of War in 1708. In 1710 he was expelled from Parliament, and even for a short while imprisoned in the Tower, on charges of political corruption brought by his opponents. However, he re-entered the Commons in 1714, and the accession of King George I, an ardent pro-Whig, to the British throne in the same year ensured Walpole of royal support.

Walpole came into prominence as a financier with the bursting of the " South Sea Bubble " in 1721. Originated as a trading concern by the South Sea Company in 1711, the " Bubble " was a financial project that was fundamentally unsound, and its eventual collapse ruined thousands of speculators. Walpole, however, had nothing to do with the Company and had warned people not to invest money in it. After the South Sea Company became bankrupt he helped the Government to devise measures to mitigate the disaster. In 1721 he became Lord of the Treasury, and

American Museum of Natural History

AN ' OLD MAN ' WALRUS OF THE ICE FLOES

Beneath the thick wrinkled hide lie folds of fat that keep him warm in the polar regions where he thrives. He prefers a quiet life, but if molested may inflict fatal wounds with those great tusks. He is a swift swimmer, but on land or ice his sprawling flippers propel him only slowly and awkwardly.

from then until 1742 was the chief adviser to George I and George II, being regarded as the first Prime Minister of Great Britain, though he did not hold that title—which, though it was first used by William Pitt (1759–1806), was not officially recognized until 1905. His policy, which proved extremely successful, was one of commercial prosperity based on sound finance and international peace. When war with Spain over trading rights in the New World broke out in 1739, Britain had a reserve of wealth which ultimately gave her victory. Walpole assumed the position of Minister of War, an office for which he was wholly unfitted, and was compelled to resign in 1742, when he received the title of Earl of Orford. He died on March 18, 1745.

Walrus. "Whale-horse" is the meaning of this creature's name, and it is also sometimes called the " morse." It is closely related to the seal and sea-lion, but has enormous down-turned tusks, or canine teeth, projecting from the upper jaw, sometimes 30 inches in length. The thick, wrinkled skin of the old animals is almost hairless, but the young ones are covered with pale brown hair.

The walrus has a thick, clumsy body, deepest at the shoulders. The head is square in front and rounded behind, with a short broad muzzle, on either side of which is a bunch of stiff, bristly whiskers. The flipper-like feet, which are adapted for swimming, are furrowed so as to hold to smooth surfaces, but do not enable the animal to move about very readily on land. Walruses normally reach a length of from 10 to 12 feet and a weight of about 2,000 lb.

There are two species, one occurring in the Atlantic and one in the Pacific. The Atlantic form, *Odobaenus rosmarus,* is found on the coast of Labrador and Hudson Bay. The Pacific form, *O. obesus,* lives farther north, being rarely found on the mainland. Both species feed largely on molluscs, which they break with their tusks, and are hunted for their hides, oil, and ivory, and, by Eskimos, for their flesh. During the breeding season walruses assemble on certain islands in huge numbers.

Walton, IZAAK (1593–1683). Although he wrote other books of considerable interest and literary merit, it is for his Compleat Angler that Izaak Walton is remembered, for this book is deservedly ranked among the classics of English literature. The book, of which the alternative title is The Contemplative Man's Recreation, is a fascinating treatise on angling, set out usually as a series of conversations between the author and his friends, full of simple philosophy and, to quote

Walton's own introduction, " innocent, harmless mirth." It contains information on how, where, and when to fish, and recipes for cooking the catch. The second part of the work was added by Walton's friend Charles Cotton in 1676.

Walton was born at Stafford on August 9, 1593, and was apprenticed to a London ironmonger. After a successful business life in London he retired about 1644, living at Farnham Castle, Surrey ; later he moved to Winchester, Hampshire, where he died on December 15, 1683, and he was buried in the cathedral there. In 1895 London anglers erected a window in his memory in the church of St. Dunstan's, Fleet Street. Walton's delightful biographies include those of the poet John Donne (1573–1631), and of the diplomat and poet Sir Henry Wotton (1568–1639).

Wandering Jew. According to legend, when Christ, bearing His heavy cross, was on His way from Jerusalem to Calvary, He paused to rest before the door of a Jew named Ahasuerus. The man struck Him, and cried out: " Go on quicker ! " For an instant Christ looked at him without speaking, then He replied, " I go, but thou shalt tarry till I come again." And from that day to this the Jew is supposed to have been wandering from place to place.

There are several versions of this medieval story, some describing the Jew as a cobbler of Jerusalem, others as the carpenter who made the cross for Christ, or as the doorkeeper of Pontius Pilate. The version given here first appeared in a pamphlet supposed to have been printed at Leiden, the Netherlands, in 1602, in which the Bishop of Schleswig is represented as having met the Wandering Jew at Hamburg, Germany. The numerous books and plays on this legend include the play The Wandering Jew by E. Temple Thurston (1879–1933), of which a film was made.

Warblers. Though these are among Britain's finest song-birds most of them are unlikely to attract attention other than by singing, for in plumage they are far from striking. The garden warbler (*Sylvia borin*), dull brown above, shading into a pale buff colour underneath, sometimes rivals the nightingale in the richness of its song. Its nest is typical of that of the warbler tribe, being a slight structure of small roots or grasses, hidden in a bush or in thick herbage; the eggs are brownish, mottled and blotched with darker shades.

Next to the garden warbler so far as singing power is concerned comes the blackcap (*S. atricapilla*), whose name betrays its most striking characteristic. This bird has a long, rambling song, which goes on and on with a number of queer phrases jumbled up in any order, and one or two notes of great beauty. Like all members of this group it feeds largely on insects and likes to creep about among the bushes rather than to show itself. It sings as it goes, not stopping to take up any particular perch.

Then there are the greater and lesser whitethroats, Britain's two commonest members of this group. The former (*S. communis*) has a red-brown top to its head, and likes to sit by the wayside, throwing itself into the air with little bursts of song. The lesser whitethroat (*S. curruca*) is a smaller bird, and prefers open, bushy places such as the outskirts of a wood. Both these are referred to as " nettle-creepers " by country-folk on account of their fondness for creeping about in thick wayside herbage, singing insistently as they progress.

The grasshopper warbler (*Locustella naevia*) is so called from its extraordinary song, often continued for some minutes at a time, all on one note. A bird of the damp moors, it is seldom seen except in the evening, when it sings a great deal; during the day it creeps about in the grass, for it is one of the shyest and most retiring of birds. This cannot be said of the reed and sedge warblers, both of them common by lakes and rivers and singing hard all day, their songs a jumble of all sorts of notes, for both are good mimics and introduce the calls of other birds into their own singing. The reed

E. J. Hosking; M. H. Crawford; Arthur Brook

THREE BRITISH MEMBERS OF THE WARBLER GROUP
To the delights of Spring in Britain are added the songs of the warblers. Those above are (left) the garden warbler, whose voice at times rivals in richness that of the nightingale ; (centre) the greater whitethroat ; and (right) the willow warbler, sometimes called the willow wren, though it is no relative of the wren. The willow warbler builds a domed nest, whilst the nests of the other two are open. These are all migrants, arriving in Britain about mid-March.

t-hog, with grotesquely curving tusks, the hideous warts below the eyes which give it its name, and a draggle of coarse hair on
d back, is indeed one of Nature's freaks. The skin is as cracked as dried mud, and the typical pig eyes, small and evil-shining,
ne generally peculiar and repulsive mien. The warts below the eyes may serve to protect them during battles between the boars.

HORRID-LOOKING HOGS

THE picture above shows a herd of wart-hogs peacefully drinking at one of the water-holes in the Kruger National Park, South Africa. There is a marked family likeness between these creatures ! On the left is another hog, almost as grotesque, and, with its lack of hair, almost as ugly; this is the babirusa, hailing from the East Indies. It is a close relative of the wart-hog, but its tusks are somewhat smaller.

To face page 334

warbler (*Acrocephalus scirpaceus*) makes a beautiful nest, slung round the stems of tall reeds, but that of the sedge warbler (*A. schoenobaenus*) is less neat and is usually hidden in the riverside vegetation.

Three members of this group are often classed together as " leaf warblers." These are the chiff-chaff (*Phylloscopus collybita*), the willow warbler (*P. trochilus*), and the wood warbler (*P. sibilatrix*). The word " wren " is sometimes used instead of "warbler" when speaking of the last two, but they are no relation of the wren. The chiff-chaff, the first warbler to reach Britain in spring, is easily recognized by its song, from which it gets its name; the willow warbler, which looks so like it as to be indistinguishable by anyone but an expert, has a completely different song, a sweet series of notes, starting strongly and bravely, then dying gradually away; it is one of the loveliest of all bird songs. The wood warbler, a pretty, yellowish bird, likes the shady oak and beech woods, and its song is a long series of shivering notes, very beautiful indeed. All these " leaf warblers " make a domed nest; that of the chiff-chaff is sometimes in thick vegetation, but others usually nest on the ground.

The warblers so far described are migrants, arriving in Britain from the middle of March onwards; the Dartford warbler (*Sylvia undata*), which is the smallest, spends its whole year in Britain. It is found chiefly in the south, where there is a good deal of dense gorse and heather. It is easy to distinguish, having very dark, almost black plumage, and a long tail which is usually held almost erect over the back. There are a number of other warblers found in Britain, some breeding in the country, some being occasional stray visitors and unfortunately rare. The nightingale (*q.v.*), although it looks like a warbler—except that it is much larger than any of this group—does not belong to their family but is related to the thrushes.

Warsaw. Crowning the heights above the left bank of the Vistula stands centuries-old Warsaw, the capital of the Republic of Poland. Almost completely destroyed in the course of the Second World War (1939–45), the city had for long been noted for its magnificent old churches and palaces, its splendid parks and public gardens, its monuments and tree-lined avenues. The heart of the city was the ancient royal castle, a vast pile built on a height overlooking the river (on the other bank of which is the suburb of Praga). To the north of the castle was the old town, later the Jewish quarter, with narrow streets and well-preserved old buildings. Here stood Warsaw's oldest church, the Cathedral of St. John, built in the 13th century. The beautiful Lazienki Park was laid out in an old bed of the Vistula by King Stanislaus Poniatowski towards the end of the 18th century. Here he built himself a small château.

Warsaw's central position in a fertile plain, with abundant transport facilities by water, rail and air, made it one of the chief commercial and manufacturing cities of eastern Europe. It manufactured machinery and metal goods, carriages, furniture, and woven goods, and had an active trade in food and animal products.

The city has been handed from one master to another since 1655. Sweden, Austria, Russia ruled in turn, with a brief period of independence—

bestowed by Napoleon, who in 1807 made Warsaw the capital of the Grand Duchy of Warsaw, which survived until 1813. During the First World War (1914–18) Warsaw was captured by the Germans, who held the city until 1919, when peace restored Polish independence. During the Second World War Warsaw suffered its worst tragedies. Heavily bombed and then shelled at the beginning of the war in September 1939, it was occupied by the Germans the following month.

Thousands of its inhabitants (especially the Jews) were later massacred, tanks and bombing aeroplanes being used against the Jewish part of the city, which was totally destroyed. In July 1944, when the advancing Russians were near Warsaw, local patriots rose against German rule. But the Russians did not reach the city, and the rising was suppressed by the Germans. It was not until January 17, 1945, that the Russians captured Warsaw and cleared the Germans from the rubble heaps that had once been a fine city. The population of Warsaw before the Second World War was 1,289,000; at the first census after the war (taken in 1946) it was only 479,000.

Wart-hog. " As ugly as sin " we sometimes say of something particularly repulsive, but we could really be as expressive if we said " as ugly as a wart-hog." For of all the wild animals there is perhaps none so unpleasant to look at as this grotesque member of the pig tribe. There are two species, *Phacochoerus aethiopicus* and *P. africanus*.

This big creature—it is one of the largest members of its family—has four of its teeth developed into tusks, which curve upwards and almost meet over its projecting snout. In addition to these " ornaments," it has two great lumps of skin growing out from under its small, beady eyes; and on top of its head, between the large ears, there is a sort of tuft of long, coarse hair.

Unlike other pigs, the wart-hogs lead a solitary life, forming at the most only small family parties. They feed on roots and similar vegetable products, digging them up from the hard soil of the African bush and jungle which is their home.

Warwickshire. From the Forest of Arden, in the northern woodland part, this midland county of England (976 square miles in area) gained the name of " leafy " or " woody " Warwickshire. Most of the county is undulating. In the south are spurs of the Cotswolds—Edge Hill, scene of the famous battle of 1642, rising to over 800 feet. Rivers include the Avon, Leam, and Tame, and roads the ancient Fosse Way and Watling Street.

The county is very important industrially, for it includes the cities of Birmingham (*q.v.*) and Coventry (*q.v.*). Birmingham is the seat of a university, and Rugby has a famous public school (the basis of the book Tom Brown's Schooldays) and a beam wireless station.

The county town is Warwick (population 14,500) on the Avon. Other important towns are Leamington, Nuneaton, Stratford-upon-Avon (*q.v.*), and Sutton Coldfield. There are several fine old castles and mansions, including Warwick Castle, Kenilworth Castle (*see* Kenilworth), and Compton Wynyates, a magnificent Tudor manor house. Shakespeare was born at Stratford-upon-Avon. The population of the county is 1,535,000.

The FATHER of the UNITED STATES

In this article we learn about Washington's immortal work as soldier, statesman, and patriot ; and how he won the War of Independence in the face of tremendous difficulties, and founded the world's greatest republic.

Washington, GEORGE (1732–99). The fame of the first President of the United States is not accounted for merely by the record of his achievements. Like another eminent American, Abraham Lincoln, the man was greater than anything he did.

Born at Bridges Creek (now Wakefield), in Virginia, on February 22, 1732, George was not quite 11 years of age when he lost his father. The boy learned arithmetic and to read and write in a school kept by the sexton of the parish church. His schooling, however, was irregular. Plantation affairs, hunting, fishing, and a little reading chiefly filled his days. It was to his mother that he owed his moral and religious training. Even when her son had become famous she would say that " George had been a good boy, and she was sure he would do his duty." A plantation on the Rappahannock river was the scene of those childhood exploits, most of them invented by his early biographer Mason Weems and narrated in his Life of Washington; this book was first published in 1866, and once thrilled adults as well as boys and girls. There, according to tradition, George cut down a cherry tree and, when challenged, explained to his father that he could not tell a lie.

When he was 14 he received two additional years of schooling, chiefly in mathematics, to prepare him for the profession of a surveyor. Through his half-brother Lawrence he won the favour of Lord Thomas Fairfax, who held enormous grants of land in Virginia, and at the age of 16 he entered his employ as land surveyor. At the age of 21 he was made major of the Virginia militia, and when war broke out with the French he served as an aide-de-camp to General Braddock (1695–1755). His advice as to methods employed by the Indians in border warfare was ignored, and Braddock suffered a big defeat. Washington was the only mounted officer in the engagement who was not killed. Two horses were shot under him, and he had four bullet-holes in his coat, but he escaped unhurt. He wrote to his mother that he had been preserved by Providence for some great duty. The Indians believed he bore a charmed life. In the later stages of the war, at the age

The history of the United States really begins with George Washington (above), who became the first President on March 4, 1789.

of 23, he was commissioned as colonel and became commander-in-chief of all the Virginia forces.

In 1758 he resigned his commission, and in the following year he married a wealthy widow, Mrs. Martha Custis. He never had any children of his own, but to hers he was devoted. The education of the children, the care of his large estate of Mount Vernon, and his duties as a member of the Virginian House of Burgesses (a local council) occupied his time for the next 15 years.

In 1774 he was chosen a delegate to the first Continental Congress. When, soon after the outbreak of the American War of Independence (*see* American Independence) the appointment as commander-in-chief of the Colonists' army was offered to him he accepted the post. Washington arrived in Boston early in July 1775, after the Battle of Bunker Hill. Beginning with an army of 14,000 untrained men, with few supplies, he had not only to attend to his military duties but also to persuade Congress and each of the 13 colonies to lend support to his operations and to furnish him with men and supplies. It was an experience to make a great man, to break a weak one. When, in March 1776, the British were driven out of Boston, Washington had become a statesman and a military commander of the first rank.

At the news of the French alliance with the Colonists in 1778, the British army evacuated Philadelphia, and Washington pursued them across New Jersey, shutting them up in New York. There he remained, watching, waiting, on the Hudson, while the main British force under Cornwallis captured Savannah and Charleston and entrenched at Yorktown, in Virginia. Then, feigning an attack on the weak garrison in New York, Washington made a forced march to the Potomac, the French fleet appearing simultaneously in Chesapeake Bay. Three weeks later Cornwallis surrendered and the actual fighting was over (1781).

WHERE GEORGE WASHINGTON LIVED AND DIED
In Virginia, overlooking the Potomac river, is Mount Vernon, where George Washington lived during much of his life and where he died on December 14, 1799. The mansion is now a national museum.

No one saw more clearly than did Washington, in the critical period from 1783 to 1789, the dangers which beset the new nation, and it was largely owing to his efforts that a convention to consider the revision of the Constitution at last met in Philadelphia in May 1787. He was called to the chair by a unanimous vote, and during the four months' session his hand guided its work.

After the convention Washington continued to work for the ratification of the new Constitution by the States. He regarded it as the best which could be had at that time, and it was largely due to the fact that he approved of the document that the people were induced to accept it.

It was to Washington, as first President (1789–97), that the American people committed the task of putting the new Constitution into operation. When he was asked in 1797 to serve a third period of four years as President he refused, thus establishing a precedent against a third term which continued to be observed until 1944, when F. D. Roosevelt (q.v.) was elected for the third time. After his retirement Washington lived the life he loved best, that of a planter " amid the mild concerns of ordinary life " at Mount Vernon. This period of

well-earned enjoyment was all too short. In less than three years on December 12, 1799, he contracted acute laryngitis as the result of a long ride on horseback in a snowstorm. Two days later he died. In accordance with his wishes he was buried in the family vault in the hill-side at Mount Vernon, overlooking the Potomac river.

So passed the man whom John Richard Green (1837–83), the historian of the British people, characterized as " the noblest figure that ever stood in the forefront of a nation's life."

Washington, Capital of the United States. In March 1791 six men stood gazing over a " wilderness " on the hills above the River Potomac, in what is now the District of Columbia, in the United States. One of the party was George Washington, President of the United States, who had come to assist in fixing the boundaries of the new " Federal District."

Major Pierre Charles L'Enfant (1754–1825), a French engineer who had fought in the War of American Independence for the Colonists against the British, prepared the plans for the new city, which was called " Washington " after the first President of the United States. On September 18,

WASHINGTON : FEDERAL CAPITAL OF THE UNITED STATES

Situated in the District of Columbia, Washington was built according to a rectangular plan but with diagonal avenues cutting across it. In this view, looking westward towards the Potomac river, the following buildings are indicated. A. The domed Capitol ; B. Offices of the House of Representatives ; C. Congressional library ; D. The Supreme Court ; E. Senate offices ; F. Federal Triangle, a triangular strip of land occupied by buildings housing the Departments of Justice and Commerce, the Bureau of Internal Revenue, the Post Office and the Archives Building ; G. Hidden by trees is the White House, the official residence of the President of the United States ; H. Washington Monument ; J. Lincoln Memorial, in the form of a Greek temple ; K. Arlington Memorial Bridge, leading to the National Cemetery.

THE CAPITOL IN THE CITY OF WASHINGTON

In a park in the centre of Washington is the massively beautiful Capitol (seen here by night), where the Senate and the House of Representatives meet in two wings at either side of the building. The rotunda under the dome is 96 feet in diameter, and its walls are decorated with paintings and statues of important events and figures in the history of the United States.

Near the Congressional Library is the home of the Supreme Court, completed in 1935.

One of the principal streets of the city is Pennsylvania Avenue, which runs diagonally toward the north-west from the Capitol to the Treasury building. Between the park known as the Mall and this avenue is an area known as "the Triangle," completely covered with magnificent government buildings, nearly all of them built since 1918. Close to the Treasury building is the White House, the official home of the President, surrounded by lawns and trees. Beyond the White House, on the west, is the building which houses the State Department. Before the First World War (1914–18) the Navy Department also occupied part of this building, but it later moved to a building in Potomac Park.

More impressive even than the view down Pennsylvania Avenue is the vista westward from the Capitol down the broad green stretches of the Mall, which extends to the banks of the Potomac. Here is another imposing array of public buildings, including those famous scientific centres the National Museum and the Smithsonian Institution. In the distance rises the Washington monument, a plain square obelisk of white marble, 555 feet high.

1793, the corner-stone of the Capitol (the United States Houses of Parliament) was laid, and in 1800 the seat of government was transferred there. It was the first city to be built as a capital.

Today the capital of the United States of America follows in its arrangement of streets and principal government buildings the plans made by L'Enfant. The general plan consists of lettered or numbered streets running at right angles to one another, and these are intersected by broad avenues, named after the States of the Union, sweeping diagonally from one corner of the city to the other. The principal avenues converge like the spokes of a wheel at the Capitol grounds.

The Capitol, crowned by a dome on which stands a statue of Freedom, the work of Thomas Crawford (1814–57), is in the centre of the city, surrounded by beautiful park-like grounds. To the left is the wing housing the House of Representatives; to the right, the wing in which are the Senate chambers. From the portico in the centre two big bronze doors lead into the rotunda, which is decorated with paintings and statues representing important scenes and figures in American history. In Statuary Hall are statues of leading citizens.

The Library of Congress, south-east of the Capitol, is considered one of the finest library buildings in the world. It contains over four million books. The walls and ceilings are decorated with many paintings, representing the arts, sciences, history, and mythology, and the march of civilization.

Looking south-west from the Capitol the eye meets the long sweep of Potomac Park, which stretches along the river for more than two miles. At the upper end stands the Lincoln Memorial, in the form of a Greek temple. South of the Capitol, where the Anacostia flows into the Potomac, is the United States War College, and about a mile up the Anacostia is the U.S. Navy Yard. In 1941 the remarkable structure known as the Pentagon was erected as the War Department's headquarters south of the Potomac, at Arlington.

From the Capitol cupola may be seen the immense bulk of the Union Station. Among educational establishments are the George Washington University, the Catholic University of America, and Howard University, renowned for the higher education of Negroes.

A characteristic feature of the city is the existence side by side of the old and the new—of the plain red-brick residences and stone buildings of President Lincoln's day alongside modern concrete structures.

The official boundaries of the District of Columbia (D.C.), which lies between Virginia and

Maryland, about 225 miles south-west of New York, are the same as those of the city and enclose 69 square miles. The government of the district is in the hands of three Commissioners appointed by the President with the approval of the Senate. The population of Washington city is 663,000, about one-third being Negroes.

Washington, U.S.A. STATE. This should not be confused with the city of Washington (*q.v.*) which is the capital of the U.S.A. Like Oregon, of which it was once a part, the State of Washington is divided from north to south by the high and broad wall of the Cascade Mountains. It is in the extreme north-west corner of the United States—far from the city of Washington in the District of Columbia.

Between the Olympic range and the Cascades is the tangle of bays and inlets called Puget Sound, forming one of the finest harbours in the world. Along its shores are most of the large cities—Seattle (population, 368,000), Tacoma (109,000), and

Olympia (13,000), the capital. The River Columbia flows south through the eastern half of the State, then bends sharply to the west and flows to the Pacific along the State's southern boundary. On a tributary is Spokane (population 122,000).

A number of peaks rise from the Cascade ridge, among them Mount Rainier. About this majestic peak (14,408 feet) Mt. Rainier National Park has been reserved, a beauty spot 377 square miles in area, famed for its fir forests.

Washington produces fruit (particularly apples) and a large variety of crops; wool; coal, magnesite, and other minerals. There are huge cattle and sheep farms, and the State is the greatest exporter of wood manufactures in the country. Its vast forests (mainly of Douglas fir) have given it the name of "Evergreen State." Water power is abundant, and is tapped by such enterprises as the Grand Coulee dam (*see* illustration facing page 961). The area of the State of Washington is 68,192 square miles. Its population is 1,736,000.

A TIGER TRIBE among the INSECTS

Wonderful indeed are the ways of living and the workmanship of the wasp. The sting which can pain us can kill or paralyse the small creatures which these swift-winged hunters mark down as their prey.

Wasps. You probably know only one sort of wasp by sight, the familiar black and yellow one that invades the house in midsummer and makes such a nuisance of itself. It is a member of a very large and important insect family.

Belonging to the same order of insects as the bees and ants, *Hymenoptera*, the wasps may be divided broadly into two groups—the social wasps and the solitary wasps. The former, including the common wasps (*Vespa*) and their close relative the hornet, live very much like bees, with queens and drones and workers. They are the original papermakers, chewing up leaves or wood fibre into pulp, out of which they build their nests, sometimes in holes dug in the ground, sometimes hanging from the branch of a tree or wedged in beneath the rafters of an old house or barn. With the exception of certain tropical honey wasps all wasps feed their young on animal food, consisting usually of other insects, or spiders. Some of the social wasps of tropical countries build huge nests. One species in Ceylon often constructs a home six feet long. Another in South America mixes earth with the paper pulp, and this makes walls as solid as stone.

Unlike the hives of bees, the wasp communities last only one summer. All the members die at the approach of cold weather, except a few queens, who

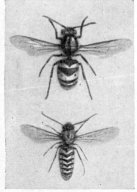

A queen (upper) and a male (lower) of the common wasp. They appear to have only two wings, but there are four.

sleep through the winter and in the spring lay the foundation for new nests and new generations. Each queen builds a few comb cells, made, like the walls of the nest, of paper. In each cell she lays an egg, which hatches in about eight days. She then feeds the legless grubs until, in about 14 days, they become pupae and 10 days later full-grown workers. These immediately take off her hands the task of enlarging the nest and providing for the new batches of young, which hatch from the eggs which she has been laying every day. As food becomes more abundant the queen produces eggs from which emerge larvae destined to become queens and males. When food is very plentiful the workers themselves often develop the faculty of laying eggs.

It is among the solitary wasps that the most astonishing habits and the highest intelligence are found. There are hundreds of species, some as large as hornets, some less than a quarter of an inch long. Their colours vary from dull black and brown to brilliant reds and yellows and blues—these are for the most part " warning colours," telling birds not to eat these dangerous little insects.

The mother solitary wasp is confronted with the fact that her offspring are very greedy and will be satisfied only with living or recently-killed prey. She must, therefore, not only build a safe nest in which to lay each egg but must stock that nest with fresh food on which the young wasp may begin feeding the moment it leaves the egg. Each species, too, demands its own particular kind of food. One eats only a certain kind of fly; another requires a carefully chosen caterpillar; a third will have only spiders; others need beetles, grasshoppers, or grubs.

Let us follow a common sand wasp (*Ammophila*) on a hunting expedition. She is a largish, red and black insect, with a very narrow waist, long spidery legs, and powerful jaws. She has built her nest in the ground. It consists of a tunnel an inch or two

H. Bastin

A SAND WASP AND ITS PREY

The long-waisted sand wasp lives in a burrow which it excavates in sand. Above, one is seen with a caterpillar larger than itself, which it has stung into insensibility and is now dragging along to replenish the sand-burrow larder in which the young wasps will hatch out.

remain alive but motionless for more than five weeks after this violent operation.

The quantity of food stored in each nest varies greatly. A single larva of a certain fly-catching wasp (*Bembex*) has been known to eat 82 flies in eight days. The mother wasp lives in the nest herself, and skilfully builds side tunnels for nurseries and storehouses, feeding and watching over her young; in this she is a step nearer to the social wasps than is *Ammophila*.

The carpenter wasps and the mason wasps show extraordinary skill in building. The former bore holes in rotten trees or old posts, or clear out the pith from the stems of certain bushes to make room for their nursery cells. The mason wasps usually construct their cradles of mortar and small stones on walls or sun-heated rocks.

long, leading down at a sharp angle to a small pocket. Before departing for the chase she may close the opening with a lump of earth and smooth it over, so that the keenest eye can hardly find it.

Presently she finds her game—a green caterpillar resting on a leaf. She attacks at once, and her strong jaws soon close over its back near the head. Standing high on her long legs, she lifts the front of the caterpillar off the ground, curves the end of her long abdomen underneath, and thrusts in her sting between two segments of her victim's body. At

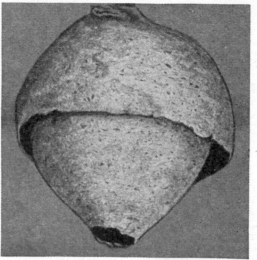

It is among the sand wasps that we find what is perhaps the only case of the use of tools by lower animals. One naturalist noticed a wasp of the genus *Ammophila* repeatedly take up in her jaws a small pebble, with which she hammered down the earth over her nest.

Although some wasps damage fruit and wood to a certain extent, the tribe as a whole do mankind a great service by destroying numbers of harmful insects and caterpillars.

once the caterpillar becomes limp and helpless. The sting is withdrawn and plunged carefully between other segments.

Now she picks up her prey and makes her way back to the nest; if the caterpillar is large the wasp will be unable to fly, and must drag it, holding it beneath her body with two legs and running with the other four. Reaching home, she opens the "front door," drags the caterpillar inside, lays an egg on one of its middle segments, comes out, closes up the hole carefully, and is off hunting again. Here is the strange thing: the caterpillar *is not dead*. The wasp has thrust her poisoned lancet into the nerve centres which control the creature's motion and has thus made sure that the food supply for her young will not decay or dry up before the egg hatches two or three days later.

There is a species of beetle-hunting wasp of Europe, described by that great French naturalist Jean Henri Fabre (*q.v.*), which is compelled to press down upon the body of its victims in order to open the one joint in their armour, through which the sting, with unerring accuracy, can reach its mark. The tarantula-killer of the south-western states of America induces her dangerous prey to rise in defence on its back pairs of legs, exposing its vulnerable spot. A quick thrust of the wasp's sting disables the great spider, which has been known to

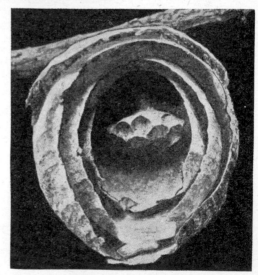

NEST OF TREE WASPS

Made of wood-fibre worked into a paste with the insects' saliva, the nest of the tree wasp usually hangs from a branch of a tree. Oval in shape (upper), it has two main walls (shown in cut-open specimen), which enclose spaces to be filled with cells. A few cells can be seen in the centre.

WATER: HOW *it* REACHES *our* HOUSES

*This familiar substance, in its three forms as liquid, solid and gas, is the wonder-
working material of the modern world. Here is an account of its properties,
and of the methods by which it is made plentifully available to us.*

Water. If by some magical process we could view in a glass of water a moving picture of the journey of its contents to our home, we should see portrayed a story of much interest.

First we might see the pure water of the mountain springs and small rivers gathered into great reservoirs. Then we should watch the water from these huge reservoirs constantly slipping into tunnels, or pipe-lines, to plunge downward through the darkness, gathering a force from gravitation that will carry it through the water mains of the city. Sometimes the water would be seen flowing rapidly into basins at the pumping stations, and then great steel pumps, working ceaselessly day and night, forcing it out through the distributing mains to all the parts of the city.

If you live in a rural neighbourhood, far from a town, the story of your water supply has to do chiefly with the work of Nature. We might begin each of these stories with the evaporation of the water from the earth and its fall in the form of rain. Perhaps the rain is caught from the roofs of buildings where smoke and dirt are not excessive, and stored in cisterns or tanks above or below ground for use in bath and laundry. In some instances this water is filtered, when it becomes fit for drinking.

Or, again, the rain falling upon the earth may continue its journey down through the ground, which is Nature's filter, to be stored in layers of porous rock or confined in rocky chambers. Wells are then dug, into which this water may percolate. It is important to dig the wells where the soil is free from contamination with harmful bacteria. Deeper wells may also be driven to tap water deeper underground. (*See* Artesian Wells).

Much water for domestic purposes and for industry is drawn from rivers. But it cannot be used " raw," and must undergo a complex process of filtering and purification. The reservoirs we spoke of earlier are situated in parts of the country uncontaminated by industries and manufactures. Thus the water of springs, streams and rivers is relatively pure; but even so it does have to be processed, though not to such a degree as water drawn, for example, from the Thames for the supply of the Greater London region.

Even though the source may be wells, provided these do not fail in a time of drought, a constant supply of water may be obtained in the country as well as in the city, for water may be pumped and stored in an elevated tank. From this tank, pipes can be installed leading to the houses, and the stored

water can be used whenever it is wanted. But wells could not supply the needs of great cities in ancient times. In Egypt, Assyria, and Babylonia the water was conducted from the river-beds through open canals to the cities.

The Romans far outstripped all other ancient peoples in the energy and engineering skill devoted to the construction of their water systems. Rome brought water clear and fresh from the distant hills and first nine and later fourteen streams flowed through aqueducts of brick and stone to supply the city's fountains, public baths, and public buildings. The aqueducts of Rome were large enough to supply 375 gallons a day for each person, and similar aqueducts were constructed throughout the Roman empire (*see* Aqueduct). The Roman systems served very few individuals and then only at great expense, for a special lead pipe was run from the reservoir out to each house served.

The cities of the Middle Ages were much less enterprising than ancient Rome, and the terrible ravages of pestilence during that period were largely due to the restricted use of water and to the pollution of the city wells. Paris in 1550 had a drinkable water supply equal to one quart a day per person ; and at the end of the 17th century the supply, if evenly distributed, would have been only 5 pints each.

For the early distribution systems hollow or bored tree trunks were used. The pipes were small, and as many as 10 separate lines were laid in some streets to furnish enough water to the customers in that street. At one time the company which supplied water for London had 400 miles of wooden-pipe water mains.

In the early systems, too, water was only pumped during a part of the day. It was not distributed under pressure, either, so that the water could be

OLD LONDON'S WOODEN WATER MAINS
At one time the water mains of London were of wood, usually of elm (which does not rot easily) like those seen in the above illustration, which shows the aqueduct over the Fleet river before the latter was built over. The wooden pipes had a very small bore and often several had to be laid in one street to ensure an adequate supply.

obtained only from taps at or near the level of the ground. As you may read in our story of the Steam Engine, the first use of these engines was for pumping water. Unless the house or city to be supplied chanced to lie *below* the level of the reservoir from which the water came—so that there was a " fall " in the pipe-line which constituted a hydraulic gradient—some form of pump had to be used to lift water from ground level and to force it up to a tank at a higher stage.

The use of iron pipes became general at the beginning of the 19th century. With these pipes for the distribution systems and with the improved steam-engine to run the pumps, the development of the modern water systems began.

In the modern distribution system water is supplied under pressure, thus overcoming the force

a "drainage area " or "gathering ground " in a mountain or forest region. Such an area is carefully guarded to prevent contamination of this supply.

Usually, however, a sufficient supply can only be obtained by drawing upon water which in its natural state is admittedly impure, and in such cases some means of purification must be adopted. River water, such as that used in London, is passed through a " slow sand filter " depending for its action on the formation, on the surface of a sand bed, of a slimy mass of organisms which acts as a bacterial filter. The " rapid sand filter " is chemical and physical rather than biological in principle. The water is first dosed with some chemical to precipitate suspended matter and bacteria, part of which settles out in suitable basins, and the remainder is removed by passing through layers of sand and gravel. Rapid

sand filters purify about 125 million gallons of water per day per acre of filter surface, which is from 30 to 50 times faster than the speed of slow sand filters. Experiments have shown that water entering the filter containing 31,200 bacteria per cubic centimetre leaves the filter with only about 120 bacteria in the same volume.

The sedimentation process uses shallow reservoirs without filter bottoms. The water is allowed to stand for a number of days in a basin before being used (intermittent system); or else it is made to flow gently

of gravity. Hence, if we live in a built-up area, it matters little whether our house be on a hill-top or in a valley: the pumps (*q.v.*) ensure that water reaches our taps. Moreover, the pressure is so great that the water gushes out with energy to spare, and an exceptional demand, as in the case of fire, finds the system ready for the emergency. A pressure of 40 lb. per square inch in the supply mains is common, so you will realize why a leak or a burst so quickly floods a room.

Because of the enormous consumption of water in modern cities, and the necessity of finding this supply within a limited area, water supply has grown to be a highly technical science. Sometimes water is drawn from

Lower, Fox

RESERVOIRS CONSTRUCTED UNDERGROUND

To ensure Constantinople's water supply in time of war, the Byzantine Emperor Justinian (A.D. 483–565) had two reservoirs built under the city, one of which (top) is still in use. The Meriden reservoir (lower), about five miles from Coventry, Warwickshire, though modern, resembles in conception the one at Constantinople (Istanbul).

FILTERING WATER FOR A GREAT CITY'S SUPPLY

Water flowing down from the hills is gathered in the reservoir, whose bottom is of fine clean sand overlying a gravel bed. The water seeps through, depositing its impurities in the sand, and is then collected through screened pipe-heads thrust up into the gravel. From there it is pumped clean and clear into the city mains. A filtering station usually has several reservoirs, so that any one can be drained and the sand changed without interfering with the regular supply.

from one to the next (continuous system). In either case, the impurities gradually sink to the bottom.

Chemical treatment consists either of coagulation or of direct destruction of bacteria. In the former process chemicals which produce a gelatinous mass are introduced into the water, and, as this mass sinks, it strains out the impurities. When only bacteria are feared, some such agent as chlorine gas is introduced and the water can be used without further delay. In cases where the only available water is particularly bad several of these processes may be used in combination.

After quantity and purity are assured, steadiness of supply must be provided for. Both drainage areas and rivers furnish most water in the spring and least in the summer. In order to preserve the spring-time excess for summer use, great dams confine water in artificial lakes. In lands which lack coal, and in others, where water-power is abundant, much use is made of flowing or falling water as a source of energy to drive machines. Today water-power is applied usually to gigantic electric generators, and the power is tapped in the form of current—to light cities, run railways, drive motors, serve as the fuel for smelting aluminium and other metallic ores, or to heat the ovens in which pottery is fired. This aspect of water supply is dealt with in our story of Hydro-Electric Installations.

Water has been the great architect and sculptor of the earth's crust, entering the cracks of rocks and splitting them apart as it freezes and expands; wearing away mountains by erosion, and rolling the fragments in its torrents to make gravel, sand and clay ; carving out valleys and filling them with rich soil; forming the rivers that are the veins of the earth's circulation; washing soluble minerals from the ground and carrying them downstream until the sea contains not only salt but also samples of most of the other earth materials, including even such precious substances as silver and gold.

Water is also the chief treasurer of the energy that pours down on the earth from the sun. As the sun's rays warm the surface of the sea, water vapour rises. This water vapour first provides the atmosphere with an extra blanket for keeping the earth warm. for it makes up from one to five per cent of the atmosphere; then, as it forms into clouds and passes over the land, it cools and falls again as rain. Rainfall provides the moisture necessary for growing plants, whose roots draw it in along with essential minerals dissolved from the soil. In returning to the ocean in rivers, water provides us with a cheap form of power. This continual movement from the ocean to the land and back is known as the " water cycle."

Of the water that falls upon the land, some evaporates; some (called the surface-water) flows quickly on or near the surface down to the rivers; some soaks into the ground and tends to sink down to what is called the " *water table*." This is the underground level where the earth is kept permanently saturated. Springs arise from the water table where gullies or slopes cut down to its level; and wells are supplied from it. If the soil above the water table dries up, moisture tends to seep upward. To hold its level, the losses of the water table must be balanced by gains of new water from above.

Water requires more heat to warm it and more cold to cool it than any other common substance. This is why the water in your hot-water bottle can supply you with more heat than the same quantity of any other easily available substance at the same temperature. This is substantially what we mean when we speak of its high *specific heat*. One calorie of heat applied to 1 gramme of water raises the temperature of the water by 1° Centigrade;

putting this another way, 1 British Thermal Unit (B.Th.U.) raises the temperature of 1 lb. of water by 1° Fahrenheit. For example, it takes five times as many calories to raise a pound of water one degree in temperature as to raise a pound of dry earth one degree; or, to put it in a more practical way, when land and sea are equally exposed to the sun's rays, it takes the sea about five times as long as the land to reach the same temperature, and similarly it takes the sea five times as long to cool down again.

As the heat of summer comes on, the oceans remain cool and send cool breezes over the hot land; but by the end of the season they have accumulated a vast amount of heat, which is slowly released again during the winter to moderate the cold atmosphere. Thus the oceans keep the earth's climate from changing season by season from deadly cold to unbearable heat. (*See* Climate).

Water, as we are all aware, can take three forms —solid (ice), liquid and gas (steam).

The expansion of water when it freezes amounts to about one-tenth of its original volume; one cubic foot of water turns into 1·09 cubic feet of ice. This is what makes ice float, since ice occupies more space than water does, without weighing any more than it did as a liquid.

The expansive force of freezing water is enormous. Many a householder finds his water-pipes torn open if they have been unprotected on cold winter nights. When the plumber thaws the pipes, he must use, for every gramme of ice melted, 80 calories (or 144 B.Th.U. for every pound of ice).

With ordinary atmospheric (sea-level) pressure water freezes at 32° F. During the process of turning to ice it remains at this same temperature, but continues meanwhile to give up " latent " heat. When the process is reversed and ice is melting, the resulting mixture of ice and water remains at 32° F. until all the ice is gone; by that time the water will have absorbed again the same quantity of heat as it lost when freezing. This definite amount of heat which is alternately given off and absorbed without change of temperature represents theoretically the energy difference between the movement of the water molecules when they are arranged in the crystal form of ice and the movement of the same molecules when they are in the liquid arrangement. The use of a mixture of ice and salt in making ice-cream illustrates the principle of latent heat. The salt melts the ice rapidly and the mixture absorbs enough heat from the liquid cream to leave it frozen.

When we boil water we encounter the latent heat of vaporization. If you put a thermometer in your kettle you will notice that the temperature rises rapidly until boiling begins at 212° F.; and there it remains until all the water has boiled away (*see* Steam). Just as when solid water (ice) turns into liquid, so when liquid water turns into gas (steam), heat is absorbed in the transformation without rise in temperature. The quantity of heat absorbed at ordinary atmospheric pressure by one gramme of water as it turns into steam is 536·7

Fox

POWER UNIT OF A WATER-PUMPING STATION
There are various types of engine in use for pumping water. This unit is one of a pair constructed in 1929 for the Kempton Park, Middlesex, pumping station. Each engine is of the vertical triple-expansion type and develops 1,008 horse-power, with a maximum pumping capacity of 19 million gallons per day.

calories. In British Thermal Units, the latent heat of vaporization is 996 B.Th.U. per pound of water.

Lowering the pressure on the water lowers its boiling point. This fact is often made use of, as, for instance, in making sugar or evaporating milk. These would be spoiled by heating to 212° F.; so they are heated in vacuum pans where the moisture boils away at about 160° F.

Boiling is evaporation artificially speeded up. A point is reached where not only the surface molecules but also those down inside the liquid move so violently that they break away from close association with their neighbours and form bubbles of vapour, which rise to the surface and escape. This is the boiling point. In an open vessel, with the surface of the liquid exposed to the atmosphere, the temperature of water at the boiling point (at sea level) is 212° F., or 100° C. Pressure on a liquid—by heating it in a closed and sealed vessel—raises its boiling point, because the vapour pressure inside the bubbles has to equal the pressure outside before the bubbles can form.

Water reaches its greatest density at 39·2° F., and at this temperature it is used as the standard of comparison for the specific gravity (q.v.) or relative density of other substances. A cubic foot of pure water weighs 62·30 lb. The pressure upon every square inch of an immersed object increases 43·3 lb. for every 100 feet of depth. At one mile the pressure increase would be more than a ton to the square inch.

Natural water is never pure. So great is water's solvent action that even the raindrops take impurities from the air as they fall. Water that passes through the soil always contains dissolved minerals. And when these are calcium or magnesium sulphates, chlorides, or bicarbonates, they prevent soap from lathering freely in the water. The water is then termed " hard." Water in which soap lathers freely is " soft." The chemical formula for water is H_2O, showing that each molecule has two atoms of hydrogen and one of oxygen. Since 1931, however, science has known that water may be a combination of either " ordinary " or " heavy " hydrogen with oxygen. " Heavy water " with double-weight hydrogen is known as Deuterium (q.v.).

Water usually is formed when a substance containing hydrogen is burned in the presence of oxygen and when acids combine with bases. It can be separated into its elements by electrolysis (q.v.).

HOW HARD WATER IS MADE SOFT

EVEN the naturally distilled rain water is not pure but contains gases dissolved from the air, including carbon dioxide and ammonia. In industrial areas traces of sulphuric acid may also be taken up. As the rain water percolates through the soil on its way to the sea it dissolves substances from the soil. If it passes through chalky soil it dissolves calcium carbonate which, although insoluble in pure water, will dissolve in water containing carbon dioxide, owing to the formation of soluble bicarbonate:

$$CaCO_3 + H_2O + CO_2 - Ca(HCO_3)_2$$
calcium   calcium
carbonate   bicarbonate

If the soil contains calcium sulphate or gypsum, this may dissolve in the water; and magnesium sulphate and the chlorides of calcium and magnesium may also be dissolved.

When water contains dissolved calcium bicarbonate it is said to be "temporarily hard" because, on boiling, the hardness disappears as the bicarbonate decomposes into calcium carbonate (which is insoluble and precipitates), and into carbon dioxide, which escapes into the air. The equation for this is the reverse of the one given above. The precipitated calcium carbonate forms the familiar "fur" in kettles when hard water has been boiled in them for some time.

Clark's process for softening water consists of adding milk of lime, so that calcium and magnesium are precipitated:

$$Ca(HCO_3)_2 + Ca(OH)_2 = 2CaCO_3 + 2H_2O$$
lime

When water contains dissolved sulphates and chlorides of calcium and magnesium it is said to be " permanently hard " because the hardness is not lost on boiling. The magnesium can be precipitated by lime, and the calcium by soda. This is known as the lime-soda process for softening water. Hard water is harmful for some purposes. It forms scale inside boilers, so that more coal is required to give the same amount of steam. It also wastes soap, since some soap has to be used to soften the water, by precipitating " calcium soaps," before any lather is formed. On the other hand, the dissolved bicarbonates prevent the corrosion of lead pipes. (See Poisons).

The hardness of water is estimated in " degrees." One degree is equal to 1 grain of dissolved calcium carbonate per gallon of water. A soft water would have a hardness of about 5 degrees; and a moderately hard water one of about 10 degrees; while a hard water would have 20 degrees of hardness.

In the " Permutit " process for softening water the latter is filtered through a bed of zeolite (sodium aluminium silicate). The calcium and magnesium ions in the water are exchanged with the sodium ions in the zeolite, and the water is left with small amounts of sodium salts which do not cause hardness. The zeolite softener, when exhausted, can be regenerated by passing strong salt solution through it: the calcium and magnesium are thus replaced by sodium again, and the softener is once more ready for use. This " ion-exchange " method of removing unwanted dissolved salts has been extended so that it is even possible on a small scale to remove the salt from seawater with a special zeolite. Apparatus for doing this is provided on lifeboats for ships at sea. Ion-exchange is also used to purify beet juice. (See Ions ; Sugar).

On a smaller scale (as in laundries), water may be softened by adding a small amount of a complex phosphate called " Calgon." (See Phosphorus).

Some water contains dissolved iron salts which give it an unpleasant taste and cause the familiar rust-coloured staining of porcelain. The presence of iron may also assist the growth of certain bacteria which cause clogging of water pipes. Iron is removed in the lime-soda process, and by an adapted zeolite process.

Water-Boatman.

Remarkable for the manner in which it rows itself about below the surface of the water, on its back, is the water-boatman (*Notonecta glauca*), a member of the bug order (*Hemiptera*), common in the ponds of Britain. In colour it is a mottled grey and black, and in size is about equal to a wasp. But it is utterly unlike that insect in shape, for in appearance it resembles an inverted boat.

Its long hind legs, fringed with stiff hairs, act as oars and under their power the water-boatman is swiftly driven along in search of the small creatures—from tiny fish to plump tadpoles—which are its food. It can dive quite deeply and steeply, and as a change from its upside-down existence in the water it can launch itself into the air and take wing, buzzing vigorously during its flight. Somewhat similar is the *Corixa*, but this is dark shiny green in colour and rows itself about right-side up.

This interesting order *Hemiptera* contains also the water-skater (*Gerris*) which conducts its hunting on the surface. Its long, narrow body, with six spidery legs, darts over the water at great speed and with hardly a ripple. The middle pair of legs act like oars, while the hind pair are used to steer. The short front legs rest lightly on the water ready to shoot out and seize any insect that fails to move out of the way.

Quite different is the behaviour of the water-scorpion, of this group. It trundles slowly about the mud at the bottom of a pond and there with its pincer-like forelegs secures its living prey and sucks the blood. This flat, dirty-brown creature has to come frequently to the surface to breathe through the two respiratory tubes at the tail-end of its body.

Water-colour Painting.

The art of painting in water-colours is perhaps the most peculiarly English of all the graphic arts, and in it the painters of England have always excelled. There are in fact few foreign artists at all who have even approached the great water-colourists of the English school, and even to the present day our own workers in this medium are the finest.

Water-colour is perhaps the most difficult of the painting arts, for it demands a very high standard of technical skill, a sureness and a patience which are less necessary in oil-painting and, to a certain degree, in other media. The water-colourist can make only the slightest of alterations to his work, and even these will be discernible to the sharp eyes of the expert ; but the painter in oils can alter his work as he goes along, perhaps even repainting a whole portion of the picture.

Water-colour was employed for practice sketches and for private amusement by many of the early masters, from the time of Dürer, whose studies of plant and animal life in this medium have become famous through reproductions; and long before this the artists of the East were working in this same medium. But water-colour as we now know it was for centuries dormant as an art, subservient to work in other media. Perhaps the first water-colourist of English birth, and certainly England's first real artist in that medium, was John White, Governor of Sir Richard Grenville's settlement in North Carolina. He executed a large number of very fine water-colour drawings of the natives, animals and plants of this newly-discovered country. Most of these are in the British Museum, London. After him the only great water-colourists in England were the foreign masters, such as Rubens,

Victoria & Albert Museum; photo, Mansell

A WATER-COLOUR OF KIRKSTALL ABBEY BY GIRTIN

The foremost early English water-colour painter was Thomas Girtin (1775–1802). No-one before him had combined with such success the work of an accurate draughtsman with the imaginative treatment which transforms a mere painting into a picture. Though the details of this lovely view of Kirkstall Abbey (now within the limits of Leeds) have been depicted with infinite care, the work can still be appreciated as a picture rather than as a reproduction of a set scene. Girtin's colouring, pure and harmonious, was also in advance of that of his forerunners in this field.

A MASTERPIECE IN WATER-COLOUR

Wallace Collection; photo, Mansell

The exquisite work of the English artist Richard Parkes Bonington (1801-28) had a lasting effect on both French and British art. He is especially noted for his water-colours. Leaning Towers, Bologna (above), is notable for bright colouring and delicate drawing.

Rembrandt and others, who used the medium for sketching rather than for finished drawings. Even their work was mainly done in monochrome wash, sometimes outlined with ink, and it was in this type of work that, in the early 18th century, Britain's own artists began to practise again.

The "father of English water-colour" was Paul Sandby (1725-80), whose studies of London and other parts of the country show his own development from a worker in monochrome to a real artist. Contemporary with him there began to work a large number of artists, most of them topographical draughtsmen at first, such as Michael Angelo Rooker (1743-1801), Thomas Holland, Alexander Cozens (died 1786) and his son John Robert Cozens (1752-99), Edward Dayes (1763-1804), and the greatest early English water-colour painter, Thomas Girtin (1775-1802), of whom Turner remarked that "had Tom Girtin lived, I should have starved."

Girtin indeed raised water-colour to a real art, and

considerably influenced Britain's whole painting, through Turner and Cotman, both of whom greatly admired his work. These two were the greatest of Britain's water-colourists, yet as different as can well be imagined: Turner, with his masterly effects of misty sunlight, and brilliant colours, his strange vision of the Mediterranean lands; and John Sell Cotman (1782-1842), a master of simple colour, of wash and pattern, whose every picture is a tapestry-like design. From them dates the greatest development of this art in England.

In succession, Peter de Wint (1784-1849), David Cox (1783-1859), Copley Fielding (1787-1855), William Hunt (1790-1864), and Birket Foster (1825-99) carried this art through the 19th century. Besides these men, all working in the direct tradition, there were others, such as William Blake (*q.v.*) and his friend Samuel Palmer (1805-91), and John Varley (1778-1842), who was a most influential teacher. John Constable (1776-1837) and R. P. Bonington (1801-28) did many glorious little masterpieces in this medium, while the Pre-Raphaelites also used it successfully.

A remarkable painter, too, was H. B. Brabazon (1821-1906), who worked largely in "body-colour"—water-colour mixed with white; while among the modern workers excelling in this medium are Sir Charles Holmes (1868-1936), J. D. Innes (1887-1914), C. A. Hunt (b. 1873), Charles Conder (1868-1909), painter of delicate Watteauesque fantasies, and Wilson Steer (1860-1942), a master of Impressionistic landscape. The whole history of the development of this great school has been recorded in the exhibitions of the Royal Society of Painters in Water-colours and the Royal Institute of Painters in Water-colours.

In the United States a strong water-colour school has long been active, remarkable for its colour and its strong broad style. Of this school Winslow Homer (1836-1910) is a good example, while John Sargent (1856-1925) worked with great distinction in the same medium.

Watercress. One of the most beneficial of salad plants—for it is especially strong in mineral salts, such as iron and sulphur, which are not found to so great an extent in other foods—watercress is grown for market in shallow "beds," which are usually levelled areas in the course of clear streams. These beds are so arranged that they can be flooded at will. The plant is found growing wild in streams in Britain.

Botanically, watercress is a hardy perennial member of the order *Cruciferae*, or "cross-bearing" flowers, so-called from the arrangement of the four sepals and four petals in the form of two crosses. Along the stems thread-like rootlets grow out, only a few of the lower ones, however, reaching the bed of the stream. The flowers, which come out in June,

H. Pickwell

WATERCRESS IN FLOWER

Found wild in streams in Britain, watercress is also extensively grown for market. Rich in mineral salts, and having a somewhat hot, biting flavour, young shoots of the plant may be eaten alone or in a salad.

are very small, and white. Its botanical name is *Nasturtium officinale*, yet it is no relation of the beautifully coloured garden nasturtium (*q.v.*), which belongs to the order *Tropaeolaceae*.

Several other wild plants bear the name of cress, among these being the common hairy bitter cress (*Cardamine hirsuta*), which has a rosette of leaves from which arises a hairy stem bearing minute white flowers ; and the very similar hairy rock-cress (*Arabis hirsuta*), which is a relative of the various species of garden *Arabis*. The " lady's smock," or " cuckoo-flower " (*Cardamine pratensis*), whose pale lilac blossoms abound in damp meadows in spring, is a member of this group.

Waterford. A county of the Province of Munster, Eire, Waterford has an area of 713 square miles. It is bounded on the north by Tipperary, on the east by Kilkenny, on the south by St. George's Channel, on the west by County Cork. It has a coastline of 50 miles, on which are the harbours of Waterford, Dungarvan and Youghal, and the natural anchorage of Tramore Bay. Chief rivers are the Blackwater and Suir.

The surface is mainly hilly ; in the west are the Knockmealdown Mountains, which reach a height of 2,609 feet. The land is more suitable for pasture than for cultivation ; cattle and sheep are bred. The main industries include brewing and flour-milling, and marble is quarried. The city of Waterford (population 28,000) is the county

town and has steamer connexion with Fish-guard, in Wales, and Bristol. Its exports are butter, bacon and cattle. Other towns are Dungarvon, Lismore, Youghal and Tramore. The population is 76,000.

Water-lily. This " queen of the water " has its home in lakes and ponds and rivers, its roots embedded in the mud. Thick stems make their way to the surface, adjusting themselves to the water's depth and serving as anchors for the flowers, which majestically float—one on

Kodak; B.N.A.

WATER-LILIES LARGE AND SMALL
The compact loveliness of the flowers and leaves in the upper photograph is more in keeping with our usual conception of water-lilies than the gigantic proportions of the species (*Victoria regia*) in the lower picture, one of whose leaves provides a seat for a boy.

each leafless stem—amidst the flat leaves. British species of this order (*Nymphaeaceae*) are the white water-lily (*Nymphaea alba*) and the yellow water-lily (*Nuphar luteum*). Two interesting points of distinction are : the fruit (seed-vessels) of the white species are round and they ripen under water, whilst those of the yellow species are flagon-shaped and they ripen above water.

To the water-lily order belongs the gigantic *Victoria regia* of the Amazon, with white flowers up to 16 inches across and leaves so vast and firm that they are capable of bearing the weight of a man. Various other species are distributed throughout the world, ranging in colour through white, pink, and yellow, to blue. The lotus of Egypt is a member of the water-lily family, as is also the sacred lotus of China and the sub-continent of India. (*See* illustration in page 2027).

Waterloo, Battle of. The history of Europe might have been very different if it had not rained in Belgium on the night of June 17, 1815. At daybreak on the 18th Napoleon Bonaparte, the commander of the French army, was scanning the battlefield of Waterloo (named after a village 11 miles south of Brussels), but it was nearly noon before the mud was dry enough for the artillery to advance. Meanwhile, the Prussians, who had been defeated by the French two days before at Ligny, Belgium, were slowly but surely making their way along the muddy roads to the aid of the British.

Only three months before Napoleon had escaped from his island prison of Elba, off the coast of Italy, whither he had been sent on his abdication in 1814. When he returned to France his old soldiers had flocked to his standard, and he had hurried north into Belgium with his army, hoping to defeat his quarrelling enemies before they could unite, a Prussian force under Blücher being at Namur, Belgium, while the British, Belgians and Dutch under Wellington (*q.v.*) were in the vicinity of Brussels. His plan seemed to be succeeding. He got between the English, who were concentrated near Brussels, and the Prussians, who were east of the road from Brussels to Charleroi. On the 16th one French force held the English engaged at Quatre Bras, while another under Napoleon attacked Blücher's Prussians at Ligny. After the battles Napoleon ordered Grouchy, one of his commanders, to follow Blücher, and turned his attention to the British and their allies. Blücher, however, drew off to the north and marched to the assistance of the British, while Grouchy wasted precious time searching for him to the east of Ligny.

The British forces had meanwhile concentrated at Waterloo, which Napoleon reached late on the 17th but could not attack until the following morning. Then, after waiting until 11 o'clock for the ground to dry, he gave the order to attack. For 10 hours the battle raged, Napoleon repeatedly hurling his columns of cavalry against the squares of British infantry. French and British infantry fought' throughout the day for possession of the farmhouses of Hougoumont and La Haye Sainte, which were the keypoints of the British front. At 6 p.m. the French seized La Haye Sainte, but were soon driven out. Late in the afternoon, Blücher's men arrived. Those hours that Napoleon had waited that morning saved the day for his enemies. The French Imperial Guard made their last desperate attack under the brave Marshal Ney, but were repulsed and counter-attacked by the British. The French were thrown into confusion ; the whole Allied line advanced and by nine in the evening Napoleon's army was in flight. So desperate was the fighting that the combined losses, including prisoners, were more than 74,000, and it is said that 45,000 killed and wounded lay in three square miles of country. Napoleon's defeat was decisive. In Paris four days later he signed his second and final abdication. (*See* Napoleon).

Water-plants. Have you ever considered the various remarkable ways in which plants have adapted themselves to a life in the water ? Those that live wholly under water in quiet depths have no need of woody tissue to support or stiffen them, but those in running water have to be tougher. Another common adaptation is the development of conspicuous air-passages, such as one may see in the stalks of water-lilies.

The roots of most water-plants are much reduced, and sometimes entirely absent. Where they exist, they serve chiefly as anchors to keep the plant in its position, and not for extracting food from the mud. The air cavities would hoist the plant from its position were it not securely fastened. Some water-plants, however, do float throughout their existence. The duckweeds (*Lemna*) form sheets of green scum on stagnant ditches, each consisting of myriads of tiny plants. Some seaweeds are kept afloat by little globular air-bladders.

The leaves, too, show interesting adaptations. Submerged leaves have no " stomata " or breathing pores. Frequently the leaves are very finely divided, especially in running water, thus presenting less resistance to the water and objects borne along in it. The slender long leaves also present a larger surface to the water whence they draw their nourishment. Some have no submerged leaves at all. In the various kinds of water crowfoot (*Ranunculus aquatilis*) you may find the whole range from perfect, five-lobed leaves which lie flat on the water, or are raised above it, to long, deeply-divided filaments which wave to and fro in the rapid parts of the stream.

Leaves that float, such as those of the water-lilies (*q.v.*), are usually thin and flat, of round or oval shape, supplied with air-filled cavities for buoyancy, and with flexible slender stems long enough to allow for changes in water level. They have breathing stomata on the upper surface.

Some water-plants bear spores, or both flowers and fruits, beneath the surface, where the pollen floats away to other plants; but in most of them the flowers either float on the water or are poised

F. R. Hinkins

QUAINT WATER CROWFOOT

Totally different in shape are the two sets of leaves of this British aquatic plant. Those below the surface of the water are almost threadlike, whilst the leaves which lie flat on the water or are raised above it are broad and glossy. The flowers are white, and appear in May and June.

on stems reaching above it. Insects and breezes are then the usual pollen-carriers. Various water-plants have buoyant envelopes for their seeds or fruits, so that when they ripen and fall on the water they can sail before the wind or ride on the current. Seeds and even tiny plants are also carried at times on the bills or muddy feet or even the plumage of waterfowl.

There are three main types of water-plants. The first type is made up of plants which are entirely sustained by water and are free to move either by locomotion or water currents. To this group belong such plants as algae and duckweeds, which float in stagnant or slow-moving water.

The second type is made up of plants that are anchored, but with their bodies submerged or floating, such as the seaweeds (*q.v.*). Moreover, seaweeds are often governed by a definite distribution, some being found at some levels, others higher or lower. Another group is that which contains the water-lilies, with broad floating leaves, and the pondweeds, with entirely submerged leaves.

The third type is made up of groups in which the plants are rooted in water or in soil rich in water, but the leaf-bearing stems rise above the surface. The conspicuous swamp " societies " are " reed swamps," characterized by tall rushes and reed grasses, which usually form a fringe about shallow margins of small lakes and ponds; " swamp moors," the ordinary swamps, bogs, etc., which are covered by coarse grass; " swamp thickets," in which there is a tangle of willows, alders, etc.; and other ecological divisions (*see* Ecology). A typical forest tree among the water-plants is the swamp cypress (*Taxodium distichum*), which has curious " knee roots " projecting above water as an additional means of securing sufficient oxygen for the root system.

Among common British waterplants are the members of the order *Alismaceae*, which are unusual in having their parts organized in threes. These include the greater and lesser water plantains and the arrowhead. The great water plantain (*Alisma plantago*) has large, simple, ovate leaves, which are reminiscent of those of the plantains found as garden weeds, borne on long stalks which raise them well above the water. The flowers are quite small, pink in colour, and borne on a very tall erect stem which rises, branching repeatedly, high above the leaves. There are three sepals, three petals, and six stamens. In the lesser water plantain (*A. ranunculoides*) the leaves are narrower in proportion to their length, and the flowers, on 18-inch stems, are smaller and paler in colour.

The arrowhead (*Sagittaria sagittifolia*) is so called because of the shape of its leaves, which are like an arrow whose barbs are as long as its blade. They are very conspicuous in sluggish streams in summer, lying flat on the surface, or standing upright. The flowers, arranged on the same system as those of the water plantains, are large, with white petals, each of which has a purple spot at its base.

Even more conspicuous than these plants, the flowering rush (*Butomus umbellatus*) has stems which rise for five or six feet from the bed of the stream, bearing an umbel of light purple flowers, which have a perianth of six parts, nine stamens and six carpels. The leaves are very long, narrow, and almost grass-like. At the other extreme from this plant is the curious frog-bit (*Hydrocharis morsus-ranae*). This has white petals, which are supported above the water, on a short stalk, by the large, heart-shaped leaves. These in fact support the whole plant, for it actually floats on the surface of the pond. At the base of the plant, however, are roots, by which the plant is lightly anchored in the mud. From these roots come off small buds, which drop to the bottom of the pond in autumn and give rise to new plants.

Water Polo.
Played without any stick or implement, water polo contests take place either in open water or in a swimming bath. The playing area is usually between 19 and 30 yards long by 20 yards wide. At either end there is a goal 10 feet wide, with a cross-bar at least three feet above the surface of the water. Seven players (three forwards, one half-back, two full-backs, and a goalkeeper) make up a team, and the object of the game is to throw an inflated ball, like a

E. J. Bedford

ARROWHEAD

A water-plant of British streams, the arrowhead derives its name from the shape of its foliage. It is strikingly attractive when in flower, July to September.

football, into the opponents' goal. There are two periods of play—seven minutes each way.

All the players wear tight-fitting caps—usually the members of one side wearing blue and those of the other white. The game is started by the referee throwing the ball into the centre of the playing area, the players then swimming at top speed from each end towards it. Fouls are given for several offences—catching the ball with both hands, kicking or splashing an opponent, or holding the ball under water when tackled. Passing the ball needs a great deal of practice, and the secret of water polo is team-work.

Waterspout.
Twisting columns of water which seem to rise from the surface of the sea and reach up into the clouds are known as waterspouts. They are caused by tornadoes which form over lakes, streams, or the ocean itself. The spout is merely the characteristic funnel-shaped cloud of the tornado.

The water in the spout is fresh and not salt, a fact which proves that the column is formed by the condensation of water vapour in the air. Waterspouts are most common in tropical waters and may be as much as 1,500 feet high. Their duration is from 10 to 30 minutes.

Watt, JAMES (1736–1819).
Everybody has heard the story of James Watt and his boyhood experiment on the lifting power of the steam under the lid of his mother's tea-kettle.

Born in the fishing-town and port of Greenock, Scotland, on January 19, 1736, Watt was a delicate, sensitive and thoughtful lad, poor in health. His first lessons were given him by his mother; later he attended the local Grammar School. Not until he got into his 'teens did he show much progress, and then it was in mathematics that the youngster began to shine. He followed his own inclinations in study and amusements. Long days were spent among the hills and lakes at the back of the town, developing physical strength and turning his thoughts toward botany, geology, and water-power.

Watt's father was a carpenter who built houses and small ships, and also did business as a ship chandler. Watt's mother died in 1753, and about the same date his father suffered heavy financial misfortunes. As a result the lad, who had become skilful in the use of tools, was sent to some relatives of his mother in Glasgow, and there was placed with an optician for training; he had made up his mind to become a mathematical instrument maker, and when he found no one plying that trade in Glasgow he decided to seek his fortune in London. After some difficulties and delays he was taken on by one John Morgan, an instrument maker with a shop near Cornhill. Morgan agreed to teach Watt for a year, on payment of a small premium.

In July 1756, having completed his year of apprenticeship, James Watt returned to Glasgow. He had been befriended earlier by Professor Robert Dick, of the College of Glasgow. Now, through Dick's aid, Watt was given the task of setting in order a number of instruments which had been left to the college by a Scotsman merchant of Jamaica. His work impressed the authorities; and when soon after Watt was seeking a small shop in which to start business as a mathematical instrument maker, he was allotted a room in the college.

One day a small model of Newcomen's steam-engine from the scientific collection was put into his hands for repair. This led him to make a thorough investigation of the whole subject of steam.

As you may read in our story of the Steam Engine, Newcomen's machine worked really by the pressure of the atmosphere, which pressed down the piston after the cylinder had been filled with steam, and this steam condensed by cold water, to lower the inside pressure. Watt's first task was to do away with the waste of heat energy due to the alternate heating and cooling of the cylinder. But later, as a result of his investigations and experiments, he built engines in which the energy of steam was used to force the pistons up and down—making an enormous advance on Newcomen's principle. Here is Watt's own recorded account of how he approached the first task—the making of a separate condenser.

" One Sunday morning," he wrote, " when I had gone for a walk in the Green of Glasgow, the idea occurred to me that, as steam is an elastic vapour, it would expand and rush into a vacuum, and if a communication was made between the cylinder and an exhausted vessel, it would rush into it and be there condensed *without cooling the cylinder* . . . The separate condenser would take care of the exhaust, and the steam-jacket keep the cylinder hot. I rushed back to the University and broke in upon Dr. Robison, lecturer on chemistry, and cried: ' You needn't trouble yourself about that any more, sir; you shall have steam boiling hot, in a boiling-hot cylinder, and not waste a single particle.' " (This was in 1765.) Watt's first changes made

big improvements, but the engine was still useful for pumping only, and did not turn wheels to drive machinery. However, it made an enormous difference in draining water-logged mines in all parts of Britain. Not till 1782 did Watt patent his " rotative " engine, which could be used to drive rolling mills, looms, and hundreds of other kinds of machine. This was a " double-acting " engine. Watt's partner, whose financial aid made the success of his inventions possible, was Matthew Boulton of Birmingham.

Watt always had some investigation to engage his inquiring mind. Now it was the composition of water, or an illuminating gas, or the fertilizing of his broad farm lands; at another time, a uniform system of weights and measures, anticipating the metric system of today. One of the chief units of electrical power, the " watt," is named in his honour. Watt died on August 25, 1819.

Lower, Science Museum, London

MEMORIALS OF JAMES WATT

The original model of James Watt's perfected steam-engine as it appeared in 1800, the year of his retirement, is seen in the upper photograph. His workshop (lower) was rebuilt at the Science Museum, South Kensington, London. Watt also invented a machine for copying sculpture, which explains the busts on the right.

Wave Motion. When you throw a pebble into a pond, the particles of water displaced by the stone rise in a ring—they must; there is no other place for them to go. Then gravitation pulls them down, displacing some of the water outside the ring, which is thus in turn compelled to rise, only to be pulled down by gravitation; and so the circle of waves or ripples goes on widening.

The production of water waves by wind is similar. Wherever the wind makes an exceptionally heavy downward thrust at the surface, it displaces the water, which is piled up in a wave. As the wind keeps pushing against the waves thus formed, they tend to increase in height and length, particularly out at sea, where there is nothing to retard or break them. In the southern Indian Ocean waves 675 feet long (length is measured from crest to crest) and from 38 to 45 feet high have been measured. Waves may run so high that two vessels of ordinary size are completely hidden from each other when lying in the troughs of adjacent waves.

Does the water move forward with the wave? Watch a bottle floating by the shore. You will see it bob up and down in nearly the same position. Shake one end of a rope extended on the ground. Waves run along it from one end to the other, but no part of the rope need move forward. So it is with the particles of water in a wave: they rise and fall, or move to and fro, only a short distance—except for the kind of wave known as a " wave of translation," which actually carries the water particles onward, as in breakers.

Let us suppose that you and a friend have gone to a lake to sail his model yacht. He sets the sails, and just as the little craft is going along nicely, you heave a great stone into the water so as to " make waves." Your friend will hardly thank you for producing the swell which rocks his little craft,

as the waves set up by the fall of the stone approach and pass under the boat. What you did was to impart the energy of the falling stone to the water particles. If the stone did not make a big splash, most of the energy was converted into waves.

Any " elastic " medium will carry wave motion, and almost all materials are elastic to some degree or other. As you may read in our stories of Light, and Heat, and Sound, these forms of energy are conducted by waves—though heat is carried by other means as well. We give the name " radiation " to the emission of electro-magnetic waves (including visible and non-visible rays from the sun, and also the entire gamut of wireless and similar waves). Sound is due to vibrations travelling through the air in waves—or through other substances by conduction. The electro-magnetic waves travel without any proved medium to carry them, other than the " ether," about the very existence of which there is controversy today. This controversy is one reason why the wave theory of light has come to be considered incomplete, since it would seem that light may be transmitted in the form of particles, although " groups " of such particles may behave as waves.

There are three main factors to bear in mind about waves, of whatever kind these waves may be. Look at our picture of sea waves: you will see two complete crests, with a steamer lying in the trough between them. The height of the wave is the vertical distance from the level of the trough to the top of the crest. The *length* of the wave is the horizontal distance between two adjacent crests. The *amplitude* of the wave is the distance to the crest, measured from a horizontal line midway between the levels of trough and crest. The *frequency* of the waves is given by the number of complete waves which pass a particular point in one second; of course this

Wind blowing in this direction

Crest

Height of wave

Trough

Water of cycle A at top of oval path

Water of cycle B at bottom of oval path

Water of cycle C approaching bottom

Water of cycle D at top of oval path

WAVE MOTION THAT IS FELT BY EVEN THE LARGEST VESSELS

Though the waves themselves travel forward, the water of any one wave really moves in an orbit. At A the particles of water are at the crest of a wave, and as the wave moves forward the water at A passes downward and then back into the trough and upward in front of the succeeding wave. At the same time the water in the trough of the wave at B passes down and up again in an orbit, a similar movement occurring also at C and D.

depends upon the velocity of propagation of the waves. As an example, wireless waves travel with the velocity of light (*see* page 2729). Since this velocity is some 300 million metres per second, wireless waves with a wave-length of six metres would have a frequency of 50 million per second.

Wax. The animal, vegetable and mineral worlds all produce useful waxes. Beeswax was known in ancient Egypt (*see* Bee), and our word wax comes from the Old English word for the material of the honeycomb.

Many crude mineral oils contain wax, and when these are distilled (producing petrol and other fractions) the wax is distilled out with the lubricating oil (*see* Oil). On strongly cooling the lubricating oil, the wax separates out. It is " sweated " to get rid of the entrapped oil, and is purified and bleached, giving the white paraffin wax used in making candles, in waxing paper, and in polishes. A wax similar to paraffin though superior for numerous purposes is ozokerite, which is mined in Central Europe and in the United States. It has probably been deposited from mineral oils during the course of ages. The crude wax is black, but it can be made white by treatment with sulphuric acid and bleaching earths.

Montan wax is extracted with benzene from lignite or brown coal. The crude wax is dark in colour and is purified by distillation with superheated steam, giving a pale yellow wax. It is used in boot polishes. A similar wax is extracted from peat.

A number of plants produce waxes—e.g. rose petals—their natural function being to restrict the loss of water. Sometimes these waxes are produced in commercial quantities. Carnauba wax is formed as a dust on the leaves of a palm native to Brazil. The leaves are cut, and the dust removed by beating, after which it is melted into cakes. This wax is valuable for furniture polishes as it forms a hard durable surface. Ouricuri wax, found on the leaves of a palm growing in Central America, is used as a substitute for carnauba and in typewriter carbon papers. Other vegetable waxes include sugarcane wax from the outsides of the canes, and Japanese wax obtained from berries of the sumac tree and used in textile and leather industries.

One of the most important animal waxes is spermaceti, obtained from the head of the sperm whale. It is used in ointments, cosmetics and candles. The standard candle on which was based the definition of candle power was made of this wax (*see* Candle). Raw wool contains about 15 per cent of wool wax. It is removed on scouring the wool. The purified form is known as " lanolin " and is used in ointments and cosmetics, its chief value being its easy absorption by the skin. The crude form of the same wax is used in lubricating greases and in anti-corrosion paints.

Beeswax is secreted on the underside of the abdomen of the worker bee. It has been used for numerous purposes, such as candles, polishes, in engraving, and in making wax models. Many other waxes are blended so as to imitate the properties of beeswax. Chinese insect wax is produced by a scale insect related to the one which gives us cochineal (*q.v.*). The larvae of this insect cover the twigs and branches of a certain tree and become embedded in the wax. The wax is used in China for candles, and is exported for electrical insulation, polishes, and for glazing paper. Crude lac produced by the lac insect (*see* Resins) contains 5 per cent shellac wax mixed with the resin. The wax can be separated, and is used in the electrical industry. The old medieval seals contained beeswax. But modern " sealing wax " is not really a wax at all ; it contains shellac, turpentine, pigments, with fillers such as chalk.

Chemically the waxes consist of long-chain molecules. Paraffin waxes are hydrocarbons similar to those in petrol and oil, only with larger molecules. Montan wax and the vegetable and animal waxes contain esters, acids and alcohols all of high molecular weight. The acids are similar to those combined with glycerol in fats. (*See* Soap).

A large variety of synthetic waxes has been produced in recent years. Some of them are made from other waxes such as montan, others from fats, while others have been synthesised from carbon monoxide and hydrogen by a Fischer-Tropsch process (*see* Oil). Some synthetic waxes have properties very different from the common waxes —e.g., the chloro-waxes, which contain a proportion of chlorine as well as carbon and hydrogen and are non-inflammable.

A. R. Thompson

BLOODTHIRSTY WEASEL
A dreaded hunter of the British countryside this ten-inch long, brown-coloured animal gets its living in a predaceous manner. It varies its meals between birds'-eggs and rats, and will even attack poultry and rabbits.

Weasel. Sometimes on a country walk you may hear a sudden piteous squealing. As likely as not the sound will lead you to a rabbit, lying paralysed with fear, while running away you see a slim, quick, pale brown little animal, with short legs and a long tail. This is a weasel (*Mustela nivalis*), a small carnivorous mammal and a member of the family *Mustelidae*. It has a remarkably slender round body with a long neck, which gives the animal the appearance of having the forelegs set back too far. The legs are very short.

The weasel, which can twist and wind its body like a snake, reaches a length of about 10 inches. It is reddish-brown above and whitish below, and in northern districts of Britain becomes more whitish in winter. It feeds on mice, moles, rats, and other small creatures, and sometimes attacks rabbits and poultry. It is never deterred by considerations of size. It also visits birds' nests, killing the birds and eating the eggs. It is distinguished from the ermine (*q.v.*) or stoat by its smaller size and by the absence of a black tip to its tail. It is less often seen than the stoat, being more nocturnal in habit.

Weather. The term weather includes the appearance of the sky, the occurrence or otherwise of rain, hail, sleet or snow, the presence of fog or mist, the direction and speed of the wind, the temperature and the humidity (dampness) of the atmosphere. As weather affects the activities of most human beings, and a number of industries, the accuracy of weather forecasts has become a matter of increasing importance.

The studied prediction of future weather was developed considerably during the Second World War (1939–45). Small balloons equipped with wireless apparatus that would automatically signal information about weather conditions in the upper atmosphere were brought into use, and radar was employed to track storms. In the forecast room of a meteorological station all the information available is plotted by an elaborate system of symbols on a large-scale chart, and the lines of equal barometric pressure are drawn. By studying this map meteorologists are able to foretell with a reasonable amount of accuracy the forthcoming weather.

With the establishment of regular trans-Atlantic air services after the Second World War the need for more accurate reports of weather conditions in mid-Atlantic became imperative, and in 1947 a number of ocean weather-ships were positioned in the North Atlantic to act as meteorological observatories. The results of their observations are transmitted to shore stations in Britain and the United States every three hours and prove valuable aids to weather forecasters.

Weaver-bird. Of all curious bird homes, those made by the weaver-birds are among the most wonderful. Though varying in size and shape, the same elaborate interweaving of grass or leaf-strips is found in nests of all the family. The weavers are small finch-like seed-eating birds, belonging mainly to Africa, some species being found in Asia and some in Australia.

W. Stokes

WEAVER-BIRDS' COLONY
In shape somewhat like a flask, with the entrance hole near to the bottom, these nests, swaying from the branches of a tree, present a pretty problem to any enemy seeking to gain entrance. The sociable nature of the weaver-birds is wonderfully developed, as this close grouping of nests shows.

The most marvellous nests are those of the sociable weaver-birds (*Philetaerus socius*) of Africa. These are community nests, usually attached to a tree in the form of a huge mushroom top. The parent birds repair and use the same nests year after year, and the young birds add their nests to the parent structure. Thus the size of the circular roof grows, until from a distance it is often mistaken for the thatched roof of a native hut. As many as 320 individual nests have been counted under one of these community roofs.

Weaving. In a single year Great Britain's output of woven goods amounts to more than £500 million in value; in normal times over a million persons are employed in those industries concerned with spinning and weaving; nearly three million horse-power is devoted to running the machinery they use. Something like £200 million is the annual value of spun and woven goods exported from Great Britain. This gives us an idea of the importance of the textile industries today.

In tracing out the early history of any of the great civilizations we come upon, quite early in the story, evidence that the manufacture of cloth by weaving was practised. In some backward countries today almost the selfsame methods as those used 50 centuries ago are still employed. Handsome carpets are still woven upon a loom consisting of little more than a pair of posts, having the warp or lengthwise threads strung between one roller above and another below. Some means of parting one set of warp threads from another is provided, and the weft (crosswise thread) is passed through the " shed " formed by the parted warp. After this " shot " of weft, the two sets of warp threads are crossed, so that those which were undermost are now brought up to form the next shed. This crossing locks in the previous horizontal thread, and provides the opening through which another line of weft is passed.

In the weaving of a plain fabric little more than this contrivance is needed ; patterns of a simple sort can be worked, even by primitive peoples, by varying the colour of the warp threads, and by varying also the hues of the weft. You yourself can make a little loom (*see* page 2025) upon which ties and similar narrow strips of material can be woven; and home weaving is a fascinating art.

The mechanism of a loom is described in pages 2024–26; the appliances there illustrated are those used for hand weaving; the worker lifts the warp and opens the shed either by moving a lever or pressing down pedals. Then he has to throw a shuttle (containing the weft) through the open shed, from one side of the warp to the other. He next raises the under set of threads, by lever or pedal, and brings back the shuttle through the new shed thus formed. It is a slow process.

In weaving broad fabric two workers were employed, one to throw the shuttle from his side, and the other to return the shuttle. The passage of the shuttle was made easier by providing a bed or guide upon which it could run, but a good amount of skill and dexterity was needed for fast and accurate work. We must not omit to mention an operation which followed every shot of weft. This was the beating of the weft by swinging back upon it a steel " reed " provided with comb-like teeth between which the warp threads ran. Beating pressed the weft against the previous line of horizontal thread, making the cloth close and compact.

In 1738 John Kay patented his fly-shuttle. This was flung to and fro by two cords connected to a handle; and the weaver no longer had to throw the shuttle with one hand and catch it with the other. Moreover, wider cloth could now be woven more quickly. Kay was mobbed by weavers in his Lancashire village, since they thought that this invention would take away their work and livelihood. (Every inventor for almost the next hundred years in the textile industry had to encounter similar opposition to new machines or improved methods. The margin between poverty and even a moderate degree of comfortable living was so narrow in those days.)

One result of loom improvements was that spinning methods could not keep up with weaving. So the progress of weaving was delayed until such inventors as James Hargreaves, Richard Arkwright and Samuel Crompton had speeded up the spinning of the yarn (see the life stories of these men in earlier volumes). But by 1785, when Edmund Cartwright patented his power loom, there was a bigger output of yarn, and within four more years the loom could be driven by the steam engine which James Watt and Matthew Boulton had meanwhile been perfecting. Prior to this the only power available for such machines was that obtained from a water wheel.

The introduction of the Jacquard Loom (q.v.) in 1804 enabled patterned fabric to be woven with speed and precision. Patterns in textile fabrics are made by arranging the warp threads in predetermined groups, each group being liftable by itself or with other groups as desired; then weft of appropriate colour is passed through the shed formed by the lifted warp. As a result, the weft threads either show at the top side of the cloth, or are hidden away beneath. A glance at a piece of woven fabric (a tablecloth for example) will make this clearer than half a page of description. Jacquard's invention used sets of cards punched with holes in a certain pattern to control the lifting or not lifting of groups of warp threads. Similar methods are used today to control automatically the weaving of figured patterns.

The final development of weaving was the rendering of looms fully automatic, once they had been provided with warp and with weft material. A small loom of this type, seen weaving handkerchiefs, is illustrated in page 920. Here then is one aspect

The Times

WEAVING A CARPET ON A GIANT LOOM
In a factory at Kidderminster, Worcestershire, a seamless carpet is being woven. This type of carpet can be made up to 12 feet wide, but not more than eight colours can be used in the pattern, which is automatically controlled by a system of punched cards, first applied to the manufacture of carpets early in the 19th century.

of weaving—the manufacture of goods by the thousand. For its opposite, look at the primitive appliance shown in page 706: two men are making a carpet, using traditional designs which perhaps are recorded only in their own memory. It will take them a long time to complete a carpet, as they tie in, knot by knot, the coloured tufts, and lock them by shots of the plain weft. But the finished article will be a thing of beauty, which will last for many years. (See Cotton; Textiles; Wool).

Week. The division of the month into weeks of seven days arose perhaps from the moon's four phases (new moon, first quarter, full moon, last quarter), each of which approximates to about seven days. The number seven was also regarded as sacred by the ancient Babylonians, among whom this division of time first arose. The Biblical story in Genesis gives six days for the work of creation, with the seventh day as a day of rest—the Jewish Sabbath (Saturday). The Christian Church adopted the first day of the week (Sunday), on which Christ rose from the dead, as its day of rest.

The seven-day week has never been universal. The Romans had an eight-day week, and five-, six- and eight-day weeks exist in various parts of Africa. The leaders of the French Revolution (1789–95) introduced the decade of 10 days, in place of the seven-day week, but this was discontinued in 1806.

Weevil. There are about 40,000. species of small beetles belonging to the weevil family (*Rhynchophora*) and nearly every one of them is a pest to Man. About 450 kinds occur in Great Britain. You may know a weevil by its head, which is lengthened out so much that it looks like a beak; in some forms this is short and thick, but in the true weevils of the family *Curculionidae* the head may be as long as all the rest of the insect together.

One of the worst offenders is the cotton boll weevil—an insect only one-fifth of an inch long, which each year causes great loss in cotton-growing countries. The damage is done by the grubs of the beetle, which hatch from eggs deposited in the buds and " bolls " (pods) of the cotton plant. If they hatch in the buds, the grubs devour the interior and prevent the formation of bolls; if the buds escape, later grubs may attack the bolls themselves.

Other members of the weevil family are known by the names of the plants that they damage. Such are the rice weevil and the corn weevil, and species attacking apple trees. The leaf-rolling weevils bite leaves partly through, roll them up, and lay their eggs inside. The pea and bean " weevils " are not true weevils, being members of the allied family *Bruchidae*.

Weimar. (Pron. vī′-mar). On the River Ilm, about 13 miles from the city of Erfurt, in Central Germany, the quiet town of Weimar is full of memories of German men of letters. The houses where lived Goethe (*q.v.*) and Schiller (*q.v.*), the two most eminent figures in German literature, are preserved as museums, and in front of the National Theatre is a monument to those two friends. For nearly 40 years Weimar was the home of Franz Liszt (*q.v.*), the composer and pianist. It was there that a National Assembly met in 1919 to draw up a Republican Constitution for Germany—the Constitution that was shattered when the German leader Adolf Hitler (*q.v.*) assumed power in 1933.

In the 18th and 19th centuries Weimar was the centre of German spiritual and artistic life. During the Second World War (1939–45) it was surrendered by the Burgomaster (mayor) to United States forces without opposition on April 12, 1945. After the capitulation of Germany to the Allies in May 1945 the town was included in the Russian zone of occupation. The population of Weimar is 52,000.

Welding. This is the process of joining metals by actual fusion of their surfaces. Thus it differs from other processes like soldering and brazing, where joints are made by adhesion between two surfaces alloyed with a metal of lower melting-point (lead-tin, silver, brass, etc.).

For centuries, blacksmiths have welded wrought iron by heating the pieces almost to melting-point and hammering them together on an anvil until they become as a single piece. This very ancient method could be used only on comparatively small pieces which could be heated in the smith's forge.

H. Bastin

A WEEVIL
Grey with black markings, this weevil (*Cionus scrophulariae*), shown magnified eight times, is found in Britain. The long ' beak ' bears the antennae.

Though portable forges are much used for such work which cannot be taken to the smith's shop, the greater part of modern welding is done not by " fire-welding " but by the use of a powerful flaming gas torch, by the electric arc, or by apparatus in which flameless electrical heating is used, accompanied by sufficient pressure to force the two parts of a joint together when the metal is made plastic by the applied heat.

Nowadays, welding of many types forms an important and widely-used method of construction, and is rapidly replacing riveting—even in ship and bridge building. Then, too, it is quite common today to " fabricate " large pieces of machinery, by building them up out of pieces of steel plate and of steel angle, instead of employing castings. In gas welding the intensely hot flame given out by burning a mixture of acetylene and oxygen is generally used. The two gases are led from separate steel cylinders to a torch similar to that shown in page 18, though here the worker is using the oxyacetylene torch to cut through steel plate and not to weld it. Extra metal is generally supplied from a stick or " filler rod " which the welder holds in the path of the joint so that, as it melts, it flows on to the joint. In addition, of course, the metal of the joint itself fuses and unites to make a portion even stronger than the rest of the article being welded. Combinations of oxygen with other gases are also used, in special torches. The great difficulty is to prevent the metal parts becoming oxidized by the heat, as this would interpose a film of oxide between the faces of the joint and prevent strong union.

The earliest form of electric welding—still very widely employed—was that using the electric arc. Later, processes came into use in which the *resistance* of the metal to an electric current flow was utilised to raise the temperature of the joint to fusion point. A short account of these methods follows.

Arc Welding. The heat required for fusion is provided by an electric arc struck between the work and a metal rod or " electrode " held in an insulated handle by the operator. In melting, this rod supplies extra metal to the weld, which is deposited in the pool of molten " parent " metal and, according to the skill of the operator, " built-up " as required. Welding electrodes are specially made according to the work for which they are required ; an electrode which would be quite suitable for ordinary " mild " steel plate would not be good for stainless steel, or for other alloy steels, cast iron, etc. Electrodes are almost invariably provided with a coating of various chemicals which fuse into a molten " slag " which floats on top of the weld, and helps to keep the metal pure and free from contamination by air or by gases from the arc.

Automatic arc welding uses a long reel of coated electrode which is fed into the arc automatically. The entire apparatus is mounted on a movable carriage which travels along, welding a long seam as it moves. This is often used in shipbuilding.

Carbon arc welding, also used, merely provides heat for melting, the additional metal being provided from a separate filler rod, as in gas welding. In " atomic hydrogen welding," the arc, instead of being struck between an electrode and the work to be jointed, is struck between two tungsten electrodes. One is hollow, and through it is blown a jet of hydrogen. This is used with a separate filler rod, like gas welding.

Resistance Welding. In this method of welding no additional metal is supplied. Joints are made by heating the metal to its softening point by passing a heavy electric current through it, so that it heats up by its own resistance (*see* Electricity), and then squeezing the joint together. The best known method is " spot welding," largely used for joining thin sheet metal together. The two sheets are laid in position between the two electrodes of a machine and, by a pedal (or by a compressed-air cylinder in large machines) the electrodes are pressed together. A heavy current passed between them makes a " hot spot " right through the metal which, under pressure unites into a solid core running right through both pieces almost like a rivet. A variation on this method is " stitch welding," where by a line of spots very close together two pieces of metal are, as it were, stitched together.

By the use of wheel electrodes in place of pointed ones, " seam " welding can be carried out, the metal being slowly passed between the wheels, and a solid seam formed. The current is not left on continuously, but is switched on and off again at a very rapid rate (on for a few cycles, and off for a few cycles), usually under electronic control.

" Flash-butt " welding is used for joining steel pipes, railway rails, and the like. The two pieces to be joined are held in the jaws of a machine, and pressed tightly together while a heavy current passes through them. Since the maximum resistance is at the joint itself, it rapidly heats up, and the metal is softened sufficiently for a perfect weld to occur. On a smaller scale, this method is used for jointing the lead-in wires of electric light bulbs.

After reading these descriptions of intense heat produced by flaming gas or by electricity, you will probably be surprised to learn that welding can be done " cold," without any heat at all. " Cold welding " has recently been developed. In this, aluminium or copper sheet is first made perfectly clean, by brushing with a metal scratch-brush. The cleaned surfaces are then placed together, and indentations are made with specially-shaped punches. No current is used, and there is no heating whatever; but, if the surfaces are properly prepared, and the punches are correctly proportioned, a perfect weld will result.

Welland Canal.

Ships cannot pass direct between Lake Erie and Lake Ontario, in North America, since the Niagara Falls interrupt the natural passage. During 1824–29, however, a small canal with 40 wooden locks was cut through the isthmus dividing the two lakes. This early canal has been gradually extended, and the Canadian Government during 1914–29 built the present Welland Canal, to take ocean-going vessels.

The Canal extends from Port Weller on Lake Ontario to Port Colborne on Lake Erie, and may be regarded as one of the finest engineering feats in the world. There is a difference of 325 feet in level between the two lakes, and this is overcome by seven locks, each with a lift of 46½ feet. At Thorold the flight locks, built double so that ships can pass each other, have a combined lift of nearly 140 feet. Each lock is 859 feet long and 80 feet wide. There are no toll charges for United States or Canadian ships, and the Canal, which is open during eight months of the year, carries 12 million tons of cargo annually.

Wellington,

ARTHUR WELLESLEY, IST DUKE OF (1769–1852). In the same year that Napoleon Bonaparte, the conqueror of half of Europe, was born in the Mediterranean island of Corsica, another boy, Arthur Wellesley, who was destined to defeat this conqueror, was born in Ireland. He was the fourth son of the Earl of Mornington, an Irish peer.

Neither the exact date of his birth nor the place can be ascertained with certainty. The " Iron Duke " (nickname given him by his soldiers on account of the very strict discipline he imposed and his own assumption of hardness) himself celebrated the anniversary on May 1. It seems more probable, however, that he was born on April 29, in Upper Merrion Street, Dublin. Little is known of his early life. His mother once said that " her ugly boy, Arthur, was fit food for powder and nothing else." Accordingly, after leaving Eton, he was sent to a military school at Angers, in France.

At the age of 17 he entered the Army as an officer, and after passing quickly through the lower ranks he

WELLINGTON : THE ' IRON DUKE '
Now in the National Portrait Gallery, London, this portrait of the Duke of Wellington was painted by the Spanish artist Goya y Lucientes (generally known as Goya) in 1812, when the British military leader was directing the campaign which resulted in the expulsion of the French from Spain.

became lieutenant-colonel in 1793. Three years later he was sent with his regiment to India. From 1796 to 1805 he conquered a series of hostile chiefs who had sworn to drive the English into the sea, and whose forces far outnumbered his own. His greatest victory in India (where his brother Richard, Marquess Wellesley, was Governor-General) was the battle of Assaye (1803), in which he destroyed the power of the Mahrattas. Arthur Wellesley, knighted and thanked by Parliament in 1804, showed himself, by the treaties which closed the war against these Mahratta tribes, a master of Indian statesmanship and diplomacy.

In 1805 he left India to fight against Napoleon in Europe. In the first campaign in the peninsula of Spain and Portugal, which the French had overrun, he won the notable victory of Vimeiro, the fruits of which were lost by the action of his superior officers, who refused to pursue the French. The next year (1809), after Sir John Moore's retreat to the sea at Corunna, he came back to the Peninsula as commander-in-chief, and in five momentous years drove Napoleon's well-trained troops back into France. His victories included Talavera (1809), after which he became Viscount Wellington; the sack of Badajoz and Ciudad Rodrigo; and the battles of Salamanca (1812), Vittoria (1813) and Toulouse (1814).

Thus he was fighting on French soil when Napoleon's first abdication brought peace to Europe in 1814. On the field of Waterloo (*q.v.*) in Belgium, and with the aid of the Prussian General Blücher, he crowned his military career by defeating Napoleon in the latter's last despairing bid for world supremacy. Honours and rewards were heaped upon the successful general, who in 1814 had been created Duke of Wellington. As commander of the international army which occupied France from 1815 to 1818, until the terms of the peace treaty were fulfilled he had immense power, and for years he was one of the most influential men in Europe.

In 1818 he began a new career as a Tory politician. For two years (1828–30) Wellington was Prime Minister, but he failed to read aright the signs of the times. The demand for the reform of Parliament—eventually carried through in the Reform Bill (1832)—he thought was the work of a few agitators. His uncompromising opposition to reform soon led to the fall of his government, and he had to protect his house (Apsley House, at Hyde Park Corner, London) from the violence of the mob. However, he again held office, being Foreign Secretary during 1834–35.

People later recognized that though Wellington was not always an able statesman he was working for what he believed to be the good of the nation. This high sense of duty and his absolute honesty, coupled with his military glory, made him in his old age venerated and beloved by all. At the age of 83 (on September 14, 1852) the old hero passed peacefully away at Walmer Castle, in Kent. He was buried in the crypt of St. Paul's, London, and there is a monument to him in the nave.

Wellington, NEW ZEALAND. The capital of New Zealand is also a seaport of considerable importance. It is on the southern extremity of North Island, on the west shore of the inlet of Port Nicholson (*see* map in page 2358). The harbour of Wellington is six miles long and five miles wide. The principal buildings of the city are Government House, the Houses of Parliament, and the town hall. The business area is largely on land reclaimed from the harbour. Among the exports are butter, cheese, meat, wool, fruit and timber. There is little heavy industry, but soap, candles, rope and woollens are manufactured. The city, the first settlement of New Zealand colonists, was founded in 1840; the seat of government was transferred there from Auckland in 1865. The population of Wellington is 183,100.

Wells, HERBERT GEORGE (1866–1946). Probably the most prolific and influential British writer since Dickens, Wells owed his position to his ability to expound his theories and opinions to high-brow and low-brow alike. In all his enormous output of works there is little that is not of importance.

The son of a professional cricketer, Wells was born at Bromley, Kent, on September 21, 1866, and was educated at Bromley, and at Midhurst Grammar School, Sussex. He was apprenticed first to a chemist and then to a draper at Hythe, in Kent, but he gained a scholarship and graduated in science at the University of London. He then became a schoolmaster for a short while, but gave this up for writing.

In 1895 came the first of the novels of scientific fantasy, in which Wells's gifts of prophetic imagination and scientific knowledge were blended to create stories of extraordinary fascination. This was The Time Machine, and was followed by The Island of Dr. Moreau (1896), The Invisible Man (1897), The War of the Worlds (1898), The First Men in the Moon (1901), and The Food of the Gods (1904).

H. G. WELLS
Author of some of the most entertaining stories in the English language, Herbert George Wells excelled as a ' visionary.'

Wells then entered on a different phase, using his own experience as a background for stories of real-life problems, such as Love and Mr. Lewisham (1900), Kipps (1905), Tono-Bungay (1909), Ann Veronica (1909), The History of Mr. Polly (1910), and Marriage (1912).

The First World War (1914–18), one aspect of which he had prophesied in The War in the Air (1908), found Wells ready with his pen. Mr. Britling Sees It Through (1916) was important as showing the war from the domestic angle. Towards the end of the war, in 1918, came Joan and Peter, and two years later was published the first part of Wells' trilogy dealing with the whole vast panorama of human activity. This was The Outline of History, subsequently published (1922) in a shorter form as A Short History of the World. It was followed in 1929 by The Science of Life, a biological survey written with the collaboration of Julian Huxley and G. P. Wells (H. G. Wells's son), and in 1932 by The Work, Wealth, and Happiness of Mankind, the tremendous scope of which is indicated by its title.

JOHN WESLEY PREACHING AT AN OPEN-AIR MEETING

Founder of the religious sect whose members performed their religious duties in such a methodical manner that they became known as ' Methodists,' John Wesley began preaching his new faith of Methodism in 1738. For some time he was not allowed to deliver his sermons in churches so he held meetings outdoors. He travelled all over England delivering his message, and in spite of opposition and persecution the new movement spread by leaps and bounds.

In 1933 came The Shape of Things to Come—which Wells himself turned into a film—and in the following year An Experiment in Autobiography. His dream of a perfectly planned world, a Utopia and World Commonwealth, found expression in all his later works. These include The Fate of Homo Sapiens (1939), The New World Order (1940) and Phoenix (1942). His last phase as a writer is represented by Mind at the End of its Tether (1946). He died on August 13, 1946.

Wells. An old-world city in Somerset, Wells is a beautiful example of an ecclesiastical cathedral city of medieval type. The present cathedral (see illustration page 728) is one of the loveliest in England and was begun in 1186. Two of its chief features are the remarkable inverted arches beneath the tower, and the clock (see illustration in page 845) said to have been constructed by Peter Lightfoot in 1392. This has astronomical indications and shows the phases of the moon as well as the date of the month. A tournament of knights, actuated by the same mechanism, is enacted every hour. The Bishop's Palace close to the cathedral is surrounded by a moat. The city owes its name to some springs dedicated to St. Andrew. It has been the seat of a bishop (now the Bishopric of Bath and Wells) since about 900. The population of Wells is 5,900.

Wesley. JOHN (1703–91). In Oxford, in the early part of the 18th century, there gathered about John Wesley, then a young curate, and his brother Charles, a student at Christ Church, a group of young men who came to be known as the " Holy Club." Their strict rules of conduct and the methodical way in which they performed their religious duties led to their being called " Methodists," the name being later applied to the religious sect which John Wesley founded.

John Wesley was born on June 17, 1703, at Epworth, Lincolnshire, where his father was rector.

John was the fifteenth of 19 children, and he was educated at Oxford, ordained deacon in 1725, and became his father's curate. In 1735, accompanied by his brother, he went to Georgia, United States, as a missionary. On the stormy voyage a deep impression was made on him by the calm faith of some simple-hearted Christians from Moravia (then a part of the Austrian Empire), who were his fellow-passengers. His stay in Georgia was not a great success. He was threatened with lawsuits for slander and for incorrect conduct of services. He studied Moravian doctrine after his return to England in 1737, and it was at 8.45 p.m. on May 24, 1738, at a Moravian meeting in London, that he felt his heart " strangely warmed " and there came to him a firm conviction of the saving power of Christ. He began preaching his new faith; and, when he found the churches closed against him, he joined George Whitefield, a celebrated revivalist, in holding open-air meetings.

Wesley travelled approximately 5,000 miles a year and preached about 15 sermons a week. In spite of opposition and persecution, the meetings were attended by thousands, and the movement spread rapidly. He organized his converts into bands for prayer, and church societies, appointed leaders to act as lay pastors, and ordained or commissioned preachers. This amounted to a break with the Church of England, although it was not recognized as such by Wesley himself. Also he was an active helper in social and charitable movements, and wrote a number of works on religious subjects. His published Journal has been called " the most amazing record of human exertion ever penned by Man." By the time of his death, on March 2, 1791, he was said to have preached 40,000 sermons.

Charles Wesley (1707–88) was associated with his brother in religious work. He is best known as a writer of over 1,000 hymns.

LANDS on AFRICA'S ATLANTIC SEABOARD

Comprising a number of districts extending from the Sahara Desert to a point hundreds of miles south of the mouth of the Congo, West Africa has become a productive area of considerable economic importance.

West Africa. The area of the continent of Africa (*q.v.*) which is included in West Africa for the purposes of this article takes in the coast lands from Cape Blanco (on the Atlantic seaboard at the southern end of the Spanish colony of Rio de Oro) to the River Kunene, which forms the southern boundary of Angola, or Portuguese West Africa, and the basins of the rivers that flow into the Gulf of Guinea. Eastward it extends to Lake Chad in French Equatorial Africa, and in the north it merges into the Sahara.

The coast, which makes a sweep to the east and then to the south, is of regular outline ; the only good natural harbours are at the river mouths. There is a narrow coastal plain, and behind this are tropical forests, the principal feature of West Africa. Trees include palms, from which oil, coconuts and other products are obtained; and ebony, mahogany, and cedar, which are valuable for their timber. The climate of this area is hot and humid.

The vast majority of the population of West Africa are Negroes. The only nominally independent state in the whole of Africa, with the exception of Abyssinia and Egypt, is Liberia (*q.v.*), a Negro republic. The other territories are all colonies of European Powers. France holds various territories comprising French West Africa; Britain, Belgium, Spain, and Portugal also have possessions there.

British West Africa is divided into four colonies—from west to east, Gambia, Sierra Leone, Gold Coast and Nigeria. Since the First World War (1914–18) Britain has also been in control of part of the former German Cameroons (*q.v.*) and Togoland.

Gambia has an area of 4,068 square miles. The capital, Bathurst (population 6,100), which stands on the island of St. Mary, exports ground-nuts, palm kernels, and hides. Formerly part of the British West African Settlements, Gambia became a separate Crown Colony in 1888. The population of Gambia (colony and protectorate) is 200,000.

Sierra Leone, bounded on the north and east by French Guinea and on the south-east by Liberia, is 30,169 square miles in extent. Freetown (population 86,000) is the capital and has the finest harbour in West Africa. The exports include iron ore, palm kernels, ginger, and diamonds. The history of Sierra Leone as a British possession dates from the sale in 1788 of a piece of land on the coast by a native chief to a party of British settlers, which was transferred to the British Crown in 1807. The population of Sierra Leone is 1,800,000.

Situated between French Togoland on the east and French Ivory Coast on the west, the Gold Coast, with Ashanti, the Northern Territories, and British Togoland—all under the Governor of the Gold Coast—has an area of 91,843 square miles. Accra (population 73,000), the capital, and Takoradi are busy ports. Principal products are palm oil and kernels, cocoa, gold, manganese ore, and timber. Established as a colony in 1874, the Gold Coast has a population of 3,963,000.

Most of the inhabitants of West Africa are Negroes: this girl lives in the British Gold Coast Colony.

POLITICAL DIVISIONS OF THE WEST COAST OF AFRICA

Britain's mandates (indicated in this map by diagonal lines) of former German territory in the Cameroons and Togoland are now held under United Nations' trusteeship. Besides Portuguese Guinea, Portugal also possesses Angola (not shown in map)

Reginald Silk

ON THE WAY TO MARKET IN NIGERIA
On their heads these women are carrying loads of the dried outer cases of
calabashes, used by the natives as bowls and receptacles for storing food.
Between the French colonies of Dahomey and the Cameroons, Nigeria is
the largest British possession on the west coast of Africa.

Nigeria, the country of the lower Niger, is by far
the largest of the British West African possessions,
with an area of 372,674 square miles. The capital
and chief port is Lagos (population 174,000). Other
centres are Ibadan (327,000), Kano (90,000), and
Ogbomosho (82,000). Products include cocoa,
ground-nuts, palm oil and kernels, tin, hides, timber
and rubber. Nigeria comprises a number of districts
formerly ruled separately by British officials ; now
the two main divisions are
Northern and Southern
Nigeria, which were united
in 1914 to form the colony
of Nigeria and were placed
under one Governor. The
population of Nigeria is
21,826,000.

French West Africa con-
sists of Senegal, French
Guinea, the Ivory Coast,
Dahomey, French Sudan,
Mauritania, and the Niger
Colony, and these terri-
tories are administered
by a Governor - General.
Senegal, which is south of
the Senegal river, has an
area of 77,730 square miles.
The exports consist mainly
of ground-nuts and gums.
St. Louis (population
49,000) is the capital. The
Governor-General has his
seat at Dakar (182,000).
The population of Senegal
is 1,720,000.

Mauritania, which lies
between Spanish Rio de

Oro on the north and Senegal on the
south, is 323,310 square miles in extent,
much of this territory being desert.
The products are chiefly cattle, gum.
and salt. The population of Mauritania
is 373,000. French Guinea, which has
Portuguese Guinea on the north and
Sierra Leone on the south, has an area
of 89,436 square miles and produces
palm oil and kernels, ground-nuts, coffee,
bananas, rubber and gum ; the capital is
Conakry (population 32,000), and the inhabitants of the colony number 2,125,000.

North of the Senegal and Niger rivers,
the French Sudan has an area of 360,330
square miles, but away from the banks
of the waterways little of it has been
brought under cultivation. Irrigation
schemes have been carried out on the
north bank of the Niger, and ground-
nuts, cotton, maize, millet and rice are
cultivated. The capital is Bamako
(population 70,500). Other towns are
Kayes and Ségou. The population of
the French Sudan is 3,778,370.

The Niger Colony is in the southern
Sahara, north of Nigeria, and has an area
of 499,167 square miles. Horses, cattle,
sheep and goats are bred. The most
important crops are ground-nuts, beans
and millet. The towns of Niamey and
Zinder are the termini of trans-Saharan motor-
routes. Population of the Niger Colony is 2,144,000.

The French Ivory Coast is between Liberia and
British Gold Coast and has an area of 180,802
square miles. Exports include cocoa, coffee, and
palm kernels. The capital is Abidjan (population
33,000), and the colony has 4,100,000 inhabitants.

Dahomey extends from Togoland on the west to
Nigeria on the east and has an area of 43,232 square

Wide World

CLAY-BUILT VILLAGE HOMES IN SENEGAL
Sitting on the flat roof of their house are two members of the Habe tribe, a little-known
people who live in the eastern highlands of the French colony of Senegal. They are
extremely independent and have almost no tribal organization, each village being ruled
by its own headman and owning allegiance to no-one else.

miles. Principal exports are palm kernels and palm oil, but the cultivation of cotton and coffee is increasing. The capital is Porto Novo (population 27,000), near the port of Cotonou. The population of the colony of Dahomey is 1,458,000. (For French and Belgian Congo, *see* Congo States).

The Spanish and Portuguese colonies are comparatively small in total extent. Spanish Guinea consists of the islands of Fernando Po and Annobon, the Corisco Islands, and the coastal strip of Rio Muni, and has a total area of 10,040 square miles. Coffee, cocoa, and fruit are the leading products. Santa Isabel (population 15,000) on Fernando Po, is the capital. The population of Spanish Guinea is 139,000.

Portuguese Guinea (13,948 square miles) includes the archipelago of Bijagoz. Rice, palm oil, and hides are among the products ; the capital and chief port is Bissau. Farther off the coast are the Cape Verde Islands (*q.v.*) and in the Gulf of Guinea are the islands of San Tomé and Principe with an area of 372 square miles. Coconut palms, coffee, and cacao (cocoa) plants are cultivated. The population of Portuguese Guinea is 351,000.

Angola, sometimes known as Portuguese West Africa, has a coast-line of over 1,000 miles, and an area of 481,351 square miles. It is ruled by a Governor-General, with headquarters at Loanda, or São Paulo de Loanda (population 23,000). Farther south are the two ports of Lobito Bay (4,000) and Benguela (4,000). From Lobito Bay there is connexion by railway with Beira in Portuguese East Africa (Mozambique). Principal crops are coffee, maize, sugar, palm oil, and palm kernels. The population of Angola is 3,738,000.

Western Australia.
A State of the Australian Commonwealth, Western Australia, with an area of 975,920 square miles, comprises nearly one-third of the island-continent. Except for a narrow coastal plain the State consists of a

Australian National Travel Association

CAPITAL OF WESTERN AUSTRALIA

On the Swan river, 12 miles from its port of Fremantle, Perth is the capital and the largest town of Western Australia. An impressive thoroughfare is St. George's Terrace (above). Some other of its streets are old and narrow.

plateau with an average elevation of 1,300 feet. The highest points are Mount Bruce (4,024 feet) and the Stirling Range (3,640 feet). The central part of the State is desert, with a rainfall of less than 10 inches a year. Rivers include the Fitzroy, Fortescue, Murchison and Swan.

Gold-mining is the chief industry ; the rich fields of Kalgoorlie and Coolgardie were discovered

---

Extent.—Area 975,920 square miles. Population 502,000 including 22,000 full-blooded aborigines.
Physical Features.—Huge inland plateau. Low, sandy coastal lands in south and west, with few good harbours. Highest points are Mt. Bruce (4,024 feet), and the Stirling Range (3,640 feet).
Principal Products.—Wheat, oats, barley, apples, meat, butter ; timber ; wool ; gold ; pearls and pearl-shell.
Chief Towns.—Perth (capital) population (including Fremantle) 272,586. Kalgoorlie (11,900).

---

in 1893. Sheep and cattle are bred. Wheat, oats and barley are grown on a large scale, as are apples. There are forests of excellent timber. At Shark Bay there is a pearl-fishery. The leading exports are wheat, flour, wool, timber, meat, butter and fruit. The Trans-Australian line links the State's railway system with those of the other States of the Commonwealth. The capital is Perth (*q.v.*), whose port is Fremantle (population 27,000). Other towns are Kalgoorlie (11,900), Boulder (7,600), Bunbury (5,700) and Geraldton (5,150).

The first settlement was established on the shores of King George Sound in 1826, and in May 1829 the territory in the basin of the Swan River was officially annexed by Great Britain. The country became self-governing in 1890, and, despite opposition from a strong minority, joined the other States to form the Commonwealth of Australia in 1901. The population of Western Australia is 502,000.

West Indies.
Geologists say that there was once in existence a land-mass called Antillia, which separated the Atlantic Ocean from the Caribbean Sea. This is now largely submerged beneath the water, the portions remaining visible being the West Indies, the first part of the New World seen by Columbus in 1492. These islands (40 of them are inhabited) curve round like a sickle from Florida in the United States to Venezuela in South America. Columbus called them the West Indies because he thought that he had sailed around the world, and reached a part of India.

Their total area is about 100,000 square miles, and they are divided into the Greater and Lesser Antilles. Of the Greater Antilles, Cuba, Haiti and the Dominican Republic are independent States ; Jamaica belongs to Great Britain, and Puerto Rico and the Virgin Islands to the United States. Most of the other islands are British possessions, though Guadeloupe, Martinique, St. Pierre and Miquelon are French, and Curaçao is Dutch.

The British West Indies apart from Jamaica are grouped into Colonies as follows : Bahamas, Barbados, Trinidad and Tobago, Leeward Islands, and Windward Islands. The two last-named, which form the Lesser Antilles, consist of the following islands : Antigua (with Barbuda and Redonda), British Virgin Islands, Dominica, St. Kitts and Nevis (with Anguilla), and Montserrat ; Grenada, St. Vincent and St. Lucia.

The archipelago has a tropical climate and vegetation. Birds, snakes, lizards, scorpions and insects abound, but there are few native mammals. Forests of valuable timber exist, but agriculture is the main industry. The chief overseas trade is in sugar, fruit, rum and tobacco. Hurricanes are frequent, and do great damage on occasion.

In 1940, during the Second World War (1939–45), sites in the Bahamas, Trinidad, Antigua, Jamaica, and St. Lucia were leased by Great Britain to the United States for use as military and naval bases. The estimated population of the islands (predominantly Negro) is 13 million. (*See* separate articles on the chief islands).

Westmeath.

An inland county of Eire, Westmeath is bounded on the north by Cavan, on the east by Meath, on the south by Offaly, on the west by Longford and Galway, and its area is 681 square miles. The most important rivers are the Shannon, Brosna, Inny, and Dale. The largest of the numerous lakes are Sheelin, Kinale, Derravaragh, Owel, Lene, Ennell, and Glore. The surface is undulating, and is boggy in parts. The pasturing of cattle, sheep, and horses is the chief industry ; flannel and coarse linens are manufactured. The county town is Mullingar (population 5,200). Other places are Athlone, and Castlepollard. The population of Westmeath is 56,000.

W. F. Mansell

ARCHITECTURAL JEWEL OF WESTMINSTER ABBEY

Begun in 1503, Henry VII's Chapel (above) in Westminster Abbey replaced an earlier Lady Chapel built by Henry III (1207–72) and was constructed in the Perpendicular style. Hanging from the walls on either side are the banners of the Knights of the Bath, who are received into the Order in the Chapel. Also in the Chapel is a memorial window to airmen who lost their lives in the Battle of Britain (1940).

Westminster Abbey.

In London's Westminster Abbey fine pillared aisles, pointed arches, fluted columns, exquisitely ornamented screens, and beautiful stained glass form an impressive background for the tombs and monuments in Britain's most renowned "temple of fame."

Not only has the Abbey been the burial-place of most of England's sovereigns, but burial there is one of the honours which Britain bestows upon the most illustrious of her sons. Around the shrine of Edward the Confessor (c. 1005–1066) are tombs of various Kings and Queens, and in the exquisite Henry VII's Chapel, along whose sides are the richly-carved stalls of the Knights of the Bath, stand the tombs of its founder, of Queen Elizabeth, and of other Sovereigns.

In the south transept, near the resting-place of numerous eminent men of letters, is the Poets' Corner (*see* illustration in page 2635). There is the tomb of Geoffrey Chaucer, over which is a window depicting the Canterbury Pilgrims. In a niche is a statue of Shakespeare; and near the bust of the dramatist Ben Jonson lies the poet Edmund Spenser.

The Abbey has been the scene of numbers of Coronations and Royal weddings. From William the Conqueror onward every Sovereign, excepting Edward V and Edward VIII, has been crowned there. The wedding of King George VI, then Duke of York, to Lady Elizabeth Bowes-Lyon took place in the Abbey on April 26, 1923, and there also their daughter, Princess Elizabeth, married Prince Philip, Duke of Edinburgh, on Nov. 20, 1947. In what is now the Chapter House the House of Commons met from 1289 to 1547, when they moved to St. Stephen's chapel.

Situated close to the Houses of Parliament, Westminster Abbey was originally the church of a Benedictine monastery, but its early history is mostly legendary. The first edifice of which records exist stood in the 8th century slightly to the west of the site of the present structure and was dedicated to St. Peter. In 1050–1065 it was rebuilt in Norman style by Edward the Confessor. Henry VII (1457–1509) rebuilt the Lady Chapel that had been added by Henry III (1207–72), who also began a reconstruction that continued until the

ENGLAND'S NATIONAL SHRINE AT WESTMINSTER

A. F. Kersting

In Westminster Abbey—officially the Church of St. Peter in Westminster—are the tombs of a number of England's most illustrious sons, and within its precincts every English sovereign, excepting Edward V and Edward VIII, has been crowned. Its early history, and that of the Benedictine monastery associated with it, is mostly legendary, but the first edifice of which records exist stood in the 8th century slightly west of the present structure. It was rebuilt in 1050–1065 by Edward the Confessor, and of this church a few fragments remain. The work of reconstruction begun in the 13th century lasted for centuries. The two towers flanking the west front (above) were completed in 1740, from Sir Christopher Wren's designs. On the right is the small 14th-century Jerusalem Chamber time of Sir Christopher Wren (1632–1723) and his pupil Nicholas Hawksmoor (1661–1736), who repaired and heightened the west towers.

The Abbey has an exterior length of 530 feet ; the towers are 225 feet high ; and there are 11 chapels. A place of worship of the Church of England, the Abbey is under the jurisdiction of neither Archbishop nor Bishop, the appointment of the clergy being made by the reigning Sovereign.

Among the tombs or other memorials in the Abbey are those of Milton, Coleridge, Burns, Samuel Johnson, Macaulay, Dickens, Livingstone, Darwin, Newton, Pitt, Fox, Gladstone, Disraeli, Hardy and Kipling. In the nave is the tomb of the Unknown Warrior of the First World War (1914–18), buried there on November 11, 1920. And in Henry VII's Chapel is a memorial window to the airmen who lost their lives in the Battle of Britain (q.v.) during the Second World War (1939–45). The Abbey suffered a certain amount of damage from German air raids in the Second World War, but no really historic feature was destroyed.

Westmorland. A northern county of England, 789 square miles in area, Westmorland consists chiefly of moorland and mountain, Helvellyn (3,118 feet) being the highest peak. In the west lies part of the lovely but very rainy Lake District, including Grasmere, Hawes Water, Rydal Water, and parts of Windermere and Ullswater. At Grasmere and Rydal lived William Wordsworth, chief of the " Lake Poets." Shap Fell, south-west of Appleby, is a notable incline on the main railway line from London to Carlisle and Glasgow.

Large numbers of sheep are raised also cattle, horses and pigs. Oats and barley are grown; graphite, marble, lead and slate are quarried. The chief manufacturing industry is the making of woollens, said to have been introduced from Flanders in the time of Edward III (1312–77).

Appleby (population 1,600) is the county town; other centres are Kendal, Ambleside and Kirkby Lonsdale. There are many old castles, and of the new ones, Lowther Castle, the seat of the Earl of Lonsdale, is notable. The population of Westmorland is 65,000.

Wexford. In south-east Eire, the county of Wexford has an area of 908 square miles. It is bounded on the north by Wicklow, on the east and south by St. George's Channel, on the west by Carlow and Kilkenny. It has 90 miles of irregular coastline on which are Wexford Harbour, Ballyteige Bay, Bannow Bay and Waterford Harbour. The surface is mainly hilly, but becomes mountainous in the north and north-east, the highest point being Mount Leinster (2,610 feet).

The chief rivers are the Slaney and Barrow. Oats, barley, potatoes and turnips are grown. Sheep, cattle, pigs and poultry are exported to Britain. The deep-sea and salmon fisheries are thriving industries. The county town is Wexford (population 12,300), where are the ruins of 12th-century Selskar Abbey. Other places are Rosslare (with a harbour constructed as a terminus for the steamer service from Fishguard in Pembrokeshire), New Ross and Enniscorthy. The population of the county of Wexford is 92,000.

MONSTER MAMMALS *that* LIVE *in the* SEA

An oddity in several ways, the whale looks like a colossal fish but is a warm-blooded mammal—though it never comes to land while alive. It has lungs, and must rise to the surface every half-hour or so to breathe.

Whales. That the very remote ancestors of the whales were land animals is known from their skeleton and breathing organs, and is especially evident in the young ones, which are born fully formed and are suckled by their mothers, like land mammals. Under the name of *Cetacea*, or cetaceans, are grouped not only the huge true whales but also their smaller relatives the dolphins, the porpoises, the grampuses, and the narwhals—one of whose front teeth grows out into a twisted spear-like tusk, extending four or five or even more feet in front of its snout.

In all these animals the shape has become fish-like. The skin is smooth, with a few traces of hair, and is usually black or black-and-white, or sometimes all white. The hind limbs have disappeared, and the fore limbs have become paddles. The tail alone is enough to show that these creatures are not fish, for it is set horizontally, not vertically.

As whales have lungs (not gills like fish) and breathe air, they must come to the surface periodically to breathe. At the instant they emerge the pent-up air is expelled from the lungs through the nostrils at the top of the nose. This discharge of warm moist breath condenses in cold air into a visible vapour, often mixed with sea-spray, but no water is expelled from the mouth when a whale " blows," as it is termed. The nostrils are connected directly with the windpipe, but not with the mouth, so that whales can swim with their mouths open without getting water in their lungs. The cetaceans are in the main fish-eaters, but the killer whale will devour porpoises and also seals, and a band of them may unite to worry a big cachalot (sperm whale) to death. Most whales go about in bands or " schools."

The whales comprise two sub-orders: the whale-bone whales (*Mystacoceti*) and the toothed whales (*Odontoceti*). Formerly the most hunted species among the first class, the right whales, have 200 or 300 blade-shaped plates of horny material (whalebone or baleen) hanging in a dense fringe from the roof of the mouth, those in the centre measuring eight or 10 feet in length.

Right whales (so called because in early times they were regarded as the only true whales), of which the Greenland species (*Balaena mysticetus*) is the best-known, are often 50 to 75 feet long. They range through all oceans, even amid Arctic ice, and live on shrimp-like crustaceans and other minute sea creatures. These are swept into the whale's mouth by the million as it swims along, the water flowing out of the sides of the mouth, and the food being caught by the fringes of the baleen and sucked down. In addition to the whalebone, these whales were hunted for the thick layer of fat (blubber) under-

S. Crook

LAST OF A FINBACK WHALE
Found stranded and battered against the rocks on the York-shire coast near Scarborough, this rorqual or finback whale was more than 70 feet long and was estimated to weigh 80 tons. Whales of this kind were formerly hunted almost to extinction for the baleen or whalebone which hangs in a dense fringe from the roof of the mouth.

lying the skin and surrounding the body, from which oil was extracted. The right whales nearly became extinct through over-hunting, and their slaughter has been forbidden by international agreement since 1935. The blue whale and the finback whale are two species still hunted, but as a precaution against over-hunting no blue whale less than 70 feet long and no finback under 55 feet in length may be killed; and the duration of the hunting season in summer, in the polar regions, is arranged internationally each year.

Similar to the right whales are the humpbacks, the grey whales, and the finbacks or rorquals. The smallest is the pygmy whale of Australasian and South American seas, which is rarely more than 20 feet long. The largest of the whalebone whales, the blue rorqual, is also the largest living animal. It sometimes reaches a length of 88 feet or more, and an estimated weight of 75 tons. A calf (young whale) whose mother was 80 feet long was 25 feet at birth and weighed about 8 tons.

The toothed whales comprise the sperm whale or cachalot, the lesser sperm whale, the small "beaked" whales, the white whale and the dolphins and porpoises.

The sperm whale (*Physeter macrocephalus*), which reaches a length of 60 to 70 feet, has a huge flat-topped, almost square-fronted, head constituting one-third of its length. There is a thin under-jaw somewhat shorter than the snout and armed with strong pointed teeth eight or 10 inches long, for these whales are hunters of squids and cuttle-fish, which form their chief food. In former times the timbers of more than one whaling boat were chewed and crushed to matchwood in their massive jaws.

The value of the sperm whale lies chiefly in the large quantity of oil that fills a cavity in the top of the head, from which spermaceti (a fat used in toilet preparations) and a fine oil are obtained. In the intestines are formed lumps of a fatty secretion called ambergris (*q.v.*) used as a base in the making of perfumes, and for which a high price is paid.

In the early days when sailing ships were engaged in whale fishing the voyages were often long—from three to five years—and the crews of the small boats in which the whales were hunted were often in danger. When a whale was sighted, the boats were lowered from the parent ship and rowed close to the quarry. Harpoons, each with a rope attached, were flung into the huge body, and the wounded beast might tow several boats over the ocean for hours. In its attempt to escape it might dive, remaining under water for some time. When it came up for air, a right whale might overturn a boat with its tail, a sperm whale might crush a boat in its jaws. As soon as possible a boat would approach so near that a long lance could be driven into the weakening mammal, to inflict a fatal wound. The dead whale would be towed back to the ship, where the blubber would be stripped off with large knives and cooked to extract the oil.

Nowadays large "factory" ships lead a fleet of small swift motor or steam vessels to Antarctic waters. Often aircraft are used to search for the beasts, whose position is wirelessed to the hunting ships, which then race to the indicated spot. Harpoons are fired from a harpoon gun mounted in the bow of each vessel. This weapon discharges a 5-foot harpoon weighing more than 100 lb. Attached to the top of the harpoon is a bomb, which a time-fuse discharges in the body of the whale. The dead animals are towed to the factory ship, where they are hauled inside up a slipway at the stern. Machinery extracts every drop of oil from blubber and flesh; some of the flesh is marketed for human consumption; chicken food and fertilizer are made from the bones and scraps; margarine and cooking fats may be made from the oil after it has been refined.

Wheat. The story of the cultivation of wheat is in essence the story of the civilization of Man. When Man ceased wandering, relying for his food almost entirely on cattle and sheep and game; when he built a home, planted grain, harvested it, and stored it away for future use, then he had taken an important step from savagery to civilization.

We do not know what people first took this momentous step, but we do know that the cultivation of wheat was being carried on at the earliest times recorded in history. Wheat is mentioned many times in the Bible. Excavations of New

MIGHTIEST OF ALL ANIMALS ON LAND OR SEA

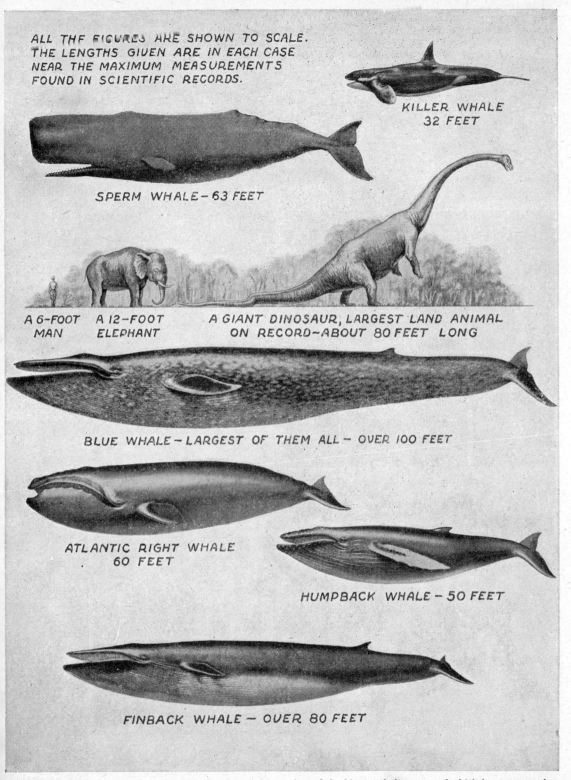

ALL THE FIGURES ARE SHOWN TO SCALE.
THE LENGTHS GIVEN ARE IN EACH CASE
NEAR THE MAXIMUM MEASUREMENTS
FOUND IN SCIENTIFIC RECORDS.

KILLER WHALE
32 FEET

SPERM WHALE — 63 FEET

A 6-FOOT
MAN

A 12-FOOT
ELEPHANT

A GIANT DINOSAUR, LARGEST LAND ANIMAL
ON RECORD — ABOUT 80 FEET LONG

BLUE WHALE — LARGEST OF THEM ALL — OVER 100 FEET

ATLANTIC RIGHT WHALE
60 FEET

HUMPBACK WHALE — 50 FEET

FINBACK WHALE — OVER 80 FEET

Even if some of the dinosaurs, as certain scientists claim, may have exceeded 100 feet in length their slender neck and tail made up the greater part of that measurement. The bulk of the largest dinosaur could not be compared to that of the bigger whales, some of which have young that are as large at birth as a full-grown elephant. The killer whale or grampus (top right) is very ferocious and several will unite to worry a sperm whale (top left) to death.

Stone Age dwellings in Switzerland have shown that at least four distinct varieties were grown there. Egypt cultivated it at a very early date in the well-watered valley of the Nile. The Chinese were

growing it 3,000 years before the Christian era.

Varieties of wheat—more than 1,000 are known—must be carefully selected to suit the soil and climate where they are to be grown, and the grain harvested from different localities is used for different purposes. Wheat has numerous enemies, the most formidable of which are the rusts (see Rust Fungus) and smuts. Methods of fighting

The ordinary cultivated wheat plant (*Triticum vulgare*) is a tall, slender annual or biennial belonging to the group of cereal grasses. It has a hollow, erect, knotted stem which grows to a height of from two to five feet, according to variety, climatic and other conditions, and bears at its summit a zigzag-shaped ear, with a number of flattened spikelets growing out of each notch. These spikelets usually bear four flowers each, which produce the grain. The grain is hard, and grooved along one side.

Spelt wheat (*Triticum spelta*) was grown by the ancient Egyptians and Romans. Kernels of this wheat thousands of years old have been found in mummy-cases. This variety is still grown in cold mountainous districts of Europe, and produces a very fine flour suitable for pastry-making.

Wheatear. In hilly parts of Britain, especially on waste land, you may sometimes startle a bird which at once attracts attention by the flash of white which is exposed as it flies away. This is the wheatear (*Oenanthe oenanthe*) and that white patch enables you at once to recognize it. It is one of the first migrants to reach Britain from Africa in the spring, arriving often at the beginning of March; but the first-comers are "passage migrants," birds that summer farther north and do not stop for more than a day or so on their way. The cock wheatear, about six inches long, is a handsome bird, with a grey back—it is bluish sometimes—black wings, white underparts, and a brilliant white patch at the base of the tail. The hen is duller, more brown than grey. It nests in rabbit burrows, holes in walls, and other similar sites; its eggs are pale blue. The food consists of insects.

The wheatear is a member of a group of the thrush family which contains several other British birds, such as the stonechat (*Saxicola torquata*) and the whinchat (*S. rubetra*). The stonechat is a partial

most of these pests have been discovered, and the farmer today feels less helpless than he once did when he found them in his wheat fields.

When the grains of wheat first reach a fairly good size they are plump and soft and filled with a milky fluid. Later they become solid, but not hard. Slowly the plant loses its green colouring and changes to lighter hues. At last comes the golden yellow, which tells the farmer that the wheat is nearly ready to be harvested. Farmers say that the wheat is ready to be cut when the grains are so hard that they cannot be crushed but are still soft enough to be dented with the finger-nail.

In olden times and in some backward countries today men cut the wheat by hand with scythes or sickles, or with a "cradle"—a large scythe with a frame-work to collect the grain as it is cut. In the 19th century an inventor fastened a number of scythes or blades to a shaft and made a reaping machine, from which has been evolved the modern machinery for swift harvesting—the self-binders, and the combine-harvesters for cutting and threshing. (*See* Agriculture).

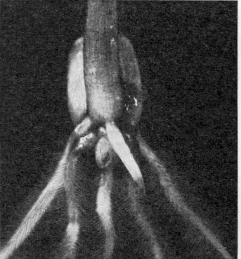

H. Bastin

A WHEAT GRAIN GROWS
The top picture shows a grain of wheat ready to germinate. In the next two photographs root development is proceeding. The fourth picture shows further root action, and extension of the young leaf-blade. The plant is now getting away strongly, and some months later ears of wheat (right) will be ripe.

migrant, as some fly south from Britain in severe winters. The cock bird is black on the upper parts, has some white on the head, wings and tail, and a dark, reddish breast; the hen is duller. The eggs are greenish-blue. The whinchat, which is found in the neighbourhood of hedgerows and furze bushes, may be recognized by its striped head; the male has a very distinctive white line above the eye. The plumage is yellowish-brown on the upper parts, yellowish-red on the breast and yellowish-white below. Like the stonechat, it nests on the ground; the eggs are greenish-blue, with rust-coloured markings. A migrant, the whinchat arrives in Britain from Africa in April.

Wheel. The oldest wheel of which we know is one discovered in Mesopotamia and probably 5,000 years old. But the wheel did not originate as such, and a long period must have elapsed from the time when Man used a rough log as a roller to place under a heavy object, so to enable the load to be dragged more easily. How many years, or centuries, elapsed before a wooden billet was shaped purposely to cylindrical form, in order to function as a roller, no one can tell. Yet the evolution of the wheel must have been in somewhat this manner.

First the load to be hauled was placed on a sledge-like frame, and then a pair of rollers was put beneath the sledge; as the latter rolled along and left the first roller behind, this was brought to the front and slipped beneath the sledge again. Today heavy machine parts are moved short distances in this manner for assembly, but we use steel rollers of small diameter, and propel the load with a steel bar, making use of leverage. We may wonder in what circumstances someone first thought of fixing the rollers on the sledge frame itself in bearings—for that was probably the next step.

A slice cut from a big roller would make a disk wheel. A pair of such disks, mounted on the ends of an axle so that they were free to rotate, and this axle fastened to a sledge frame beneath, would make a simple cart. An enormous improvement would result from thus changing the rollers into wheels, however rough and crude these wheels might be. In some lands wheels little better than solid disks are still used, and we need not leave Europe to find them, on bullock-drawn carts.

We must remember that, all through the history of transport, it was the road which set the pattern for the wheel. It was no use making light and swift-running wheels if the roads were rough and rutty ones. In the early days of stage coaches and private carriages, the wheels were made big so that the height would still raise the carriage above the levels of the deep ruts into which the wheels sank. If you visit a museum where there is a collection of carriages you will note the gradual progression of the wheels, until you come at last to the fragile-looking spidery wheels on the very light vehicles which were used in trotting races.

The craft of the wheelwright was one of the most skilled of the woodworking crafts. He made wheels to suit all kinds of vehicle—from the hay-wain and the manure cart to the sprightly dog-cart in which the farmer drove to market, or took his family out.

So much for road wheels. When the early clockmakers (who were among the first engineers and mechanics) sought for a mechanism to convert the energy from a falling weight into motion of

E. J. Hosking

THE MALE WHEATEAR
Often the earliest spring migrant to reach Britain, the wheatear settles for the summer on hills or downs, where it is familiar until autumn. The cock is a handsome bird, whose grey-blue upper parts and black wings contrast with the white rump, here hidden from view.

wheels and levers, to strike bells and tell the hours, they found the wheel as a ready-made pattern. All they had to do was to provide it with " cogs " or teeth. They would see what they needed in the wooden wheels of the hoisting gins used at mines, or in those of windmills and watermills. The cogs of such wheels were wooden pegs driven into mortises cut in the rim of the wheel ; and for centuries all large iron wheels were made on the same principle, until the casting of iron cog wheels was achieved. Outside the house of William Murdock at Handsworth was preserved a cast iron gear wheel made in 1760—the earliest of this kind.

The clockmakers used brass for small wheels, and iron for those of tower clocks. They devised a kind of lathe or " wheel-engine " for cutting the teeth in brass disks and so making these disks into gear wheels. But until the 18th century such work, when required to be particularly accurate, demanded many hours of labour.

What greater contrast can we imagine than that between the tiny wheels of a wrist-watch and the enormous steel ones used in powerful machinery? Yet both have developed from the primitive roller, as have all the wheels of railway engines, coaches and wagons, and those on which we ride so swiftly along the roads in motor-cars.

One of the " mechanical powers " (see Mechanics) is the wheel-and-axle—i.e. a wheel fixed on the end of an axle so that both turn together. If we wish to raise a bucket of water from a well we can employ a simple winch : this may consist only of two uprights with holes in which the ends of the axle can turn. We call these holes bearings, and if our uprights are wooden ones we line the bearings with brass or iron, to save wear and reduce friction. Fixed on the axle is a wooden cylinder about three inches in diameter; to this cylinder we attach one end of the rope which suspends the bucket. First of all let us imagine that the wheel has been taken off the end of the axle (which is squared here, and fits into a square hole in the centre of the wheel).

Having let down the bucket and filled it with water, we attempt to hoist it by seizing the end of the wooden cylinder and turning it with our hands. We shall find it a difficult task. So we now fix the wheel on the axle end and proceed to turn the wheel, grasping it by the rim. At once we find the work much easier, for we have employed the mechanical advantage of leverage. Suppose that the diameter of the wheel is 24 inches; the " lever arm " is half this diameter, divided by half the diameter of the wooden cylinder upon which the rope is coiled.

$$\text{Then} \quad \frac{24}{2} \div \frac{3}{2} = 8$$

and it is eight times more easy to turn the wheel than to turn the wooden cylinder. But, as we explain in the article on Pulley, the amount of " work " done, in the scientific sense, is the same in both cases. We have to move any point on the wheel rim through a distance eight times as great as that traversed by a point on the wooden cylinder in the same time.

In order to demonstrate that the principle employed is indeed that of the lever, let us replace the wheel by a cranked handle, the length of the crank arm (known as the " throw " of the crank) being 12 inches. We find that we can raise the bucket as easily as we did with the wheel, so that we can regard the latter as a many-spoked crank, with an imaginary handle screwed into the rim.

White, GILBERT (1720–93). If ever an example were needed of a man who became eminent through living a quiet existence and observing what went on around him, Gilbert White would surely come to mind. His book, Natural History of Selborne, a series of letters written to several of his friends, has become a classic of the English language. In it are to be found numerous entertaining observations on birds and beasts, and much curious folklore.

The son of a barrister, Gilbert White was born at Selborne parsonage in Hampshire — his grandfather was vicar of the parish—on July 18, 1720. After attending a local school he studied at Oriel College, Cambridge. He entered the Church of England in 1747, and for the next few years held curacies in various places in the southern counties of England. He settled in Selborne in 1755, and, save for visits to friends and exploratory tours of the countryside, remained there until his death on June 26, 1793. Here is his own recorded opinion of his work :

" If the writer should at all appear to have induced any of his readers to pay a more ready attention to the wonders of the Creation, too frequently overlooked as common occurrences; or if he should by any means, through his researches, have lent an helping hand towards the enlargement of the boundaries of historical and topographical knowledge; or if he should have thrown some small light upon ancient customs and manners, and especially on those that were monastic, his purpose will be answered.

" But if he should not have been successful in any of these his intentions, yet there remains this consolation behind—that these his pursuits, by keeping the body and mind employed, have, under Providence, contributed to much health and cheerfulness of spirits, even to old age."

Whitebeam. Growing on the chalk downs and limestone hills of Britain, and also found in North Africa and Asia, the whitebeam (Pyrus aria) is easy to recognize by the white undersides of its broad grey-green leaves. In May and June it has clusters of small white flowers, which are followed in autumn by masses of round, red berries of which birds are extremely fond. The tree seldom attains a height of more than 40 feet ; the wood, hard and fine-grained, is used in cabinet-making. Its relative the mountain ash (Pyrus aucuparia) or rowan, also grows in hilly places and has similar blooms and berries; but its leaves are of the form known as pinnate (see illustration in page 1916). Both these trees are members of the family Rosaceae.

Whitman, WALT (1819–92). Numerous critics consider Walt Whitman to be the foremost poet of the United States. Born at West Hills on Long Island, United States, on May 31, 1819, Whitman was the son of a carpenter. After receiving an elementary education he was in turn office boy, printer, teacher and journalist before the first small volume of his poems, Leaves of Grass, was published in 1855. This attracted little or no attention until the poet Ralph Waldo Emerson (q.v.) characterized the work as " the most extraordinary piece of wit and wisdom yet contributed to American literature." These poems had neither rhyme nor metre but a magnificent cadence. By many literary men they were challenged for their irregular form and unconventional ideas.

Out of his experiences as an army nurse in the American Civil War (1861–65), Whitman wrote Drum Taps, in which occurs his poignant lament on the death of Lincoln. After the war

Painting by J. W. Alexander; Metropolitan Museum of Art, New York

WALT WHITMAN

Not appreciated at his true worth during his lifetime, Walt Whitman is now considered by some as the foremost North American poet. His first volume of poems, Leaves of Grass (1855) was written in irregular, unrhymed lines.

he worked in a government department until 1873, when, partly disabled by a paralytic stroke, he retired to Camden, New Jersey, where he lived for nearly 20 years the free unworldly life of a poet. He died on March 26, 1892.

Whittington, RICHARD (died 1423). One of the most popular of legends and pantomime " plots " is the story of Dick Whittington, the poor orphan boy who, hearing that the streets of London were " paved with gold," journeys to the great city from the west of England, gains employment as a scullion in a rich merchant's household, and lends his cat to his master's ship.

Ill-treated by the cook, Dick runs away, but, while resting at Holloway, turns back on hearing Bow Bells ringing : " Turn again, Whittington, thrice Lord Mayor of London."

On his return he finds that the king of a country on the Barbary coast, whose palace was overrun with rats and mice, has paid a fabulous sum for the cat—and Dick marries his master's daughter, succeeds to the business, prospers greatly, and eventually becomes " thrice Lord Mayor of London." This popular tale seems to have been first told in 1605.

The real Whittington of history does not appear ever to have been poor. The son of a Gloucestershire knight, and a mercer by trade, he flourished exceedingly, and after holding several civic offices was appointed by the king to be Lord Mayor of London, in 1397, to complete the term of a mayor who had died. In 1398 he was elected Lord Mayor, and again in 1406 and 1419. He gave liberally to charities, and frequently helped Richard II, Henry IV and Henry V with loans. On his death, in March 1423, he bequeathed his vast fortune to charitable and public objects. It is uncertain whether he was ever knighted.

Wicklow. Known for long as the " Garden of Ireland," Wicklow is an eastern county of Eire, with lovely glens, beautiful valleys and tranquil lakes. It is bounded on the south by Wexford, on the west by Carlow and Kildare, on the north by Dublin, on the east by the Irish Sea, and it has an area of 780 square miles.

Traversing the county is a range of granite mountains (the Wicklow Mountains), 40 miles in length and with peaks reaching 2,000 feet or more. The coastline extends for 36 miles. Wicklow, the county town (population 3,500), stands on the side of a hill overlooking the sea; other centres are Bray and Arklow. Bray is a favourite holiday resort; and Greystones, another seaside town, is a popular centre for tourists. The picturesque vale of Glendalough is one of many beauty spots. Sheep, cattle and pigs are bred; copper, lead and other minerals are worked. The population of the county of Wicklow is 60,000.

Wight, ISLE OF Half way along the south coast of England is one of her best-known islands— the Isle of Wight. It is separated from the mainland of Hampshire, of which it is a part, by the busy waterways of the Solent and Spithead. In the summer months its seaside resorts—Ryde, opposite Portsmouth and Southsea ; Cowes, directly opposite the entrance to Southampton Water ; Freshwater Bay, Shanklin, Sandown, Ventnor, and others—are filled with visitors. Cowes is the headquarters of yacht-racing in Britain. Chines—

Fox

THE NEEDLES OFF THE ISLE OF WIGHT
At the western extremity of the Isle of Wight are the Needles, a series of rocks, with a lighthouse at the outermost point. Forming part of the county of Hampshire, from which it is separated by the Solent and Spithead, the island contains a number of holiday resorts, including Cowes, the headquarters of British yacht-racing.

ravines running inland from the shore—add to the attraction of the island, as do the rolling downs of the interior. Newport (population 11,000), an inland town, is the " capital." Although part of Hampshire, the island is separately administered.

The ancient Vectis of the Romans, the Isle of Wight was often visited by Queen Victoria in her later years, and not far from Cowes is Osborne House, where she died. Lord Tennyson (q.v.) lived at Farringford. The area of the island is 147 square miles, and the population is 88,000.

Wigtownshire. The most south-westerly of all the counties of Scotland, Wigtownshire forms part of the district of Galloway. Its double peninsula, thrust out into the North Channel, which connects the Irish Sea and the Atlantic Ocean, is known as the Rhinns of Galloway.

The south-eastern portion of the peninsula also has a name—the Machers or Machars—and the county itself is known as the Moors. The coast is rugged and rocky. The main rivers are the Cree, Bladnoch and Luce. The chief occupations are the breeding of cattle, horses, pigs and sheep, and the growing of oats. Wigtown (population 1,200) is the county town. The Scottish terminus of the Irish cross-channel steamer service to Larne is at Stranraer (6,000). The area of Wigtownshire is 487 square miles, and the population is 31,000.

Wilhelmina, QUEEN OF THE NETHER-
LANDS (born 1880 ; ruled 1890–1948). The daughter of William III of Orange-Nassau, king of the
Netherlands, by his second wife Emma of Waldeck-
Pyrmont, Wilhelmina Helena Pauline Maria was
born at The Hague, the Netherlands, on August
31, 1880, and was educated privately. Her
father's two sons by his first marriage dying in
1879 and 1884, she succeeded him on his death
on November 23, 1890. Queen Emma acted as
Regent until the Princess's 18th birthday, when she
officially came of age. Wilhelmina was enthroned
on September 6, 1898.

On February 8, 1901, she married Henry, Duke
of Mecklenburg-Schwerin (1876–1934), and their
only child, Princess Juliana, was born on April 30,
1909. Of simple tastes, Queen Wilhelmina lived
a quiet life, chiefly at The Hague, where she was
often to be seen riding through the streets on a
bicycle. She managed to keep her country neutral
during the First World War (1914–18) and had
hoped to maintain neutrality again in the Second
World War (1939–45); but the Netherlands was
overrun by German forces in May 1940.

An attempt to capture Queen Wilhelmina by
German paratroops failed and she escaped to
England in a British warship. She remained in
Britain during the war as head of the Dutch
Government in exile, and broadcast on a number
of occasions to her people. The Queen returned
to the Netherlands immediately after its liberation
in May 1945 and was accorded an enthusiastic
welcome. Failing health caused her to abdicate
on September 4, 1948, in favour of her daughter
Princess Juliana, and she retired into private life
as the Princess of the Netherlands.

Will. The act of " leaving " one's property
at death to certain persons or institutions, etc.,
is called making a will. All wills must be in
writing (or typewritten) except that a member of
the armed forces on active service may make a
verbal will; and all written or typewritten wills
must be signed by the maker of the will, called the
" testator." Two witnesses must sign the will,
declaring that they were both present together
when the testator signed the document, and it is
usual for the testator to name a friend or solicitor
as " executor," i.e., a person to see that the provisions of the will are executed, or carried out.
Persons receiving property under a will are called
" legatees." The witnesses to a will may not be
also legatees.

A " sole legatee " is one receiving all the property owned by the testator, as when a man leaves
everything he possesses to his wife. A " residuary
legatee " receives what is left of the property, usually
called the estate, after other legacies have been
made—as when a man leaves certain sums of money
or articles of property, to several of his friends and
relations, and the remainder of his belongings
to his wife, child, or other close relative.

When a second or later will is made it should
explicitly state that earlier ones are " hereby
revoked " or cancelled. A " codicil " is a clause
added to a will at a later date, usually altering
some provision ; it has to be dated, signed, and
witnessed, in the same way as the original will.

The most important aspect of making a will
is to make one's wishes perfectly clear, so that no
lawsuits or quarrels need arise among relatives
after one's death. It is wisest to have the will
drawn up by a solicitor. If it can be proved that
the wife, husband or children of a testator have
been unfairly dealt with—as, for instance, when
no money has been left to them, and large sums
have gone to some institution—the Courts of Law
can alter the provisions of a will so as to ensure that
relatives do not become penniless.

William. GERMAN EMPERORS. Two
monarchs of the former kingdom of Prussia of
this name and members of the House of Hohen-
zollern have borne the title " German Emperor."

WILLIAM I (1797–1888), the first German Emperor
(Kaiser), was born on March 22, 1797, at a time
when his country was of small importance. As
second son he was not expected to ascend the
throne, and he devoted himself entirely to the
army. During the Prussian revolution of 1848
he was obliged to leave Berlin, but the following
year, in command of the Prussian troops, he defeated the revolutionary army and effectively
quelled the rebellion.

His elder brother, King Frederick William IV,
was childless, and in his later years insane. As
Regent and then as King of Prussia (from 1861),
William I devoted himself to the re-organization of
the Prussian army. After 1862 the history of
William's reign is mainly the history of Otto von
Bismarck, who became the King's chief Minister
and who controlled the State. William would have
preferred to remain simply King of Prussia, but
Bismarck and the Crown Prince Frederick persuaded
him to accept the title of German Emperor in
1871. The proclamation took place at Versailles,
near Paris, during the Franco-Prussian War.

WILLIAM II (1859–1941), the son of the Emperor
Frederick III and of the eldest daughter of Queen
Victoria of England, was born in Berlin on
January 27, 1859, and ascended to the throne
after the brief reign of his father (March to June
1888), determined to rule as well as to reign. This
became sufficiently plain in 1890, when he quarrelled
with Bismarck and dismissed him.

From the first William II placed his reliance on
the army as the main instrument for the expansion
of Germany. Amid the constructive work of
statesmen, financiers, and industrialists—which
raised Germany within a period of 40 years from
the position of one of the backward countries of
Europe to one of the most progressive—was to be
heard, in crisis after crisis of European affairs, the
ominous sabre-rattling of this Prussian " war lord,"
which often made war seem likely.

To put himself into a position to win for Germany
the place among the World Powers which he
desired, he needed a strong navy as well as an
army, so he turned with energy to the development
of the German fleet. The British Government
viewed this with alarm, a feeling which was soon
to be justified when the Kaiser, in 1914, thinking
that the other nations would not fight, took the
fatal steps that led to the First World War (1914–18).
On November 9, 1918, when Germany itself had
risen in revolt against him, William II abdicated,
and the following day he fled to the Netherlands.
First at Amerongen, and later at Doorn, near
Utrecht, the ex-Kaiser lived in seclusion. He
died at Doorn on June 4, 1941.

The FOUR crowned WILLIAMS of ENGLAND

Nearly eight centuries are spanned in the interval between the crowning of the first, and the death of the last King William of England. Two were invaders of the country, but they ruled none the less well for that.

William. KINGS OF ENGLAND. Four kings of England have borne this name, which was introduced with the Norman Conquest of 1066.

WILLIAM I, THE CONQUEROR (1027–87) who ruled England from 1066 to 1087, was the sixth Duke of Normandy in descent from Rolf (c. 860–932), or Rollo, the first Duke, and had many of the qualities of his Viking ancestor. He was still a boy when he inherited the Duchy of Normandy from his father Duke Robert, but by the time he was 24 he had not only established his authority over his rebellious nobles but had made himself one of the most powerful rulers in France.

But William's ambitions went further. Across the Channel reigned his father's cousin, the childless Edward the Confessor, from whom William was said to have obtained a promise that he should succeed Edward on the throne of England. So when Edward died in 1066 William claimed the throne, despite the fact that Earl Harold, who had also promised William the crown of England, was chosen king by the English. When Harold himself accepted the crown, in January 1066, William prepared a large expedition, which set sail for England in October 1066.

Landing on the Sussex coast at Pevensey, William defeated the forces of the English king at the battle of Hastings on October 14, 1066, leaving Harold dead on the field. Tradition has preserved a characteristic anecdote. As William landed he is said to have stumbled and fallen on the beach—an unlucky omen. With ready wit he clutched a handful of sand and, holding it aloft, said : " By the splendour of God, I have taken possession of England! " Hailed as king by the people of London, William was crowned in Westminster Abbey on Christmas Day, 1066.

Five years of warfare were needed to subdue the turbulent English nobles, notably Hereward " the Wake " (q.v.) who resisted the Conqueror from his stronghold in the Isle of Ely. William, stern and pitiless, laid waste rebellious districts and at strategic points erected castles

with royal garrisons to keep the people in subjection. He seized the lands of those who had fought against him and gave them to his followers, or allowed their original holders to regain them on payment of heavy fines. He thus established the feudal principle that every foot of the soil was the property of the Crown, and granted it to his vassals only on condition of an oath of fealty (loyalty) and the promise to supply him with money and men. William further strengthened the power of the Crown against the nobles by demanding an oath of personal allegiance from all freemen, which took precedence of the service they owed their lords.

His wise policy of retaining the old Anglo-Saxon laws, courts, and customs, with only a few innovations, gained him the loyalty of the mass of the people. Thus the principle of local self-government, which lies at the root of the political system of the English-speaking peoples, was preserved and strengthened. At the same time William taught his people of England the advantages of a central government, powerful enough to secure justice for all.

Among his new measures was the compilation of the Domesday Book (q.v.). " So very narrowly did he cause the survey to be made," complains the Anglo-Saxon Chronicle, " that there was not a single rood (quarter of an acre) of land, nor an ox, or a cow, or a pig, passed by and that was not set down in the accounts."

William the Conqueror was a tall, heavy man, with a tremendous voice. Though he was despotic and grasping, such was the good order he established that " any man, who was himself aught, might travel over the kingdom with a bosom of gold unmolested, and no man durst kill another, however great the injury he might have received from him." William was thrown from his horse after sacking the French town of Mantes, and died from his injuries at Rouen on September 9, 1087.

Before his death he divided his possessions, giving Normandy to his eldest son, Robert, and

Donald McLeish

WILLIAM THE CONQUEROR

In the town of Falaise in Normandy, France, where he was born in 1027, this monument was erected to William I, the ' Conqueror.' He succeeded his father as Duke of Normandy in 1035; and in 1066, after winning the battle of Hastings or Senlac, he became King of England.

England to William, his next son. To his youngest son, Henry, he left 5,000 pounds of silver, saying—so the story goes—that in due time he would get all that his father had.

WILLIAM II, RUFUS ("Red") (1056?–1100), ruled from 1087 to 1100. The Norman barons revolted in favour of the eldest son, Robert, but were crushed by William, who received ready aid from the English. He was ungrateful, greedy and cruel, and soon earned the hatred of his subjects. He angered the clergy by his shameless practice of selling Church offices or keeping them unoccupied in order that he might seize their revenues for himself. Once, when he thought that he was dying, he vowed that he would turn from his evil ways and fill the Archbishopric of Canterbury, which he had kept vacant for four years. His choice fell on Anselm, Abbot of Bec, in Normandy.

Anselm accepted with the greatest reluctance, and his forebodings proved only too well justified, for when William II recovered he returned to his old ways. Contrary to established custom he insisted upon conferring the symbols of office upon the Archbishop himself, instead of allowing this to be done by the Pope. On this question of "lay investiture" of the clergy, as the consecration of priests by civil rulers is called, Anselm took a determined stand against the king, and there was a long series of disputes. When, tired of quarrelling with William, he went to Rome to ask the Pope to settle the matter, the king seized and retained the revenues of Canterbury.

In 1096 William II received Normandy from his elder brother Robert, to whom he had lent large sums of money for the First Crusade. Desirous of extending his French possessions still further, William prepared an expedition to Normandy but was slain by an arrow when hunting in the New Forest, Hampshire, on August 2, 1100. Whether the shooting was accidental or intentional no one knows. He was hastily buried, without religious rites, at Winchester, and was succeeded by his younger brother, who became Henry I (*q.v.*).

WILLIAM III (1650–1702), who ruled Britain from 1689 to 1702, came to the throne by the revolution of 1688 which cost James II his crown. He was the great-grandson of William the Silent, Prince of Orange, and was "stadtholder" (ruler) of the United Provinces of the Netherlands. He was also the son of one English princess, Mary, daughter of Charles I, and the husband of another, Mary, the elder daughter of James II. As William was the chief defender of the Protestant interests on the continent of Europe, and Mary was regarded by most as the lawful heir to the British throne, it was only natural that the English nobility and clergy should turn to him with an invitation to save them from the tyranny of James II, who was a Roman Catholic. He had but to land in Torbay, Devonshire, on November 5, 1688, with an expedition of 14,000 men, and almost the whole of England and Scotland rallied to his support. In February 1689, William and Mary were proclaimed joint sovereigns: Ireland did not submit until James II had been defeated at the battle of the Boyne on July 1, 1690.

Although William III was never very popular with his British subjects, his reign was one of considerable progress in real liberty and constitutional government. In the judgement of historians, he ranks as one of our ablest kings. His chief aim was to curb the power of France in Europe. He led the Netherlands at a time when Louis XIV (1638–1715) was embarking on plans to make himself the overlord of Europe, and William had already (1672–78) won fame for his skill in generalship and in building up alliances to resist French aggression. After eight years of war (1689–97) Louis XIV was forced to accept the treaty of Ryswick (1697), which left him with only slight gains and bound him to give no further assistance to James II. Five years later, just when he had formed a powerful alliance against France, William died from the effects of a chill and a fall from his horse, on March 8, 1702. Queen Mary had died several years before—in 1694. The throne passed to her sister, the Princess Anne (*q.v.*).

WILLIAM IV (1765–1837), who reigned for only seven years (1830–37) was the third son of George III, and was known before his accession as the Duke of Clarence. He was born at Buckingham Palace, London, on August 21, 1765, and entered the Royal Navy as a midshipman in 1779, enjoying some popularity as the "sailor prince." Entering the House of Lords in 1789, he left the Navy

MYSTERIOUS DEATH OF WILLIAM RUFUS
William II, who was called Rufus, was slain by an arrow on August 2, 1100, while hunting in the New Forest, Hampshire. Whether the shooting was accidental or not no one knows, but a certain Walter Tirrel, who fled the country, was said to have loosed the fatal arrow. The incident is depicted in the above engraving after the painting by E. F. Burney.

important duties and had sent him on diplomatic missions. It was on one of these missions that William won his name "the Silent" by his taciturnity and discretion in diplomacy.

When the brutal persecutions of Philip's general, the Duke of Alva, drove the Dutch to armed revolt, William put himself at the head of the movement. At the same time he abjured his Roman Catholic faith and became a Calvinist. At first William was defeated and was obliged for a time to take refuge in Germany. But he went on doggedly, until in 1581 the seven northern provinces of the Netherlands issued a formal declaration of independence. Holland was now a separate nation under the leadership of William of Orange, who was the "father of his country." William then settled at Delft, and with the remnants of his former wealth supported himself in a simple and quiet style. Meanwhile King Philip had put a price on William's head. In 1584 an assassin shot and mortally wounded the heroic leader. William did in the following year, but he took little part in public life until his accession to the throne in 1830. The most important event of his reign was the passing of the Reform Bill in 1832, by which the right to vote was considerably extended. William IV died on June 20, 1837, and was succeeded by his niece as Queen Victoria (q.v.).

William the Silent,

PRINCE OF ORANGE (1533–84). When Charles V, with impressive ceremonies, laid down his office as ruler of the Netherlands (1555), he leaned on the arm of a tall young man, William, Prince of Orange. On the other side of him stood his son, Philip II. In a few years these two young men were to be bitter enemies, and William of Orange was to be the leader of the Dutch armies in their struggles for independence. (See Philip II, King of Spain).

At the time of Charles's abdication William was 22 years old. At the age of 11 he had succeeded to the little principality of Orange in southern France, and to possessions in the Netherlands. From early youth he had been brought up at the court of the emperor, who had given him

TWO ROYAL WILLIAMS OF GREAT BRITAIN
The landing of William of Orange (later William III) at Brixham in Devonshire on November 5, 1688, is depicted in a portion of a painting (lower) by an unknown artist in Hampton Court Palace, Middlesex. The upper illustration is a reproduction of Sir Martin Archer Shee's (1769–1850) painting of William IV in naval uniform; he served in the navy from 1779 to 1790.
Upper, National Portrait Gallery; lower, by permission of the Lord Chamberlain

G. Bird

ROSE-BAY WILLOW-HERB

Reaching a height of about four feet, this plant blooms in woodland clearings in Britain in July and August when the rose-hued flowers form a wide mass of colour. The seeds terminate in long tufts of fine filaments, and when the wind releases them they are sown far and wide.

not live to enjoy the fruits of the struggle to which he had given his life, but his sons, Maurice and Frederick Henry, continued the fight, and their father's place as creator of a nation is firmly fixed.

Willow. Those big, puffy, silvery-coloured or golden catkins which are common round about Easter-time and are generally called " palm " are the flower-clusters of a species of willow, known as the goat or pussy willow or sallow (*Salix caprea*), a tree of common occurrence in Britain. It is the golden catkins which produce the pollen needed to fertilize the female flowers, which are silvery at first and later pale green in colour.

The wood of which cricket bats are made comes from the bat willow (*S. alba coerulea*). The long whippy shoots used for making hampers and baskets are produced by the osier willow (*S. viminalis*). The weeping willow (*S. babylonica*) is so called because of its drooping branches. There are several other species which though not native to Britain are now quite at home in the country.

Willow-herbs. Close-packed stems of the rose-bay willow-herb (*Epilobium angustifolium*) rising to four feet, and at their summits bearing racemes (spikes) of rosy coloured flowers each about an inch across, make a handsome sight in woodland clearings in Britain during July and August.

Especially where the ground has been burnt-over does this attractive plant seem to thrive. After the Second World War (1939–45) it took

possession—as the result of wind-borne seeds—of quite large areas of London where fires had raged among the city buildings and had left seared and scattered ruins. Hence its alternative name " fire-weed." The freely produced seeds terminate in long tufts of fine filaments, and when the wind plucks them from their open capsules they sail away to quite long distances. Also this perennial plant spreads by means of underground stems.

Other British species include the rosy-purple flowered great willow-herb, or codlins-and-cream (*E. hirsutum*) which grows beside streams and ditches, and the rose-lilac marsh willow-herb (*E. palustre*) of bogs and marshy places generally.

Willow Pattern. Most people have seen sets of china bearing an attractive design in blue and white, obviously of Chinese origin, showing a river, houses, trees, a bridge, birds and human figures. The pattern was copied from Chinese pottery and first produced in England about 1780 by Thomas Turner (1749–1809) at Caughley, Shropshire, and in due course was imitated by other makers of chinaware. (*See* illus. opposite.)

The legend depicted on the surface of a Willow Pattern plate is this. A mandarin had an only daughter named Li-Chi, who fell in love with Chang, a young man who had once been her father's secretary. The mandarin, who lived in the big house on the right, heard they were in love, and he forbade their engagement. They eloped and escaped by

R. St. Barbe Baker

CRICKET-BAT WILLOWS

A hybrid between the Bedford and the white species is the cricket-bat willow, which is grown commercially. Straight-grained and with slender boles, they are quick growers and yield suitable timber for bat manufacture—tough yet light and free from knots—in about 15 years.

WILLOW PATTERN WARE

Copied from the Chinese, willow pattern pottery was first produced in England about 1780 by Thomas Turner at Caughley, Shropshire, since when it has been imitated by other makers of chinaware. (*See* text).

boat to Chang's home. The enraged mandarin pursued them with a whip, and would have beaten them to death had the gods not changed the lovers into the pair of turtle-doves which are seen flying at the top of the pattern.

Wilson, THOMAS WOODROW (1856–1924). Twice President of the United States, and the founder of the League of Nations (*q.v.*), Woodrow Wilson was born at Staunton, Virginia, on December 28, 1856, and was educated at Davidson College, North Carolina, and at the universities of Princeton and Virginia. He became a lawyer, practised for a time at Atlanta, Georgia, and in 1885 he was chosen associate Professor of History at Bryn Mawr College. From 1902 to 1911 he was President of Princeton University, and was elected Governor of the State of New Jersey in 1910. This brought him to the notice of the public, and in 1912 he was elected President of the United States.

When the First World War began, in 1914, Wilson was determined that the United States should remain neutral, and his policy led to his re-election as President in 1916. But in 1917 the sinking of United States shipping by German submarines forced him to declare war on Germany. On January 8, 1918, he outlined his Fourteen Points for world peace, which not only largely formed the basis of the terms offered to Germany and which brought the war to an end but also led to the formation of the League of Nations.

In December 1918 Wilson went to Paris as the head of the United States delegation to the Peace Conference. Returning to the United States, he found that Congress and the Senate were opposed to the entry of his country into the League. This disappointment may have been responsible for the nervous breakdown that he suffered in September 1919, and which caused his retirement from public life. Wilson was awarded the Nobel Peace prize in 1920 He died in Washington on February 3, 1924.

Wiltshire. An inland county of southern England, Wiltshire has an area of 1,345 square miles. It is bounded by Gloucestershire on the west and north, by Berkshire and Hampshire on the east, by Dorset on the south. It is divided into two portions by the Vale of Pewsey ; the northern and more fertile section contains the Marlborough Downs, while the southern includes Salisbury Plain, with the prehistoric remains of Stonehenge (*q.v.*) and Avebury (*q.v.*).

The highest point is Inkpen Beacon (975 feet), which is on the Berkshire boundary. Savernake Forest and parts of Cranborne Chase and the New Forest are in the county. The chief rivers are the Bristol Avon, the Wiltshire Avon, Kennet, Ebble, and Nadder. The main industries are sheep-breeding, dairy-farming, cheese-making and bacon-curing. Wheat and oats are the principal crops.

Salisbury (*q.v.*) is the county town ; but the largest is Swindon (population 65,500), where is one of the biggest locomotive works of British Railways. Other centres are Marlborough (with a noted Public School), Chippenham, Calne, Devizes, Trowbridge, Warminster, Malmesbury and Wilton (famed for its carpets). The population of the county of Wiltshire is 303,000.

Winchester. In former times the capital of England, Winchester is now the county town of Hampshire. Situated on the Itchen, the city is 12 miles north of Southampton and is the market for the surrounding agricultural district. The Cathedral is largely Gothic, but some Norman work survives ; its length of 526 feet makes it the longest in England. In the County Hall is the so-called Round Table of King Arthur (*q.v.*). Winchester College, founded by William of Wykeham in 1382 and one of the oldest of the notable Public Schools, is in the city.

First a Celtic and later a Roman settlement, Winchester became the capital of the kingdom of

PRESIDENT WOODROW WILSON

Having fought for the establishment of the League of Nations at the Allied Peace Conference of 1919, President Wilson was bitterly disappointed when the United States refused to join the League. He was twice President of the United States (1912–16 and 1916–20).

A. F. Kersting

WINCHESTER CATHEDRAL
Largely Gothic, but with traces of the original Norman work, St. Swithin's Cathedral at Winchester, Hampshire, of which the west front is seen above, is the longest cathedral in England, with a length of 526 feet. It is noted for its Perpendicular nave, constructed in the 14th century.

Wessex, and under King Edward the Elder (died 924) was recognized as the capital of England, but after the Norman Conquest of 1066 it was gradually supplanted by London. The population of Winchester is 23,000.

Wind. Have you ever thought how different the world would be without wind ? The ocean would have no waves ; windmills could never turn. Columbus could never have sailed across the ocean. Not merely this, for the winds are now remaking, scouring and sculpturing the face of the earth, as they have done for ages past. Next to water, wind is the greatest erosive force in wearing down rocks and hills and scooping out gorges and valleys with strong blasts of sand. It transports sand and dust for miles, sometimes making, sometimes destroying, fertile soil.

To see what winds can accomplish, look at the northern part of China, an area larger than the whole of France, overlaid with deep rich *loess*, or fine soil, brought by winds from Central Asia ; then glance at the Desert of Gobi, where great cities lie buried under sand heaped by the wind.

Of all the mysteries the movements of the air have long been among the most baffling. " The wind bloweth where it listeth, and thou hearest the sound thereof, but canst not tell whence it cometh and whither it goeth," expresses about all that it was thought possible to say on the subject until comparatively recent times. But today we know that all winds, from gentle breezes to raging

hurricanes, are caused by differences in atmospheric pressure. A simple example is found in land-and-water breezes.

Sunshine pours down upon land and water alike, and warms them. Over oceans and lakes most of the heat energy is consumed in evaporation, or is absorbed by the water ; the air does not become greatly heated. But land absorbs only six-tenths as much heat as water does, and evaporation is less. Hence over land the air receives a greater share of the heat than over water.

Heated air expands, and exerts less pressure than before. When this occurs over the land soon after sunrise, the sea air, which has greater pressure because it is colder, forces its way landward. This movement is the day sea breeze. At night land cools more quickly than water, and the breeze is reversed. Similar day-and-night pressure changes cause mountain-and-valley breezes. By day the greatest heating takes place along mountain sides. Pressure from below then starts a breeze blowing up the valleys. At night this action also is reversed.

Pressure differences likewise cause world-wide air movements known as planetary winds. Throughout the year the most intensely heated portion of the earth is the tropical zone, which is centred upon the Equator. The abundant heat there keeps the air pressure low, and denser air continually pushes in from both sides. But the central part of this zone has little wind, because the chief air movement is upward, as the heated air is forced up by the incoming cooler air. As the ascending air cools, its moisture condenses into clouds and keeps the zone drenched with steaming showers. Sailors were often becalmed for weeks in those latitudes, which are called the " doldrums," from an old word meaning " dull " or " stupid."

Fox

HOW WIND IS RECORDED
An appliance used for recording the pressure or velocity of the wind, the anemograph (above) utilises the difference of pressure set up between two pipes, one of which is kept facing the wind by a wind vane, the other connected to a system of ' suction holes ' on a vertical tube. The difference in pressure causes a float, to which a pen is attached, to trace on the upper part of a record (left) the gusts and lulls of the wind. The shaft on the right, connected to the wind vane, operates a pen which records changes in the direction of the wind at the base of the chart (lower left).

The flow of air from each side constitutes the trade winds, so called from the old meaning of " trade," viz., a steady track. The trade winds, however, do not blow directly toward the Equator. They are deflected by the earth's rotation. On the average, they blow inwards, from the N.E. in the N. hemisphere and from the S.E. in the S. hemisphere.

Beyond the regions of the trades on each side of the Equator is another calm belt called the " horse latitudes "—some say because becalmed ships laden with horses often ran short of water, and the sailors had to throw the horses overboard. Two specific pressure conditions cause these calms. The first of these conditions is the behaviour of the air which is driven upward at the Equator. After ascending, the air flows toward both poles at a level well above the trade winds. It becomes cooled, acquires higher pressure, and returns to the earth near the parallels of 30° north and south. Since this settling is very nearly straight downward, these high pressure belts have little wind. After settling, the air continues its poleward movement and becomes deflected to constitute the prevailing westerlies of the middle latitudes (temperate zones). This entire movement in the upper atmosphere and in the region of the westerlies is called the anti-trades, as it is contrary to the trades.

The second condition arises in summer. Less heat is received from the sun as distance from the Equator increases. Air pressure therefore tends to become higher. But the greater the distance from the Equator, the longer the day in summer and the greater the number of hours of sunlight. In the middle latitudes, this increase in hours of sunshine more than makes up for its lessened intensity. Hence, pressure decreases in summer in these latitudes, leaving areas of semi-permanent high pressure near the Tropics of Cancer and Capricorn. This pressure reinforces the anti-trades. At the same time, the persistent trade winds represent the circulation of the air at the eastern and equatorial sides of these great anticyclones.

The characteristic planetary wind of middle latitudes is the prevailing westerly. At sea the westerlies are so strong that the 40th degrees of latitude are called " the roaring forties." In the northern hemisphere, the influence of the continents breaks up the regularity of these winds. They are disturbed also by depressions and anticyclones. The southern hemisphere, however, has few great land masses ; so here the westerlies blow without interruption. They are especially strong, as are the trade winds, in the South Indian Ocean.

THE ' TRADES ' AND ' PREVAILING WESTERLIES '
The great wind currents are here flowing in toward the equator to form the ' trades,' and the high return currents settling to earth beyond 30 degrees north latitude. Along the equator, where the air is rising, is the region of the ' doldrums,' where sailing ships lie in the torrid heat for lack of wind ; while between the belt of trades and ' westerlies ' are the ' horse latitudes,' likewise regions of feeble winds. The reason why the trades and westerlies do not blow due south and north is given in the text. This system of winds is duplicated in the Southern Hemisphere, with, of course, corresponding differences in direction.

In Asia the seasonal difference of temperature between land and sea areas is so great as to produce the famous " monsoons " blowing from land to sea in winter and from sea to land in summer. The changes are most marked in the sub-continent of India, Siam, and the Malay Archipelago. In winter, cold north-east winds from a region of high pressure in northern Siberia blow over India ; this is the dry or winter monsoon. During the summer the heated air over the land rises, and cooler winds from the Indian Ocean flow in to take its place, delivering their moisture in the form of heavy torrents of rain. This is the wet or summer monsoon. Similar summer and winter reversals of wind directions take place also on the east coast of Africa, the north coast of Australia, in Texas, U.S.A., and Chile.

Among notable irregular local winds are the Siberian " buran," a high north wind with snow ; the " sirocco " of Italy and Spain, a hot south wind ; a warm dry wind which blows down from higher regions into mountain valleys, becoming heated by compression during its descent, so that it melts the snow—called " föhn " in Switzerland and " chinook " in the Rocky Mountains ; and the cold " mistral," a strong north-west wind which blows from the Alps through southern France.

Wind velocities as high as 200 miles an hour or more in gusts have been recorded by anemometers (instruments for measuring wind speeds and directions), the highest at the earth's surface being 231 m.p.h. at Mount Washington Observatory (6,284 feet), U.S.A., on April 12, 1934.

Windmills. So few of the old-type windmills which we see about the country are in working order that not many people have a clear idea how these machines carry out their work of grinding corn or pumping water. The mill appears to have reached the rest of Europe from the regions bordering the Mediterranean, early in the Christian era. In Britain it is first mentioned towards the end of the 12th century. In our own country it was chiefly used for grinding the grain which local farmers brought to the miller. The only other means of doing this work by power was the water mill ; but whereas a sizeable stream was needed for the latter, a windmill could be erected on any lofty piece of ground where it could obtain a fair amount of its motive power, in steady winds.

Windmills are an uncertain source of power. If the wind is too strong, the sails or sweeps must be set for the time being so that they present their *edges* to the gale; if this were not done the sweeps would be whirled round so furiously that the machinery inside the mill would be broken. Assuming a fair wind, then the mill-head, bearing the four or more sweeps, must be turned so that the sweeps face the wind.

The "post" mill is turned round bodily by pressing against a long wooden lever, so that the entire building rotates on a vertical post which serves as a pivot. The "tower" mill is a bigger and more massive erection, constructed of brick or masonry and often having a wooden "smock" or outer covering to the upper part. Other names for this type are smock mill or cap mill. The "cap" is a separate part at the top of the tower, which can rotate on rollers. The cap holds the mill-head, with the main horizontal shaft for the sweeps, and the cogwheel which drives the vertical shaft from which power is taken for the millstones.

At the opposite side of the cap to that at which the sweeps are situated there is a boom which carries a smaller vaned wheel, this structure being known as the "fantail." The fantail wheel is set on a short shaft which is at right-angles to the shaft on which the sweeps are fixed. This means that when the fantail wheel is facing the wind, the main s w e e p s are presenting their edges to the wind, and are not driven round. T h e fantail w h e e l is geared to a rod which, by other cog wheels, moves the cap of the mill around on rollers on top of the tower. Consequently the wind, blowing against the fantail, gradually moves this until it comes *edge* to wind, bringing the sweeps *face* to wind, and the sails turn merrily. Should the wind change direction, the fantail wheel will be driven once more, and will move the cap around until the sweeps are again fronting t h e w i n d. A system of rods and gears enables the cap to be moved round by hand so as to take the mill-head out of the wind when needed.

The face of the sweeps is set at a slight slope, so that wind blowing between them gives them a

HOW THE WINDMILL WORKS TO GRIND THE CORN
On the left is a tower mill, of which only the head rotates ; it is also called a Dutch mill, because it is the kind most often seen in the Netherlands. On the right is a post mill, so called because the whole structure revolves on a stout post. Either the mill or the top of it must be able to turn in order that the sails may face into the wind. Power is transmitted by the sails through toothed wheels to revolve the millstones.

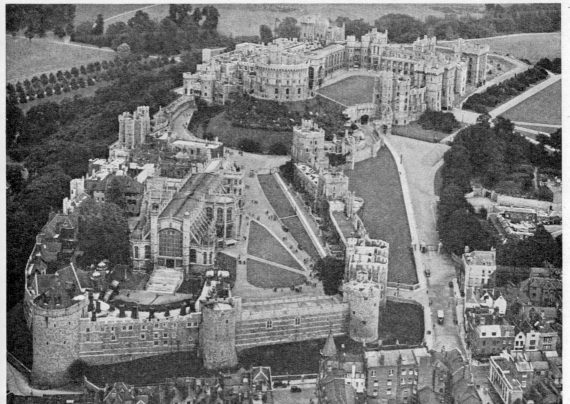

Central Press

WINDSOR CASTLE : A HOME OF BRITAIN'S SOVEREIGNS

Founded by William the Conqueror (1027–87), the royal palace of Windsor, in Berkshire, stands on a hill overlooking the Thames. In the left foreground is St. George's Chapel, a beautiful example of Perpendicular Gothic dating from the 15th century, in which several British kings are buried. In the choir of the Chapel are the seats and banners of the Knights of the Garter. On a mound in the middle distance is the Round Tower or Keep, which was added by Edward III (1312–77). In the immediate foreground and on the right are some buildings of the town of Windsor.

sideways thrust, which drives them round. The air pressure is not *directly* proportional to the velocity of the wind, but *varies as the square* of wind velocity. The actual power derived varies as the cube of the velocity. Consequently, as the wind drops, the turning force it exerts falls off more quickly still. The use of wind for power would never have been worth while except that the upkeep of the mills was low, and there was generally no alternative means of power. The coming of the steam engine spelt the doom of the windmill.

Windmills of the old type are still employed for pumping water to drain low-lying regions—notably in Holland. But today a light steel lattice tower structure is commonly used, 50 to 70 feet high, and having a ring-shaped windmill of six to 30 feet in diameter set at the top. There is a fantail arrangement not unlike that which we have already described. The windmill drives a vertical shaft which in turn transmits reciprocating motion to the rod of a pump. Automatic mechanism takes the main wheel out of the wind when wind pressure becomes too great.

Similar windmills, generally somewhat smaller than the pumping machines, are used to generate electricity for low-power requirements. In this case the wheel drives a dynamo, and the dynamo charges batteries in which current is stored. A simple modification of this device uses merely a two-bladed " airscrew " formed rather like the propeller of an aircraft. Any youngster with a mechanical turn of mind could rig up a miniature model of one of these, using a model aeroplane propeller and a toy dynamo.

Windsor. Its grey towers and battlements reflected in the waters of the Thames, the royal palace of Windsor Castle, in Berkshire, covers with its grounds 12 acres. It was founded by William the Conqueror (1027–87) on the site of an earlier fortress; the Round Tower or Keep was added by Edward III (1312–77). The castle was extended and renovated by George III (1738–1820), George IV (1762–1830) and Queen Victoria (1819–1901).

St. George's Chapel, a beautiful example of Perpendicular Gothic, was begun in the 15th century and completed by Henry VIII (1491–1547), who was buried there, as were Jane Seymour (one of Henry VIII's wives), Charles I, George III, George IV, William IV, Edward VII and George V. The Albert Memorial Chapel, built by Henry VII, was converted to a memorial of the Prince Consort by Queen Victoria.

In the residential parts of the castle is a marvellous collection of artistic and other treasures. In the Upper Ward are the Royal private apartments, the visitors' rooms and the State apartments, which include the throne room and St. George's Hall, where meetings of the members of the Order of the Garter are held. Also at Windsor Castle is Queen Mary's Doll's House—a miniature house, perfect in every detail, designed in 1924 by Sir Edwin Lutyens (1869–1944) for Queen Mary, and furnished and decorated by leading commercial firms and notable artists.

In the Home Park is Frogmore House, with the mausoleum built by Queen Victoria over the tomb of her husband Prince Albert, by whose side she herself was buried. The Great Park, 1,800 acres in extent, is noted for its Long Walk—a magnificent avenue nearly three miles long which leads towards Virginia Water, a lovely artificial lake. To the west of the castle lies what is left of Windsor Forest, a hunting ground of William the Conqueror and originally 180 miles in circumference.

The market town of Windsor (New Windsor) is on the right bank of the Thames, in Berkshire, about 22 miles west of London. It is connected by bridges with Eton (q.v.) and Datchet. The Town Hall was built by Sir Christopher Wren (1632–1723) in 1686, and there is a museum with Shakespearian relics. The population of the town is 20,000. About two miles south-east of the town is the village of Old Windsor, where Edward the Confessor (c. 1005–66) had a palace.

Windsor is the family name of the Royal House of Great Britain which was adopted in place of that of Saxe-Coburg-Gotha in 1917 during the First World War (1914–18). After his abdication in 1936, Edward VIII assumed the title of the Duke of Windsor.

There is also a Windsor in Ontario, Canada, situated on the Detroit river opposite the town of Detroit in the United States, with which it is connected by the Ambassador Bridge and a tunnel. Its products include motor-vehicles, machinery, iron and steel goods, flour and bricks. The population of this Windsor (Ontario) is 105,000.

Wines. Alcoholic drinks that are made from the fermented juice of grapes are known as wines. Common in early ages, wine was drunk by the Egyptians, Jews, Assyrians, Greeks and Romans. Though the practice differs in various wines, the general method of production is the same. Grapes are gathered when ripe, and are pressed to extract the juice. With red wines the skins of the grapes are not removed. The juice thus procured is allowed to ferment, the process taking several months.

Wines vary greatly in taste and price, and certain types are associated with particular countries. Thus claret, burgundy and champagne come from France, port from Portugal, sherry and malaga from Spain, hock (a general name for the Rhine wines) and moselle from Germany, tokay from Hungary, and chianti from Italy.

Winnipeg. The growth of Winnipeg from a frontier trading-post in 1871 to the fourth city of Canada, a huge metropolis and railway centre, the country's chief live-stock market, and one of the world's largest grain markets, is due primarily on its geographical situation. Standing at the junction of the Red and Assiniboine rivers, midway between the southern boundary of Canada and Lake Winnipeg, the city of Winnipeg is the centre through which pass the cattle and grain of the prairie

provinces, and the point from which the manufactures of the industrial East are distributed to the smaller cities and farms of the West. Foodstuffs, flour, farm implements, confectionery, clothing, structural steel and leather goods are among the leading products. Water is brought to the city by an aqueduct nearly 100 miles long from the Lake of the Woods.

The capital of the Province of Manitoba and the seat of the University of Manitoba, Winnipeg is a city of wide straight streets and boulevards, with many parks and playgrounds. The site has been occupied since the early days of the Canadian fur trade, the first post (1738) being known as Fort Rouge. Fort Garry, the nucleus of the colony established by Scottish settlers sent out by Lord Selkirk (1771–1820) in 1812, gave its name to the settlement until 1873, when the city was named Winnipeg (an Indian word meaning " Murky Water ") from the lake 50 miles to the north. The population of the city is about 220,000. (See illustration in page 682).

Winter Moths. Three species known as winter moths are remarkable for the fact that in each case the females have wings so small that they are quite unable to fly, their general appearance being almost that of a bloated spider. The male moths are normal.

The male of the true winter moth (*Operophtera*, or *Cheimatobia*, *brumata*) is greyish brown and measures up to 1¼ inches across the forewings. From October to the end of December both males and females are to be seen, having emerged from chrysalids in the soil around the trees or bushes which the destructive caterpillars infested the previous spring. The females crawl up the stems and trunks and lay their numerous eggs. From these the caterpillars appear in March, and at once commence to feed on the leaves, unopened flower buds and, later, on the tiny fruit if their ravages are being conducted on a fruit tree or bush. The caterpillars of this winter moth and of the March moth generally spin two leaves together before proceeding to eat holes in them. When they are full-fed they let themselves down to the ground by silken threads, burrow into the soil and there become chrysalids.

The March moth (*Erannis*, or *Anisopteryx aescularia*), usually appearing in that month, has much the same life history (as also has the third species). The male March moth is about the same size as the true winter moth, but the forewings are grey-brown. The third species, the mottled umber moth (*Hybernia defoliaria*), is about during the last three months of the year. The male is somewhat larger than the true winter moth, and

J. J. Ward
A WINTER MOTH
The male mottled umber moth measures about 1¼ inches across the forewings. The female, which is unable to fly, is responsible for caterpillars which sometimes strip oaks and other trees bare of leaves.

the forewings are brown or brownish-yellow, banded and mottled with dark brown. The caterpillars sometimes strip oaks and other trees of every scrap of foliage, leaving the branches bare.

Fruit-growers and others fight these three pests with poison sprays, and by trapping the wingless females (on their journey up the trunks or stems and before they can lay their eggs) on greasy bands of stout paper tied around the stems or trunks low down.

Winter's Tale, THE. The King of Bohemia, in this romantic drama by Shakespeare, is a guest at the Court of Leontes, King of Sicilia (Sicily), and enjoys such hospitality from Queen Hermione that Leontes becomes madly jealous. Leontes forces his guest to flee for his life, casts the Queen into prison, and commands that her new-born babe, a girl, be carried to a foreign shore and left to die. Hermione, put on trial on a charge of high treason, appeals to the oracle of Apollo at Delphi, in Greece, and to her husband's confusion the oracle declares that " Hermione is chaste, Leontes a jealous tyrant, and the King shall live without an heir if that which is lost is not found." Almost immediately word is brought that Mamilius, the young Prince of Sicily, Leontes's heir, is dead, whereupon Hermione falls down as if she, too, were dead.

For 16 years Leontes lives a lonely life without wife or children. Then there arrives at his Court a pair of runaway lovers, and these prove to be the King of Bohemia's son, Prince Florizel, and his bride, the daughter of a shepherd of Bohemia. The Bohemian king reaches the Court soon afterwards.

Fearing the King's rage, the shepherd produces a jewelled chain and a letter. These prove Florizel's bride to be not the shepherd's daughter but Perdita, the lost princess of Sicilia !

One of the ladies of the Court now invites the company to view a wondrous statue. As they gaze in admiration the " statue " comes to life, being indeed Hermione, who has lived in seclusion until the oracle should be fulfilled and Perdita found.

One of the most charming scenes in the play is the sheep-shearing feast, where Perdita makes the well-known speech about the flowers. A notable minor character is the light-hearted and light-fingered pedlar, Autolycus, with his songs.

Wire. When you wake up in the morning perhaps it does not occur to you that one of the chief reasons for your comfortable slumber is the fine wire network of the springs on which your mattress rests—or those embedded in little pockets in the mattress itself. It may be a dark winter morning : then the electric light which you turn on is charged with power transmitted to you over steel and copper wires. Perhaps you travel to school in a tram or a trolley-bus; the power current reaches the motors through other wires. You may cross a suspension bridge, hung from its towers by thousands of strong wires grouped into cables. The fence that surrounds your home may be made of woven steel wire. Every time you use a pin or needle, and often when you drive a nail, the wire industry supplies you with the instrument. The music of your piano is largely the result of vibrations of a number of finely attuned wires.

The improvement in the manufacture of wire is one of the greatest steps forward that industry has taken in the last century. Many of the most wonderful inventions of our age could never have reached their present high efficiency had it not been for the discovery of the method of making machine-drawn wire.

Wire drawing was known in the 14th century, but the machinery now used in this process was not perfected until the 19th century. Wire was known in Egypt at least as early as 800 B.C. It was made then, and for many centuries afterwards, by first beating metal into plates, then cutting the plates into strips, and finally rounding these strips by further hammering.

The Company of Gold and Silver Wire Drawers, of the City of London, dates back to 1693.

Metals used for wire must be ductile—capable of being drawn out—and of sustaining weight or bending without snapping. Platinum and gold possess these qualities in the highest degree; platinum has been drawn into wire one fifty-thousandth of an inch thick. The commonest wires used are made of steel or copper or alloys of both, other metals employed being nickel, silver, iron and aluminium.

In making steel wire the bars or billets are heated and conveyed to a set of rollers to be reduced in size. For ordinary sizes of wire the billet is rolled down to a rod smaller than a lead pencil. The heated rod is carried through a pipe to a device which coils the rod. The coiled metal is cooled and taken to the drawing plant, where it is drawn into wire of all sizes.

First, the scale which has accumulated is removed by an acid bath, the acid being then removed in an alkali bath. Next, the rod, with its point made small enough, enters a bell-mouthed hole in a draw-plate or die made of hard steel or, in some cases, of a diamond or ruby. Its protruding end is gripped by tongs and pulled by hydraulic or other power, so that it emerges from the smaller end of the hole reduced in size. The process of drawing the wire through smaller and smaller holes continues until the desired size is reached.

As the metal is drawn finer, it becomes harder and more brittle, so that from time to time it must be annealed to make it soft and tough. It must also be constantly oiled as it is drawn through the dies. Fine wire may require from 20 to 30 drawings.

Small wire of iron, steel, or steel alloy is often drawn through diamond dies with holes ranging from 0·040 to 0·002 inch in diameter, sometimes passing through as many as 12 dies in one draw. The dies are made of " industrial " diamond, a form of mineral worthless for gem-stones. An 0·040-inch wire requires a diamond of some 3½ carats. Dies for drawing copper wire are usually made of chilled steel, and last about a year before they become too large. Diamond dies are made originally with holes of 0·002 inch, which are redrilled as occasion demands until they are too large for further use.

Larger wire goes into the high-grade spring steel coils used in most internal combustion engines to close the valves. Enormous quantities of special heat-resisting wire are used as the centre wire electrodes of sparking plugs. Electric irons, heating elements, and other appliances employ resistance wire, made from high-resistance metals or alloys which glow red when heated, and so radiate warmth. (*See* Alloys).

Electricity is carried by high-tension transmission lines of aluminium wire containing steel centres

HOW WIRE IS MADE AND PUT TO WORK

1. Coarse wire is drawn from reels on the floor through holes in dies on the bench. The holes squeeze the wire down to smaller size. Then the wire is wound around the spools behind the dies. 2. Thousands of small wires are packed together to make one of the suspension cables to support the George Washington Bridge between New York City and New Jersey.

3. Two sets of sheaves (wheels) draw stainless steel wires through dies between the sheaves. Smaller and smaller hole in the dies squeeze each wire to almost threadlike size. The finely drawn wire is wound around the big spool at the back 4. This machine makes barbed wire. As two strands pass through, it wraps short pieces of wire (the barbs) around them

which bear the weight of the wires and the strain imposed by winds.

Dredgers, excavators, derricks, cranes, ships, and tug boats use wire hawsers or cables. These are twisted around hemp cores, layer on layer, each layer composed of many strands of small wire. In many power-houses wire rope is used to transmit power from engines to machinery.

Huge suspension bridges depend on giant wire cables to carry the load. These are remarkable for their enormous size, and because they are usually made as the bridge is being built.

Barbed wire was invented about 1875 to fence in cattle. As a defence in war it was used in the Spanish-American and other wars, but the full development of barbed-wire entanglements did not come until the First World War (1914-18), in which the various combatants are said to have used more than a million miles of barbed wire.

Steel wire and wire mesh have come into wide use in recent years among the materials for reinforcing concrete for roads and buildings.

Wire is made to certain standard diameters, the gauging system in Britain being the Imperial Standard Wire Gauge. The numbers run from 7/0 downwards to 1/0 (0·500 inch to 0·324 inch); and then from 1 to 36, the diameter decreasing as the Gauge Number grows higher. The diameter of Gauge 1 wire is 0·300 inch, and that of Gauge 36 is 0·0076 inch. The same gauging system (abbreviated I.S.W.G., or S.W.G.) is used to measure the thickness of some sheet metals.

How WORDS and MUSIC FLY through SPACE

In conjunction with other articles in our pages, this story describes the marvels of radio transmission and reception—for communication, for entertainment, and for information. There is no more enthralling story of science.

Wireless. The discovery and development of wireless are among the most wonderful achievements of modern science. As early as 1827 Savart (1791–1841) showed that iron needles become magnetized if they are held near a spark discharge. In 1840 Joseph Henry (1797–1878) succeeded in producing high-frequency oscillations and showed their effects over small distances. In the same year Samuel Morse (1791–1872), inventor of the telegraph, actually sent signals across a canal in America, by stringing two parallel wires on the banks and using electro-magnetic induction—not quite the same as wireless, but close to it.

When James Clerk-Maxwell (*q.v.*) laid down his famous theory of electro-magnetism between 1867 and 1873, he predicted the discovery of radio waves. This prediction was realized in 1887 by Heinrich Hertz (*q.v.*), who, for the first time, actually demonstrated wireless transmission by the spark method. He showed that when a heavy spark was discharged from a Leyden jar (*q.v.*), a corresponding small spark would leap across the narrow gap of a loop of wire 15 feet away. He proved that the "Hertzian waves," as they are still called by research scientists, were of the same type as light and heat waves. Then, in 1896, followed the first patent of Guglielmo Marconi on wireless telegraphy by the modern method, and he was able to operate his sets over a distance of a mile or more. While Marconi, of course, built largely on the work of Hertz, and adapted ideas from various other

sources, he made many original contributions. (*See* Marconi).

Meanwhile, in 1883, Thomas Alva Edison (1847–1931) had noticed that the filament of his incandescent lamps gave off electrified particles. In this he had really discovered the principle of electronic emission, which is the basis of the wireless valve, but Edison did not recognize its importance. Not until 1904, when Sir John Ambrose Fleming (1849–1945) produced his valve with two electrodes—the filament and the plate—was the principle applied to wireless. Then, in 1906, came Lee De Forest (b. 1873), who invented a grid between the filament and plate, producing the triode valve.

Since that time improvements in the details and methods of wireless and the extension of its use

Marconi's Wireless Telegraph Co., Ltd

MARCONI'S WIRELESS TRANSMITTER IN CORNWALL
In 1901 the Italian Guglielmo Marconi established a wireless transmitting station (above) at Poldhu in Cornwall. And from there on December 12, 1901, operators sent the first signals—in Morse by spark transmitter—across the Atlantic Ocean, which Marconi himself received at St. John's, Newfoundland. (*See also* illustration in page 2099)

have been so rapid that it is almost impossible to keep track of them. Beyond this, the methods and principles employed are today basic ones for a great variety of apparatus ranging from radar to navigational aids for ships and aircraft. For reasons such as this you must look in other pages for the story of the thermionic valve and for portions of general electrical theory concerning—for example —inductance, capacity, the behaviour of high-frequency currents, and so on. By appropriate cross references we indicate where this additional information is to be found.

When we speak of wireless telegraphy and telephony (or radio-communications, as they are sometimes termed) we mean the transmission of messages or speech between two or more points without the use of connecting wires. Instead of wires, we use electro-magnetic waves as a connecting medium. In our story of Radiation we tell how Clerk-Maxwell prophesied the existence of these waves, and how Hertz, Marconi, and others produced them. It is explained also that wireless waves can range in wavelength from only a little longer than heat waves (infra-red) to lengths of several

miles, the corresponding frequencies varying from thousands of millions to only a few thousand cycles per second. Now we have to see how these waves are produced, and how we are able to make them carry our messages.

The production of wireless waves is a comparatively simple affair—we need an " aerial " (called in America an " antenna ") and an " earth " connexion, which act as the two plates of a condenser (*see* Electricity). Into this condenser we feed a high-frequency current. This, flowing in the aerial circuit, sets up a strain in the lines of force associated with the electrons, and an electromagnetic wave travels outwards—much as a stone cast into a pond causes ripples to travel in everwidening circles until they reach the bank.

We must not imagine that the current rushes off the aerial into space—for it does no such thing. To use a simple analogy, think of a long rope tied at one end and lying along the ground. If you take the free end, and jerk it up and down, a ripple will travel along the rope until it reaches the fixed end ; and if you do this quite quickly the rope will appear to be moving along. But your hand has not

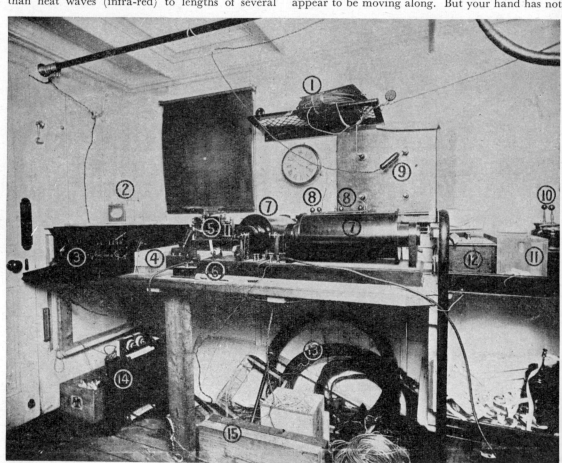

Marconi's Wireless Telegraph Co., Ltd.

EARLY MARCONI WIRELESS RECEIVER FITTED IN A STEAMER

To prove that it was possible to receive wireless messages over a greater distance than that from Cornwall to Newfoundland, between which points he had established communication in 1901, Marconi had the above set installed in a ship in 1902. The components are : 1. Loading coil ; 2. Galvanometer and coil ; 3. Two coherer receivers ; 4. Aerial tuning inductance for very long waves ; 5. Morse inker ; 6. Key ; 7. Two 10-inch induction coils ; 8. Leyden jars ; 9. Jigger ; 10. Spare Leyden jars ; 11. Travelling box for Morse inker ; 12. Primary inductance for coils, and mains circuit ; 13. Spare aerial wire ; 14. Charging resistance ; 15. Condensers to prevent sparking at coil contacts.

moved forwards, and you are merely oscillating the rope, thus causing certain strains in it.

Oscillatory Circuits. As we know from the story of Electricity, every current-carrying conductor has a magnetic field around it (*see also* Magnetism) which gives it " inductance." (If wound into a coil, the conductor will produce a much greater field, and have a much higher inductance.) The combination of the inductance and capacity of our aerial system forms an " oscillatory circuit "—i.e. one which resonates at a particular frequency. To get a simple idea of resonance, think of a spring hanging from a hook, and supporting a weight at the lower end. If you give the weight a small push downwards the spring will pull it up again, and it will commence to vibrate up and down.

Every spring, and, in fact, everything capable of vibrating, has what is known as a natural frequency which will depend on the inertia of the weight and the " stretchability " of the spring. If you give the weight small pushes at fixed intervals (say two a second) you may sometimes push down as the weight is moving up, and thus you will damp down and check the vibrations. If, on the other hand, you time the pushes so that they coincide with the natural frequency of the system, you will find that quite a large movement can be produced for quite a small amount of power. The spring is resonating, or is in resonance with, the frequency of the pushes you are providing. You may have noticed that a certain note on the piano will cause a glass on the table to " ring." When this occurs it is because the frequency of the piano note is the same as the natural frequency of vibration of the glass. It is, in fact, possible to break a wineglass by playing its natural frequency on a violin, or by singing—the amplitude of vibration of the glass gets so large that it overstresses the material, which may fly into fragments.

To return now to our aerial circuit, if we think of capacity as the " stretchability " of the spring, and of inductance as the inertia of the weight, we can see how to " tune " our aerial to oscillate at a given frequency. If we feed it with current at that frequency, it will oscillate very strongly, and will radiate strong signals for a given amount of power supplied to it. Since the capacity of an aerial itself, and the inductance of the wires leading to it, are fixed, we can tune our aerial by adding more capacity in the form of a variable condenser, or by using additional inductance in the form of a coil.

An aerial system may vary from the small rod you sometimes see on the top of a motor-car to an elaborate array of conductors slung on steel masts hundreds of feet high and covering an area as large as a small town. The apparatus for producing the high-frequency current may be small enough to be held in the hand, or may be large enough to fill a church; but the fundamental principles remain

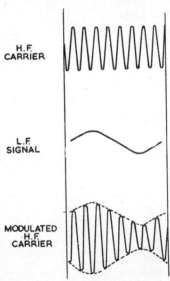

Fig. 1. In order to modulate wireless waves the low-frequency signal is superimposed on the high-frequency carrier (top), thereby causing a variation in amplitude (lower).

unchanged. " Wireless waves " are radiated at a certain power and a certain frequency, depending on the actual details of the transmitter.

At some distant point, we have our wireless receiver, where we set up another aerial system. This, again, may vary from a high wire slung on a pole to a small coil of wire inside the set. The electro-magnetic waves radiated by the transmitter affect this receiving aerial, tending to induce an E.M.F. (electromotive force) in it, by the ordinary rules of electro-magnetic induction. If the aerial is " tuned " (by proper proportion of inductance and capacity) to resonate at the frequency of the waves sent out by the transmitter, high-frequency oscillations will be set up of sufficient magnitude to affect a wireless receiver attached to the receiving aerial.

Modulation. So far, we have considered only the broad principles of the generation of wireless waves, and their reception at a distance. Now let us see how we make them convey some useful information. In the first place, let us consider the generation of high-frequency currents. There have in the past been several methods of doing this, but the only one which we need mention now is the production of continuous oscillations by the use of the thermionic valve (*q.v.*). This can be made to act as a generator of high-frequency currents, in addition to its uses as an amplifier (or magnifier) and a rectifier. If we set up a valve in an *oscillatory circuit*, and couple this to an *aerial circuit*, we have a transmitter which will send out continuous wireless waves. We can either " key " these waves, interrupting them in the dots and dashes of the Morse code (*see* Telegraph), or use them uninterrupted as a " carrier " for telephony.

The most generally used system for telephony is that of amplitude modulation. In effect, what we do is to superimpose on the high-frequency carrier a low-frequency signal, so that the carrier wave has its amplitude (i.e., the amount by which it varies either side of a zero value) altered to correspond with the low-frequency signal (Fig. 1). The way this is done is shown in Fig. 2, which is correct in principle, but takes no account of detail. It will be seen that the output from the microphone is taken to a " modulator " where it is coupled to the high-frequency output of the oscillator. No amplifiers are shown, but they would, of course, be used.

Reception of Wireless Signals. So far we have considered sending out either a " keyed " (Morse code) interrupted wave, or a modulated carrier wave (telephony) which will affect the receiving aerial by inducing currents which are faithful (although very tiny) copies of the currents in the transmitting aerial. Now, let us consider the actual reception of the signals. To begin with, the voltages induced in the receiving aerial are, in most cases, much too tiny to use directly ; therefore we introduce one or more stages of high-frequency amplification, using thermionic valves connected as amplifiers. Again, the frequency of the waves is much too high for the diaphragm of a telephone receiver or loud-speaker to follow them.

If we wish to receive telegraphy, we must reduce the frequency to one which we can usefully employ. The simplest method is that of " heterodyne " or " beat " reception. For this we put a small oscillator in our receiver, and tune it to oscillate with a frequency fairly near to that of the received oscillations, and mix the two. The result will be a beat frequency—equal to the

Even a beat frequency is still too high to be useful in wireless. If we connected a telephone receiver to the output, the diaphragm could not possibly vibrate fast enough to follow the waves. What we want is something which will take account of the *average value* of each little " parcel " of waves. The average value of an alternating current wave is zero, because it alternates equally on the positive and negative sides of a zero line. If, however, we " rectify " the wave (*see* Rectifier ; Thermionic Valve ; Electronic

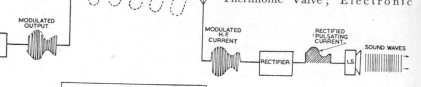

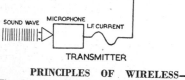

PRINCIPLES OF WIRELESS—
Fig. 2. High-frequency currents generated by the oscillator are ' modulated ' by the high-frequency current produced by the sound waves acting on the microphone. The modulated current is fed to the aerial, causing electro-magnetic waves to be produced. The reception side of the diagram is shown opposite (Fig. 4).

difference between that of the other two oscillations—which will vary in amplitude as the two sets of waves add together at one instant, and are opposed to each other at the next (Fig. 3).

An understanding of beat frequency is so important that it is worth while to spend a little more time on it. Imagine two series of sound waves, of the same frequency. If we direct them at the ear *one after the other*, the interval between being equal to the frequency of one oscillation, we can produce not sound but *silence*. The crest of one wave in the *second series* will coincide with the trough of a wave in the *first series*, and will cancel out the pulsation. We have produced " interference." If the two series of sound oscillations are sent out *simultaneously*, in step, the sound will be strengthened, for crests in both series will coincide.

The sounds in such laboratory experiments are produced by tuning forks. Suppose that one fork has a tiny piece of sealing wax affixed to one prong: this will alter its oscillation period, and we will suppose that the loaded fork makes 249 vibrations per second, while the unloaded fork makes 250 in the same time. Sound the two forks at exactly the same time. The unloaded one will send out quicker oscillations, and will " gain " on the other fork; after one second of time the oscillations coincide, as they did at the start. Midway in a second, the forks will be out of step, producing silence. This one-per-second differential pulsation is a " beat."

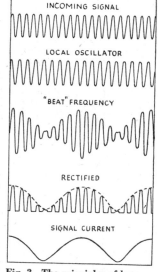

Fig. 3. The principles of heterodyne or 'beat' reception of telegraphy are illustrated. The incoming signal oscillation is mixed with that produced by a local oscillator of slightly different frequency. The 'beat' frequency oscillation thus produced is then rectified, giving a unidirectional pulsating current in a series of small 'parcels.'

—TELEPHONY TRANSMISSION
Fig. 4. Wireless waves cause a current to flow in the aerial circuit which is a weak replica of the transmitted current. This is rectified to form a unidirectional pulsating current which, after amplification (not shown), is applied to a loudspeaker, causing sound waves reproducing those made into the microphone.

Devices), suppressing one-half of the alternations, we can get what is, in effect, an average value of each little parcel of the beat frequency oscillations, and thus obtain something which can be heard in our ears (within the audible range), as shown in Fig. 3.

So much for telegraphy reception. In telephony, we are not interested in the carrier wave at all. What we want to do is to " skim off " the information the wave is carrying. By using a rectifier we do just this, since the current we get out of the rectifier is a measure of the modulation which the transmitter applied to the carrier. This is shown in diagrammatic form in Fig. 4, which represents the receiver working in conjunction with the transmitter shown in Fig. 2. Again, it will be noticed that no amplifier is shown, for the sake of simplicity. In actual fact there would be both high and low-frequency amplifiers, the h.f. or " radio-frequency " one being connected directly on the incoming side of the set (before the rectifier) ; and the l.f., or " audiofrequency " amplifier would be placed between the rectifier and the telephone or the loud-speaker.

In the early wireless sets, the rectifying stage or " detector " was a " crystal detector." It had been found that certain mineral crystals, in conjunction with a needle-point known as a " cat's whisker," possessed the property of unidirectional conductivity or rectification. Nowadays it is more usual to have a valve for the purpose, although the crystal detector (in a vastly more sensitive form) is coming into use for certain applications.

Super-Heterodyne Receivers. Perhaps you may have wondered why many wireless receivers are referred to as "superhets." This is a type of receiver which is very widely used, and is an extension of the heterodyne principle described earlier. A local oscillator is used of such a frequency that, mixed with the incoming signal-frequency, a radio-frequency beat is produced, instead of a low-frequency beat. This beat oscillation is then amplified and rectified as in an ordinary radio set. The

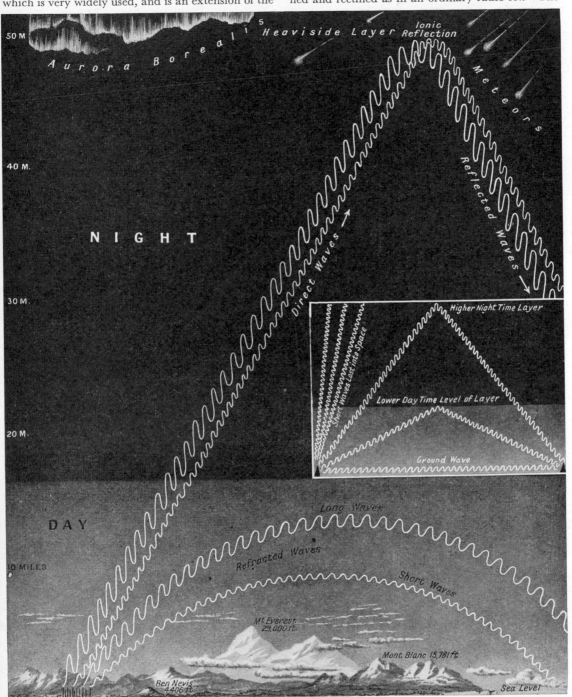

WHY SOME STATIONS FADE AT NIGHT AND ARE OUT OF RANGE BY DAY

How differently wireless waves behave by day and by night is shown in this illustration. Obeying the laws of refraction and reflection, wireless waves are unequally refracted in the lower atmosphere and equally reflected by the Heaviside Layer, which is at a greater altitude at night than during the day (see inset). If the reflected waves are 'out of phase' with the direct ones fading will occur; also the reflected waves are weak by day, which limits the range.

great advantage of the superhet circuit is that the amplifier has to work at only one frequency (the beat frequency), and not over a large range of frequencies as it would in an ordinary receiver circuit. The superhet can be made more efficient in design, and is easier to use for short-wave work, since the amplifiers can be designed for a convenient frequency, and do not have to work at the enormous frequencies which are inseparable from short-wave reception. The superhet also simplifies tuning arrangements, and is more selective. This means that there is not so much interference between two transmitters working on nearly the same frequency.

Wave Propagation—Short Waves. Wireless waves are propagated in straight lines, like light beams; but, in exactly the same manner, they can be refracted or reflected. There are two paths by which the waves can travel from one point to the other—the "ground wave," which keeps fairly close to the earth (and gradually dies out owing to absorption, etc.); and the "sky wave." This last is a wave which has been sent out in an upward direction and reflected by the "Heaviside layer." This layer, named after Oliver Heaviside (1850–1925), is one of ionised gas, lying high above the earth, which possesses reflecting properties. At night time the absence of the sun's rays causes ionisation to disappear except at a much higher level; and in fact the Heaviside layer seems to rise considerably. This has the effect of reflecting

Marconi's Wireless Telegraph Co., Ltd.
'WALKIE-TALKIE'
Receiving and transmitting sets, complete with aerial, are now made so small that they can be carried around by one man.

the waves back at a different point— farther along—so that the night-time range of a transmitter is longer than the day-time range.

In the early days of wireless it was found that signals having wavelengths round about 200 metres seemed to be absorbed very readily. This was discovered to be due to a phenomenon concerned with the movement of electrons in the upper atmosphere; and if this critical point were passed, and still shorter wavelengths used, efficient transmission could once more be obtained. It was discovered also that short waves were very much more efficient than long waves. The ground wave here is negligible, but the sky wave, by successive reflections between the earth and the Heaviside layer, will travel enormous distances for the amount of power used.

The chief merit of short waves is that advantage can be taken of reflecting properties to "beam" them in a required direction, much as the light from a small bulb in the headlight of a motor-car can be collected, focused and thrown as a dazzling beam by a mirror. All wireless waves can be reflected, of course, but it is not practicable to build a reflector for waves several miles in length. By the use of a vertical aerial, surrounded with reflector wires in the form of a parabola, some astonishing results have been obtained; and commercial transmission, including radio links for trans-Atlantic telephony (*see* Telephone), is regularly carried on to the most remote parts of the world.

Ultra-Short Waves. With progress in wireless research, definitions of short waves have altered very considerably. At one time 200 metres was considered too short for practical purposes; now 200 metres is considered a "medium" wave. Most of the commercial short-wave transmission takes place on wavelengths between 100 and 10 metres. Below about 10 metres, however, another peculiar change takes place in that, so far as is known, the waves are not reflected at all from the Heaviside layer, and pass through into outer space. Transmission is therefore limited, roughly, to "line of-sight" paths. For short distances, up to a few miles, it is possible to build transmitters and receivers of low power and astonishing compactness; and two-way radio communication is possible between motor-cars (such as police patrol cars, taxicabs, and the like). During the Second World War (1939–45) soldiers in the field were provided with "walkie-talkie" radio sets small enough to be carried on the back, for communication with headquarters.

Marconi's Wireless Telegraph Co., Ltd.
TWO-WAY RADIO COMMUNICATION IN A TAXI
In Great Britain some taxi-cabs are fitted with short-wave wireless transmitters and receivers of low power, to enable the driver to communicate with his garage over short distances. Wireless sets of this type are also fitted to British and American police cars.

Short waves are also used for the remote radio control (i.e. from a distance) of mechanisms, such as pilotless aeroplanes, guided missiles and ships.

When we get down to " centimetric " waves (i.e., waves of only a few centimetres in length), further great changes take place—not in the principles of transmission, but in the actual design of sets. The frequencies in this region are extremely high (a wave one centimetre in length has a frequency of thirty thousand million cycles per second), and as you can read in the story of High Frequency Currents, some peculiar things happen, including insulators heating up, and other odd effects. The ordinary methods of constructing a transmitter could not possibly be used for centimetric waves. The inductance of a single foot of wire would be sufficient to prevent the set working, and therefore unconventional methods of construction had to be adopted. The " aerial " becomes a short piece of wire coupled directly to one of the special types of valve used for these frequencies. At these low wavelengths, reflection is a very simple business, and ordinary metallic reflectors of a few inches in diameter are used. The waves produced by the aerial are " piped " to this reflector in a kind of rectangular tube made of metal—a "waveguide." A diagrammatic representation of this method is shown in Fig. 5.

The use of tubular waveguides to convey electro-magnetic waves (instead of using conductors to carry currents) has given rise to the nickname of " plumber's radio " for these " microwave " regions. Uses of centimetric waves include radar (q.v.) and telephone links. Instead of using a telephone cable, it is possible to line up two reflectors on towers 50 or 60 miles apart, and to transmit a beam which will carry a number of telephone conversations. Micro-waves have also been suggested for industrial work on the lines of photo-cell equipment (see Photo-Electric Devices), using a radio beam and a simple crystal receiver, instead of a light beam and a photo-electric cell.

Direction-Finding. In addition to the sending of messages, wireless is also used for navigational work and direction-finding. This must not be confused with radar (q.v.) in which a beam is sent out and reflected from various objects. Direction-finding consists in finding one's position by taking the bearings of two or more fixed stations, and plotting them on a chart, when the intersection of the lines showing the direction of these fixed stations will give one's own position (see Navigation). In principle, direction is found by the use of a rotatable " frame " aerial (i.e., one composed of several turns of wire mounted on a pivot so that it can be turned). When the frame is revolved, the signal strength of any given station will vary from a maximum (when the frame is pointing directly at the station) to zero (when it is at right angles to the station). By fixing a pointer to the frame, and using a degree scale, the direction of a known station can be determined. In practice, there are very many more refinements than this, but all operate on the same basic principles.

Interference. Radio reception suffers from both fading and interference. The fading is due to many causes, all connected with reflection from the Heaviside layer, and is particularly noticeable with short waves. Interference may be caused by " static " electricity due to thunderstorms or to various types of atmospheric disturbance, all of which themselves radiate electro-magnetic energy. Or it may be man-made interference, since almost every form of electrical device radiates energy to a greater or lesser extent. A trolley-bus with a sparking trolley-shoe will radiate wireless " noise "; and so will your neighbour's vacuum cleaner. The cure for static is not easy—because the interfering radiation is on a broad band of wavelengths, and is not sharply tuned. It cannot easily be tuned out. Man-made interference can be sup-

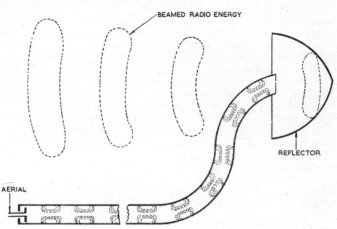

BEAMED RADIO ENERGY

REFLECTOR

AERIAL

ULTRA-SHORT WAVE TRANSMISSION

Fig. 5. In micro-wave transmission the ultra-short wireless waves set up by the aerial are conducted by a tubular ' waveguide ' to a reflector, from which they emerge in a narrow beam.

pressed at the source by fitting " suppressors " (combinations of condensers and chokes) to the offending apparatus. The ignition circuits of cars are a very considerable trouble on the shorter waves, particularly to television.

A system which is said to overcome the noise problem very considerably is that known as " frequency modulation (F.M.). In this, the signal fed into the transmitter modulates the carrier wave not by varying its amplitude but by shifting its frequency by a certain amount either side of its normal frequency. This, of course, requires totally different types of receiving circuits to re-translate the signal, for an " ordinary " wireless set will not receive F.M. signals. Since it requires a large range of frequency shift without a large change in wavelength, it can be used only on high frequency or short wavelengths. This means that it is, practically speaking, confined to optical or line-of-sight paths, and a large area must be served by a number of small stations. There can be no question here of a single large high-power station broadcasting over a wide area. Frequency modulated wireless is remarkably free from background noise, and suitable for extremely high quality reproduction of sounds.

Facsimile Transmission. Not to be confused with television, which shows a moving picture of something which is actually happening, facsimile transmission is the transmission of pictures, handwriting, etc. The principles for the transmission of photography by wireless are the same as those used by ordinary telegraphy, which are described under Photo-Electric Devices.

Another system uses a photo-electric cell which "scans" the copy to be transmitted (pictures, print or writing). The original is mounted on a revolving drum, and is scanned slice by slice by the cell, which feeds appropriate "black" or "white" signals into the transmitter. At the receiving end, a roll of paper is fed upwards, line by line, between a metal blade and a drum which has a skewed blade on it—rather like a lawn mower with only one blade. As this squeezes the paper, the point of contact moves along the line, in synchronism with the signals sent out by the transmitter. The paper is specially sensitised so that a black spot is formed wherever current passes through it. Thus, at every "black" signal sent, a small black dot is made at the appropriate spot on the line. The result is a facsimile of the material being scanned, in a kind of dot pattern rather like a fine-screen newspaper half-tone illustration. Sets available in America—looking like wireless sets—will produce a 16-page "newspaper" in an hour or less.

As soon as it became clear that it was possible to transmit sounds by wireless—that is to say, that wireless telephony, as distinct from telegraphy, was possible—there were attempts to use this discovery commercially. Some firms making wireless receivers sent out occasional "broadcasts," as these telephonic transmissions were known, and in the

Radio Inventions Inc.
'PRINTED' BY WIRELESS
Pages of a journal reproduced by wireless are being withdrawn from the receiver, which is capable of 'printing' on sensitized paper 16 pages in about an hour.

United States broadcasting stations were soon set up, which sent out programmes of music and other entertainment, together with a good deal of commercial advertising.

In Great Britain an experimental station had been started in 1919 by the Marconi Company, but soon the Government decided that there could be only one way of carrying on broadcasting in a small country—by granting a monopoly to one firm, which would be in effect a branch of the group of makers of sets. The British Broadcasting Company was accordingly formed and began to broadcast regularly from London, Birmingham and Manchester in November 1922. The Government, through the General Post Office, sold licences for receiving sets, and the sale of these licences covered the company's running costs.

For a few years this worked reasonably well, though it soon became clear that broadcasting was a new kind of entertainment which was very rapidly to grow in popularity. By 1927 the Government came to the conclusion that the British Broadcasting Company, though it had accomplished good work, was doing something which ought no longer to be left to any private company. The public body —the British Broadcasting Corporation—which was now formed was thus a new type of organization. It took over the studios, staff, and so on, of the company, and the fees from licence-holders were also at the disposal of the Corporation. The Postmaster General was made answerable in Parliament for any questions which might arise about the running of the "B.B.C.," though he does not interfere with its day-to-day arrangements or with the planning of its programmes. The Corporation is run by a Director-General, who is appointed by seven Governors, themselves appointed by the Crown.

In the course of the years the B.B.C. developed in several directions. It is now a publisher of considerable importance, and its Radio Times, which contains details of programmes, sells millions of copies a week. The B.B.C. also publishes The Listener, which is mainly concerned with reprints of broadcast talks ; and issues a variety of books and pamphlets. It has organized a series of broadcasts to schools, which are sent out in mornings and afternoons during term-time. It has a first-rate symphony orchestra and several smaller orchestras ; and a repertory company who perform in many plays, some adapted from stage successes and many especially written for broadcasting.

The main function of the B.B.C. is to provide a satisfactory service of broadcast programmes for home listeners; but it also maintains a series of short-wave programmes (started in 1932), directed at all parts of the Commonwealth. In 1937, when the international misunderstandings which eventually led to the Second World War (1939–45) were coming to a head, the B.B.C. started broadcasting information in foreign languages for the benefit of listeners overseas. During the war regular news-bulletins in nearly 50 languages were being sent out, and some of these were continued after the end of the war in 1945.

The original charter, by which the Government gave the B.B.C. the right to carry on broadcasting, was for 10 years; when this expired in 1937 it was renewed for a further 10 years; in 1947 a new charter for five years was granted the Corporation.

From 1926 onwards the B.B.C. helped in experiments on television (*q.v.*); and in 1936 it established a television station at the Alexandra Palace in North London, which gave much entertainment until it closed down at the outbreak of the Second World War. This closure was because it was thought that the waves sent out from the station might give direction to German aeroplanes raiding London. After the war the television programmes were started again, and remained the responsibility of the B.B.C. Originally, a single licence was sufficient for either television or an ordinary radio receiving set; but in 1947 the licence fee was increased for television, though the holder of a television licence might use a wireless set as well.

The principal transmitting stations of the B.B.C. are situated in various parts of the British Isles, with the result that listeners in most areas get satisfactory reception. There are also regional offices and studios in several of the larger provincial cities, these being responsible for the production of programmes of special interest in their own regions of Great Britain and Northern Ireland.

Most of the more important programmes (symphony concerts, plays, news bulletins, and so on) are broadcast from all the regions simultaneously; but there are other less important programmes originating in London. When these are being broadcast from the London stations, special programmes for local listeners are broadcast from the provincial or regional stations.

In some other countries (most of the British Dominions, for example) broadcasting has developed very similarly to the way it has evolved in Britain. In Australia, however, there are private

British Broadcasting Corporation

NEWS READER AND CONTROL ENGINEER

Seated at the table in the foreground is the reader of a news bulletin, with the microphone hanging in front of him. Behind the glass panel is the engineer who listens to the broadcast, switches in other programme items and controls the quality and volume of sound sent out over the network.

broadcasting stations which accept advertising, as well as the official stations corresponding to those of the B.B.C. In the United States the whole development has been different; and private stations, depending for their costs on the money paid by advertisers, are in full operation in all parts of the country. One inevitable result of this is that wireless in the United States has tended to concentrate more and more on light entertainment, since an advertiser is mainly interested on getting a large audience, and there is generally a larger audience for a programme of comedy and dance music than there is for the more serious fare which the B.B.C. presents to British listeners.

British Broadcasting Corporation

CONTROL ROOM OF A B.B.C. TRANSMITTING STATION

At Ottringham in the East Riding of Yorkshire is the British Broadcasting Corporation's transmitting station which broadcasts European Service programmes in some 24 languages. Above is the central control room, with the chief engineer (centre foreground) seated at the panels on which are dials that indicate whether the broadcast is being transmitted satisfactorily. In the background is an official who keeps a record of any mechanical defects or failures.

Wisconsin. A north-central state of the United States, Wisconsin is bounded on the north by Lake Superior, on the east by Lake Michigan, on the south by Illinois, on the west by Iowa and Minnesota. Its area is 56,154 square miles, and it is mainly an undulating plateau from 600 feet to 1,000 feet in height. The chief rivers are the St. Croix, Wisconsin, Chippewa and Black (all tributaries of the Mississippi) and the Fox. Winnebago is the largest of numerous lakes.

Manufacturing is the leading industry, the most important products being machinery, motor vehicles, furniture, paper, leather goods, clothing, rubber goods and cheese. Dairy-farming and agriculture are among the leading occupations. Maize, hay, oats, barley, rye, potatoes, flax, tobacco and sugar beet are the principal crops. The mineral wealth includes iron, zinc and lead. There is a valuable mineral water bottling industry at Waukesha, about 20 miles from Milwaukee.

Milwaukee (population 587,000), on Lake Michigan, is by far the largest city and the most important industrial centre. The State capital is Madison (population 67,000). The population of the State of Wisconsin is 3,138,000.

Witchcraft. There is of course no such thing as witchcraft, and what really concerns us is the belief that people used to have in the supernatural powers of witches. Witches were women who were thought to have made a contract with an evil spirit—a contract sealed with blood—to serve him, and who in return for that promise were given power to accomplish things beyond ordinary human abilities. It was believed they could bring sickness and death to whom they wished, could go through locked doors, could ride through the air on broomsticks, and transform themselves into animals.

Their greatest delight, so it was said, was to bring harm and suffering to those who incurred their displeasure. This they did in many ways. Sometimes they made waxen representations of those they sought to harm or kill, and pricked these images or slowly melted them, hoping thereby to cause suffering and bring death to the persons represented.

Furthermore, it was believed that at certain times of the year there were assemblies of witches, known as Witches' Sabbaths, at which the witches met with the devil, performed elaborate ceremonies, and were instructed by him in the evil that they should accomplish. It was supposed that the devil left certain marks upon the persons of the witches, which could be detected only by experts.

Most of the women suspected as witches were old, mumbling crones, without friends or influence, usually women who had incurred the ill-will of neighbours in some way. Often the old crone had merely threatened someone who had made fun of her. The curious thing is that when such women were accused of having bewitched a cow or child or neighbour, they would often confess their " guilt."

All through the ages there has existed a belief in magic and evil spirits. From about the middle of the 15th century down to the 17th century, and in some places as late as the 19th century, witches were persecuted and often executed for their supposed misdeeds. Thousands of women have been put to death—usually by burning at the stake—because they were alleged to be witches. But by the latter half of the 17th century the more intelligent people were beginning to suspect that witchcraft was a delusion. Today few people, save those who live in barbaric or savage communities in such places as the African jungle, believe in witchcraft. (*See also* Magic).

Wolf. Numerous authorities think that the common wolf (*Canis lupus*) is very similar to the beast from which domestic dogs are descended, and for this reason the animal is of especial interest.

When cornered, the wolf fights savagely and proves itself a formidable antagonist, but by nature it is a cowardly beast. As a rule in summer wolves go about singly or in couples, running down their prey by night. In the winter they hunt in packs, and, emboldened by hunger, become very fierce, sometimes penetrating into towns and attacking people. Wolves can run for miles without tiring, and display amazing cunning in avoiding traps, detecting poison, and keeping out of rifle range.

The wolf is found in Europe, Asia, and North America, but not in Africa or South America. The British Isles were formerly infested with wolves, until special measures were taken against them, and in the latter half of the 18th century they were exterminated. Although they vary greatly in size and colour in different regions, it is now generally considered that all the varieties represent merely local races of the same species. The colour of the fur ranges from whitish to tawny-grey (the prevailing colour) and even black. The typical European wolf is brownish-grey and about three and a half feet long, while the huge, blackish-brown Alaskan wolf has been known to measure nearly six feet from the muzzle to the tip of the tail. In North America the best-known form is the timber or grey wolf ; the smaller coyote or prairie wolf (*C. latrans*) is still considered a separate species. In the sub-continent of India is found another type, *C. pallipes.*

WOLVES IN ENGLAND *Fox*
In days gone by Britain was infested with wolves ; now only in a Zoo can one be seen in these islands. These fine grey or timber wolves, native to North America, roam a large enclosure at the Zoo at Whipsnade in Bedfordshire.

After Benjamin West, R.A.

DEATH OF WOLFE ON THE PLAINS OF ABRAHAM

One phase of the Seven Years' War (1756–63) was the struggle between Great Britain and France for possession of Canada. General Wolfe was given command of a British force with orders to capture Quebec. He led his army at night up the heights overlooking the St. Lawrence river and on September 13, 1759, routed the French under General Montcalm on the Plains of Abraham. Wounded in the battle, Wolfe is here seen dying in the hour of victory.

Wolfe, JAMES (1727–59). Slender, frail and studious, the conqueror of the French on the Plains of Abraham outside Quebec, Canada, was little like the usual ideal of a military hero. Yet when, in 1759, after it had been decided to send an expedition against Quebec, William Pitt, the British Prime Minister, needed a commander to give the finishing blow to French power in North America, he entrusted the command of the British forces to this young soldier.

Born at Westerham, Kent, on January 2, 1727, Wolfe was educated at Greenwich, Kent, and was commissioned in the Marines in 1741. In 1758 he was sent to North America with the rank of brigadier-general, to assist in the expedition against Louisburg, Nova Scotia, one of the French strongholds. His brigade effected a landing under heavy fire and played an important part in the memorable siege, which resulted in the capture of the fortress (1758). A few months later, when Pitt resolved on the capture of Quebec, then held by the French, he gave Wolfe the command of the expedition with the rank of major-general.

The taking of Quebec has been styled " one of the epics of modern military history."

For three months Wolfe tried in vain to capture the almost impregnable position of the French, who were entrenched below the town. At last, depressed by his failures and enfeebled by disease, Wolfe embarked on the exploit which brought him fame.

He crossed the river above the town in the early hours of September 13, 1759, surprised the French sentinels at the cove which now bears his name, climbed the steep heights, and by daybreak had 4,000 men drawn up in battle array on the Plains of Abraham. As he led his men in the ensuing engagement General Wolfe was wounded three times. He died before the pursuit of the French was ended, but when he knew that all was well he murmured " I die contented." His body was brought to England and buried in the church of St. Alfege, Greenwich. A bronze statue of Wolfe stands on the green at Westerham, near the house where he was born. (*See* Seven Years' War).

Wolsey, CARDINAL (1475–1530). " The proudest prelate that ever breathed," as he has been called, Cardinal Wolsey (pron. wool′-zi) shaped England's policy in the field of foreign affairs, and was the leading figure in

CARDINAL WOLSEY

Winning the confidence of King Henry VIII, Cardinal Wolsey was made Lord Chancellor in 1515. His failure to persuade the Pope to annul the king's marriage to Catherine of Aragon brought about his downfall in 1529.

Church and State at home for more than a decade during the early years of the reign of Henry VIII.

The son of a well-to-do citizen of Ipswich, Suffolk, Thomas Wolsey was educated at Magdalen College, Oxford, where he is said to have taken his degree at the age of 15. After becoming a priest he was appointed chaplain to Henry VII and later to Henry VIII. His powers as a diplomat won for him rapid advancement and in 1511 he was appointed a member of Henry VIII's Council. He was made Archbishop of York in 1514 and Lord Chancellor as well as a Cardinal and Papal Legate (Pope's ambassador).

Soon all authority was concentrated in the hands of the Cardinal. England became too narrow a field for his vast ambition: he aspired to be the controller of Europe. He threw England's influence into the scale on the side of Charles V of Spain in the latter's rivalry with Francis I of France, expecting thereby to enlist Spanish support for his own aspirations to the Papacy.

Prodigiously able, indefatigably industrious, he ruled with a firm hand, doing swift justice, ruthlessly sweeping away the feudal powers of the nobility and initiating that policy of dissolution of monasteries which was to be carried to completion by his royal master, Henry VIII. Some of the proceeds of the confiscated religious property

he used to found Christ Church College at Oxford. He built Hampton Court Palace, Middlesex, and later presented it to the King.

His greed, his arrogance and his insatiable lust for power outweighed his numerous fine qualities. His more than regal state was sustained not by the revenues of his several offices alone but also by pensions from foreign sovereigns, bribes from people seeking justice, and the misappropriated revenues of the suppressed religious foundations. His policies and his haughtiness earned him the enmity of churchmen and laymen alike. Charles V had judged it prudent to see that Wolsey should not become Pope, and the British statesman's power had no more stable base than the king's favour.

Henry VIII was developing a taste for the power so long monopolized by the mighty Chancellor. The costliness of Wolsey's foreign policy was added to other grounds for popular murmurings against him. When, having made himself responsible for the success of Henry's appeal to Rome for a divorce from Catherine of Aragon, the Cardinal committed the unpardonable crime of failure, his doom was sealed. Enraged and disappointed, the King stripped Wolsey of all his civil offices, leaving him only the Archbishopric of York.

He retired to his diocese which he had never visited—but this did not place him beyond the

King

WOLSEY'S WEST FRONT OF HAMPTON COURT PALACE

The gatehouse and west front of Hampton Court Palace, Middlesex, were built by Cardinal Wolsey in 1515. The moat, and the bridge over it, were added in 1535-36 by King Henry VIII, to whom the Cardinal presented the mansion in 1525. Wolsey lived in regal state, and his wealth and pride earned him the envy and dislike of churchmen and nobles alike. In 1529 he was disgraced and charged with high treason, but he died in 1530 before his trial.

reach of the king's unsated anger. Summoned to London to answer a charge of treason, he died on the way at Leicester Abbey, on November 29, 1509, where he was buried the following day.

Woodcock. Besides being noted for its zigzag flight, which makes it as difficult to shoot (it is highly esteemed for the table) as its relative the snipe, the woodcock (*Scolopax rusticola*) has two other remarkable characteristics. While the hen bird is hatching her eggs the male performs a kind of sentry-go day after day at dusk and dawn, flying slowly round and round along exactly the same course. Nets used to be hung up in the woods to catch woodcocks when they were "roading," as this is called. Then, when the young birds are hatched, the mother bird will sometimes tuck them between her legs and carry them one by one to another spot, safer or nearer a supply of food.

A. Brook

WOODCOCK'S PROTECTIVE COLOURING

Few birds have such efficient protective markings as the woodcock, and when it is sitting on its nest, on the ground, as here, the bird is so hard to see that one might accidentally tread on it. Only the very large, brown eye stands out, fixed in an unwinking stare at any suspicious object, and quick to pick out movement of any sort. The woodcock needs this large eye, for it is mainly a nocturnal bird.

A winter migrant to Britain, the woodcock is a native of the pine forests of northern Europe and Asia and is about 14 inches long, with beautifully mottled plumage of warm brown, black, grey, and buff. During the day it hides in secluded parts of the woods. In the evening it emerges to probe damp ground with its long, straight, slender beak in search of worms and grubs, its feeding habits indicating its membership of the wader group (*see* Waders). Its eggs, usually four in number, are yellowish, streaked with reddish-brown.

Woodlouse. Unattractive is the word that describes this small, crawling creature. It shuns the sunlight, and is at home in the dank darkness of crevices in rotting timber and under stones—whence it creeps at night to feed upon seedlings and small plants in general ; so that every man's hand is turned against it.

Of the 24 species common in Britain—belonging to the order *Isopoda* of the class *Crustacea*—the one most frequently encountered is *Oniscus ascellus*. It is about one-half inch long, oval in shape, bluish-grey in colour and, like all other woodlice, it is armoured with a covering of shelly plates. Very closely resembling it is *Armadillidium vulgare*, distinguished by its ability to roll itself instantly into a tight, pill-like ball—a most useful accomplishment when danger threatens.

Woodlice have 14 legs, and the female lays her eggs in a pouch between the bases of the front 10 legs. In this pouch the eggs hatch, and the miniature woodlice resemble their elders in

ARMOURED WOODLOUSE

With all its fourteen legs in action this common species of woodlouse (shown life-size) still does not get up much speed when it comes out at night to feed.

all respects save that they have only 12 legs. The other two legs make their appearance at the first moult (change of skin).

Woodpecker. The woodpecker goes up and down the side of a tree with a *rap, rap* of its stout chisel-shaped beak against the bark, drilling holes or prising off the bark until its long tongue can reach and bring forth the insects which make up a large part of its food. When a pair of woodpeckers want a home, their pick-like bills and strong neck muscles enable them to make a deep hole in the trunk of a tree, and on the chips that fall to the bottom of this hole the glossy white eggs are laid and the young reared.

All the members of the woodpecker family (*Picidae*) are characterized by short stout legs with two toes pointing forwards, two pointing backwards, and stiff tail feathers, which are pressed against the bark in climbing and also help to support the bird in an upright position while it works. The most peculiar point about these birds is the tongue. This is cylindrical and terminates in a hard point, with barbs upon the sides. It can be thrown out to great length, and it is a most effective instrument for dislodging grubs from trees, as well as for picking up ants, of which these birds are especially fond.

Most of the woodpeckers have a distinctive undulating flight, rising as they beat their wings, falling as with wings closed. Though they do not sing, they have distinctive and in some cases musical calls. The laughing call of the green woodpecker

A. Brook

LESSER SPOTTED WOODPECKER
Rarest and smallest of the three British species of wood-pecker, this bird is about three inches shorter than the green species shown in the colour plate opposite. Its plumage is mainly black and white, with some crimson.

(*Picus viridis*) is responsible for its country name "yaffle." This species (*see* colour plate) is about 12 inches in length, and may be heard—if not actually seen—in many parts of Britain.

The other British species are the greater spotted woodpecker (*Dryobates major*), about nine inches long, and the lesser spotted (*D. minor*), about six inches long. Both are chiefly black and white, with some crimson. Their feeding habits—they consume mostly insects—put them high on the list of birds beneficial to the farmer.

Wood-wind Instruments. A very early type of wood-wind instrument is the *flute*. Flutes made of the hollow leg-bones of birds have been found among the relics of the ancient cave dwellers. The breath of the flautist, blown across a hole drilled into the side of the bone, caused the air

in the hollow tube of the bone to vibrate and produce a tone, just as in the flute of the present day.

Modern flutes and similar instruments are made of carefully finished wood or of artificial materials which are less affected by climate and moisture. The flute is furnished with a set of keys which make it possible to produce all the tones of any scale. The smallest type, the *piccolo*, sounds the shrillest notes of the orchestra. The *fife*, which resembles the flute except that it has six finger holes instead of keys, is used chiefly in military bands.

Other instruments in the wood-wind group are the *oboe*, *cor anglais*, *clarinet*, and *bassoon*. These differ from the flute in that the characteristic tone and " colour " are given by the vibration of a single or a double reed fitted into the mouthpiece.

The *oboe* has a double reed. Unlike the flute, it is held vertically and is slightly conical in shape. Its tone is somewhat like that of the violin, but shriller and more penetrating. The *cor anglais* (literally " English horn ") is a larger oboe, having a tenor tone. It has a bent upper part made of metal. The tone is rich and beautiful.

The *bassoon*, the bass of the oboe, is sometimes called the clown of the orchestra, because when its deep tones are produced with extreme agility they are irresistibly grotesque. In ordinary use it supplies the bass of the entire wood-wind group. It is so long (nine feet) that its tube has to be bent back upon itself, bringing what we would naturally call the lower end to a position above the mouthpiece. The double reed is fixed to a crooked mouthpiece several inches in length coming from the side. There is a still larger (and lower toned) form called the *contra-bassoon*, or double bassoon.

The *clarinet* is larger than the oboe, and its mouthpiece is cut into almost the shape of a chisel, to take a single thin flat reed which is clamped over the opening. Its voice has three distinct qualities, the lower tones being dark and gloomy, the middle tones full and liquid like a soprano voice, and the highest fierce and shrill. In fullness and variety of tone it is the chief of wind instruments. The *bass clarinet* is larger and deeper in tone. (*See* Musical Instruments; Orchestra).

How the SHEEP'S COAT gets on YOUR BACK

Here we follow the story of wool, and the garments made from it, from the shearing of the sheep to the weaving of the cloth. From beginning to end it is a revelation of hard-won knowledge and considerable skill.

Wool. Because it effectively keeps in the heat of the body, woollen clothing is the most comfortable in northern climes, and wool has become the characteristic clothing of the Western world, as cotton is of the warmer East.

The presence of a proportion of cotton in woollen cloth is not always a disadvantage, since it is useful in strengthening cheap and tender woollens. " Shoddy " is wool cloth containing reclaimed fibres from old materials. Such fibres are shorter than those of new wool, and being worn and weaker, the material does not wear so well.

Why do we say that wool is " warm," compared with cotton, for example ? It is because wool fibres, and clothing made from them, act excellently

as an insulating material, on account of air entrapped in the spaces between the fibres. When a wool garment becomes impregnated with moisture (even up to 30 per cent), it still keeps its open structure. A cotton garment, on the contrary, tends to lose its rigidity and to cling to the skin when wet, the fibres collapsing and the air " pockets " closing up. Wool fibres are naturally wavy, or crimped, which helps to keep the open structure of a cloth. Again, wool will stretch more than cotton without losing its elasticity.

There is a difference in chemical composition between these two natural fibres, for cotton is cellulose, whereas wool is made up mainly of keratin, which is a protein. Even a proportion of

urful and handsome is the sprightly green woodpecker, one
ae gayest in plumage of British birds. Besides the crimson
green and yellow seen here it has a yellow-green back and
w rump. Often, indeed, it is mistaken for an escaped

parrot. In this photograph by Capt. C. W. R. Knight we see
how the bird uses its stiff tail for support whilst clinging to the
side of a tree-trunk or branch. About twelve inches in length,
this is the largest of the three British species of woodpecker

WOODPECKERS' WORK

ALTHOUGH woodpeckers spend a lot of time in drilling neat round holes in standing timber, they are not harmful birds. They make the holes principally in search of food; the creatures they are after are the large, soft grubs of wood-boring beetles, which themselves are real enemies of the forester and timber merchant. The thoroughness with which these birds go over a badly attacked tree can be gathered from the specimen on the left, riddled with holes. The upper picture shows a greater spotted woodpecker, one of Britain's three species, just about to enter its nesting hole with food for its young family. This is a brilliantly marked bird, being black and white with red on its head and beneath its tail; but the colour-scheme is very effective camouflage, helping to " break up " the bird's contours so that it is often most difficult to see in its natural surroundings.

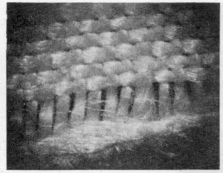

hot weather. Nowadays, the shearing is done largely by machine clippers. With these expert shearers can clip 150 to 200 sheep a day, while a man using hand-shears will have done a good day's work in clipping 30.

The first and finest clip, called "lamb's wool," may be taken at about the age of eight months. Fleeces from sheep shorn for the first time, at about the age of 12 or 14 months, are known as "hogg wool." Fleeces from sheep that have already been shorn are called "wether wool," and are of relatively less value. Wool taken from the pelts of sheep in slaughter-houses is known as "skin" wool, and is inferior to the shorn wool obtained from live sheep.

wool in a cotton fabric will endow the material with many of wool's advantages, so that mixed cotton-wool cloths, and those which the trade calls "union" materials, have many uses. Some of these advantages of woollen clothing themselves lead to drawbacks. Clothing must not merely keep us warm in cold weather: it must also allow the body to lose warmth comfortably in hot weather. Since wool gives up absorbed moisture only slowly, it is inclined to have a "poultice effect" when worn next to the skin. Therefore it is often better to wear under-garments of other materials than wool, and to keep in the bodily warmth by means of an outer

WOOL, LINEN AND COTTON

Often mixed with other fabrics, wool (lower), which is both absorbent and heat retaining, endows the resulting material with some of its properties. Linen (upper left) is light but does not retain heat. Cotton (upper right) absorbs moisture but is not as warm as wool.

woollen or wool-containing garment, which can be doffed, or unbuttoned, readily.

The magnified photographs of pieces of linen, woollen and cotton fabrics shown at the top of this page illustrate the characteristics of these fabrics.

The name wool is properly given only to the fibre of the domestic sheep. Other fibres so closely resemble it, however, that they are also called wool in commercial usage—for example, mohair, from the Angora goat; cashmere, from the Cashmere goat of India; and alpaca, from the alpaca of the Andes—but these are in general rather coarser and stiffer than the fleece of the domestic sheep.

The difference between wool and hair is one of degree rather than of kind, wool fibres being commonly finer, softer, and curlier, with innumerable minute scales which overlap one another. The curl keeps the yarn from unwinding, and the scales interlock and hold the fibres together. These properties are also used in making felt, which is done by rolling or pressing a pulpy mass of wool into a flat mat (see Hats and Caps). The elasticity of wool is another distinctive quality, giving woollens pliability and softness.

Much attention, too, has naturally been paid to breeding sheep for wool, the finest being produced by Merino sheep. Wool is shorn from the sheep ordinarily once a year, sometimes twice a year in places of continuous

After shearing, the fleeces are rolled up in bundles and sent to the mill, where they are sorted. Not only do the various kinds of sheep furnish widely different qualities of wool, but different qualities are obtained from the same

WOOL WASHED AND DRIED

When they have been sheared from the sheep the fleeces go to a mill to be torn apart, washed, and dried. The clean, white wool (above) is then ready for the processes shown in the next page.

stage. Usually, however, they are twisted with the wool yarn after spinning, or combined in the weaving.

The wool is now oiled to restore its natural pliancy, and is ready for carding, an operation which pulls the fibres apart so that they lie loosely, separated in a uniform film. This is done by revolving cylinders covered with leather strips fitted with numerous fine long wire teeth.

If the wool is to be used for "worsteds," it must be combed in addition to being carded, to make the fibres lie parallel to one another, so that the threads when spun will be regular in shape, and hard and

animal. The best quality wool is obtained from the sides and shoulders.

Although the fleece may have been washed on the live sheep's back, it still has to be scoured to rid it of stains of earth and dust which it has picked up, and of the greasy matter secreted by the skin of the animal. The wool is then dried and is ready for blending, to produce cloth of the desired quality. If other materials are to be mixed with the wool—such as silk, cotton, or shoddy— they may be added at this

Australian News and Information Bureau

PREPARING THE FIBRES OF THE WOOL

In the carding machine (top) the fibres of the cleaned wool are disentangled by passing it between rollers fitted with small teeth, the fibres then being delivered in the form of a 'rope.' Short fibres are removed from the wool of the 'rope' in the comber (middle) and the long ones straightened. Shorter-fibred wool is combed in another type of machine (bottom), which does similar work.

compact. The wool for "woollens" is not combed, but after emerging from the carding machine in light strands, called rovings, goes directly to the spinning-room, where the mixed and matted fibres are spun into a soft, loose, irregular thread. (*See* Spinning.)

In the spinning-room the fibres are drawn out, twisted, and spun into a single yarn. The yarns are then twisted into two, three, or four strands, or used singly, according to the coarseness or fineness of fabric desired. Soft, fragile yarn is often used for weft or filling, but the warp threads must be able to bear much greater strain, and are twisted harder. Formerly nearly all woollen goods were

Australian News and Information Bureau

HOW THE WOOL FIBRES ARE SPUN

In the spinning-room the combed wool is run through a machine which twists and draws it into a loose, irregular thread suitable for spinning. The long spinning-machine (above) converts this thread into a single yarn of the required size. The yarn may then be twisted into a strand of three or four yarns or used singly, according to the type of fabric.

The soil is fertile, that in the Vale of Evesham being especially so. A large area is devoted to the growing of plums, apples and pears. Hops are cultivated, also wheat, oats and potatoes, and there are numerous market gardens. The manufacturing district in the north around Stourport and Kidderminster forms part of the so-called Black Country.

The county town is Worcester (population 61,000), noted for its porcelain and its 13th-century Cathedral. Other centres include Kidderminster, where carpets are made ; Redditch, known for its needles and pins; Droitwich, celebrated for its brine baths. At Malvern, which is a holiday resort, there is a Public School. The population of the county of Worcestershire is 420,000.

dyed soon after leaving the loom, but now the practice is more general of dyeing the yarn before spinning. (*See* Loom; Weaving).

After the cloth leaves the loom, any defects of knotted or broken yarns are made good. Then the cloth is saturated with hot water and soap, and rubbed between slowly-revolving rollers to give the desired shrinkage (and so to prevent shrinkage later). The soap is then washed out and the cloth is stretched so that it may dry evenly.

Next the nap is raised in a " teaselling " machine by means of thousands of little steel hooks, which scratch the surface and give the cloth its characteristic " woolly " look. This process gets its name from the teasel (*q.v.*) plant, whose prickly heads are still used for this work to some extent. The nap may be trimmed by a very fine machine, which acts on the principle of the lawn-mower. After being pressed between hot plates and dry-steamed to impart lustre, the cloth is ready for market. Australia, South America and South Africa are the largest wool producing areas. Yorkshire is the centre of the great woollen industry of England.

Worcestershire.

An English county in the West Midlands, with an area of 700 square miles, Worcestershire is bounded on the north by Shropshire and Staffordshire, on the east by Warwickshire, on the south by Gloucestershire, on the west by Herefordshire. Much of the surface is hilly. On the Herefordshire border the Malvern Hills rise to 1,400 feet; in the south-east is Bredon Hill, a spur of the Cotswolds; and in the north and north-east are the Clent Hills and Lickey Hills. The Severn flows through the county from north to south, and its tributary the Avon waters the south-east portion. The only other rivers of importance are the Teme and Stour.

J. Dixon-Scott

WORCESTER CATHEDRAL

Overlooking the Severn at Worcester is the 13th-century Cathedral of Our Lord and the Blessed Virgin Mary. Its central tower, completed in 1374, is 196 feet high. Under the choir and aisles is a crypt built in 1084.

Wordsworth, WILLIAM (1770–1850).
As the British poet and critic Matthew Arnold
(1822–88) said: "Wordsworth's poetry is great
because of the extraordinary power with which

From a miniature by Margaret Gillies

WORDSWORTH AND HIS WIFE
In 1802 Wordsworth married Mary Hutchinson, his sister's
friend and the subject of his lyric beginning : ' She was a
phantom of delight When first she gleamed upon my sight.'

Wordsworth feels the joy offered us in Nature,
the joy offered us in the simple affections and
duties, and because of the extraordinary power
with which he shows us this joy, and renders it so
as to make us share it."

Born on April 7, 1770, at Cockermouth, among
the Cumberland hills, Wordsworth came of a
family of landowners, and from his earliest days
had a deep love for simple country life and for
the beautiful region in which he lived. He was
educated at Hawkshead Grammar School
and St. John's College, Cambridge.

His life was singularly uneventful, save for
visits to the Continent. On the second of
these, made in 1791, he threw himself fervently
into the cause of the French Revolutionists,
and was just about to join the Girondins (the
moderate party) when his disapproving family
stopped sending him money, and he was compelled to return home towards the end of 1792.
For three years he lived in an unsettled
fashion, without prospects or profession, until,
on receiving a legacy, he took a cottage at
Racedown in Dorsetshire with his sister
Dorothy, resolved to devote his life to poetry.

In 1797 Wordsworth moved to Alfoxden,
in Somersetshire, where he enjoyed the friendship of Samuel Coleridge (*q.v.*). The two
poets wandered, talked, and worked together,
producing in 1798 their collection of Lyrical
Ballads. In the second edition of this anthology Wordsworth startled and enraged the
literary world by declaring that poets should
rely on simple scenes, everyday words, truth

to Nature, and imagination. In the book
itself were such splendid applications of this
viewpoint as Coleridge's Ancient Mariner, and
Wordsworth's Lines Above Tintern Abbey.

Wordsworth made his home for the last 50 years
of his life first at Grasmere and then at Rydal
Mount, in the Lake District. In 1802 he married
his sister's friend, Mary Hutchinson. Gradually
he won public favour, and seven years before
his death on April 23, 1850, he was made Poet
Laureate. (*See* illustration in page 1214.)

In his long poem The Prelude he gives an
account of his mental growth, and tells how his
boyish love of Nature's physical beauty changed
to an appreciation of the tranquillizing spiritual
kinship between Nature and Man. He is un-
dramatic and lacks broad sympathy with human
nature. But his best Nature poems, a number of
his exquisite sonnets—e.g., those on Westminster
Bridge and on Milton—and several of his simple
peasant poems, in which he lifts the commonplace into genuine poetry, are immortal.

Wordsworth's works include The Evening Walk,
and Descriptive Sketches (1793); his contributions
to Lyrical Ballads (1798); The Prelude (1805);
Poems, including the Ode on the Intimations of
Immortality (1807); and The Excursion (1814).

Works, Ministry of. A department
of the British Government, the Ministry was
formed in 1832 as the Office of Works to perform
duties previously carried out by the Office of
Woods and Forests, which had charge of all royal
palaces and parks, public offices and other buildings
belonging to the nation, and remained under the
control of a First Commissioner until 1940, when
it was raised to the status of a Ministry and the
chief official became a Minister of Cabinet rank.

The Ministry retained its old functions, and in
addition is responsible for the promotion of the
efficiency of the country's civil engineering and
building industries, and it issues licences for private
building. The Ministry of Works also has charge
of certain ancient monuments and is responsible
for their preservation.

WORDSWORTH'S HOUSE AT RYDAL
With his family Wordsworth went to live at Rydal, a Westmorland
hamlet at the east end of Rydal Water, in 1813. The house,
Rydal Mount, was the poet's home until his death in 1850. He
was made Poet Laureate in 1843.

TWO WARS *that* SHATTERED *the* WORLD

Neither the First World War (1914–18) nor the Second (1939–45) brought a prospect of lasting peace. More had been destroyed than Mankind could hope to build up again in many lifetimes.

World War of 1914-18. The year 1914 saw the outbreak of a war on a scale unknown and undreamed of in all history. Of all the countries of the world, the only ones to remain out of the conflict were Holland and her Empire, Spain, Norway, Sweden, Denmark, Switzerland, Argentina, Colombia, Venezuela, and Mexico—comprising less than one-fourteenth of the world's population. The First World War was the first real clash not between professional armies and navies but between whole peoples in arms against one another and equipped with scientific and terrible weapons for mass slaughter.

The number of killed and wounded reached about 30 million ; the British Empire's dead numbered 1,104,890. Aeroplanes and submarines made their appearance (*see* Aeroplane ; Submarine). Guns of every size, some able to throw shells for 70 miles, were used in gigantic numbers (*see* Artillery). The wide use of machine-guns made infantry attack hopeless without crushing artillery preparation beforehand.

In 1916 the first tanks (*q.v.*) lumbered into action—to secure mastery of attack over defence. All these developments, in their infancy in the First World War, were to come to terrible maturity in the Second. There was one new weapon, however, which made no reappearance in the war of 1939–45, and that was perhaps the most frightful of all : poison gas, first employed by the Germans in 1915 and thereafter freely used by both sides.

Europe in 1914 was very different from the Europe we know today. There was no Poland; its lands were divided between Germany, Austria and Russia. The country we now know as Yugoslavia was then the two nations of Serbia and Montenegro; but a part of it, together with the whole of modern Czechoslovakia, was also included in the Dual Monarchy of Austria and Hungary.

Murder of an Archduke

Francis Ferdinand, heir to the throne of Austria-Hungary, was murdered on June 28, 1914, at Sarajevo in what is now Yugoslavia, by Gavrilo Princip. The assassin was one of the millions living in Austria-Hungary who longed to throw off the Austrian yoke and to join with their kinsmen in Serbia. Austria accused the Serbian government of complicity in the crime, and presented an ultimatum. The terms were impossibly severe: Serbia suggested reference to The Hague Tribunal or arbitration by the great Powers, but Austria's immediate answer was to declare war (July 28, 1914).

Serbia appealed to Russia, who came to her assistance. Germany, whose government had blocked British attempts to find a peaceful settlement, then entered on the Austrian side; and France ranged herself with her ally, Russia.

On August 2, 1914, in order to strike France from behind, Germany demanded the right to march through Belgium—this despite repeated previous undertakings to respect Belgian neutrality. The demand was refused, but Germany nevertheless invaded Belgium. This brought Great Britain into the struggle, and three weeks later Japan joined her in fulfilment of treaty obligations.

Causes of the First World War

The murder of the Archduke was thus the spark that set the world on fire. But it was the excuse for the war rather than its cause. For years Austria-Hungary had sought to dominate the Balkans. Resenting the increased power which had been gained by Serbia in the war of the Balkan allies against Turkey in 1912–13, she still would never have dared to fight unless assured of German support. Rather was it Germany who, by encouraging Austria-Hungary to make unacceptable demands on Serbia, was the true instigator of the war.

Jealous of Great Britain's trade and colonies, Germany, who already had the greatest army in the world, began to build a navy to challenge British sea-power. The German Emperor, or Kaiser as he was called, spoke often of Germany's " mission " and of her " place in the sun "—much as, a quarter of a century later, Adolf Hitler (*q.v.*) was to claim Germany's need of " living space." The mutual rivalries of the Powers created such a strained atmosphere that cool and reasonable discussion became impossible.

Belgium resisted the Germans' assault, holding their armies' onslaught long enough for the French commander, General Joffre, to reorganize his troops to face attack from this unexpected direction; while the British were able to send over an expeditionary force of 100,000 men, which fought bravely at Mons and Charleroi.

But Joffre was forced to retire behind the River Marne. There he launched his counter-attack. In the First Battle of the Marne, September 6–10, 1914, the Germans were flung back; and Paris—which they had made their main objective (rejecting the wiser counsel to concentrate first on capturing the Channel ports)—was saved.

The Germans retired to a line roughly parallel with the River Aisne. There both armies " dug themselves in." This was the beginning of the trench warfare, so exhausting and costly, that lasted throughout most of the remaining four years of the Western Front fighting.

The British army saved Boulogne, Calais, and the northern coastline of France at the First Battle of Ypres (October–November 1914). But the Germans had captured Ostend, Zeebrugge and Antwerp, and the Belgians only retained a few square miles in the extreme western corner of their country by cutting the dykes and flooding the lowlands. In the following spring, when the Germans used poison gas in their counter-attack after crushing a British offensive in Belgium, it looked for a time as if the Channel ports would go:

but the defence, after losing some ground, held fast and prevented a German break-through.

By the end of 1915 Britain had 36 divisions on the Western Front. The introduction of conscription in January 1916 brought the total strength of the British army to five million men; and both Britain and France pressed on with the production of war materials ready for a great offensive in 1916. But that year began badly. In February the Crown Prince, the Kaiser's eldest son, launched a great attack on the fortress of Verdun, the key to the entire French defence. Some of the city's forts fell; but General (afterwards Marshal) Pétain rallied the defenders, and though the Germans sacrificed 500,000 men Verdun remained secure.

With Verdun safe the Allies began an offensive on the River Somme, north-east of Paris. The First Battle of the Somme began on July 1, 1916, and lasted until November 18. Sir Douglas (afterwards Earl) Haig, the British commander, attacked on a line extending north of the river on an 18-mile curve facing the German-held town of Bapaume. The French had an eight-mile front straddling the river opposite Péronne.

The " big push," as it was called, failed to break through the German line. The British lost

G.P.A.
A BATTERED FORT AT VERDUN : 1916
In February 1916 (during the First World War) the Germans began an offensive against Verdun, key to the French positions in France, and though some of the surrounding forts, including Fort de Vaux (above), were captured by the Germans the French retained possession of the city.

60,000 in the first day's fighting; and by November 1916, though a wedge nine miles deep had been driven into the German positions, neither Bapaume nor Péronne had fallen, and the Allied casualties amounted to 800,000. It was in September 1916 that the Allies first used the newly invented armoured fighting vehicles we know as " tanks."

Russian Advance and Retreat

On the Eastern Front, Russia had surprised Germany by the speed of her mobilization, and quickly penetrated deep into East Prussia; but at Tannenberg and in the Battle of the Masurian Lakes (August and September 1914) the Russian armies were crushingly defeated. A second Russian invasion in the spring of 1915 also came to grief among the Masurian Lakes; Hindenburg, the German commander, became the idol of his country.

Farther south the Russians overran the Austrian province of Galicia and began to cross the Carpathian Mountains into Hungary; but in the summer of 1915 German and Austrian forces drove them many miles back. Between this push and an offensive launched by Hindenburg in the north the Russians found themselves in the jaws, as it were, of giant pincers, and were at length driven out of the whole of Russian Poland. In 1916 Russia again invaded Austria, capturing 500,000 prisoners; but the Russian commander was unable to exploit his early successes.

Serbia was not invaded until November 10, 1914. The Austrians, successful at first, were later flung back across the Danube. A year later they attacked again, reinforced this time by German troops; and at the same time Bulgaria, their ally since October 13, 1915, launched an offensive from the south-east. Serbia and Montenegro were crushed. A remnant of the Serbian army, suffering terribly from cold and hunger, escaped with their aged King Peter through the mountains to the Albanian coast, and there the Allies took them off in warships and sent them, re-equipped, to Salonika (now named Thessaloniki), in Greece.

Italy had been bound to Germany and Austria in the Triple Alliance, but refused to join them in 1914 because the war was an aggressive and not a defensive one. On May 23, 1915, receiving a secret promise of the Austrian districts of Trentino, Trieste and Dalmatia, she came in on the Allied side. By August 1916 her forces had advanced across the River Isonzo as far as Gorizia and were threatening the great seaport of Trieste.

In 1916 Rumania, encouraged by the Allies' successes, determined to liberate the thousands of Rumanians included in the Hungarian kingdom. But her forces invading Hungary were attacked in the rear by the Bulgarians, and in a disastrous retreat lost all the western half of their country, with its oil and agricultural produce.

Turkey had cast in her lot with Germany and Austria in October 1914. After beating off attacks on the Suez Canal the British, in April 1915, landed an expedition on the narrow Gallipoli peninsula, the Dardanelles' western shore. Casualties were enormous, and in January 1916 the Allied force was withdrawn. A British force that advanced from the Persian Gulf up the Tigris into Mesopotamia (now called Iraq) was besieged by the Turks at Kut-el-Amara, and forced to surrender

Imperial War Museum

HEROIC LANDING OF BRITISH TROOPS AT GALLIPOLI : 1915
On April 25, 1915, British forces landed at Gallipoli, a peninsula of Turkey on the European side of the Dardanelles. Some of the troops disembarked from the transport River Clyde, of which the forepart is shown close to ' V ' beach in the above illustration from a diorama by Mr. Denny C. Stokes. Though a foothold was gained, the Allied forces could not overcome the stubborn resistance of the Turks, and the peninsula was abandoned in January 1916.

merchant fleet had suffered severely.

The year 1917 began with a German retirement in the west. The wedge which the Allies had driven into the German lines on the Somme during the previous summer had seriously menaced the German positions. So a regrouping of forces was called for. By evacuating a large area from Arras to Soissons the Germans shortened their line by some 40 miles. British and French attacks on the new positions—the "Hindenburg Line"—had some early success, but soon it was clear that the Germans could not be beaten by a frontal attack—the only kind open to the Allies in the Western Front trench warfare.

(April 29, 1916). Only Russia scored a success against the Turks, capturing most of Armenia.

In other parts of the world the Allies were generally successful. German possessions in China fell to the Japanese; Germany's Pacific colonies were taken by the Australians and New Zealanders. By the end of 1916 the German territories in Africa were under British control, the Allied forces being commanded by two South African generals, Botha in the south-west and Smuts in the east.

The War at Sea

On the outbreak of war Germany's merchant ships had run for home, while her high-seas fleet remained securely bottled-up in the Kiel Canal. A few German commerce raiders led a spectacular career in eastern waters before being captured or destroyed; three British cruisers were sunk by submarines in the North Sea; a German squadron defeated a British force at Coronel in the south Pacific before itself being destroyed in the Battle of the Falkland Islands (December 8, 1914).

On May 1, 1916, came the decisive Battle of Jutland, in which the German high-seas fleet met the British Home Fleet off the Danish coast. British losses were the heavier, but the German warships were so battered that they never again ventured beyond their protecting minefields.

Germany's chief weapon at sea was the submarine. With sufficient under-sea craft the Germans hoped to destroy Allied commerce and to starve the Allies into submission. In February 1915 Germany proclaimed a blockade of the entire British and French coasts : any vessel, Allied or neutral, was to be in danger of sinking if found within the forbidden zone. Nearly a hundred vessels, many of them neutral, were sunk within three months; and by the end of 1916 the British

In shell-torn, boggy Flanders the British attacked from July to November 1917, threatening Germany's hold on western Belgium by the capture of Passchendaele Ridge. This prolonged assault under appalling conditions cost staggering casualties, and Field-Marshal Haig's refusal to break off the battles when little material gain could be looked for from them has been much criticized. The British gained a valuable advantage at Cambrai, where tanks were used on a large scale for the first time; but in a surprise counter-attack the enemy re-took all that had been gained. Meanwhile, however, the French had won important victories north of the Aisne.

The Italian Rout at Caporetto

The Italians advancing on Trieste failed adequately to guard the upper Isonzo; and at the end of October 1917 the Austrians and Germans struck like an avalanche at Caporetto. The Italian armies broke; the rout was not halted until it reached the River Piave, and for the next year this remained the battle-line.

Some Allied successes in the Middle East offset this disaster: General Maude took Baghdad, and General Allenby captured Jerusalem.

On March 11, 1917, a revolution broke out at Leningrad—then called Petrograd—the Russian capital. Four days later the Tsar (Emperor) abdicated. At first the republican government planned to continue the war; but soon military discipline collapsed, thousands of Russian soldiers deserted and fled to their homes, and the cry was raised that the peoples should not fight one another in a "capitalistic and imperialistic" war.

The first Bolshevik Government came into power in November 1917. In December they arranged an armistice with the Germans, and the following

Imperial War Museum

IN THE NIGHTMARE SWAMPS OF PASSCHENDAELE: 1917

Heavy rain, continuous shelling and destruction of the drainage system converted the terrain over which the British fought the battle of Passchendaele in Flanders in 1917 into a swamp, dotted with water-filled shellholes. These Canadian machine-gunners are manning positions in ground captured from the Germans during the action at Broodseinde on October 4, 1917, before the final assault on the Ridge. Rough causeways were built over the mud, but these were often destroyed by shellfire, and men and mules were engulfed in the seemingly bottomless ooze.

March their delegates signed the harsh Treaty of Brest-Litovsk. The Germans were now able to transfer many thousands of troops to the Western Front, and henceforth Britain and France bore the brunt of the German attacks.

The United States Enters the War

The sinking of the British liner Lusitania on May 7, 1915, with the loss of 1,198 lives—124 of them American—caused a wave of indignation throughout the United States. For a time the Germans relaxed their blockade; but in January 1917 their Ambassador at Washington announced that the following day . German ships would resume the policy of sinking without warning all vessels found in the "war-zone." America would be " permitted " to send one passenger vessel a week to England, under strict conditions.

American indignation was further aroused by the revelation that Germany was planning an alliance with Mexico. With German financial support Mexico was to reconquer her " lost territory " in New Mexico, Texas and Arizona. War now became inevitable. The United States declared war on Germany on April 6, 1917, and on Austria-Hungary eight months later. On June 26, 1917, the first American troops reached France.

Hindenburg (now the German commander in the West) and his chief of staff, Ludendorff, planned a final decisive attack for the spring of 1918. On March 21 a great offensive was launched in the devastated region of the Somme. In a few days the Germans recaptured all the ground gained by the Allies during the previous summer.

In front of Amiens the Allies held fast. In the critical situation it was agreed to make Marshal Foch, now commanding the French forces, commander-in-chief of all the Allied armies on the Western Front.

By April 6 the German advance had been blocked to the north, west and south. A few days later Ludendorff succeeded in breaking through the British line towards the Channel ports. The British, as Haig said in a historic signal, " had their backs to the wall "; they rallied, and the vital coastline was saved.

On May 27 it was the turn of the French. Attacked on the Aisne by a force under the personal command of the German Crown Prince they were forced back to the line of the Marne, less than 50 miles from Paris. But a second German blow gained little ground, and American troops at Belleau Wood and Château Thierry barred the way. The Germans struck again on July 15, and succeeded in crossing the Marne. Foch, however, had bided his time, and now at last was the moment for his counter-offensive, which was to turn the tide.

On July 18, 1918, French and American forces attacked the Germans and chased them back across the Marne. The assault continued east and west of Château Thierry. Small "whippet" tanks climbed across the German trenches and broke up enemy machine-gun nests. The Germans retreated across the River Vesle and the French captured Soissons. Now the British launched a great offensive in the region of the Somme. Albert and Bapaume were speedily recovered. In little over a month the Allies took over 100,000 prisoners; the Germans were in full retreat on a front of 140 miles.

Blow followed blow in quick succession at different parts of the German line. The French and Americans straightened out the salient that so long had threatened Verdun. The British advanced in the neighbourhood of Cambrai; a combined British and Belgian drive won more territory in a few days than the British had been able to gain in four months during the previous year. The

Belgian coast towns were now recovered; Lille, La Fère, and Laon—in north east France—were surrendered by the retreating Germans.

The Americans were fighting hard in the Argonne forest north of Verdun, the sector that covered the railway communications to Germany, and had finally reached the railway when, on November 11, 1918, an armistice was signed. By this time the

Imperial War Museum

BRITISH TROOPS IN ACTION ON THE SOMME IN 1916

The first battle of the Somme, in France, began on July 1, 1916, when the British and French attacked German positions protected by wide belts of barbed wire and concrete machine-gun emplacements, after a week's artillery bombardment. The initial British onslaught met with considerable success except in the north of the sector, where the Germans retained Beaumont-Hamel, against which men of the 16th Battalion the Middlesex Regiment are seen advancing (upper). Lower, howitzers of the Royal Garrison Artillery are seen in action during the Somme engagement.

Germans had virtually been driven out of France, and were retreating all along the line.

Germany's downfall had been hastened by the sudden collapse of her three allies: Bulgaria, Turkey and Austria. For three years an Allied army composed of detachments of British, French, Italian and Serbian troops, with a force of revolutionary Greeks under their Prime Minister, Venizelos, had been stationary at Salonika (later named Thessaloniki), hesitating to advance for fear of being attacked in the rear by Greece's King Constantine (who had German sympathies). But Constantine had been forced to abdicate on June 12, 1917, and Greece rallied to the side of the Allies.

Suddenly, on September 15, 1918, the Allied army here moved forward. In less than two weeks most of southern Serbia had been won back. Bulgaria, threatened with invasion, obtained an armistice on September 29. The Serbian army continued its triumphant progress northward, and the Austrians fled from Albania and Montenegro. In less than seven weeks Serbia was wholly cleared of Austrians, and the Serbians had recaptured Belgrade.

Shortly after this Balkan campaign began, General Allenby's Palestine army recommenced hostilities in conjunction with the Arab force led by the Emir Feisal and the famous Colonel T. E. Lawrence. The Turkish army was overwhelmed; Damascus, Acre, Beirut, and Aleppo were captured. On October 31, 1918, Turkey surrendered.

Even more dramatic was the fall of Austria. An advance by the Italians begun on October 24, 1918, took them across the Piave, virtually cutting the Austrians in two. Within ten days over 300,000 Austrians surrendered, and their commander begged for an end to the fighting. The collapse of the Austrian army was accompanied by the fall of their government at home. Bohemia and other parts of the Austro-Hungarian Empire joyfully proclaimed their independence. The heads of the proud and ancient House of Hapsburg fled to Switzerland.

All these events had their effect in Germany. On November 3, 1918, disorders broke out in the German fleet at Kiel and spread rapidly to Hamburg and Bremen. The Socialists in Berlin refused to support the government any longer; the rulers of Bavaria and Württemberg abdicated. Then, on November 10, the Kaiser himself abdicated and fled to Holland. Everywhere the princes of the German states resigned their crowns or were deposed. A temporary government in Berlin arranged for a national convention to determine the form of the future republic of Germany.

As early as October 6, 1918, the German Government, realizing how hopeless was the military position, had informed the Allies it would accept their peace terms. After some preliminary negotiations, terms for an armistice were agreed among the Allies; and at daybreak on November 11, in a railway carriage drawn up in the Forest of Compiègne, Marshal Foch handed these terms to the Germans. They were accepted and six hours later, at 11 o'clock in the morning, the guns ceased to fire.

FATEFUL YEARS BETWEEN THE TWO WORLD WARS

THE First World War—in those days they called it simply the Great War—was over. It had been described as a war to end wars. Was an era of peace really dawning for the world?

In the forefront of the Treaty of Versailles was the Covenant of the League of Nations, by which the victorious countries and some which had been neutral set up an international organization for the settlement of disputes. Provision was made for the entry of ex-enemy countries after they had proved their goodwill. The number of member nations at the beginning was 48; at its highest it reached 62.

But the United States, which had been the principal sponsor of the League, now repudiated its spokesman, President Wilson, and declined to join. Without the United States the League never enjoyed the prestige it required to fulfil the task of preserving peace in the world.

The map of the world that took shape after 1918 was greatly changed. Poland reappeared as a sovereign state; and on the Baltic coast, Estonia, Latvia and Lithuania were recognized as independent. In central Europe the great patriot Thomas Masaryk (q.v.) became president of the new republic of Czechoslovakia, comprising Bohemia, Moravia, Ruthenia and Slovakia Serbia and Montenegro were fused into another new State as Yugoslavia. Albania became independent. With the end of the Turkish Empire, Syria and the Lebanon appeared as French mandated territories; while Britain received the mandate to administer Palestine, as well as Iraq and Transjordan.

Unfortunately the wholesale redrawing of frontiers, though with good intentions, was no guarantee of future peace. The liberation of one set of minority peoples only created a new set, and the new Europe was no less inflammable than the old.

Drawing Up the Treaties

The Peace Conference assembled at the Palace of Versailles in January 1919. The terms handed to the Germans were severe. Alsace and Lorraine were to become French; the Saar coalfields were ceded to France for 15 years. Belgium was awarded Eupen and Malmédy. Much of Posen and West Prussia were given to Poland. Danzig became a Free City; Memel and the surrounding territory were handed over to the Allied powers, and later were incorporated in Lithuania. Germany lost all her colonies.

Germany also had to admit her full responsibility for the war, and to make reparation in cash and goods for the damage she had caused. German territory west of the Rhine was to be occupied by Allied troops for 15 years. On June 28, 1919, the German delegates signed the Treaty of Versailles, but owing to various disputes it was not until January 1920 that the Treaty was brought into force and the Allied blockade lifted.

A treaty with Austria-Hungary was handed to the delegates on June 2, 1919. It reduced Austria to a small country with six or seven million people, and required her to recognize the independence of Bohemia, Hungary and the southern Slavs, to cede a large area to Italy, and to make reparation for war damage. The Austrians signed on September 10, 1919. Later treaties fixed the new frontiers of Turkey and Bulgaria. Turkey was stripped of the whole of her Empire by the Treaty of Sèvres, August 10, 1920.

It early became clear that the League of Nations was not a strong enough instrument to maintain peace among the nations. Poland, which in March 1921 had forced on the Russians (still struggling with the opponents of the Revolution) a treaty by which Russia ceded a great stretch of border territory, openly defied the Peace Treaty by occupying Upper Silesia, the inhabitants of which by a considerable majority had voted to remain German. The League weakly acquiesced, and awarded Poland the greater part of this area.

Greece, hoping to secure and enlarge her gains, started a war with Turkey. The Allies, finding the Turks too strong to handle, consented to replace the Treaty of Sèvres with another, drawn up at Lausanne, and signed on July 25, 1923, by which Greece gave up all claims in Eastern Thrace and Asia Minor. An Italian dispute with Greece in the same year, over Corfu, also proved too difficult for the League to settle.

All over the world wars broke out, or were threatened. Japan invaded Manchuria in 1932, and set up a puppet state there. Finding the League of Nations' feeble attempt to discipline her distasteful, Japan withdrew from the League in March 1935. In the following year Japan invaded China, the start of a long undeclared war that only found an end on Japan's signature of the armistice with the Allies, in August 1945, which ended the Second World War.

Ambitions of Italy and Germany

Italy had been in a state of political chaos since her representative had left the Peace Conference in a huff on the grounds that Italy was not receiving her due rights. In 1922 Benito Mussolini (q.v.), a journalist and once a Communist, gathered together a band of " blackshirts " called the Fascisti and, marching on Rome, seized power. The King of Italy found it expedient to invite him to form a government. This government of the Fascists, once in, made certain that it could never be removed; and all other parties were suppressed by force.

The Fascisti began by achieving a praiseworthy degree of efficiency in the public services; but before long the desire for expansion, for aggrandizement, turned the thoughts of the dictator (Duce or " Leader " was his official title) to conquest overseas. On October 2, 1935, Abyssinia, which had thoroughly beaten the Italians a quarter of a century earlier, was attacked with tanks, aircraft and poison gas. The campaign was a short one, and in the following May the King of Italy became Emperor of Abyssinia.

Italy was now in a mood of assertive self-confidence. The western nations had made a half-hearted attempt to check her aggression against Abyssinia by imposing economic " sanctions," designed to cut off supplies of commodities needed for warfare, but had boggled at military action. In 1937 the Italians left the League of Nations.

Germany had found it hard to form a stable government after the creation of the new republic in 1918. Communism was strong, and the general

poverty and misery was a breeding ground of unrest. Money lost any real value, and the mark was devalued until at one time there were 10 billion of them to the pound. In 1923 an unknown ex-corporal, Adolf Hitler, led a rising against the authorities in Munich. It was easily put down, and Hitler was imprisoned for nine months. While in prison he wrote a remarkable book, entitled Mein Kampf (My Struggle), in which he set forth his aims should he ever come to power. They contained the repudiation of the Treaty of Versailles, the sending of troops to the Rhineland, which by treaty had been de-militarized, the union of Austria and Germany, the " liberation " of the German minorities in Czechoslovakia, Poland, Danzig and Memel, the recovery of Alsace-Lorraine and of the ex-German colonies.

After his release Hitler set to work to gain power; and because his National Socialist (or " Nazi ") party appealed to the beaten and bewildered Germans to regain their former greatness, he soon secured a powerful following. In January 1933 Hitler became Chancellor, and in August 1934, on the death of the aged President Hindenberg, he combined the offices of President and Chancellor as Fuehrer (" Leader ").

Gambling on the western nations' reluctance to oppose force with force, Hitler began to put his aggressive programme into effect. He built up armies and sent troops into the Rhineland in 1936. In October 1936 he made an agreement with Mussolini

Central Press

HITLER GIVES THE NAZI SALUTE
Founder of the National Socialist (Nazi) party, Adolf Hitler became German Chancellor in 1933 ; above he is seen giving the Nazi salute at a military display. In 1934 he succeeded Hindenburg as President of the German Republic and at once began to pursue the policy of aggression that led to the Second World War (1939–45).

by which Germany and Italy were linked by what was called the Rome-Berlin Axis. In October 1935 Germany had left the League of Nations.

One of the first undertakings of the Rome-Berlin Axis was the provision of aid to the insurgents in the Spanish Civil War in 1936. In the first place the two dictators recognized in General Franco, the insurgents' leader, one of like mind to themselves ; in the second place, and certainly more important, Spain was a ready-made testing ground for the newly built-up forces of Germany and Italy. The German army made great use of tanks and motor-borne infantry; and the German air force, or Luftwaffe, was ahead of all others in the technique of close support of ground troops with bombers. All this was perfected in Spain.

Hitler's next blow was at Austria. The National Socialist movement was already strong in this country, and had been responsible for the murder of the Chancellor, Dollfuss, in 1934. In March 1938 the Austrian Nazis seized power, and Hitler's columns streamed over the frontier. Austria was incorporated into " Greater Germany," and the Chancellor, Schuschnigg, was sent to a concentration camp.

Hitler was now certain that nothing would rouse the French and British to action. He demanded of the president of Czechoslovakia the cession of the Sudetenland, a border region with a large German population. President Benes̆ refused, and France and Britain supported him. The French and British prime ministers flew to Germany for a conference with Hitler, but failed to reach agreement. War seemed inevitable, but at the last moment a conference was called at Munich, and conflict was averted (September 29, 1938)—but at the cost of yielding to all the German demands on the Czechs. Neville Chamberlain, the British Premier, said that he believed he had won " peace in our time "; but there were few who really thought that. At best a little time had been gained to prepare for a war that could now scarcely be avoided.

The dictators were now scornful of the risk of war. On March 15, 1939, Hitler marched into what was left of Czechoslovakia and declared himself Protector of Bohemia and Moravia. On April 7 Mussolini landed troops in Albania, and annexed it to the Italian crown.

On March 31 Britain and France gave Poland guarantees of military aid in case of German aggression; and on April 13 these guarantees were extended to Rumania. Conscription was introduced in Britain. Meanwhile Germany had annexed Memel from Lithuania, and was demanding Danzig and a road through the Polish Corridor. This " corridor " was a strip of land, formerly German, which had been handed over to Poland by the Peace Treaty of Versailles in order to give Poland an outlet to the Baltic. It cut off East Prussia from the rest of Germany.

The " balance of power " at this time might well lie with the unknown quantity, Soviet Russia. But Britain and France had been slow to approach her, and in the event the Germans got in ahead of them. Despite their often declared hostility, a non-aggression pact between Germany and the Soviet Union was signed in Moscow on August 23, 1939.

THE SECOND WORLD WAR, 1939-1945

THIS time war was certain. Hitler presented his terms to Poland, and Col. Beck, the Polish Foreign Minister, refused them. At 5.30 a.m. on September 1, 1939, notwithstanding last-minute appeals by the Pope and by President Roosevelt of the United States, the German army marched into Poland. In fulfilment of their pledges, Britain and France declared war on Germany on September 3, together with Australia and New Zealand. Canada and South Africa joined the Allies within a week; and on September 10 the British Expeditionary Force under General Lord Gort began to move to France.

The German armoured columns streamed over the Polish border, and the bombers attacked towns and railways, soon disrupting the Polish defence organization. In a little more than a fortnight the resistance of Poland had been crushed, except for Warsaw, which held out until September 27, 1939. The Poles had received an unforeseen and crushing blow in the rear. Soviet troops marched in on September 17 and the Germans and Russians signed an agreement for the partition of Poland on September 28. A week later Hitler made known his conditions for peace; he demanded the return of the ex-German colonies and declared he had no claims to make on France. This offer was ignored.

While the British and French in the west built up their forces and waited for Germany to take the initiative—France trusting in the Maginot Line while British troops manned the Franco-Belgian frontier—the Soviet Union struck another blow. Demands on Finland for the cession of Hangö and the grant of naval bases were refused, and Soviet troops invaded Finland on November 30. The League of Nations expelled the Soviet Union from membership, and the Allies sent such arms as they could; but by mid-February the Finns had been forced back in the Karelian Isthmus to their main defence line; and on March 12, 1940, a Finnish delegation agreed to the Russian terms.

In April 1940 came the long-expected German blow which opened the real campaign against Britain and France, but it was aimed in an unexpected direction. On April 9, 1940, Germany invaded Denmark and Norway. Denmark offered virtually no resistance, but Allied forces were hastily embarked for Norway, and the Norwegian King and Government called on their people to fight. But the surprise that the Germans had achieved, aided by a good deal of treachery, gave them too great an advantage. The Allies, failing to capture Trondheim, were without a good port; moreover they had no air cover, and the German bombers attacked them without respite. Early in May 1940 the Allies withdrew from all of Norway except Narvik; and within a month the last of them had gone, together with a number of Norwegians.

Still the uneasy lull persisted for a few days on the Western Front. Then, on May 10, 1940, the Germans struck: not at the fortified French frontier, but into Holland, Belgium and Luxembourg. A series of hammer-blows took them over the River Maas at Arnhem, over the Albert Canal and the Ijssel which the Allies had relied on to hold them up, and by May 15 they were across the River Meuse. The tiny Dutch air force was annihilated. Rotterdam was systematically bombed to ruins. On May 15 the Dutch laid down their arms.

British and French forces had advanced into Belgium on May 10 to meet the German drive. But they were no match for the German armoured columns. In quick succession the Germans took Brussels, Amiens, Antwerp; soon they were across the River Aisne and had reached the old battlefield of the Somme. By May 23 Boulogne had fallen, and on the night of May 26–27, after a valiant fight, Calais was in enemy hands. The Allied force in Flanders was cut in two by the German thrust to the sea; and with the capitulation of the Belgian army on May 28 the British determined to evacuate as many as possible of their men from Dunkirk (q.v.).

On June 4 Winston Churchill, who had succeeded Neville Chamberlain as British Premier, announced the " hard and heavy tidings." He affirmed Britain's determination to fight to the last: " We shall fight on the beaches, we shall fight on the hills. . . . We shall never surrender."

Opening on June 5, there followed what has come to be called the Battle of France. The Germans crossed the Somme and the Marne in quick succession and were soon threatening Paris. The French Government was evacuated to Tours. On June 12 the Germans were over the Seine. Allied operations were hampered by the streams of refugees who blocked the roads.

Next the Germans attacked farther south. Crossing the Rhine above Strasbourg (June 15), they took Verdun and broke through into the Champagne district. The Maginot Line, which had already been turned by an outflanking movement, was now breached.

The French Premier, Paul Reynaud, resigned on June 16 and his successor, the aged Marshal Pétain—hero of Verdun in the First World War—now sued for peace. Winston Churchill, in a last effort to retain France as an ally, offered political union with Britain. But Pétain preferred an armistice, and the remaining British troops were withdrawn from ports in the west of France.

On June 10 Italy, regarding the Allies (Britain and France) as already beaten, had declared war on them. On June 21, a day after the French had asked for an armistice with Italy, the Italian armies in the south launched an attack upon France.

But France was finished. Hitler had planned a dramatic revenge. The railway-carriage in which Marshal Foch had dictated the terms of the armistice to the German delegates in 1918 was taken from the museum in Paris where it had been lodged, and was drawn up again in the Forest of Compiègne; and there the French now signed the German terms (June 22, 1940). A separate armistice with Italy was signed at Rome two days later.

The British Isles were now besieged. This was the great test of British sea power. Germany had

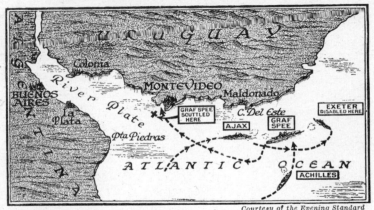

Courtesy of the Evening Standard

FIRST SEA BATTLE OF THE SECOND WORLD WAR: 1939
In December 1939 the British cruisers Achilles, Ajax and Exeter forced the German battleship Admiral Graf Spee into the neutral harbour of Montevideo, Uruguay. Rather than come out and fight, the Graf Spee's crew scuttled their badly-damaged vessel at the entrance to the River Plate.

no high seas fleet as she had had in 1914, but relied on attacks on Allied shipping by bombers, submarines and single warships. In November 1939 the Germans began to employ magnetic mines, sown from aircraft; but British scientists soon found a defence against them. (See Atlantic Battle).

In December 1939 had come the war's first sea battle, when the Graf Spee, cornered by the British cruisers Ajax, Achilles, and Exeter, was forced to put into the neutral port of Montevideo, and later scuttled herself in the approaches to the River Plate.

Britain at Bay

All through the late summer of 1940 the British lived in expectation of an attempted German invasion. A strict black-out was imposed after dark, and air-raid shelters were built. Food rationing was already in force.

British men too old or too young for military service had since May been able to join the Local Defence Volunteers (the name was soon changed to Home Guard), and the whole population stood ready. In July the German air force began the series of bombing attacks which have come to be known as the Battle of Britain (q.v.), but they never achieved control of the air ; and, as is now known, the invasion plan, timed for September 21, 1940, had to be postponed and eventually cancelled.

The autumn of 1940 saw the beginning of the mass air raids on British towns that were to continue with varying intensity throughout the war. The City of London was severely damaged by fire on December 29, 1940 (see illustration in page 3418). But despite great damage and high civilian casualties, the bombers did not cripple Britain's industry nor destroy her will to fight. And Britain was fighting back in the air; the night of August 25–26 saw the first British raid on Berlin.

The French General de Gaulle raised a legion of " Free French." The French Government, now established in Vichy, condemned him; but soon Frenchmen overseas, in the Pacific colonies, French Equatorial Africa, and the Cameroons, rallied to the Allies' cause. The Allies had appreciated the danger that the Germans might make use of captured French warships, and early in July British

THE MORNING AFTER A GERMAN FIRE-RAID : 1940

Associated Press

A particularly severe raid on London occurred on the night of December 29, 1940, when German aircraft showered incendiary bombs upon the square mile of the City. Fierce fires raged, and next day when people went to their work as usual thoroughfares such as Fore Street (above) showed blackened shells of buildings, masses of fallen debris, and pools of water left by the fire brigades.

part of Libya) fell to an Australian assault; while an armoured column went across the desert to El Agheila, the strategic point at the "bottle-neck" between Cyrenaica and Tripolitania, to cut off the retreating Italian army. Italian losses in men and material had been crippling.

A campaign in East Africa won Italian Somaliland and Eritrea for the Allies by early in April 1941. British Somaliland was reoccupied. The Italians were pursued into Abyssinia; the capital, Addis Ababa, fell on April 5, and the Emperor returned to his throne. At sea, too, the Italians had taken some hard blows; a Fleet Air Arm attack on Taranto had damaged seven Italian warships, including three battleships; and in the Battle of Cape Matapan on March 4 the Italians had seven ships sunk, while the Allies lost two aircraft.

The end of March brought a reverse on land. German troops had reinforced the Italians in Libya, and their counter-attack from El Agheila sent General Wavell's force racing back to the Egyptian frontier, leaving an isolated garrison in Tobruk.

On April 6, 1941, came Germany's invasion of Greece and Yugoslavia. General Wavell, his forces already dangerously stretched, sent help to Greece; but Yugoslavia's surrender on April 18 made the situation untenable. In response to a Greek request the British Empire forces withdrew from Greece to Crete on April 22. On May 20 the Germans invaded Crete, making great use of large numbers of parachute troops, and the forces of the Allies were taken off with heavy losses by the Royal Navy.

During the summer of 1941 Britain had also to deal with a short-lived revolt in Iraq. In June, too, when it became certain that German aircraft were using airfields in Syria, a British, Australian, and Free French force marched into Syria and the Lebanon, and after some bitter fighting took over control of these regions from the Vichy French.

units, after due warning, attacked French battleships lying in Oran and put them out of commission.

Meanwhile fighting flared up in Africa. On July 4, 1940, the Italians attacked in the Sudan. On August 4 they invaded British Somaliland. The British, enormously outnumbered and with their supplies now forced to come by way of the Cape, had to give ground for the time being, and British Somaliland was evacuated.

In September 1940 the Italians concentrated in the Libyan Desert to the west of Egypt launched their offensive. Advancing cautiously along the coast, they took Sollum on the frontier on September 13, and Sidi Barrani on September 17. Inland their patrols penetrated to points south of Mersa Matruh. But reinforcements for the heavily-outnumbered British armies were arriving from India, Australia and New Zealand.

On October 28, 1940, Mussolini invaded Greece from Albania. But the Greeks did not find the Italian soldiers so redoubtable, and before long had driven them far back across the frontier.

With the situation in Greece at least temporarily secure, General Wavell (*see* Fact-Index) launched his whirlwind counter-offensive in the Desert. By December 11, 1940, after two days' fighting, the British, Indian, and Australian forces had reached Sidi Barrani. Sollum and the frontier posts inland were taken within the next week. Tobruk and Derna fell in quick succession ; Italian prisoners were coming in by the thousand. On February 6, 1941, Benghazi, the capital of Cyrenaica (the eastern

Germany Invades Russia

The Soviet Union had all this time been building up its strength. The partition of Poland had been followed in July 1940 by the incorporation of Estonia, Latvia, and Lithuania in the U.S.S.R. About the same time, Rumania was forced to cede the greater part of Bessarabia to the Soviets. Gradually it became clear that the understanding between Russia and Germany had no firm foundation; that each side was building up for a conflict.

Flushed with her victories elsewhere, Germany took the plunge on June 22, 1941, invading Russia without warning at dawn. Italy and Rumania cast in their lot with Germany ; while Finland took the opportunity to regain the territory wrested from her a year earlier. In London, Winston Churchill made it clear that Britain would give to Russia all the aid in her power.

The Germans, Finns and Rumanians attacked all the way from Petsamo to the Black Sea. Brest Litovsk, Vilna, Kaunas and Lwow soon fell ; but the retreating Russians left behind them, in Joseph Stalin's phrase, nothing but " scorched earth." There was bitter fighting for Smolensk, on the direct path to Moscow. By the end of August the Soviet forces had evacuated the Karelian Isthmus, and Leningrad was threatened ; Smolensk had fallen ; German columns had reached the River Dnieper. October 1941 saw the opening of a two-pronged German drive on Moscow. In the Ukraine, Kiev and Kharkov had to be evacuated ; while along the shore of the Sea of Azov the Germans advanced steadily until they reached Rostov and were in control of the Crimea.

December 1941 saw a Russian counter-offensive along the whole front. Rostov was re-taken, then Mariupol. Opposite Moscow the Russians advanced into Smolensk province: farther south they crossed the upper Donetz and penetrated 30 miles into the Ukraine. Losses on both sides were enormous. Great Britain made haste to send tanks and fighter aircraft to the Russians, and the British convoys to Murmansk and Archangel suffered from German bomber and submarine attacks.

Meanwhile there had been another flare-up in the Western Desert. An Allied attack on November 18, 1941, on a line from Sollum south to Jarabub, synchronised with a break-out from Tobruk, had considerable success, but the German General Rommel's forces managed again to escape beyond El Agheila. Then once more the enemy counter-attacked, and early in 1942 the front was stabilised on a line running south from Gazala.

War Spreads to the East

Japan had been fighting in China—though war had never been declared—since 1937. Now, towards the end of 1941, relations between Japan and the Allies grew rapidly worse. In December 1941 Japan dispatched a special envoy to Washington, and under the " smoke-screen " of these talks sent a naval and air force to Hawaii. At dawn on December 7 this force attacked the U.S. base of Pearl Harbour (q.v.), causing immense damage which included the putting out of action of eight

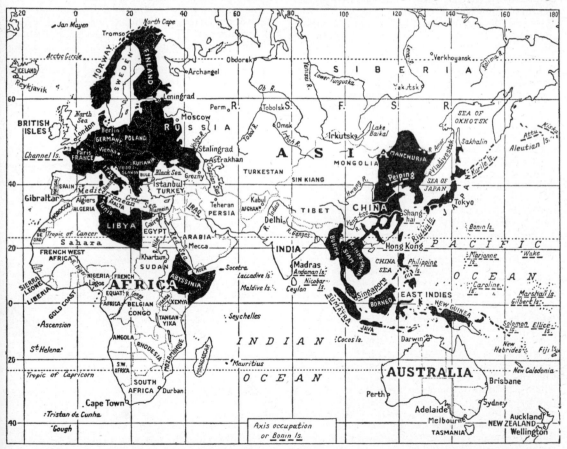

FARTHEST LIMITS OF ADVANCE OF GERMANY, ITALY AND JAPAN : 1939–45

Before the outbreak of the Second World War in September 1939 Germany had annexed Austria and Czechoslovakia, and Italy had added Abyssinia to her African possessions. Japan held parts of China and controlled Manchuria. About three years later Germany and Italy dominated territory in Europe from the Atlantic to the Volga and were threatening Egypt. The Japanese were on the threshold of India, and even menaced Australia with invasion from New Guinea.

battleships. Only after this did the Japanese Government declare war. The British Empire countries, the Netherlands and some of the Central and South American countries immediately declared war on Japan. China declared war not only on Japan but also on the Axis powers, who in their turn declared war on the U.S.A.

Japan had been preparing war for some time. Large forces had been concentrated in French Indo-China, on the pretext that this region must be defended from the British and Free French. On December 7 and 8, 1941, these forces moved into Siam, which quickly ceased to resist; and landings were made on the east coast of the Malay Peninsula. Next the Japanese landed on Luzon, in the Philippine Islands; on December 15 they attacked Hong Kong; on December 17, North Borneo.

The next week saw further landings in the Philippines, and a landing at Kuching, capital of Sarawak. The jungle-trained Japanese soldiers progressed quickly down the Malay Peninsula, while their aircraft bombed Penang and Singapore. By the end of January 1942 the whole peninsula was in Japanese hands ; on February 15 Singapore fell to the Japanese, with the loss of 70,000 prisoners. Hong Kong had been forced to surrender on Christmas Day, 1941; Japanese troops were by now fighting also in New Guinea.

At the same time as they made the above-mentioned invasions the Japanese advanced into Burma. There the British, Indian, and Burman troops constituted scarcely more than a skeleton force; and, after stubborn rearguard actions, a long, arduous retreat through the difficult country towards the Indian frontier was begun. On May 1, 1942, all British and Imperial forces were withdrawn north of the Irrawaddy river; and by May 15 they reached Assam in India.

The Japanese Hordes Sweep On

Meanwhile the Japanese had attacked Java and Sumatra. Dutch and British naval forces fought with the utmost bravery to drive off Japanese convoys in the China Sea, sustaining terrible losses; British naval strength in the East had already been crippled by the sinking at the outset of the Japanese war of the battle-cruiser Repulse and the battleship Prince of Wales. Before long the whole of the Malay Archipelago, from Sumatra as far as Bali and Timor, was under Japanese control, as well as the Philippine Islands, the Solomon Islands, New Guinea, and some islands in the Western Pacific. Towns in the north of Australia began to be raided by Japanese bombers, and Australia began to prepare for a Japanese invasion.

The war was now in truth a world war : only Sweden, Switzerland, Spain, Hungary, and some of the South American States were not involved in it. On New Year's Day of 1942, representatives of 26 Allied nations in Washington signed a declaration, proclaiming their determination to use their full resources to defeat the German-Italian-Japanese alliance, to co-operate to the full, and in no circumstances to make a separate peace with any of the enemy countries.

In Europe the British and Americans were making increasing use of their heavy bombers. British four-engined aircraft attacked by night, while American Fortresses and Liberators carried out raids by day.

On the night of May 30, 1942, a thousand British bombers attacked Cologne.

May 26 saw the opening of another round in the Western Desert campaign. Fighting was even and severe for a month, and then the British were compelled to retire to the frontier. An attempt was again made to leave a holding garrison in Tobruk, but this time the Germans made certain: an attack in great force on June 20 overwhelmed Tobruk's defenders. The retreat of British and Imperial troops did not stop at the frontier this time: the Germans pursued them to Mersa Matruh and beyond, and the retirement was halted only at El Alamein, on July 1, 1942. There successive German-Italian attacks were driven off, and the enemy, who had proclaimed themselves " at the gates of Alexandria," were destined to come no nearer to it. In August 1942 the reinforced Allied troops in the Middle East were reorganized ; General Alexander took supreme command, while General Montgomery assumed command of the 8th Army in the field. German attacks during September were successfully held.

British 8th Army at El Alamein

October saw the turning of the tide in the Desert. On the night of October 23–24, 1942, General Montgomery launched a terrific offensive against the German and Italian forces facing him at El Alamein. His well-equipped army included many new tanks, among them " flail " tanks that cleared a way through the minefields, and artillery mounted on tank chassis; and his air superiority was complete. The fighting was intense for a week, and then the enemy cracked. By November 5 the 8th Army had advanced 100 miles; a week later it had taken Tobruk; by November 20 Benghazi, and by November 23 El Agheila, had been recaptured from the Germans.

The enemy was now attacked from a new quarter. On the night of November 7–8 a great Anglo-American convoy, 500 ships with a naval escort of 350 warships, arrived off the coast of French North Africa, and American and British troops landed in French Morocco and Algiers. The French resisted them, but not strenuously, and by November 11, 1942, the Allies had occupied the ports of Casablanca and Bougie.

The Germans and Italians hastily landed in Tunisia, and for a while the Allied advance was checked. Admiral Darlan, the Vichy Vice-Premier, who had been in North Africa at the time of the landings, came over to the Allies, calling on the French fleet in Toulon to join him ; but the Germans intercepted this move. A little later, Darlan was assassinated.

The British 8th Army, after a triumphant race through Tripolitania, was held up at the fortified Mareth Line; but in March 1943 these troops blasted a way into Tunisia, and joined up with an Anglo-American force there. Tunis and Bizerta fell, and the last German and Italian resistance in North Africa ceased in mid-May.

In Russia, too, the tide had turned by now. The Soviet offensive of December 1941 had come to a standstill, and the following summer had seen another German thrust in the southern sectors. Opposite Moscow the Russians held fast; but the Germans reached Rostov in July, and advanced

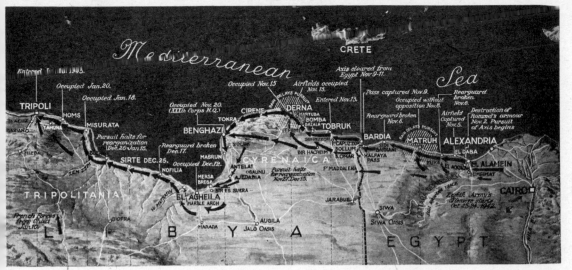

BRITISH 8TH ARMY'S ADVANCE FROM ALAMEIN TO TRIPOLI: 1942–43

After defeating the Germans and Italians at Alamein in Egypt in October-November 1942, the British 8th Army under General (later Field-Marshal) Montgomery took only 80 days to drive the disorganized remnants of the enemy's once-mighty force to Tripoli, about 1,400 miles away. No serious resistance was encountered, but rain, minefields and damaged roads hindered the advance. The dates when Allied units reached successive places are given on the map.

into the Caucasus. By September German forces were along the River Volga, and were fighting in the outskirts of the great industrial city of Stalingrad. (See map and article in page 3073).

This was to be the limit of their advance, however. November 1942 brought a colossal Soviet counter-offensive north and south of Stalingrad. Other Russian attacks followed, west of Moscow, on the middle Don, in the Caucasus. On January 1, 1943, it was announced that the long siege of Leningrad had been raised (though the blockade was not fully broken for another year). On January 31 the capture of a German field-marshal and 16 generals at Stalingrad was made known. Great tank battles were taking place all along the line, the Russians aiming all the time to encircle the German forces and to mop them up at leisure.

The Germans struck back fiercely, repulsing the Russians in the bend of the River Donetz, striking hard west and south-west of Moscow. (The Russian seat of Government had been moved east to Kuibishev.) All through that summer the ding-dong battles raged. Kharkov changed hands for the last time when the Red Army took it on August 23, and from this time on the Germans were fighting a grim but losing battle. Smolensk was retaken early in September, and by the end of the year the Russians had swept westwards beyond Kiev.

Counter-Offensive in the East

By the end of 1942 the Japanese were strongly established in the Pacific, from the Aleutian Islands in the north to the Solomon Islands and New Guinea. Most of Burma was in their hands, and they held all the Malay Archipelago. The Chinese, too, were hard pressed. But Allied strength was being built up. Australian troops in Papua had stopped the enemy's drive on Port Moresby, the town that faces Australia, and had gone over to the offensive. There was fighting in the Solomon Islands and some tremendous battles were fought out in the waters of the Western Pacific, in which the Japanese suffered huge losses of ships and aircraft.

It was clearly impossible to seize each island successively ; but it was possible, by occupying strategic islands from which Japanese communications could be attacked, to isolate the Japanese garrisons; and this was the Allied strategy.

In May 1943 the Japanese were cleared from Attu, in the Aleutians. The American reconquest of Guadalcanal in the Solomon Islands took from August 1942 to February 1943. New Georgia was cleared of the enemy in August 1943. By September the Australians had cleared the northern coastline of New Guinea. November saw the capture of Japanese positions in the Gilbert Islands; December witnessed a landing in New Britain. Early in 1944 U.S. forces obtained complete control of the Marshall Islands. Japanese strong points and convoys were continually pounded from the air and the sea, and as these thrusts approached closer to Japan itself, the communications of the Japanese troops (who had to be supplied over many miles of ocean) grew more insecure.

The Invasion of Italy

With North Africa clear of the enemy, the next step towards a foothold in Western Europe was Italy. The first blow fell on Sicily, invaded on July 10, 1943, and finally in Allied hands by August 17. On September 3 British and Canadian forces landed in the "toe" of Italy.

Italy was now in a turmoil. Mussolini had been deposed and arrested in July; and his successor, Marshal Badoglio, negotiated an armistice. But the strong German armies in Italy fought on. An Allied landing near Salerno met hard resistance; but by October Naples had fallen, and in November the Germans' "winter line" on the River Sangro was penetrated. While Badoglio's Government declared war on Germany, German parachutists rescued Mussolini from his mountain prison in the

British Official

CANADIAN TROOPS INVADE THE ITALIAN MAINLAND: 1943

On September 3, 1943, the fourth anniversary of the beginning of the Second World War between Great Britain and Germany, the Allies once again set foot on the mainland of Europe in strength, units of the British 8th Army crossing the strait of Messina from Sicily to land on the ' toe ' of Italy. Canadians went ashore at Reggio (above) in vehicles equipped with both wheels and propellers so that they could manoeuvre equally well through the water and on land.

Abruzzi, and put him at the head of a new government in the north. Throughout 1944 the struggle continued. A sea landing by the Allies in the Anzio area, south of Rome, fought off three counter-attacks; and in May a sortie by its columns linked up with a great assault from the south, where the Allies had been held at Cassino since February. Rome fell on June 4, and the enemy retreated northwards.

The ' Second Front ' in Europe

But this was not the Second Front which everyone, Russians, British and Americans alike, anticipated. Another blow, still harder and more damaging, was being prepared against Hitler's armies; and on June 6, 1944, it fell. After an enormous preliminary air bombardment, and the landing of airborne forces, a gigantic convoy carried the Anglo-American invasion armies over the Channel from England, and put them ashore on the beaches of Normandy between Cherbourg and Le Havre. The operation was completely successful, and by June 10 General Montgomery, who commanded the land forces under the supreme command of the American General Eisenhower, established his headquarters in France. (See Normandy Invasion; Mulberry Harbours).

The invasion armies once established, Allied strategy was to attract the main German forces, including the bulk of their armour, to the Caen sector on the left, held by the British and Canadians. With the Germans deeply engaged here, American mobile formations broke out west of St. Lô (July 27, 1944), quickly sealed off the Brest peninsula, and headed for Le Mans and Nantes. A German counter-attack towards Avranches led to a big German force being surrounded and destroyed. Then it was the turn of the British and Canadians to advance. By the end of August 1944 they were crossing the Seine; on September 1 the British entered Arras, and the Canadians took Dieppe, while U.S. forces captured Verdun. The Germans were now in retreat.

Hitler had still one card to play. On the night of June 13-14 the first " flying bomb " (q.v.) landed in England; it was a new and terrifying weapon for bombardment. The anti-aircraft batteries eventually mastered them, however, and before long the invasion forces in France had captured their launching sites. But September 1944 brought a second long-range weapon, the V-2 rocket (see Rocket-Bomb). Launched from Germany and Holland, these did great damage before the overrunning of the sites put a stop to them.

Meanwhile another Allied force had landed in France, in the south, and was advancing up the Rhône valley; all over France the patriot movement called the " maquis " was attacking the Germans on every opportunity. It was the citizens of Paris who freed that city on August 23; a French armoured division arrived two days later.

Brussels and Antwerp fell in September 1944. The British crossed the Albert Canal, while Canadians mopped up the Channel coast, where the Germans had left behind garrisons to deny the use of the ports to the attackers. Farther south the Americans were over the German border and advancing on Aachen. Then a great airborne force was dropped in Holland, to seize bridge-heads over the rivers Maas, Waal, and lower Rhine; in an epic stand at Arnhem (see page 2320) the British 1st Airborne Division was almost wiped out.

In December 1944 the Germans made their last effort in the west. A counter-offensive penetrated 40 miles through the Ardennes, but was contained by British and American armies and was squeezed out. Hard fighting now brought the Allies to the bank of the Rhine. Cologne was captured on March 6, 1945, and on March 7 the U.S. troops found a bridge over the Rhine at Remagen which had not been destroyed, and quickly established a bridge-head there on the farther bank.

On March 23–24 British and Canadian formations crossed the lower Rhine in strength between Rees and Wesel and fanned out, the Canadians clearing the enemy from flooded Holland, while the British advanced into Germany. At the same time the Americans advanced from Remagen. German resistance was cracking. Germany itself was over-run in a few weeks, the advancing troops finding gruesome evidence of Nazi barbarity in the concentration camps at Belsen, Dachau, and Buchenwald. An offer made through Count Bernadotte of Sweden, of a German surrender to the Western Powers alone, was refused on April 27; but on May 4 all German armies in Holland, north-west Germany, and Denmark capitulated to the Allies.

The Russians had been advancing almost continually, though against bitter opposition, since the beginning of 1944. A series of drives, now in one

INVASION OF GERMANY FROM WEST AND EAST: 1945

Keystone; British Official; S.C.R.

In the spring of 1945, while the Russians were advancing through eastern Germany, British, Canadian, United States and French armies were penetrating into the Reich from the West. 1. United States infantry and tanks about to enter Geilenkirchen, captured in a combined action by the British 2nd and American 9th Armies. 2. U.S. troops passing through anti-tank defences in the German Siegfried Line—a system of fortifications in western Germany. 3. Russians advance through Gleiwitz in German Silesia. 4. British tanks and men of the 15th Scottish Division on the road to the River Elbe. 5. Men of the Cheshire Regiment land on the east bank of the Rhine near Wesel.

sector, now in another, had taken them across the Dniester in March, and into Rumania in April. They took Vilna and crossed the Bug in July, also capturing Lublin and Brest Litovsk.

Rumania made peace with Russia on August 23, 1944, and joined the Allies in the war against Germany. Finland signed an armistice on September 10. The Red Army entered Yugoslavia on October 1, crossed into Hungary from Rumania on October 6, entered Czechoslovakia on October 18, and crossed the frontier of East Prussia on October 23, 1944. June of this year had seen a renewed offensive in Poland, where the Red Army had stopped short before Warsaw and, unaccountably, had allowed the Polish resisters to be rounded up by the Germans. On February 6, 1945, Russian troops crossed the River Oder near Breslau. On April 7 they were fighting in Vienna; by April 21 they had reached the eastern suburbs of Berlin. On April 30, 1945, Adolf Hitler shot himself in the air-raid shelter of his Berlin Chancellery.

In Italy the German armies had capitulated on May 2, 1945. Mussolini was captured by Italian partisans, and shot on April 28. On May 7, at his headquarters at Reims, General Eisenhower with representatives of the Allied powers received the unconditional surrender of Germany.

The war in the East lasted another five months. In March 1944 the Japanese in Burma had crossed the Chindwin river and attacked the British, Indian, and African forces in the area of Kohima and Imphal, near the Indian border. For a time these towns were isolated, and the situation looked menacing. But by May the position had been restored.

The spring of 1945 saw the final assault here. The Japanese were utterly out-manoeuvred and out-fought by the British 14th Army under General Slim; and with the fall of Rangoon, on May 3, after a rapid advance, the Japanese in Burma were trapped.

British units had reinforced the U.S. fleets in the Pacific, and the attacks on Japanese positions were intensified. American forces had landed on Leyte in the Philippines in October 1944, and later seized Iwojima and Okinawa, from which they directly threatened Japan. Bombers were now attacking Japanese cities constantly. August 6 saw the beginning of the end, and the opening of a new and frightful era in warfare—when the first atom bomb was dropped on Hiroshima. This single bomb killed 70,000 Japanese. A second bomb, on Nagasaki, finally broke the Japanese resolution. On August 8 the Soviet Union entered the war against Japan, in Manchuria, but encountered virtually no resistance. On August 14 the Japanese cabinet agreed to accept the Allied terms of surrender (signed on September 2).

So the Second World War ended. The armed forces of the British Empire had suffered 1,128,315 casualties, of whom 307,210 were killed; while civilian casualties in air raids on the United Kingdom were 60,585 killed, and 86,175 seriously hurt. What were the total casualties of all belligerents has not been computed, and perhaps never will be; it is certain that German and Russian losses on the Eastern Front ran into some millions.

The signing of treaties did not bring world peace. Hitler had spoken truth for once when he said: " In a modern war there are no victors; only survivors." A history of the Second World War cannot go on to tell of the many conflicts that broke out and those that threatened to break out, in the years that followed; fighting in Indo-China, in Java and Sumatra, and in Palestine; civil war in China and Greece; revolt in Malaya; and political persecution in many countries in eastern Europe.

The organization called the United Nations, replacing the League of Nations, had not much greater success in maintaining the peace, and some of its delegates were more concerned with furthering their own political theories than with setting up a satisfactory world order. Only the growth of a movement for a United Europe, and the assurance with the signing of the Atlantic Pact in 1949, that the United States would never again withdraw into isolation from world affairs, brought a ray of hope.

VICTOR AND VANQUISHED AT LÜNEBURG
At Lüneburg Heath, south of Hamburg, on May 3, 1945, German emissaries led by General-Admiral von Friedeburg (back to flagstaff) vainly tried to arrange an armistice with Field-Marshal Montgomery (wearing black beret). The following day all German forces in north-west Europe surrendered unconditionally.

Worms. To most people the word "worm" means the earthworm, but to a zoologist it includes a vast variety of creatures, belonging in fact to a number of different groups in the lowlier ranks of the animal kingdom. Of these the earthworm is one of the highest forms, for it belongs to the phylum *Annelida*, or ringed worms, its body being composed of a series of rings. (*See* Earthworm).

Several sorts of earthworm are found in Britain, including the little red " brandling " worm, which is a favourite bait of fishermen. The most interesting members of the ringed-worm group are found on the seashore. These comprise the strange " rag " and " lug " worms, which are an important item of bait with sea anglers, and certain other worms which live in wonderful tubes of sand-grains. One of these is *Terebella*, whose curious tube projects above the surface of the sand like a small tree, being crowned with diminutive " branches " and " twigs" of sand-grains.

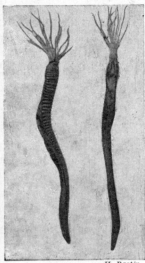

H. Bastin

SEA-WORMS

Tube-homes made of sand and projecting a little above the surface of the seashore are the abiding places of these creatures.

The *Annelid* group contains the leeches. These creatures are mostly parasites, and some of the foreign species may cause fatal injuries to Man. In Britain they live in ponds, attacking newts and frogs and small fish. A remarkable thing about a leech is the way in which it can contract itself into a small lump, or stretch out to many times its original length. At one end is a sucker with a mouth, at the other another sucker used for attaching the leech to its host. When it has had its fill of blood, it drops off and swims away. Some tropical sorts may be two feet in length.

Other sorts of worms are the *Nematodes* (round worms and thread worms), which are long, usually whitish objects, often without any distinguishable head or tail; these include some deadly parasites, responsible for diseases not only in Man and in all classes of the animal kingdom but even in plants. The tapeworms or *Cestodes* and the flatworms and flukes are also important, one of the last-named being the " liver fluke," which is a scourge of sheep farms in parts of the world. In old classifications these creatures, together with several other primitive invertebrate forms, were classed as worms into one great group, *Vermes*. Now, however, they are all in their own classes.

Wren. Like a nimble little brown mouse scurrying through the hedgerow, the wren (*Troglodytes troglodytes*) is no bird of the open country. No long flights for this four-inch long feathered mite with the stubby, cocked-up tail, but the security of quiet retirement both for itself and its nestlings. The dainty nest, domed and with the entrance at one side, is wonderfully concealed in a hedge, or in tangled ivy; sometimes it will be in a hole in an old tree.

Where song is concerned the wren is a rather astonishing performer, for its notes are sweet and melodious and loud for a bird of such small size. Common in Britain, the wren is found in Europe generally, and in Asia and North Africa. Its food consists of insects.

No relative of the common wren, the so-called golden-crested wren, more properly goldcrest (*Regulus anglorum*), is Britain's smallest bird. It is about three and a half inches in length, and has golden-streaked feathers on its head which can be erected as a crest. The willow warbler (*see* Warblers) is sometimes called willow wren.

Wren, SIR CHRISTOPHER (1632–1723). " If you seek a memorial look around." No more fitting epitaph could have been chosen for the architect of St. Paul's Cathedral, London, than this, which is inscribed in Latin inside that building.

For Sir Christopher Wren the Great Fire of London (1666) provided a wonderful opportunity. Only four months before he had submitted designs for remodelling the old cathedral of St. Paul's, but in that terrible calamity the church was almost destroyed, so that he was able to plan an entirely new building. His own favourite design was very different from that eventually adopted in 1675.

Besides St. Paul's, Wren drew up the plans for 50 City churches to replace those burnt down in the Great Fire. Among the other buildings designed by him are the Ashmolean Museum and Sheldonian Theatre at Oxford, the Chapel of Pembroke College and the Library of Trinity College, Cambridge, the Monument in London which commemorates the Great Fire, and Chelsea Hospital. In his official capacity of surveyor-general he also submitted a scheme after the Fire for the rebuilding of the entire city on an ordered plan. This scheme,

E. J. Hosking

WREN AND NESTLINGS

The beady, bright eye of the wren finds full employment searching high and low for insect food when beaks gape from the well-concealed nest in spring. This tiny bird seems to be the embodiment of good cheer and tireless activity.

which would have completely changed the face of London, was unfortunately rejected.

Wren was a man of wide attainments. For his skill in geometry he had been praised by Sir Isaac Newton (*q.v.*), and in 1660 he became Savilian professor of astronomy at Oxford. There, too, he proved himself very proficient in applied mathematics, his excellence as an architect being as outstanding from an engineering point of view as it was artistically.

The son of a clergyman, Wren was born at East Knoyle, Wiltshire, on October 20, 1632, and was educated at Westminster School, London, and Wadham College, Oxford. As an astronomer and mathematician he won the admiration of the scientific men of the day long before he was known as an architect. It is rare for a genius to win more than

National Portrait Gallery

SIR CHRISTOPHER WREN

Mathematician and scientist, and designer of St. Paul's Cathedral, London, Sir Christopher Wren is in the forefront of British architects. This portrait was painted by Sir Godfrey Kneller.

praise, but Sir Christopher (he was knighted by Charles II in 1672) gained everyone's affection. He was a simple, kindly, and pious-minded man whose life was devoted to the pursuit of learning, and his modesty was undoubted. He had a hand in the formation of the Royal Society (the premier scientific society in Britain) and was President of that body from 1680 to 1682. He died in London on February 25, 1723, and was buried in the crypt of St. Paul's cathedral.

Wrestling. Of the numerous kinds of wrestling one of the most popular is the catch-as-catch-can or Lancashire style, which is the descendant of the ancient Greek and medieval forms of the sport. It allows the wrestlers to do almost anything, including struggling on the ground and tripping. At the beginning

of a catch-as-catch-can match the two opponents face each other, and at the signal to start each tries to secure a hold that will enable him to throw his opponent and pin his shoulders to the ground.

A fall consists in forcing both of the opponent's shoulders to the ground. Some of the holds are the half-, three-quarter-, bar-, and locked half-nelsons, used simply or combined with leg holds. In recent years the " scissors " hold, which consists in getting an opponent between one's legs and then crossing the ankles and locking the feet, has come into favour. The " flying mare " is a spectacular means of throwing an opponent. It consists in seizing his wrist, turning quickly, and swinging him over one's shoulder with a sudden jerk.

In the Cumberland and Westmorland or North Country style a firm hold is taken by each contestant before the bout begins. The loser is the one who first touches the ground with any part of his person except his feet. Wrestling on the ground is forbidden in the West Country or Cornwall and Devon style, and the match is won when two shoulders and a hip or two hips and a shoulder touch the ground at the same time.

The so-called Graeco-Roman style differs from the catch-as-catch-can in forbidding tripping and catching hold of legs; also all holds must be secured above the waist. In spite of its name it bears hardly any resemblance to classic wrestling and was developed in France. The so-called " all-in " wrestling, introduced into Britain about 1930 from the United States of America, is performed in an ordinary boxing ring. It is

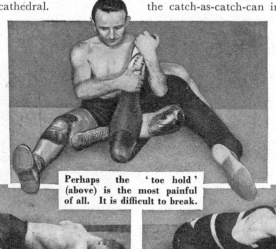

Perhaps the ' toe hold ' (above) is the most painful of all. It is difficult to break.

THREE WAYS OF OBTAINING A FALL IN WRESTLING
Another agonizing hold is the ' body scissors ' (left), though a fall may be averted for a time by bridging—holding up the shoulders from the floor by supporting the body on the head and feet. In the ' three-quarter nelson ' (right) the opponent's head is forced down and towards oneself, at the same time raising his shoulders so that he will roll over.

Some of the tricky 'Holds' and
'Locks' of an ancient sport

The rear man has secured the hold known as the 'full nelson,' which will enable him to force his opponent to the ground.

The man swung off his feet is gripped in a 'half nelson.'

The 'headlock' (right) is painful and difficult to counter.

regulated by a minimum of rules, and can scarcely be classed as a sport, as it is brutal and sordid.

In Ireland the national style of wrestling is the " collar and elbow " method. In this the two opponents seize each other with one hand on the collar and the other on the elbow, and neither must let go his hold until a fall has been gained.

Jujitsu, judo, or ju-jutsu, is a Japanese style of self-defence. In some respects jujitsu resembles what is generally known as wrestling, but in it mere strength is easily countered by the scientific use of leverage and balance and by an intimate knowledge of anatomy. (*See* Jujitsu).

Wright, WILBUR (1867–1912) and ORVILLE (1871–1948). Probably no men in history ever enjoyed a greater thrill than these two brothers experienced when on December 17, 1903, they made the first successful man-carrying aeroplane flights. Orville Wright, who was born at Dayton, Ohio, on August 19, 1871, made the first flight, covering about 120 feet in 12 seconds. Later that day Wilbur, who was born at Millville, Indiana, on April 16, 1867, flew 852 feet in 59 seconds, then crashed and wrecked the machine ; but the brothers returned to the bicycle shop they owned at Dayton, Ohio, quite happy. For this was the first occasion on which a man had been carried from the ground in an aeroplane flying under its own power. (*See* illustration in page 45).

A biplane glider, with a petrol engine fitted to it, was the first aeroplane. For years the Wrights had followed the experiments of Lilienthal, Langley, Chanute, and other pioneers of flight. They studied the soaring of birds, and the action of larger and larger box-kites. Then they built gliders, much like long box-kites with two wings and a rudder to guide the machine. In 1900 and for two years after they practised gliding at Kitty Hawk in North Carolina, a district which provided favourable winds, and sandy hills for a jumping-off place. Repeated glider flights showed that accepted formulae used in the design of aircraft were wrong, and in the winter of 1901–02 they built a wind tunnel to measure air currents for themselves. In this tunnel, 16 inches square and 6 feet long, they observed the air's action against 200 miniature wings of varying proportions and set at a number of angles. They discovered how to maintain lateral (sidewise) stability by warping or twisting the wings. Then they determined to see if such a machine could be propelled by a motor, and built a four-cylinder petrol motor of 12 horse-power.

In September 1903 the brothers went to Kitty Hawk to assemble a new glider, larger than any previous one. The wings were 40 feet 4½ inches in span and 6½ feet wide. They built a 60-foot monorail track to enable them to start with the least possible friction. When all was ready they tossed a coin to see who should fly first. Wilbur won, but failed; and two days were spent repairing the damage. Then Orville made his historic flight. From 1903 to 1908 the Wrights improved their designs, working mostly in secret. Failing to arouse interest in their invention among government officials in the United States, they went abroad to exploit their great invention. In 1908 Wilbur toured Europe, demonstrating their machine, and sold the French rights for about £20,000.

At Dayton, Ohio, they established an aircraft factory, which had become highly successful by the time Wilbur died on May 30, 1912. Orville, who continued to manage the business, lived until January 30, 1948. (*See* Aeroplane).

Wycliffe, JOHN (about 1320–84). Almost six centuries ago an English priest stood on trial in London before the Archbishop of Canterbury and the Bishop of London. A tall figure, clad in a simple black gown, pale and thin, with keen, sharply cut features that bore the marks of earnest study and of self-denial, he faced his accusers resolutely. This clergyman was John Wycliffe (pron. wik'-lif), Oxford scholar and teacher, called to account for criticizing the Church.

At that time the Pope was claiming the right to impose taxes and to make appointments to Church offices without interference from the king. John Wycliffe protested against this and against the evil and worldly lives of the clergy. Moreover, he declared that every man was responsible directly to God, and that the Bible, not the Church, was the supreme authority.

It might have gone hard with this defiant clergyman, whom his enemies called "John Wicked-believe," had not the people, who had learned to love him for his kindness and the holiness of his life, come to his rescue. A crowd of Londoners caused such a commotion that Wycliffe was allowed to go, with a warning to be careful what he preached.

Wycliffe was supported by John of Gaunt, the Duke of Lancaster (who was one of the most influential men in England) and by other nobles, so long as he denounced rich Churchmen. So he continued to preach as fearlessly as ever, though the Pope himself issued Bulls or Papal decrees denouncing him, and his teachings were condemned at the University of Oxford. He sent out "poor priests"— Lollards, as they, like all his followers, came to be called— who travelled throughout the country calling men back to faith in the simple gospel of Christ (*see* illustration in page 425). The name Lollard is derived from the Dutch *lollen*, to sing in an undertone, and was first applied to the members of an association founded in Antwerp *c.* 1300, who sang thus and were suspected of heresy.

Wycliffe lost the support of the nobles after the Peasants' Revolt in 1381. His teachings that overlordship and property were held only by God's grace and were forfeited if the holders fell into mortal sin had contributed not a little to that movement. In order that the people themselves might be able to read and understand the Bible, his followers made the first full translation of it into English (1382). To this important work Wycliffe's name was attached, although his direct part is a matter of uncertainty. Not only did this translation have a tremendous influence on people, but it set the standard of their language and earned for Wycliffe the title "father of English prose."

A native of Hipswell near Richmond, Yorkshire, Wycliffe went to Balliol College, Oxford, of which he became Master *c.* 1360. Later he was parish priest at Fillingham, Wiltshire, and in 1374 at Lutterworth, Leicestershire. Fearless in his efforts to effect religious reform in England, he has been called the "Morning Star of the Reformation." Although he failed to bring about any notable change in the Church, his teaching had a powerful influence on John Huss, the Bohemian reformer, and through him on Martin Luther. Wycliffe died on December 31, 1384. (*See* Luther, Martin ; Reformation).

Wyoming.
A mid-western State of the United States, with an area of 97,914 square miles, Wyoming is bounded on the north by Montana, on the east by South Dakota and Nebraska, on the south by Colorado and Utah, on the west by Utah and Idaho. It is traversed by branches of the Rocky Mountains, the highest point being Fremont Peak (13,790 feet). But not all of the State is mountainous : in the east there is a vast plain, and wide valleys lie between the mountain ranges. The North Platte, Big Horn, Powder and Green rivers are the longest, but none of them is navigable. In the north-west of Wyoming is the Yellowstone National Park, with its sanctuary for wild animals, its geysers, petrified forests and Grand Canyon.

The average annual rainfall is about 14 inches, and agriculture has to be assisted by irrigation. The chief crops include lucerne, sugar-beet, beans, maize, potatoes, wheat and oats. The breeding of sheep and cattle is an important industry, but is slowly being displaced by dairy farming. The mineral wealth includes coal, oil, natural gas, iron, sodium salts and limestone. The State is sparsely populated and contains few towns of any importance. The capital is Cheyenne (population 22,000). Casper, with 18,000 inhabitants, is the next largest. The population of the State of Wyoming is 251,000.

Top, British Museum, Egerton MS. 617

WYCLIFFE AND HIS BIBLE
The Reformation owed more to John Wycliffe, depicted in the lower illustration after the engraving by R. Houston, than is generally realized. To enable the people to read and study the Bible he and his followers in 1382 made the earliest full translation of it into English ; a portion of a page from the first version is seen above.

X

Xavier, FRANCIS (1506-52). In the long and glorious annals of Christian missions there is perhaps no more inspiring page than that which tells of the labours of St. Francis Xavier (pron. ză'-viä), the "Apostle of the Indies." The hardships he underwent in 11 years of travel through India, the East Indies and Japan, and the results he achieved entitle him to be regarded as one of the greatest Christian missionaries.

He was born at Xavier in Navarre, France, on April 7, 1506, and was educated at the University of Paris, where after a few years he became a lecturer in philosophy. He at first scorned but later succumbed to the influence of Ignatius Loyola, with whom he was associated in the founding of the Society of Jesus in 1534. (*See* Loyola, Ignatius de).

Ordained priest in 1537, Francis Xavier studied medicine, tended the sick in hospitals, and preached wherever men would listen to him. In 1541 he began the missionary career to which he was to devote the remaining years of his life. He was sent to preach the Gospel in India.

Landing at Goa, on the west coast of India, he laboured there for several months, then began a series of remarkable journeys through India, the scattered islands along the coast, Malacca, and the Moluccas or Spice Islands far to the east. Then he went to Japan, where he remained more than two years, penetrating into all parts, and winning a number of converts. His next plans were for the conversion of China, but he fell ill of fever on the way and died on the island of Sancien near Macao, China, on December 2, 1552. He was canonized in 1622 by Pope Gregory XV.

Xenon. This, the rarest of the inert gases of the atmosphere, is present in air to the extent of one part by volume in 10 million. The inert gases helium, neon, argon, krypton and xenon form Group O in the Periodic Table (*see* page 768). The last member of the group, radon, does not occur in the air but is formed in radio-active changes. (*See* Radium).

Xenon is obtained by fractionating (fractional distillation) liquid air. It is a colourless, odourless gas five times as dense as nitrogen. It condenses to a liquid at $-109°$ C., and freezes to a solid at $-112°$ C. Like the other inert gases it is unreactive, and forms no chemical compounds. Xenon, so called from the Greek *xenos*, "strange," is element No. 54, and has an atomic weight of 131·3. The chemical symbol is Xe. The gas is not likely to be used commercially, as it is so rare. (Pron. zen'-on).

Xenophon (*c.* 430–355 B.C.). To anyone who has studied Greek, mention of the name Xenophon (pron. zen'-o-fon) calls to mind the Anabasis (Greek, *anabasis*, going up), of which he is the author. Therein one may read of the long, hazardous retreat of 10,000 Greeks who had entered the service of the Persian Prince Cyrus the Younger against Artaxerxes, King of Persia, and of the cry, "Thalassa! Thalassa!" (The sea! The sea!) with which the weary and sadly reduced band greeted the waters of Bosporus after five months' marching along the road home. This retreat was mainly directed by Xenophon, who assumed command of the Greek contingent after the death of Cyrus at the battle of Cunaxa (401 B.C.).

The son of an aristocratic Athenian family, Xenophon was a pupil of Socrates. After his return to Athens in 399 from the Persian campaign he found his old teacher condemned to death for introducing new divinities in place of those recognized by the State, and Xenophon wrote the Memorabilia in vindication of the philosopher.

Xenophon was so enraged by the Athenians' treatment of Socrates that he entered the service of the Spartans and fought against his fellow-citizens at the battle of Coroneia in 394, for which treasonable act he was banished from Athens. For some years he lived on an estate given him by the Spartans in Elis, where he wrote, and cultivated the land. After the Anabasis, Xenophon's chief work is Hellenica, a history of Greece from 411 B.C. (when the history of Thucydides ended) to 362 B.C. He died in 355 B.C., probably in Corinth.

Bruckmann

ST. FRANCIS XAVIER PREACHING

In 1541 St. Francis Xavier began his missionary career in India. This portrait, part of a huge canvas by the Flemish painter Rubens (1577-1640), shows the saint preaching to the natives on one of his many journeys in the east. He was canonized by Pope Gregory XV in 1622.

SEEING *through* SOLIDS *with* X-RAYS

Among the most remarkable scientific discoveries to date is that of the wonderful X-rays that pass through most solids as light passes through glass. Here we see how they are generated and used.

X-Rays. Near the end of the 19th century some leading men of science had begun to think that all the really important discoveries in physics had been made. But the discoveries that followed in the next few years upset almost every idea then held about the constitution of matter and the nature of electricity. The vacuum tube, invented by Heinrich Geissler (1814–79) and perfected by Sir William Crookes (1832–1919), was the centre of the whole disturbance.

The German physicist Röntgen announced in 1895 the discovery of the invisible rays that bear his name.

The Crookes tube was a glass tube from which air had been exhausted; it had two metal electrodes, held by wire connexions fused through the glass at opposite ends of the tube. It was later superseded by improved forms of cathode ray tube. When the air is exhausted from a Crookes tube gradually while an electric current is passed through, beautiful luminous phenomena, arranged in definite order with reference to certain dark spaces or bands, appear in the tube one after the other as the exhaustion proceeds. Just before exhaustion of the air reaches a point at which the tube resists completely the passage of the electric current, the glow within becomes extinguished as the dark space enlarges, and the walls of the tube begin to shine with a weird green phosphorescence.

In the tube walled with light, something is travelling like rays from the cathode or negative plate to the anode or positive plate at the opposite end of the tube. If a piece of mica coated with phosphorescent powder be placed edgeways in the path of the supposed rays it glows brightly, and a suitable screen placed in the path of these " rays " casts a shadow on the bright end-wall of the tube. So far these seemed much like rays of light, and they were called " cathode rays " because they appeared to stream out from the cathode.

One early investigator found that cathode rays, unlike light rays but like an electric current, could be bent out of their straight path by a magnet. Others (Heinrich Hertz and his pupil P. E. A. von Lénard) discovered that the new rays, again unlike light, could pass through gold or aluminium foil. At length Sir William Crookes suggested that the cathode rays consisted of something the discovery of which Faraday had long ago foreshadowed— matter in a fourth state, neither solid, liquid, nor gaseous, but radiant " matter."

Later Sir J. J. Thomson and others showed that Crookes's " radiant matter " consisted of streams of fine particles, and that these particles were the " atoms " of electricity, or, as they are now called, " electrons."

For what is known and conjectured regarding electrons *see* the articles on Atom; Electron; Electricity ; Physics ; Radiation ; Radium. The practical importance of the rays arises out of the next discovery in regard to them.

In 1895 Professor Wilhelm Röntgen (1845–1923) of Munich, while experimenting with a Crookes tube, noticed that some crystals of a barium salt which were near glowed brilliantly. Knowing that cathode rays themselves could not pass through the glass to produce this effect, he immediately suspected that some other kind of ray was present. He exposed photographic plates near the tube and found they became fogged. Plates wrapped

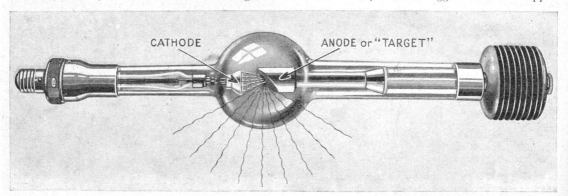

CATHODE   ANODE or "TARGET"

DETAILS OF THE MODERN HIGH-POWER X-RAY TUBE

The cup-shaped cathode focuses a stream of electrons, called the cathode rays, against the tungsten anode, or 'target.' This causes the target to produce the penetrating X-rays. A 'Coolidge' tube of this kind is made with the highest possible vacuum, and the electrons have to be supplied by a filament behind the cathode and heated by an independent low-voltage current. The potential difference between cathode and anode often exceeds 100,000 volts.

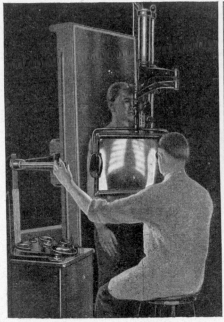

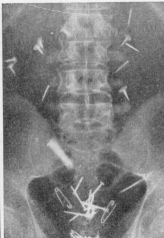

REVEALING X-RAYS

Left, penetrating the man's body from behind, X-rays throw shadows of bones and organs on to a screen. Above, the shadow picture (radiograph) reveals safety pins, nails and tacks swallowed by a child.

substances were diffracted (*see* Spectroscope). This was acceptable proof that X-rays were radiant energy very similar to light, and not streams of electrons like cathode rays. These diffracted rays can be focused on a photographic plate, where they produce patterns as characteristic of the crystalline substances used as are the patterns furnished by the spectroscope. These patterns depend upon the atomic structure of the substance, and by carefully measuring and analysing them, scientists have been able to learn much about atomic arrangement. This method of analysing the structure of various atoms is called "X-ray spectroscopy." The valuable property of the rays here is their extremely short wave-length.

Other practical uses of X-rays turn upon their penetrating power, which is shared to a lesser degree by the longer ultra-violet rays and to a greater degree by the shorter cosmic rays. This penetrating power of X-rays can be demonstrated by the same phenomenon that led Röntgen to discover them. Certain chemicals have the quality of *fluorescing*, or glowing, when X-rays strike them. If a plate covered with zinc sulphide, for instance, is held on one side of a human hand, and an X-ray tube is operating on the other side, the bones of the hand will be outlined on the plate as shadows. Such a device is known as a *fluoroscope*. The X-rays do not penetrate the denser bone structure as intensely as they do the flesh, and consequently the bones show up as shadows on the plate. Another way to demonstrate this penetrating power is the other method used by Röntgen—letting the X-rays fall on a photographic plate after passing through the object. These plates are sensitive to X-rays as well as to visible light, and when developed disclose a shadow picture, called a *radiograph*.

The density of a substance determines the depth to which X-rays will penetrate it. The rays pass readily through organic tissues such as flesh, the soft green tissue of plants, and smooth-grained wood, because the molecules and atoms forming them are packed loosely, making it easy for the short waves of the X-rays to pass *between* the particles. Other substances such as bone, teeth, and knots of wood have a closer structure and the rays are partially blocked. Substances like rock and metal offer still greater resistance. Some materials, like lead, are so dense, the molecules being so closely packed, that the X-rays pass through them only if the metals are in thin sheets. Consequently metals such as these are used as safety shields to block the passage of X-rays.

X-radiation consists of waves of widely differing properties. Long or so-called " soft " X-rays do not penetrate things as easily as the shorter or " hard " rays. The faster the speed of the electrons

in black paper were affected just as if no paper were round them. Astonished by this result, Röntgen decided that here was an invisible ray, hitherto unknown, differing in important respects both from the cathode ray which produced it, and from light. He named this newly-discovered form of radiation " X-rays "—the " rays of an unknown nature."

The story of Röntgen's amazing discovery was spread over the world immediately by telegraph and cable. Its medical value was at once recognized when experiments showed that these rays would penetrate flesh; and the use of X-rays in this and other fields developed amazingly, as will be told later. Meanwhile, scientists attempted to learn what these mysterious rays might be; but it was not until 1912, when investigators obtained X-ray spectra by using crystals, as explained in the story of the Spectroscope, that scientists considered the problem as at all settled. But meanwhile discoveries in other fields were suggesting the answer, based on the nature of cathode rays—which consist of streams of millions of electrons, travelling to the anode at enormous speeds. When these streams of electrified particles struck the atoms of the target, some of the target's atoms were disrupted momentarily, and electrons were jarred loose. These electrons probably fell back again, while the electronic disturbance caused radiation similar to light. The fact that X-rays were invisible to the eye could be explained by saying that their wavelength was much shorter, lying between the wave-lengths of ultra-violet and gamma rays (*see* Radiation). This supposition was strengthened by the fact that X-rays were more like light waves than cathode rays, in that the X-rays could not be deflected by magnetic fields.

The problem was considered settled in 1912, at least in broad outline, by the work of such scientists as the Braggs, von Laue, and Moseley. They found that X-rays falling upon crystalline fired from the cathode of the tube the more powerful are the X-rays produced.

The chief use of these wonderful X-rays is to enable physicians, surgeons, and dentists to examine the inside of the body in diagnosing disease. A doctor, wishing to know, for example, the exact facts about the digestive condition of a patient, gives him a meal of a harmless bismuth or barium compound. This inert material is so dense that it shows clearly on both the fluoroscope and the radiograph. The shape and position of the stomach and intestines can plainly be seen as this opaque meal moves through the body. By a series of pictures, taken at intervals, the passage of food and the muscular processes may be watched and the doctor can detect any abnormality of the organs or their functions. X-rays also help surgeons, especially when the operation is a case of bone injury, or involves removal of bullets.

Dentists take X-ray pictures to determine the condition of teeth and jaws. They help to find abscesses and other infections, to decide exactly which teeth should be extracted or treated, and often provide information long before the tooth itself gives warning pains. By long experience radiologists are able to detect abnormalities in deeply-seated organs merely by the slight differences in the shadows made by them.

For some time after the discovery of X-rays it was not fully understood that they have profound and marked effect on living tissues. On the one hand, they have been used to destroy cancer tissue and to treat other diseased conditions; on the other hand, when applied too long or too intensely they have caused great damage. In the early days, many of those who experimented with X-rays were overtaken, months and even years later, by the effects of terrible " burns," usually in the form of skin cancers on hands, arms, and face. Today, fortunately, it is possible to minimize and in most cases entirely avoid these dangers, both by surrounding the X-ray apparatus with metal shields and by regulating the exposure.

Outside medicine and surgery the field for utilizing X-rays is continually expanding. Especially is this true in industry, where they are used to inspect the internal quality of products. For instance, manufacturers of wireless valves examine the assembled valves to determine if the delicate hidden parts are in correct position and the lead-in wires properly sealed. X-rays will reveal inner cracks, air-holes, cavities, and strains in castings, and are being used to improve foundry practice. X-ray testing of castings for aeroplane and motor-car engines is now general, not only for safety but to avoid machining and grinding a casting that might be found to have a flaw at some later operation. Radiographic tests are now employed to examine pneumatic tires for imperfect binding between the tread and the cords. X-rays will also show up foreign metallic bodies embedded in reclaimed rubber. Similar methods are used on other rubber products to examine them for faulty fabrication. In electrical apparatus, X-rays will show broken conductors inside insulated wires, and bring to light air bubbles or foreign metal bodies that might cause failure in operation at high voltages. In short, the X-rays provide the only means of definite inspection short of actual destruction or actual use of the material, etc.

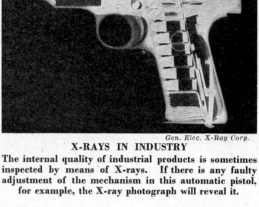

Gen. Elec. X-Ray Corp.

X-RAYS IN INDUSTRY

The internal quality of industrial products is sometimes inspected by means of X-rays. If there is any faulty adjustment of the mechanism in this automatic pistol, for example, the X-ray photograph will reveal it.

Coal samples can be examined for the presence of slate and other impurities. In the field of art, the under layers of old paintings can be inspected to determine authenticity, and detect retouching or alterations. Sculpture, inlays, and furniture offered to collectors and museums as antiques, can often be classified by this method, and many frauds that formerly deceived the best experts have been uncovered. Police and customs inspectors may use X-rays for searching out stolen or contraband articles concealed in luggage or in bales of apparently innocent merchandise.

Progress in the technique of using X-rays has been rapid. In the early days the experimenters could obtain high-voltage electrical currents only by the old-time induction coil (*q.v.*), and these voltages were comparatively low by modern standards. In those early days they had to depend on batteries for the current. Today we have the limitless power furnished by the electric mains, and make it adaptable for X-ray generation by using transformers (*q.v.*) capable of stepping-up current to enormous voltages.

The type of generating tube used today is based on one introduced by Dr. W. D. Coolidge (born 1873), of Schenectady, U.S.A. A diagram is printed in page 3056; also illustrations of the effects produced when X-rays are employed for analysis. (Coolidge also invented and applied ductile tungsten for use as electric lamp filaments.)

The bombardment of high-velocity electrons released by such high potentials has a profound effect upon many substances, often disrupting their structure and changing their form. It converts some solids to gases or fine powders, sometimes changing their colour, and makes some colourless crystals fluoresce even after the bombardment by the X-rays has ceased.

Specially small X-ray sets are made for dentists. This valve —about two inches long—was manufactured for such a unit.

Y

Yak. No large animal habitually lives at such high altitudes as the yak (*Bos grunniens*), a member of the ox family. Found in a wild state on the high plateaux of Tibet and in parts of China, the animal is characterized by long hair which grows from the legs, tail and underparts and often reaches the ground. The colour of the wild species is blackish or dark brown. Both the male and female have long horns, and a bull may stand nearly six feet high at the shoulder and weigh more than 1,000 lb.

This beast has been domesticated for centuries in Tibet, where some of the breeds are brown and white or wholly white. Besides being used as a beast of burden it provides milk (which makes excellent butter) and meat; the long hair is spun into ropes and woven into cloth; and the hides are used as tent coverings. The long hairs from the tip of the tail are made into tassels and fly-whisks.

Yangtze, RIVER. "Ta-kiang" (great river) is the name which the Chinese usually give to this their longest and most important waterway. The name "Yangtze-kiang" (which means Yangtze river) is used by them only for the lower part; other portions have different names.

Rising in the Kuenlun Mountains of Tibet and flowing into the Yellow Sea, the river traverses the central regions of China from west to east for a distance of some 3,400 miles, forming with numerous canals and tributaries a wonderful system of communication unparalleled in the world. Its basin, which has an area of about 650,000 square miles, includes the greater part of China proper.

From Shanghai, the commercial outlet for the whole of the basin, 12 miles south of the mouth, ocean-going vessels can travel as far as Hankow, a port about 620 miles inland. As the Yangtze is 30 to 40 miles wide at its mouth, land is not visible from shipping in the middle of the waterway. Above Hankow the volume of water diminishes considerably, but by changing to a river steamer one may go 500 miles farther inland, through a fertile, lake-studded country. In flood time the lakes on the course of the Yangtze take much of its surplus water, so that, unlike the Hwang-ho (*q.v.*), it rarely causes widespread destruction. Occasionally, however, the Yangtze overflows; the floods of 1931 were particularly disastrous.

Above Ichang steam navigation ceases, for there are the Yangtze gorges and rapids. This is by far the most beautiful part of the river, if we except its upper course in Tibet. In its lower course the flow is not so rapid, and carries along a vast amount of silt, which it deposits in the Yellow Sea at a rate which has been estimated at about 6,000,000,000 cubic feet a year.

Yankee. When the Red Indians first tried to pronounce the French word *Anglais*, meaning "English," the nearest they could get to it was "Yenghees." This is one explanation of the origin of the name Yankee, which was used by the British soldiers in derision of the untrained North American troops who fought beside them in the Seven Years' War (1756–63). There is a theory that a Dutch nickname *Yankey* is the source, because as early as 1683 it was used by Dutch sailors. *Yankey* may have been derived from *Janke*, a diminutive of the Dutch name *Jan* (John).

Applied at first only to New Englanders, the term Yankee was given by the Confederates (Southerners) in the American Civil War (1861–65) to all Northerners. Since that time the name has been popularly but erroneously given to all citizens of the United States.

"Yankee Doodle," a national American air, dates from about the middle of the 18th century, and its origin is obscure.

Yeast. This mysterious substance, which seems to grow and spread out of nothing, is really a mass of microscopic fungus plants. Each plant is a single, simple cell, which produces new cells by budding. Usually the cells thus produced cling

Fox

YAK FROM TIBET AND ITS BABY CALF
Both bull and cow yaks have long horns, and in the wild state are usually black or dark brown. The domesticated species is valuable to the Tibetans, for these ox-like animals with long hair provide them with food and clothing and also serve as beasts of burden.

together in short chains. Of the various kinds of yeast-plants those used by bakers and brewers are the best known.

The usefulness of these tiny yeast plants consists in their ability to produce fermentation in starch and sugar solutions. They do this in the process of extracting oxygen (indispensable to their existence) from almost any substance which contains sugar. The chief products of this fermentation are alcohol and carbon dioxide gas. The alcohol-making properties are employed in brewing and the manufacture of wines, and the gas-making properties in making bread. The carbon dioxide bubbles produced by the yeast makes the bread light, since the gas produces innumerable little " pockets " in the baking dough. The alcohol which is formed in the process evaporates.

In brewing, the solution of malt—known as the " wort "—is fermented with yeast, about one

Natural History Museum

A FINE OLD BRITISH YEW

Although it bears no cones the yew is classed with the *Coniferae*, and the leaves (which are poisonous to livestock) resemble those of the firs. The small fruit is red when ripe. Native to Britain, it is a slow-growing and long-lived tree. Some specimens are estimated to be over 1,000 years old. The wood, strong and elastic, was formerly used in the making of bows and is still valued for cabinet-making.

pound of yeast being added to the barrel of wort. The yeast multiplies until a foaming creamy " head " four feet high covers the surface of the liquor in the fermenting vessel. When this head thickens and settles down, the surplus yeast is skimmed off and kept in cold storage for sale or for future use. In doing its work the yeast gives off much energy in the form of heat, so that the wort has to be cooled by circulating water through copper pipes suspended in the solution. The chemical changes that yeast produces are due to substances called *invertase* and *zymase*, secreted by the yeast plants. (*See* Fermentation).

If we leave any moist substance containing sugar or starch open to the air, yeast spores are almost certain to fall upon it and start fermentation. But some of these " wild " yeasts may create, along

with alcohol and carbon dioxide, other substances, which have unpleasant tastes and odours. So bakers and brewers use pure standard cultures of yeast, which are free from these characters.

In favourable circumstances the yeast plant grows very rapidly, the full-size cell putting out a bud; when this bud reaches maturity, it in turn buds, and so on. But in conditions unfavourable for growth, the yeast cell forms four spores (*see* Seeds and Spores) within itself, and then shrivels. The cell wall breaks, and the spores are carried hither and thither by the winds, and transported also on the bodies of insects and other animals. This accounts for the yeast fermentation of sugar or starch containing substances left in the open. Yeast belongs to the class of fungi known as *Ascomycetes*. (*See* Fungi).

Yew. Before firearms had taken the place of bows and arrows, the strong and elastic wood of the evergreen yew tree was in great demand in England for the making of bows. Probably this is one of the reasons why yews are found in so many English churchyards. They were planted to ensure a good supply of bow-staves as well as to provide the greenery used at Easter and other festivals. Later, the practice arose of training and clipping yew and other trees into pyramids, or into complicated geometrical shapes, and into figures bearing a resemblance to beasts and birds, a form of gardening known as topiary.

Native to Great Britain, the yew (*Taxus baccata*) is a very slow-growing and very long-lived tree. Some of the oldest specimens in Britain are about 30 feet in circumference and estimated to be over 1,000 years old. Yew wood is highly valued for cabinet-making, being close-grained, of a reddish colour, and capable of taking a brilliant polish.

The yew is a member of the family *Taxaceae* of the coniferous group, but it has no cones. The small fruit is red and was long believed to be poisonous, but the fleshy part is not so; the seed, however, is poisonous. The leaves are flat, about half an inch long, yellowish-green on the under side, and are poisonous to livestock.

Yogi. There are innumerable religious sects in India, and one of them consists of Hindu ascetics known as yogis. *Yoga* is a Sanskrit (ancient language of India) word meaning " effort," and the yogis are so called because by the suppression of all worldly desires and the development of intense self-concentration they strive after union with God. The practice of the sect is, by means of fasting, concentration, and penances, to reach a state of ecstasy in which the soul is thought to be united with the divine spirit. Yogis claim to have special knowledge of the secrets of Nature, and influence over their fellow creatures beyond that of most men.

Yokohama.

(Pron. yō-ko-hah'-ma). The principal seaport of Japan, Yokohama is on the east coast of Honshu Island, on Tokyo Bay, about 15 miles from Tokyo, with which it is connected by the oldest railway line in the country. Much of the city was destroyed by bombing raids carried out by the United States Air Force during the Second World War (1939–45), but the massive breakwaters protecting the spacious harbour remain. Silk was one of the chief articles of export; others were coal, copper and tea. The leading industries included shipbuilding, oil refining, and the manufacture of food-stuffs, bicycles, motor-cars and general electric equipment.

In 1859 the fishing village of Yokohama was opened by the Japanese Government to foreign trade, and merchants of several nations settled there in large numbers. Thenceforward the city grew rapidly, and numerous fine buildings were constructed in the town itself and in the foreign residential settlement on the " Bluff," a wooded hill overlooking Tokyo Bay. In 1923 almost the whole city was destroyed either in an earthquake or in the fire that raged after it. When the Japanese rebuilt the port they laid out wide avenues of fire-breaks and erected fire-proof buildings; but in 1945 vast areas were bombed into ruins. At the outbreak of the Second World War the population of Yokohama was 968,000. It was Japan's fifth largest city, with an area of about 70 square miles.

York.

The city of York, county town of Yorkshire, stands on the Ouse at the junction of the county's three Ridings (see Yorkshire). It is one of the few cities in England of which the old walls still stand; four of the original gates or "bars," as they are called, also remain.

The most noble building in York is the Minster, or cathedral church of St. Peter, which was begun in 1230. It is especially noted for its stained glass and its chapter house, and includes examples of three styles of architecture (see illustration, page 725). In the north-west tower is the bell known as Great Peter. The castle, of which the oldest part is Norman, and St. Mary's Abbey, dating from the 11th century, are two of York's other ancient buildings.

The city is an important railway centre, and its industries include chocolate-making and flour-milling. York was an early British settlement, and as Eboracum was an important place under the Romans. The Archbishop of York bears the title of Primate of England. The population is 106,000.

Yorkshire.

A county of moors and dales, Yorkshire is the largest in the United Kingdom—6,077 square miles in area. It is the only county in which the ancient division of the riding (Scandinavian *thriding*, a third) still exists, being split up into East Riding, North Riding, and West Riding. It is bounded on the north by Durham, on the east by the North Sea, on the south by Nottinghamshire and Derbyshire, on the west by Lancashire and Westmorland.

To the west is the Pennine Chain, the highest point being Mickle Fell (2,591 feet). In the north-east is the moorland district of Cleveland and the Hambleton Hills. In the east are the chalky Yorkshire Wolds. Eastward from the Pennines run such well-known and beautiful dales as Swaledale, Airedale, Wensleydale, Nidderdale and Wharfedale. The coastline is generally high and rocky from the Tees southward to Flamborough Head, but thence to Spurn Point it is low. The county is mainly drained by the Ouse and its tributaries. Other rivers include the Tees, Ribble, Derwent and Esk.

The North and East Ridings are largely agricultural. Sheep farming and horse breeding are the leading activities; oats, barley and wheat are principal crops. Yorkshire ham has long been noted, as has Wensleydale cheese. Coal is the most important mineral product, and most of the south-west is highly industrialised, with such manufacturing centres as Sheffield (*q.v.*), Leeds (*q.v.*), Barnsley, Rotherham and Dewsbury. Iron ore, as well as coal, is worked in Cleveland, with Middlesbrough the centre of the industry and its seaport. Bradford and Huddersfield are engaged in the manufacture of woollen goods, which is the main industry of a large part of the West Riding.

York (*q.v.*), the county town, and Ripon (*q.v.*) are cathedral cities, as is Bradford. Popular coastal holiday resorts include Scarborough, Whitby, Filey, and Bridlington. Harrogate is an inland spa. Doncaster is famed for its railway works and racecourse. Northallerton, Wakefield and Beverley are the capitals of the North, West and East Ridings respectively. Among several abbey ruins are those of Fountains, Jervaulx, Rivaulx, Bolton, Whitby and Byland. The population of Yorkshire is 4,305,000.

B. C. Clayton

RUINS OF FOUNTAINS ABBEY IN YORKSHIRE
In the West Riding of Yorkshire, three miles from Ripon, are the ruins of Fountains Abbey, which was begun about 1132 and completed 200 years later. They are considered to be the finest and most complete of those of the ruined abbeys in England. The architectural styles vary from the Norman to the Perpendicular.

Young, THOMAS (1773–1829). This remarkable man, who won renown by his researches into optics and became famous as an Egyptologist, showed early promise of his genius. Young was born at Milverton, Somerset, on June 13, 1773; by the age of two he could read well, and was sent to school at six years. He made the acquaintance of a land surveyor, with whom he went out into the country and soon learned to use the theodolite and the surveyor's level.

From the age of nine he went to a school at Compton in Dorset, where he was taught Greek and Latin; but by the time he was 14 he had made progress also in French and in Oriental languages by self-teaching. He studied natural science and mathematics, and worked so hard that he suffered in health. After a rest he took up his studies

Courtesy of the Youth Hostels Association
IN THE COMMON-ROOM OF A YOUTH HOSTEL
Established throughout the United Kingdom to encourage walking and cycling holidays, the Youth Hostels offer simple, cheap, and clean accommodation to members of the Youth Hostels Associations of England and Wales, Scotland, and Northern Ireland. Above is the common-room of one of the most modern hostels in Surrey ; it has electric cooking, built-in bunks, and central heating.

again, this time at Youngerbury in Hertfordshire. His uncle on his mother's side was a physician, and Young chose medicine as his own profession, studying at Cambridge, London and Edinburgh, and taking his degree of M.D. at the University of Göttingen in Germany.

Young was not much more than 20 when he contributed a paper on the working of the eye to the " Transactions " of the Royal Society; in this he gave his view of the manner in which the lens of the eye " accommodated " itself to focus objects at different distances—by changing the curvature of the lens. This is commonplace today, but in Young's time it was hotly disputed by many men of science. He had ideas about the interference of light, and the wave theory of its propagation. In 1801 he was appointed Professor of Natural Philosophy to the Royal Institution. Seventeen years later he became secretary to the Board of Longitude, in which post he had to supervise the Nautical Almanac (*see* Chronometer; Navigation). He

then gave up the practice of medicine, which up till now he had continued despite his other work.

It was at this period that Young utilized his familiarity with Oriental languages to decipher the name " Ptolemy " in hieroglyphics on the Rosetta Stone (*q.v.*). This black basalt stone, inscribed in two Egyptian versions and in Greek, had been brought to the British Museum from Lower Egypt in 1801; it had defied the efforts of scholars to read its hieroglyphics. The French savant Champollion followed up Young's discovery, and eventually was able to translate the entire inscription. Young died on May 10, 1829.

Youth Hostels. After the First World War (1914–18) there was a big increase on the continent of Europe in the number of young people who spent their holidays on walking or cycling tours. This led to the establishment of hostels, at which accommodation could be obtained very cheaply. In Britain the Youth Hostels Associations for England and Wales, for Scotland, and for Northern Ireland were founded in 1930 and 1931 to help people, especially young persons of limited means, to a greater appreciation of the countryside; to encourage walking and cycling holidays; and to provide simple accommodation for travellers.

Hostels are maintained throughout the United Kingdom, and their use is restricted to members of the Youth Hostels Associations. The annual membership fee ranges from one shilling to seven shillings, according to age. The nightly charge at a hostel varies from one shilling and sixpence to ninepence, according to age, and includes the provision of bed, pillow and blankets, and washing and cooking facilities. The head office of the Youth Hostels Association for England and Wales is at Midland Bank Chambers, Howardsgate, Welwyn Garden City, Hertfordshire.

Ypres. (Pron. ē′-pr) One of the place-names connected with the First World War (1914–18) that will live long in men's minds is that of Ypres —familiarly called " Wipers " by the British soldier —a fine old city in West Flanders, Belgium. During that war the town was defended by British troops against numerous German attacks, and continuous German bombardment reduced it to ruins. The beautiful Cloth Hall and Cathedral were destroyed, but were reconstructed after the war (*see* illustrations in page 407). The Menin Gate (*see* illustration in page 403) is a memorial to 58,600 British soldiers.

By the 13th century Ypres had become one of the most important cities in western Europe and the centre of the manufacture of woollen cloth. With the decline of that industry it lost much of its prosperity and became a quiet market town, of which the chief occupation was the production of hand-made lace. There remained, however, as remainders of its former greatness the Cloth Hall, one of the finest examples of Gothic municipal architecture in Europe; the old Gothic Butchers' Hall, with a museum of antiquities and paintings, and the medieval Cathedral of St. Martin. The population of Ypres is 17,000.

Ypres, JOHN DENTON PINKSTONE FRENCH, 1ST EARL OF (1852–1925). Born at Ripple, Kent, on September 28, 1852, John French served for four years in the Royal Navy as a cadet and midshipman before he joined the Army. In 1874 he was commissioned in the 8th Hussars, and first saw active service in 1884, when he went to Egypt with the force sent to relieve General Gordon besieged in Khartum. It was in the Boer War (1899–1902) that he made his name as a brilliant cavalry commander. For his services there he was knighted and promoted to the rank of Lieutenant-General. In 1912 he was appointed Chief of the Imperial General Staff, and in 1913 was made Field-Marshal.

In 1914, at the outbreak of the First World War, he was chosen to lead the British Expeditionary Force which was sent to France. His name is especially associated with the retreat of the British Army from Mons and the defence of the town of Ypres (q.v.) during the winter of 1914–15. He was much criticized for his failure to co-operate with the French Generals, and the costly and unsuccessful actions fought at Neuve Chapelle, Festubert and Loos in 1915 caused dissatisfaction with his leadership. At the end of 1915 French gave up his command to General Haig (q.v.) and returned to England to take charge of the forces in the United Kingdom. In 1916 he was created a Viscount. Lord Lieutenant of Ireland from 1918 until his retirement in 1921, he was made an Earl in the latter year, assuming the title of Earl of Ypres. He died on May 22, 1925.

Ytterbium. In 1878 the Swiss chemist Jean Charles de Marignac (1817–94) separated a compound of a new element from the mixture of yttrium group rare earths, and it was named after the Swedish village which also gave its name to several of the rare earth elements (see Terbium; Yttrium). Ytterbium is one of the rarer of the rare earths. It is element No. 70 in the Periodic Table (see page 768); its atomic weight is 173. The symbol is Yb.

Ytterbium differs from most of the rare earth elements in forming two series of salts, one with a valence of 2, and the other with a valence of 3 (see explanation of valence in pages 770 and 771). By electrolytic reduction of the sulphate a lower sulphate is formed which, like barium sulphate, is insoluble in water. This property can be utilized to separate the element in the form of its sulphate from the other yttrium group sulphates, but as it was not discovered until 1929, it was of no use to Marignac in his original separation. The free metal ytterbium has never been obtained. The ordinary salts are colourless, but the lower series of salts are coloured.

Yttrium. The complex mixture of elements known as the rare earth metals (see Terbium) includes two, Scandium and Yttrium, which do not belong to the rare earths proper (elements 57 to 71), but they generally occur with them in Nature. In separating the mixture into its constituent elements, yttrium and scandium have to be separated too. So these elements are often classed with the rare earths. In the initial separation they are often divided into two groups, the cerium earths and the yttrium earths, on the basis of the solubility of the sodium double sulphates.

Mosander in 1843 separated yttria from the oxide of the new "element" discovered by Gadolin in 1794. It was named after the Swedish village Ytterby, as were the fractions terbia and erbia from which, later, other rare earth elements were isolated.

Yttrium occurs in minerals with the other rare earths, especially those, such as gadolinite, which are rich in the yttrium group earths. It also occurs in monazite sand (see Sand). Yttrium is element 39 in the Periodic Table (see page 768), and occurs in the same group as scandium and the rare earths proper. It has an atomic weight of 88·9 and is given the symbol Y. The metal itself has been prepared by heating the chloride with potassium metal, and is an iron-grey powder with a metallic lustre. It has a relative density of 4·5, and melts at 1,490° C. It is oxidised in air and reacts with boiling water. The oxide (Y_2O_3) is white, and absorbs carbon dioxide from the air. Yttrium salts are colourless.

Yucatan. A peninsula of Central America, separating the Gulf of Mexico from the Caribbean Sea, Yucatan is about 400 miles long and 200 miles wide. It comprises the States of Yucatan (23,926 square miles) and Campeche (19,670 square miles) in Mexico, and parts of British Honduras and Guatemala. Its eastern coast is indented with numerous bays, some of which form excellent harbours. The climate is hot and generally dry. There are forests of rosewood and mahogany, and the soil in parts is extremely fertile, yielding crops

MAYA RELIC FROM YUCATAN
A number of astonishing remains of the Mayas have been discovered in Yucatan. The Mayas were a people who attained a high standard of civilization and were living in fine cities in A.D 300. Above is a limestone figure of one of their gods.

of sisal hemp, maize, cotton, tobacco and sugar-cane. Most of the world's supply of chicle, the basis of chewing-gum, comes from the sapodilla plum trees of Yucatan.

Mérida (population 120,000) is the chief city of Mexican Yucatan and is the centre of the sisal hemp industry. It is connected by railway and by road with its port of Progreso (population 15,000). Campeche (20,000) on the bay of the same name is the largest town in the chicle-producing area.

The people are mostly Indians and half-breeds, in part the descendants of the ancient race called the Mayas, a highly civilized people who have left many interesting remains. The Mayas attained a standard of civilization far beyond that of the other early peoples of America, and then a long period of civil war followed by their conquest by the Spaniards early in the 16th century destroyed their culture. Their cities were abandoned and were soon over-grown by the jungle.

According to their records these talented folk were flourishing more than 2,000 years ago; by A.D. 300 they were living in beautiful cities. They devised a calendar which can be related to the modern European system; art of all kinds flourished. They had books written on deerskin or paper made from hemp fibre in a hieroglyphic script, which dealt with history, religious rites and magic.

The typical building material of the Mayas was faced concrete, the limestone in the region yielding abundant material for both mortar and stone. Two-storey or three-storey houses were common, and ruins of five-storey structures have been found. These buildings were ornamented with intricate carvings, which reveal a keen artistic sense, as well as skilled workmanship. Although metals suitable for tools were rare, gold and copper were used in the fashioning of ornaments. The Mayas were expert potters and have left numerous exquisite products of their skill. In 1947 an American expedition discovered in the jungle near Bonampak in south-east Yucatan the remains of 11 temples, also pottery, wall-paintings, jade carvings and three remarkable stones on which Mayan records had been carved. Some of the relics date from the 5th century of the Christian era.

The REPUBLIC of the SOUTHERN SLAVS

A patchwork State which was established (first as a kingdom) after the First World War (1914–18), Yugoslavia is a Balkan country which for years has been sorely troubled by internal strife.

Yugoslavia. Among the nations created in Europe after the First World War (1914–18) was the Kingdom of the Serbs, Croats, and Slovenes, or Yugoslavia (Land of the South Slavs). It was, and still is, a patchwork of various peoples, some semi-Oriental and others more akin to western Europeans. With an area of 99,720 square miles, Yugoslavia is the largest of the Balkan countries. The country is bounded on the north by Austria and Hungary, on the east by Rumania and Bulgaria, on the south by Greece and Albania, and on the west by the Adriatic Sea and Italy.

Much of the country lies within the fertile Danube basin. Across this plain flows the River Save, which joins the Danube at Belgrade and is navigable over nearly the whole of its course; other rivers of importance are the Morava, Bosna and the Narenta. South and west of the Danube plain there rises a maze of highlands, culminating in the Dinaric Alps, of which the highest point is Mount Triglav (9,450 feet). Along the Adriatic coast the mountains fall sharply to the island-fringed shore. The coastline, known as Dalmatia, has a sunny Mediterranean climate; the interior has hot summers and long, very cold winters.

In soil and forests, in mineral deposits and potential water power, Yugoslavia has rich natural resources. Copper, iron and coal are worked; lead, zinc, antimony, chrome, aluminium ore and salt are found. The forests are beech, oak and fir.

Agriculture is the most important industry; about four-fifths of the people are farmers or shepherds. Principal crops include maize, wheat, oats and barley, sugar-beet, hemp, hops, tobacco and flax. Orchards and vineyards flourish in the valleys, and sheep, goats and cattle are pastured in the uplands. The majority of the industries are centred in the north-west of the country; manufactures include iron and steel goods, chemicals, fertilizers, textiles, food products and clothing.

The harbours on the Adriatic coast are almost inaccessible from the interior owing to lack of communications through the mountains, but some commerce passes through the ports of Fiume and Trieste (placed under the control of the United Nations). There are 6,700 miles of railway, about the same mileage of State highways, and 14,000 miles of second-class roads. Belgrade has an international air port, and internal air services link the principal towns. The capital is Belgrade (population 267,000). Other centres are Zagreb (186,000), Subotica (100,000), Ljubljana (79,000), Sarajevo (78,000), Skoplje (68,000), and Novi Sad (64,000).

The Croats, Slovenes and Serbs are all related by blood; but they have developed widely differing ways of living. The Croats and Slovenes are mostly Roman Catholics. The Croats' language is almost identical with that of the Serbs, but they use Latin letters, as do the Slovenes, for their closely-allied

---

Extent.—Area 99,720 miles. Population 15,325,000.

Natural Features.—Rivers: Danube, Save, Drave, Morava, Bosna and Narenta. Mountains: Dinaric and Julian Alps, Karst Plateau and Shar. Climate: hot summers and very cold winters in interior with typical Mediterranean mildness on Dalmatian coast.

Products.—Maize, wheat, barley, oats, rye, grapes, sugar-beet, hemp, flax, tobacco, plums, pears; horses, cattle, sheep, pigs and goats; silk; timber, coal (chiefly lignite), iron ore, bauxite (aluminium ore), copper, lead, chrome, and antimony; flour, textiles, iron and steel goods, chemicals, clothing, and food products.

Chief Cities.—Belgrade (capital, population 267,000); Zagreb, Subotica (more than 100,000); Skoplje, Sarajevo, Ljubljana and Novi Sad (more than 60,000).

Dorien Leigh; M. O. Henchoz

IN RUGGED YUGOSLAVIA TODAY
Part of the western barrier separating the interior of
Yugoslavia from the Adriatic Sea is formed by the rugged
Velebit Mountains (above). The hardy-looking peasant
(lower right) lives in the district of Bosnia, where there are
a number of Mahomedans who still wear a turban or a fez.

tongue. The Serbs, nearly half the population,
belong to the Serb Orthodox Church and use a
Cyrillic alphabet resembling that of the Russians.
Ten per cent of the people are Mahomedans.
Elementary education is compulsory and free; there
are universities at Belgrade, Zagreb and Ljubljana.

The Kingdom of the Serbs, Croats and Slovenes
was created at the end of the First World War by
the amalgamation of the former Austro-Hungarian
provinces of Bosnia-Herzegovina, Dalmatia, Croatia-
Slavonia and parts of Carniola (Slovenia), with
the kingdoms of Serbia and Montenegro. Though
the different races had worked together to create
an independent nation, friction soon arose between
them once their aim had been achieved. The
Croats and Slovenes wanted a large measure of
self-government, which the Serbs, who dominated
the Government, were not prepared to grant them.

In 1929 it seemed that the Croats and Slovenes
were determined to break away from the kingdom,
when King Alexander I established a military
dictatorship and changed the title of the country
to the Kingdom of Yugoslavia. Though parliamentary government was nominally restored in
1931 the king continued to rule autocratically until
1934, when he was assassinated at Marseilles,
France, on October 9.

His 11-year-old son succeeded as King Peter
II, with Alexander's younger brother Prince Paul
as Regent. The occupation by the Germans of
Austria and Czechoslovakia in 1938 and 1939

respectively, and the establishment of a pro-German Government in Rumania, rendered Yugoslavia very vulnerable to attack by German forces, so that when, in the spring of 1941, the German leader Adolf Hitler demanded that Yugoslavia should enter the Second World War (1939–45) on the side of Germany, the Regent agreed to do so.

That act so enraged the Yugoslav armed forces and the mass of the people that the Regent was forced to flee the country, and King Peter assumed the throne in his own right. Hitler soon took his revenge, and Yugoslavia was subjugated by the Germans in April 1941, after a fortnight's campaign. But many of the more stalwart people carried on a fierce resistance, and the country was the scene of guerrilla fighting during the rest of the war.

At first Colonel (later General) Mihailovitch led the partisan troops, but in 1942 guerrillas led by Josip Broz, who was generally known as Tito, took an ever more active part in the fighting. In December 1943 Tito was recognized as a full Allied commander by the Allied nations, who helped him with supplies of food, money and munitions. In 1944 Tito aided Russian armies in the expulsion of the Germans from Yugoslavia, and on November 29, 1945, the State was proclaimed by Tito a republic under the name of the Federal People's Republic of Yugoslavia, comprising the republics of Serbia, Croatia, Slovenia, Montenegro, Macedonia and Bosnia-Herzegovina, with two self-governing provinces— Vojvodina and Kossovo-Metohija. King Peter, who had returned to Yugoslavia after its liberation from the Germans, now left the country.

Under the terms of the Peace Treaty between the Allied nations and Italy, signed in February 1947, Yugoslavia received from Italy the greater part of the province of Venezia Giulia at the head of the Adriatic, the district of Zara and the island of Pelagosa, a total of 3,500 square miles. The population of Yugoslavia is 15,325,000.

Yukon Territory. To most people "the Yukon," as this Canadian territory is popularly called, means two things—gold and cold. With an area of 207,076 square miles, it is bounded on the north by the Arctic Ocean, on the west by Alaska, on the south by British Columbia, and on the east by the North-West Territories. Its climate is intensely cold in winter, temperatures of $-68°$ F. having been recorded. In the summer it is often very hot, the temperature sometimes reaching 95° F. The sun shines for 20 hours a day. Some crops, like potatoes, turnips, oats and rye are grown.

Before the discovery of rich surface deposits of gold in the Klondike river region, in 1896, the North-West Territories of Canada extended to the boundary of Alaska. When the metal was first found prospectors poured in, and a local government system was needed to maintain order. As it was found impossible to control the district from Ottawa, the capital of the Dominion, the Yukon was organized as a Territory, governed by a Commissioner appointed by the Governor-General. The Commissioner is assisted by a Council of three elected members. The people also elect a representative to the Canadian House of Commons.

Dawson City (population 1,000) is the capital. It was named after G. M. Dawson (1849–1901), director of the first geological survey of Canada. White Horse, a mining settlement in the south, has an airport, which helps to link east with west.

The prosperity of the Territory depends almost entirely on the gold mines. At first the mineral could be obtained from the beds of creeks, but now the deposits have to be worked with expensive equipment. Since 1900 the output of gold has considerably declined; and the population (27,000 in 1900) is now only about 4,900.

The Yukon river, which has its source in the Chilkoot Pass Mountain in British Columbia, flows for part of its 1,800-miles' course to the Behring Sea through Yukon Territory. Dawson lies at the point where the Yukon and Klondike rivers join.

Dorien Leigh

OLD WALLED CITY OF DUBROVNIK IN YUGOSLAVIA
On the Adriatic coast of Yugoslavia, Dubrovnik is surrounded by a wall with numerous towers. It was a thriving port and commercial centre in the 16th and 17th centuries, but its prosperity was destroyed by an earthquake and plague in 1667. The entrance to the harbour is obstructed by sandbanks, and large vessels use Gruz, four miles to the north.

Z

Zambezi. Although the lower course of the River Zambezi, for a distance of at least 300 miles from its mouth, has nominally been in the possession of the Portuguese since the beginning of the 16th century, it is only since the last half of the 19th century, through the reports of David Livingstone (*q.v.*) and other explorers, that any definite knowledge of this vast region has been gained.

The Zambezi is the fourth longest river of Africa, with a length of about 1,600 miles, and its headstreams rise in Northern Rhodesia, Belgian Congo and Portuguese West Africa (Angola). It flows mainly south and east to its mouth in Mozambique, discharging its waters into the Indian Ocean through a delta with an area of 2,500 square miles. The watershed of the Zambezi covers an area of about 475,000 square miles, most of which is in Northern Rhodesia. The Shiré is its chief tributary.

In its upper course dense forests alternate with open bush country, and there are extensive plains subject to floods. In Southern Rhodesia are the Victoria Falls (*q.v.*). From the Kebrabasa Rapids it is navigable for 400 miles to its mouth. Opened in 1935, the Lower Zambezi railway bridge at Sena connects Nyasaland with Beira, the capital of Mozambique or Portuguese East Africa; it has a length of 4,021 yards and is a notable engineering feat.

Zanzibar. A speck of an island close to the east coast of Africa, Zanzibar was for centuries the leading African trading centre on the Indian Ocean. Sailing vessels stopped there on their way to the East Indies, and a valuable trade in ivory and slaves was carried on by the Arab traders who dominated the island.

The island of Zanzibar, which has an area of 640 square miles, was conquered by the Portuguese early in the 16th century, but passed again into the possession of the Arabs in 1730. In 1832 the Sultan of Oman, who controlled much of the east coast of Africa, made the town of Zanzibar the capital of his empire. The commerce of the island declined when France, Germany and Great Britain divided the Sultan's possessions in East Africa between them at the end of the 19th century, and built ports on the mainland which absorbed a very large proportion of Zanzibar's trade.

Today Zanzibar and Pemba, its sister island to the north, are noted for cloves (dried, unopened flowers of the clove tree, used as a spice), which the Arabs introduced into the islands from the East Indies. Plantation owners were compelled to cultivate clove trees, and the industry prospered so long as the Arabs could use slave labour. When slavery was abolished in 1897, most of the plantations were bought by people who were prepared to work hard themselves—something the Arabs would not do. Copra (dried "meat" of the coconut) is the next most important product of Zanzibar. Ivory is still exported from the island, but not in such large quantities as formerly.

The town of Zanzibar, on a triangular peninsula on the west coast of the island, is more Oriental than African in appearance, largely owing to the

E.N.A.

WHERE THE JUNGLE COMES DOWN TO ZAMBEZI'S BANK
Largest of the African rivers flowing into the Indian Ocean, the Zambezi is about 1,600 miles long. Its headwaters rise in Northern Rhodesia, Belgian Congo and Portuguese West Africa. Despite its size it is navigable only for some 400 miles from its mouth, the Victoria and Kebrabasa Falls preventing its development as a commercial waterway.

Arab style of architecture. The towers of Mahomedan mosques rise from narrow streets lined with white-walled, red-roofed houses. Richly carved doors in blank walls open to offer glimpses of fountains playing in gardens ablaze with tropical flowers. The city's population (50,000) is very varied, for members of numerous African tribes have come to work on the clove plantations. In the harbour, one of the finest in the world, may be seen

Kenneth Comyn

A STREET IN ZANZIBAR

Latticed windows, massive portals and tortuous stairways
impart a touch of mystery to the winding streets of Zanzibar
city, accentuated by deep, dark shadows thrown by the
brilliant sunshine through its narrow lanes.

craft of all kinds—warships, mail steamers, cargo
ships and Arab dhows (sailing boats).

Zanzibar, Pemba and the adjacent small islands
have been a British Protectorate since 1890, though
the Sultan continues to exercise some authority.
The area of the Protectorate is about 1,020 square
miles, and the population is 250,000.

Zebra. On grassy African tablelands from
Abyssinia south to the Union of South Africa graze
the fleet and wary zebras, those members of the
horse family that wear stripes. Though hunted by
men and lions, Grant's zebra (*Equus granti*) still
roams East Africa in large herds. It stands four and
a half feet at the shoulders; its general colour is
pale yellow-brown, with dark brown to black stripes
on head, body, legs and tail. Burchell's zebra
(*E. burchelli*), found from Abyssinia to South Africa,
and Chapman's zebra (*E. chapmani*) of Tanganyika,
have less distinct stripes between the large ones.
Burchell's species resembles the quagga, now
extinct, and has spotted sides, with legs and under
parts white and free from stripes.

In Abyssinia and Somaliland lives the largest
species, Grévy's zebra (*E. grevyi*), five feet at the
shoulders. It is noted for its enormous ears and its
numerous narrow stripes, jet black on a pure white
background. Only about four feet high, the mountain zebra (*E. zebra*) of South Africa is the smallest
of the family. The general colour is tawny, with

broad black stripes on the body, legs and tail.
Once plentiful, it has been hunted until only a few
scattered herds survive, which are not now allowed
to be shot. Though the zebra can be driven in
harness it has never been properly domesticated
and is very difficult to tame. The flesh is eaten by
natives; the hide makes excellent leather.

Zeppelin, FERDINAND, COUNT VON (1838–
1917). One night in January 1915, during the
First World War (1914–18), a long, cigar-shaped
airship flew over the North Sea, and crossing the
Norfolk coast dropped bombs on the defenceless
towns and villages below. Some months later
more raiding airships came, and yet again, so that
soon " The Zepps are here! " became a familiar cry
in London and a number of other places.

" Zepp " was short for Zeppelin, the name of the
designer of these airships. He was born at Constance, Germany, on July 8, 1838, was educated at
Stuttgart, and joined the German army in 1858.
When he retired from military service, with the rank
of General, in 1891 he turned his attention to
aeronautics, and in 1900 his first airship was built
at Friedrichshafen on Lake Constance and flown.

He suffered numerous disappointments, but,
aided by the German Government, he continued
his experiments, and in 1906 one of his airships flew
60 miles in two hours, a remarkable achievement
for that time. At the outbreak of the First World
War Zeppelins were capable of flying long distances
with fair loads, but they were frail and defenceless,
and proved of little military value. Count Zeppelin
died on March 8, 1917. (*See also* Airship).

G.P.A.

ZEBRAS IN A ZOO

Though the zebra's stripes are very conspicuous when seen
under these conditions, the animals are difficult to see when
standing motionless in the light-and-shadow-flecked shade
of trees on the plains or mountains of Africa.

Zeus. (Pron. zūs). The supreme deity in classical mythology was called Zeus by the Greeks, and Jupiter or Jove by the Romans. He was regarded as the father of the human race, protector of kings and supporter of law and order, the avenger of broken oaths and other offences; he watched over the State and the family and over strangers and suppliants; his hands hurled lightning and guided the stars; he it was who ordained the changes of the seasons, and regulated the whole course of Nature.

The son of Kronos, the king of the gods, and of Rhea, according to legend Zeus dethroned his father and drove the Titans, a family of giants, out of heaven. Zeus then assumed the sovereignty of the world, and successfully resisted the attacks of the giants and the conspiracies of the gods (*see* Uranus). After the expulsion of the Titans Zeus was allotted the empire of heaven and air, Hades (Pluto) that of the infernal regions, and Poseidon (Neptune) that of the sea, while the earth was left under the joint power of the three. Zeus, however, was supreme over all. At his palace on Mount Olympus in Greece the gods met to settle the affairs of men. Hera (Juno) was his wife.

The highest achievement in Greek sculpture was said to have been the statue of Zeus by Pheidias (*c.* 490–432 B.C.). It was a colossal image of ivory and gold, occupying the place of honour in the temple of Zeus at Olympia, Greece. (*See* colour plate facing page 1524).

Zinc. Brass, an alloy of zinc and copper, was known in antiquity, although the ancients probably included copper and bronze under that name. It was made by smelting copper with the ore cadmia and charcoal. The zinc from the ore alloyed with the copper, giving it a yellow colour reminiscent of gold. That zinc itself was not obtained in the smelting is understandable as it is volatile and also burns in air.

When zinc was finally obtained it was probably found in the flues of brass furnaces, where it had distilled. Georg Agricola (1490–1555) mentioned the formation of "zincum" in the furnaces of Silesia. The art of smelting zinc was known several centuries earlier in China. The first zinc smelting works in Europe was set up by John Champion at Bristol in 1743, and the metal was later smelted in Belgium and in Silesia.

The chief ore is zinc sulphide, or blende, found in America, Europe, Rhodesia and Australia. Calamine, or zinc carbonate, was used for smelting before blende, and occurs in the United States and in Europe. In extracting zinc from its ores they are roasted to give the oxide, which is then heated with powdered coal in fireclay retorts ; the metal then distils over and is condensed. Impure zinc is known as spelter. Zinc dust forms in the condensers, contaminated with oxide. Granulated zinc is made by pouring the molten metal into tanks of cold water.

Zinc is placed with cadmium and mercury in the Periodic Table (*see* page 768), the three metals having certain properties in common. The atomic number is 30, the atomic weight 65·38, and the

symbol is Zn. It is a hard, brittle, bluish-white metal, with a relative density of 7·14 , It melts at 100° C. and boils at 920° C. It burns in air with a green flame, forming the oxide (ZnO) as a voluminous white powder that is known as "philosophers' wool."

Zinc dissolves readily in dilute acids, although when very pure a trace of impurity such as copper is

Palermo Museum

MARRIAGE OF ZEUS AND HERA
Probably dating from the 5th century B.C., this relief from a Greek temple in Sicily depicts the wedding of Zeus (right), the supreme god in classical mythology, and Hera (left). The bride is pulling aside her veil at the conclusion of the ceremony.

required to start the reaction. The salts of zinc are white or colourless. The soluble salts are poisonous, although a very dilute solution of the sulphate (white vitriol) is used as an eye lotion. The carbonate (calamine) and other salts are used in medicine. Zinc sulphide is white, and is used in fluorescent screens (*see* Radium). A mixture of the sulphide with barium sulphate is very important as a paint pigment under the name lithopone. Zinc oxide is also an important white pigment. These zinc pigments are notable because, unlike lead pigments, they do not blacken on exposure to the hydrogen sulphide present in the atmosphere of industrial centres.

The most important use of zinc is the coating of iron or steel with the metal. The zinc exerts a protective action on the iron, which was early recognized as being electrical in nature. For this reason zinc-coated iron became known as "galvanized iron." Today, when steel plate has replaced iron for many uses, the name is even less appropriate. Zinc coating may be done by dipping the iron (after cleaning the surface in hot dilute acid and passing through a flux) into a bath of molten zinc. Or the metal may be deposited on the iron in an electrolytic bath containing a solution of a zinc salt. The zinc coating in galvanized iron is about 1/500 of an inch thick. Small articles are also coated with zinc by a process known as " sherardizing." The articles to be treated are packed in fine zinc dust in a container which is heated to 300 to 400° C. The zinc forms a fine coating on the iron. Protection of an iron surface against corrosion is also provided by incorporating zinc dust in paints.

There is another way in which zinc is used to prevent corrosion. By attaching sheets or blocks of zinc to boiler plates or propeller shafts the zinc is corroded in preference to the iron or copper. The zinc can be easily replaced from time to time, while the other metal, forming a part of machinery not so easily replaced, is protected.

Zinc is also important in its alloys with other metals. Brass contains 30–40 per cent zinc and 60–70 per cent copper, although special brasses may contain small amounts of other metals such as iron, aluminium or tin. Delta metal, harder than brass and used for ships' propellers, contains 1–3 per cent iron. Brass can be drawn, rolled, stamped and extruded. Until the middle of the last century brass was made by the calamine process, in which copper was heated with calamine and carbon : the zinc produced from the last two ingredients alloyed with the copper. Now brass is made from copper and high-purity zinc.

German " silver " is an alloy of zinc, copper and nickel. Zinc is very important, in its alloys with copper, tin, lead and other metals, in anti-friction alloys for bearings. By itself zinc is used for producing metal castings. Other uses of the metal include the negative poles of certain electric cells (e.g. Leclanché cells), and the precipitation of gold and silver from the cyanide solutions used in extracting these metals from their ores.

Zirconium.
In 1789 the German chemist M. H. Klaproth found the oxide of a new element in a mineral, zircon, from Ceylon. The metal zirconium was first obtained by Berzelius. The two principal minerals containing zirconium are zircon, a silicate of the metal ; and baddeleyite, the oxide (ZrO_2). Zircon is found in Australia, India and Brazil ; and baddeleyite occurs in Ceylon and Brazil. Zirconium is also present in monazite sand (see Sand). Zircon is found in gem varieties such as hyacinth or jacinth and jargoon.

After separating other metals from the ores by chemical methods, zirconium is still difficult to obtain as the free metal. This is because it reacts with hydrogen, oxygen, nitrogen, carbon and silicon. The metal powder is prepared by heating a complex fluoride of the metal with sodium in a " bomb " (a strong, securely sealed metal casing). The compact

metal has been made by heating a tungsten filament electrically in a vacuum into which zirconium iodide vapour is passed. The iodide decomposes, and the zirconium is deposited on the tungsten.

Zirconium is placed in the same group in the Periodic Table (see page 768) as titanium and silicon. The atomic number is 40, the atomic weight 91·2 and the symbol Zr. Powdered zirconium has to be kept wet, as otherwise it catches fire. The compact metal has a relative density of 6·5, and melts at about 2,000° C. It is unaffected by most acids and alkalies. The powdered metal is used in ammunition primers, and is mixed with magnesium in smokeless flashlight powders. Zirconium steel (an alloy) is very tough, and has been used for armour plating. Zirconium oxide is used in pottery, to render a coating opaque ; and is employed in making refractory furnace linings (which withstand intense heat). The carbide is very hard, and is used as an abrasive.

Zodiac.
The apparent annual path of the sun in the sky runs through 12 constellations or groups of stars, and the zone which these stars occupy is called the zodiac (Greek *zodion*, little animal). Within this zone, likewise, are found the paths of the moon and principal planets. The zodiac was regarded with superstitious awe by the ancients ; and the various movements of the sun, moon and planets through it still form the basis upon which astrologers claim to be able to predict the future and to cast horoscopes.

The following rhyme makes the list of the 12 signs given to the constellations of the zodiac easy to remember :

> The Ram, the Bull, the Heavenly Twins,
> And next the Crab the Lion shines;
> The Virgin, and the Scales,
> The Scorpion, Archer, and the Goat,
> The Man that Bears the Watering Pot,
> And Fish with glittering tails.

Usually they are known by their Latin names : Aries (Ram), Taurus (Bull), Gemini (Twins), Cancer (Crab), Leo (Lion), Virgo (Virgin), Libra (Balance or Scales), Scorpio (Scorpion), Sagittarius (Archer), Capricornus (Goat), Aquarius (Water Bearer), and the twelfth, Pisces (Fishes).

As a result of the shifting of the equinoxes, the sun is now a whole constellation behind the appropriate sign. For example, at the beginning of spring the sun is said to enter the sign of Aries, but it is still in the constellation Pisces. Two thousand years ago the signs and the constellations exactly corresponded, but this will not again happen for nearly 26,000 years. (See also Astronomy ; Constellation).

Zola,
ÉMILE (1840–1902). In a way this French novelist resembles wise men of ancient times who tried to write down the knowledge

Signs of the zodiac, from a 16th-century MS.

ÉMILE ZOLA : NOVELIST OF REALISM
The principal work of this French writer was the Rougon-Macquart series of 20 novels, which were intended to cover the whole field of human activity and thought. Published between 1870 and 1893, they won him recognition as a genius.

of the whole world as they knew it. Zola was not quite so ambitious, but he set out to represent the workings of the laws of heredity in human society, and to this end produced some 20 volumes, composing what are called the Rougon-Macquart series of novels. In these he sought to show how a character who had inherited certain tendencies must develop and flourish or perish according to the strength or weakness that he had received by birth and the circumstances in which he was placed. He belonged to the " naturalist " or " realist " school of French writers—that is, writers who tried to show life just as it is without any comment from themselves.

Born in Paris on April 2, 1840, Zola had a French mother, and an Italian father who was a distinguished engineer. He was educated at Aix-en-Provence, Paris, and Marseilles University, but failed to take a degree. In 1861 he started work as journalist, writing novels and short stories in his spare time. His novel Thérèse Raquin was published in 1867. His Rougon-Macquart series, begun in 1870 and completed in 1893, place him among the creative geniuses of fiction.

Zola was accidentally poisoned by gas fumes on the night of September 28-29, 1902, and in 1908 his body was placed in the Panthéon — a temple of honour to eminent Frenchmen in Paris.

His chief works include L'Assommoir, dealing with the drink problem (1877) , Germinal, descriptive of coal-mining (1885) ; La Débâcle, a story of the Franco-Prussian War of 1870–71 (1892). In Lourdes (1894), Rome (1896), and Paris (1898) Zola traced the mental transition of a priest from Roman Catholicism to an independent form of religious thought.

Zoological Gardens. Although we may regard these establishments, housing a collection of wild animals, as places mainly of popular resort and amusement, the zoological garden is properly an institution where interested persons can study the ways and life of wild animals. The proper name for such a collection of living animals is " menagerie."

Thus the " zoo " is an adjunct to the study of zoology (q.v.), and behind the scenes, in a zoo's laboratories, there goes on much research which enriches the world's knowledge of animal life. In the menagerie itself, rare animals of all kinds can be studied in a manner which would be impossible if scientists had to observe them solely in their native haunts. Modern zoos house their collections in open-air cages as far as the climate will allow ; and, indeed, avoid cages or similar structures by letting their charges live in comparative freedom amid surroundings resembling the natural ones.

A menagerie is kept up usually by a zoological society whose members contribute towards the cost. The receipts from admission of the public form a larger part of the financial support needed for what is necessarily an expensive establishment.

London has its famous Zoological Gardens in Regent's Park ; there are zoos also in many of our great cities, as well as all over the continent of Europe, and, in fact, in all the great cities of the

TEA FOR TWO AT THE ZOO
Sometimes the inmates of zoos, especially if bred in captivity, become extraordinarily tame and fond of their keeper, who may be able to teach them tricks. This cockatoo at the London Zoo has learned to imitate its friend and drink out of a cup—having discovered that there is always a lump of sugar or some other tit-bit at the bottom.

world. The first authenticated zoological garden was that of a Chinese emperor, in 1100 B.C., and from that date in civilized countries there have been collections of animals, for the most part out of doors.

Perhaps the first English zoo was that kept by Henry I, at Woodstock near Oxford. Later, this royal collection of animals was kept in the Tower of London, which it used to be fashionable to visit " to see the lions." The present London Zoo is the private property of the Zoological Society of London, and dates from 1826. It has the most comprehensive collection of birds, beasts and reptiles in existence. In addition, there is the famous " Park " at Whipsnade, in Bedfordshire, also belonging to the Zoological Society, where wild animals of all sorts live out in the country, a number of smaller birds and beasts having complete freedom within the park. Other notable zoos are at Edinburgh, Dublin and Bristol. In Europe the zoos of Paris, Marseilles, Berlin, and Amsterdam have been famous, while at Stellingen near Hamburg was for long the world-renowned collection of Carl Hagenbeck.

One of the features of the London Zoo is the former " Pets' Corner," now known as the Children's Zoo, where young people can handle and make friends with all manner of other young creatures.

Zoology. (Pron. zō-ol´-oji). Animal life is the subject of zoology, which is one of the two main divisions of the science of biology (q.v.). In the present-day study of zoology attention is directed less to morphology—the external appearances of animals, such as shape, colour, differences in horns, hoofs, etc.—than to anatomy and physio-

logy, their internal structure and life processes. An attempt is made to analyse the vital activities of animals and to determine their proper position in the history of the universe.

The Greek philosopher Aristotle (384–322 B.C.) has been called the " Father of Natural History," and as such he was perhaps the first zoologist. He was a man of truly scientific mind, and made many original observations on the structure and development of animal life. The Roman scholar Pliny the Elder (A.D. 23–79) also wrote on zoology, but in a far less scientific spirit.

The revival of interest in anatomy (q.v.) by Vesalius in the 16th century helped zoology by giving a knowledge of structure, the study of which was gradually extended downward from the higher animals to other forms, including the invertebrates. In due time came the study of comparative anatomy. The development of the microscope, from the 17th century onwards, was of especial importance in the study of minute animal forms and structures.

The systematic classification of animals (as well as plants) owes much to the Swedish naturalist Carl von Linné (q.v.) or Linnaeus (1707–78). The French zoologist George-Louis Leclerc, Comte de Buffon (1707–88), who was a man of more philosophical mind, created a popular interest in the subject by his writings, and also opened up new fields and led the way in some matters of great importance. His countryman Georges Cuvier (1769–1832) laid the foundation of the comparative study of the structure of animals (comparative morphology); and another countryman, Jean-

Fox

TROPICAL AND ARCTIC ANIMALS 'AT HOME' IN ENGLAND

Three miles south of Dunstable in Bedfordshire is Whipsnade Zoological Park. A private estate when it was purchased by the Zoological Society in 1927, it has been developed as a ' home ' for foreign wild animals and as a sanctuary for British wild creatures and plants. It was opened to the public in 1931. The animals live amid unspoilt country scenery, and the necessary fences and ditches have been made as unobtrusive as possible. The chimpanzees (left) have an isolated site with trees on which they can perform acrobatics to their hearts' content ; polar bears (right) revel in the snow.

THE UNTAMED AND THE TAME

Fox

Unlike most of the cat family tigers are good swimmers and are fond of playing about in water in hot weather, as the one above is doing at Whipsnade. The Indian elephant is more docile than its larger African relative ; the one at the right, giving rides at the London Zoo, is accepting a bun.

Baptiste Lamarck (1744–1829), was the most noteworthy of the predecessors of Charles Darwin in working out a theory of evolution.

Microscopic study of animal tissues by Theodore Schwann (1810–82) founded the science of histology (study of organic tissues) and led to the establishment of the cell theory (*see* Cell). The study of embryology, or the development of the individual organism, was founded by Karl Ernst von Baer (1792–1876); and at the same time the foundations of animal physiology were laid by Johannes Müller (1801–58).

Zoology up to 1860 was thus the product of the concurrent growth of knowledge in regard to these subjects—the structure of animals (morphology), their development (embryology), and their vital activities (physiology). Then an additional element was introduced which has illuminated the whole field—the doctrine of organic evolution, as set forth by Charles Darwin in 1859. (*See* Darwin ; Evolution).

From that time zoology has been dominated by the idea of evolution, and animals have been studied broadly—in the light of their ancestral history. Progress is dependent still upon advance in anatomy, physiology, and embryology, but the point of view from which the facts are considered has been changed. As in the case of botany (*q.v.*) new lines of study have been developed, such as ecology (*q.v.*), now ranked as a most important branch of zoology. The study of animal structure, or morphology, together with that of microscopic anatomy (histology) and embryology, makes up what is called structural zoology. The general description and classification of animals is systematic zoology, or taxonomy. The geographical distribution of animals has been widely studied and raised to the rank of a special department, linked with ecology. The great field of morphology is supplemented by physiology, which, broadly speaking, concerns itself with the vital processes of all living organisms. Studies of the mental powers and the mental phenomena in animals lead to animal psychology, which may be considered a part of zoology. (*See* Animal Kingdom).

Zoroaster. (Pron. zor-ō-as′-ter). Perhaps 1,000 years before the birth of Christ the Persian Zoroaster, also known as Zarathustra, founded the religion known as Zoroastrianism, which is still practised by about 9,000 Persians and some

115,000 Parsees living in the sub-continent of India. The Parsees, whose name means " inhabitants of Pars (Persia)," emigrated from their homeland to India to escape religious persecution by the Mahomedans in the middle of the 7th century, most of them settling in Bombay.

Zoroaster regarded life as a battle, in which the forces of good and evil, or of light and darkness, were struggling for mastery. The forces of good were led by Ahura Mazda or Ormuzd, and those of evil by Ahriman. Zoroaster taught that good must eventually triumph; but every one has to fight on one side or the other and will receive reward or punishment hereafter according to whether he fights for good or evil.

Fire, the symbol of the spirit, plays an important part in the religion, though its followers are not really " Fire Worshippers " as they are sometimes called. The doctrines and teachings, embodied in a book called the Avesta or Zend-Avesta, may be summed up in the words " good thoughts, good works, good deeds."

Zulus. A South African race of Bantu stock, the Zulus live mostly north of the Tugela river in Natal. Noted for their fine physique and fighting qualities they became the most powerful people in South Africa early in the 19th century, when after a series of victorious campaigns by their chief Chaka (1783–1828) they made themselves masters of the country from the Zambezi river to the Cape of Good Hope.

In 1879 the Zulus under Chief Cetewayo (c. 1836–84) came into conflict with the British, and at Ulundi, Natal, on July 4, 1879, their hitherto invincible army was defeated and their power broken. Zululand, area 10,427 square miles, was declared British territory in May 1887, and was annexed to Natal in 1897. The population of Zululand is 260,000.

Zürich. (Pron. zūr'-ikh). Capital of the canton of the same name, and the largest city of Switzerland, Zürich stands on both banks of the River Limmat at the point where it flows from the lake of Zürich. The stream separates the *Grosse* (big) from the *Kleine Stadt* (small town) and is crossed by the Münster bridge. Near by is the Grossmünster, a Romanesque church with Gothic

features, built between the 11th and 13th centuries. Another fine edifice is the Frau Münster, erected in the 13th and 14th centuries.

The Swiss National Museum, opened in 1898, contains a valuable collection of antiques and art treasures. Among other notable buildings are the Town Hall, dating from 1694, and the University, which is the intellectual centre of German-speaking Switzerland.

The foremost commercial and industrial city in the country, its products include silk and cotton goods, paper, chemicals and machinery ; it is also the Swiss banking centre. Zürich was the capital of Switzerland until 1848, when it was displaced by Berne (q.v.). The population is 336,000.

Zwingli, ULRICH (1484–1531). The Protestant Reformation, which was begun in Germany by Martin Luther (q.v.), was carried out in Switzerland by Ulrich Zwingli (pron. tsving-lē), and although his influence on the movement was perhaps not so great as that of Luther he made an important contribution to the Protestant doctrine.

Born at Wildhaus, near St. Gall, Switzerland, on January 1, 1484, Zwingli was educated at Berne, Vienna and Basle. He entered the Roman Catholic Church, became a parish priest in 1506, and later for a time acted as an army chaplain, during which period he seems to have acquired some doubts about the tenets of the Roman Catholic Church.

Basing his teaching on the Gospel, Zwingli publicly denounced the authority of the Pope and attacked abuses in the Church. In 1518 he was appointed pastor in Zürich, where, under the influence of Luther, he broke completely with the Pope. When Pope Adrian VI asked the people of Zürich not to listen to Zwingli's sermons, the City Council held a public debate at which the reformer defended his views so aptly that the whole canton of Zürich decided to support the reformer and to leave the Roman Catholic Church.

Dorien Leigh

TOWERS OF ZURICH'S MINSTER

The finest of the old buildings in Zürich is the Gross Münster, or Great Minster (church formerly associated with a monastery), a Romanesque edifice with Gothic features. On the right bank of the Limmat river, building was begun about 1090 but the main structure was not completed until 1300. The twin towers date from 1779.

Other Swiss cantons gradually adopted the Protestant religion, until only five remained Catholic. When fighting broke out between the rival cantons, Zwingli fought with the Protestants and was killed at the battle of Cappel on October 11, 1531.

STORIES and RHYMES in COLOUR

3 1M 7

ALADDIN *and the* WONDERFUL LAMP

LONG, long ago there lived in the capital of China a young boy, Aladdin, the son of a very poor widow. One day as he played in the street with his companions, a stranger who was passing stopped and spoke to him.

"Child, was not your father called Mustapha the tailor?" he asked.

"Yes, sir," answered Aladdin, "but he has been dead a long time."

At these words the stranger threw his arms about Aladdin's neck, kissed him several times, and with tears in his eyes said:

"I am your uncle; your worthy father was my own brother. I knew you at first sight, you are so like him."

He then gave the boy a handful of money, saying:

"Go, my son, to your mother. Give my love to her and tell her that I will visit her to-morrow, that I may see where my good brother lived so long and ended his days."

Aladdin's mother was much surprised to learn that her husband had a brother, but she rejoiced with her son at the good fortune which had come to him, for the stranger promised to buy Aladdin a shop, and to dress him as handsomely as the best merchants in the city.

Early the next morning the stranger called to take Aladdin into the country to spend the day. After walking some distance they reached a narrow valley between two mountains. Here Aladdin's companion paused and bade him gather up all the dry sticks he could find. These the stranger set on fire. Then, pouring some incense into the blaze, he pronounced several magical words, and immediately the earth opened, disclosing a stone with a brass ring fixed in it. Aladdin was greatly frightened, and would have run away; but the stranger caught hold of him and said:

"Do not be afraid. Under this stone there is hidden a treasure destined to be yours, and which will make you richer than the greatest monarch in the world. Take hold of the ring and lift up the stone."

A STORY FROM THE ARABIAN NIGHTS

Aladdin did as he was told; and there appeared under the stone a staircase leading down to a door.

"Descend those steps, my son, and open that door," said the stranger. "It will lead you into a palace divided into three great halls. Before you enter the first hall be sure to tuck up your robe and wrap it about you, for if your clothes so much as touch the wall you will die instantly. Then pass through the second and third halls without stopping. At the end of the third you will find a door which opens into a garden, planted with fine trees loaded with fruit. Walk directly across the garden to a terrace, where you will see in a niche a lighted lamp. Take the lamp and put it out. When you have thrown away the wick and poured out the oil, put it in your waistband and bring it to me."

The stranger then drew a ring off his finger and putting it on one of Aladdin's said: "This is a talisman against all evil, so long as you obey me. Go, therefore, boldly, and we shall both be rich all our lives."

Aladdin followed the stranger's instructions; but as he was returning with the lamp, he noticed that the fruit of the trees was composed of what he imagined to be coloured glass, though in reality these bits of glass were beautiful jewels of every description. He filled his purse and his skirts with them; and, loaded with riches of which he little realized the value, he returned to the mouth of the cave and cried out: "Pray, uncle, lend me your hand to help me out."

The stranger, however, insisted that Aladdin give him the lamp first. But Aladdin, whose hands were filled with jewels, refused. At that the stranger flew into a passion, threw some incense into the fire, and spoke two magical words—at which the stone rolled back into place, imprisoning the boy in the gloomy cave.

Aladdin then realized that the stranger was no uncle of his, but a wicked magician who designed him evil. And this indeed was true, for he was known as the African magician and had come from his native land for the express purpose of obtaining the magic lamp. An oracle had revealed to him its whereabouts, and had further stated that the lamp must be given to him as a gift from the hands of another if he would obtain favours from it. It was for this reason that he had prevailed upon Aladdin to secure his prize.

Aladdin's cries for help echoed and re-echoed through the dark cave, unheard by anyone. Worn out at last he joined his hands to pray, and in doing so rubbed the ring which the magician had placed on his finger. Immediately there rose from the earth a frightful Jinn or spirit bearing a torch in his hand, who said:

"What wouldst thou have? I am ready to obey thee. I serve him who possesses the ring on thy finger; I, and the other slaves of the ring."

Although greatly frightened, Aladdin replied: "Whoever thou art, deliver me from this place."

No sooner had he spoken when he found himself on the very spot where the magician had left him, while no sign of the cave remained. He quickly made his way home, and after relating to his mother all that had happened he asked for some food.

"Alas, child," she replied; "I have not a bit of bread in the house, nor have we money to buy any."

Aladdin thereupon suggested selling the lamp, and his mother agreed, but wished first to clean it. No sooner had she begun to rub it when there appeared another hideous Jinn who roared in a voice of thunder:

"What wouldst thou have? I am ready to obey thee as thy slave, and the slave of all those who have that lamp in their hands."

Greatly terrified, Aladdin's mother fainted; but Aladdin quickly seized the lamp and said boldly:

"I am hungry. Bring me something to eat."

The Jinn disappeared, and presently returned bearing a large silver tray holding 12 covered silver dishes filled with delicious food, two flagons of wine, and two silver goblets. In their humble cottage the mother and son then partook of a feast fit for a king.

In spite of the fact that they had an inexhaustible source of riches in the lamp, and that Aladdin had come to realize the value of the

"glass stones" which he had brought home, he and his mother continued to live very simply. One day, however, as Aladdin was strolling about the town he chanced to see the beautiful Princess Buddir al Buddoor, the daughter of the sultan. Charmed by her grace and beauty, he fell in love with her, and resolved to win her.

Hastening home, he eagerly told his mother to take all his jewels as a gift to the sultan and

One day as Aladdin was strolling about he chanced to see the beautiful Princess Buddir al Buddoor, the daughter of the sultan, being carried through the town, and fell deeply in love with her.

ask of him the hand of the Princess for her son. The sultan was amazed at the beauty of the gems, and replied without hesitation:

"Go tell your son that I wait with open arms to embrace him; and the more haste he makes to come and receive the Princess from my hands, the greater pleasure he will do me."

Aladdin, overjoyed at his mother's success, summoned the Jinn of the lamp and said:

"Jinn, build me a palace of porphyry, jasper, agate, lapis lazuli, and the finest marble. Let its walls be of massive gold and silver bricks, and let the lattices of the windows be enriched with diamonds, rubies, and emeralds. Let there be an inner and an outer court, and beautiful gardens. But above all things provide a safe treasure-house and fill it with gold and silver. Let there be also kitchens and storehouses, stables full of the finest horses, with their masters and grooms, and hunting equipage, officers, attendants and slaves, both men and women, to form a retinue for the Princess and myself."

The next day the marriage was celebrated with great splendour, and Aladdin led his Princess to the palace built overnight by the Jinn.

Several years later the magician, who had returned to Africa after imprisoning Aladdin in the cave, decided to learn whether Aladdin had perished. He set out for the capital of China and soon after arriving learned of the boy's wealth and happiness. Filled with rage, he bided his time until Aladdin one day went hunting. Then purchasing 12 bright new lamps, he walked past the palace crying:

"New lamps for old! Who will exchange old lamps for new?"

The Princess, who heard him, sent one of her slaves to fetch an old lamp which she had noticed in her husband's robing room, and bade her exchange it for a new one. Little did she realize that this old lamp was the source of all their wealth and prosperity! The

Filled with rage, the magician bided his time until one day Aladdin was out hunting. Then, with his bright new lamps, he walked past the palace crying, "New lamps for old! Who will exchange old lamps for new?"

magician snatched the lamp, summoned the Jinn, and ordered the palace and all its occupants to be transported into the heart of Africa.

Aladdin was frantic when, upon his return, he learned that his palace and his Princess had disappeared with a clap of thunder. The sultan, very angry at the disappearance of his daughter, at first ordered Aladdin to be executed; but finally agreed to allow him 40 days in which to find her. In his grief Aladdin forgot the magic ring upon his finger, until he accidentally rubbed it, whereupon its attendant spirit appeared.

"Transport my palace to the place where it first stood," commanded Aladdin.

"Only the Jinn of the lamp can do that," replied the spirit of the ring.

"Then I command thee to transport me to the spot where my palace now stands."

At once Aladdin found himself in the presence of Princess Buddir al Buddoor, who told him all that had befallen. Learning that the wicked magician kept the lamp always in his waistband, Aladdin got the Princess to invite the magician to dine with her. Then, purchasing a powder which would mean instant death to anyone who swallowed it, he gave it to the Princess to put in her guest's wine goblet. Aladdin hid under the table during the repast, and as the magician drank his wine and instantly fell forward senseless, he snatched the lamp, and quickly rubbed it.

"Jinn," he cried, "I command thee to transport this palace instantly to the place from which it was brought hither!"

Immediately the palace and its occupants were carried back to China, and the happy sultan, as he embraced his daughter, begged Aladdin's forgiveness for distrusting him.

Within a few years the old sultan died. The Princess Buddir al Buddoor succeeded him, and she and Prince Aladdin reigned together in great prosperity for many years. — *Retold from The Arabian Nights.* (See also page 202).

The TADPOLE who WANTED to be a FROG
A Story of Life in the Pond

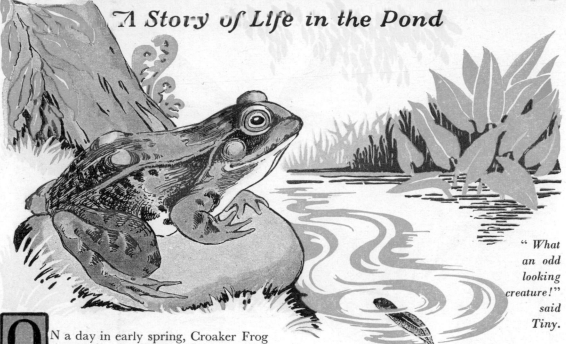

" What an odd looking creature!" said Tiny.

ON a day in early spring, Croaker Frog sat under the drooping branches of a willow tree near the edge of Shady Stream. He was a fine looking young frog, with his coat of green and his white vest. On this spring morning he felt very happy, as he sat there enjoying the feel of the warm air and the sound of the wind in the trees.

All through the long cold days of winter he had slept in the mud at the bottom of Shady Stream. When the first warm wind came down the hills, and the snow and ice began to melt, he had wakened. He was very glad that spring had come, and very glad indeed to be hopping about once more.

This morning he had hopped up and down the bank of Shady Stream for quite a while. By and by he grew tired, so he sat down on a large flat stone under the willow tree and closed his eyes.

He had not been sitting there long when three little black tadpoles came swimming by. Catching sight of Croaker Frog, they stopped to look at him.

"Dear me!" said Tiny, the smallest tadpole. "What an odd looking creature! I wonder what it is."

The two other little tadpoles stared at Croaker Frog for a moment. "I don't know," said the second little tadpole. "I don't know at all."

"I don't either," said the third little tadpole.

"Just look how his throat trembles whenever he breathes!" said Tiny Tadpole. "And just look at his long hind legs! What can he ever do with legs like that, I wonder."

Just then Croaker Frog opened his big round eyes so suddenly that two of the little tadpoles were frightened and swam away as fast as they could. But Tiny Tadpole was not frightened. He stayed just where he was and said politely: "Good day, sir! Would you mind telling me who you are?"

Croaker Frog looked down at the little tadpole in the water, and croaked, in his deep voice: "I'm Croaker Frog, and I live here in Shady Stream."

"Do you?" Tiny Tadpole said in surprise. "Why, I live here, too, but I'm sure I never saw you before."

"Have you lived here long?" Croaker Frog asked.

"No, I haven't," Tiny Tadpole answered. "I haven't lived *anywhere* very long, because I'm only a few weeks old."

"Well, I have lived here a long time," Croaker Frog said. "I'm sure I've seen you before. Aren't you a tadpole?"

"Yes," Tiny Tadpole answered, "that's what I am. Now, *I* would like to ask you a question."

"What is it?" said Croaker Frog. "I will answer it if I can."

"I would like to know what you do with your long hind legs," Tiny Tadpole said. "I never saw legs like those in all my life."

"I use them to swim with, and I use them to hop with," Croaker Frog told him. "I can hop very far and very fast," he added proudly.

*Suddenly he drew himself together
and gave a mighty leap!*

"Can you indeed?" said Tiny Tadpole. "Let's see you do it!"

Croaker Frog hopped along the bank and back again so fast that it almost took the little tadpole's breath away. "Oh!" he said. "I wish I could do that. What else can you do?"

"Well, for one thing," Croaker Frog said, "I can sing, because I am a male frog. Female frogs can't sing. I often sit here in the evening and sing with the other frogs."

"And what else can you do?" Tiny Tadpole asked eagerly.

"I can catch flies and gnats with my tongue," said Croaker Frog, swelling out his sides proudly. "Look!"

He shot out his long notched tongue and caught a fly which was buzzing by.

"Did you see that?" he asked proudly. "Did you see my tongue shoot out? Did you notice that it is hinged at the front end, so that I can make it go ever such a long way?"

"Indeed, I did," answered Tiny Tadpole. "I wish I could do that. The only thing I do is swim."

"I can swim too," Croaker Frog replied, "and I can dive from that high bank away out into the water."

"I never heard of anyone who could do so many things!" exclaimed Tiny Tadpole. "But I don't understand about diving. How do you do it?"

"I can't tell you very well," said Croaker Frog, "but I can show you. Would you like to see me dive?"

"Of course I would," said Tiny Tadpole. "I want to find out how it is done."

Croaker Frog hopped up the steep bank. When he had reached the top he sat for a moment, high above Shady Stream. Tiny Tadpole watched him closely.

Suddenly Croaker Frog drew himself together and gave a mighty leap!

Out through the air he went, his long hind legs spread far apart! Tiny Tadpole, looking up at him as he passed high overhead, gave a little wiggle of excitement. "Dear me!" he said. "That's almost like flying!"

Splash! Croaker Frog landed in the middle of Shady Stream, sending up a great spray of water all around him. He made such large waves that the little tadpole was almost washed out on the bank.

"Goodness gracious me!" said Tiny Tadpole. "That was the most wonderful thing I ever saw!"

"It was a fine dive, wasn't it?" said Old Turtle, who came swimming lazily along. "Young Croaker Frog is a splendid jumper."

"I do wish I could jump like that," Tiny Tadpole said.

"Do you?" Old Turtle asked, blinking his eyes slowly.

"Yes, I do," Tiny Tadpole answered. "I wish I could jump the way Croaker Frog does. I wish I could hop about on the bank. I wish I could catch flies with my tongue. I wish I could sing. I'm just a little tadpole. I can't do anything but swim."

"Well, now, I wouldn't feel too bad about it if I were you," Old Turtle said kindly. "Maybe the day will come when *you* will do all these things too."

"What do you mean, Old Turtle?" Tiny Tadpole asked eagerly. "Do you really think I will be able to?"

"I shouldn't wonder," said the turtle. "I'll tell you what; suppose you come with me for a little swim. I think I can show you something that will surprise you very much."

"Let's go right away!" cried Tiny Tadpole.

"All right," answered Old Turtle. "Come along!"

They swam slowly away, down—down—down, to the very bottom of Shady Stream. Old Turtle stopped beside the roots of some water weeds.

"Look around you, young Tadpole," he said, "and tell me what you see."

"I don't see anything," said Tiny Tadpole, "except a lot of little tadpoles."

"Do you see anything queer about them?" Old Turtle asked.

Tiny Tadpole looked at them closely. "Why, they haven't any eyes or any mouths, have they, Old Turtle?"

"No," answered Old Turtle, "they haven't."

"But how do they eat?" Tiny Tadpole asked in surprise.

"They don't eat. They aren't hungry, so they don't eat. They just lie here at the bottom of Shady Stream and wait. But in a day or two their eyes and mouths will grow—just as yours did."

"What! Didn't I have any eyes or mouth at first?" Tiny Tadpole asked.

"No, you had no eyes and no mouth. You came out of an egg, you know, just as all little tadpoles do, and at first you didn't do anything. You lay here on the bottom of Shady Stream and just waited, like these little fellows."

"Did I?" asked Tiny Tadpole. "I've forgotten all about it. Isn't that strange?"

"Yes, it is," said Old Turtle, "but something even stranger than that is going to happen to you soon, young Tadpole."

"Do you see anything queer?" Old Turtle asked.

"What is it? What is it?" Tiny Tadpole said, wiggling his little tail very fast. "Please tell me quick, Old Turtle!"

"I will show you what is going to happen to you if you will come with me," answered the turtle, and he swam away.

Tiny Tadpole swam after him as fast as he could, and presently the turtle stopped again.

"*Now* tell me what you see," he said.

Tiny Tadpole looked around him. There, among the water weeds, were the oddest little creatures he had ever seen. He stared at them for a moment without speaking. "Why," he said at last, "you are tadpoles, aren't you?"

"I suppose we are," one of the odd little creatures answered. "At least we *were* tadpoles only a few days ago. But see what is happening to us now! It *is* something very strange; something we don't understand at all. Look at us closely. See! Each one of us is growing a pair of hind legs!"

"So you are!" cried Tiny Tadpole. "Why are you doing that?"

"I'm sure I don't know," the little creature said slowly. "Do you know, Old Turtle?"

"Yes," said Old Turtle, "I know why you are growing hind legs; you are turning into frogs, that's why. Pretty soon your front legs will grow too, and then you will lose your tails."

"Lose our tails!" cried the little creature. "Won't it hurt?"

"Not a bit," said Old Turtle. "They will just get a little shorter and a little shorter each day, and then you will be frogs and be able to hop and dive and swim."

"Oh!" cried Tiny Tadpole. "How wonderful! I wish I could be a frog."

"You will, because you are a tadpole," Old Turtle said. "One of these days you, too, will lose your tail and your legs will grow. Then you will be just like Croaker Frog."

"Will I?" asked Tiny Tadpole eagerly. "And will I be able to hop very far and very fast?"

"Yes," Old Turtle told him.

"And will I be able to dive?"

"Yes, you will do that too."

Tiny Tadpole swam very close to Old Turtle. "And will I be able to *sing*?" he asked anxiously.

"Yes," Old Turtle said, "of course you will."

"Oh! Oh! Oh!" Tiny Tadpole wiggled all of his little body. "Do little tadpoles always turn into frogs? Do they, Turtle?"

"Yes," Old Turtle answered.

"Well, that is the very most wonderful thing I ever heard," Tiny Tadpole said. "I am going straight away to tell all the other little tadpoles."

Tiny Tadpole turned around and waved his tail politely. "Good-bye, Turtle; and thank you very much for telling me," he said.

"Good-bye," said Old Turtle, and swimming to the bank of Shady Stream he climbed out on a log and went sound asleep.

Tiny Tadpole turned around and waved his tail politely. "Good-bye, Turtle," he said.

Arithmetic

"Arithmetic just makes me sick,"
Cried our poor little Mary,
The figures never act the same,
They're always so contrary."

That night, when Mary fell asleep,
A dream so wondrous came,
That afterwards Arithmetic
Was never quite the same.

Mary's Dream

Quite suddenly a funny man
Was standing by her side,
"Arithmetic has made you sick;
Just take this pill," he cried.

He held out such a great big pill
She screamed out, "Never, never!"
But down it went and then, said he,
"You're just as well as ever."

And next he gave a whistle clear.
The door flew open wide,
And in a lot of figures rushed
And stood there by his side.

"My name is Mr. Arithmetic"
He said: "I came to-night
To introduce these figures here
And do it truly right.

"The first is Zero as you see,
And then right down the line
Are One Two Three and Four Five Six
Then Seven Eight and Nine

"Now here you see our cousin Plus,
And all must understand
That Plus is just another way
Of saying little 'and.'

"Then Equal, too, I'll introduce;
  She has another name.
It's 'Make', and both of them you see
  Mean just the very same."

"He clapped his hands and music came
  From somewhere out of sight.
The figures marched in perfect time
  Left, right-left, right-left, right

Then Two and Three marched from the line
  And Plus stepped in between.
When Equal took her place like this
  A question could be seen........

"Two plus three make what", they said.
  "We're waiting to find out."
Five took his place, for Three and Two
  Make Five without a doubt.

Then marching to the music gay,
New questions form in line;
They showed in just a minute more
That Seven And Two Make Nine.

And Four Plus Three Make Seven, too,

The figures form with care;
Then quickly Five Plus Four Make Nine;

Just see them standing there.

"And Five And One Make Six, of course;

And Three Plus One Make Four

And Five And Three Make Eight as well

And Oh, so many more.

"These figures are like Washington

And I will tell you why;

It really is exactly true

That figures never lie."

Subtraction

"O please dear Mr. Arithmetic
    I'm 'Minus,' Take Away,
Do let your figures every one
    Come out with me and play."

Soon out they ran—the figures gay—
    And Equal, also, came.
And then with Minus managing
    They planned a lively game

"Just watch me! Watch me!" Minus cried
    Before the game began.
"I'll take my place, then you take yours
    As quickly as you can."

She called for figures Nine and One
    And then skipped in between;
And like a flash, to end the line,
    Equal and Eight were seen.

"Nine Minus One Equal Eight," they cried
With all their might and main;
Then broke the line with a whoop and yell
And began all over again.

And Minus then looked around and said,
"I next choose Five and Three;
Five Minus Three Make Two, of course
As plain as plain can be."

Next Six Minus Four stood in a row,
Then Equal came—and Two,
For Six Minus Four Make Two each time
You know they always do.

And Eight Minus One Equal Seven, Yes

And Nine Minus Five Equal Four.

They formed these lines with a merry rush
And then called out for more.

And Eight Minus Two Make Six, dear me

How fast the figures run!

And now—just look—they've formed again
Nine Minus Eight Make One

And Mr. Arithmetic stood by
And clapped his hands in glee;
"My figures never tell a lie"
He cried   out joyously.

STORY of the BLUE BIRD

IT was the happiest evening in the year! You know what *that* is. Christmas Eve! Tyltyl and his little sister Mytyl should have been fast asleep. Mummy Tyl had tucked them into their beds and turned out the lamp. But the rich children who lived in the Big House across the way were having a party. Gay music could be heard, and a thin line of light shone in round the wooden shutters which closed the windows.

Tyltyl and Mytyl jumped out of bed. They climbed on a stool and opened a shutter to see. There was a sparkling Christmas tree. Little boys and girls dressed like fairy princes and princesses were dancing around it. A big table was loaded with all kinds of sweets, jellies, creams, and iced cakes.

"Oh, how lovely! Oh, how lovely!" cried dear little Mytyl, clapping her hands with delight. Tyltyl and Mytyl were children of Daddy Tyl, a poor woodcutter. They had not been invited to the party, but they were not envious. It made them happy just to look and listen. They danced merrily around their small, dark room and pretended that they had some of the iced cakes to eat.

Transformation Scene!

A sudden knocking at the door made them jump. Before they could run to open it the latch was lifted. The funniest little old woman, in a bright green dress and red cap, hurried in. She was bent nearly double and leaned on a cane. Her nose and chin almost met over her puckered mouth. Bright mouse-like eyes peered from under her shaggy brows. She might be a witch or a cross old fairy.

"Have you the Bird that is Blue?" she asked impatiently. "My little girl is sick. Nothing will make her well but the Blue Bird."

Now Tyltyl had a turtle dove in a cage, but he wouldn't part with his pet for anything. Besides, it was grey.

"Well, then, you'll have to go in search of the Blue Bird," said the funny little old woman. She gave Tyltyl a bright green hat, with a magic diamond button on it. "Turn the diamond," she ordered, almost before he had time to look at it.

Tyltyl put on the hat and turned the diamond. Instantly the poor little dark room grew big and bright and splendid.

"Oh, how lovely!" cried dear little Mytyl.

"It's just the same as it always was, only you couldn't really see it," said the fairy, for the funny little woman had turned into the beautiful Fairy Berylune.

Out Through the Window

Then the clock door flew open and all the laughing hours danced out. The crusty brown soul of Mummy Tyl's good bread hopped from the pan. The soul of sugar appeared as a polite gentleman who broke off his candy fingers and handed them to the children, the soul of milk as a pale maiden. Water was a dripping green lady, fire a flame-coloured, hot-tempered man. Light, a dazzling rainbow sort of angel lady, streamed from the lamp. Last of all, Tylette the Cat found his soul and turned into a very polite but rather critical and unfriendly person with a cat face. And Tylo the Dog became a noisy, loving dog-boy. He nearly went out of his wits with happiness when he could speak to his little master.

"My little god, I love you, I love you, I love you!" he cried.

The Fairy Berylune smiled at the surprised and delighted children. "Now you see all the good things in your home as they really are. But hurry! You must find the Blue Bird before morning. We can go out by the door or the window, just as you please."

It was much more exciting to whisk out through the window. In a moment they were off, through the white and frosty air of Christmas Eve, to the palace of the Fairy Berylune. There they were dressed like fairies, or like people and animals in story books. Tylette the Cat was dressed as Puss in Boots.

Before they set out on the journey Tylette the Cat secretly told Water, Bread and the rest that great danger awaited them if they joined in the search for the Blue Bird.

"If Tyltyl and Mytyl find the Blue Bird, then men will know all our secrets. They will have power over us, and take away our liberty. Let us kill the children," he advised.

"No!" snapped Tylo the Dog. "I will guard my master and his good little sister with my life."

"And I will guard them, too," said Light. "While I shine around them danger cannot come near."

So Light and Tylo the Dog went everywhere with Tyltyl and Mytyl. They had many adventures, but nothing harmed them. The Fairy Berylune thought the Blue Bird might be in the Land of Memory. The children went there; and whom do you think they found? Why, their grandfather and grandmother, Gaffer Tyl and Granny Tyl, and seven little brothers and sisters who had died and gone to heaven.

They weren't changed at all. They were all fast asleep by the door of a dear little cottage; but they woke up at once. "We just went to sleep, but we always wake up when our loved ones on earth think of us, and have a fine time with them," said Granny Tyl.

They had a lovely time, talking and playing and laughing, and eating the good old-fashioned dinner that Granny Tyl cooked. They were all so happy that the black bird which Gaffer Tyl had in a cage turned blue. He gave it to Tyltyl, and the children hurried away with it to the Fairy Berylune. But when they left the misty Land of Memory behind the bird turned black again.

Light was sure that the Blue Bird was hidden in the dreadful Palace of Night. Tylette the Cat overheard her. He was a great friend of Night and knew all her dark secrets. So he went on ahead and warned Night that the children were coming. Night tried to frighten them with stories of the Fears and Terrors, Diseases, Troubles, and Ghosts that lived behind great doors in her dark caverns.

But Tyltyl was a brave boy, and Tylo the Dog was brave; and Light stood outside waiting for them, for she was not allowed to enter the Palace of Night.

Tyltyl cautiously opened the first door, and at once five or six Ghosts escaped from the cavern into the hall. Night ran after them and endeavoured, with the aid of a whip formed of snakes, to drive them back to their prison. Assisted by Tyltyl and Tylo the Dog the Ghosts were herded back into the cavern, where they had been living a very boring existence ever since Man had ceased to take them seriously.

In the next cavern Tyltyl discovered the Sicknesses, who were very miserable and poorly, because the doctors were so unkind to them. Only one of the Sicknesses managed to slip out and that was Cold-in-the-Head, who was one of those least persecuted by the doctors and who enjoyed the best health; but he returned to the cavern when told to do so by Night.

Despite Night's entreaties Tyltyl insisted on opening the next door to see the Wars, who exerted their terrible strength in an attempt to gain their freedom. Night, Tyltyl and Mytyl only just contrived to shut the door upon them.

Tyltyl also looked into the cavern of the Shades and Terrors, who were more afraid of the boy than he was of them. Since Man had ceased to believe in them, they had become extremely timid. In the adjoining chamber were several mysteries, and there Tyltyl was nearly captured by the giant Silence.

The last and biggest door of all he pushed wide. For

The two children went to the Land of Memory; and whom do you think they found? Why, their grandfather and grandmother, Gaffer Tyl and Granny Tyl, and seven little brothers and sisters.

Tyltyl and Mytyl stared into the vast cavern in the Palace of Night. It was flooded with moonlight and filled with birds of the Moon—millions of them, as blue as the sky. The real Blue Bird was there, too, perched high on a ray of light. But how was Tyltyl to know that, when it looked just like the others?

the vast cavern was flooded with moonlight and filled with birds of the Moon. There were millions of them, as blue as the sky!

The real Blue Bird, who could live in the sunlight, was there, perched high on a ray of light. But how was Tyltyl to know that, when it looked just like the others? He gathered his arms full of birds and they all hurried away through the brightening dawn to the Fairy Berylune. But with the first ray of the morning sun the blue birds turned grey and died.

Tyltyl and Mytyl were so disappointed that they nearly cried. Then Tylette the Cat persuaded Tyltyl to go to a forest at night to look for the Blue Bird hidden there by the trees, and then treacherously went on ahead to warn the trees that the children were coming. The trees decided that the only way to prevent Tyltyl and Mytyl obtaining the Blue Bird was to kill them.

Surrounded by Enemies

In the depths of the forest Tyltyl turned his diamond button and immediately the spirits of the trees appeared in the form of men, who surrounded the brother and sister. The spirit of the Oak was a very old man, who carried the Blue Bird perched on his shoulder. Tyltyl implored the old man to give him the Blue Bird, but as Tyltyl was the son of a woodcutter the trees regarded him as an enemy and the Oak angrily refused his request.

Presently the spirits of a horse, a bull, a cow, an ox, a wolf, a sheep, a pig, a cock and an ass appeared and sat down amongst the trees and listened to a speech from the Oak, in which he told them that unless the children were killed the Blue Bird would be taken from the trees.

Tylo the Dog, enraged by the Oak's words, wanted to attack the trees and the animals, but before he could do so Tylette the Cat tricked Tyltyl into having the faithful beast bound with ivy. All the trees and all the animals agreed that Tyltyl and Mytyl must die, but when Tyltyl drew a knife to defend himself they hesitated to attack him until the wolf sprang upon the boy from the rear.

Down on one knee, Tyltyl used his body as a shield to protect his sister, while he defended himself as best he could. Almost overwhelmed, he cried for help to Tylo, who broke his bonds and joined in the fray. A blow on the head half-stunned Tyltyl, and Tylo was handicapped by a broken paw. The trees and animals tried to persuade the dog to desert his master, but, exhausted as he was, he preferred to fight.

Tyltyl, beaten and battered, fell to the ground, and their enemies were gathering themselves for a final rush when suddenly Light appeared and bade Tyltyl turn his diamond button. As he did so the spirits of the animals and trees disappeared and the forest became harmless once more. But when they looked around they realized that the Blue Bird had vanished, too.

Then Light happened to think that there must be a Blue Bird in the Land of Unborn Children. There they found millions of tiny babies waiting to be born. Those who were all ready for the journey to the earth, with their little boxes packed with talents, good luck, gold, measles, whooping-cough, sweet tempers, or odds and ends, hurried on to a ship at dawn and sailed away. Tyltyl and Mytyl were listening to the sweet singing of the mothers on earth greeting their new babies, when Light flew past.

"I have the Blue Bird! Turn the diamond. Time is after us and we must fly to escape!"

In a twinkling they were at home, in the woodcutter's poor little cottage. Light was gone, and Fairy Berylune. The hours trooped back into the clock. The souls of things took their old forms. Tylette the Cat curled up on the warm hearth and went to sleep. Only the heart of Tylo the Dog was nearly broken because he could never speak to his little master again.

"Wake up, sleepy heads! Merry Christmas!"

Tyltyl and Mytyl sat up in their beds and blinked their eyes. Daddy Tyl and Mummy Tyl were laughing at them for being so hard to awaken. Tyltyl flung his arms round the neck of Tylo the Dog, who licked his face.

"Oh, how lovely!" cried little Mytyl. "How nice it is to be home. It's so big and bright and beautiful. How good the bread and milk and sugar are. And the clock is full of lovely hours to play with."

Yet Another Miracle!

The children said and did such queer things and were so wildly happy that Daddy and Mummy Tyl thought they were out of their heads. When Madame Berlingot, a funny little old neighbour, who was so bent that she walked with a cane, came in, she told them that her little girl was sick.

"Fairy Berylune, Light has the Blue Bird, but your little girl can have my grey dove," said Tyltyl, at once.

"Why, what is the child talking about? I'm not a fairy." But Mytyl chuckled, and Tyltyl took down the cage.

The grey dove had turned blue!

"Take it! It will make your little girl well!"

In a moment Madame Berlingot was back. A miracle had happened. The little girl was well and strong and happy. For a moment the Blue Bird had nestled in her arms. Then in a flash it was gone.

Tyltyl and Mytyl told me to ask you if you ever find the Blue Bird please send it back, for they need it for their happiness. But if you did return it they would give it away again to the first person who asked for it. And where do you think you should look for the Blue Bird?

Adapted from the story of The Blue Bird by Maurice Maeterlinck, by permission of and special arrangement with the late M. Maeterlinck and his publishers, Messrs. Methuen & Co., Ltd., holders of the English copyright.

ROBIN HOOD *and* HIS MERRY MEN

How Little John Got His Name

"NO sport have we seen for fourteen days," said Robin Hood one bright spring morn, "so now I will go abroad to seek adventures forthwith. But tarry ye, my merry men all, here in the greenwood; only see that ye mind well my call. Three blasts upon the bugle horn I will blow in my hour of need; then come quickly, for I shall want your aid."

So saying, he set off and strode along until he came to a narrow bridge that spanned a little stream. At one end of it there stood a man, a good seven feet tall, who carried a staff that looked like a small tree trunk.

"Now stand thou back," quoth Robin, "and let the better man cross first." "Nay," answered the stranger, "then stand back thine own self, for the better man am I."

"That we shall presently see," said Robin Hood, "for if thou movest one step forward, I will send a good Nottingham shaft betwixt thy ribs."

"Thou pratest like a coward," said the stranger, "to talk of shooting with thy bow, when I have only this staff to defend myself."

"Faith, never have I had a coward's name in all my life before," replied Robin, and so saying he went to the wood and cut himself a stout oak staff, six feet in length. Then taking

---

Here are two adventures of the valiant and light-hearted

OUTLAWS OF SHERWOOD FOREST

who, when Plantagenet kings ruled in England, plundered the wealthy oppressors and shared their spoils with the poor and needy.

You can read more about famous Robin Hood in page 2790.

---

their staffs by the middle with the two hands wide apart, Robin and the stranger stepped upon the narrow bridge and gave blow for blow in one of the stoutest quarterstaff bouts that ever man saw. Robin smote the stranger upon the ribs until his jacket smoked like a damp straw thatch in the sun, and the stranger gave Robin a crack on the crown that caused the blood to flow, and still both kept their footing. But at last the stranger gave Robin such a blow that he fell head over heels into the water as a pin falls in a game of skittles.

"And where art thou now, good lad?" cried the stranger, roaring with laughter. Robin laughed too as soon as he could get his breath, and as he scrambled out on to the bank he said: "I needs must own thou art, a brave soul as well as a stout fellow with the quarterstaff, and hast fairly won the fight."

Then he set his horn to lip and blew a loud blast. Scarcely had the echo died away when his men appeared, a score or two of stout bowmen, all clad in Lincoln green.

"Good master, how is this?" cried Will Stutely, seeing Robin Hood dripping from head to foot.

"Yon fellow hath tumbled me in the brook," replied Robin.

"Then in he shall go, too." And the lads made for the stranger, and would have given him a good ducking and also a drubbing, had not Robin cried out, "Nay, forbear! He hath beaten me in fair fight, and if he will stay with us and be one of our men he is right welcome."

"What name goest thou by?" he asked as the stranger gave him his hand.

"John Little," answered the stranger solemnly, at which all the men laughed heartily, and Will Stutely cried out:

"Little art thou indeed, and small of bone and sinew, and therefore shalt thou be christened Little John!"

"Then come, my merry men," quoth Robin Hood, "and we will prepare a christening feast for this fair infant."

So through the forest they went until they came to a great oak tree with broad-spreading branches and 'neath it a seat of green moss where Robin was wont to sit at feast and merry-making with his good men about him. A brace of fat does from the king's fine herd was brought forth and a barrel of humming ale was broached.

At last the stranger gave Robin such a blow that he fell into the water.

Then whilst great fires crackled and the savoury smell of sweetly roasting venison filled the glade, some of the men stood forth and contended with the quarterstaff, whilst others set up garlands on the branches of trees and shot at them in archery practice. When the feast was ready, all sat down, and Robin Hood placed Little John at his right hand.

And thus, amid jest and song and good cheer, the men of the greenwood christened their new comrade Little John, who was to win renown second only to that of Robin Hood himself.

The Shooting-Match at Nottingham

NOW you must know that all this time the proud Sheriff of Nottingham was trying in vain to bring Robin Hood to justice. So many times had he tried and failed that the king had spoken harsh and scornful words. Then at last he bethought himself how he might use guile to capture the daring outlaw.

"It is of no avail," thought the Sheriff, "to seek out that evil knave Robin Hood in his woodland haunts. But if I could persuade him to come nigh to Nottingham Town, I warrant I would lay hands upon him so stoutly that he would never get away from us again."

So he bethought him to proclaim a great shooting-match to which everyone who could draw a longbow should be bidden. An arrow of gold was to be the prize and the one who gained it fairly and squarely should be hailed by all as the greatest archer throughout the length and breadth of the land.

"If I know aught of Robin Hood," quoth the Sheriff, who was Robin's greatest enemy, "he will never

"John Little" answered the tall stranger solemnly, at which the others laughed heartily.

itherto the ragged stranger had shot so quickly that one could scarce take breath between the drawing and the
ooting; and men marvelled that one blind of one eye could shoot so well.   Now he shot with greater care...

submit to see that title of champion archer won without making trial to win it himself."

When Robin Hood heard of the Sheriff's proclamation he called his men about him and said : "I fain would have one of us win this fair prize that our sweet friend the Sheriff offers ; and therefore will we take our bows and shafts and go to Nottingham Town. What say ye, lads ? "

"Have a care, good master," said one of his followers. "I have heard it said that this same shooting-match is but a trap whereby the knavish Sheriff would draw thee into the town and so beguile thee."

"Then," said Robin, "must we meet guile with guile. We shall lay aside our suits of Lincoln green and go in disguise—some as shaven friars, some as rustic peasants, and some as tinkers or as beggars. How like you the plan, my merry men all ? "

"Good, good ! " cried all the band right heartily.

The great day was arrived, and at the appointed time the Sheriff took his place in the seat of honour near the target. Leaning forward he scanned the crowd of archers that had come from far and near throughout merry England, but he saw none clad in Lincoln green, such as was worn by Robin Hood and his men.

An arrow with a scroll attached came through the window. The Sheriff grew red with rage as he read the scroll and learned that he had given the prize of the golden arrow to Robin Hood.

And now the archers began to shoot, each in turn; and never had the good folk seen such archery as was shown that day. After the first contest the ten best men were chosen to shoot again.

"Seest thou Robin Hood amongst those ten ? " asked the Sheriff of a man-at-arms who stood near him.

"Nay, that I do not, your worship," answered the man. "Six of them I know right well and of the others none is of Robin Hood's size except perhaps that tattered beggar in scarlet, and he has a beard of brown instead of yellow, besides being blind in one eye."

Each of the ten now shot again, and then from these the three best were chosen for the final contest. One of these was the tattered stranger in scarlet with the patch over one eye ; another was Gilbert o' the Red Cap, one of the Sheriff's own archers. Twice they shot, all three, and it was soon seen that the match lay between Gilbert and the tattered stranger. On the third shot Gilbert's shaft lodged close beside the spot that marked the very centre.

"Well done, Gilbert ! " cried the Sheriff joyously. "Now, thou ragged knave, let us see if thou canst shoot a better shaft than that."

All held their breath as the ragged stranger stepped forth. Hitherto he had shot so quickly that one could scarce take breath between the drawing and the shooting; and men marvelled that one blind of one eye could shoot so well. Now he shot with greater care, holding his trusty yew drawn for a moment before loosing the string. Straight flew the arrow and so true that it smote a feather from off Gilbert's shaft and lodged in the very centre.

"Here, good fellow," quoth the Sheriff as he stepped down in silks and velvets to where the tattered archer stood. "Take thou the prize, for well and fairly hast thou won it. I trow thou drawest better bow than that same coward knave Robin Hood, that dared not show his face here this day."

That afternoon, in the depths of Sherwood Forest, Robin Hood's men feasted merrily, but the soul of their leader was vexed. He it was who had won the prize from the Sheriff's own hands, and the Sheriff's words rankled in his heart. "I would fain let him know who it was that won the golden arrow from out his hand," at last said Robin to his men.

Then up spoke Little John : "Let me but go to Nottingham Town, and I will send yon Sheriff news of this by a messenger such as he does not expect."

That night as the Sheriff sat at meat in his great hall talking of the shooting-match and wondering who might be the bold archer who had won the prize, a blunted grey goose shaft with a small scroll attached came through the window and fell upon the table.

The Sheriff opened the scroll and grew red with rage, for on it he read :

> Now Heaven bless thy grace this day,
>   Say all in sweet Sherwood,
> For thou didst give the prize away
>   To Merry Robin Hood.

—*Retold from Howard Pyle's Merry Adventures of Robin Hood.*

How SCREECHER LEARNED to HUNT
The Story of a Young Owl

moon peeped over the edge of the hills. "It has been a long time since I had anything to eat—an awful long time."

His parents had been flying about since dusk, hunting for food. Each night they hunted like this, through the darkness. They ate great quantities of mice and insects that lived in the fields around the apple orchard. Screecher was sure that, by and by, they would bring him something to eat, too. So he sat there on the branch and turned his round head first toward the orchard and then toward the meadow, looking for them. Owls must turn their whole head when they want to look around, for their eyes are placed in front and do not move at all. As Screecher turned his head this way and that he looked very grave and solemn, and a little angry, too, for he was getting hungrier and hungrier.

Presently he saw his mother flying toward him, her wings moving slowly and silently. For a moment he watched her in admiration. He loved to watch his parents fly. The soft feathers on their wings were tipped with a downy fringe, so that they could move through the air without making any sound at all. And because they flew so silently, they could hear the little creatures moving about through the grass, and could pounce upon them so noiselessly that it made young Screecher very proud of them. He, too, would fly like this some day, he knew; and he hoped he would have fine reddish brown feathers, like his father's. Many screech owls are grey, and Screecher thought his father was much more splendid than the grey owls.

"What did you bring me for supper?" he asked eagerly, when his mother alighted on the branch beside him.

"Nothing," she told him. "Your father and I think it is high time you were learning to catch your own food."

"But I am so hungry, mother," Screecher complained in surprise. "Won't you please catch me something to eat?"

"No," his mother answered. "Not one mouse, not one bird, not even one beetle, will I ever catch for you again. You must look out for yourself from now on, Screecher. You are plenty old enough to do this."

T HE old apple orchard was very peaceful and quiet in the twilight. Most of the birds had gone to rest, and only an occasional sleepy note broke the evening stillness. On a branch of an apple tree at the edge of the orchard, Screecher, a young American screech owl, sat blinking his great eyes. He was waiting for his parents to return with food for him.

Most of the day Screecher had been asleep in the family nest—a bare hole inside the apple tree. Like most owls, he slept in the daytime. Now that the sun had gone down, he was wide awake and very hungry for his supper.

He was lonely, too, because the three other little owls who had been hatched there in the family nest had already flown away. They had wanted Screecher to fly away with them, but he was not yet ready to go. It was pleasant to stay here in the old apple tree, sleeping through the day, and waking at evening to eat the beetles and other insects, or the fine fat field mouse, that his parents brought him. And it was pleasant to sit here in the darkness and listen to the cries of other owls, as they flew softly about in search of food. So, although the other little owls had made fun of him, young Screecher had stayed on in the old apple tree in the peaceful orchard.

"I wish my father and mother would hurry back with my supper," he thought now, as the

The father owl had pounced upon a field mouse.

"Oh dear!" Screecher cried, in his high quavering voice. "Oh, dear! Whatever shall I do?"

Just then his father alighted on the apple tree, and the young owl stopped his crying at once. "Father," he begged, "*you* will catch a mouse for me, won't you? You won't let me go hungry, I know."

"There is no need for you to go hungry, Screecher," the father owl said pleasantly. "There is plenty of food to be found on the ground. You have only to fly a little way to get all you want."

"Oh, father!" Again Screecher raised his voice. "I don't want to get my own supper! I want you to bring it to me. Pl—e—ase!"

The father owl did not wait for Screecher to say anything more, but flew softly to the ground. "Now," thought the young owl, "he will bring me my supper. I knew he would if I coaxed him."

The father owl had pounced upon a field mouse and, holding it in his claws, he flew back to the branch beside Screecher. But to the young owl's dismay, his father at once began to eat the mouse.

"Oh, father!" Screecher cried sharply, "you are eating my mouse!"

"No," his father replied, "this is my mouse. I caught it, you know. If you want food, you must catch it for yourself now. You have good sharp ears, and if you will only listen you will hear any number of small creatures moving about on the ground. They will make a fine meal for you."

Screecher was disappointed, but he obeyed his father and, sure enough, he heard something stirring in the grass. Without waiting a moment he flew down and caught a fine fat beetle!

"There! That's right," said his father, when Screecher was once more beside him on the branch. "A little later, you can practise catching mice. You will soon be able to do it as well as I do."

With this, the father owl gave his long quavering cry and flew away. The mother owl, with only a glance to see that Screecher was all right, flew after him.

"Well," thought Screecher, as he watched them go, "it is plain to be seen that if I want any more supper, I must catch it for myself." And then hearing another beetle he flew down and seized it.

All night long he flew about, finding all kinds of dainties in the grass—earthworms, moths, spiders, and even an occasional snail. He ate so many of them that at last he could not eat another thing.

The east was now growing pale with the coming dawn. The young owl decided to go back to his nest and sleep until another night should come. But, as he looked about, he found that his own apple tree was nowhere to be seen. He had flown so far from home in his search for food that he could not find his way back! He was lost!

At first this frightened him, for the day was coming fast, and he did not see very well in the daylight. But after a moment he wisely decided to seek shelter in the thick branches of a near-by tree. "I will wait here until darkness comes again," he thought, "and then I can find my way home."

When he was settled on a leafy branch, he turned his round head from side to side to look about and be sure that he was well hidden. Then he contentedly shut his eyes and went soundly off to sleep.

Higher and higher rose the sun. The birds sang gaily all around him, but Screecher did

"You horrid creature!" cried the woodpecker.

not hear them. He was dreaming of the fine supper he meant to have when night came again.

Presently a jay flew on to a branch just above his head. Seeing the owl, it screamed loudly at him. "So there you are, Young Owl," it cried, "hiding yourself away among the leaves, hoping I would not see you! But I do see you, and I mean to fly at you and peck you with all my might. I certainly don't like any of you owl people."

The jay had screamed so loudly that several other birds came flying to the tree to see what was wrong.

"You horrid creature!" cried the woodpecker. "With your great round eyes, and your short sharp beak, and your cruel claws! What do you mean by flying around at night, frightening our children? We will teach you a lesson, we will!"

"You're a screech owl!" piped a titmouse, flying close to Screecher's face, "and you make dreadful cries in the night that wake us up. Aren't you ashamed of yourself?"

Poor young Screecher was now thoroughly alarmed. What should he do? He must frighten these birds away if he could. So he snapped his beak with a chattering sound, and spread his wings, and ruffled up his feathers, trying to make himself as terrifying as he could.

But still the birds flew about him, darting closer and closer. A cardinal had come to the tree, and now added its cries to those of the jay, the woodpecker, and the titmouse, so that their noise was fairly deafening.

"Go away from this tree!" they screamed. "We don't like those funny bunches of feathers that stand up on your head like horns. Why should you have horns, anyhow? We don't!"

"They are not horns!" Screecher answered angrily. "They are tufts of feathers that grow above my ears. And good sharp ears I have, too. I can hear better than any of you other birds."

Screecher knew now that he could stay here no longer. So, without waiting another moment, he spread his wings and flew away. The birds screamed at him as he went, but the young owl landed safely in a tree a long way off and there he quickly hid himself in the heavy foliage.

For a long time he sat there, not daring to go to sleep. To add to his discomfort, he began to feel hungry once more. Ever since he had been hatched from a round white egg, Screecher had always had food in the daytime, for his parents had left worms and insects in the nest where he could find them when he woke up from time to time. Now there was no food for him unless he flew to the ground and caught it for himself. But screech owls do not hunt in the daytime, and he knew he must wait until the darkness came. So he closed his eyes and went to sleep again, and this time he slept in peace.

The twilight had come again when he woke, refreshed by his sleep. The other birds had gone to rest, and as he sat blinking his eyes and looking about he felt very contented and happy. It was fine, he thought, that he was now old enough to catch his own food, instead of having to wait for his parents to bring it to him. And as for the birds who had scolded him, he would take good care after this to hide himself where they could not find him. One of these days, when his feathers had grown a little longer, he would be able to fly about through the night without fear. He would be able to frighten his enemies and drive them away by flying at them, flapping his wings, and even pecking them with his strong curved beak, as he had often seen his parents do. Yes, it was a good thing to be a young owl who could go where he pleased and catch his own food.

Tightening his eight strong toes around the branch on which he sat, he looked down at the ground. Down there, somewhere in the grass, was all the food that he could eat; but, although he was hungry, he was in no hurry to begin his hunt. He had the whole long night before him.

An old screech owl flew silently past his tree. He could see its body outlined against the twilight—its round head covered with soft brown feathers, out of which its two great eyes gleamed. He could see the soft brown feathers that covered its body thickly, and he watched with admiration as its wings rose and fell without a sound.

Another screech owl, farther off, sent up its long shivering cry. Perhaps it was his mother, Screecher thought, or his father, he did not know. And it did not matter much, for now the dark had come and owls were flying everywhere. He, too, would fly presently.

Again he looked down at the ground, listening intently. All of a sudden he swooped. Straight down he went, softly and surely. And in a moment his claws had closed around a fine fat field mouse.

He had done it! He had caught a mouse! He was able now to look after himself, as his parents had said he must. How proud they would be!

Flying up to a low branch of the tree, he raised his voice in a long thin cry that rose and fell with a trembling sound. From not far away there came an answering cry, and Screecher knew that it was his father's voice.

"I will go along now," he thought, "and tell him about the mouse I caught!" And, spreading his wings, he flew happily away into the night.

All of a sudden he swooped.
Straight down he went,
softly and surely.

PRICKLES LEARNS *to* LIKE HIS QUILLS
The Story of a Young Porcupine

*A large porcupine
squeezed through the hole
and stood in front of Prickles.*

PRICKLES, the young porcupine, lived in a little cave by the edge of a wood. He was called Prickles because his back and sides were covered all over with long, prickly quills—white quills with black tips. Even his tail was covered with quills. His head was small and his legs were short and stumpy.

"Oh, dear!" he would often say to himself. "I wish I had a nice soft fur like the squirrels. Fur would be much nicer than quills." But he could not change his quills, because all porcupines have them.

Prickles usually slept all day, but this afternoon he was very hungry. So he got up bright and early to look for his breakfast. There was plenty of bark on the trees for him to eat, but he was tired of eating bark. There were plenty of nice juicy twigs, but he was tired of eating twigs, too.

"I wish I could find something new to eat," he thought, "something I have never tasted before in my life."

All at once he saw a dark hole under the roots of a big tree. "I wonder what is in that hole," thought Prickles. He went a little nearer—something moved inside the hole. He went still nearer—and saw two small eyes looking out at him. "Oh!" cried Prickles. "Who are you? What is your name? Do you live here?"

The two eyes blinked back at him for a moment and then, very slowly, a large porcupine squeezed through the hole and stood right in front of Prickles.

"You ask a lot of questions," said the porcupine, "but that's all right. You are young and you have many things to learn. My name is Old Quills," he went on politely, "and this is my den. I usually sleep through the day and hunt at night."

"I have a den, too," said Prickles, "but it is smaller than yours. Have you lived here very long?"

"I have lived here a long time, little porcupine," answered Old Quills, "for I am very old. I have seen six summers and six winters."

"My goodness!" said Prickles, "you *are* old, aren't you!"

Old Quills shuffled slowly off to look for his breakfast, and left Prickles standing all alone.

"Wait a minute!" cried Prickles. "I want to go with you!" He couldn't walk very fast because his legs were so short, but he walked as fast as he could. A saucy chipmunk scurried past him and called back, "What a slow walker you are, porcupine! Don't you wish you could run as fast as I can?"

Prickles knew he was slow; but he couldn't

go faster, no matter how hard he tried. So he just walked on and didn't answer the chipmunk, but his feelings were hurt. Pretty soon he saw Old Quills waiting for him by a hemlock tree.

"Come along, little porcupine," said Old Quills. "I will show you where there are a lot of fine lily pads. They are tender and green and very good to eat."

"Oh, good!" cried Prickles. "I am so hungry that I could eat them all."

As they shuffled along on their stumpy legs, the little creatures of the woods peeped out from their nests and burrows to look at them.

"See the clumsy porcupines!" said a rabbit. "Did you ever see such awkward creatures in all your life?"

"Shhh!" whispered a squirrel. "They might hear you and stick you full of quills."

"Pooh," laughed the rabbit, "they won't hear me. Porcupines can hardly hear at all. Anyhow, I am too fast for them."

At last Prickles and Old Quills came to a little pond covered with the loveliest lily pads. "Here is our breakfast," said Old Quills, pulling out a lily pad and munching it slowly. "There is enough here for both of us, and more too."

"I am going to eat all I can hold," said Prickles. "My! they look good!"

He grabbed the nearest one in his mouth and ate it greedily. *Mmmm*—it was tenderer and juicier than anything he had ever eaten. He ate another, and then another How good they were! He munched and crunched.

Then Prickles saw the biggest lily pad of all.

It was round and green and smooth, and he wanted it very much.

"Maybe if I stretch hard, I can reach it," he thought. So he leaned out as far as he could and tried to seize it with his sharp teeth. The big lily pad was just out of his reach. He leaned out a little farther and—splash! he fell right into the water!

Prickles was so frightened that he splashed and kicked with all his might. "Old Quills! Old Quills!" he called, when at last he caught his breath. "Come quick and help me out!"

But Old Quills just stood on the bank and chewed his lily pads.

"Don't be frightened, little porcupine," he said. "Your hollow quills will keep you up and make you float like a piece of wood. We porcupines don't have to swim if we don't want to," he added proudly. "We just float."

Prickles stopped his splashing and kicking and, sure enough, his quills held him up, just as the old porcupine had said!

"What fun it is to float about on the water like this!" thought Prickles. "I like to float," he said aloud, "it really is great sport."

"You had better get out of the water now, young porcupine, if you want to come with me," said Old Quills. "I am going to my hemlock tree up on the hill."

"Oh, I do want to go with you, Old Quills!" cried Prickles, as he paddled to the shore. "Please wait for me!"

So the old porcupine waited until Prickles had climbed out on the bank.

"Did you ever see such awkward creatures in all your life?" said a rabbit.

"I'm going to eat all I can hold," said Prickles.

"Now then," said Old Quills, "let us go!"

"Ha! Ha!" screamed a bluejay, as the two porcupines shuffled clumsily along. "Look at the funny porcupines! *They* can't fly or run. They can't even walk very fast."

"I don't like to be made fun of," little Prickles said to Old Quills. "I know I can't walk fast and I know I look clumsy, but I wish the other creatures wouldn't laugh at me."

"Don't pay any attention to them," said Old Quills, "we porcupines can do some things that they can't do."

"What?" asked Prickles.

"Well, we can float for one thing," said Old Quills.

"Yes, and that's fun; but we can't run like the squirrels and chipmunks," said the little porcupine. "They think we are terribly slow and clumsy."

"We don't have to run," replied Old Quills. "Other creatures run when they smell danger, because they are afraid. We aren't afraid of anything, because we know how to protect ourselves."

"How do we protect ourselves, Old Quills?" cried Prickles eagerly. "Do please tell me, won't you?"

"It's very simple," the old porcupine said. "Your sharp quills are your weapons. You haven't any quills on your nose, so if a creature tries to harm you, turn your back to it, put your nose between your forepaws, and then thrash about with your tail as hard as you can. If the creature tries to touch you then, he will get his nose stuck full of your sharp needles. That will teach him to leave you alone, because a nose full of your needles hurts. Most creatures have learned not to bother us."

"Oh," said Prickles, "then we *are* as clever as the other forest creatures, aren't we? Is there anything else we can do?"

"Yes," said Old Quills, "there is another very useful thing."

"What is it? What is it?" cried Prickles.

"Well," said Old Quills, "whenever I get sleepy or tired I crawl into the first little hole I see and curl up with my prickly back in the mouth of the hole. I won't be bothered, because if any other creature tries to get into the hole, he gets stuck with my quills."

"Oh," cried Prickles, "I want to try that! It sounds fun!"

"You will have to find a hole first," said Old Quills. "*I* am going to my hemlock tree at the top of the hill. There is nothing I like better to eat than bark and twigs, and that hemlock tree has the nicest bark and twigs to be found in the whole forest."

While Old Quills climbed slowly up the hill, Prickles looked around for a hole to sleep in.

"I'm afraid there are no holes in this hill," he thought, after he had looked and looked. "What shall I do? I am so tired and sleepy."

Just then Prickles saw something black a little farther up the hill. " It looks like a fine sleeping hole," he said. " Hurray! There's just room for me." He crawled into it as fast as he could and put his prickly back right up against the opening of the hole.

"Now nobody can bother me, or make fun of me," he thought. " I can sleep just as long as I want to."

By and by he was awakened by a noise outside. He couldn't see out, but he knew from the grunting noise that it was a young groundhog or woodchuck.

"What do you mean by lying in my hole!" the groundhog scolded. " The very idea! Come out this minute!" But Prickles lay very, very still. The young groundhog tried to push his way in. Foolish groundhog!

"Oh me! Oh my!" he cried. " What have you done, porcupine! You've stuck me full of quills. My poor nose! My *poor* nose!"

"Oh, I'm sorry, groundhog," said Prickles. " Why weren't you more polite? You should have known better than to start pushing a porcupine about."

"I will surely know better the next time," said the groundhog, as he tried to pull the quills out of his nose. " I will never make fun of a porcupine again as long as I live."

"You may have your hole now," Prickles said. " I've had a good sleep and I must go and find Old Quills. Good-bye, I'm sorry I hurt you." The groundhog didn't answer. He was too busy rubbing his nose.

Prickles had not gone far before he saw Old Quills coming toward him. " Did you find a hole, little porcupine?" Old Quills asked.

"Yes," said Prickles, " I found a groundhog's hole. He came home and started to push in. When I left him he was busy pulling my quills out of his nose."

"Ho—ho!" chuckled Old Quills. " You are learning fast. All the creatures will soon learn not to make fun of *you*. And now let's go home. You have had an exciting day for a little porcupine, and we have a long walk."

So Prickles and Old Quills started home. Prickles was very happy.

"I would rather be a porcupine than any other creature in the forest," he told Old Quills, as they shuffled along. " Porcupines can do so many, many things."

" You should have known better than to push a porcupine about."

BLACKFACE MEETS HIS NEIGHBOURS

The Story of a Young Raccoon

Bright black eyes saw everything.

BLACKFACE was a little raccoon, and he lived in a hollow high up in a big tree. He had four little brothers and sisters. They lived in the hollow tree, too, and so did his father and mother.

The little raccoons looked just alike. Their faces were black and their noses were sharp. They had bright black eyes that saw everything that was going on around them. All of them had fine coats of grey fur and beautiful bushy tails with black rings around them right to the very end.

Blackface was the liveliest in the family. He was full of mischief, and he liked to romp and play better than anything in the world. He was very curious, too, and he sometimes let his curiosity get him into trouble.

" Dear, dear! " his mother would often say. " I don't know what I am going to do with you, Blackface, if you don't learn not to meddle with things you do not understand. Ask all the questions you like, but don't be nosing and touching everything that comes along." This was very hard for Blackface to learn. Every time he saw anything new he always wanted to touch it or grab it with his slender little paw to find out what it was.

Another thing that was hard for him to learn was to sleep all day. His brothers and sisters lay on the floor of the den and slept the whole day through as their mother and father did ; but Blackface was too lively for that. He liked to poke his little head out at the doorway and see what was going on in the forest. Most of all, he liked to climb down the tree and play about on the ground, though he did not do this very often because his father and mother would not let him.

" I don't see why we have to sleep in the daytime, when nearly all the other creatures are awake," he said to his father one day. " Why do we, father ? "

" It is a thing raccoons have always done," his father told him. " We stay in our dens in the daytime to rest and sleep. At night we go out and hunt for our food. It is much the safest way."

Blackface didn't say anything more, but he still thought it was silly to sleep in the daytime when there was so much to see and do. He made up his mind that *he* would stay awake, no matter what other raccoons did.

So one summer afternoon, when his father and mother and brothers and sisters were fast asleep, Blackface very quietly slipped out of the den

For a moment he stood on a big branch, just outside the doorway, and looked about him. Then he started down the tree.

He went down head-first, as all raccoons do, digging his little sharp claws into the bark to keep from falling. Pretty soon he reached the ground.

"Now," he thought, "I will go wherever I like, and do whatever I please. This is a lot more fun than sleeping."

He started off through the woods. He hadn't gone far, when he heard a queer noise up in a tree. *Tap—tap—tap*, *tap—tap—tap*. Blackface looked up. He saw a bird tapping its long bill against a tree as hard as it could.

"I wonder why he's doing that," he thought. "I'd better try to find out." So he started to climb up the tree.

The woodpecker was getting his dinner. He was very much annoyed at being interrupted and flew away with a loud scream. Blackface continued climbing. "Maybe he will come back," he thought. "I'll just wait, because I *must* find out why he tapped like that."

Soon the woodpecker came back and flew very near to the little raccoon. "What are you doing in my tree?" he asked angrily. "Go away this minute!"

Blackface was surprised, but he was not frightened. He answered: "I just came up here to find out why you were tapping on the tree like that."

"Go away! go away, I tell you!" the woodpecker screamed louder than ever. "Go away, or I will peck you with my bill!"

"I won't go away," Blackface said stubbornly, "until I have found out what I want to know!"

The woodpecker darted at him and pecked him on the head!

"Ouch!" cried Blackface. "That hurt!"

"Of course it did!" screamed the woodpecker; "and if you don't go away I will peck you again!"

Once more it darted towards him, and this time Blackface didn't wait a second. He turned and scrambled down the tree as fast as ever he could go.

"Dear me!" he said when he was on the ground once more, "what a cross old bird! And I didn't find out what I wanted to know, after all."

He wandered on through the woods and soon forgot about the woodpecker, because there were so many other things to see. All kinds of creatures scampered about—up and down trees and through the grass—but none of them paid any attention to the little raccoon.

"I do wish someone would talk to me," he thought, "but everyone seems to be too busy."

So he started up the tree.

Just then a black beetle came running along the path where Blackface was standing. Blackface had never seen such a queer looking thing, and without thinking he reached out to touch it. Quick as a flash, the beetle fastened its pincers in the little raccoon's paw and pinched it sharply!

"Oh! Oh! Oh!" cried Blackface, shaking his paw. "Let go! You're hurting me! *Please* let go!"

The black beetle opened his pincers and dropped to the ground. "There! I hope that will teach you not to meddle with me another time!" he said as he scurried away.

"Oh, dear me!" Blackface thought as he licked his paw. "Everyone in the woods seems cross. But surely if I walk far enough I'll find *someone* who will talk to me." So he kept on walking.

At last he came to an open place where bright-coloured flowers bloomed in the tall grass. "Isn't this pleasant!" Blackface thought. "I'm glad I found this place."

The sun was getting low in the sky now, and the little raccoon lay down in the grass to rest. His head was sore where the woodpecker had pecked it; his paw was sore where the beetle had pinched it; and he was tired and sleepy after his long walk.

He hadn't been lying there very long when something said *buzz—buzz—buzz*, close to his ear. Blackface turned quickly. He couldn't see anything except a little creature with wings, sitting on a flower.

"That will teach you!" said the black beetle.

"Was it this little fellow who made all the racket?" he wondered. Forgetting about the woodpecker and the beetle, Blackface put out his paw to touch the little creature.

Zoom! The bumblebee darted at his nose and stung it as hard as he could.

"Oh, dear me! Oh, dear me!" cried Blackface, rubbing his nose on the ground. "That hurt! Why did you do that?"

"It's the only way I have to make you stop bothering me," said the bumblebee. "Haven't you learned not to annoy others?"

"But I only wanted to find out about you," answered Blackface, unhappily.

"Well, you found out that I can sting, didn't you?" the bumblebee said. "And now I must hurry and gather all the nectar I can before it is dark."

Blackface was very uncomfortable. His head was still sore where the woodpecker had pecked him. His paw was still sore where the beetle had pinched him. His nose was still sore where the bumblebee had stung him. He was tired and he wanted his mother.

Blackface shut his eyes. The sky grew dark. "Blackface! Blackface! Blackface!" he heard. Blackface jumped up. There stood his mother! "Blackface," she said, "I have been looking everywhere for you! Where in the world have you been?"

"I have been walking through the woods to see what I could see," Blackface said, trying to be brave.

The bumblebee darted at his nose.

"Well, it was very wrong of you to run away when you should have been asleep in the den. Something might have happened to you."

"Something *did* happen to me," Blackface answered quickly. And then he told his mother all about the woodpecker and the beetle and the bumblebee. And when he had finished telling her, he whimpered a little and said: "I'm awfully hungry, too, mother."

His mother did not scold him any more. She only rubbed his fur with her nose and said: "You will feel better when you have something to eat. We will go down to the stream and fish for our supper. Your father and the rest of the family are already down there."

Blackface followed his mother down to the little stream. "Hello, Blackface!" called his sister Greypaws. "Come and fish with us—we're catching crayfish."

The cool water felt very good as he waded out into it. He began to feel about on the sandy bottom of the stream with the slim fingers of his forepaws. He turned over several stones before he found what he wanted, but by and by he caught a fine crayfish.

He was so hungry that he put it to his mouth at once, but his mother called sharply: "Blackface! Don't eat your food until you have washed it! I have told you that a great many times already."

"But I am so hungry, mother," the little raccoon told her. "Must I wash all the food I eat tonight?"

"Yes," answered his mother. "Raccoons always wash their food when they can, so of course you must do it too."

Blackface grumbled a little, but he dabbled the crayfish about in the water for a moment or two, and then, going out on the shore, he sat down and ate it greedily.

All night long the raccoon family fished and gathered berries and dug up tender roots. At last it was time for them to go back to their home in the hollow tree.

Blackface felt very sleepy. As he trotted along through the woods behind his mother he said:

"I thought it would be fun to go out into the forest in the daytime, but it wasn't as much fun as I thought it would be."

"No," his mother answered. "The safest place for raccoons in the daytime is inside their hollow tree."

"After this, I'm going to stay in the tree in the daytime, and sleep as you and father do," he said. "But I will go out at night, won't I? I will go out every night for the rest of my life and fish in the stream for my supper."

"Not *every* night," his mother told him. "You will fish and eat all summer, but when the cold comes you will go to sleep in the hollow tree and you will sleep there all winter long."

"Won't I fish at all, then?" the little raccoon asked.

"No," his mother answered, "you will only sleep. Raccoons always sleep when winter comes, so you will lie safe and snug in the den through the cold weather. You will not wake until the warm spring is here again."

Blackface thought about this for a little while, but he soon forgot it, for winter would not be here for a long time yet.

Safe up in the den once more he thought only about the fun he would have when he went fishing again for the tasty crayfish.

All night long the raccoon family fished in the stream.

How GOLDENWINGS LEARNED to FLY
The Story of a Baby Woodpecker

*He went out alone
and sat on a
branch.*

GOLDENWINGS, a little flicker (American woodpecker), woke early one fine morning and opened wide his mouth.

"I'm hungry! I'm hungry!" he called. He made so much noise that his five little brothers and sisters opened their eyes. Then they all began to call for their breakfast as loud as they could.

The nest in which the six little flickers lived was in a hole in a tree near the edge of a wood. The mother and father flicker had made this nest with their sharp round bills. They had pecked out a small round hole for the doorway, and then made a larger room inside. It had taken them more than a week to hollow out the nest, because they had been careful to carry all the chips away. They didn't want a pile of chips at the foot of the tree, telling everybody where their nest was.

Now mother flicker put her head in at the doorway and looked at the six noisy little flickers.

"Oh! So you are awake and hungry again as usual," she said. "It seems to me your voices grow stronger each morning. Well, snuggle down a minute, and father and I will bring your breakfast very soon."

She flew away as she spoke and the six little flickers settled down once more in the nest and closed their eyes.

"Let's all go out and sit on a branch of the tree, the way we did yesterday," Goldenwings said after a while. "It is so nice out there."

"We don't want to! We want our break-fast!" cried the other little flickers. So Goldenwings went out alone and sat on a branch in the sunshine.

He liked to sit out here and watch the other birds flying past him. For a little while he sat very still. After a bit, because he was getting hungrier every minute, he began to call as loud as he could: "Mother! Father! Come and feed me! Come quick! Come quick! Come quick!"

"What is all this noise?" said a voice. A screech owl poked his head out of a hole farther up the tree. "How do you suppose I can get to sleep?"

Goldenwings looked up. There, right above his head, he saw two eyes staring down at him. They were very large eyes. They frightened Goldenwings because they looked so fierce. Just then mother and father flicker flew back. Goldenwings forgot all about the screech owl, as he stretched his bill wide open. His father stuffed a fat caterpillar down his throat.

Mother flicker flew inside the tree to feed the other little birds. When they saw her each little flicker cried louder than ever. Once again the screech owl poked his head out of his door.

"Can't you woodpeckers keep your children quiet?" he scolded. "They make so much noise that I can't get a wink of sleep."

"You should sleep at night, the way we do," father flicker said. "Then these children wouldn't bother you."

"*Night* isn't the time for owls to sleep!" The screech owl was surprised. "Owls always sleep in the daytime."

"Well," said father flicker, "I'm afraid you won't get much sleep today, screech owl. It's going to be pretty noisy here at my tree."

The screech owl poked his head still farther out of his door. "What do you mean by calling this *your* tree?" he asked, ruffling his feathers. "This is *my* tree! My home is just here in this hole."

"Yes, but we made it for you," mother flicker told him, putting her head out of her own door. "You wouldn't have that hole to live in if father flicker and I hadn't made it."

The screech owl looked down at her and blinked his eyes. "Did you woodpeckers make this hole?" he asked.

"Of course we did," she said. "We dug it out last year. We made most of the holes in this tree. It was hard work, too!"

"Well, I declare!" the screech owl said in surprise. "If I had known that, I wouldn't have scolded just now. I am much obliged to you for the hole. It makes a very comfortable home, and I certainly couldn't have dug one like it myself."

"Oh, that's all right," father flicker said. "I know the children are noisy when they are hungry. But soon we are going to teach them to get their own food. Then they won't bother you any more."

The screech owl drew his head back in his hole. Goldenwings was glad to see him close his two great staring eyes.

Goldenwings watched his father and mother as they flew away. He hoped he would soon grow as big as they were. And he hoped, very hard, that when he *did* grow up, he would be just like them. He wanted to have a bright

"I'm much obliged to you for this hole," said the owl.

scarlet band on his head, and bands of black across his back.

Most of all, he wanted to have a bright yellow colour under his wings, as his mother and father had. It looked so pretty when they flew in the sunshine. " I think I will have it, too," he said to himself. " Mother says my wings are already getting yellow—that's why she calls me Goldenwings."

Father and mother flicker were now out of sight, and Goldenwings was beginning to grow a little tired of sitting still. He looked around for something to do. Just then his sharp eyes spied a number of tiny insects running over the bark of the tree. Quick as a wink his long, round tongue darted out and caught one of them on its sticky tip.

" Why," he said in surprise, " it's food! Who would have thought that I'd find food right here in my tree! "

He was so pleased with himself that he caught another and another and another. Presently he dug his sharp little claws into the bark and began to creep slowly around the tree, eating insects as he went.

" This is just the way father and mother do," he thought. He was very proud of himself. " I wonder if I could fly like them, too? " He sat on a branch to think about this for a while. Just to see how it would feel to fly, he began to move his little wings up and down . . . up and down.

At first he moved them slowly. By and by he made them go faster and faster, and then, all at once, his little claws let go the branch . . . and down Goldenwings fell!

Down—down—down! He flapped his little wings as hard as he could. " I'm flying! " he said. " I'm flying, just like my father and mother! "

But Goldenwings wasn't really flying as well as he thought he was. He landed on the ground with a thump, right beside a fat robin, who was looking for a worm in the grass.

" Mercy! " said the robin. " What do you mean by landing on the ground like that? "

Goldenwings was frightened. He had never been on the ground before, and everything looked so strange down here that he began to call: " Mother! Father! Come and get me! Come and get me! "

" You mustn't make a noise like that when you are on the ground," the robin told him. " If you do, some creature will hear you and come along and eat you up! "

The little flicker stopped calling. " Who will eat me up? " he asked quickly.

" A cat, maybe," said the robin, as it hopped away. " Cats love to eat little birds who are learning to fly."

This scared Goldenwings so badly that for a while he didn't make a sound—he didn't even move. Presently he saw some tiny creatures running along through the grass. He caught one of them on the end of his long, sticky tongue.

" More food! " he cried, hopping a little in his excitement. " It's good food, too! "

Then he went on catching ants as fast as he could. He was so busy that he didn't even see his mother until she spoke to him. " Well, Goldenwings," she exclaimed, " you are really finding your own food, aren't you? "

" Who will eat me up? "
he asked quickly.

"It's fun!" Goldenwings cried. "I like this sort of food."

"Yes, ants are good," she said, shooting out her long tongue and catching a few herself. "There is nothing we flickers like better, though we are very fond of beetles and caterpillars and grasshoppers and other insects."

"But, mother," interrupted Goldenwings, "won't I hunt some of my food in trees? When you were gone I caught some funny little things that tasted awfully good."

"Oh, yes," she answered. "Have you noticed what a sharp point your bill has? Soon you will be strong enough to drill holes in trees with it and catch fat little grubs, if you want to. But we flickers prefer to get most of our food on the ground. You will like to eat berries, too."

"What else will I do, mother?" Goldenwings asked, hopping nearer.

He kept
hopping up
the tree.

"Well, some day you will dig the biggest hole of all in a tree," she told him, "and it will be your home. There you and your mate will raise a family of your own."

"Aren't there lots of things to do?" Goldenwings cried. "I hope I can very soon do all of them."

"You must learn to fly well, first," his mother said quickly. "I think you had better try it now for a little while."

So Goldenwings fluttered his wings and flew a few feet just above the ground. He was pleased. He tried it again. This time he didn't watch where he was going and he flew right against a tree. At first he was terribly frightened, but he held on to the bark with his claws and called for his mother.

"That's fine, Goldenwings!" she told him, alighting on the tree beside him and propping herself up with her strong tail. "Now watch me and see if you can climb up the tree the way I do. Come on."

Goldenwings wasn't frightened any more. He flattened his tail feathers against the rough bark and gave a hop, and sure enough he was a little farther up the tree.

He just loved this. It was more fun than being on the ground. He kept hitching himself up the tree until, at last, his mother said:

"Here we are! Here we are at home again, Goldenwings!"

And there was the little round doorway to the nest right before them!

Goldenwings had flown down to the ground; he had found food for himself; and now he was safely back home again! He was so excited at the thought of all this that he called loudly to his brothers and sisters: "I know how to fly! I know how to fly!"

But they had all gone to sleep again and didn't hear him.

Tired out with all the things he had done that morning, Goldenwings hopped into the nest and snuggled down. "Tomorrow," he thought, "I will try to peck a hole in the tree and find a fat little grub to eat!"

ADVENTURES of BLACKIE and GINGER
The Story of two Little Bears

He gave her a push that sent her sprawling.

ON a day in summer two little bears were playing together on a hillside. "What can we do, Blackie?" Ginger asked her brother. "There must be lots of things we've never done yet."

"I'll tell you," Blackie answered. "Let's hide in the bushes so that mother can't find us when she comes back."

"You know very well that mother will find us!" Ginger said. "She'll smell us right away."

"*I* can hide so mother won't find me," Blackie boasted. "I can hide so she couldn't *ever* find me!"

"No you can't!" Ginger said quickly. "Mother can find anything anywhere just by smelling it."

Blackie did not answer. Going over to his sister he gave her a push that sent her sprawling on her little back. Ginger got to her feet and rushed at Blackie as hard as she could. She loved a rough-and-tumble just as much as her brother did.

Blackie saw her coming and was ready for her. Rising to his hind legs, he gave her a smack. This time Ginger did not fall; instead, she rose to her hind legs too and cuffed Blackie soundly on the ear.

The two little bears were so busy scuffling that they did not see the mother bear coming toward them. Suddenly her big paw reached out and . . .

"*Wooff!*" said Blackie, sitting down on the ground very hard.

"*Whuff!*" said Ginger, landing near him.

"Stop it!" said the mother. "Listen to me! I have a treat for you. I know where there is something specially good to eat—something that you both like very much."

"What is it? What is it?" cried both little bears excitedly.

"It is honey!"

"Oh—Oh—Oh!" Blackie and Ginger stood on their hind legs and waved their paws joyfully. "Where is it, mother? Where is it? How did you find it?"

"I smelled it," she answered. "I think it is in an old tree on the other side of the hill. It won't take us long to get there. Come along! Single file!"

She started off, rolling her great body from side to side. The little bears followed, trying to walk just as she did. They lifted both feet on one side at the same time, first the right and then the left, then the right and then the left. And they put their feet down flat, just as she did, leaving tracks that showed the prints of their claws.

"Look, mother!" Ginger called out. "Blackie isn't coming! He's back there looking for grubs under a stone!"

Mother bear stopped and turned her head. "Blackie!" she called sharply. "Come along! You can hunt for grubs any time, but you don't get honey every day."

"But I'm hungry *now*," Blackie said, turning over a large stone with his front paw, "and it's a long way to the honey tree."

The mother bear started back toward Blackie. He gulped down a large fat grub and came running toward her. "I'm coming, mother," he called. "I'm hurrying as fast as I can."

The bees buzzed and swarmed angrily.

"You don't remember that at all, Blackie Black Bear! Mother told you that—I heard her! And I heard her tell you that we didn't go out of the den until we were three months old! I don't believe you really remember anything about the den."

"But I do!" Blackie said crossly. "I remember that it was cold."

"That's because we didn't have nice thick fur then," Ginger said. "Mother told me that we didn't have much fur at all when we were born. We weren't very big, either—we weren't much bigger than squirrels!"

"I was *never* as little as a squirrel!" Blackie said, very angry at the thought of this. "Was I, mother?" he called. "Was I ever as little as a squirrel?"

"Yes, you were," his mother said, "but you children had better hurry up. We are getting near the honey now. It's in that old hollow stump right over there."

The two little bears forgot everything else and ran to catch up.

"Um-m!" Blackie said, sniffing the air. "Doesn't it smell good?"

"Yes," Ginger answered. "Only I hope the bees won't sting us the way they did last time."

The mother bear went straight to the stump. The bees buzzed and swarmed angrily, but she paid no attention. She began to scratch and tear at the rotting wood to make a hole big enough for her paw.

"Oh, dear!" cried Ginger, holding her paws to her tender little nose, "a bee stung me right on my nose!"

"Ouch!" Blackie cried at the same time, "a bee stung me on my head!"

The mother bear kept on tearing at the stump with her strong claws. Her fur was so thick that the bees couldn't sting her easily. Even though one or two did sting her nose, she didn't mind much; she was so eager to get at the honey.

When the hole was big enough, she put in her paw and brought it out dripping with honey. "Delicious!" she said, as she licked off the sweet sticky stuff. Blackie and Ginger stretched up on their hind legs and put in their paws too.

Then for a while the two little bears followed her without a word.

Presently Ginger whimpered. "It's hot and I'm tired. We've walked such a long way, haven't we?"

"I'm not tired," Blackie said. "I can walk ever and ever so far and not get tired."

"I wish the honey tree wasn't so far away," Ginger complained. "I wish we were back in our nice den, with mother to feed us."

"Ho! I don't," Blackie said scornfully. "We're too old to drink milk now. And anyhow, I like grubs and fruit and berries better—and honey," he added. "I like honey better than anything."

"I do too, only I don't like to walk so far to get it. Do you remember how dark the den was, Blackie?"

"Of course I do. I remember all about it. We were born there, and for a good many days we didn't open our eyes."

"I like honey better than anything," said Blackie.

By and by each of them caught a handful of little fish.

They gobbled down the honey as fast as they could. The angry bees stung them and the little bears whined and whimpered but still kept on eating.

"Wasn't it good?" Blackie said when all the honey was gone. "I wish we had delicious honey every day."

"Well, I wish the bees wouldn't sting so hard," Ginger said, rubbing her sore nose.

"Come, children," their mother said. "We will go over to the shade, away from the bees, and take a nap."

The little bears were so full of honey that they were glad to lie down. Ginger dropped off to sleep at once. Suddenly Blackie raised his head.

"What's that, mother? What's that queer scratching sound I hear?"

"That is something you ought to know about. Come with me and I'll show you."

They waddled over to a clump of bushes near a tall smooth tree. The little bear looked through the bushes and saw a strange sight.

A huge bear was standing on his hind legs scratching on the tree as high as he could reach.

Blackie watched him a moment in silence. He couldn't understand what the bear was doing. He wanted to know. So he walked straight through the bushes and called out: "What are you scratching that tree for, Black Bear?"

The black bear stopped his scratching and looked down at little Blackie. "This is a scratching tree," he said in a big gruff voice. "Don't you know what a scratching tree is?"

"No, I don't. What is it?"

"It is a tree that he-bears scratch on."

"Why do you scratch on it?"

"So that other bears that come along will know who has been here. Look! That is my mark—the one that is highest up on the tree. No other bear who has scratched this tree is as big and strong as I am."

Blackie stared at him with big eyes. "He's a terribly big bear, isn't he, mother?" he said. "I'd like to be as big as he is."

"Maybe you will be one of these days," his mother said.

When they got back to where they had left Ginger she was awake and ready to play again.

"Now what can we do, mother?" she said. "I'd like to do something I've never done before."

"How would you like to catch some fish?" her mother asked.

"Is it fun?" asked the little bears.

"Lots of fun, and besides, fish are tasty and good to eat."

"As good as honey?" Ginger asked eagerly.

"They have a different taste," her mother answered, "but they're good."

Their mother took them down the hillside, along a path that other bears had made when they went to fish. Presently they came to a little stream. "Now watch me," she said, "and do just as I do."

She stood at the side of the stream and put her front paw in the water. For a long time she stood perfectly still, waiting. All of a sudden she scooped it through the water with a splash and brought out a handful of little fish.

" Oh, let me taste them ! " Blackie cried.

" No! You will never learn to fish if I feed you. You must catch your own food."

So the two little bears stood beside the stream and tried to do just as their mother had done. At first they only brought up water in their paws, but by and by each of them caught a handful of little fish. They felt very proud of themselves.

Suddenly the mother bear rose to her hind feet and moved her head from side to side, sniffing the air.

" Climb this tree, children! Quick! " she said. " I smell danger ! "

" I'm too tired to climb," Ginger said.

" Go up this tree, as I tell you! " the mother said sharply.

Ginger moved so slowly that her mother gave her a push. Blackie followed a little more quickly. The mother bear, behind him, prodded him on with her nose until at last they were all safely up.

For a while they lay very still on a high branch and waited. The mother bear kept sniffing the air. Presently she said: " I think it was that cross old lynx we saw last week. But he's gone now. Let's go down."

Then they all three climbed down again—tail first. Blackie and Ginger were even slower coming down than they had been going up, because they kept looking down over their shoulders to see where they were going.

" I don't like to climb trees," Ginger said. " It's too hard for little bears."

" Coming down is worse," said Blackie. " I can't see where I'm going."

" You must always climb a tree when you smell danger," their mother said. " Remember that, both of you."

The sun had set and the air was getting chilly. Blackie and Ginger were sleepy.

" Can't we go back to the den tonight, mother? " Ginger asked.

" No," their mother said. " We will sleep out in the woods all summer. When it gets cold we will go to our old den or find a new one and stay there until it is spring."

" What will we eat ? " Blackie asked quickly.

" We will not eat," his mother told him. " We won't be hungry. Before we go into the den we will eat and eat and eat until we are very, very fat. Then we won't need food all the long winter."

" I like fish," Ginger said sleepily.

" I like honey better," said Blackie.

" Enough talking, children! Go to sleep! "

The two little bears were so tired with all they had done that day, that they were glad enough to cuddle close to their mother and close their eyes. And soon they were fast asleep.

*"Climb this tree! Quick!
I smell danger ! "*

WHITE TAIL and the OLD STAG'S LESSON
The Story of a Young Deer

" What a fine fellow!" said the Squirrel.

"HOW good everything smells this morning," thought White Tail, the young deer, as he went along a forest pathway.

It was a fine morning late in summer, and White Tail was on his way to a near-by stream to breakfast on the rushes and water weeds that grew there. His small pointed hoofs made scarcely a sound as he walked, and his long ears were pointed forward, alert and listening. Those ears caught every small sound and warned him of danger while it was yet a long way off.

Though the sun had only just risen, many of the forest creatures were already abroad. They looked at him admiringly. He was a handsome young deer, with his slim legs and his rich brown summer coat that glistened almost red where the sun reached it.

"Good morning, White Tail," a squirrel called out from a tree. "What a fine fellow you are growing to be ! "

"Thank you, Squirrel," White Tail answered. "I have grown a good bit lately, haven't I ? "

"Indeed you have," said the squirrel. "Why, last year you were only a little fawn. You couldn't go anywhere without your mother."

"Yes," White Tail answered quickly, "I used to be afraid to leave her. But now I go about alone whenever I like."

"Well, don't let it make you too proud, or you will get into trouble," said the squirrel, as it whisked down the tree and scampered away.

White Tail was greatly pleased that the squirrel had noticed how much he had grown, and he held his small head high as he went along through the forest.

Presently, as he stopped to nibble at a bush beside the path, a pair of branching antlers was suddenly lifted, and there stood an old stag looking right into his eyes.

"Excuse me," the young deer said politely, "I didn't know you were feeding here. I am White Tail, and I only wanted to eat a few leaves from this bush. I didn't mean to startle you."

"You didn't startle me," the old stag said. "I knew you were coming. I heard a squirrel chattering with you; and once I heard you paw the ground when you stopped to browse."

White Tail was ashamed at the old stag's words, for he knew that one of the first things a young deer should learn was to pass through the forest without making any noise. "I will be more careful next time," he thought. Then, looking curiously at the old stag, he asked, "Aren't you a stranger here ? I don't remember seeing you before."

"Yes, I am a stranger," the old stag told him, "and I have come from a great distance. I wonder if you could tell me where I can find some salt," he went on. "I do not know the country around here, and I am longing for some salt."

"Yes, sir," White Tail answered. "I know where there is plenty of salt. If you will come along with me, I will show you."

The two deer set off together, through the forest. At first, White Tail felt a little shy, but presently he ventured to say, "What a fine pair of antlers you have, Old Stag ! I never saw such huge ones before."

"There are plenty of antlers as large as mine," the old stag told him. "Some are even larger. But my antlers have served me well in many a fight."

White Tail felt a new respect for this old stag who had come from such a distance, and who spoke so quietly about the fights he had had. "I wish my antlers were larger," he said. "It must be fine to have big antlers to fight with."

"It is," the old stag answered. "But there are times when I have no antlers. Did you know that, White Tail?"

"No," said White Tail, in amazement. "What happens to them?"

"Each year, in winter, they fall off," the old stag replied. "And then for a while I have no antlers at all."

"Will mine do that, too?" asked White Tail, anxiously.

"Yes, your antlers will fall off in the winter, and new ones will grow again in the spring. For a long time after the antlers begin to grow, they are tender and easily hurt. So they have a soft, velvety covering to protect them. But when the time comes, we rub the covering off against a tree or bush, and then our antlers are fine and hard again, and we are ready to fight with them."

"I hope my antlers will soon be hard," White Tail said, "and then I will fight with them."

The old stag looked at the two small spikes

"A fine pair of antlers!"

growing out of White Tail's head, and he was a little amused at the young buck who was in such a hurry to grow up. "You will have plenty of fights when you are older," he said, "but there are many things that you must learn before your antlers are ready to fight with."

"What things?" White Tail asked.

"Well," said the old stag, "I noticed a moment ago that you stepped on a dead twig and snorted when it snapped under your feet. You must learn to be quiet in the forest. You must not snort. You must not make any noise at all. For if you do, some day the Hunter will find you, and then you will be sorry!"

White Tail stopped in his tracks. "What is the Hunter?" he asked. "I do not know him."

"The Hunter is a danger," the old stag said. "He comes into the forest to look for us, and if he sees us he tries to kill us."

"Tell me more about him," White Tail said anxiously. "Won't you?"

"No," replied the old stag, "I want to hurry along to that salt lick. You ask your mother. She will tell you all you need to know about life in the forest."

Now they had reached the edge of a shallow ravine. White Tail turned from the path they had been following and led the way through dense underbrush out into a wide, well-beaten runway. "This is the road to the salt lick," he said. "We'll soon be there now."

The old stag had seen such paths before.

Their white spots looked like patches of sunshine on the grass.

" It has taken a long time to make a runway like this," he said. " The feet of many deer have passed this way."

Soon they were in a rocky glade, where a number of other deer were eagerly licking the soft, salty earth at the edge of a little stream. White Tail and the old stag at once began to lick up the salt that tasted so good.

After a little while the young deer raised his head and looked about him. The old stag had not yet had his fill of salt; so White Tail went over to some scrubby bushes and peeped through them. At first he saw nothing to interest him, but a moment later he caught sight of two small fawns on the ground not far away. Pushing his way through the bushes, he spoke to them.

" Hello, little fawns ! I didn't see you at first, because the white spots on your bodies fooled me. They look like patches of sunshine on the grass."

" Our mother says that is why we have these white spots," one of the little fawns answered shyly. " They help to hide us from sight."

" I know," White Tail said. " I had them too, when I was as small as you. But mine have gone now, and yours will go before winter comes. You will have another coat for winter. It will be beautifully thick and warm, and it will not be spotted."

" I don't want another coat," said one of the little fawns. " I like my coat just as it is."

" Well," White Tail replied, " you will have a dull brown coat for winter, whether you want it or not. All deer change their coats

He ran, his small head held high.

before winter gets here. You have never seen a winter, and you don't know what it is like It is a cold time, and the deer live together in the forest. Last winter the snow was piled so deep on the ground that we could not walk through it at all, and we had to keep paths open everywhere. I was hungry most of the time, for there was nothing to eat except a few small berries and the young branches of trees, and now and then a little dry grass and moss that we pawed up from under the snow."

" That seems very strange," said the fawns. " We have always had all we wanted to eat. We don't understand such things at all. But we must not talk any more now Mother told us to keep very quiet until she came back to us."

" Where is your mother ? " White Tail asked.

" She is over at the salt lick, but she will be back soon. She never leaves us very long."

" Don't you wish you were big enough to go about alone, the way I do ? " White Tail asked. " Watch me now ! See how fast I can run ! "

He gave a leap into the air and ran a little distance, his small head held high, his short white tail erect. Then he turned and ran back; and this time he did not stop beside the little fawns, but ran past them on into the rocky glade.

" Aren't you forgetting what I told you about keeping still ? " the old stag scolded him. " You run about making as much noise as though there were no such thing as a Hunter in all the world."

" I forgot," White Tail said. " I only wanted to show the fawns how fast I could run."

" You mustn't be too proud, or you will get into trouble," said the old stag, just as the squirrel had said earlier in the morning.

" I'm sorry," White Tail answered. " I'll try to remember next time."

" All right," said the old stag. " And now suppose we look for something green to eat."

" I would like that," White Tail told him. " I know a stream where water lilies and rushes grow. Shall we go there now, Old Stag ? "

" Yes," the old stag replied, " that will be fine. There is nothing better to eat than rushes and water plants. Besides," he added, " the flies are beginning to bother me, and I shall be glad to splash about in the cool water for a while."

When they reached the stream the two deer swam at once to the other side, where the rushes grew thickest.

White Tail liked to swim almost as well as he liked to run. After they had eaten all they wanted of the fresh green leaves and the tender stems, he swam about in the cool water, while the old stag rested on the shore and

" There is nothing better to eat than rushes and water plants."

chewed his cud. The young deer would have liked to stay there all day. He was sorry when, by and by, it was time for them to return. "The sun is getting high," the old stag said, "and we are not safe out here. Night is the best time to come to the stream to eat."

Crossing to the other side, they made their way back along the forest path. They had not gone far when the old stag suddenly stopped and listened. "Keep very still, White Tail!" he whispered. "I hear the Hunter!"

In spite of the old stag's warning, White Tail took a few quick steps forward, as though he were about to run. "Keep still!" the old stag repeated sharply. "He may see you if you move. The wind is blowing toward us, so I can smell him plainly. I can tell just where he is each moment. I will warn you if there is any need to run."

White Tail sniffed the air anxiously, and there came to his nostrils a strange new smell, a smell that he would never forget for the rest of his life.

In a moment the old stag whispered again. "Do you hear the cawing of the crows and the screaming of the jays? It is their warning to the forest creatures. They have seen the Hunter. Keep your head low behind the bushes, White Tail."

The young deer did as he was told. It seemed a long time that he stood there, trembling, not daring to move. "You can see him now, White Tail, if you peep through the bushes," the old stag said at last.

White Tail had never seen a man before. At the first sight of the Hunter, coming down the hillside, he was so frightened that, in spite

of all the old stag had said, he turned and ran as fast as he could. He did not stop until he reached the middle of the forest.

For a long time he stood there, tired and panting. But though he strained his ears he heard nothing, and he knew that for this time he was safe.

"I should not have run so soon," he said to himself. "The Hunter might have seen me."

Presently White Tail saw the old stag coming along the forest pathway. "I am sorry I ran, Old Stag," he said. "Are you very angry with me?"

"No, I would have done the same thing at your age, I suppose. And I have seen older deer than you run from the Hunter. But the next time you see him you must keep as quiet as you can, until you are sure which way he is going. Do not let him see you if you can help it, White Tail, for the Hunter is the greatest enemy we have. Always remember that."

"I will," White Tail promised. "Next time I won't forget a thing you have told me."

"I shall not be with you the next time you see the Hunter," the old stag told him, "for I must be going on now. But you are a fine young buck and will soon know how to take care of yourself. I hope I shall see you again some day."

Without another word the old stag went off into the forest, his head held high and his long ears pointed forward, listening for danger. White Tail stood watching him until at last he disappeared from sight. Then he turned and went back the way he had come, thinking of the exciting story he had to tell his mother and the many questions he wanted to ask her.

What SINBAD FOUND OUT in the DESERT
The Story of a Young Camel

" I want to go out in the desert," said young Sinbad.

SINBAD was a baby camel. He lived with his mother in the far-off land of Arabia, away across the sea. Arabia is very hot and dry. There are deserts there, where the yellow sand stretches away for miles and miles. It was at the edge of one of these deserts that little Sinbad lived.

He was only a few weeks old, but he had already learned to walk on his long thin legs. At first they were so wobbly that he could scarcely stand up on them at all; but now, although they still felt a little queer, he could walk about without once falling down. This made him very proud.

This morning little Sinbad stood in the sand, looking contentedly out across the desert. The hot sun beat down on him, but he did not mind. He liked the sun, and he liked the sand, so he was very happy.

Not far away from him knelt his mother, blinking her eyes sleepily as she chewed her cud. She had a long neck, a small head, and a big body covered with shaggy brown hair. On her back was a great hump. Little Sinbad thought she was a wonderful creature.

" Mother," he said to her, " will I ever be as big as you are ? "

" Of course you will," she told him. " You are a fine young camel and you are growing very fast "

" I'm glad," he said happily. " I want to be big, for then I can walk out there on the sand that stretches away so far, and I will see what the desert is like."

The mother camel looked at him for a moment, working her lower jaw from side to side as she chewed. " Yes," she said, " I suppose you will want to get out in the desert as soon as you are old enough. But you will not find much out there to see. In the desert there is nothing green—only sand and rocks and a few prickly shrubs."

" But I want to see it, anyhow," Sinbad said. " I want to go out in the desert."

" You will," his mother said. " You will cross the desert many times when you are older, and carry loads on your back for our master. Sometimes our master himself will ride on your back. There he comes now," she added. " He is bringing me my breakfast."

Sinbad saw a man come out of a tent, carrying an armful of fodder. He was a tall man with a brown skin. Instead of a hat, he wore a bright red and white striped turban wound about his head.

The little camel moved nearer to his mother. " Our master brings you your breakfast every morning, doesn't he ? " he asked. " He is a kind master."

" Yes," answered his mother, " he is kind, but he only feeds me so that I will be strong enough to work for him. Our master could not get along without his camels to carry burdens for him across the desert. There is no other creature that can travel in the desert the way we can. We have soft pads on the bottoms

*" You must always groan when
our master puts anything
on your back."*

of our feet that spread out wide and flat when
we walk and keep our feet from sinking in the
deep sand. We can go without food and water,
too, if we have to. And we often *do* have to,
out there in the desert where no green thing
grows, and where there are no pools or
streams of water."

"But what do you do when you get hungry
and thirsty, mother?" little Sinbad asked.

"We are well fed and watered before we
start on a journey," his mother told him, "so
we do not get hungry or thirsty very soon. We
can live for a while on the fat in our big humps,
and we can store enough water in our stomachs
to last us for days and days."

"We are wonderful creatures, aren't we?"
little Sinbad said.

"We are very wonderful creatures," his
mother answered. "You should be proud that
you are a camel."

She got slowly up, lifting herself first on her
hind feet and then on her front feet, as camels
always do. Now little Sinbad could see the big
leathery pads that grew on his mother's knees
and chest. He would have pads like that, too,
he knew, when he was a little older. All
camels have them so that they can rest softly
when they kneel on the ground.

He stood beside his mother while she ate her
breakfast. When she had finished, her master
made her kneel down and put a strange looking
saddle across her back. At once she began to
groan so loudly, as if in pain, that little
Sinbad was frightened.

"No—o—o—o—o—o!" she groaned.
"No—o—o—o—o—o!"

"Does the saddle hurt you badly, mother?"
Sinbad asked anxiously.

"No," she answered, "it does not hurt at all,
but I groan just the same. You must always
groan when our master puts anything on your
back. No matter whether it is light or heavy,
you must groan as loudly as you can."

"What for?" little Sinbad asked in surprise.

"It is the way we camels do," she answered.
"Perhaps if we did not, our masters would put
loads on our backs that are too heavy to carry—
I do not know. But I *do* know that we always
groan. You must remember this when you
are old enough to travel."

"I will," little Sinbad promised. "I will
groan with all my might. But, mother, why
has our master put that big saddle on your
back? Do you know why?"

"I suppose we are going to make a journey,"
his mother told him. "A journey out into the
desert."

"Oh!" cried little Sinbad happily. "Then
I will walk far out on the sand, as I have always
wanted to!"

"No, Sinbad," she answered. "You are too
young to walk far. You will have to be carried.
Baby camels always have to be carried when
they make a long journey."

She was about to say something more, but just
then their master led up one of his biggest
camels and made it kneel down. Across his
back he put a saddle and on each side of this he
fastened a heavy load.

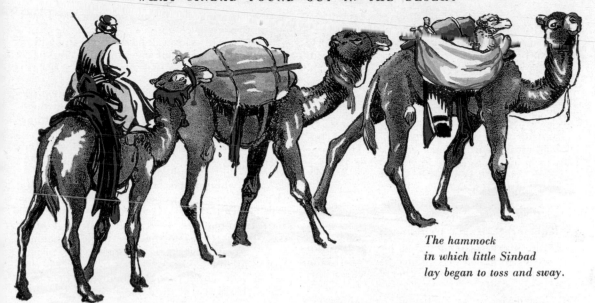

The hammock
in which little Sinbad
lay began to toss and sway.

When he had finished doing this, he picked little Sinbad up in his arms and put him into a sort of hammock that swung from one side of the big camel's saddle.

Sinbad was surprised and frightened. He kicked and squirmed as hard as he could, but his mother called to him and tried to quiet him.

"Be still, Sinbad!" she said. "They are not going to hurt you. You will ride in your hammock and I will walk just behind you. All baby camels ride like that."

"But I'd rather ride on *your* back, mother," little Sinbad cried. "Why can't I?"

"Because I must have you where I can see you all the time," she told him. "Be still now, and you will be all right."

So Sinbad lay still in his hammock while their master fastened a great load on his mother's back. "Maybe this will be fun after all," he thought, now that he knew his mother would be close to him. "I will see the desert that I have wondered so much about."

"*Goom!*" their master cried suddenly. "*Goom!*" This was his way of saying to his animals "Get up!"

Sinbad's mother and the big camel got slowly to their feet, groaning and grumbling. The hammock in which little Sinbad lay began to toss and sway, for a camel has a very queer way of walking. It moves on two feet on one side of its body at the same time and then the two feet on the other side of its body at the same time, so that its body rolls from side to side. But little Sinbad did not mind this; indeed, he liked the motion.

Soon they came to where there were a great many other camels with loads upon their backs. They were being formed in a long line, one camel behind another. Sinbad's big camel took his place in the line, and Sinbad's mother followed close behind.

It was all very new and strange and exciting. It was exciting to see the desert, like a great ocean of sand, all round him, and to watch his mother plodding patiently along behind him, holding her head high and looking at him all the time with her big soft eyes. And it was exciting to hear the tinkling of the little silver bells that many of the camels wore.

For a long time they travelled on under the hot sun. When noon came, the caravan stopped for a rest. Sinbad's master lifted him down from his hammock. The little camel ran quickly to his mother and greedily drank the milk that he was so hungry for.

When he had finished, he walked about for a while. It was wonderful, he thought, to be out in the desert like this! He would have liked to walk on and on, but his mother was kneeling down, half dozing, and he did not dare to get far away from her.

The other camels were kneeling, too, resting quietly until the time came to start on again. Most of them had crossed the desert many times before, and such a journey as this was nothing new to them. But to little Sinbad it was all very strange and exciting.

He looked curiously at the camel drivers sitting about on the sand and talking to each other. When would they be ready to go on across the desert? he wondered.

Suddenly he saw some of them spring to their feet. Then others jumped up, and still others, until all of them were running about, calling excitedly to each other. The camels were excited, too, and the men were very careful not to get too close to them. For no one can tell when a camel may lose its temper and begin to kick and bite anyone who happens to be near it.

Little Sinbad raised his head and listened. He heard a low roaring sound that rolled across the desert, growing louder every minute. "The wind! The wind!" he heard an old camel say. "The wind is coming!"

Sinbad had heard the wind blow before, but he had never heard it roar like this! He ran as fast as he could to his mother's side. "What is it?" he cried. "What is it, mother?"

"A sand storm is coming," she told him. "You must lie down here beside me, Sinbad. Stretch your head flat on the ground! See how the other camels are doing!"

Little Sinbad at once did as he was told, for something in his mother's voice frightened him. "What is a sand storm, mother? Will it hurt me?" he asked.

"Not if you do as I tell you," she answered. "You must close your eyes. Your long eyelashes will help keep the sand out of them. And you must close your nostrils tight so that the sand will not get into your nose. Then you must lie as still as you can lie."

The hot wind came with a mighty rush and roar, and the sand beat against Sinbad's body like sharp little needles. He closed his eyes and he closed his nostrils as tight as he could; and he waited.

The camel drivers huddled behind the kneeling camels for protection. The camels lay very still, their heads flat on the ground, their eyes and nostrils closed, while great clouds of sand came sweeping in across the desert.

It seemed a very long time to little Sinbad that he lay there, trembling with fright. After a while the storm died down and the wind stopped roaring. Then in the silence he heard his mother's voice again.

"The storm is over, Sinbad," she told him. "You can open your eyes now. You have been brave."

"Have I, mother?"

"Yes," his mother said. "Not many little camels as young as you are have gone through a sand storm like this. You did everything exactly right."

"The camel drivers had to hide behind their camels to get away from the storm, didn't they, mother?" little Sinbad said.

"Yes," his mother answered, touching him with her queer soft upper lip; "but we camels didn't have to hide. It is better to be a camel than anything else when a sand storm comes. We camels belong to the desert and it belongs to us. You have good reason to be proud, little Sinbad!"

The little camel thought about this for a long time. He was still thinking about it when the camels moved off again on their journey. High up in his little hammock, he looked across the desert that stretched on and on as far as he could see. He was happier than he had ever been before.

As the camels swayed along on their way, little Sinbad thought: "I am glad that I am a camel. I am glad that I belong to the desert. I would rather be a camel than anything else in the world!"

*It seemed
a long time
to little Sinbad
that he lay there,
trembling with fright.*